ONE-DAY INTERNATIONAL CRICKET

The Ultimate Guide to Limited-overs Internationals

ONE-DAY INTERNATIONAL CRICKET

Compiled by Stephen Samuelson, Ray Mason & David Clark

Introduction by Christopher Martin-Jenkins

Robinson

LONDON

Acknowledgements

In compiling this volume, we are indebted to:

- Charlie Wat and Graham Dawson whose landmark work *Test Cricket Lists*, first published in 1989 and now in its fourth edition, inspired *One-day Intermational Cricket* .
- Cricket statistician Ross Dundas for providing the tables and statistics beyond the reach of three mortal cricket authors.
- *International Limited-overs International Cricket: The Complete Record*, compiled by Bill Frindall and published by Headline Book Publishing, London, 1997.
- Erica Sainsbury, official statistician for women's cricket in Australia, for providing the most comprehensive set of women's one-day international statistics ever published. Also thanks to Marian Collin, Bronwyn Calver and women's cricket's greatest fan, Don Miles.
- Zaheer Abbas, Jeffrey Archer, Dickie Bird, Greg Chappell, Belinda Clark, Bryce Courtenay, Peter Roebuck, Sir Richard Hadlee, Kim Hughes, Clive Rice and Tony Greig for providing their best one-day elevens of all time.
- Michael Browning, Event Manager for the 1999 Cricket World Cup for permission to reproduce the tournament schedule.
- Roger White, UK Director of Marketing Communications and Rob Eastaway for permission to reproduce the PricewaterhouseCoopers one-day international cricket ratings.
- Clive Hitchcock, International Cricket Council for permission to reproduce ICC Code of Conduct breaches in limited-overs internationals.
- Melissa Samuelson for all her support and assistance.
- George Simnos for his advice and encouragement.
- And Sonya Plowman at The Five Mile Press for her painstaking efforts as Editor of this book.

Robinson Publishing Ltd
7 Kensington Church Court
London W8 4SP

Published, with additional material, in the UK by Robinson Publishing Ltd 1999
This edition first published in Australia by The Five Mile Press Pty Ltd 1998

A copy of the British Library Cataloguing in Publication Data
for this title is available from the British Library.

ISBN 1-84119-038-1

Printed and bound in the EC

Authors' Note

Like many youngsters, we idolised cricket's sporting heroes; they were who we wanted to be when we grew up and we emulated their glorious deeds in the backyard.

Although in time our hopes faded to reality, we were left with a wonderful passion for the game, yearning for the latest Test scores on radio or that scarce piece of television footage from exotic places such as Mumbai, Lahore or Bridgetown. We were also part of the explosion of limited-overs international cricket and learnt to love that game as well.

From its origins in 1971 in a match that came about only by accident, few would have predicted the enormous impact limited-overs international cricket would have on the game. Whilst the abbreviated version and its innovations upset many traditional followers, few could argue that one-day cricket has breathed new life into the sport and increased its popularity through improved television coverage and match attendances. Countries new to the game such as Bangladesh and Kenya now play at international level and seem destined to achieve Test status within the next decade. Neutral venues such as Sharjah, Singapore and Toronto regularly host matches. Other innovations include day/night matches, coloured clothing, the white ball and fielding restrictions, as well as a host of tournaments, many involving three or more nations. Cricket's great quadrennial contest, the World Cup, is also played in the abbreviated format.

Whilst there is an abundance of literature on cricket, surprisingly few books have addressed the history and statistics of limited-overs internationals. Inspired by Charlie Wat and Graham Dawson's outstanding *Test Cricket Lists*, also published by The Five Mile Press and by Robinson Publishing, *One-day International Cricket* completes the cricket enthusiast's collection of a comprehensive reference for the sport at international level.

We hope *One-day International Cricket* is informative and enjoyable, throwing a spotlight not just on the records, but the greats and not so greats, the highs and lows, the curious and the unbelievable of the game. Most of all we hope you enjoy it both as an entertaining read and a handy reference for answering those nagging questions or solving the lively arguments that flow from the seemingly endless statistics associated with cricket.

Stephen Samuelson, Ray Mason and David Clark
February 1999

About the Authors

Stephen Samuelson
Stephen Samuelson was the principal researcher on *Australian Sport Through Time*, a chronology of Australian sport since 1870. A cricket aficionado, Steve is the sports editor for the *Sydney Morning Herald's* entertainment-based internet site CitySearch (www.citysearch.com.au), and also runs regular sports trivia quizzes at Sydney's Harold Park Hotel.

Ray Mason
Ray Mason was a principal writer on *Australian Sport Through Time* published in 1997 and is a columnist with *Inside Sport Magazine*. He has also been a major contributor to the *Australian Sports Almanac* since 1994. Ray is a cricket fanatic, having played the game at various levels for over 30 years.

David Clark
David Clark has been the editor of the annual *Australian Sports Almanac* since 1994 and was a researcher and consultant on a number of recently published books including *Campese, Australia at the Olympics*, and *Australian Sport Through Time* in both its book (1997) and CD-ROM (1998) versions. David has worked in sports marketing and publishing for his entire career.

Dedication

To our wives: Melissa, Robyn and Roslyn for the
patience and understanding that helped
make this book possible.

Contents

Contents Expanded

The Players

Batting

Batting Partnerships

Introduction

It was beguiling at first. We took to one-day cricket like innocent teenagers discovering champagne. But there are always those for whom moderation in all things does not seem to be a good idea. Frankly, the world of cricket has over-indulged on the considerable pleasures of the one-day international during the last 20 years. The habit has become ingrained and there seems no going back.

Since the experiment at Melbourne in 1971 which had such extraordinarily far-reaching consequences, one-day internationals have simply got out of hand. They happen with such bewildering frequency these days that the closest student of the game, whether amateur or professional, gets dizzy trying to keep up. For the cricketers of India, Pakistan and Sri Lanka, especially, it seems to be a case of playing in Sharjah one week, Toronto the next, and then Colombo the week after that.

One must never forget, however, that the players generally enjoy these games, not least the ones played at night in coats of many colours, and that they have encouraged a young, often family-based audience. Professionals want to play before full houses and naturally they get a buzz from doing so. Moreover, like the cricketers themselves, those who stage these matches often laugh all the way to the bank, with television companies and sponsors always eager to jump on the bandwagon. There is a simple reason for this: in most cases one-day internationals are good fun for all concerned, producing in particular fielding and batting feats of a spectacular quality seldom seen before.

In England, the last country to retain a certain rarity value for these games (no more than six matches a year until 1998, and virtually always played to a guaranteed full house), there will from the year 2000 be ten internationals a season, with three sides playing each other three times to determine a finalist. There is a danger apparent to me, that while these games will continue to be supported by the public and commercial interests, Test match tickets, let alone those for County Championship games, will become harder to sell.

Thank goodness, then, for the World Cup every four years; a competition which really means something and which everyone wants to win. I shall never forget the excitement and quality of the first World Cup final at Lord's in 1975 when the ground was bursting at the seams when the Duke of Edinburgh presented the trophy to Clive Lloyd as a golden evening descended into twilight after an outrageous last wicket stand by Jeff Thomson and Dennis Lillee.

That day Lloyd had produced the first of many great individual performances that have made each final special. John Arlott, watching from his commentary box as the 'supercat' with long-armed strokes both languid and ferocious, plundered a high-class Australian attack, observed with typical wit: 'It now seems impossible not only to bowl a maiden over but to bowl a maiden ball.'

Expectations rise and these days a maiden ball is often the occasion for a hearty round of applause for the bowler. But one-day cricket is not necessarily a batsman's game. Like all games of cricket, it is the pitch and its conditions that usually dictate who has most fun.

Viv Richards, who fielded so superbly in the first World Cup final, won the second for the

West Indies with another memorable century against England, completed when he stepped outside the off stump to Mike Hendrick's last ball and lifted it off the very gateway to his stumps high into the Mound Stand. Yet four years on, the West Indies' strokeplayers were strangled mainly by very straight and steady Indian medium-paced bowling on the slow pitch at Lord's.

When England and Australia got through to the final of the next event at Eden Gardens in Calcutta (much to the disappointment of all citizens of India and Pakistan, the joint host countries) the key performances again came from the bowlers, this time on a pitch full of runs. Neil Foster for England, and Simon O'Donnell and Steve Waugh for Australia were the men who keep the bowling tight when it mattered. Australia squeezed home by seven runs and Waugh's subtle changes of pace showed the way for bowlers in future: often the secret has been to slow the ball down and make the batsmen do the work. However, try telling that to Mushtaq Ahmed and Wasim Akram, both by nature aggressive and expansive cricketers who are better suited to Test cricket than one-day internationals. They were the ones who sliced through England in the final at Melbourne in 1992 after Javed Miandad and Imran Khan had rescued a Pakistan innings faltering against another notable one-day specialist, Derek Pringle.

Pakistan provided the venue, Lahore, for the final of the next World Cup in 1996, but the pressure of living up to the expectations of their followers proved too much and it was Australia and Sri Lanka who reached the final after much drama in the qualifying games. Sri Lanka's cricket had been brilliant throughout, based upon uninhibited attack from the first ball by the dazzling opening pair of Sanath Jayasuriya and Romesh Kaluwitharana. It was the old masters, however, the genius Aravinda de Silva and the durable captain, Arjuna Ranatunga, who eventually did for Australia.

No wonder expectations are so high for the seventh World Cup, back in England in 1999. Thank goodness, too, for statisticians with the energy and interest to chronicle everything that has happened in between. For those who attempt from time to time to put the history of cricket into some sort of perspective a book like this is an invaluable reference work as well as being a fascinating volume to dip into at bedtime.

The story of the one-day international has been the perfect example of the oak that grows from an acorn. That first match at Melbourne came about by accident. England and Australia had attempted to start a Test match on 31 December 1970. But it rained. It kept on raining for two more days and the solution was to stage a limited-overs game to entertain the public. And ever since then, the entertainment has hardly stopped.

Christopher Martin-Jenkins

Statistical Note and Abbreviations

STATISTICAL NOTE

Terminology
The authors recognise that the correct terminology is 'limited-overs internationals', however we use this phrase interchangeably with the less cumbersome and more colloquial 'one-day international'.

Contents
One-day International Cricket Lists includes statistics and records from all 1406 limited-over internationals played from 5 January 1971 to 13 Feb 1999. The women's cricket section also covers all limited-overs internationals up to 8 Feb 1999.

Overs
The scheduled number of overs for limited-overs internationals for each team often varied between 40 and 60, depending on the agreed conditions of the tournament or series. This has now been standardised to 50 overs. Some early limited-overs internationals also featured eight-ball overs. A number of matches have featured a reduced number of overs owing to factors such as rain delays, and these differing conditions have been noted in the statistics where appropriate.

Matches
In referring to the matches, the home country is listed first. Where the match is being played at a neutral venue, the teams are listed in alphabetical order.

Ties
Although the team losing fewer wickets has been declared the winner in a number of tied matches, these have still been regarded as ties in the Team statistics.

Indian cities
A number of cities in India that have hosted limited-overs international matches underwent name changes in 1996/97. They include: Mumbai (formerly Bombay), Vadodara (formerly Baroda), Margao (formerly Goa), Chennai (formerly Madras), Kochi (formerly Cochin) and Visag (Vishakhapatnam).

Early matches
There are some instances where full details of some early games such as balls faced were not recorded by the scorers, meaning some information such as strike-rates and fastest innings may not be definitive. However it is unlikely that the information contained herein has been unduly affected by these minor omissions.

ABBREVIATIONS

Ave.	average	R	runs
b	byes	RO	run out
Bwld	bowled	RPO	runs per over
Ct	caught	R-R	run-rate
DNB	did not bat/did not bowl	St	stumped
Ec Rt	economy rate (runs per over)	Stk Rt	strike-rate: batting (runs per 100 balls)
FoW	fall of wicket		strike-rate: bowling (balls per wicket)
HS	highest score	Ttl	total
Inns	innings	v	versus
lb	leg byes	Wkts	wickets
LBW	leg before wicket	W	wides
M	matches	*	denotes captain in scorecards, and a not out
Mdns	maidens		or unbroken partnership in the records.
nb	no-ball	†	wicket-keeper or revised target
NO	not outs	%	percentage
No.	number	4wi	four wicket innings
NR	no result	5wi	five wicket innings
O	overs		

PART 1

MATCHES, MOMENTS AND MILESTONES

One-day Cricket Timeline

The following timeline gives a brief rundown of the most important events that have shaped one-day cricket history.

1971

5 January 1971 — The first one-day international is played, between Australia and England at the Melbourne Cricket Ground. Australia wins by five wickets.

1972

24 August 1972 — The first one-day international is played in England, at Old Trafford, Manchester. Dennis Amiss scores the first century and England defeats Australia by six wickets.

28 August 1972 — England defeats Australia by two wickets at Edgbaston, Birmingham, wrapping up the inaugural three-match series for the Prudential Trophy 2-1.

1973

11 February 1973 — New Zealand and Pakistan appear in a one-day international for the first time, at Lancaster Park, Christchurch. New Zealand wins by 22 runs.

20 June 1973 — The inaugural women's one-day international, a World Cup preliminary match between Jamica and New Zealand, is washed out at Kew. The first matches of the tournament are completed three days later.

5 September 1973 — The West Indies team plays their first match, losing to England at Headingley, Leeds, by one wicket.

1974

13 July 1974 — India appears in their first one-day international, losing to England by four wickets at Headingley, Leeds.

31 August 1974 — England opener David Lloyd (116 not out) becomes the first player to bat throughout a completed innings, during a Prudential Trophy match against Pakistan at Trent Bridge, Nottingham.

1975

7 June 1975 — Four matches are played involving all eight participating nations on the opening day of the first World Cup: England defeats India by 202 runs at Lord's; Australia defeats Pakistan by 73 runs at Headingley; West Indies defeats Sri Lanka by nine wickets at Old Trafford; and New Zealand defeats East Africa by 181 runs at Edgbaston.

21 June 1975	West Indies defeats Australia by 17 runs in the final of the inaugural World Cup at Lord's.
20 December 1975	Australia defeats West Indies by five wickets at Adelaide Oval in the only one-day international between the two sides of the 1975/76 season.
1976	
16 October 1976	Pakistan hosts their first one-day international at Jinnah Park, Sialkot. New Zealand wins by the closest possible runs margin for the first time — one run.
1977	
16 March 1977	The first match is played in the Caribbean, between Pakistan and West Indies at the Albion Sports Complex in Berbice, Guyana. West Indies wins by four wickets.
1978	
3 November 1978	Indian captain Bishen Bedi calls his batsmen from the field in protest against the bowling of Pakistan's Sarfraz Nawaz, the first and only time a team has conceded a match after it started.
1979	
18 June 1979	Sri Lanka defeats India by 47 runs in a World Cup match at Old Trafford, Manchester, the first victory by an ICC associate-member nation over a full-member nation.
23 June 1979	West Indies defeats England by 92 runs in the final of the second World Cup at Lord's.
27 November 1979	Australia and West Indies play the first official limited-overs international under lights at the Sydney Cricket Ground. The match is also the first for the Australian team reunited after the World Series Cricket split.
1980	
22 January 1980	West Indies defeats England by eight wickets in the second final of the inaugural three-nation World Series Cup at the Sydney Cricket Ground.
23 November 1980	New Zealand substitute fieldsman John Bracewell bags four catches against Australia in Adelaide, the first non wicket-keeper to hold four catches in an innings.
9 December 1980	New Zealand and India meet in the 100th one-day international, the first match to be held at the WACA Ground in Perth.
1981	
1 February 1981	With seven runs required for victory by New Zealand at the Melbourne Cricket Ground, Australian captain Greg Chappell orders his brother Trevor to bowl the final ball underarm in order to prevent a possible tie. The incident causes an international furore and the rules are changed by the Australian Cricket Board the following day.

8 June 1981	Australia defeats England by 71 runs at Headingley, Leeds, to win the best-of-three Prudential Trophy for the first time.
25 November 1981	The first one-day match is played in India at Sardar Patel Stadium in Ahmedabad. England defeats India by five wickets.

1982

7 February 1982	Australia defeats England by three wickets in the final of the third women's cricket World Cup at Lancaster Park in Christchurch, New Zealand.
13 February 1982	Sri Lanka hosts their first one-day international at the Sinhalese Sports Club in Colombo. England wins by five runs.
20 September 1982	Pakistan's Jalaluddin takes the first hat-trick in a one-day international, dismissing Australia's Rod Marsh, Bruce Yardley and Geoff Lawson at Hyderabad in the first match between the two sides in Pakistan.

1983

9 June 1983	Zimbabwe, playing their first one-day international, defeats Australia by 13 runs at Trent Bridge on the opening day of the 1983 World Cup. It is one of the biggest upsets in the history of the game.
9 June 1983	New Zealand's Martin Snedden concedes 105 runs off 12 overs in a World Cup match against England at The Oval, the only bowler to have been hit for a century in a one-day international.
10 June 1983	West Indies loses their first World Cup match in three tournaments, to India by 34 runs at Old Trafford, Manchester.
25 June 1983	India upsets defending champions the West Indies by 43 runs in the final of the third World Cup at Lord's.

1984

11 February 1984	Australia and West Indies produce the first ever tie in a one-day international, at the Melbourne Cricket Ground. Both teams finish on 222 runs, but West Indies loses fewer wickets.
6 April 1984	The first match is played at Sharjah, United Arab Emirates, between Pakistan and Sri Lanka. Sri Lanka wins by five wickets.
13 April 1984	India wins the inaugural three-nation Asia Cup in Sharjah, defeating Pakistan by 54 runs.
31 May 1984	Viv Richards hits a record 189 not out against England at Old Trafford, Manchester, which remained the highest individual innings in a one-day international until 1997.

3 October 1984	Australia's Allan Border becomes the first player to make 100 appearances, in a match against India in Jamshedpur.
1985	
28 January 1985	Australia defeats Sri Lanka by 232 runs in a World Series Cup match in Adelaide, the largest ever runs victory in a one-day international.
10 March 1985	India wins the World Championship of Cricket at the Melbourne Cricket Ground, defeating Pakistan by eight wickets in the final of the seven-nation tournament to celebrate the 150th anniversary of Victoria. During the tournament the MCG became the second stadium to host day/night cricket under lights.
1986	
9 February 1986	In a match against Australia at the Melbourne Cricket Ground, India's Mohinder Amarnath becomes the first batsman to be given out for handling the ball in a one-day international.
31 March 1986	Bangladesh appear in their first one-day international, against Pakistan in the second Asia Cup tournament at Moratuwa, Sri Lanka. The match is retrospectively awarded official international status.
18 April 1986	Pakistan wins the inaugural Austral-Asia Cup in Sharjah, their first success in a tournament involving more than two nations.
1987	
20 March 1987	India and Pakistan play the second tied match, at Lal Bahadur Stadium in Hyderabad.
8 November 1987	Australia wins the fourth World Cup in India, defeating England by seven runs at Eden Gardens, Calcutta. The margin remains the narrowest in World Cup finals.
1988	
20 January 1988	Australia and New Zealand meet in the 500th one-day international, a World Series Cup match at the Sydney Cricket Ground. Australia wins by 78 runs.
4 February 1988	Australia and England play a one-off game at the Melbourne Cricket Ground to celebrate Australia's bicentenary. Australia wins by 22 runs.
27 October 1988	Bangladesh hosts its first one-day international, with matches in Dhaka (Pakistan v Sri Lanka) and Chittagong (Bangladesh v India) on the opening day of the Asia Cup.

1989

27 May 1989 — England and Australia play a thrilling tie at Trent Bridge, Nottingham, with both teams finishing on 226 runs.

1 November 1989 — Pakistan wins the final of the Nehru Cup at Eden Gardens, Calcutta, defeating the West Indies by four wickets. The seven-nation tournament was held to celebrate the centenary of the birth of the nations' first Prime Minister Jawarhalal Nehru.

1990

20 February 1990 — Australian captain Allan Border becomes the first player to appear in 200 one-day internationals, in a match against Pakistan at the Sydney Cricket Ground.

1991

20 March 1991 — Australia completes a 4-1 series victory over the West Indies in Georgetown. It is the first and only home series loss for the West Indies.

23 October 1991 — Kapil Dev becomes the first player to reach the 200-wicket milestone, against Pakistan in Sharjah.

25 October 1991 — Pakistan's Aaqib Javed captures seven wickets for 37 runs in a match against India in Sharjah, the best bowling analysis in a one-day international.

10 November 1991 — South Africa, captained by Clive Rice, returns to the world cricket stage against India at Eden Gardens, Calcutta before an estimated 90,000 people, the largest attendance at a one-day international. India wins by three wickets in the first of the three-game series.

1992

22 February 1992 — The fifth World Cup begins with the opening match between the two host nations, Australia and New Zealand, at Eden Park, Auckland. Hasty rescheduling allows South Africa a berth in the tournament and all nations play each other for the first time.

22 March 1992 — A controversial ruling because of a rain interruption robs South Africa of any chance of winning the World Cup semi-final against England at the Sydney Cricket Ground.

25 March 1992 — Pakistan defeats England by 22 runs in the final of the fifth World Cup at the Melbourne Cricket Ground.

25 October 1992 — Zimbabwe's first home international is played at the Harare Sports Club, a one-off match against India.

7 December 1992	Newlands in Cape Town hosts South Africa's first one-day international. The host nation defeats India by six wickets in the first of a seven-game series eventually won by South Africa 5-2.
1993	
25 February 1993	Pakistan is dismissed for 43 runs off 19.5 overs by the West Indies at Newlands in Cape Town, the lowest ever team total and the least balls faced in a completed innings of a one-day international.
27 February 1993	West Indies' Desmond Haynes becomes the first player to reach 8000 runs in one-day internationals, against Pakistan in Johannesburg.
1 August 1993	England defeats New Zealand by 67 runs in the final of the fifth Women's World Cup at Lord's.
14 November 1993	South Africa's Jonty Rhodes takes five catches in a match against the West Indies in Bombay, the most catches by a fielder (not including wicket-keepers) in a one-day international.
1994	
8 April 1994	Australian captain Allan Border plays his 273rd and final match, against South Africa in Bloemfontein. Border had appeared in all but 35 of Australia's games.
20 April 1994	Pakistan's Aamir Sohail and Inzamam-ul-Haq add 263 runs for the second wicket against New Zealand at Sharjah, the highest ever partnership (since broken) in one-day matches.
24 August 1994	Pakistan's Wasim Akram becomes the highest wicket-taker in one-day cricket when he takes his 253rd wicket, against Sri Lanka in Colombo. The previous record was held by India's Kapil Dev.
1995	
26 February 1995	Australia defeats New Zealand by six wickets at Eden Park, Auckland to win a four-nation series celebrating the centenary of New Zealand cricket.
26 May 1995	England wins the 1000th one-day international, defeating West Indies by 25 runs at The Oval, London.
26 November 1995	A wall collapses, killing 12 people during a match between India and New Zealand at Vidarbha Stadium in Nagpur.
1996	
6 March 1996	Sri Lanka reaches 5 for 398 against Kenya in a World Cup match in Kandy, the highest ever team total in a one-day international.
17 March 1996	Sri Lanka defeats Australia by seven wickets in the final of the sixth World Cup in Lahore. As one of the three countries where the tournament is played, Sri Lanka became the first host nation to win the World Cup.

2 April 1996	In the opening match of a three-nation tournament in Singapore, Sri Lanka's Sanath Jayasuriya produces the fastest hundred (48 balls), the most sixes in an innings (11) and the most runs off an over (29 off Aamir Sohail) in a one-day international. The match against Pakistan also produces a record aggregate (664 runs).
7 April 1996	Sri Lanka's Sanath Jayasuriya breaks another one-day record in the final against Pakistan in Singapore, the fastest 50 ever (17 balls).
14 April 1996	Sharjah Cricket Association Stadium becomes the first venue to host 100 matches, a Sharjah Cup game between India and South Africa.
16 September 1996	Canada hosts its first one-day international, the first of a five-match series for the Sahara 'Friendship' Cup between India and Pakistan at the Toronto Cricket, Skating and Curling Club. India wins the series 3-2.
28 September 1996	Kenya hosts its first one-day international in Nairobi, a match between the host nation and Sri Lanka at the Nairobi Gymkhana Ground. Kenya is the fourteenth country, Nairobi the 103rd city, and three days later Nairobi's Aga Khan Ground becomes the 114th ground to host a one-day international.
4 October 1996	Pakistan's Shahid Afridi blasts a century off only 37 balls against Sri Lanka in Nairobi, to break Sanath Jayasuriya's record for the fastest century.
30 October 1996	Pakistan's Hasan Raza, aged 14 years and 233 days, becomes the youngest player to appear in a one-day international, against Zimbabwe in Quetta. In the same match, Wasim Akram becomes the first bowler to capture 300 wickets.
1997	
21 May 1997	Pakistan's Saeed Anwar scores 194 against India at Chennai, the highest individual innings in a one-day international, beating Viv Richards' previous record of 189 against England at Manchester in 1984.
18 June 1997	Bangladesh and Kenya are awarded official limited-overs international status by the International Cricket Council.
16 December 1997	Australian captain Belinda Clark scores 229 not out against Denmark in a Women's World Cup match in Mumbai, the only player to reach a double century in a one-day international.
29 December 1997	Australia wins the sixth Women's World Cup, defeating New Zealand in the final by five wickets at Eden Gardens, Calcutta.

1998

1 April 1998	India's Mohammed Azharrudin plays his 274th match, eclipsing Allan Border's record for the most appearances in limited-overs internationals.
9 April 1998	India's Mohammed Azharrudin (153 not out) and Ajay Jadeja (116 not out) hit an unbeaten 275 runs for the fifth wicket in a match against Zimbabwe in Cuttack, breaking the previous record (263) for the highest partnership in a one-day international.
11 April 1998	Pakistan's Wasim Akram takes his 350th wicket in one-day internationals, in a match against South Africa in East London.
17 May 1998	After a record 22 consecutive losses, Bangladesh record their first victory in a limited-overs international, defeating Kenya by six wickets in Hyderabad, India.
18 June 1998	The International Cricket Council awards the 9th World Cup in 2007 to the West Indies, with the possibility of some matches being played in the USA, Canada and Bermuda.
7 July 1998	India's Sourav Ganguly and Sachin Tendulkar set a new opening partnership world record of 252 runs, against Sri Lanka in the final of the Independence Cup in Colombo.
20 August 1998	Sri Lanka defeats England by five wickets in the final of the Emirates Triangular Tournament. This series, which also included South Africa, is the first to feature players wearing coloured clothing in England.
27 September 1998	Sachin Tendulkar breaks West Indian Desmond Haynes' long-standing record for the most centuries in limited-overs internationals when he notches up his 18th ton (127*) against Zimbabwe at Bulawayo.
28 October 1998	India's Mohammed Azharuddin makes his 300th appearance against Australia in the quarter-final of the Wills International Cup in Dhaka, Bangladesh. He is the first player to reach this milestone.
1 November 1998	South Africa, led by Hansie Cronje, win the inaugural Wills International Trophy (mini World Cup) defeating the West Indies in the final by four wickets. The knockout tournament featured all nine Test-playing countries and was staged to raise money for the development of cricket worldwide.
6 November 1998	During his innings of 94 against Sri Lanka at Sharjah, Indian captain Mohammed Azharrudin passes Desmond Haynes (8,648 runs) as the highest run-scorer in limited-overs internationals.

Great Matches

Australia v England — 1971

Melbourne Cricket Ground, 5 January 1971
Australia won by 5 wickets
England 190 (39.4 overs) (J.H. Edrich 82, A.A. Mallett 3-34, K.R. Stackpole 3-40)
Australia 5-191 (34.6 overs) (I.M. Chappell 60, R. Illingworth 3-50)

Acknowledged as the first official one-day international, this game was hastily put together to give Melbourne fans some cricket after rain had forced the abandonment of the Third Test. After meetings between Australian Board of Control Chairman Sir Donald Bradman and President of the MCC Sir Cyril Hawker, it was agreed the teams would be called Australia and England. The format of the match was based on the flourishing one-day competitions in England, with each side to face 40 eight-ball overs.

A crowd of over 46,000 saw Australian captain Bill Lawry win the toss and send England in to bat. Australia took the initiative with a great fielding display, and despite a magnificent 82 by John Edrich in 119 balls, England was dismissed for 190 in 39.4 overs, their last seven wickets falling for only 46 runs.

Australia chased the total aggressively, with Doug Walters (41 from 51 balls) showing a return to form and Ian Chappell (60 from 103 balls) tormenting the visitors after a scratchy start. Australia made the required runs in 34.6 overs with five wickets to spare, but the $200 Man of the Match award rightfully went to Englishman John Edrich.

England v West Indies — 1973

Headingley, Leeds, 5 September 1973
England won by 1 wicket
West Indies 181 (54 overs) (R.B. Kanhai 55, C.M. Old 3-43, D.L. Underwood 3-30)
England 9-182 (54.3 overs) (M.H. Denness 66, A.W. Greig 48)

Mike Denness began his reign as England captain with an exciting one-wicket victory over the West Indies at Headingley.

Captain Rohan Kanhai (55 from 75 balls) and Clive Lloyd (31 from 32 balls) ensured the tourists had a good platform, but from 2 for 100 after 25 overs the innings fell away and they were all out for 181 in 54 overs. Chris Old (3 for 43) and Derek Underwood (3 for 30) combined to see the West Indies lose their last seven wickets for only 49 runs, including a duck by Garfield Sobers in his only one-day appearance.

England started badly, losing Boycott for a duck, before Denness (66 from 117 balls) and Mike Smith (31 from 71 balls) added 71 in 22 overs. England then suffered a batting collapse before Tony Greig, with a quick-fire 48 in 54 balls, seemingly rescued the innings. But the lower order panicked in the face of some tight West Indian bowling, and it was left to tail-ender Bob Willis to score the winning runs with just three balls to spare. Denness was named Man of the Match.

England v Pakistan — 1974

Trent Bridge, Nottingham, 31 August 1974
Pakistan won by 7 wickets
England 4-244 (50 overs) (D. Lloyd 116* C.M. Old 39)
Pakistan 3-246 (42.5 overs) (Majid Khan 109, Sadiq Mohammad 41)

Majid Khan compiled a majestic 109 to lead Pakistan to a relatively easy seven-wicket victory, after England had put together a formidable total of 4 for 244 when the match had been reduced to 50 overs a side following morning rain. This was the first one-day international to contain two centuries.

England decided to bat and David Lloyd scored 116 not out to become the first player to bat throughout a one-day international innings. He added 103 for the third wicket with captain Mike Denness (32) in very good time, before Chris Old (39 from 31 balls) launched a late onslaught, relishing a promotion in the order. At the close, the England score of 244 looked very good, especially given the heavy ground conditions.

In response, Pakistan openers Majid Khan (109 from 93 balls) and Sadiq Mohammad (41 from 52 balls) attacked the England bowling from the outset, with a stand of 113 in just over 18 overs. When Majid Khan was dismissed in the 31st over with the score at 187, the visitors were almost home. The Pakistan middle order finished the match off in a more sedate manner, capitalising on the great start. Majid Khan was named Man of the Match after scoring the first one-day international century by a Pakistani.

Pakistan v West Indies — 1975

Edgbaston, Birmingham, 11 June 1975
West Indies won by 1 wicket
Pakistan 7-266 (60 overs) (Majid Khan 60, Mustaq Mohammad 55, Wasim Raja 58)
West Indies 9-267 (59.4 overs) (C.H. Lloyd 53, D.L. Murray 61*, Safraz Nawaz 4-44)

Pakistan was eliminated from the 1975 World Cup after the West Indies pulled off a thrilling last-over victory with one wicket to spare.

A controlled innings by stand-in captain Majid Khan (60) and erratic bowling and fielding by the West Indians left Pakistan well placed for a huge score. However, a number of the senior players were dismissed just as the final assault was about to be launched and the innings fell away. Fortunately, 17-year-old Javed Miandad (24) showed more composure than some of his more experienced team-mates, taking the score to 7 for 266 from their 60 overs.

The West Indies began in an aggressive fashion, but Sarfraz Nawaz took early wickets to have them in trouble at 3 for 36. The wickets continued to fall regularly, and when Clive Lloyd (53) was dismissed with the score at 7 for 151 a West Indies victory looked unlikely. However, keeper Derryck Murray had other ideas and he combined with Vanburn Holder to take the score to 9 for 203. With 64 runs needed to win and 14 overs to be bowled, Andy Roberts joined Murray and the pair calmly went about the chase. Pakistan had their chances in the last overs, but were unable to take the elusive last wicket. Roberts scored the winning runs with two balls to spare. Pakistan's Sarfraz Nawaz was named Man of the Match following his superb bowling effort of 4 for 44.

Australia v West Indies — 1975

Lord's, London, 21 June 1975
West Indies won by 17 runs
West Indies 8-291 (60 overs) (R.B. Kanhai 55, C.H. Lloyd 102, G.J. Gilmour 5-48)
Australia 274 (58.4 overs) (I.M. Chappell 62, K.D. Boyce 4-50)

The West Indies defeated Australia by 17 runs to win the inaugural World Cup at Lord's. West Indies started slowly, losing 3 for 52 after 19 overs, but Clive Lloyd (102 from 85 balls) and Rohan Kanhai (55) took advantage of a number of dropped catches to add 149 for the fourth wicket. The lower order continued in an aggressive fashion, lifting the score to 8 for 291 from their 60 overs. Gary Gilmour starred for Australia, finishing with 5 for 48 in only his second match of the tournament, after taking 6 for 14 in the semi-final against England.

The unfancied Australians knew they would be hard-pressed to make the runs, but went about the task in a confident manner. But the West Indian fielding, especially that of Viv Richards, was magnificent and the continued pressure led to a number of run-outs.

The Australians were best served by captain Ian Chappell (62) and Alan Turner (40 from 24 balls), but found themselves still 58 behind when the ninth wicket fell. Dennis Lillee and Jeff Thomson took up the challenge of reaching the target in the seven overs remaining, but fell 17 runs short when Thomson became the fifth run-out victim. Earlier their partnership had been interrupted by an invasion of a jubilant crowd when Lillee was 'caught' off a no-ball. West Indies' captain Clive Lloyd was named Man of the Match and had the honour of receiving the World Cup from HRH Prince Philip.

Pakistan v New Zealand — 1976

Jinnah Park, Sialkot, 16 October 1976
New Zealand won by 1 run
New Zealand 8-198 (35 overs) (G.M Turner 67, G.P. Howarth 43)
Pakistan 9-197 (35 overs) (Javed Miandad 47, Mushtaq Mohammad 46)

New Zealand held on to beat Pakistan before a frenzied crowd at Sialkot in the first one-day international in Pakistan and the first by the narrowest of margins — one run.

New Zealand captain Glenn Turner won the toss for the first time on tour and opted to bat. The visitors lost two wickets with the score on 48, but Turner and Geoff Howarth consolidated with an 87-run partnership against some loose Pakistani bowling. The rest of the New Zealand contributions were patchy, although Lance Cairns' quick-fire 24 boosted the total to 8 for 198 from 35 eight-ball overs.

Pakistan's openers struggled against a tight New Zealand bowling attack and Majid Khan (20) fell trying to force the pace. Sadiq Mohammad (17) and Zaheer Abbas (23) also succumbed to the need for quick runs, before Javed Miandad (47) and Mushtaq Mohammad (46) put Pakistan back on course. Despite Mushtaq's dismissal, Miandad continued to take toll of the bowling, although with only six overs left Pakistan still needed 56 runs with six wickets in hand. Pakistan was scoring runs but losing wickets in the process and was 7 for 191 with an over remaining. Sarfraz Nawaz was run out the second ball, while two singles and two leg byes reduced the deficit to four. Asif Masood was then run out, before Wasim Bari's effort on the last ball yielded only two to give New Zealand the narrowest of victories.

England v Australia — 1977

The Oval, London, 6 June 1977
Australia won by 2 wickets
England 242 (54.2 overs) (D.L. Amiss 108, J.M. Brearley 78, L.S. Pascoe 3-44)
Australia 8-246 (53.2 overs) (G.S. Chappell 125*, R.D. Robinson 70)

Australia survived driving rain and a fierce hailstorm to defeat England by two wickets in the third Prudential Cup match of the 1977 Ashes tour.

Australian captain Greg Chappell won the toss and sent England in to bat, but Mike Brearley and Dennis Amiss took command, moving the score to 136 at lunch without loss. Shortly after, however, with the score on 161, Brearley (78) was stumped from the bowling of leg spinner Kerry O'Keeffe to trigger a collapse, with all 10 wickets falling in just an hour and a half. Amiss went on to make 108, but received little support, with Chris Old the next best on 20. The Australian bowling was patchy

Australia v England - 1970/71

Melbourne Cricket Ground, 5 January 1971

Result: Australia won by 5 wickets
Umpires: T.F. Brooks and L.P. Rowan

Toss: Australia
Man of the match: J.H. Edrich

England innings			Runs	Balls
G. Boycott	c Lawry	b Thomson	8	37
J.H. Edrich	c Walters	b Mallett	82	119
K.W.R. Fletcher	c G.S. Chappell	b Mallett	24	47
B.L. D'Oliveira	run out		17	16
J.H. Hampshire	c McKenzie	b Mallett	10	13
M.C. Cowdrey	c Marsh	b Stackpole	1	5
*R. Illingworth		b Stackpole	1	7
†A.P.E. Knott		b McKenzie	24	31
J.A. Snow		b Stackpole	2	16
K. Shuttleworth	c Redpath	b McKenzie	7	19
P. Lever	not out		4	6
Extras	(b 1, lb 9)		10	
Total	**(all out, 39.4 overs)**		**190**	

FoW: 1-21, 2-87, 3-124, 4-144, 5-148, 6-152, 7-156, 8-171, 9-183, 10-190

Bowling	O	M	R	W
McKenzie	7.4	0	22	2
Thomson	8	2	22	1
Connolly	8	0	62	0
Mallett	8	1	34	3
Stackpole	8	0	40	3

Australia innings			Runs	Balls
*W.M. Lawry	c Knott	b Illingworth	27	49
K.R. Stackpole	c & b Shuttleworth		13	15
I.M. Chappell	st Knott	b Illingworth	60	103
K.D. Walters	c Knott	b D'Oliveira	41	51
I.R. Redpath		b Illingworth	12	14
G.S. Chappell	not out		22	29
†R.W. Marsh	not out		10	18
Extras	(lb 4, w 1, nb 1)		6	
Total	**(5 wickets, 34.6 overs)**		**191**	

DNB: A.A. Mallett, G.D. McKenzie, A.N. Connolly, A.L. Thomson

FoW: 1-19, 2-51, 3-117, 4-158, 5-165

Bowling	O	M	R	W
Snow	8	0	38	0
Shuttleworth	7	0	29	1
Lever	5.6	0	30	0
Illingworth	8	1	50	3
D'Oliveira	6	1	38	1

Prudential World Cup, 1975, Final   Australia v West Indies

Lord's, London, 21 June 1975

Result: West Indies won by 17 runs
Umpires: H.D. Bird and T.W. Spencer

Toss: Australia
Man of the match: C.H. Lloyd

West Indies innings

			Runs	Balls
R.C. Fredericks	hit wicket	b Lillee	7	13
C.G. Greenidge	c Marsh	b Thomson	13	61
A.I. Kallicharran	c Marsh	b Gilmour	12	18
R.B. Kanhai		b Gilmour	55	105
*C.H. Lloyd	c Marsh	b Gilmour	102	85
I.V.A. Richards		b Gilmour	5	11
K.D. Boyce	c G.S. Chappell	b Thomson	34	37
B.D. Julien	not out		26	37
†D.L. Murray	c & b Gilmour		14	10
V.A. Holder	not out		6	2
Extras	(lb 6, nb 11)		17	
Total	**(8 wickets, 60 overs)**		**291**	
DNB:	A.M.E. Roberts			

FoW: 1-12, 2-27, 3-50, 4-199, 5-206, 6-209, 7-261, 8-285

Bowling	O	M	R	W
Lillee	12	1	55	1
Gilmour	12	2	48	5
Thomson	12	1	44	2
Walker	12	1	71	0
G.S. Chappell	7	0	33	0
Walters	5	0	23	0

Australia innings

			Runs	Balls
A. Turner	run out (Richards)		40	24
R.B. McCosker	c Kallicharran	b Boyce	7	54
*I.M. Chappell	run out (Richards/Lloyd)		62	93
G.S. Chappell	run out (Richards)		15	23
K.D. Walters		b Lloyd	35	51
†R.W. Marsh		b Boyce	11	24
R. Edwards	c Fredericks	b Boyce	28	37
G.J. Gilmour	c Kanhai	b Boyce	14	11
M.H.N. Walker	run out (Kallicharran/Holder)		7	9
J.R. Thomson	run out (Kallicharran/Murray)		21	21
D.K. Lillee	not out		16	19
Extras	(b 2, lb 9, nb 7)		18	
Total	**(all out, 58.4 overs)**		**274**	

FoW: 1-25, 2-81, 3-115, 4-162, 5-170, 6-195, 7-221, 8-231, 9-233, 10-274

Bowling	O	M	R	W
Julien	12	0	58	0
Roberts	11	1	45	0
Boyce	12	0	50	4
Holder	11.4	1	65	0
Lloyd	12	1	38	1

and the fielding inconsistent, with England their own worst enemy as they threw wickets away in the chase for quick runs.

In reply, Australia lost opener Rick McCosker with the score on 33, but Greg Chappell and Richie Robinson had taken the score to 1 for 88 when the heavens opened up. Most of the crowd left, believing that there would be no further play, but organisers were so keen to avoid playing on the following day (Queen's Silver Jubilee Day), that when the clouds cleared an hour later, play resumed. Robinson and Chappell put on 148 for the second wicket, before the rangy Victorian fell for 70 to a catch by Brearley. With Australia needing 62 runs from 14 overs, the light began to fade and Kim Hughes, Doug Walters and David Hookes went in quick succession. The rain returned, followed by hail, but the match continued under these farcical conditions. However, Chappell remained resolute, scoring 125 not out in 137 balls to lead the Australians to victory through the dark and damp.

India v Pakistan — 1978

Ayub National Stadium, Quetta, 1 October 1978
India won by 4 runs
India 7-170 (40 overs) (M. Amarnath 51, S. Amarnath 37, Sarfraz Nawaz 3-34)
Pakistan 8-166 (40 overs) (Majid Khan 50)

India snatched a narrow four-run victory over Pakistan, the first time the two countries had met since the 1960/61 Test series.

The Indians lost Chetan Chauhan to be 1 for 7, but they got back on track after Anshuman Gaekwad (16) and Surinder Amarnath (37 from 41 balls) added 53 for the second wicket. A collapse then saw the home side slump to 4 for 72 before Dilip Vengsarkar (34) and Mohinder Amarnath (51) rebuilt the innings with 76 for the fifth wicket. In the end, India was restricted to 7 for 170, with Sarfraz Narwaz (3 for 34) the pick of the Pakistan bowlers.

Pakistan appeared set for victory in their run chase, but a restrictive fielding strategy by Indian captain Bishen Bedi, and tight bowling by Kapil Dev and Venkat, made the task difficult. When Mohinder Amarnath captured the wicket of Majid Khan (50 from 64 balls), and then Zaheer Abbas (26) a short time later, the home side were in trouble. At 8 for 165, Sarfraz Nawaz needed to hit a six from the last delivery to win the match, but his sweep shot yielded only one run to give the Indians victory.

England v West Indies — 1979

Lord's, London , 23 June 1979
West Indies won by 92 runs
West Indies 9-286 (51 overs) (I.V.A. Richards 138, C.L. King 86)
England 194 (60 overs) (J.M. Brearley 64, G. Boycott 57, J. Garner 5-38)

The West Indies retained their World Cup title with an impressive 92-run victory over England in the final at Lord's.

England captain Mike Brearley sent the West Indies in to bat on a pitch that gave the England quicks a deal of assistance. England had some degree of success too, before Collis King joined Viv Richards with the score at 4 for 99. The pair added 139 in 121 balls, with King scoring 86 from 66 deliveries as they launched an assault on the bowling of part-timers Geoff Boycott, Graham Gooch and Wayne Larkins. Richards finished on 138 not out off 157 balls as the West Indies tail fell away, but the final score of 9 for 286 was always going to be tough.

Geoff Boycott (57) and Mike Brearley (64) put on 129 runs for the first wicket, but the pace was slow and both were dismissed trying to slog. England began to take chances as the run-rate grew above seven an over, and the desperation led to calamity. From 2 for 183, England lost their last eight wickets for just 11 runs, as Joel Garner ripped the heart out of the England line-up. Garner took five wickets for four runs in eleven balls, and was twice on a hat-trick, as the English challenge crumbled. Richards was named Man of the Match, after making what remains the highest score in a World up Final.

Australia v West Indies — 1979

Sydney Cricket Ground, 27 November 1979
Australia won by 5 wickets
West Indies 193 (49.3 overs) (A.I. Kallicharran 49, L.S. Pascoe 4-29, A.R. Border 3-36)
Australia 5-196 (47.1 overs) (G.S. Chappell 74* K.J. Hughes 52)

Both sides replaced the traditional whites with new clothing featuring coloured striped sleeves, as the feuding World Series Cricket and Australian Cricket Boards were reunited in the first official one-day international under lights.

The West Indies lost early wickets to Dennis Lillee, but recovered to reach 2 for 89. However, after Border bowled Haynes to capture the first of his three wickets, the visitors struggled to regain any momentum. Alvin Kallicharran (49 from 94 balls) was the pick of the West Indies batting but he just failed to reach his half-century, as Len Pascoe cleaned up the lower order with his second spell to finish with four wickets. The West Indies eventually set the Australians 194 for victory.

Australia was in trouble at 3 for 52, but former captain Kim Hughes (52) joined current skipper Greg Chappell in putting on 92 runs in 68 minutes for the fourth wicket. There was a brief stutter, before Chappell (74* from 100 balls) and Rod Marsh (18* from 22 balls) added 52 to see the Australians to victory. Chappell rightfully won the Man of the Match for his dominant batting display.

England v West Indies — 1979

Sydney Cricket Ground, 28 November 1979
England won by 2 runs (revised target)
England 8-211 (50 overs) (P. Willey 58* D.W. Randall 49,
D.I. Gower 44, J. Garner 3-31)
West Indies 196 (47 overs) (L.G. Rowe 60, A.I. Kallicharran 44,
D.L. Underwood 4-44)

Note: England's score was adjusted to 6 for 198, after rain prevented the West Indies from receiving their full complement of 50 overs.

England survived a scare in this rain-shortened replay of the World Cup Final, eventually winning by just two runs after the West Indies lost batting time due to rain. Controversial field settings by England captain Mike Brearley in the last overs of the match were the catalyst for changes to one-day international rules.

England's openers got off to a confident start, reaching 79 before Mike Brearley (25) fell to a reflex catch by Gordon Greenidge. Fellow opener Derek Randall (49) went shortly after, before David Gower (44) and then Peter Willey (58 not out) put the innings back on track, as the West Indies' fielding fell below their usual standard. Still, England frittered away some of their early advantage, falling from 3 for 160 to finish with 8 for 211.

The West Indies lost Desmond Haynes early, but Greenidge (42) and Lawrence Rowe (60) put them back in a strong position. When the rains came, they were well placed at 2 for 122, however after the resumption the middle order panicked and while Alvin Kallicharran scored 44, he saw five wickets fall at the other end. The time lost had reduced the target to 199 from 47 overs and the Windies seemed unable to adjust to the situation. With the West Indies needing three runs from the last ball, England captain Mike Brearley pushed all his fielders, including wicket-keeper David Bairstow, back onto the fence to deny the victory. Amid some confusion, Colin Croft was bowled by Ian Botham, going for glory.

Australia v New Zealand — 1981

Sydney Cricket Ground, 13 January 1981
New Zealand won by 1 run
New Zealand 8-220 (50 overs) (J. G. Wright 78,
L.S. Pascoe 3-37)
Australia 7-219 (50 overs) (K.D. Walters 50*, R.W Marsh 49)

With a run-out off the last ball, New Zealand sealed a remarkable victory over Australia.

New Zealand had recovered from a shaky start, as opener John Wright anchored the innings with a determined 78 from 135 deliveries. He received good support from Geoff Howarth (20), John Parker (23) and Ian Smith (23*), who launched a late attack on the otherwise economical Dennis Lillee.

Australia lost wickets regularly to be 5 for 123 with only 18 overs remaining, before Rod Marsh teamed up with Doug Walters to rescue the innings. A young fan came close to changing the result of the match after he jumped the fence to field a Walters' pull shot as it headed towards the mid-wicket boundary. Bruce Edgar raced to intercept, but was forced to back off, before the umpire ruled that he would have stopped the ball and awarded only three runs. The tension was momentarily broken when, to the amusement of most, Rod Marsh broke his bat as he attempted a lofted drive off the bowling of Lance Cairns. When Marsh (49) was eventually out, the Australians needed 20 runs from as many balls, but tight bowling saw the pressure mount with Shaun Graf run out attempting a second to force the tie on the last ball. John Wright was named Man of the Match.

Australia v New Zealand — 1981

Melbourne Cricket Ground, 1 February 1981
Australia won by 6 runs
Australia 4-235 (50 overs) (G.S. Chappell 90, G.M. Wood 72)
New Zealand 8-229 (50 overs) (B.A. Edgar 102*,
J.G. Wright 42, G.S. Chappell 3-43)

Australia defeated New Zealand by six runs in a match that will always be remembered as the game of the 'underarm delivery'.

Australia lost Allan Border early, but recovered when Greg Chappell and Graeme Wood scored 145 for the second wicket. However the partnership was marred by controversy over a disputed catch by Martin Snedden when Chappell was on 58. Television replays indicated the Australian captain was out, but he was given the benefit of the doubt by the umpires and went on to make 90 from 122 balls before he was caught off Snedden's bowling. Australia eventually finished on 4 for 235.

New Zealand started confidently and looked in good shape after an opening stand of 85 by John Wright and Bruce Edgar. Edgar was the backbone of the innings, but wickets began to fall regularly and the task was becoming more difficult. With the score on 6 for 221 and one over remaining, Greg Chappell gave his brother Trevor the job of keeping the New Zealanders at bay. Richard Hadlee hit the first ball for four before falling LBW, then keeper Ian Smith made consecutive twos before being bowled. Enter Brian McKechnie, one ball to go, six runs to tie. Much to the dismay of some of his team-mates, Greg Chappell then gave the instruction for Trevor to bowl underarm, a delivery not then banned under tournament conditions. McKechnie blocked the delivery and then threw his bat away in disgust, as New Zealand captain Geoff Howarth raced onto the field to remonstrate with the umpires. Controversy reigned on both sides of the Tasman, with politicians wading into the fray. However the ball was legal and stood, leaving the Australians as victors, but not victorious.

Prudential World Cup, 1979, Final   England v West Indies

Lord's, London   23 June 1979

Result: West Indies won by 92 runs   Toss: England
Umpires: H.D. Bird and B.J. Meyer   Man of the match: I.V.A. Richards

West Indies innings			Runs	Balls
C.G. Greenidge	run out (Randall)		9	31
D.L. Haynes	c Hendrick	b Old	20	27
I.V.A. Richards	not out		138	157
A.I. Kallicharran		b Hendrick	4	17
*C.H. Lloyd	c & b Old		13	33
C.L. King	c Randall	b Edmonds	86	66
†D.L. Murray	c Gower	b Edmonds	5	9
A.M.E. Roberts	c Brearley	b Hendrick	0	7
J. Garner	c Taylor	b Botham	0	5
M.A. Holding		b Botham	0	6
C.E.H. Croft	not out		0	2
Extras	(b 1, lb 10)		11	
Total	**(9 wickets, 60 overs)**		**286**	

FoW: 1-22, 2-36, 3-55, 4-99, 5-238, 6-252, 7-258, 8-260, 9-272

Bowling	O	M	R	W
Botham	12	2	44	2
Hendrick	12	2	50	2
Old	12	0	55	2
Boycott	6	0	38	0
Edmonds	12	2	40	2
Gooch	4	0	27	0
Larkins	2	0	21	0

England innings			Runs	Balls
*J.M. Brearley	c King	b Holding	64	130
G. Boycott	c Kallicharran	b Holding	57	105
D.W. Randall		b Croft	15	22
G.A. Gooch		b Garner	32	28
D.I. Gower		b Garner	0	4
I.T. Botham	c Richards	b Croft	4	3
W. Larkins		b Garner	0	1
P.H. Edmonds	not out		5	8
C.M. Old		b Garner	0	2
†R.W. Taylor	c Murray	b Garner	0	1
M. Hendrick		b Croft	0	5
Extras	(lb 12, w 2, nb 3)		17	
Total	**(all out, 51 overs)**		**194**	

FoW: 1-129, 2-135, 3-183, 4-183, 5-186, 6-186, 7-192, 8-192, 9-194, 10-194

Bowling	O	M	R	W
Roberts	9	2	33	0
Holding	8	1	16	2
Croft	10	1	42	3
Garner	11	0	38	5
Richards	10	0	35	0
King	3	0	13	0

Benson & Hedges World Series Cup, 1980/81   Australia v New Zealand

Melbourne Cricket Ground, 1 February 1981

Result: Australia won by 6 runs   Toss: Australia
Umpires: P.M. Cronin, D.G. Weser

Australia innings

			Runs	Balls
A.R. Border	c Parker	b Hadlee	5	8
G.M. Wood		b McEwan	72	114
*G.S. Chappell	c Edgar	b Snedden	90	122
M.F. Kent	c Edgar	b Snedden	33	38
†R.W. Marsh	not out		18	13
K.D. Walters	not out		6	5
Extras	(b 8, lb 3)		11	
Total	**(4 wickets, 50 overs)**		**235**	

DNB: K.J. Hughes, G.R. Beard, T.M. Chappell, D.K. Lillee, M.H.N. Walker

FoW: 1-8, 2-153, 3-199, 4-215

Bowling	O	M	R	W
Hadlee	10	0	41	1
Snedden	10	0	52	2
Cairns	10	0	34	0
McKechnie	10	0	54	0
McEwan	7	1	31	1
Howarth	3	0	12	0

New Zealand Innings

			Runs	Balls
J.G. Wright	c Kent	b G.S. Chappell	42	81
B.A. Edgar	not out		102	141
*G.P.J. Howarth	c Marsh	b G.S. Chappell	18	20
B.L. Cairns		b Beard	12	10
M.G. Burgess	c T.M. Chappell	b G.S. Chappell	2	5
P.E. McEwan	c Wood	b Beard	11	18
J.M. Parker	c T.M. Chappell	b Lillee	24	19
R.J. Hadlee	lbw	b T.M. Chappell	4	2
†I.D.S. Smith		b T.M. Chappell	4	3
B.J. McKechnie	not out		0	1
Extras	(lb 10)		10	
Total	**(8 wickets, 50 overs)**		**229**	

FoW: 1-85, 2-117, 3-136, 4-139, 5-172, 6-221, 7-225, 8-229

Bowling	O	M	R	W
Lillee	10	1	34	1
Walker	10	0	35	0
Beard	10	0	50	2
G.S. Chappell	10	0	43	3
T.M. Chappell	10	0	57	2

England v Australia — 1981

Edgbaston, Birmingham, 6 June 1981
Australia won by 2 runs
Australia 8-249 (55 overs) (G.N. Yallop 63, G.M. Wood 55)
England 247 (54.5 overs) (M.W. Gatting 96, J.D. Love 43,
D.K. Lillee 3-36, G.F. Lawson 3-42)

Australia held on for a thrilling two-run victory in their Prudential Trophy match against England, ensuring that the best-of-three series went down to the final match at Headingly, two days later.

Australia began slowly, losing Trevor Chappell in the second over, before Graeme Wood and Graham Yallop provided a steady 86-run partnership in trying conditions. With the fall of Wood (55), Yallop continued the good work with captain Kim Hughes (34), adding 64 for the third wicket before wickets began to tumble. Pace bowler Geoff Lawson contributed a valuable 29 not out from only 26 balls, including consecutive sixes, as the Australians compiled a respectable score of 8 for 249 from their 55 overs.

England was in trouble early, losing Graham Gooch, Geoff Boycott and David Gower with only 36 runs on the board. The scenario improved when Mike Gatting celebrated his twenty-fourth birthday with a courageous innings to rescue the England cause. After good partnerships of 75 with Jim Love (43), 66 with Peter Willey (37) and 47 with Ian Botham (24), England started their last over needing six runs with three wickets in hand. However, Robin Jackman was run out off the first ball in his desperation to get Gatting on strike, and then Gatting holed out the next ball to a diving catch by Geoff Lawson in the deep. Runs from the next two balls gave England some respite, but when Mike Hendrick's big drive found the edge and was caught behind, the Australians had brought off a remarkable victory.

Pakistan v West Indies — 1981

Adelaide Oval, 5 December 1981
Pakistan won by 8 runs
Pakistan 140 (49 overs) (Zaheer Abbas 46, Sarfraz Nawaz 34*)
West Indies 132 (38.5 overs) (S.F.A.F. Bacchus 37,
Wasim Raja 4-25)

Pakistan recorded a stunning eight-run victory, after setting the West Indies a seemingly easy target of only 140 runs.

Pakistan slumped to 7 for 68 before Zaheer Abbas found someone willing to stay with him. Abbas and bowler Sarfraz Nawaz added 57 in 46 minutes to give some respectability to a Pakistan innings that had wilted before a tight West Indian pace barrage. Still, 141 runs did not seem nearly enough, despite the fact that the West Indians had gone into the match with only five recognised batsmen.

When Gordon Greenidge, Desmond Haynes and Viv Richards went cheaply, the Pakistanis might have given themselves some hope, but Faoud Bacchus (37) and Clive Lloyd (28) appeared to turn the innings around with a partnership of 47. However, part-time leg spinner Wasim Raja took four wickets to tear through a fragile West Indian middle order and capture a remarkable Pakistan victory.

Sri Lanka v England — 1982

Sinhalese Sports Club, Colombo, 14 February 1982
Sri Lanka won by 3 runs
Sri Lanka 7-215 (45 overs) (S. Wettimuny 86*,
A. Ranatunga 42)
England 212 (44.5 overs) (G.A Gooch 74, K.W.R. Fletcher 38)

Sri Lanka gained an exciting three-run victory over England before a capacity crowd of 20,000 at the Sinhalese Sports Club in Colombo. The match was the second of two one-day internationals that preceded Sri Lanka's debut as a Test playing nation, coming only three days before their first Test against England.

Sri Lanka floundered early, losing 2 for 5 before Sidath Wettimuny was joined by dashing strokemaker Roy Dias. However, with the score on 43, Dias swayed to avoid a short ball from John Lever, losing his helmet onto his stumps. Eighteen-year-old Arjuna Ranatunga then joined Wettimuny in a crucial partnership of 87, before the youngster was run out trying to beat a throw from Chris Tavare. Wettimuny then took over the innings, guiding the lower order to a respectable total and batting through the innings for 86 not out from 109 balls.

Although the scoring was slow, Gooch and Cook looked in complete command as they took the score past the century without loss. However, when both were stumped shortly after off the bowling of Ajit De Silva, and were then quickly joined in the pavilion by David Gower, England's task looked a little tougher. With 10 overs to go England still needed 74 to win, although they had seven wickets in hand. The light was beginning to fade as Keith Fletcher and Mike Gatting plundered some easy runs from the spinners to get England to 5 for 202 with two overs remaining. However, when Gatting and then Fletcher were run out from the first three balls of the next over, England lost their way completely. The visitors lost five wickets for nine runs in eleven balls, four of them to run-outs, to see Sri Lanka victors by three runs.

Pakistan v Sri Lanka — 1982

Gaddafi Stadium, Lahore, 29 March 1982
Sri Lanka won on a superior run rate
Pakistan 4-239 (40 overs) (Zaheer Abbas 123, Haroon
Rashid 63*)
Sri Lanka 4-227 (33 overs) (R.L. Dias 81, L.R.D. Mendis 52)

Sri Lanka beat Pakistan on a faster run-rate in a run-fest at Lahore in the second of a three-match series between the two sides in Pakistan.

Pakistan was sent in by Sri Lanka and lost both openers and captain Javed Miandad cheaply on an easy-paced wicket. However, Zaheer Abbas survived some early good fortune to completely dominate the Pakistan innings. He was joined by Haroon Rashid (63 not out) and the pair added 123 runs for the fourth wicket in only 18 overs. Abbas was eventually out with the total on 215, having made 123, hitting 3 sixes and 15 fours from a tidy, if not threatening, Sri Lankan attack.

Imran Khan and Sikander Bakht gave Pakistan a good start, bowling tight early, but when their spells ended the Sri Lankan run-rate exploded. Roy Dias clubbed 81 from 59 balls, and together with Duleep Mendis (52) put on 73 in only 10 overs. Ranjan Madugalle (36 not out) continued to plunder quick runs, and the scoring wasn't stemmed by the re-introduction of Imran and Sikander. Sri Lanka scored 21 runs for their last two overs before bad light stopped play, needing only 13 runs from the remaining seven overs. In the end, the Sri Lankan scoring rate of 6.87 runs per over was too hot for Pakistan to handle.

England v New Zealand — 1983

Adelaide Oval, 29 January 1983
New Zealand won by 4 wickets
England 5-296 (50 overs) (D.I. Gower 109, I.T. Botham 65, T.E. Jesty 52*)
New Zealand 6-297 (48.5 overs) (R.J. Hadlee 79, J.J. Crowe 50, B.L. Cairns 49, J.V. Coney 47*)

England lost to New Zealand by four wickets, despite scoring 296 runs and both teams breaking the then record for the highest total in the Australian World Series Cup competition.

Ian Botham set the standard for the match, chancing his arm for 65 runs off 54 balls, before falling to Ewen Chatfield. David Gower then took over, scoring an elegant 109 from only 85 balls and putting on 83 runs with Derek Randall (31) and 74 with Trevor Jesty (52 not out). In the end, England's total of 5 for 296 passed the previous competition record of 3 for 289 scored by Australia against New Zealand in the 1980/81 season. Richard Hadlee (0 for 36) was the pick of the New Zealand bowlers, with Martin Snedden, Gary Troup and Chatfield all going for more than one run a ball.

New Zealand's run chase was made even tougher after they had lost Glenn Turner and Geoff Howarth with 10 overs gone and only 33 runs on the board. Poor fielding by England allowed the Kiwis back into the match, as John Wright (30) and Jeff Crowe (50) put on 63 runs for the third wicket in 12 overs and Lance Cairns (49 from 24 balls) joined Crowe to plunder 70 in only eight overs for the fourth wicket. However when Crowe and Cairns were both dismissed with the score on 166, the pendulum had swung back to England. Jeremy Coney (47 not out) and Richard Hadlee (79) had other ideas

and the pair punished England, scoring 121 in only 18 overs to ensure a remarkable New Zealand victory. Coney was left to hit the winning runs and Hadlee was rewarded with Man of the Match.

Australia v Zimbabwe — 1983

Trent Bridge, Nottingham, 9 June 1983
Zimbabwe won by 13 runs
Zimbabwe 6-239 (60 overs) (D.A.G. Fletcher 69, I.P. Butchart 34*)
Australia 7-226 (60 overs) (K.C. Wessels 76, R.W. Marsh 50, D.A.G. Fletcher 4-42)

In their very first one-day international, Zimbabwe brought off one of the biggest upsets in international cricket after defeating Australia by 13 runs on the opening day of the 1983 World Cup.

After being sent in to bat, Zimbabwe struggled to get any early momentum into their innings and when their main run-scorer Dave Houghton was dismissed for a duck, they had slumped to be 5 for 94. Then the Zimbabwean captain Duncan Fletcher took charge, adding a further 70 runs in 15 overs with Kevin Curran (27) and 75 in 12 overs with Iain Butchart (34 not out). Fletcher went on to make 69 not out, and the score of 6 for 239 appeared to be at least a challenge for the Australians.

Graeme Wood and Kepler Wessels got Australia off to a steady start, adding 61, but the innings lacked urgency and the required run-rate began to grow. When Graham Yallop was out to a freak catch on the boundary by Andy Pycroft to make the score 5 for 138, the target had grown to nearly eight an over and the unthinkable looked likely. Rod Marsh (50 not out) took up the challenge, adding 50 with Rodney Hogg (19 not out) for the eighth wicket, but the task proved to be too great and the tournament minnows celebrated a win over one of cricket's big fish. Fletcher took 4 for 42, including Wood, Kim Hughes, David Hookes and Yallop, to go with his half-century to win the Man of the Match award.

India v Zimbabwe — 1983

The Nevill Ground, Tunbridge Wells, 18 June 1983
India won by 31 runs
India 8-266 (60 overs) (Kapil Dev 175*, P.W.E. Rawson 3-47, K.M. Curran 3-65)
Zimbabwe 235 (57 overs) (K.M. Curran 73, R.D. Brown 35, Madan Lal 3-42)

India, on the back of an astonishing innings from Kapil Dev, managed a 31-run victory over Zimbabwe at the 1983 World Cup.

Zimbabwe looked set to add to their upset win over Australia only eight days earlier, when India, after winning the toss, slumped to 4 for 9 after 10 overs. Kapil Dev then strode to the wicket, determined to show the way the game should be played. While the Indian score improved, 8 for 140 was clearly still not enough as Dev

Prudential World Cup, 1983, Final India v West Indies

Lord's, London, 25 June 1983

Result: India won by 43 runs
Umpires: H.D. Bird and B.J. Meyer

Toss: West Indies
Man of the match: M. Amarnath

India innings			Runs	Balls
S.M. Gavaskar	c Dujon	b Roberts	2	12
K. Srikkanth	lbw	b Marshall	38	57
M. Amarnath		b Holding	26	80
Yashpal Sharma	c sub (A.L. Logie)	b Gomes	11	32
S.M. Patil	c Gomes	b Garner	27	29
*Kapil Dev	c Holding	b Gomes	15	8
K.B.J. Azad	c Garner	b Roberts	0	3
R.M.H. Binny	c Garner	b Roberts	2	8
Madan Lal		b Marshall	17	27
†S.M.H Kirmani		b Holding	14	45
B.S. Sandhu	not out		11	30
Extras	(b 5, lb 5, w 9, nb 1)		20	
Total	**(all out, 54.4 overs)**		**183**	

FoW: 1-2, 2-59, 3-90, 4-92, 5-110, 6-111, 7-130, 8-153, 9-161, 10-183

Bowling	O	M	R	W
Roberts	10	3	32	3
Garner	12	4	24	1
Marshall	11	1	24	2
Holding	9.4	2	26	2
Gomes	11	1	49	2
Richards	1	0	8	0

West Indies innings			Runs	Balls
C.G. Greenidge		b Sandhu	1	12
D.L. Haynes	c Binny	b Madan Lal	13	33
I.V.A. Richards	c Kapil Dev	b Madan Lal	33	28
*C.H. Lloyd	c Kapil Dev	b Binny	8	17
H.A. Gomes	c Gavaskar	b Madan Lal	5	16
S.F.A.F. Bacchus	c Kirmani	b Sandhu	8	25
†P.J.L. Dujon		b Amarnath	25	73
M.D. Marshall	c Gavaskar	b Amarnath	18	51
A.M.E. Roberts	lbw	b Kapil Dev	4	14
J. Garner	not out		5	19
M.A. Holding	lbw	b Amarnath	6	24
Extras	(lb 4, w 10)		14	
Total	**(all out, 52 overs)**		**140**	

FoW: 1-5, 2-50, 3-57, 4-66, 5-66, 6-76, 7-119, 8-124, 9-126, 10-140

Bowling	O	M	R	W
Kapil Dev	11	4	21	1
Sandhu	9	1	32	2
Madan Lal	12	2	31	3
Binny	10	1	23	1
Amarnath	7	0	12	3
Azad	3	0	7	0

Benson & Hedges World Series Cup, 1984   Australia v West Indies

Melbourne Cricket Ground, 11 February 1984

Result: Match tied   Toss: West Indies
Umpires: R.A. French, M.W. Johnson

West Indies innings			Runs	Balls
D.L. Haynes	c Hogan	b Border	18	53
R.S. Gabriel	c Smith	b Rackemann	19	35
R.B. Richardson	c Marsh	b Lawson	43	70
I.V.A. Richards	c Hogan	b Wessels	59	70
*C.H. Lloyd	c Hogg	b Wessels	11	19
H.A. Gomes	not out		25	34
†P.J.L. Dujon	not out		33	24
Extras	(lb 10, w 3, nb 1)		14	
Total	**(5 wickets, 50 overs)**		**222**	
DNB:	M.D. Marshall, E.A.E. Baptiste, M.A. Holding, J. Garner			

FoW: 1-33, 2-54, 3-116, 4-137, 5-173

Bowling	O	M	R	W
Lawson	10	4	26	1
Rackemann	10	4	52	1
Hogg	9	1	40	0
Hogan	10	2	31	0
Border	6	0	34	1
Wessels	5	0	29	2

Australia innings			Runs	Balls
K.C. Wessels	c Marshall	b Holding	77	109
D.M. Jones	c Dujon	b Holding	12	29
*K.J. Hughes	LBW	b Marshall	53	89
A.R. Border	c Dujon	b Garner	14	31
G.M. Ritchie	c Dujon	b Garner	4	6
†R.W. Marsh		b Garner	16	13
G.F. Lawson	not out		21	19
T.G. Hogan	c sub (A.L. Logie)	b Holding	6	8
R.M. Hogg	run out		3	3
C.G. Rackemann	run out		1	1
Extras	(b 2, lb 8, w 1, nb 4)		15	
Total	**(9 wickets, 50 overs)**		**222**	
DNB:	S.B. Smith			

FoW: 1-23, 2-132, 3-161, 4-169, 5-176, 6-192, 7-209, 8-218, 9-222

Bowling	O	M	R	W
Holding	10	0	39	3
Garner	10	1	39	3
Baptiste	10	0	44	0
Marshall	10	1	27	1
Richards	3	0	26	0
Gomes	7	0	37	0

was joined by wicket-keeper Syed Kirmani. The pair added 126 in the last 16 overs, Dev making 175 not out and taking only 72 balls to make India's first century in a one-day international. The Indian captain hit 16 fours and 6 sixes and batted for 181 minutes, turning the game around single-handedly in the highest score in a one-day international to date.

Undaunted by Dev's onslaught, Zimbabwe took up the challenge, although they steadily lost wickets to the tight bowling of the Indian medium-pacers. A sparkling late-order innings by Kevin Curran (73) gave them some chance of victory, but when he was finally out in the fifty-sixth over, the Indians could relax, safe in the knowledge that their captain's knock had not been in vain.

India v West Indies — 1983

Lord's, London, 25 June 1983
India won by 43 runs
India 183 (54.4 overs) (K. Srikkanth 38, S.M. Patil 27, A.M.E. Roberts 3-32)
West Indies 140 (52 overs) (I.V.A. Richards 33, P.J. Dujon 25, S. Madan Lal 3-31, M. Amarnath 3-12)

India turned around their earlier patchy form of the tournament to pull off a stunning victory against the West Indies by 43 runs in the final of the 1983 World Cup and thus deny them the hat-trick of finals wins.

Despite losing Sunil Gavaskar for 2, the Indians built a solid innings, with eight of their players making double figures. However the Indian batsmen struggled to make a really big score against the West Indian pace quartet of Marshall, Garner, Holding and Roberts, with Kris Srikkanth (38), Mohinder Amarnath (26) and Sandeep Patil (27) the most proficient. Andy Roberts was the pick of the bowlers, but the other three all proved hard to get away in a display of controlled hostility.

The West Indian innings did not start well either, with Gordon Greenidge bowled without playing a shot for one. Desmond Haynes and Viv Richards then took the score along to 50, but when both went shortly after to Madan Lal, the tournament favourites quickly collapsed to be 6 for 76. Jeff Dujon and Malcolm Marshall arrested the tide, putting on 43 for the seventh wicket, but Mohinder Amarnath took the last three to mop up the tail. Amarnath was named Man of the Match for his fine all-round display.

Pakistan v West Indies — 1984

Adelaide Oval, 28 January 1984
West Indies won by 1 wicket
Pakistan 8-177 (50 overs) (Wasim Raja 46, Qasim Omar 26, M.D. Marshall 3-28)
West Indies 9-180 (49.1 overs) (M.D. Marshall 56*, Wasim Raja 3-33, Abdul Qadir 3-34)

The West Indies defeated Pakistan by one wicket, in a match where the innings of both sides were rescued by rearguard actions.

The Pakistan team was nearing the end of a frustrating summer and it showed when they struggled to 4 for 59 after Mudassar Nazar (18) and Mansoor Akhtar (20) gave them a 40-run opening stand. A 68-run partnership in only 49 minutes by Qasim Omar (26) and Wasim Raja (46) got them back on track, only to see the innings stutter again as they lost four wickets for only nine runs. Ijaz Faqih and Rashid Khan gave them some hope with an unbroken stand of 41 for the ninth wicket, Pakistan finishing with 8 for 177.

As Pakistan was still without the injured Imran Khan, the West Indies' task looked simple, but their top order lost their way against a tight, if not threatening, attack. Champion leg spinner Abdul Qadir shrugged off some of his recent disappointing form, capturing Richard Gabriel, Viv Richards and Jeff Dujon, while he received solid support from Wasim Raja and Mudassar Nazar. The West Indies limped to 7 for 92, before Malcolm Marshall and Eldine Baptiste (24) added 53 runs for the eighth wicket. Marshall (56 not out) was again the major partner as he and Wayne Daniel put on 21 for the last wicket to see the Windies through to victory. Marshall was the clear choice for Man of the Match.

Australia v West Indies — 1984

Melbourne Cricket Ground, 11 February 1984
Match tied
West Indies 5-222 (50 overs) (I.V.A. Richards 59, R.B. Richardson 43, K.C. Wessels 2-29)
Australia 9-222 (50 overs) (K.C. Wessels 77, K. J. Hughes 53, M. Holding 3-39, J. Garner 3-39)

The second final of the World Series Cup between the West Indies and Australia ended in a thrilling tie, the first in a one-day international. The result left officials to pore over the rules to decide if both sides needed to front up for a third match on the following day to decide the outcome of the series.

Clive Lloyd won the toss and decided to take advantage of both the easy batting conditions and the good form his team had shown in their nine-wicket victory in the first final in Sydney. Viv Richards (59) and Richie Richardson (43) added 62 runs in 40 minutes for the third wicket, before Kepler Wessels chipped in with the wickets of Richards and Clive Lloyd to slow down the Windies charge as they finished at 5 for 222 from their 50 overs.

However, the total looked more imposing after injuries during the West Indies innings weakened the Australian batting line-up. Dean Jones was promoted to replace opener Steve Smith, who had dislocated his shoulder trying to stop a cover drive from Richardson, but the Victorian's stay at the crease was short-lived. Kepler Wessels (77) and captain Kim Hughes (53) then put the innings on track, adding 109 runs in only 102 minutes before Hughes was trapped in front by Malcolm Marshall. The Australians then struggled as Joel Garner tore the heart out of the middle order, with Allan Border, Rod Marsh and the injured Greg Ritchie, batting with a runner, all falling to 'Big Bird'. When the last over commenced, Australia needed 11 runs as Geoff Lawson (21 not out) tried to keep their hopes alive. Rodney Hogg was run out off the third ball and Carl Rackemann off the last, as the sides tied the match and lived to fight another day.

England v West Indies — 1984

Old Trafford, Manchester, 31 May 1984
West Indies won by 104 runs
West Indies 9-272 (55 overs) (I.V.A. Richards 189*,
E.A.E Baptiste 26, G. Miller 3-32)
England 168 (50 overs) (A.J. Lamb 75, N.A. Foster 24,
J. Garner 3-18)

The West Indies beat England by 104 runs, in a match totally dominated by a magnificent innings of 189 not out by Viv Richards, which remained the highest individual innings in a one-day international until it was broken by Pakistan's Saeed Anwar (194) in Chennai 13 years later.

The West Indies had chosen to bat and were in total disarray at 7 for 102 after 26 overs before Richards took absolute control. He added 59 with Eldine Baptiste (26) for the eighth wicket and then an unbeaten stand of 106 runs for the last with Michael Holding (12 not out) off only 14 overs — still the highest 10th-wicket partnership in one-day internationals. Richards faced 170 balls, hitting 21 fours and 5 sixes, one right out of the ground at the Warwick Road end.

If England was not demoralised by Richards, having a similar batting slump to their opponents brought an end to their chances. Only Allan Lamb (75 from 89 balls) showed any resistance, as England's seemingly strong batting line-up limped to 8 for 115. Neil Foster provided some late-order entertainment with Lamb, but the match belonged to Richards and 'The Master Blaster's' awesome display of power.

West Indies v England — 1986

Queen's Park Oval, Port-of-Spain, 4 March 1986
England won by 5 wickets
West Indies 3-229 (37 overs) (I.V.A. Richards 82,
R.B. Richardson 79*, D.L. Haynes 53)
England 5-230 (37 overs) (G.A. Gooch 129*, W.N. Slack 34,
J. Garner 3-62)

England defeated the West Indies off the last delivery of a rain-shortened match at Port-of-Spain, with both sides scoring better than a run a ball.

The West Indies innings began slowly, and after a mix-up that saw Carlisle Best run out with the score on 37, the scoring rate was below three an over. Richie Richardson soon found touch, and he and Haynes increased the tempo after half an hour was lost to rain. They took the score to 106 before Haynes' (53) dismissal brought Viv Richards to the crease. Sensing the need for urgency, the pair added 117 runs for the third wicket in only nine overs, scoring at will off Ian Botham and Richard Ellison. Richards made his 82 from only 39 balls, setting England a target of 230 at 6.21 per over.

Ian Botham opened with Graham Gooch but England's plan for quick runs faded when Botham fell to Joel Garner with the score on nine. Wilf Slack gave Gooch valuable support and the pair added 89 in 17 overs, before Slack (34) was caught as he tried to lift the England scoring rate. However Gooch remained the cornerstone of the England innings, as with 12 overs left England required a further 100 runs. David Gower (9) fell with six overs remaining and the score on 4 for 170, which left the visitors needing 10 runs an over for victory. Gooch was magnificent, making 129 not out from 126 balls as England gained a thrilling last-ball victory to keep the four-game series alive at one all.

India v Pakistan — 1986

Sharjah Cricket Association Stadium, 18 April 1986
Pakistan won by 1 wicket
India 7-245 (50 overs) (S.M. Gavaskar 92, K. Srikkanth 75,
D.B. Vengsarkar 50, Wasim Akram 3-42)
Pakistan 9-248 (50 overs) (Javed Miandad 116*,
Chetan Sharma 3-51)

Pakistan pulled off an amazing one-wicket victory over India in the final of the inaugural Austral-Asia Cup in Sharjah.

India was sent in to bat, and Kris Srikkanth (75) and Sunil Gavasker put on 47 before Srikkanth fell to Abdul Qadir. Dilip Vengsarkar (50) and Gavaskar (92) combined to keep the scoreboard moving and they added 99 before two wickets fell with the score on 216. The re-introduction of Imran Khan and Wasim Akram to the attack reaped further benefits for Pakistan, as the Indians lost four more quick wickets to finish with 7 for 245 from their 50 overs.

Pakistan struggled to keep in touch with the target of just under five runs an over, falling to 4 for 110 as the chase for victory drifted. Javed Miandad was the one shining light and he found a willing, if unlikely, ally in leg spinner Abdul Qadir (34). They added 71 runs for the fifth wicket, as Pakistan began the last 10 overs needing 90 for victory. Noted big hitters Imran Khan and Wasim Akram came and went, but Miandad kept the target in sight with exciting running between the wickets. With one ball remaining Pakistan needed four to win and Miandad clubbed Chetan Sharma over the fence to bring about an astonishing victory. Miandad's innings of 116 not out included only 3 fours and 3 sixes and he was rightfully named Man of the Match. Ironically the tournament was organised as part of the Cricketers' Benefit Fund Series, with Dilip Vengsarkar and Miandad as two of the four beneficiaries.

Australia v Pakistan — 1987

WACA Ground, Perth, 2 January 1987
Pakistan won by 1 wicket
Australia 6-273 (50 overs) (D.M. Jones 121, S.R. Waugh 82)
Pakistan 9-274 (49.5 overs) (Qasim Omar 67, Asif Mujtaba 60*, S.R. Waugh 4-48)

Pakistan defeated Australia by one wicket, in the second match of a four-nation tournament that was organised as part of the celebration of the America's Cup Yachting Challenge in Fremantle.

Australia had lost Geoff Marsh, Glenn Bishop and Allan Border to be 3 for 70 before Dean Jones found a willing ally in Steve Waugh. Together the pair added 173 runs in 175 deliveries, in a partnership highlighted by some dazzling running between the wickets, before Waugh was bowled by Imran Khan. When Jones was out for 121 from only 113 balls, he became the first player to score a hundred on successive days in one-day international cricket. The Australians finished with an impressive 6 for 273, forcing the Pakistanis to use seven bowlers to try to contain the damage.

When Pakistan had slumped to 5 for 96 in the twenty-fourth over, it looked like the locals had finally turned around a disappointing season. Javed Miandad and Imran Khan were back in the pavilion, and the prospects looked bleak, with opener Qasim Omar (67 from 80 balls) playing the only innings of substance in the top order. Seizing the initiative, Manzoor Elahi (48 from 44 balls), Saleem Yousuf (31 from 27 balls) and Asif Mujtaba (60 not out from 56 balls) all scored at better than a run a ball to put the home side on its heels. The Australian attack was on the receiving end of some savage hitting, especially from the 19-year-old Mujtaba, as the Pakistanis clawed their way back into the match. Mujtaba found the target of 28 runs from the last three overs of little concern, chipping Steve Waugh over mid-wicket with a ball to spare. Dean Jones won the Man of the Match award.

Australia v England — 1987

Sydney Cricket Ground, 22 January 1987
England won by 3 wickets
Australia 8-233 (50 overs) (D.M. Wellham 97, G.R. Marsh 47, J.E. Emburey 3-42)
England 7-234 (49.5 overs) (A.J. Lamb 77*, D.I. Gower 50, S.P. O'Donnell 3-39)

England grabbed an improbable three-wicket victory over Australia, after Allan Lamb took 18 runs from the last over of the match. Dirk Wellham and Geoff Marsh got the Australians off to a good start, with a 109-run opening stand spiced with spirited running between the wickets. When Marsh (47) was dismissed, Dean Jones (34) and Wellham (97) continued the aggressive running to have Australia well placed for a big total. But after both were dismissed the Australian innings faltered and 8 for 233 was well short of what had originally seemed likely.

The English innings began cautiously on a wicket that was playing low and slow. Allan Border juggled his bowlers and used attacking field placements to try to frustrate the England batsmen, although Chris Broad (45) and David Gower (50) provided early runs. Allan Lamb was struggling but surviving, as he seemed unable to come to terms with the bowling as wickets fell around him. England began the last over at 7 for 216, not looking likely to reach the target, before Lamb took to the otherwise economical Bruce Reid. Lamb had not hit a boundary in his innings before hitting Reid's first delivery for six and then scored a four, a two, a two, and another four for a rousing finish to the match.

India v Pakistan — 1987

Eden Gardens, Calcutta, 18 February 1987
Pakistan won by 2 wickets
India 6-238 (40 overs) (K. Srikkanth 123, M. Azharuddin 49, Wasim Akram 3-49)
Pakistan 8-241 (39.3 overs) (Salim Malik 72*, Ramiz Raja 58, Younis Ahmed 58, R.J. Shastri 4-38)

Pakistan staged a late fight-back, scoring 78 runs from the last seven and a half overs for a thrilling two-wicket victory before a crowd of 90,000 at the first one-day international at Eden Gardens.

India was asked to bat by Imran Khan and then lost two wickets for 12 before Kris Srikkanth received some support from Dilip Vengsarkar (13) to add 45 for the third wicket. Srikkanth then added 145 with Mohammad Azharuddin (49) in rapid time before both fell within a run of each other. Srikkanth scored 123 from 103 balls, including 14 fours and a six, savaging the Pakistani bowling. Wasim Akram was the pick of the bowlers, capturing the wickets of Srikkanth, Azharuddin and Kapil Dev, as India made 6 for 238 from their 40 overs.

Pakistan got off to a solid start with Ramiz Raja (58) and Younis Ahmed (58) scoring 106 for the first wicket in 22 overs. They then lost a steady stream of wickets as Ravi Shastri cut a swathe through the Pakistan middle order to have them faltering at 5 for 161 with only 7.3 overs to go. With 78 runs still needed Salim Malik took over, scoring 35 from the thirty-fifth and thirty-sixth overs and moving to 46 from only 21 deliveries. By the time the last over had arrived, Malik had reduced the target to 12 and got them from only three balls from Kapil Dev, finishing with 72 not out from only 36 deliveries.

India v Pakistan — 1987

Lal Bahadur Stadium, Hyderabad, 20 March 1987
Match tied (India declared winners after losing fewer wickets)
India 6-212 (44 overs) (R.J. Shastri 69*, Kapil Dev 59)
Pakistan 7-212 (44 overs) (Salim Malik 84, Gopal Sharma 3-29)

The match ended in controversy after India was awarded victory after the teams finished level on runs for only the second time in one-day internationals.

India's innings started badly when Kris Srikkanth retired hurt after he edged a delivery from Wasim Akram into his forehead and Sunil Gavaskar was caught off Akram with only six runs on the board. The score moved along to 53 before Mohammad Azharuddin (18) and Shadanand Viswanath (1) both fell in quick succession. When Raman Lamba (41) was out with India on 95, the innings looked in deep trouble, before Ravi Shastri (69 not out from 74 balls) and Kapil Dev (59 from 52 balls) combined for 112 runs, a new fifth-wicket record for India. A very slow over rate restricted the Indian innings to only 44 overs, with the home side finishing with 6 for 212.

Ramiz Raja (23) was out with the Pakistan total on 39, while Younis Ahmed took 97 minutes to make 26. Salim Malik then took over the running, making 84 from 89 balls and adding 64 with Javed Miandad (25) and 41 with Manzoor Elahi (27 not out from 24 balls) to give Pakistan some chance. With two runs needed for victory from the last delivery, Qadir ran himself out trying to steal the second run, giving India the match because it had lost one less wicket. Pakistan later protested unsuccessfully, saying that the last ball should have been a no-ball, as India had only three players instead of four in the circle.

England v West Indies — 1987

Municipal Stadium, Gujranwala, 9 October 1987
England won by 2 wickets
West Indies 7-243 (50 overs) (R.B. Richardson 53, A.L. Logie 49, P.J. Dujon 46, N.A. Foster 3-53)
England 8-246 (49.3 overs) (A.J. Lamb 67*, G.A. Gooch 47, C.L. Hooper 3-42)

England got off to a grand start in their opening match of the 1987 World Cup, passing the West Indian total with two wickets to spare. England sent the West Indies in to bat and Foster and DeFreitas bowled tidily to restrict the early scoring. Carlisle Best (5) was out with the score on 8, before Desmond Haynes (19) and Richie Richardson added 45 for the second wicket. Richardson (53) and Viv Richards (27) then added 52 for the third, before both went in quick succession as the Windies slumped to 4 for 122 in the thirty-first over. Jeff Dujon and Gus Logie began slowly, adding only 32 runs in the next 12 overs, before they took to the bowling of Derek Pringle (0 for 83). Logie and Dujon added 83 for the fifth wicket, then Roger Harper slammed 22 from Pringle's

last over as the West Indies added 84 in the last eight overs to lift their total to 7 for 243.

England's response was slow, before Graham Gooch (47) and Mike Gatting (25) added 58 for the third wicket, both then falling to Carl Hooper for only one run. Hooper then claimed Pringle, and Downton was run out, to have England good as gone at 6 for 131. Allan Lamb steadied the innings, though England still needed 91 runs from their last 10 overs. John Emburey (22 from 15 balls) did well, and when Phillip DeFreitas (23 from 21 balls) fell, England required 35 from the last three overs. Lamb smashed 15 off the next over, before Patterson restricted England to six from the next. But the pressure and heat got to Courtney Walsh, as he conceded four wides and a no-ball, before Lamb (67 not out from 68 balls) and Foster earned the required runs with three balls to spare.

India v Australia — 1987

M.A. Chidambaram Stadium, Madras, 9 October 1987
Australia won by 1 run
Australia 6-270 (50 overs) (G.R. Marsh 110, D.C. Boon 49, D.M. Jones 39)
India 269 (49.5 overs) (N. Sidhu 73, K. Srikkanth 70, C. J. McDermott 4-56)

Australia brought off a stunning one-run victory over India in their opening game of the 1987 World Cup, in a match where a show of sportsmanship by captain Kapil Dev cost India dearly.

After Kapil Dev won the toss and sent the Australians in David Boon (49) and Geoff Marsh made an opening stand of 110 runs in 25 overs. Dean Jones carried on the good work following Boon's dismissal, scoring 39 from only 35 balls, but the Australian middle order struggled to maintain the momentum. However Geoff Marsh was a tower of strength, scoring 110 from 141 balls in just over three hours, battling extreme heat and stifling humidity. In a crucial decision during the break between innings, Indian captain Kapil Dev agreed with Australia's contention that one of Dean Jones' sixes had only been counted as a four, and the Indian target was increased by two runs.

It seemed to matter little, as Sunil Gavaskar and Kris Srikkanth set about the task of scoring 5.4 runs an over with some relish. Craig McDermott felt the brunt of the assault, his first four overs costing 31 runs, before Gavaskar was out for 37 from only 32 balls, with the total on 69. Navjot Sidhu took up where Gavaskar had left off, blasting the bowling to all parts of the ground before Srikkanth (70 in 83 balls) departed to make it 2 for 131. Sidhu hit 5 sixes in his innings of 73, before he was bowled during McDermott's second spell with the score on 207 and it was here that the tenor of the game changed. India had looked in total command, but McDermott claimed Vengsarkar, Azharuddin, and Shastri in a telling comeback. With four overs remaining, four wickets in hand and only 15 runs to get, India was still in the box seat. But casual shots and run-outs would cost the defending World Cup holders dearly, and when Maninder Singh was bowled by Steve Waugh, Australia had won with a ball to spare.

New Zealand v Zimbabwe — 1987

Lal Bahadur Stadium, Hyderabad, 10 October 1987
New Zealand won by 3 runs
New Zealand 7-242 (50 overs) (M.D. Crowe 72, M.C. Snedden 64)
Zimbabwe 239 (49.4 overs) (D.L. Houghton 142, I.P. Butchart 54)

New Zealand and Zimbabwe continued the thrills in the fourth match of the 1987 World Cup, with Zimbabwe wicket-keeper Dave Houghton just failing to claim a remarkable victory for his team.

New Zealand surprised by opening their batting with Martin Snedden, a bowler not renowned for his exploits with the bat. However, Snedden added 59 with John Wright (18) and 84 with Martin Crowe (72) to underline the success of the experiment. Then the New Zealand innings lost its way, with four wickets falling in the space of only 26 runs. At the end, Jeff Crowe (31 from 35 balls) and Ian Smith (29 from 20 balls) managed to put some form in the lower order, as New Zealand made 7 for 242.

Zimbabwe started badly, losing 2 for 10, before Dave Houghton was joined by Andy Pycroft in a partnership worth 51 runs for the third wicket. After Pycroft was run out for 12, Houghton struggled for partners as the next four batsmen failed to reach double figures and Zimbabwe slumped to 7 for 104. When Houghton was joined by Iain Butchart the pair put on 117, which is still a World Cup record for the eighth wicket. Houghton fell in the forty-seventh over, having scored 142 from 137 balls, including 6 sixes and 13 fours, and Zimbabwe needed 22 to win. Butchart (54) almost completed the fairytale, but he was run out on the fourth ball of the final over with Zimbabwe still three runs behind.

Pakistan v West Indies — 1987

Gaddafi Stadium, Lahore, 16 October 1987
Pakistan won by 1 wicket
West Indies 216 (49.3 overs) (I.V. A. Richards 51, P.V. Simmons 50, Imran Khan 4-37)
Pakistan 9-217 (50 overs) (Salim Yousuf 56, Ramiz Raja 42, C.A. Walsh 4-40)

The close finishes in the 1987 World Cup continued, as Pakistan pipped the West Indies on the last ball with only one wicket to spare. West Indies won the toss and decided to bat, giving newcomer Phil Simmons (50 from 57 balls) a chance to show his wares. He and Desmond Haynes (37) put on an opening stand of 91, but then the Windies lost both openers, as well as Richie Richardson (11) and Gus Logie (2) in the space of only 30 runs. Viv Richards (51 from 52 balls) provided an innings of quality, but only Carl Hooper (22) provided any support,

as Imran Khan and Wasim Akram swept away the last six wickets.

Pakistan did not look entirely convincing in its chase of the West Indies total of 216, and lost 2 for 28 before Ramiz Raja (42) and Javed Miandad (33) stemmed the tide with 64 runs for the third wicket. When Ramiz fell with the score on 92, and was quickly joined back in the pavilion by Ijaz Ahmed and then Miandad, Pakistan looked in trouble again at 5 for 110 with only 15 overs to go. Imran Khan (18) was joined by Salim Yousuf, and the pair added 73 runs in only 11 overs, with Imran's dismissal leaving Pakistan 21 runs to get in the last three overs. When Yousuf's charmed life came to an end with the score on 200, after the wicket-keeper had scored 56 from only 49 balls, and Wasim Akram and Tauseef Ahmed fell for the addition of only three more runs, the Pakistan cause again looked gone with 14 to get off the last over. However, Abdul Qadir calmly gained the required runs, including a straight hit for six on the fourth ball of Courtney Walsh's over, to record a last gasp victory.

Australia v New Zealand — 1987

Nehru Stadium, Indore, 18 (no play) & 19 October 1987
Australia won by 3 runs
Australia 4-199 (30 overs) (D.C. Boon 87, D.M. Jones 52, A.R. Border 34)
New Zealand 9-196 (30 overs) (M.D. Crowe 58, J.G. Wright 47, K.R. Rutherford 37)

Australia continued their heart-stopping run through the 1987 World Cup with a three-run victory over New Zealand. New Zealand needed a win to stay in the race for a semi-final berth, and after rain prevented play on October 18, both sides agreed to play 30 overs for a result rather than share the points. New Zealand won the toss and sent the Aussies in, with David Boon and Dean Jones making up for the early loss of Geoff Marsh (5). The pair took toll of spinners Dipak Patel and John Bracewell, adding 117 in 98 balls for the second wicket, before Jones fell to Patel for 52 from 48 balls as he tried to hit his fourth six of the innings. Boon was joined by Allan Border (34 from 28 balls) and the pair continued to wreak havoc before Boon was caught in the deep for 87 from 96 deliveries. Australia finished on 4 for 199, setting New Zealand a target of 6.66 runs per over.

John Wright (47) and Ken Rutherford (37) got New Zealand off to a great start, scoring 83 in 12 overs, before both fell to Simon O'Donnell. The Kiwis lost some wickets in the chase but were always within the target, starting the last over needing seven runs and with four wickets still in hand. With the in-form Martin Crowe on strike, victory looked likely but that ignored the resolve of last-over bowler Steve Waugh. Crowe was caught off the first ball after making 58 from 48 balls, Ian Smith was yorked by the next and Waugh bowled with deadly

Reliance World Cup, 1987, Final   Australia v England

Eden Gardens, Calcutta, 8 November 1987

Result: Australia won by 7 runs
Umpires: R.B. Gupta and Mahboob Shah

Toss: Australia
Man of the match: D.C. Boon

Australia innings			Runs	Balls
D.C. Boon	c Downton	b Hemmings	75	125
G.R. Marsh		b Foster	24	49
D.M. Jones	c Athey	b Hemmings	33	57
C.J. McDermott		b Gooch	14	8
*A.R. Border	run out (Robinson/Downton)		31	31
M.R.J. Veletta	not out		45	31
S.R. Waugh	not out		5	4
Extras	(b 1, lb 13, w 5, nb 7)		26	
Total	(5 wickets, 50 overs)		**253**	
DNB:	S.P. O'Donnell, †G.C. Dyer, T.B.A. May, B.A. Reid			

FoW: 1-75, 2-151, 3-166, 4-168, 5-241

Bowling	O	M	R	W
DeFreitas	6	1	34	0
Small	6	0	33	0
Foster	10	0	38	1
Hemmings	10	1	48	2
Emburey	10	0	44	0
Gooch	8	1	42	1

England innings			Runs	Balls
G.A. Gooch	lbw	b O'Donnell	35	57
R.T. Robinson	lbw	b McDermott	0	1
C.W.J. Athey	run out (Waugh/Reid)		58	103
*M.W. Gatting	c Dyer	b Border	41	45
A.J. Lamb		b Waugh	45	45
†P.R. Downton	c O'Donnell	b Border	9	8
J.E. Emburey	run out (Boon/McDermott)		10	16
P.A.J. DeFreitas	c Reid	b Waugh	17	10
N.A. Foster	not out		7	6
G.C. Small	not out		3	3
Extras	(b 1, lb 14, w 2, nb 4)		21	
Total	(8 wickets, 50 overs)		**246**	
DNB:	E.E. Hemmings			

FoW: 1-1, 2-66, 3-135, 4-170, 5-188, 6-218, 7-220, 8-235

Bowling	O	M	R	W
McDermott	10	1	51	1
Reid	10	0	43	0
Waugh	9	0	37	2
O'Donnell	10	1	35	1
May	4	0	27	0
Border	7	0	38	2

accuracy to concede only three singles and effect a run-out, as New Zealand fell short by three runs.

Australia v England — 1987

Eden Gardens, Calcutta, 8 November 1987
Australia won by 7 runs
Australia 5-253 (50 overs) (D.C. Boon 75, M.R.J. Veletta 45*,
D.M. Jones 33)
England 8-246 (50 overs) (C.W.J. Athey 58, A.J. Lamb 45,
M.W. Gatting 41)

Australia bounced back from recent poor form to claim their first and only World Cup, with a narrow seven-run victory over England.

Australia won the toss and followed the trend of the tournament by batting first. David Boon and Geoff Marsh made 52 from the first 10 overs, taking advantage of an inaccurate spell from Phillip DeFreitas and Gladstone Small, before the introduction of Neil Foster slowed the scoring. Foster then claimed the wicket off Marsh (24) with the score on 75 in the eighteenth over. Dean Jones and Boon added 76 for the next, but with Jones' dismissal for 33, Craig McDermott was sent in to increase the scoring rate. He gave the innings some momentum, scoring 14 from eight balls, but it was Allan Border (31 from 31 balls) and Mike Veletta (45 not out from 31 balls) who put Australia back on track. The pair added 73 in 10 overs to help Australia post 5 for 253, the first time in the tournament that England had conceded greater than 250 runs.

Tim Robinson fell off the third ball of the England innings, appearing to walk before umpire Gupta gave the plum LBW decision. Graham Gooch (35) and Bill Athey steadied the ship, adding 65 in 17 overs, before Mike Gatting and Athey made 69 runs in 13 overs. Gatting (41) had taken risks and enjoyed some luck, but his audacious attempted reverse sweep to Allan Border's first ball was not the shot of a captain trying to set an example, especially as England appeared to be getting on top. His dismissal allowed the England innings to drift and then some indecisive cricket saw Athey run out, after others had failed to take the initiative. Steve Waugh claimed the two remaining dangermen Allan Lamb (45 from 45 balls) and Phil DeFreitas (17 from 10 balls), as Australia ran out victors by seven runs. David Boon claimed his third Man of the Match award of the tournament.

Australia v New Zealand — 1988

WACA Ground, Perth, 3 January 1988
New Zealand won by 1 run
New Zealand 9-232 (50 overs) (A.H. Jones 87, M.D. Crowe 45)
Australia 231 (49.4 overs) (D.M. Jones 92, D.C. Boon 44,
R.J. Hadlee 3-35)

Australia suffered its only defeat of the 1987/88 season, losing the second match of the World Series Cup to New Zealand by one run in a thrilling encounter. New Zealand opted to bat first and Andrew Jones and Martin Crowe set the side up with 106 runs in 117 balls for the second wicket. The New Zealanders lost direction after Crowe's (45) dismissal, although Jones' fine 87 from 107 balls ensured they were always going to set a respectable total. Richard Hadlee (23) and Tony Blain (16) also showed some lower-order fight to get the visitors to 9 for 232.

Geoff Marsh (24) and David Boon (44) gave Australia a solid start, adding 78 in 21 overs, their sixth 50-plus opening in their last seven one-day matches. However, Australia then lost five wickets for 27, as Richard Hadlee and John Bracewell set the home side on its heels. Dean Jones, who had endured the carnage from the other end then took over, scoring 92 from only 91 balls as he guided the lower order to within sight of victory. Jones was the ninth wicket to fall and Australia still needed 12 from the last 10 balls. With Australia still one run behind, Mike Whitney fell trying to loft Snedden over mid-off, to give New Zealand a victory by the narrowest margin with two balls to spare.

Pakistan v Australia — 1988

Gaddafi Stadium, Lahore, 14 October 1988
Match tied (Pakistan declared the winner having lost fewer wickets)
Australia 8-229 (45 overs) (G.R. Marsh 89, D.C. Boon 38,
J.D. Siddons 32, Wasim Akram 3-38)
Pakistan 7-229 (45 overs) (Mudassar Nazar 76, Salim Malik 44,
Ijaz Ahmed 39)

After finishing level on runs, Pakistan was deemed to have beaten Australia as they had lost one less wicket, in the only one-day match of a troubled series.

Javed Miandad won the toss and asked the Australians to bat on the same pitch that had been used for the third test that had finished three days earlier. David Boon and Geoff Marsh brought up Australia's 50 in the eleventh over, with the pair going to make 71 before Boon was out LBW to Mudassar for 38 in 41 deliveries. Allan Border (11) and Mike Veletta (18) helped Marsh get the score to 146, before Jamie Siddons (32 from 37 balls) joined the opener in a partnership of 50. However from there wickets fell cheaply and Australia lost 5 for 21 in the quest for quick runs, eventually finishing at 8 for 229.

Ramiz Raja and Mudassar Nazar posted an opening stand of 53 before Ramiz (24) was caught off the bowling of Tim May. Mudassar was joined by Salim Malik and they took advantage of a depleted Australian attack to add 88 in 93 balls for the second wicket. Malik made 44 in better than one run per ball, while Mudassar hit 9 fours in his splendid innings of 76. Pakistan then lost 3 for 29 before Ijaz Ahmed scored a rapid-fire 39 from only 36 balls to take the home side within sight of victory. With an over to go, Pakistan needed two to win and Salim Yousuf gained a single from the first ball. Wasim

Akram couldn't get the next three deliveries from Tony Dodemaide away and was then caught in close by Border, before Abdul Qadir survived an enthusiastic LBW appeal on the last ball to leave Pakistan on 7 for 229.

Australia v West Indies — 1988

Sydney Cricket Ground, 13 December 1988
West Indies won by 1 run
West Indies 220 (48 overs) (D.L. Haynes 78, C.G. Greenidge 52, M.G. Hughes 3-48, P.L. Taylor 3-50)
Australia 8-219 (50 overs) (D.C. Boon 71, S.R. Waugh 40)

The West Indies defeated Australia by one run after they scrambled to a last ball victory in their first encounter of the 1988/89 World Series Cup. West Indies won the toss and decided to take the initiative, with Gordon Greenidge and Desmond Haynes scoring 90 for the first wicket in 20 overs. Greenidge (52) was caught off the bowling of Peter Taylor, who also picked up Richie Richardson (12) and Viv Richards (12), as the Windies innings faltered. Merv Hughes and Allan Border squeezed the West Indies middle order to have them fall from 3 for 182 to be all out for 220 in the space of nine overs.

David Boon and Geoff Marsh made 50, before Marsh (19) fell to Courtney Walsh and was quickly joined back in the pavilion by Dean Jones. Steve Waugh joined Boon in a third-wicket partnership of 87, before Boon was bowled by Malcolm Marshall after scoring 71 runs in 120 deliveries. The first partnership for Australia between twins Mark and Steve Waugh lasted only three runs before Steve was run out for 40. Then Mark Waugh and Allan Border both went cheaply, as Australia slumped to 6 for 177 and fell behind the required run rate. The match turned again as Peter Taylor and Ian Healy added a stylish 30 for the seventh wicket, before it all came down to the last ball. Australia needed two runs for victory as Curtly Ambrose delivered a full toss to Craig McDermott, who clouted it to mid-wicket only to see Viv Richards take the catch.

India v New Zealand — 1988

Moti Bagh Stadium, Baroda, 17 December 1988
India won by 2 wickets
New Zealand 3-278 (50 overs) (M.J. Greatbatch 84, J.G. Wright 70, A.H. Jones 57)
India 8-282 (47.1 overs) (M. Azharuddin 108*, S.V. Manjrekar 52, Ajay Sharma 50, D.K. Morrison 3-50)

The home side proved too good in the fourth and final game of their series, despite New Zealand hitting their highest score against India in a one-day international. New Zealand won the toss and John Wright (70) and Andrew Jones (57) made it worthwhile, adding 140 runs in 27.2 overs before both openers fell to Venkataramana. Ken Rutherford and Mark Greatbatch added 56 for the third wicket in good time, before Rutherford fell to Chetan Sharma for 32. Greatbatch was joined by Tony Blain (11), but the partnership was dominated by Greatbatch who scored 84 in only 67 deliveries to see New Zealand finish with an impressive 3 for 278.

India looked in some trouble as they slumped to 3 for 50, before Dilip Vengsarkar (28) and Sanjay Manjrekar added 68 for the fourth wicket. But after Manjrekar was out for 52 after completing his first one-day half-century, India was 5 for 133 and still needed 146 at better than seven runs an over. Mohammed Azharuddin and Ajay Sharma took up the challenge, as the pair added 127 in 83 balls for the sixth wicket. Sharma made his 50 from 35 balls, his dismissal leaving India a target of 19 from their last five overs. Despite losing two more wickets, India passed the target with 17 balls to spare, as Azharuddin completed his century in only 62 balls. This was the fastest century in one-day internationals, beating the previous quickest by Javed Miandad against India six years earlier. Azharuddin finished with 108 not out from only 65 balls, including 3 sixes and 10 fours, as India got home with 17 balls to spare.

Australia v West Indies — 1989

Melbourne Cricket Ground, 14 January 1989
Australia won by 2 runs
Australia 9-204 (50 overs) (A.R. Border 78, D.M. Jones 36, S.R. Waugh 33, C.E.L Ambrose 5-26)
West Indies 9-202 (50 overs) (C.L. Hooper 33, I.R. Bishop 33)

Australia took a 1-0 lead in the 1988/89 World Series Cup Finals after defending a modest total for a two-run victory over the West Indies.

Australia opted to bat and captain Allan Border must have been ruing the decision after Curtly Ambrose and Malcolm Marshall had them reeling at 3 for 34. Australia recovered somewhat when Border had his best innings of the summer against the West Indies, scoring a fine 78 just when his side needed it most. Border's innings took 103 balls, and included a six over mid-wicket off Viv Richards, as he and Dean Jones (36) added 99 for the fourth wicket. Steve Waugh then compiled a handy 33 before he joined Border as one of Ambrose's victims. In his first year of international cricket, Ambrose finished with a remarkable 5 for 26, which should have been enough to win the game as the Australians set the Windies a modest target of 205.

But it was not to be. Pace bowlers Merv Hughes and Terry Alderman combined to see the West Indies slump to 4 for 41. The middle order provided some hope, with Richie Richardson (24), Carl Hooper (33) and Jeff Dujon (27) all passing 20, but at 8 for 148 the West Indies cause looked lost. Curtly Ambrose and fellow paceman Ian Bishop (33) resurrected the Windies hopes, as they added 48 in 62 balls for the ninth wicket. When Ambrose fell for 23, though, the target was nine runs off the last over, with victory going to Australia when a Courtney Walsh cover drive failed to yield the necessary last ball boundary.

England v Australia — 1989

Trent Bridge, Nottingham, 27 May 1989
Match tied
England 5-226 (55 overs) (A.J. Lamb 100*, M.W. Gatting 37)
Australia 8-226 (55 overs) (S.R. Waugh 43, A.R. Border 39, G.R. Marsh 34)

Australia and England played out a controversial tie in the second match of the 1989 Texaco Trophy series. England won the toss and David Gower and Graham Gooch gave them a slow start, Gooch falling for 10 off 35 balls with the score on 30. Mike Gatting and Gower then took the score to 57, before the England captain was bowled for 28 from 59 balls. Enter Allan Lamb, who rightfully decided that the pace of scoring was too slow and set himself to do something about it. He added 62 in just over an hour with Gatting, before dominating an unbeaten sixth-wicket partnership of 88 in 12 overs with Derek Pringle (25) to record a fine century. Lamb's 100 not out took 105 balls and saw England set the target of 227.

Australia's response was slightly more positive, with David Boon making 28 from 35 balls in an opening stand of 59 runs with Geoff Marsh. The Australian top order all made starts, and modest partnerships for each wicket saw them reach 6 for 205. The wheels came off when Ian Healy injured his knee turning for the third run, leaving Steve Waugh stranded. Still with four wickets left, 18 runs needed and three overs to get them, Australia looked best placed. Geoff Lawson departed 13 runs later and, with Healy clearly in trouble, Dean Jones was called in as a runner. The adrenalin took over shortly after and controversy reigned when Healy hared off for two, beating his runner home. Gower ruffled some feathers as he rightfully queried Healy's need for Jones' help and the runner was despatched to the pavilion. The last over saw a wide, four singles, a wicket and then a cheekily-run bye off the last ball, leaving the scores level on 226.

England v Australia — 1989

Lord's, London, 29 May 1989
Australia won by 6 wickets
England 7-278 (55 overs) (G.A. Gooch 136, D.I. Gower 61, T.M. Alderman 3-36)
Australia 4-279 (54.3 overs) (G.R. Marsh 111*, A.R. Border 53, S.R. Waugh 35)

Australia brought off a stunning six-wicket victory in the last game of the 1989 Texaco Trophy series.

England decided to bat and Graham Gooch and David Gower carved up the bowling, making 123 in 127 minutes to give the home side a great start. Gower fell for 61, then Gooch and Mike Gatting put on 57 in 46 minutes for the second wicket, before Gatting was run out and Allan Lamb left without scoring. At 3 for 182 and with 12 overs to go, England went into overdrive. Ian Botham clouted 25 not out from only 11 balls, before Gooch's dismissal started a flurry of late wickets. Gooch was bowled by Alderman for 136, his seventh one-day hundred and the highest in matches between the two countries. Alderman was easily the pick of the bowlers and finished with 3 for 36, as Australia faced an imposing target of 279 for victory.

David Boon was out with the score on 24, having made 19 from 17 balls, before Geoff Marsh and Dean Jones guided the score to 80 at the tea break. This session may best be remembered for an exuberant female streaker, who did a long tour of the ground and finished off with a cartwheel. Faced with 199 runs from the last 30 overs, Jones was out shortly after, then Allan Border joined the fray.

The Australian captain blasted 53 from 46 balls in a 17-over stand of 113 with Geoff Marsh, before he was bowled by Derek Pringle. However, Pringle turned from hero to villain as he dropped both Marsh and Steve Waugh in successive overs. With three overs to go, Australia needed 36, but Waugh hit consecutive sixes off Neil Foster to swing the balance. His dismissal proved to be only a minor hiccup, as Australia won in the last over on the back of Marsh's 111 not out, to join Gooch with seven one-day hundreds.

Pakistan v West Indies — 1989

Eden Gardens, Calcutta, 1 November 1989
Pakistan won by 4 wickets
West Indies 5-273 (50 overs) (D.L. Haynes 107*, P.V. Simmons 40, Imran Khan 3-47)
Pakistan 6-277 (49.5 overs) (Salim Malik 71, Ijaz Ahmed 56, Imran Khan 55*)

Pakistan proved to be too strong for the West Indies in the final of the Nehru Cup, a six-nation tournament organised to celebrate the centenary of the birth of Jawaharlal Nehru, the first Prime Minister of India after independence.

West Indies was held to only 17 runs from the first 10 overs by tight bowling from Aaqib Javed and Wasim Akram. However when Pakistan opted for leg spin from both ends, Desmond Haynes and Phil Simmons cut loose, adding 83 before Simmons holed out for 40. Richie Richardson (27), Viv Richards (21) and Jeff Dujon (28) all got a start, but Haynes was the mainstay, making 107 not out from 137 balls.

Imran Khan bowled nine overs straight at the end of the innings and claimed the last three wickets to fall, keeping the Windies in some check as they finished with 5 for 273.

Unlike their opposition, Pakistan started in a blaze of glory, with Ramiz Raja (35 from 31 balls), Ijaz Ahmed (56 from 66) and Salim Malik (71 from 62) all scoring around one run a ball, as the West Indies strove for wickets. The fifth-wicket partnership between Salim and Imran Khan yielded 93 from 95 balls, as Pakistan kept up with the required run-rate. Viv Richards' gamble to bowl Marshall and Ambrose to try to snuff out the Pakistan charge failed and after that he was left to bowl at the end of the innings. Wasim Akram ended the match by hitting the first ball he faced over the mid-wicket fence.

Pakistan v Sri Lanka — 1990

Adelaide Oval, 17 February 1990
Pakistan won by 27 runs
Pakistan 3-315 (50 overs) (Saeed Anwar 126, Ramiz Raja 107*, Wasim Akram 34)
Sri Lanka 8-288 (50 overs) (R.S. Mahanama 72, A. Ranatunga 64, D.S.B.P. Kuruppu 37)

Pakistan beat Sri Lanka by 27 runs in this World Series Cup match where 603 runs were scored, a then record aggregate for a 50-over international.

Sri Lanka won the toss and sent Pakistan in, a decision they would have been ruing as Saeed Anwar and Ramiz Raja took their attack apart. The opening pair added 100 runs in 75 minutes and were 159 at the start of the thirtieth over. The partnership was finally broken in the thirty-third over, when Anwar fell for 126 from 99 balls. He hit 6 sixes and 8 fours, equalling Shoaib Mohammad's record score for Pakistan, while the partnership fell just 10 short of the best opening stand in one-day cricket. Salim Malik (25 from 25 balls) and Wasim Akram (34 from 23 balls) continued the assault, while Ramiz finished unbeaten on 107 from 154 deliveries as Pakistan compiled 3 for 315.

Sri Lanka faced the challenge bravely, but the pursuit of better than six runs an over caused the steady loss of wickets. At 4 for 123 the match looked over before Arjuna Ranatunga and Roshan Mahanama took up the challenge. They added 128 runs from 120 balls in only 78 minutes before the fight-back faltered in the face of the tight bowling of Waqar Younis. After both Ranatunga (64 from 70 balls) and Mahanama (72 from 79) fell, the Sri Lanka innings challenge ended, the innings finishing at 8 for 288.

New Zealand v India — 1990

Basin Reserve, Wellington, 6 March 1990
India won by 1 run
India 221 (48.2 overs) (Kapil Dev 46, M. Prabhakar 36, S.V. Manjrekar 36, S.R. Tendulkar 36, D.K. Morrison 3-33)
New Zealand 220 (48.5 overs) (M.J. Greatbatch 53, R.J. Hadlee 46, K.R. Rutherford 44, M. Prabhakar 3-37)

India defeated New Zealand by one run on the second last ball of their Rothmans Cup match in Wellington.

India decided to bat after rain reduced the game to 49 overs. After losing Wookeri Raman for a duck, Manoj Prabhakar (36) and Sanjay Manjrekar (36) added 58 runs in good style for the second wicket to get them back on track. However from there the Indians struggled in the heavy conditions to be 5 for 122 in the thirty-fifth over, before Sachin Tendulkar (36 from 39 balls) and Kapil Dev (46 from 38) lifted the run-rate with 41 runs in seven overs for the sixth wicket. India was eventually all out in the forty-ninth over for 221.

The home side lost captain Martin Crowe with the score on 33 and the Kiwis slumped to 3 for 68 before Mark Greatbatch and Ken Rutherford took over. The pair gave New Zealand the upper hand before tight bowling and desperate fielding saw Greatbatch's (53) dismissal after they had added 80 for the fourth wicket. Even when Rutherford (44) became the fifth player out at 174, New Zealand still looked likely winners. But wickets began to fall regularly and it was left to Richard Hadlee to try to win the game. With 11 runs required from the last over, Hadlee made a four, a two, and another two before Martin Snedden was run out attempting a second. Hadlee (46) was then yorked by Kapil Dev, with India one run in front with one ball to spare.

India v Sri Lanka — 1990

Sharjah Cricket Association Stadium, 25 April 1990
Sri Lanka won by 3 wickets
India 8-241 (50 overs) (M. Azharuddin 108, N.S. Sidhu 64, J.R. Ratnayeke 3-31)
Sri Lanka 7-242 (49.2 overs) (A. Ranatunga 85*, P.A. de Silva 34)

Sri Lanka came back from the dead to beat India by three wickets in the opening game of the 1989/90 Austral-Asia Cup in Sharjah. Sri Lanka sent the Indians in and had them in some trouble after they captured dangerous openers Kris Srikkanth (19) and Wookeri Raman (7) to have them 2 for 35. Then Navjot Sidhu and Mohammed Azharuddin took control, adding 114 in good time before Sidhu fell for 64 from 73 balls. Azharuddin played a great captain's knock as the rest of the batting line-up failed to respond to the good platform that he and Sidhu had given them. Azharuddin made 108 from 116 balls, while four other batsmen fell without any of them reaching double figures. Joseph Ratnayeke took three wickets for 31 in an economical spell, as the Indians finished with 8 for 241.

The Sri Lankan top order all got starts, but wickets fell steadily, with Aravinda de Silva's 34 the best effort. In the thirty-sixth over, Sri Lanka had slumped to 6 for 134 with the required run-rate well over six an over, before Arjuna Ranatunga found an ally in Joseph Ratnayeke. They steadied the ship, but the run-rate still continued to blow out, with 55 needed from the last five overs. When Ratnayeke fell with the score on 203, the pair had put on 69 in 66 balls for the seventh wicket, before his brother

Rumesh joined his captain to finish the job. Ranatunga was unbeaten on 85 from only 77 balls, as the Sri Lankans took 44 runs from the last 20 balls to record a miraculous win with four balls to spare.

England v New Zealand — 1990

Headingley, Leeds, 23 May 1990
New Zealand won by 4 wickets
England 6-295 (55 overs) (R.A. Smith 128, G.A. Gooch 55, A.J. Stewart 33)
New Zealand 6-298 (54.5 overs) (M.J. Greatbatch 102*, J.G. Wright 52, A.H. Jones 51, C.C. Lewis 3-54)

After looking likely to cruise to an easy victory with 12 overs to go, New Zealand fell over the line with a four on the second last ball of their Texaco Trophy match against England.

A run of injuries had forced New Zealand to recruit Chris Pringle from the local league, but they still sent England in to bat. An early success was made when Richard Hadlee snared David Gower, but the decision looked dubious as Graham Gooch and Robin Smith put 113 in 27 overs. The pair had started to accelerate when Gooch was out for 55 just before lunch. Smith then dominated a 50-run partnership with Allan Lamb (18), before receiving valuable support from Alec Stewart in reaching his first century in this type of cricket. They had added 57 in 33 minutes before Stewart was out for 33, with Smith later holing out for 128 from 168 balls. Derek Pringle (30 from 17 balls) added some sparkle at the end, hitting Hadlee's last four balls to the fence as England made 6 for 295.

If New Zealand thought the task beyond them, John Wright's elegant four off the first ball must have lessened the doubts. Wright (52) and Andrew Jones (51) tamed the new ball, adding 97 for the first wicket at a run a minute before both fell to Graham Gooch in quick succession. Then Martin Crowe and Mark Greatbatch took over, adding 118 in 20 overs, with Greatbatch particularly brutal on the bowling as the target fell to 72 from the last 12 overs. However with Crowe's dismissal for 46 with the score on 224, the match took another twist. Chris Lewis took another quick wicket and suddenly the Kiwis needed 37 from the last four overs. Greatbatch found a willing ally in Ian Smith, with Greatbatch (102) making his century from 104 balls and Smith (17 from 11 balls) clubbing the second last ball for four.

Australia v New Zealand — 1990

Bellerive Oval, Hobart, 18 December 1990
New Zealand won by 1 run
New Zealand 6-194 (50 overs) (B.A. Young 41*, R.T. Latham 38, J.G. Wright 37)
Australia 193 (50 overs) (G.R. Marsh 61, D.M. Jones 25)

After dominating the World Series Cup with five easy wins, Australia fell apart before a spirited New Zealand display to lose by one run.

Allan Border asked New Zealand to bat and they were always off the pace, losing wickets regularly and unable to get the tight Australian bowling away. John Wright (37 from 56 balls) tried to hold the innings together, but at 5 for 112 in the thirty-eighth over the New Zealand cause looked hopeless on a good batting track. However, Rod Latham (38 from 44 balls) and replacement wicket-keeper Bryan Young took over, adding 57 in rapid time as New Zealand plundered 74 in the last 10 overs. Young finished unbeaten with 41 from 37 balls, as the tourists made 6 for 194.

It still didn't look like enough runs, especially in view of Australia's strong batting line-up. Border decided to shuffle the order to give everyone a hit, a decision usually rejected as unwise in cricketing history, but even at 3 for 93 in the twenty-fifth over the task still looked in hand. Geoff Marsh made 61 in his usual sheet anchor role, but others failed to capitalise on their opportunities. At 6 for 153 in the fortieth over, and with Border and Dean Jones at the crease, the Australians started to panic. First Jones, then Border and finally Terry Alderman were run out as the tension mounted. The scenario for the last over consisted of Bruce Reid on strike, with two runs to win. But the lanky West Australian failed to get bat on ball before he was run out off the last delivery for an improbable New Zealand victory.

Pakistan v West Indies — 1991

Sharjah Cricket Association Stadium, 21 October 1991
Pakistan won by 1 run
Pakistan 7-236 (50 overs) (Ramiz Raja 90, Imran Khan 77, C.E.L. Ambrose 5-53)
West Indies 235 (50 overs) (R.B. Richardson 122, P.J.L. Dujon 53, Aqib Javed 3-54, Waqar Younis 4-39)

Pakistan held on for a thrilling one-run victory over the West Indies in the Wills Trophy tournament at Sharjah.

Things began badly for Pakistan. They lost Sajid Ali with the score on 17 and Javed Miandad was forced to retire hurt shortly after. Finally opener Ramiz Raja (90 from 129 balls) found a willing partner in captain Imran Khan (77 from 100 balls) and the pair added 137 in 28 overs for the third wicket. But both fell victim to Curtly Ambrose to leave Pakistan at 4 for 202, while Miandad returned at the fall of the sixth wicket only to become the paceman's fifth victim as Pakistan finished with 7 for 236.

Aqib Javed cut a swathe through the West Indies top order, claiming Phil Simmons, Clayton Lambert and Brian Lara to have them 3 for 32. Richie Richardson stood firm, but when Carl Hooper fell for 13 and Gus Logie was run out one run later, the Windies had slumped to 5 for 57. However Jeff Dujon joined Richardson to turn things around, adding 154 for the sixth wicket. Richardson made 122 from 121 balls, but his dismissal and Dujon's run-out for 53 saw the fortunes swing again. At the start of the last over the Windies were 9 for 227, the last pair getting eight from three balls, including a six from Ian Bishop, before he was unable to get the next two away and was bowled by the final delivery.

India v South Africa — 1991

Eden Gardens, Calcutta, 10 November 1991
India won by 3 wickets
South Africa 8-177 (47 overs) (K.C. Wessels 50, A.P. Kuiper 43)
India 7-178 (40.4 overs) (S.R. Tendulkar 62, P.K. Amre 55, A.A. Donald 5-29)

South Africa marked their historic return to international cricket with a one-day international against India before a crowd of over 90,000 in Calcutta, the biggest crowd ever for a one-day international. South Africa's first official game for nearly 22 years, and their first ever match in a non-white country, resulted in a three-wicket loss.

India won the toss and sent South Africa in, with Andrew Hudson falling for a duck off the last ball of the first over with the score on three. The visitors were clearly frustrated by the lack of pace in the wicket and found themselves 3 for 49 before Adrian Kuiper joined Kepler Wessels in a partnership of 60 in 14 overs. Wessels became the first person to play one-day internationals for two countries and marked his debut for his homeland with a determined 50 from 95 balls. Kuiper went on to make 43 from 64 balls, and after both he and captain Clive Rice fell to Manoj Prabhakar, the South African innings fell away, setting the Indians 178 to win.

The task looked simple enough, but Allan Donald made it more challenging, removing Ravi Shastri, Navjot Sidhu and Sanjay Manjrekar to have the Indians 3 for 20. However, he received little support from the other bowlers and 18-year-old Sachin Tendulkar suddenly made batting look easy. After losing captain Mohammad Azharuddin, the debutant Pravin Amre joined Tendulkar to put the home side on track. Tendulkar (62 from 73 balls) and Amre (55 from 74 balls) became Donald's fourth and fifth victims giving him 5 for 29, but it wasn't enough to deny the Indians victory.

India v South Africa — 1991

Nehru Stadium, New Delhi, 14 November 1991
South Africa won by 8 wickets
India 4-287 (50 overs) (R.J. Shastri 109, S.V. Manjrekar 105, K. Srikkanth 53)
South Africa 2-288 (46.4 overs) (K.C. Wessels 90, P.N. Kirsten 86*, A.P. Kuiper 63*)

South Africa took only four days and three games to record their first victory after their return to international cricket, with an eight-wicket win over India.

India decided to bat and Kris Srikkanth and Ravi Shastri gave them an 86-run opening stand. Srikkanth was stumped for his usual quick-fire 53 from 61 balls, giving Peter Kirsten his first international wicket, before Sanjay Manjrekar joined Shastri in a partnership of 175. Shastri had been dropped after the first one-day match of the series but returned to this match because captain Mohammed Azharuddin was resting with a stomach strain. He rewarded the selectors' faith by scoring 109 from 149 balls, but Manjrekar was the dominant batsman, making 105 from only 82 balls as India finished with an imposing score of 4 for 287.

If South Africa had doubts about their chances, Jimmy Cook (35) and Kepler Wessels gave them plenty to be optimistic about with 72 from the first 16 overs. Peter Kirsten then joined Wessels in an entertaining partnership of 111 from 19 overs, before Wessels was out for 90 from 105 balls, his third half-century in as many matches. Adrian Kuiper took to the purposeless Indian bowling as he and Kirsten added 105 for the third wicket in only 12 overs. Kuiper finished with 63 not out from 41 balls, while Kirsten was also unbeaten on 86 from 92 balls, as South Africa celebrated the first win of their comeback to world cricket.

Pakistan v West Indies — 1991

Gaddafi Stadium, Lahore, 22 November 1991
Match tied
West Indies 5-186 (39 overs) (D.L. Haynes 69, P.A. Wallace 32)
Pakistan 9-186 (39 overs) (Imran Khan 51, M.D. Marshall 3-39)

Pakistan and the West Indies tied the second game of their three-match series, after Mushtaq Ahmed was run out off the last ball of the match.

Imran Khan asked the West Indies to bat and Desmond Haynes and Philo Wallace put on a quick-fire 53 for the first wicket, before Wallace fell to Imran. The West Indies' middle order all got starts but didn't go on with it, as Haynes again proved to be the mainstay of the innings, eventually fifth out for 69 in 169 minutes. Imran Khan and Mustaq Ahmed proved to be difficult to get away, both conceding less than three an over, as the Windies set Pakistan a target of 187 to win.

Like most others, the Pakistan top order looked uncomfortable at times against the West Indies pace onslaught, but managed to get the score to 1 for 69 before Inzamam-ul-Haq fell in the sixteenth over. However, Salim Malik and Ramiz Raja were dismissed for the addition of only one run, before Imran Khan steadied the ship with a solid 51. With Imran's dismissal Pakistan needed 16 from nine balls with three wickets in hand and Waqar Younis took over. However he lost the strike for the last ball and Mustaq Ahmed's shot to cover yielded only one run before he was run out with the scores level.

India v West Indies — 1991

WACA Ground, Perth, 6 December 1991
Match tied
India 126 (47.4 overs) (R.J Shastri 33, P.K. Amre 20,
C.E.L. Ambrose 2-9)
West Indies 126 (41 overs) (A.C. Cummins 24,
S.T. Banerjee 3-30)

India and the West Indies tied the first match of the World Series Cup for the 1991/92 season, after the game appeared destined for an early finish when India was bowled out for 126. This match was the first tie where both sides were dismissed.

India lost opener Kris Srikkanth with the score on eight and then struggled to score against an accurate West Indian pace attack. This frustration led to indiscrete shots, with only Ravi Shastri standing firm, although his 33 runs took over two hours. Praveen Amre was next best with 20, with Curtly Ambrose (2 for 9 from 8.4 overs) the pick of a pace quartet that all conceded less than three an over.

Although facing a target of 127 for victory, the Windies got a less than ideal start when Desmond Haynes was caught behind off the first ball of the innings. Richie Richardson and Philo Wallace were out shortly after to have them 3 for 25, before Brian Lara and Carl Hooper added 30 for the fourth wicket. However, when both fell with the score on 55 and Keith Arthurton went for a duck to make it 6 for 61, the Indians started to look likely winners. At 8 for 76, the pair of Curtly Ambrose and Anderson Cummins became unlikely batting heroes, adding 37 for the ninth wicket before Ambrose (17) was run out. India had bowled out their four specialist bowlers to try to get wickets, before Mohammad Azharuddin snapped up Cummins at second slip off Sachin Tendulkar to bring an at times seemingly uneventful match to an astonishing end.

Australia v West Indies — 1991

Melbourne Cricket Ground, 12 December 1991
Australia won by 9 runs
Australia 9-173 (50 overs) (T.M. Moody 51, G.R. Marsh 43,
M.D. Marshall 4-18)
West Indies 164 (49.1 overs) (D.L. Haynes 62,
C.J. McDermott 3-23)

After setting a modest target, Australia restricted the West Indies to 164 and squeezed out an enthralling nine-run victory.

Allan Border won the toss and decided to take first use of the dry wicket. But the Australians struggled against the tight bowling of Curtly Ambrose and Malcolm Marshall, with Marshall (4 for 18) taking the wickets of David Boon and Dean Jones to have the home side 2 for 29. Geoff Marsh (43 from 111 balls) and Border (37 from 71 balls) rescued the innings with a partnership of 68 in 80 minutes, but it was tough going and both fell three runs either side of the hundred. Tom Moody then played a lone hand as wickets fell at the other end, scoring 51 from 45 balls and lifting the Australian innings out of the mire.

Carlisle Best was the first of the West Indians to fall, as Steve Waugh began a memorable night of top class fielding. Waugh lunged forward, touching a ball up for Border to snare at first slip to have the Windies 1 for 9. Waugh then caught Richie Richardson, took another catch off his own bowling to dismiss Brian Lara and had Hooper LBW to see the visitors slump to 4 for 64. Desmond Haynes remained resolute at the other end and he and Keith Arthurton (28) added 55 in 50 minutes before Haynes fell for 62 with the score at 5 for 119. Waugh then ran out both Arthurton and Malcolm Marshall, as the West Indies tail wagged a little to tighten the game before Craig McDermott claimed his third victim and Steve Waugh the Man of the Match award.

Sri Lanka v Zimbabwe — 1992

Pukekura Park, New Plymouth, 23 February 1992
Sri Lanka won by 3 wickets
Zimbabwe 4-312 (50 overs) (A. Flower 115, A.C. Waller 83,
K.J. Arnott 52)
Sri Lanka 7-313 (49.2 overs) (A. Ranatunga 88*,
M.A.R. Samarasekera 75, R.S. Mahanama 59, E.A. Brandes 3-70)

Sri Lanka stunned everyone, successfully chasing Zimbabwe's highest ever one-day score to make the highest total by a team batting second in a one-day international.

Zimbabwe didn't hint at what was to follow when they reached 3 for 82 in fairly sedate fashion. Opener Andy Flower held the innings together in his debut match, before Kevin Arnott (52 from 56 balls) and then Andy Waller set the innings alight. Waller reached his 50 in 32 balls, a World Cup record, going on to make 83 not out from only 45 deliveries. He and Flower scored 145 in 13 overs for the fifth wicket, as Flower carried his bat and made 115 not out on debut in this World Cup run-fest.

The dining wasn't over though as Roshan Mahanama and Athula Samarasekera put on an opening stand of 128 from 134 balls. Samarasekera made 75 in 61 balls, including 50 in 33 balls, before the dismissal of the two openers led to a middle-innings slump. The oldest player in the tournament, 41-year-old John Traicos, put the brakes on, taking 1 for 33 to be the only player in the match to go for fewer than five runs an over. With 15 overs to go Sri Lanka needed nine an over, before Arjuna Ranatunga, celebrating his status as the first Sri Lankan to play 100 matches, clubbed a superb 88 from only 62 balls. Aided by Sanath Jayasuriya (32 from 23), Ranatunga clubbed 88 not out from 61 balls to give the Sri Lankans an amazing three-wicket victory with 4 balls to spare.

Australia v India — 1992

Woolloongabba, Brisbane, 1 March 1992
Australia won by 1 run (target adjusted due to a rain delay)
Australia 9-237 (50 overs) (D.M. Jones 90, D.C. Boon 43,
Kapil Dev 3-41, M. Prabhakar 3-41)
India 234 (47 overs) (M. Azharuddin 93, S.V. Manjrekar 47,
T.M. Moody 3-56)

India just failed to peg back Australia in their run chase during the fifth World Cup, as the Cup holders recorded their first victory after three games in the tournament.

The Australian openers struggled, with Geoff Marsh taking 29 balls to make eight, before Mark Taylor's dismissal at 2 for 31 brought Dean Jones to the crease. He set the scene for his innings, opening with a four and a six, before sharing a 71-run partnership with David Boon (43). Steve Waugh (29) and Tom Moody contributed (25 from 23 balls), but it was Jones with 90 from 109 balls that gave the innings some life, although a stumble at the end saw the last four Australian wickets fall for only seven runs.

India also had a slow start after losing dashing opener Kris Srikkanth for a duck, and was 1 for 45 in the seventeenth over when rain interrupted their innings. They resumed needing 191 from only 30.4 overs and lost three wickets to the run chase before Mohammad Azharuddin found a willing ally in Sanjay Manjrekar. The pair added 66 runs in quick time before Azharuddin was run out for 93 in 103 balls. Manjrekar (47 from 42 balls) kept going before his dismissal left India at 7 for 216, 20 short of the target with just on two overs to go. Tom Moody was left to defend 13 from the last over, but his first two balls were too full and Kiran More helped himself to boundaries. More was then bowled, Prabhakar run out and India needed four from the last ball. Javagal Srinath swung lustily, Steve Waugh dropped the catch in the deep and Venkatapathy Raju was run out by stand-in wicketkeeper David Boon just short of the tieing run.

South Africa v Sri Lanka — 1992

Basin Reserve, Wellington, 2 March 1992
Sri Lanka won by 3 wickets
South Africa 195 (50 overs) (P.N. Kirsten 47, K.C. Wessels 40,
S.D. Anurasiri 3-41)
Sri Lanka 7-198 (49.5 overs) (R.S. Mahanama 68,
A. Ranatunga 64, A.A. Donald 3-42)

Sri Lanka recorded an upset victory over South Africa in the first clash between the two countries during the preliminary rounds of the 1991/92 World Cup.

South Africa lost Adrian Kuiper with the score on 27, but Kepler Wessels (40) and Peter Kirsten (47) consolidated with a second-wicket partnership of 87. However South Africa had taken 36 overs to reach 114 and when both fell on that score they were in trouble. Wessels took 94 balls to make 40 and left his team-mates little

time to get set. Wickets fell rapidly, as the South Africans desperately tried to remedy the situation, with only Jonty Rhodes (28 from 21 balls) making any real impression. South Africa lost their last 9 wickets for 81 in 85 balls to be all out for 195 on the last ball of their 50 overs.

Sri Lanka got off to a bad start, losing 3 for 35 under a blistering spell from Allan Donald, before Roshan Mahanama and Hashan Tillekeratne (17) added 52 for the fourth wicket. Arjuna Ranatunga then joined Mahanama in a 67-run stand, before the opener fell for 68 from 121 balls, after he had importantly survived the early onslaught of Donald. Ranatunga finished with an unbeaten 64 from 73 balls getting the Sri Lankans home with a ball to spare, as the South Africans proved to be their own worst enemy conceding 13 wides and four no-balls.

England v Zimbabwe — 1992

Lavington Sports Ground, Albury, 18 March 1992
Zimbabwe won by 9 runs
Zimbabwe 134 (46.1 overs) (D.L. Houghton 29, I.T. Botham 3-23,
R.K. Illingworth 3-33)
England 125 (49.1 overs) (A.J. Stewart 29, E.A. Brandes 4-21)

Zimbabwe recorded only their second win in a World Cup match, after bundling England out for 125 for a nine-run victory in the first one-day international at Albury.

Zimbabwe was asked to bat and looked unlikely to cause England any trouble after they slumped to 3 for 30. Boundaries were few and far between, as captain David Houghton tried to rescue the innings with a patient 90-minute stay at the crease. His 29 from 74 balls was Zimbabwe's top score, followed by Iain Butchart's comparatively breezy 24 from 36, as England's bowlers relished the opportunity to boost their economy rates. Zimbabwe was all out in the forty-seventh over for 134.

Graham Gooch's comeback from injury was short-lived when he fell LBW first ball to Eddo Brandes. The Harare chicken farmer then plucked the England top order, taking 4 for 21, including his old school mate Graeme Hick for a duck. England had slumped to 5 for 43 in the fifteenth over, before Alec Stewart and Neil Fairbrother tried to repair the damage in a 94-minute partnership that yielded 52 runs. Stewart's dismissal for 29 left the ailing Fairbrother to battle on, as wily veteran John Traicos tied up an end, conceding only 16 runs from his 10 overs. The end for England came when Gladstone Small was caught by Andy Pycroft in the fiftieth over, as Zimbabwe celebrated their unexpected victory.

New Zealand v Pakistan — 1992

Eden Park, Auckland, 21 March 1992
Pakistan won by 4 wickets
New Zealand 7-262 (50 overs) (M.D. Crowe 91,
K.R. Rutherford 50)
Pakistan 6-264 (49 overs) (Inzamam-ul-Haq 60,
Javed Miandad 57*, Imran Khan 44, Ramiz Raja 44)

Pakistan defeated New Zealand by four wickets to win their semi-final of the 1991/92 World Cup.

New Zealand opted to bat first and got off to a slow start, losing both openers and taking nearly an hour to reach 2 for 39. Martin Crowe joined Andrew Jones and the pair added 48 before Jones became Mustaq Ahmed's second victim. While Crowe crafted an innings based on all that is best in cricket, Ken Rutherford took 22 balls to get off the mark before launching into a gem of an innings. They added 107 for the fourth wicket in 68 minutes, with Rutherford (50 from 68 balls) scoring freely after his slow start. Crowe required a runner after pulling a hamstring, but still made 91 in only 83 balls, as New Zealand added 161 runs in their last 20 overs to finish with an imposing 7 for 262.

Pakistan lost Aamir Sohail with the score on 30 and Imran Khan batted next to try to keep them on track. Although Ramiz Raja compiled a handy 44 from 55 balls, Imran struggled to score quickly and Ramiz was caught in the deep trying to increase the run-rate. Javed Miandad then joined his captain in adding 50, before Imran fell for 44 from 93 balls, while Salim Malik came and went after scoring one. At 4 for 140 in the thirty-fifth over, Pakistan looked under pressure, but Inzamam-ul-Haq didn't show it, scoring 60 from 37 balls in a partnership of 87 with Javed in only 43 minutes. Javed finished with 57 not out in 69 balls, as he and Moin Khan (20 from 11 balls) took Pakistan home with an over to spare.

Pakistan v England — 1992

Melbourne Cricket Ground, 25 March 1992
Pakistan won by 22 runs
Pakistan 6-249 (50 overs) (Imran Khan 72, Javed Miandad 58,
Inzamam-ul-Haq 42*, D. Pringle 3-22)
England 227 (49.2 overs) (N.H. Fairbrother 62, A.J. Lamb 31,
Wasim Akram 3-49, Mustaq Ahmed 3-41)

Pakistan claimed the fifth World Cup with a 22-run victory over England before a crowd of 87,182, after losing four of their first five qualifying matches and looking unlikely to make the finals.

Pakistan won the toss and got off to a shaky start, losing Aamir Sohail and Ramiz Raja to be 2 for 24, but Imran Khan and Javed Miandad dug in to steady the innings. With Pakistan 2 for 30 in the twelfth over, the captain and vice-captain had every reason to be concerned, but the pair re-built the innings and then accelerated as they added 139 runs in 188 balls. After many close calls

Miandad fell for 58 from 98 balls, while Imran made 72 from 110 balls, before Inzamam-ul-Haq (42 from 35 balls) and Wasim Akram (33 from 19 balls) took over. They added 52 for the fifth wicket in 39 balls, before both fell in the last over, leaving England a target of 250 to win.

England lost Ian Botham for a duck, with Alec Stewart following not long after for 7 with the score on 21. England never seemed to fully recover from these setbacks slumping to 4 for 69 before Neil Fairbrother and Allan Lamb combined for a 72-run stand for the fifth wicket. But the game was as good as over when Wasim Akram came back to dismiss Lamb (31) and Chris Lewis with successive deliveries. Fairbrother made a valiant 62 from 70 balls, and the tail gave him honourable support, but England fell 22 runs short before the Lion of Lahore led his Pakistan team in a well-deserved lap of honour after receiving the new World Cup Trophy from ICC President, Sir Colin Cowdrey.

Australia v West Indies — 1992

Sydney Cricket Ground, 8 December 1992
Australia won by 14 runs
Australia 9-101 (30 overs) (D.M. Jones 21, P.V. Simmons 3-11,
C.E.L. Ambrose 3-18)
West Indies 87 (29.3 overs) (A.L. Logie 20, P.R. Reiffel 3-14)

Australia defeated the West Indies by 14 runs on a pitch severely affected by rain. Both captains had said that the wicket was unfit, but the umpires ordered that a 30-over match be played after a four hour delay.

The West Indies won the toss and not surprisingly asked Australia to bat. The home side made it to 31 before Phil Simmons claimed three wickets in 12 balls to have Australia reeling at 3 for 34. Dean Jones battled the bowling and a gastric attack to make 21 from 54 balls, the highest score in the match, as only Mark Waugh (17) and Greg Matthews (11) made double figures. Curtly Ambrose claimed three wickets as a rather handy first change bowler, as the Australians struggled to make 9 for 101.

Having beaten Australia by nine wickets only two days earlier, the West Indies must have felt that they were about to do it again. However those hopes were dashed when Desmond Haynes, Brian Lara, Phil Simmons and Richie Richardson were all back in the pavilion by the time the Windies had reached 22. Keith Arthurton then fell to a brilliant slips catch by Mark Taylor to make it 5 for 31, with Taylor celebrating his debut as Australian captain by taking three more catches in succession, a record for an Australian in a one-day international. Gus Logie top-scored with 20, while Ian Bishop (11) and Curtly Ambrose (13 not out) were the next best scorers. Mark Taylor was named the Man of the Match for his fielding and leadership.

Australia v Pakistan — 1992

Bellerive Oval, Hobart, 10 December 1992
Match tied
Australia 7-228 (50 overs) (D.M. Jones 53, M.A. Taylor 46)
Pakistan 9-228 (50 overs) (Salim Malik 64, Asif Mujtaba 56*,
C.J. McDermott 4-42)

Australia and Pakistan tied their World Series Cup match in Hobart, after Asif Mujtaba hit the final delivery of the day for six.

Australia won the toss and decided to bat, but struggled to score quickly on a wicket with uneven bounce. Local hero David Boon (14) was the first wicket to fall, but Mark Taylor and Dean Jones put on 92 for the second wicket to provide a solid foundation. Taylor made 46, but took 107 balls, while Jones made 53 from 73 balls in a return to form. Jones was to be the first of three vital run-outs by Aamir Sohail, while Ian Healy (24 from 23 balls) and Paul Reiffel (23 from 25) added handy late runs to lift the Australian total. Australia's score was further boosted during the lunch break, after discussions between the official scorer and those scoring for radio and television agreed that the total should be increased by one run to 7 for 228.

Both Aamir Sohail (6) and Ramiz Raja (4) started with a boundary, but both fell shortly after. From 2 for 10 it became 3 for 41 when Javed Miandad was adjudged LBW after making 14 from 50 balls, before Salim Malik and Inzamam-ul-Haq (22) added 50 for the fourth wicket. Pakistan then slumped to 6 for 129, and after Malik (64 from 99 balls) and Wasim Akram (3) were dismissed and with just over 10 overs to go things looked decidedly grim. Asif Mujtaba and Rashid Latif thought otherwise and added 68 in 57 balls before Rashid was run out for 39 from 35 balls. With 46 to get from four overs, Mujtaba then got it down to 17 from the last, which saw Steve Waugh take a wicket, concede 2 fours, two singles and a six off the last ball by Mujtaba to force a tie. Mujtaba finished with 56 from 51 balls to win Man of the Match.

Australia v West Indies — 1992

Melbourne Cricket Ground, 15 December 1992
Australia won by 4 runs
Australia 8-198 (50 overs) (M.E. Waugh 57, D.R. Martyn 40,
C.E.L. Ambrose 3-25)
West Indies 194 (50 overs) (B.C. Lara 74, R.B. Richardson 61,
M.E. Waugh 5-24)

Australia held on for a narrow win before a crowd of nearly 75,000, after a late-order West Indies collapse saw them lose their last seven wickets for 21 runs.

Australia decided to bat, but lost Mark Taylor and David Boon to be 2 for 17 on a pitch that gave variable bounce at both ends. Dean Jones survived a vicious spell from Curtly Ambrose, only to fall to Anderson Cummins for 22, while Steve Waugh's (34) run-out had Australia at 4 for 86. Mark Waugh survived a number of fielding lapses before finding a willing ally in Damien Martyn and the pair added 74 for the fifth wicket. Australia found scoring difficult and managed only 7 fours in their innings, but Mark Waugh got five off them in his score of 57 from 70 balls while Martyn made 40 from 49 balls. However from 5 for 160 the rest of the innings faded away and the home side finished with 8 for 198.

West Indies lost Desmond Haynes for four and Phil Simmons for 24, but Brian Lara and Richie Richardson survived some early trouble to take the score from 2 for 66 to 158 in only 115 balls. The partnership was finally broken when Mark Waugh bowled Lara for 74 from 123 balls, but as the Windies had cruised to 3 for 173 their win seemed inevitable. But on that score Richardson (61 from 73 balls), who had earlier become the seventh player to make 5000 runs in one-day internationals, slashed a Mark Waugh delivery to cover and the collapse began. In 29 deliveries, Mark Waugh took 5 for 16, to rout the Windies' batting, becoming the third player to score 50 and take five wickets in a one-day international.

West Indies v Pakistan — 1993

Bourda Ground, Georgetown, 3 April 1993
Match tied
Pakistan 6-244 (50 overs) (Basit Ali 57, Inzamam-ul-Haq 53,
Wasim Akram 39*)
West Indies 5-244 (50 overs) (D.L. Haynes 82, C.L. Hooper 69*,
R.B. Richardson 41)

The match referee decided that the game between Pakistan and the West Indies would be declared a tie, after an invasion by a jubilant crowd who thought the West Indies had won put the result in some doubt.

Pakistan opted to bat first, with Aamir Sohail (33) and Ramiz Raja (26) racing to 50 in seven overs, before the visitors suffered a mini collapse to be 3 for 85. The Pakistan innings ground to a halt and the second 50 runs took nearly 23 overs before Inzamam-ul-Haq (53 from 91 balls) and Basit Ali (57 from 69 balls) put the foot down. They added 103 in 123 balls before they were parted on 188 when Courtney Walsh removed them both. Wasim Akram then clubbed 39 runs in 27 balls to add 55 with Rashid Latif (15 from 13 balls), to give Pakistan a finish of 6 for 244.

Brian Lara continued his recent run of outs, bowled by Aamir Nazir for 15 with the score on 24. Phil Simmons (12) fell with the score 54, before Desmond Haynes combined with Richie Richardson (41 from 37 balls) to put on 63 in 10 overs. Haynes and Carl Hooper continued the onslaught adding 106 in 116 balls, before Haynes fell for 82 from 131 balls. The home side began the last over needing 12 to win and hit 10 from the first five of Wasim Akram's deliveries, before Ian Bishop drove

Benson & Hedges World Cup Final, 1991/92 England v Pakistan

Melbourne Cricket Ground (day/night), 25 March 1992

Result: Pakistan won by 22 runs
Umpires: B.L. Aldridge (NZ) and S.A. Bucknor (WI)

Toss: Pakistan
Man of the match: Wasim Akram

Pakistan innings

			Runs	Balls
Aamir Sohail	c Stewart	b Pringle	4	19
Ramiz Raja	LBW	b Pringle	8	26
*Imran Khan	c Illingworth	b Botham	72	110
Javed Miandad	c Botham	b Illingworth	58	98
Inzamam-ul-Haq		b Pringle	42	35
Wasim Akram	run out		33	19
Salim Malik	not out		0	1
Extras	(lb 19, w 6, nb 7)		32	
Total	**(6 wickets, 50 overs)**		**249**	
DNB:	Ijaz Ahmed, †Moin Khan, Mushtaq Ahmed, Aaqib Javed			

FoW: 1-20, 2-24, 3-163, 4-197, 5-249, 6-249

Bowling	O	M	R	W	
Pringle	10	2	22	3	(5nb 3w)
Lewis	10	2	52	0	(2nb 1w)
Botham	7	0	42	1	
DeFreitas	10	1	42	0	(1w)
Illingworth	10	0	50	1	
Reeve	3	0	22	0	(1w)

England innings

			Runs	Balls
*G.A. Gooch	c Aaqib Javed	b Mushtaq Ahmed	29	66
I.T. Botham	c Moin Khan	b Wasim Akram	0	6
†A.J. Stewart	c Moin Khan	b Aaqib Javed	7	16
G.A. Hick	LBW	b Mushtaq Ahmed	17	36
N.H. Fairbrother	c Moin Khan	b Aaqib Javed	62	70
A.J. Lamb		b Wasim Akram	31	41
C.C. Lewis		b Wasim Akram	0	1
D.A. Reeve	c Ramiz Raja	b Mushtaq Ahmed	15	32
D.R. Pringle	not out		18	16
P.A.J. DeFreitas	run out		10	8
R.K. Illingworth	c Ramiz Raja	b Imran Khan	14	11
Extras	(lb 5, w 13, nb 6)		24	
Total	**(all out, 49.2 overs)**		**227**	

FoW: 1-6, 2-21, 3-59, 4-69, 5-141, 6-141, 7-180, 8-183, 9-208, 10-227

Bowling	O	M	R	W	
Wasim Akram	10	0	49	3	(4nb 6w)
Aaqib Javed	10	2	27	2	(1nb 3w)
Mushtaq Ahmed	10	1	41	3	(1w)
Ijaz Ahmed	3	0	13	0	(2w)
Imran Khan	6.2	0	43	1	(1nb)
Aamir Sohail	10	0	49	0	(1w)

to cover and set off hoping for the two runs to win the game. However as Bishop played the shot the crowd surged over the fence, and the Pakistan captain dropped the return from substitute fielder Zahad Fazal, with Hooper out of his ground, to seemingly hand the game to the West Indies. After much deliberation, match referee Raman Subba Row decided that the game should be declared a tie, leaving the series a two-all draw.

England v Australia — 1993

Edgbaston, Birmingham, 21 May 1993
Australia won by 6 wickets
England 5-277 (55 overs) (R.A. Smith 167*, G.P. Thorpe 36, C.J. McDermott 3-29)
Australia 4-280 (53.3 overs) (M.E. Waugh 113, A.R. Border 86*)

Australia defeated England by six wickets, despite a phenomenal batting display by Robin Smith.

Australia won the toss and England struggled early after being asked to bat in damp conditions. Alec Stewart made a duck, Graham Gooch (17) was Craig McDermott's second victim with the score on 40 and Graeme Hick (2) was caught behind leaving the home side on 3 for 55. Neil Fairbrother joined Robin Smith and they added 50 for the fourth wicket, before Fairbrother fell for 23. Smith flayed the bowling after lunch, getting his century, then clubbing the next 50 in only 20 balls, as he and Graham Thorpe put on 142 in 21 overs for the fifth wicket. Smith finished with 167 not out in 163 balls, beating David Gower's previous record for a one-day international score by an Englishman, as England made 5 for 277.

Australia lost Matthew Hayden (14) and Mark Taylor (26) to be 2 for 55, and had dropped well behind the required run-rate when David Boon fell just before the tea break to have them 3 for 95. Australia needed better than a run a ball, but Mark Waugh and Allan Border didn't panic, playing the ball into the gaps for ones and twos to keep the visitors in touch. When Mark Waugh fell for 113 from 122 balls, Australia was as good as home on 4 for 263 after he and Border had added 168 runs for the fourth wicket. Border remained unbeaten on 86 from 97 balls, as Australia passed the target with nine balls to spare.

India v Zimbabwe — 1993

Nehru Stadium, Indore, 18 November 1993
Match tied
India 5-248 (50 overs) (M. Prabhakar 91, V.G. Kambli 55, M. Azharuddin 54*, S.G Peall 3-54)
Zimbabwe 248 (50 overs) (A. Flower 56, A.H. Shah 37, G.J.Whittall 33, A.C. Waller 32, J. Srinath 3-44)

India and Zimbabwe tied their match in the Hero Cup, after Heath Streak was run out off the last ball of the match.

Zimbabwe asked India to bat and claimed Woorkeri Raman for a duck before Manoj Prabhakar and Vinod Kambli added 122 for the second wicket. Kambli fell for 55 from 96 balls with the score on 128 and then Yadav went for a duck on the same score, before Mohammad Azharuddin joined Prabhakar in a 69-run partnership. Prabhakar had anchored the innings but sadly fell nine short of his century, while skipper Azharuddin finished with 54 not out from 56 balls as the Indians made 5 for 248.

Zimbabwe didn't get off to a good start, losing Grant Flower (2) and Alistair Campbell (7) to be 2 for 23. David Houghton joined Andy Flower to stabilise the innings, but after the pair had taken the score to 67, Houghton fell for 22 to Kapil Dev. Flower and Andy Waller then added 64 for the fourth wicket, but Zimbabwe lost both within the space of 12 runs to totter at 5 for 143. Guy Whittel and Ali Shah put them back on track with 64 for the sixth wicket, with the lower order getting them closer to the target but losing wickets as well. The last over began with Zimbabwe 9 for 239. Heath Streak and John Rennie managed eight from the first five balls, before Streak hesitated going for a second leg bye off the last and was run out by the throw from Azharuddin. The match was declared a tie, as the competition rules stated that only total runs mattered for the result.

India v South Africa — 1993

Eden Gardens, Calcutta, 24 November 1993
India won by 2 runs
India 195 (50 overs) (M. Azharuddin 90, P.K. Amre 48, R.P. Snell 3-33)
South Africa 9-193 (50 overs) (A.C. Hudson 62, B.M. McMillan 48)

India held on to beat South Africa in the first semi-final of the Hero Cup and Calcutta's first match under lights.

India decided to bat first and struggled to 3 for 18 after losing Manoj Prabhakar and Vinod Kambli to run-outs from Daryl Cullinan. Kambli's run-out was the first time that TV replay had been used in India. Mohammed Azharuddin was again the rock on which the innings was based and he added 35 with Sachin Tendulkar (15), before Praveen Amre helped the Indian captain to put on 95 for the fifth wicket. Amre (48) became the third player run out, while Azharuddin made 90 from 118 balls before the lower order faded as the Indians were dismissed off the last ball for 195.

It was the first time that a day/night match had been played at Eden Gardens and local authorities tried smoke bombs to clear the insects attracted by the lights, causing delays as the smoke, and a local mongoose, cleared the ground. After losing Kepler Wessels for 5, Andrew Hudson and Hansie Cronje (13) added 35 before Cronje joined the list of those run out. The South African middle order all got starts but struggled to make any real impact and got behind the required run-rate. Brian McMillan and Dave Richardson came together with the score on 145, eventually needing 45 to win from the last five overs. In the end, they added 44 for the eighth wicket, losing Richardson (15) towards the end of the forty-ninth over. Needing six to win off the last over, Sachin Tendulkar restricted them to three and forced the run-out of Fanie De Villiers, the seventh for the match, to give India a two-run victory.

New Zealand v Pakistan — 1994

Eden Park, Auckland, 13 March 1994
Match tied
Pakistan 9-161 (50 overs) (Basit Ali 34, Saeed Anwar 25, G.R. Larsen 4-24)
New Zealand 161 (49.4 overs) (K.R. Rutherford 47, C.L. Cairns 39, Waqar Younis 6-30)

New Zealand had their first tie in a one-day international after losing their last six wickets for 19 to finish level with Pakistan.

Pakistan decided to bat and Aamir Sohail (24 from 28 balls) and Saeed Anwar (25 from 54 balls) put on an opening stand of 38, which proved to be the best partnership of the innings. From there wickets fell regularly, and only Basit Ali, with 34 from 60 balls, made any real impression. Gary Larsen did the early damage, taking the first three wickets to fall and finishing with 4 for 24, but all the bowlers did well as Pakistan could only manage 9 for 161.

Waqar Younis gave Pakistan the start they were hoping for when he dismissed openers Bryan Young and Blair Hartland to make the score 2 for 9, but Andrew Jones and Ken Rutherford rescued the situation by adding 56 in just over an hour for the third wicket. Jones went for 21 with the score on 65 and Rutherford followed 20 runs later after making a match-high score of 47 from 76 balls. Chris Cairns and Shane Thomson then took control to put New Zealand in a very strong position, adding 57 in 64 balls before the re-introduction of Waqar Younis turned the game. He had Thomson caught behind for 24 to make it 5 for 142 and Tony Blain followed the same way two runs later. At 152, Chris Cairns was run out for 39 from 62 balls and then Larsen became Waqar's fourth victim on the same score only two balls later. New Zealand now needed 10 runs from the last two overs and got seven off the forty-ninth, but Waqar claimed 2 for 2 in the last over to tie the match. Waqar finished with 6 for 30, including 4 for 8 off his last 20 deliveries.

South Africa v Australia — 1994

Springbok Park, Bloemfontein, 8 April 1994
Australia won by 1 run
Australia 6-203 (50 overs) (D.C. Boon 45, S.R. Waugh 42, I.A. Healy 41*, C.R. Matthews 3-40)
South Africa 8-202 (50 overs) (A.C. Hudson 84, K.C. Wessels 28)

Australia and South Africa shared their eight-match series 4-4, after Australia held on to beat the home side by one run in Bloemfontein and Allan Border retired after 273 one-day internationals.

Australia decided to bat and got off to a slow start, losing Mark Taylor and Mark Waugh to be 2 for 31. When Michael Slater was stumped for 34 from 75 balls, Australia was in some trouble at 3 for 69 in the twenty-sixth over. David Boon (45) and Steve Waugh (42) began a rescue mission, adding 71 for the fourth wicket in 91 balls, before both fell within three runs of each other to leave the score at 5 for 143. Allan Border and Ian Healy then added 41, with Border ending his last international match with only 11 next to his name. Healy finished with 41 not out from 31 balls to give the visitors some chance with 6 for 203.

South Africa got off to a great start, with Andrew Hudson and Kepler Wessels putting on an opening stand of 82, before Wessels (28) was bowled by Steve Waugh. South Africa got to 3 for 158 and was seemingly in charge at the end of the forty-first over, when they lost their way. Three wickets fell for six runs and suddenly the pressure was back on the home side. Hudson made the only half-century of the match and his 84 from 132 balls should have been enough to ensure a South African victory. Damien Fleming, in his first match of the tour, was given the honour of the last over, with the South Africans 7 for 198 and needing six to win. Wicket-keeper Dave Richardson (18 from 18 balls) was run out off the last ball and Australia had victory by a single run.

New Zealand v Sri Lanka — 1994

Sharjah Cricket Association Stadium, 18 April 1994
New Zealand won by 2 runs
New Zealand 8-217 (50 overs) (S.A. Thomson 50, A.C. Parore 37, B.A. Young 34)
Sri Lanka 9-215 (50 overs) (A.P. Gurusinha 117*, D.J. Nash 3-43, C. Pringle 3-46)

New Zealand just held on to defeat Sri Lanka by two runs to reach the semi-final of the Austral-Asia Cup.

Sri Lanka sent the Kiwis in and had them 1 for 12 before Bryan Young and Adam Parore (37) added 56 for the second wicket. Just as the Kiwis seemed to be getting on top a rush of blood by Young (34) saw him caught at deep mid-wicket and from there the middle order lost direction to slump to 5 for 135. Shaun Thomson rescued the situation, scoring 50 in 41 balls, but tight bowling from Asanka Gurusinha (1 for 30) and newcomer Chaminda Vaas (1 for 31) restricted New Zealand to 8 for 217.

Roshin Mahanama and Maitipage Samarsekera had moved the score to 24, but the innings ground to a halt after both openers fell on the same score. Sri Lanka lost two more to be 4 for 41, when Gurusinha was joined by Chandana in a vital partnership of 88 to take them to 129. Chandana's dismissal for 27 led to another collapse that saw them slump to 7 for 152. Gurusinha kept his single-handed effort going, recording his maiden one-day century, but Sri Lanka still needed 10 runs to win off the last two balls. He hit a six from the second last delivery, but could only manage a single off the last, finishing with 117 not out and collapsed at the boundary after being clapped from the field by his opponents for his astounding effort.

Australia v South Africa — 1994

Shahi Bagh Stadium, Peshawar, 24 October 1994
Australia won by 3 wickets
South Africa 6-251 (50 overs) (W.J. Cronje 100*, D.J. Cullinan 36)
Australia 7-252 (49.4 overs) (M.J. Slater 54, M.G. Bevan 45, M.E. Waugh 43, D.C. Boon 39)

Australia got home for a narrow victory over South Africa in a match marred by crowd violence that tested the resolve of the local police. It was Peshawar's first international match since 1987 and fieldsmen were bombarded with firecrackers, metal spikes and padlocks in an ugly display.

South Africa won the toss and elected to bat, but got off to a poor start losing Kepler Wessels for 4 with the score on 7. However Hansie Cronje and Gary Kirsten got the South Africans back on track, adding 85 for the second wicket before Kirsten fell for 45. Daryl Cullinan scored an enterprising 36 from 35 balls in his partnership of 65 with Cronje, before he was bowled by Shane Warne with the score on 3 for 157. South Africa then lost their way a little, falling to 6 for 207 before Cronje took control of a 41-run partnership with Eric Simons (10 not out), bringing up his second one-day century off the last ball of the innings. Cronje finished unbeaten on 100 from 124 balls, South Africa setting Australia 252 for victory.

Mark Taylor (17) was first to go with the score on 38, then Mark Waugh joined Michael Slater to add 69 runs for the second wicket. Slater's 54 from 82 balls proved to be the highest of the innings and his dismissal with the score on 107 was followed 12 runs later by Waugh's (43). David Boon and Michael Bevan then combined to stem the tide, but with 10 overs to go Australia still needed 76 runs. Boon was dismissed for 39 from 44 balls, before Bevan (45 from 56 balls) became another to get a start but not go on with it. Then Justin Langer clubbed 33 from 19 balls in one of his rare innings of the tour, hitting three consecutive fours to bring Australia level

with an over to spare. Tight bowling from Craig Matthews raised the tension before Craig McDermott's single gave Australia victory with two balls to spare.

India v West Indies — 1994

Sawai Mansingh Stadium, Jaipur, 11 November 1994
India won by 5 runs
India 5-259 (50 overs) (S.R. Tendulkar 105, V.G. Kambli 66, A.D. Jadeja 31)
West Indies 254 (49 overs) (C.L. Hooper 84, J.C. Adams 50, B.C. Lara 47, S.L.V. Raju 4-46)

India had a narrow five-run victory over the West Indies, after the visitors lost their last 7 wickets for 39.

Brian Lara lost the toss on his debut as West Indian captain and then dropped a catch in the first over, as Ajay Jadeja and Sachin Tendulkar posted an opening stand of 95. Jadeja was caught and bowled by Hooper for 31 from 63 balls and then Vinod Kambli joined Tendulkar in a second-wicket run-fest, adding 117 in rapid time. Kambli made 66 from 64 balls and Tendulkar 105 in 134 balls for his third one-day international century in two months, but after the pair were dismissed the innings fell away a little as India finished with 5 for 259.

Phil Simmons went cheaply, but the West Indies recovered before Lara threw his wicket away on 47 to leave them on 3 for 90. Then Carl Hooper (84 from 88 balls) and Jimmy Adams (50 from 55 balls) took over, adding 126 in 125 balls to take the score to 216, leaving the West Indies needing only 44 from the last seven overs. However, after being in the box seat the innings fell apart when both players were dismissed within two runs of each other. West Indies crumbled before spin, as Venkatapathy Raju (4 for 46) and Anil Kumble (2 for 44) ran through the visitors. In the end, the last seven West Indies wickets added only 39 runs to hand India an improbable victory.

Zimbabwe v Sri Lanka — 1994

Harare Sports Club, 5 November 1994
Zimbabwe won by 2 runs
Zimbabwe 5-290 (50 overs) (A.D.R. Campbell l31, A. Flower 76, W.P.U.J.C. Vaas 3-59)
Sri Lanka 8-288 (50 overs) (R.S. Mahanama 108, P.A. de Silva 97*, H.H. Streak 4-44)

Zimbabwe recorded its first win in a one-day international at home, after recording a tight two-run victory over Sri Lanka.

Zimbabwe won the toss and elected to bat, with the Flower brothers putting on an opening stand of 60.

Grant was run out for 21, before Andy was joined by Alistair Campbell in a 92-run second-wicket partnership. Zimbabwe was 2 for 152 when Andy Flower was dismissed for 76 from 98 balls, but Campbell continued to attack the Sri Lankan bowling, bringing up his first one-day international century off only 96 deliveries. Campbell went on to make an unbeaten 131 from 115 balls, as Zimbabwe added 138 runs from the last 17 overs to finish with a creditable 5 for 290.

Sanath Jayasuriya and Roshin Mahanama got Sri Lanka off to its usual flying start, before Jayasuriya fell for 37 from only 24 balls with the score on 66. After Sanjeeva Ranatunga was dismissed for 15, Mahanama and Aravinda de Silva added 122 runs for the third wicket, to have the visitors well placed at 2 for 233 in the forty-third over. However, Mahanama's dismissal for 108 saw the Sri Lankans panic, with three more wickets falling in the next three overs. De Silva remained 97 not out from 89 deliveries and, despite hitting a four from the last ball, was unable to get the Sri Lankans over the line.

Zimbabwe v Pakistan — 1995

Harare Sports Club, 22 February 1995
Match tied
Zimbabwe 9-219 (50 overs) (G.W. Flower 41, G.J. Whittall 33, Aamir Sohail 3-33)
Pakistan 219 (50 overs) (Saeed Anwar 103*, B.C Strang 4-36, G.J. Whittall 3-46)

Zimbabwe and Pakistan tied the first game of their three-match series, after an injured Wasim Akram was dismissed off the second last ball of the match.

Zimbabwe won the toss and batted, with Andy and Grant Flower adding 45 before Andy was bowled for 25. Grant Flower made a painstaking 41, as all the top order made starts, but the batting was slow before Dave Houghton (32 from 40 balls) gave the innings some impetus. Later, Guy Whittall clubbed 33 from as many balls, including 14 from the last over, to have Zimbabwe finish with 9 for 219. In a crucial incident late in the innings, Pakistan bowler Wasim Akram split the webbing of his right hand in a wound requiring six stitches, after he attempted a return catch off Stephen Peall.

Pakistan lost both Aamir Sohail and Inzamam-ul-Haq to Bryan Strang to be 2 for 13, before Salim Malik (22) joined Saeed Anwar in a steady partnership of 55 for the third wicket. Ijaz Ahmed then rattled off 25 runs in 20 balls, but after he was dismissed Pakistan had faltered to be 4 for 107. Anwar and Shakil Ahmed (25) set about re-establishing the innings and with 10 overs to go Pakistan needed only 51 runs with six wickets in hand. Two run-outs put the game back in the balance, before Mansoor Elahi hit a quick-fire 21. Strang came back to claim two more wickets, but Saeed remained the constant and he hit a four off the third ball of the last over to record his eighth one-day century. However a leg-bye off the next tied the scores and brought last man Wasim Akram in on strike. His injury only allowed him one hand to grip the bat and he was caught and bowled by Guy Whittall to complete the match. Saeed finished with 103

from 131 balls to become only the second player to carry his bat in a completed innings of a one-day international.

Sri Lanka v West Indies — 1995

Sharjah Cricket Association Stadium, 16 October 1995
West Indies won by 4 runs
West Indies 7-333 (50 overs) (B.C. Lara 169, S. Chanderpaul 62*, P.V. Simmons 30)
Sri Lanka 329 (49.3 overs) (H.P. Tillekeratne 100, R. S. Mahanama 76, U.C. Hathurusinghe 45)

The West Indies just held on to beat Sri Lanka in a match yielding 662 runs, breaking the previous record for the highest aggregate for a one-day international.

The West Indies won the toss and lost both openers to be 2 for 37, before Brian Lara and Richie Richardson set the innings back on track with a third-wicket partnership of 96. Richardson fell for a slow 29, but Lara had only just begun to dominate the innings before he fell with the score on 5 for 282. He finished with 169 from 129 balls, including 15 fours and 4 sixes, to fall 21 short of adding the one-day international record to his record test score. Shivnarine Chanderpaul finished off the innings in grand style, making 62 not out from 45 balls, with the West Indies amassing 7 for 333.

Sri Lanka made 46 from the first five overs, but lost Sanath Jayasuriya and Aravinda de Silva (20 from 12 balls) in the process. Romesh Kaluwitharana joined Roshin Mahanama in adding 55 runs for the third wicket in only six overs, but Kaluwitharana's dismissal for 31 from 20 balls triggered a collapse that saw them lose three wickets in nine balls to slump to 5 for 103. Hashan Tillekeratne took over, adding 68 with Mahanama (76 from 78 balls) and then 86 with Hathurusinghe (45 from 43 balls) to give them some chance at 7 for 257. An eighth-wicket stand of 49 with Dharmasena (24 from 18 balls) made it a real contest, and when Tillekeratne brought up his hundred in just on a run a ball, the match was evenly poised. The match ended when Tillekeratne's (100 from 106 balls) attempted six midway through the last over just failed to clear Williams and the fence, leaving Sri Lanka four runs in arrears.

New Zealand v Pakistan — 1995

Lancaster Park, Christchurch, 17 December 1995
New Zealand won by 1 wicket
Pakistan 9-232 (50 overs) (Inzamam-ul-Haq 80, Salim Malik 58, D.K. Morrison 5-46)
New Zealand 9-236 (49.5 overs) (C.L. Cairns 54, S.P. Fleming 48, A.C. Parore 45. Waqar Younis 3-55)

New Zealand brought off a stunning one-wicket victory over Pakistan, scoring the winning runs off the second last ball of the match.

Pakistan opted to bat and struggled to 3 for 61 before

Inzamam-ul-Haq and Salim Malik took control to rescue the visitors. The pair added 114 in quick time, the partnership broken when Inzamam was bowled by Nathan Astle after making 80 from 95 balls. Unfortunately Malik (58 from 82 balls) followed shortly after, as Pakistan slumped to 5 for 185. Although five different bowlers from New Zealand had taken wickets, Danny Morrison returned to mop up the tail and record his best figures. Morrison snatched four wickets from his last 15 balls to finish with 5 for 46 and 100 one-day wickets, as Pakistan ended with 9 for 232.

New Zealand got off to a poor start, losing both Craig Spearman and Nathan Astle to Aaqib Javed to be 2 for 21. Bryan Young (34) and Stephen Fleming (48) decided to consolidate, adding 77 for the third wicket in slow time, and just when it appeared that they had seen off the danger both fell to Aamir Sohail to have New Zealand at 4 for 107. Adam Parore and Chris Cairns then lifted the run-rate, taking the home side to 204 before both fell to Wasim Akram. Then Waqar Younis took three wickets in four balls to leave New Zealand needing 15 runs from the last seven balls with only one wicket left. Morrison survived Waqar's last ball, then Gary Larsen contrived 15 runs from Wasim's last over to bring off an unlikely victory.

Australia v West Indies — 1996

Sydney Cricket Ground, 1 January 1996
Australia won by 1 wicket
West Indies 9-172 (43 overs) (C.L. Hooper 93*, P.R. Reiffel 4-29, S.K. Warne 3-30)
Australia 9-173 (43 overs) (M.G. Bevan 78*, P.R. Reiffel 34, C.E.L. Ambrose 3-20)

Australia brought off a remarkable victory by one wicket after Michael Bevan hit the required boundary off the last ball of the match.

Australia sent the West Indies in under threatening skies and Paul Reiffel took three wickets to have the visitors in trouble at 3 for 28. Sherwin Campbell and Carl Hooper then steadied to take them to 3 for 54 before the heavens opened, with officials forced to reduce the match to 43 overs per side. The Windies resumed their innings only to see Shane Warne claim Campbell (15) and Jimmy Adams (0) without addition to the score with 25 overs still to be bowled. Roger Harper (28) then helped Hooper resurrect the innings, as they added 81 for the sixth wicket. Hooper was magnificent, showing a mixture of control and aggression to finish unbeaten with 93 from 99 balls, giving his side a chance of victory as they finished with 9 for 172.

Australia started badly when Mark Taylor was run out with the score on four, but worse was to come. Ambrose tore the heart out of the Australian top order, taking three wickets, while Otis Gibson removed Mark Waugh and

Shane Lee to have the home side reeling at 6 for 38. Ian Healy helped Michael Bevan add 36 for the seventh wicket, but Healy's dismissal for 16 left the home side's hopes looking forlorn.

Paul Reiffel helped Bevan get Australia back on track, the pair adding 83 for the eighth wicket before a gallant Reiffel was dismissed for 34 from 45 balls. Another wicket brought last man Glenn McGrath to the crease with five balls left and six runs needed for victory. Plenty of tension, a wide and then a single, left Bevan on strike for the last two balls, Australia still four runs from victory. The penultimate ball failed to yield a score, but the last saw Bevan drive Hooper up the ground for the boundary and the win. Bevan finished on 78 from 89 balls, while Reiffel claimed Man of the Match with a brilliant all-round performance.

Kenya v West Indies — 1996

Nehru Stadium, Pune, 29 February 1996
Kenya won by 73 runs
Kenya 166 (49.3 overs) (S.O. Tikolo 29, H. Modi 28, C.A. Walsh 3-46)
West Indies 93 (35.2 overs) (S. Chanderpaul 19, R. Ali 3-17, M. Odumbe 3-15)

Kenya pulled off a stunning victory in their first World Cup, defeating the West Indies by 73 runs in one of cricket's greatest upsets.

West Indies won the toss and sent the Kenyans in and quickly had them in trouble, despite Curtly Ambrose conceding two boundaries in his first over. Courtney Walsh did the early damage, removing the first three Kenyans, but to their credit they continued to try to attack the bowling. However, at 6 for 81 the Kenyans looked gone, despite the West Indian bowling being wayward and conceding 14 wides and 13 no-balls in the match. Stephen Tikolo (29 from 51 balls) managed 2 fours and a six off Walsh to lead the Kenyan scoring, but the partnership of 44 by Hitesh Modi (28 from 74 balls) and 17-year-old Thomas Odoyo (24 from 59 balls) was crucial in setting the West Indies a reasonable target. Windies keeper Jimmy Adams equalled the one-day international record of five dismissals in an innings as the Kenyans made 166, however the total did not look big enough to challenge their more vaunted opponents.

The West Indies reply was nothing short of disgraceful. The Windies batsman scratched around, getting more frustrated and finally throwing their wickets away. Despite slumping to 4 for 35, it was always possible that the middle order could rescue the situation, but Maurice Odumbo claimed Chanderpaul (19), Jimmy Adams (9) and Roger Harper (17) to finish with 3 for 15 from his 10 overs of off-spin to put paid to that theory. Only Chanderpaul and Harper made double figures as the West Indies folded for 93, their second lowest score in a one-day international and lowest in a World Cup match. The Kenyans celebrated with a much-deserved victory lap, jubilant with claiming a prize scalp.

India v Sri Lanka — 1996

Feroz Shah Kotla Stadium, Delhi, 2 March 1996
Sri Lanka won by 6 wickets
India 3-271 (50 overs) (S.R. Tendulkar 137, M.A. Azharuddin 72*, S.V. Manjrekar 32)
Sri Lanka 4-272 (48.4 overs) (S.T. Jayasuriya 79, H.P.Tillekeratne 70*, A. Ranatunga 46*)

Sri Lanka claimed an exciting victory in this World Cup clash between two of the three host nations.

Sri Lanka won the toss and gained early success claiming Manoj Prabakhar (7) in what proved to be his last one-day international with the score on 27. However further wickets were hard to come by, as Sachin Tendulkar and Sanjay Manjrekar (32 from 46 balls) added 66 for the second wicket, before the fireworks really started. Tendulkar and Mohammed Azharuddin clubbed 175 in 156 balls, a record partnership for any Indian wicket in this type of cricket. Tendulkar made 137 from 135 balls to become the first Indian to score six one-day international hundreds, while Azharuddin remained 72 not out from 80 deliveries as the Indians finished with 3 for 271.

Sanath Jayasuriya and Romesh Kaluwitharana got Sri Lanka off to a blistering start, adding 53 in just over four overs, before Kaluwitharana fell for 26 from 16 balls. Manoj Prabhakar particularly felt the brunt of the onslaught, conceding 33 from his first two overs, before Asanka Gurusinha continued the run-fest with Jayasuriya, adding 76 for the second wicket. The Sri Lankan hundred came up in the fourteenth over, but the dismissal of both Gurusinha (25 from 27 balls) and Jayasuriya (79 from 76 balls) caused Sri Lanka to stumble to 4 for 141. However Arjuna Ranatunga (46 from 63 balls) and Hashan Tillekeratne (70 from 98 balls) safely guided the Sri Lankans to victory with eight deliveries and six wickets to spare.

Australia v New Zealand — 1996

M. A. Chidambaram Stadium, Chennai, 11 March 1996
Australia won by 6 wickets
New Zealand 9-286 (50 overs) (C.Z. Harris 130, L.K. Germon 89)
Australia 4-289 (47.5 overs) (M.E. Waugh 110, S.R. Waugh 59*, S.G. Law 42*)

Despite scoring their highest ever total against Australia, New Zealand was unable to prevent them from advancing to the semi-finals of the 1996 World Cup before a crowd of over 50,000 in the first day/night international in Chennai.

New Zealand won the toss but lost both openers early to be 2 for 16, with Nathan Astle (1) failing again, his last five innings yielding only 10 runs after he scored a century in the opening game against England.

New Zealand then slumped to 3 for 44, but captain Lee Germon backed his good fortune and joined with Chris Harris in a rousing comeback. Germon, who had not previously made a one-day half-century, took to the Australian attack, and Shane Warne in particular. Harris was no less severe and the pair clubbed 168, a fourth-wicket record for both New Zealand and World Cups. Germon made 89 from 96 deliveries and his dismissal saw the New Zealand middle order falter. Harris fell for 130 from 124 balls, his first one-day international century, and New Zealand had set an imposing total of 9 for 286.

Recurring injuries to Danny Morrison and Gavin Larsen forced New Zealand to revert to an old tactic and Dipak Patel's gentle spin claimed Mark Taylor for 10 with the score on 19. Mark Waugh and Ricky Ponting then consolidated, before Ponting fell for 31. Shane Warne was promoted to number four as a 'pinch hitter' and made 24 from 14 balls to give the innings some impetus. Steve Waugh then joined his brother at 3 for 127 and the pair took control, before Mark fell for a magnificent 110 from 112 balls, making him the first player to score three hundreds in one World Cup as well as passing Graham Gooch's record (471) for most runs in a World Cup (subsequently passed by Tendulkar). From there Steve Waugh (59 from 71) and Stuart Law (42 from 28) made it look easy, as Australia won by a comfortable six wickets.

Australia v West Indies — 1996

Punjab Cricket Association Stadium, Mohali, 14 March 1996
Australia won by 5 runs
Australia 8-207 (50 overs) (S.G. Law 72, M.G. Bevan 69, I.A. Healy 31)
West Indies 202 (49.3 overs) (S. Chanderpaul 80, R.B. Richardson 49, B.C. Lara 45, S.K. Warne 4-36)

In a match where both teams experienced amazing turnarounds, the West Indies managed to lose this World Cup semi-final, wrenching defeat from the jaws of victory.

Australia won the toss and crashed to be 4 for 15 in the tenth over, before Stuart Law and Michael Bevan rescued the situation, adding 138 in 32 overs for the fifth wicket. However both Law (72 from 105 balls) and Bevan (69 from 110 balls) fell when much of the hard work had been done and well-deserved hundreds beckoned. Then Ian Healy's timely 31 from 28 balls allowed Australia to set the Windies a modest total of 208 for victory.

The West Indies lost Courtney Browne (10) with the total on 25, before Shivnarine Chanderpaul and Brian Lara carried them safely into the nineties. On 93, Lara fell for a run-a-ball 45, but the runs continued to flow as

Richie Richardson and Chanderpaul took the West Indies to 2 for 165, leaving them only 43 runs to get from the last nine overs. Chanderpaul's dismissal for 80 from 126 balls started an astonishing collapse with eight wickets falling for 37 in 8.3 overs. Richardson was left stranded on 49, as Shane Warne, backed up by great fielding, swept away the West Indies World Cup dream.

Australia v Sri Lanka — 1996

Gaddafi Stadium, Lahore, 17 March 1996
Sri Lanka won by 7 wickets
Australia 7-241 (50 overs) (M.A. Taylor 74, R.T. Ponting 45,
M.G. Bevan 36, P.A. de Silva 3-42)
Sri Lanka 3-245 (46.2 overs) (P.A. de Silva 107,
A.P. Gurusinha 65, A. Ranatunga 47)

Sri Lanka defeated Australia to become the fifth different team in succession to win the World Cup, also becoming the first team to win a World Cup final when batting second.

Sri Lanka won the toss and sent the Australians in after heavy rains on the previous night made for damp conditions. Mark Waugh (12) fell with the score on 36, but Mark Taylor and Ricky Ponting kept the run-rate at five an over to make a big total likely. Australia was 1 for 72 after only 13 overs and Sri Lankan captain Arjuna Ranatunga resorted to spin, but the free scoring continued. Taylor was eventually dismissed for 74 from 83 balls after adding 101 in 115 balls with Ponting, leaving Australia well placed at 2 for 137 in the twenty-seventh over, but from here their fortunes declined. Ponting (45) fell four overs later and Australia had two relatively new batsmen at the crease as the spinners tightened their grip. Aravinda de Silva turned the game, capturing Taylor and Ponting with his off-spin, catching Steve Waugh and Stuart Law and then returned to bowl Ian Healy. Michael Bevan made 36 not out to hold the innings together, but 7 for 241 appeared short of what was required.

The Sri Lankan innings started poorly, losing both openers cheaply to be 2 for 23 after six overs. However, Asanka Gurusinha and Aravinda de Silva consolidated then took control, being particularly brutal on Shane Warne and Damien Fleming. Gurusinha was dropped just after passing his fifty and fell shortly after for 65, but the damage had been done as he and de Silva had added 125 in good time. Moreover, de Silva was just getting going and he and Arjuna Ranatunga took advantage of a loose over by Mark Waugh to bring the required rate down to 51 from the last 10 overs. De Silva finished with 107 not out from 124 balls, only the third century in a World Cup final after Clive Lloyd (1975) and Viv Richards (1979), while the Sri Lankan captain Ranatunga remained unbeaten on 47 from 37 balls. De Silva was named Man of the Match and Ranatunga received the World Cup trophy from Pakistan Prime Minister, Benazir Bhutto.

Pakistan v Sri Lanka — 1996

Padang Ground, Singapore, 2 April 1996
Sri Lanka won by 34 runs
Sri Lanka 9-349 (50 overs) (S.T. Jayasuriya 134,
H.D.P.K. Dharmasena 51, Waqar Younis 4-62)
Pakistan 315 (49.4 overs) (Salim Malik 68, Inzamam-ul-Haq 67,
Aamir Sohail 46)

Sri Lanka defeated Pakistan in the opening match of the Singer Cup in Singapore, after Sanath Jayasuriya scored the fastest one-day international hundred and the game broke the record for the highest match aggregate.

Pakistan sent Sri Lanka in and were rewarded with the wicket of Romesh Kaluwitharana in the third over, however he had made a quick-fire 24 from only 10 balls and Sri Lanka was 1 for 40. Jayasuriya then set about the bowling, taking 31 balls to register his 50 and a further 17 to bring up his hundred. He was eventually out for 134 from 65 balls in the twenty-first over with the score 2 for 196, having broken the record for the fastest hundred previously held by Mohammed Azharuddin at 62 balls. As well, Jayasuriya broke the records for the most sixes in an innings (11) and the most runs off an over (29), as the Sri Lankans went on to make 9 for 349 at just under seven an over.

In any other game, Pakistan's reply would have been sensational, with the Pakistan top six all making runs in very good time, but after losing their fourth wicket at 247, the challenge fell away. Despite scoring at better than a run a ball, with half-centuries to Salim Malik (68 from 77 balls) and Inzamam-ul-Haq (67 from 54 balls), Pakistan still fell 34 runs short in a game totally dominated by Sanath Jayasuriya.

Pakistan v Sri Lanka — 1996

Nairobi Gymkhana Ground, 4 October 1996
Pakistan won by 82 runs
Pakistan 9-371 (50 overs) (Saeed Anwar 115, Shahid Afridi 102, Salim Malik 43, S.T. Jayasuriya 3-94)
Sri Lanka 289 (50 overs) (P.A. de Silva 122, A. Ranatunga 52,
H.D.P.K. Dharmasena 51, Waqar Younis 5-52,
Saqlain Mushtaq 4-33)

Sanath Jayasuriya's record for the fastest one-day international century lasted only six months, with Pakistan prodigy Shahid Afridi taking only 37 balls to better Jayasuriya's record of 48 deliveries. In a touch of irony, Afridi took 43 runs from two overs by Jayasuriya on his way to the record.

Sri Lanka won the toss and asked Pakistan to bat, with Saeed Anwar and Salim Elahi (23) putting on 60 for the first wicket. Then Afridi came to the crease, scoring his 50 in 18 balls and then taking 19 to add his second 50 and capture the record. He and Saeed added 126 runs, with the normally free-hitting Pakistani captain totally over-shadowed by the youngster Afridi in only his second international. Afridi was out for 102 from 40 balls, while

Saeed went on to add 92 with Salim Malik for the fourth wicket before falling for 115 in 120 deliveries. Jayasuriya captured three late wickets after receiving a mauling from Afridi, finishing with 3 for 94, however all the Sri Lankan bowlers came in for punishment as Pakistan made 9 for 371.

The Sri Lankan innings started dismally, as Waqar Younis fired out four of the top five to have them reeling at 4 for 27. De Silva found an ally in his captain Ranatunga and the pair added 124 runs for the fifth wicket before Afridi, who had originally been added to the tour party to replace injured bowler Mushtaq Ahmed, claimed Ranatunga for 52 from 46 balls. De Silva and Kumara Dharmasena added 110 for the seventh wicket, but after de Silva was stumped off the bowling of Saqlain Mushtaq for 122 from 116 balls, the game was as good as over. Saqlain finished with 4 for 33, while Waqar came back to claim his fifth, as Sri Lanka's 289 all out left them 82 runs short.

India v Australia — 1996

Punjab Cricket Association Stadium, Mohali,
3 November 1996
India won by 5 runs
India 6-289 (50 overs) (M.A. Azharuddin 94, S.R. Tendulkar 62, R. Dravid 56)
Australia 284 (49.I overs) (M.A. Taylor 78, M.J. Slater 52, M.G. Bevan 40, A. Kumble 3-42)

India just held on to beat Australia as the tourists slumped to a record sixth successive defeat in one-day internationals.

Mark Taylor won the toss, but as if haunted by the conditions from the World Cup, broke with his recent practice and sent the Indians in to bat. Navjot Sidhu and Sachin Tendulkar posted a 54-run opening stand before Sidhu was run out for 11, while Tendulkar's dismissal for 62 from 60 balls after propping up the innings left India struggling at 3 for 95. However, Mohammed Azharuddin and Rahul Dravid rescued the situation with a fourth-wicket partnership of 110. Dravid made 56 from 67 runs, while Azharuddin fell with the score on 6 for 253 having made 94 from 104 deliveries. Ajay Jadeja and Nayan Mongia then added an unbeaten 36 for the seventh wicket at better than one run per ball to give India 6 for 289.

Mark Taylor and Mark Waugh made an opening stand of 84, before Waugh fell for 37 and Stuart Law was dismissed on the same score. Taylor was joined by Steve Waugh and the pair added 67 before Waugh fell for 33 and Taylor followed four runs later for 78 from 92 balls. At 4 for 155, Michael Bevan and Michael Slater put on 86 in only 71 balls, before Bevan's dismissal for 40 from 43 balls triggered Australia's slide. Despite having five wickets in hand and needing only a run a ball, the Australians panicked and Slater's demise for 52 from

38 balls with the score on 7 for 250 virtually signalled the end. Australia got to the last over needing six to win, but a run-out off Tendulkar's only ball of the match gave India victory.

New Zealand v Sri Lanka — 1996

Sharjah Cricket Association Stadium, 11 November 1996
Match tied
New Zealand 8-169 (50 overs) (N.J. Astle 66, M.J. Greatbatch 35, S.C. de Silva 3-18)
Sri Lanka 169 (48 overs) (S.T. Jayasuriya 53, A. Ranatunga 34. D.K. Morrison 5-34)

New Zealand held on to tie with World Cup Champions Sri Lanka after an inspiring last over by Danny Morrison.

New Zealand won the toss and batted and were soon in trouble, losing Craig Spearman and Adam Parore to be 2 for 8. Sanjeeva de Silva claimed his third wicket and then Chris Cairns was run out to have the Kiwis reeling at 4 for 61. However Nathan Astle remained resolute and combined with Mark Greatbatch (35) to bring them back into the match with a 75-run fifth-wicket partnership. Astle was the backbone of the innings, making a painstaking but necessary 66 from 130 balls, before falling to the tight bowling of Muthiah Muralitharan. New Zealand ended their 50 overs with 8 for 169.

Sri Lanka also got off to a shaky start, losing Kaluwitharana, Atapattu and Aravinda de Silva to be 3 for 31. Sri Lanka then recovered when Sanath Jayasuriya and Hashan Tillekeratne added 43, but Jayasuriya's dismissal for 53 from 64 balls was quickly followed by Tillekeratne and Roshin Mahanama to have them reeling at 6 for 98. Their situation was rescued by Arjuna Ranatunga and Chandana who added 42 for the seventh wicket, before some clean hitting by Chaminda Vaas had Sri Lanka needing eight to win with three overs left and two wickets in hand. Morrison began the forty-eighth over with two wides. Vaas hit the third delivery straight up the ground for four and then a wild leg side bye brought the scores level. However, he then bowled Sanjeeva de Silva and had Muralitharan caught off the last ball of the over to capture 5 for 34 and a remarkable victory.

Zimbabwe v England — 1997

Harare Sports Club, 3 January 1997
Zimbabwe won by 131 runs
Zimbabwe 7-249 (50 overs) (A.D.R. Campbell 80*, G.W. Flower 62, A. Flower 35)
England 118 (30 overs) (R.B. Croft 30*, A.J. Stewart 29, E.A. Brandes 5-28)

Zimbabwe capped a dark phase of English cricket history with an astonishing 131-run victory in Harare giving the home side a 3-0 series win.

England won the toss and sent Zimbabwe in, with Grant

Wills World Cup 1996, Final   Australia v Sri Lanka

Gaddafi (Lahore) Stadium, Lahore (D/N), 17 March 1996

Result: Sri Lanka won by 7 wickets
Umpires: S.A. Bucknor (WI) and D.R. Shepherd (Eng)
Match Referee: C.H. Lloyd (WI)

Toss: Sri Lanka
TV Umpire: C.J. Mitchley (SA)
Man of the Match: P.A. de Silva

Australia innings

			Runs	Balls
*M.A. Taylor	c Jayasuriya	b de Silva	74	83
M.E. Waugh	c Jayasuriya	b Vaas	12	15
R.T. Ponting		b de Silva	45	73
S.R. Waugh	c de Silva	b Dharmasena	13	25
S.K. Warne	st Kaluwitharana	b Muralitharan	2	5
S.G. Law	c de Silva	b Jayasuriya	22	30
M.G. Bevan	not out		36	49
†I.A. Healy	b de Silva		2	3
P.R. Reiffel	not out		13	18
Extras	(lb 10, w 11, nb 1)		22	
Total	(7 wickets, 50 overs)		241	
DNB:	D.W. Fleming, G.D. McGrath.			

FoW: 1-36 (M.E. Waugh), 2-137 (Taylor), 3-152 (Ponting), 4-156 (Warne),
5-170 (S.R. Waugh), 6-202 (Law), 7-205 (Healy)

Bowling	O	M	R	W	
Wickremasinghe	7	0	38	0	(2w)
Vaas	6	1	30	1	
Muralitharan	10	0	31	1	(1w)
Dharmasena	10	0	47	1	(1nb)
Jayasuriya	8	0	43	1	(5w)
de Silva	9	0	42	3	(3w)

Sri Lanka innings

			Runs	Balls
S.T. Jayasuriya	run out		9	7
†R.S. Kaluwitharana	c Bevan	b Fleming	6	13
A.P. Gurusinha		b Reiffel	65	99
P.A. de Silva	not out		107	124
*A. Ranatunga	not out		47	37
Extras	(b 1, lb 4, w 5, nb 1)		11	
Total	(3 wickets, 46.2 overs)		245	
DNB:	H.P. Tillekeratne, R.S. Mahanama, H.D.P.K. Dharmasena, W.P.U.C.J. Vaas, G.P. Wickremasinghe, M. Muralitharan			

FoW: 1-12 (Jayasuriya), 2-23 (Kaluwitharana), 3-148 (Gurusinha)

Bowling	O	M	R	W	
McGrath	8.2	1	28	0	
Fleming	6	0	43	1	(4w)
Warne	10	0	58	0	(1nb, 1w)
Reiffel	10	0	49	1	
M.E. Waugh	6	0	35	0	
S.R. Waugh	3	0	15	0	(1nb)
Bevan	3	0	12	0	

Flower and Andy Waller adding 58 before England tasted success with Waller's run-out for 19. Flower and Alistair Campbell then compiled a productive 73-run partnership for the second wicket, with Flower making 62 from 87 balls. Andy Flower then replaced his older brother, giving the innings a boost with 35 runs from 30 balls in a 50-run partnership with Campbell. At 3 for 181 Zimbabwe was well placed and Campbell paced himself for a top score of 80 not out from 103 deliveries to see Zimbabwe finish with 7 for 249.

England began poorly with Nick Knight falling to Eddo Brandes for 9, before John Crawley and Nasser Hussain then became part of Zimbabwe's first ever hat-trick to make the score 3 for 13. Alec Stewart (29) and Mike Atherton (18) played with patience to add 32 in 10 overs for the fourth wicket, but both fell to Brandes to give the part-time cricketer and full-time chicken farmer five wickets for the match. Stewart's dismissal saw five wickets fall cheaply to have England in complete disarray at 8 for 77, before Robert Croft (30 not out) and Allan Mullally (20) put on 41 runs in eight overs, the highest partnership of the innings. England were all out for 118 in only 30 overs, not their lowest total, but surely their most soul destroying.

Zimbabwe v India — 1997

Boland Park, Paarl, 27 January 1997
Match tied
Zimbabwe 8-236 (50 overs) (A.D.R. Campbell 61, P.A. Strang 47, C.N. Evans 40, B.K.V. Prasad 3-49)
India 236 (49.5 overs) (R.R. Singh 48, S.C. Ganguly 38, S.S. Karim 38, E.A. Brandes 5-41)

Zimbabwe and India played their second tied match, leaving Zimbabwe still to register a win over India in 13 clashes.

Zimbabwe won the toss and decided to bat, with Andy Waller and Andy Flower falling cheaply to have them 2 for 32. After Grant Flower went for 28 from 48 balls, Paul Strang and Alistair Campbell set the innings on track with a 94-run partnership for the fourth wicket. Strang fell first after making 47 in fairly slow time, while Campbell went on to make 61 from his 71 deliveries. At 5 for 172 the innings lost a little direction, before Craig Evans clubbed 40 from 32 balls to have Zimbabwe finish with 8 for 236.

India also had a shaky start to their innings, losing Sachin Tendulkar, Javagal Srinath and Mohammed Azharuddin to be 3 for 40. Sourav Ganguly added 45 for the fourth wicket with Rahul Dravid, the partnership ending when Dravid (23 from 43 balls) was run out to leave the Indians at 4 for 85. Ganguly fell 25 runs later after taking 79 balls to make 38, before Ajay Jadeja and Syed Karim gave the innings a boost with a 56-run sixth-wicket stand. Karim's dismissal for 38 was followed by Jadeja's (32 from 58 balls) 10 runs later and it was left to some hard

hitting from Robin Singh to get them back in the match. Needing two runs to win from the last ball, the match ended in bizarre circumstances when Singh was run out for 48 from 31 balls at the bowler's end after the delivery had been called wide. Eddo Brandes, who bowled the last over and finished with 5 for 48, and Singh were declared joint Men of the Match.

New Zealand v England — 1997

McLean Park, Napier, 26 February 1997
Match tied
New Zealand 237 (49.4 overs) (B.A. Young 53, N.J. Astle 34, C. White 4-37)
England 8-237 (50 overs) (G.P. Thorpe 55, N.V. Knight 39, C. White 38, C.Z. Harris 3-20)

New Zealand and England finished level on scores, in New Zealand's third tie in one-day internationals.

New Zealand won the toss and Nathan Astle got them off to a bright start with 34 in 32 balls before he departed with the score on 50. Bryan Young was then joined by Lee Germon and the pair added 53 before Germon was stumped for 22. New Zealand lost their way at this point, falling to 5 for 145 when Young was bowled for 53 from 82 balls by Andy Caddick. Fortunately the lower order contributed, with Adam Parore (24), Chris Harris (19), Gary Larsen (19) and Simon Doull (22) carrying the total to 237. Craig White picked up three of those players to finish with 4 for 37, but took some punishment in his 5.4 overs.

England got off to a rousing start with Nick Knight and Mike Atherton taking 52 from the first six overs. However, the momentum slowed and then Knight fell for 39 from 48 balls to put England under some pressure. Chris Harris (3 for 20) bowled 10 overs with great control to capture Atherton (23), Alec Stewart (17) and Nasser Hussain (13) as England slumped to 5 for 127 with 19 overs remaining. Graham Thorpe batted with great Composure, and he and Craig White added 47 before Thorpe fell for 55 from 89 balls. White and Dominic Cork then came together with England needing 64 from the last 10 overs, finally needing eight to win as the last over began. After a bye and a run, White was run out for 38 from 47 balls, before Robert Croft hit a four, was bowled and then Darren Gough scrambled a bye to bring up the tie. Cork remained unbeaten on 31 from 35 balls.

South Africa v Australia — 1997

Centurion Park, Pretoria, 10 April 1997
Australia won by 5 wickets
South Africa 7-284 (50 overs) (D.J. Cullinan 89, W.J. Cronje 80, H.H. Gibbs 33, S.M. Pollock 33)
Australia 5-287 (49 overs) (M.G. Bevan 103, S.R. Waugh 89, S.G. Law 31, S.M. Pollock 3-40)

Australia overhauled an imposing South African total to take an unbeatable 4-2 in their best-of-seven series.

With the series evenly poised, South Africa won the toss and opted to bat, with Adam Bacher and Herschelle Gibbs batting cautiously despite bringing up the 50 in only 39 minutes. Bacher (15) was first to go with the score on 52 at the start of the eleventh over and Gibbs (33) followed 25 runs later, but from here Hansie Cronje and Daryl Cullinan took over. The pair added 149 runs from 166 balls to set a new record for South Africa in one-day internationals for the third wicket, the partnership broken when Cronje was run out for 80 from 81 balls. South Africa had a minor slump with Cullinan (89 from 96 balls) and Jacques Kallis (3) both falling to Shane Warne only six runs later. Shaun Pollock put the innings back on track with 33 from 23 balls to give South Africa 7 for 284, their highest score against Australia and their second highest ever score in a one-day international.

Australia lost Mark Waugh for a duck, then Greg Blewett (21) and Stuart Law (31), bringing Steve Waugh and Michael Bevan together with the score at 3 for 58. Australia needed 227 runs from 211 balls and Waugh took up the challenge early before Bevan took over, building through his innings. He made his 50 from 54 balls, but took only 39 more to reach his first one-day international hundred, before he was out LBW for 103 with the score on 247. At the other end Waugh got 89 from 102 balls before he fell the same way, their partnership worth 189 from 162 balls, a record for one-day internationals. Adam Gilchrist and Ian Healy finished off the job with an over to spare, Australia's score then their highest batting second.

India v Sri Lanka — 1997

Wankhede Stadium, Mumbai, 17 May 1997
Sri Lanka won by 5 wickets
India 7-225 (50 overs) (A. Jadeja 72, R. Dravid 61, R.R. Singh 51, K.S.C. de Silva 3-59)
Sri Lanka 5-229 (40.5 overs) (S.T. Jayasuriya 151*, M.T. Atapattu 38)

Sanath Jayasuriya hit 151 to claim the record for the highest score by a Sri Lankan, as well as already having Sri Lanka's best bowling figures (6 for 29).

India won the toss and lost Saurav Ganguly with the first ball and Sachin Tendulkar shortly after to be 2 for 4. Then Vinod Kambli made a painstaking four before he was dismissed to leave India 3 for 29 in the twelfth over. Rahul Dravid and Ajay Jadeja rescued the innings, scoring 95 in 21.5 overs for the fourth wicket, before Dravid was bowled for 61 from 103 balls. With the run-rate at just over 3.5 per over, Jadeja and Robin Singh then increased the tempo in a fifth-wicket partnership that yielded 58 runs in 10 overs. Jadeja fell for 72 from 102 balls, then Singh took over making 51 from 52 balls in an entering partnership of 42 with Nayan Mongia (21 not out from 17). India slogged 41 from the last five overs

to finish with 7 for 225 — very respectable given their poor start.

Sri Lanka lost Romesh Kaluwitharana for a duck to be 1 for 8, but it didn't seem to affect Sanath Jayasuriya. He clobbered the Indian attack, taking 41 balls to reach 50 and 85 to reach his hundred, adding 138 in 23.5 overs for the second wicket with Marvan Atapattu, before Atapattu fell for 38 from 69 balls. At times it seemed like the other batsmen were just there to hold up an end, as Jayasuriya quickly gathered in the Indian total. He went to finish with 151 not out from 120 balls, with 17 fours and 4 sixes, beating his country's previous best of 145 scored by Aravinda de Silva against the Kenyans in 1995/96. Sri Lanka passed the Indian total with 9.1 overs and five wickets to spare.

India v Pakistan — 1997

M.A. Chidambaram Stadium, Chennai, 21 May 1997
Pakistan won by 35 runs
Pakistan 5-327 (50 overs) (Saeed Anwar 194, Ijaz Ahmed 39, Inzamam-ul-Haq 39)
India 292 (49.2 overs) (R. Dravid 107, V.G. Kambli 65, R.R. Singh 35, Aaqib Javed 5-61)

In this match, Saeed Anwar (194) broke the record for the highest score in a one-day international, previously held by Viv Richards (189 v England, Old Trafford, 1984).

Pakistan captain Ramiz Raja decided to bat, losing Shahid Afridi (5) with the score on 8, before Saeed Anwar started his assault on the Indian attack. He and Ramiz added 89 for the second wicket, but his captain was just along for the ride, making 22 from his 51 balls. Anwar was joined by Ijaz Ahmed, with the opener still blazing runs to all parts of the ground as the heat took its toll and he was forced to use a runner. Still, Anwar brought up his hundred off 84 balls, before Ijaz fell for 39 from 55 deliveries with the score on 213. Inzamam-ul-Haq came to the crease and Anwar brought up his 150 by scoring six, six, six and a four off consecutive balls from Anil Kumble. Anwar was finally out for 194 from 146 balls with the score at 4 for 297, scoring 22 fours and 5 sixes, while Inzamam made 39 from 33 balls to leave Pakistan with 5 for 327.

India faced a daunting task, made worse when Sachin Tendulkar fell for 4 with the score on 9. Saurav Ganguly and Rahul Dravid brought the score to 61, before Ganguly threw away a good start to be out for 33 from 28 balls. Vinod Kambli and Dravid then gave the Indians some hope, despite Dravid requiring a runner after suffering cramp. They added 134 for the third wicket in 24 overs, before Kambli fell for 65 off 80 balls. Dravid went on to make his first century in a one-day international, but his dismissal for 107 from 116 balls left India 5 for 247 and from there the challenge faded, the home side finishing with 292.

Sri Lanka v India — 1997

R. Premadasa (Khettarama) Stadium, Colombo, 17 August 1997
Sri Lanka won by 2 runs
Sri Lanka 4-302 (50 overs) (M.T. Atapattu 118, S.T. Jayasuriya 73, R. S. Mahanama 53)
India 7-300 (50 overs) (A. Jadeja 119, M. Azharuddin 111*, W.P.U.J.C. Vaas 3-63)

Sri Lanka held on for a thrilling two-run victory over India in this run bonanza in Colombo.

India won the toss and sent the home side in and was able to contain Sanath Jayasuriya and Marvan Atapattu to only 16 runs from the first five overs. However, the next five conceded 45 and Sri Lanka was on their way. Jayasuriya was first out with the score on 91, but not until after he had blazed 73 from only 52 balls. Atapattu played the sheet anchor role, adding 108 for the second wicket with Mahanama (53 from 58 balls) and 80 for the third wicket with Aravinda de Silva (34 in 34 balls). Atapattu was last man out for 118 from 153 deliveries, his maiden century, as Sri Lanka made an imposing 4 for 302.

Sachin Tendulkar and Saurav Ganguly took to the challenge, before Ganguly fell for 31 from 26 balls after the pair added a rapid 58. However from there India slumped to 4 for 64, after Tendulkar was out for 27 from 28 deliveries in the eleventh over. Then as all appeared lost Mohammed Azharuddin and Ajay Jadeja came together in an astonishing fight-back that saw them add 223 to break the previous fifth-wicket world record held by Ricky Ponting and Michael Bevan. After taking them to the edge of victory, Jadeja was out for 119 from 121 balls in the forty-ninth over, with India needing nine from the last to clinch the win. However, the Sri Lankans claimed two wickets and the match, leaving Azharuddin dejected on 111 not out from 117 balls as the Indians finished on 7 for 300.

Zimbabwe v New Zealand — 1997

Queens Sports Club, Bulawayo, 1 October 1997
Match tied
Zimbabwe 8-233 (50 overs) (G.W Flower 66, D.L. Houghton 40, A. Flower 35)
New Zealand 9-233 (50 overs) (C.Z. Harris 77, M.J. Horne 55)

Zimbabwe and New Zealand played out a thrilling tie in the first match of the three-game series.

Zimbabwe won the toss and batted, losing Gavin Rennie and Alistair Campbell cheaply to be 2 for 24. The Flower brothers combined for a 77-run third-wicket partnership from 19 overs, before Andy was bowled for 35 from 53 balls to leave the home side 3 for 101. Guy Whittall made a quick-fire 24 before he was caught on the fence and was quickly followed by Grant Flower (66) to leave Zimbabwe in some trouble at 5 for 139. David Houghton and Chris Evans rescued the situation, although Evans

was needlessly run out after making 21 at a run a ball. Houghton went on to make 40 from 36 balls, as tradesman-like performance by New Zealand restricted Zimbabwe to 8 for 233.

John Rennie gave Zimbabwe a great start by removing both openers to have New Zealand reeling at 2 for 14. Captain Stephen Fleming steered the visitors to 49 before he tried a cross-bat slash and was caught behind for 19. Chris Cairns felt the best form of defence was attack, and he proceeded to take 26 from 18 balls before he attacked once too often. He was quickly followed by Craig McMillan (2) and Adam Parore (1) and New Zealand crashed to 6 for 100. Throughout the turmoil Matt Horne had stayed resolute, and he and Chris Harris added 37 before Horne fell for 55 from 75 deliveries. Harris and Daniel Vettori had previously denied Zimbabwe a Test win and now joined in a 41-run stand for the eighth wicket before Vettori was run out for 18. Gavin Larsen joined Harris at 8 for 178, and the pair had taken the score to 219 when the last over began. One wide, two quick singles and then Harris hit four, two, four, leaving one run to tie, two to win. Harris hit the last ball up the ground as the crowd burst on to the oval. Craig Evans beat a number of spectators to the ball and his return found Larsen short of his ground attempting a second run to leave the match tied.

New Zealand v South Africa – 1998

Brisbane Cricket Ground, 9 January, 1998
South Africa won by 2 runs
South Africa 6-300 (50 overs) (G. Kirsten 103,W.J. Cronje 55, L. Klusener 50)
New Zealand 9-298 (50 overs) (A.C. Parore 67, C.L. Cairns 64, A.A. Donald 4-43)

This was the first match played after the 1997/98 Christmas/New Year break. South Africa were down 1-0 in their test series with Australia and New Zealand returned from a short break at home. Hansie Cronje won the toss and the South African openers got off to a flying start, with Gary Kirsten and Lance Klusener smashing 100 before Klusener (50 from 55 balls) was bowled by Dion Nash in the 19th over. Jacques Kallis (31 from 40) helped Kirsten to a 67 run second wicket stand, before the skipper and Kirsten then added 64 in 9 overs. Kirsten (103 from 113) was the first of Chris Harris' two wickets, with Harris finishing with the best bowling figures both in terms of wickets (2) and runs per overs (4.1). Cronje made 55 from 47 balls, as Jonty Rhodes (23), Shaun Pollock (14 not out) and Pat Symcox (12 not out) all scored better than a run a ball to help South Africa finish with 6-300.

Needing to make the highest successful run chase in Australia, New Zealand were well in it despite losing their first wicket at 24. Nathan Astle (29 from 45 balls) and Matthew Horne (42 from 66 balls) added 60 for the second wicket before Allan Donald claimed 3-1 in 10 balls to have the Kiwis reeling at 5-97. Then the loss of the Chris Harris 27 runs later in the 31st over seemed to toll the death knell. However New Zealand had a deep batting line-up and Chris Cairns and Adam Parore took to the challenge adding 71 in 8 overs before Cairns was run out for 64 from 53 balls. Dion Nash joined the keeper and they added 69 in 46 balls before Parore (67 from 46 balls) became Donald's fourth victim. Nash took New Zealand to 8-289 at the start of the last over, then nearly claimed the game when his shot to fine leg hit the rope for a four rather than six. Needing three to win, Nash clipped the final delivery to mid-wicket only to see Lance Klusener hold the catch just inside the fence to deny New Zealand a courageous victory.

Pakistan v India — 1998

Bangabandhu National Stadium, Dhaka, 18 January 1998
India won by 3 wickets
Pakistan 5-314 (48 overs) (Saeed Anwar 140, Ijaz Ahmed 117, Harvinder Singh 3-74)
India 7-316 (48 overs) (S.C. Ganguly 124, R.R. Singh 82, S.R. Tendulkar 41, Saqlain Mushtaq 3-66)

India made the highest score batting second in a one-day international, after successfully chasing Pakistan's total of 5 for 314 in the third final of the Independence Cup.

Pakistan was asked to bat and lost Shahid Afridi for 18 with the score on 30, before Aamir Sohail and Saeed Anwar took the score to 66 in the twelfth over. Sohail's dismissal for 14 opened the floodgates, as Ijaz Ahmed joined Saeed Anwar in adding 230 for the third wicket in 33 overs. The Indian fielding fell away, as Ijaz and Anwar pummelled the opposition into submission in an onslaught interrupted by bad light which reduced the match to 48 overs per side. Anwar was out for 140 from 132 balls in the forty-sixth over with the score on 296, while Ijaz (117 from 112 balls) followed five runs later in the next over. Pakistan finished with 5 for 314, setting the Indians a target of 6.56 runs per over.

Sachin Tendulkar and Saurav Ganguly made a bright start of 71 in the ninth over, before Tendulkar fell after blasting 41 from only 26 balls. Robin Singh's promotion to add some aggression to the top order was a masterstroke, as he and Ganguly added 179 for the second wicket in 29.5 overs. Robin Singh made 82 from 83 balls, but then India lost four more wickets, including Ganguly for 124 from 139 balls, to slump to 6 for 296. They needed 18 runs from the last 14 balls, and nine from the last over, before Hrishikesh Kanitkar clouted the fifth ball to the mid-wicket boundary to give India an astonishing victory.

New Zealand v Zimbabwe — 1998

Bangabandhu National Stadium, Dhaka 24 October, 1998
New Zealand won by 5 wickets
New Zealand 5-260 (50 overs) (S.P. Fleming 96, A.C. Parore 52, C.Z. Harris 37*)
Zimbabwe 7-258 (50 overs) (A.D.R. Campbell 100, A. Flower 77, G.I. Allott 3-54)

New Zealand and Zimbabwe, two of the lower ranked nations in Test cricket, got the Wills International Cup off to a rousing start in Bangladesh with a last ball finish.

Alistair Campbell won the toss and led by example, as Zimbabwe added 93 in the first 15 overs despite losing the wickets of Grant Flower, Neil Johnson and Murray Goodwin. Campbell then found an able ally in Andy Flower, the keeper scoring 77 in their partnership of 118 before falling to Nathan Astle. Just as Zimbabwe looked likely to make a score in the order of 270 to 280, they lost valuable wickets and momentum, including Campbell as soon as he had reached his hundred. Craig Wishart finished the innings in style, hitting Geoff Allott down the ground for six to leave Zimbabwe with 7-258.

Zimbabwe debutant Neil Johnson claimed the wicket of fellow newcomer Mark Bell for 2 at the end of the 4th over, and when Nathan Astle went 6 overs later, New Zealand were struggling. Craig McMillan and Stephen Fleming steadied the ship, but it was the arrival of Adam Parore that gave New Zealand the lift they required as he and Fleming added 125 for the fourth wicket in 24 overs. However Fleming fell for 96 near the end of the 45th over, with New Zealand still needing 54 runs. Parore (52) was out shortly after with the Kiwis still needing 42 from 18 balls. Chris Harris and Alex Tait took up the challenge, taking 18 from the 48th over and from the next, before Campbell entrusted Johnson with the last over. He opened with a no-ball, then conceded nine from the next five balls before Harris (37 from 22) drove the last delivery to the cover boundary to get New Zealand home for a five-wicket victory.

Pakistan v Australia — 1998

Gaddafi Stadium, Lahore. 10 November, 1998
Australia won by 6 wickets
Pakistan 8-315 (50 overs) (Ijaz Ahmed 111, Yousuf Youhana 100, Shahid Afridi 40)
Australia 4-316 (48.5 overs) (R.T. Ponting 124*, A.C Gilchrist 103, S.R. Waugh 30*)

In this match, Australia set a record by successfully chasing the highest ever target in a one-day international.

Pakistan captain Aamer Sohail opted to bat, losing opening partner Asif Mahmood for a duck in third over. Sohail (21) and Ijaz Ahmed added 43 in 5 overs, then Malik (2) struggled before being run out by Ricky Ponting to make the score 3-72. Ahmed was joined by Yousuf

Silver Jubilee Independence Cup 1997/98, Third Final   Pakistan v India

National Stadium, Dhaka, Bangladesh (D/N), 18 January 1998

Result: India won by 3 wickets
Umpires: R.B. Tiffin (Zim) and R.E. Koertzen (SA).
Match Referee: M.H. Denness (Eng)

Toss: India
TV Umpire: D.B. Cowie (NZ)
Man of the Match: S.C. Ganguly

Pakistan innings

			Runs	Balls
Shahid Afidi	c R.R. Singh	b H. Singh	18	20
Saeed Anwar	c Azharuddin	b H. Singh	140	132
Aamir Sohail	c Mongia	b H. Singh	14	17
Ijaz Ahmed	c Sidhu	b Srinath	117	112
Azhar Mahmood	c Azharuddin	b Tendulkar	10	6
Mohammad Hussain	not out		2	2
Extras	(lb 7, w 6)		13	
Total	**(5 wickets, 48 overs)**		**314**	

DNB: *†Rashid Latif, Inzamam-ul-Haq, Manzoor Akhtar, Saqlain Mushtaq, Aaqib Javed

FoW: 1-30 (Afridi), 2-66 (Sohail), 3-296 (Anwar), 4-301 (Ijaz Ahmed),
5-314 (Azhar Mahmood)

Bowling	O	M	R	W	
Srinath	10	0	61	1	(2w)
H.Singh	10	0	74	3	(1nb, 4w)
R.R. Singh	8	0	47	0	
Ganguly	2	0	5	0	
Kanitkar	6	0	33	0	
Tendulkar	7	0	49	1	
Sanghvi	5	0	38	0	

India innings

			Runs	Balls
S.C. Ganguly		b Aqib	124	138
S.R. Tendulkar	c Azhar	b Shahid	41	26
R.R. Singh	c Aqib	b Mohammad	82	83
*Mohammed Azharuddin	c Aamir	b Saqlian	4	11
A.D. Jadeja		b Saqlain	8	9
N.S. Sidhu	LBW	b Saqlain	5	4
H. Kanitkar	not out		11	12
†N.R. Mongia	run out		9	6
J. Srinath	not out		5	3
Extras	(b 1, lb 11, w 13, nb 2)		11	
Total	**(7 wickets, 47.5 overs)**		**316**	

DNB: R. Sanghvi, Harvinder Singh

FoW: 1-71 (Tendulkar), 2-250 (R.R. Singh), 3-268 (Azharuddin), 4-274 (Ganguly),
5-281 (Sidhu), 6-296 (Jadeja), 7-306 (Mongia)

Bowling	O	M	R	W	
Aaqib Javed	9.2	0	63	1	(2nb, 2w)
Azhar Mahmood	8	0	56	0	(1nb, 3w)
Shahid Afridi	6.4	0	56	1	(2nb, 2w)
Saqlain Mushtaq	9.5	0	66	3	(4w)
Mohammad Hussain	10	0	40	1	

Youhana and the pair took command of the Australian attack, adding 163 in 167 balls as the visitors were forced to use eight bowlers to try to break the partnership. Ahmed made 111 from 109 balls, eventually bowled by part-timer Darren Lehmann's second ball, with Youhana (100) falling 53 runs later after having made his maiden one-day hundred. Shahid Afridi made a rapid-fire 40 from 26 balls as Pakistan amassed an imposing 8-315, their highest ever score against Australia.

Despite losing Mark Waugh (13) early, Australia were undaunted by the task and Adam Gilchrist and Ricky Ponting set about destroying the Pakistan bowling. They added 193 runs in 177 balls, a record for Australia for any wicket against Pakistan. Gilchrist was eventually stumped for 103 from 104 balls in the 34th over, his third century in one-day internationals. Darren Lehmann went for eight, then Steve Waugh and Ponting added 69 in 57 balls before Waugh fell for 30 from 29 balls with the visitors in sight of victory. Michael Bevan and Ponting completed the task with seven balls to spare, the Tasmanian making 124 not out from 129 and earning the Man of the Match award. It was the first time that four centuries were scored in a limited-overs international.

England v Sri Lanka – 1999

Adelaide Oval, 23 January, 1999
Sri Lanka won by 1 wicket
England 3-302 (50 overs) (G.A. Hick 126*, N.H. Fairbrother 78*, N.V. Knight 44)
Sri Lanka 9-303 (49.4 overs) (D.P.Mde.S, Jayawardene 120, S.T. Jayasuriya 51)

The scorecard would suggest that this game should be included as a classic match. However, it will more likely be remembered for controversy rather than cricket.

Sri Lanka asked England to bat and Alec Stewart and Nick Knight took up the challenge with an opening stand of 64 from 62 balls. Stewart (39 from 33) gave way to Graeme Hick who was lucky to survive a confident appeal for caught behind when he was on 11. Mutiah Muralitharan's introduction into the attack sent a buzz through the crowd, but the anticipated action by umpire Ross Emerson seemed to have passed until he called the spinner for an illegal delivery in his second over. Arjuna Ranatunga led his team to the boundary, as heated discussions took place between Ranatunga, the Sri Lankan manager, the match referee and the umpires. After a 14-minute delay, the game resumed but the finger-pointing and dissent continued to mar the tone of the match. Hick and Knight (44 from 74) added 75 for the second wicket, and Nasser Hussein quickly came and went, before Neil Fairbrother helped Hick put Sri Lanka to the sword. The pair added an unbeaten 154 from 21 overs, with Hick making 126* from 188 balls and Fairbrother 78* from 71, as England reached 3-302, the highest score so far in the Australian summer.

Sri Lanka's effort to make the highest successful run chase in Australia began badly when Romesh Kaluwitharana (0) was run out in the second over and Marvin Atapattu (3) was dismissed shortly after. Sanath Jayasuriya then launched a one-man rescue mission, scoring 51 from 36 balls before he fell with the score on 68 in the 11th over. Hashan Tillekeratne and Mahela Jayawardene kept the scoreboard ticking over with determined running until Tillakeratne was dismissed for 28. Then Arjuna Ranatunga joined Jayawardene and they added a quick-fire 89 to keep the Sri Lankans in sight of their target. The skipper went for 41 from 51 deliveries, but the youngster kept going, making 120 from 11 balls, until he fell with the score at 7-269. Sri Lanka needed 34 from their last 28 balls, but a six from Chandana brought the equation closer. However the mood of the match darkened when Roshan Mahanama appeared to obstruct English paceman Darren Gough during a quick single. As the tension grew, Chandana (25 from 18 balls) and Mahanama (13 from 11) were both dismissed, leaving Sri Lanka needing 5 runs from the final over with the last pair as the crease. In the end, Muralitharan became the hero, slicing Vince Wells just over the head of Adam Hollioake at cover with two balls to spare.

Firsts

The Teams

First game	Australia v England, Melbourne Cricket Ground, on 5 January 1971.
First women's game	The first women's international, on the opening day of the inaugural Women's World Cup, was scheduled to take place on 20 June 1973 between Jamaica and New Zealand at Kew, however the match was washed out. Three matches were successfully completed three days later.
100th game	India v New Zealand, WACA Ground, Perth, on 9 December 1980.
500th game	Australia v New Zealand, Sydney Cricket Ground, on 20 January 1988.
1000th game	England v West Indies, Trent Bridge, Nottingham on 24 and 25 May 1995.
First tie	West Indies (5 for 222) and Australia (9 for 222) both finished with the same number of runs in the second final of the World Series Cup in Melbourne on 11 January 1984.
First victory by one run	New Zealand (8 for 198) defeated Pakistan (9 for 197) by one run, at Jinnah Park, Sialkot on 16 October 1976. The game was the first international played in Pakistan.
First victory by one wicket	England (9 for 182) overhauled the West Indies' total of 181 with one wicket in hand in the first game ever played between the two sides, a Prudential Cup match played at Headingley, Leeds on 5 September 1973.
First victory with one ball to spare	New Zealand's John Bracewell hit a boundary off the penultimate ball of the match bowled by England's Paul Allott at Edgbaston, Birmingham on 15 June 1983.
First victory off the last ball	Ian Botham's cover drive for four helped England to a three-wicket victory over Pakistan at Sahiwal on 23 December 1977, the first victory off the last ball of the innings by the team batting second.
First victory by 10 wickets	India's openers Sunil Gavaskar (65 not out) and Farouk Engineer (54 not out) kept their wickets intact (0 for 123) reaching the target set by East Africa of 120 in a preliminary game of the inaugural World Cup on 11 June 1975 at Headingley, Leeds.

First match played over two days	The second Prudential Trophy match between England and India at The Oval was the first match to be played over two days — 15 and 16 July 1974. England won by six wickets to wrap up the series 2-0.
First no result	Rain forced the first no result in a match between England (8 for 167) and New Zealand, who did not bat, at Old Trafford, Manchester on 20 July 1973. The game was only the seventh one-day international.
First forfeit	Australia was the first team to forfeit a match, refusing to play their 1996 World Cup preliminary game against Sri Lanka in Colombo on 17 February 1996 after a terrorist bombing in the Sri Lankan capital a fortnight earlier raised concerns about security for the players. The West Indies also refused to play their match in the Sri Lankan capital one week later.
First conceded match	India conceded a match to Pakistan in Sahiwal on 3 November 1978 after Indian captain Bishen Bedi ordered his batsmen off the field in protest against short-pitched bowling.
First default	Sri Lanka was awarded the World Cup semi-final against India by default in Calcutta on 13 March 1996 due to crowd rioting.
First victory by an ICC associate member nation over a full member nation	Sri Lanka recorded the first victory by an ICC associate member nation over a full member nation when they defeated India by 47 runs in a World Cup match at Old Trafford, Manchester on 16 and 18 June 1979.
First team to play 50 games	England played its 50th match on 21 January 1980 at the Sydney Cricket Ground against the West Indies.
First team to play 100 games	Australia played its 100th game on 21 January 1984 at the Melbourne Cricket Ground against Pakistan.
First team to play 200 games	Australia played its 200th game on 15 December 1988 at the Melbourne Cricket Ground against the West Indies.
First team to play 300 games	Australia played its 300th game on 25 January 1994 at the Sydney Cricket Ground against South Africa.
First team to play 400 games	Pakistan played its 400th game 15 April 1998 at the Willowmoore Park, Benoni, against Sri Lanka. Six days later Australia played its 400th match at Sharjah against New Zealand.

The Players

First appearance	The 22 players who appeared in the first one-day international between Australia and England at the Melbourne Cricket Ground on 5 January 1971 were: Australia — Bill Lawry (captain), Keith Stackpole, Ian Chappell, Doug Walters, Ian Redpath, Greg Chappell, Rod Marsh, Ashley Mallett, Graham McKenzie, Alan Connolly, Alan Thomson. England — Ray Illingworth (captain), Geoff Boycott, John Edrich, Ken Fletcher, Basil D'Oliveira, John Hampshire, Colin Cowdrey, Alan Knott, John Snow, Ken Shuttleworth, Peter Lever.
First player to make 50 appearances	Australian captain Greg Chappell played his 50th match against the West Indies on 19 January 1982 in Sydney.
First player to make 100 appearances	Australia's Allan Border played his 100th match against India at Jamshedpur on 3 October 1984.
First player to make 200 appearances	Australian captain Allan Border played his 200th match against Pakistan at the Sydney Cricket Ground on 20 February 1990.
First player to make 300 appearances	Indian captain Mohammed Azharuddin played his 300th match against Australia at the Bangabandhu National Stadium, Dhaka, during the Wills International Cup, on 28 October, 1998.
Longest gap between appearances	England batsman Wayne Larkins played against the West Indies at the Sydney Cricket Ground on 22 January 1980, then next appeared in a Nehru Cup game against Sri Lanka in Delhi, India on 15 October 1989, nine years and 267 days later. England had played 110 matches in between.
Only player to represent two countries	Kepler Wessels is the only player to play for two countries in one-day internationals. South African-born Wessels played 54 matches for his adopted country, Australia, between 1983 and 1985. His first match for South Africa was against India at Calcutta on 10 November 1991 and he played a total of 55 games for South Africa between 1991-94.
First player to be suspended under the ICC Code of Conduct	Pakistani fast bowler Aqib Javed was suspended for one match after he called umpire Brian Aldridge 'a f***ing cheat' during a game against New Zealand in Napier on 28 December 1992.

First player to be given out with the aid of a television replay	South African captain Kepler Wessels became the first player in a one-day international to be given out with the aid of a television replay (the so-called 'third umpire'), on 7 December 1992. Wessels was adjudicated run out for 43 against India at Newlands in Cape Town.
First player to appear in a one-day international but destined never to play a Test	Opening batsman Peter Coman made his one-day debut for New Zealand against Pakistan on 11 February 1973 in Christchurch and played two games against Australia the following year, but never appeared in a Test match.
First brothers	Australian brothers Ian and Greg Chappell appeared in the first one-day international against England in Melbourne on 5 January 1971.
First twin brothers	Australia's Steve and Mark Waugh are the only twins to appear in one-day internationals. They first played together on 11 December 1988 against Pakistan in Adelaide, when neither batted and Steve took 1 for 27 off 7.4 overs.
First three brothers	New Zealand brothers Richard, Dale and Barry Hadlee all appeared in a match against England on 8 March 1975 at Dunedin. Richard and Dale recorded identical bowling figures of 2 for 21 and opening batsman Barry was not out on seven in a run chase that was abandoned because of rain.
First four brothers	Following earlier appearances by Arjuna, Dammika and Nishantha, Sanjeeva Ranatunga made his debut for Sri Lanka on 3 August 1994 against Pakistan in Colombo, the first instance of four brothers appearing in one-day internationals.
First player to make his debut on his birthday	New Zealand's Bevan Congdon was the first player to make his debut on his birthday, playing his first one-day international against Pakistan at Christchurch on 11 February 1973, as he turned 35.
First player to be knighted	West Indies' Garfield (Gary) St Aubrun Sobers became the first player to be knighted in 1975. Sobers played one match against England on 5 September 1973.

Batting

First half-century	English batsman John Edrich scored the first half-century (82), during the inaugural match against Australia at the Melbourne Cricket Ground on 5 January 1971. Edrich also won the Man of the Match award.
First century/First century on debut	Dennis Amiss scored the first century in a one-day international, 103 off 134 balls against Australia at Old Trafford, Manchester on 24 August 1972. Amiss' innings was also the first century on debut.
First century by a left-hander	West Indian opener Roy Fredericks (105) was the first left-hander to score a century, against England at The Oval in London on 7 September 1973. It was only the third century in a limited oversk;Inv c wrgpjopoi[g international.
First score over 150	New Zealand captain Glenn Turner batted throughout the innings to score 171* against East Africa in their opening World Cup match at Birmingham on 7 June 1975.
50th century	English left-hander David Gower (109) scored the 50th century in limited-overs internationals, against New Zealand at Adelaide on 29 January 1983.
100th century	West Indian opener Gordon Greenidge (100) scored the 100th century in limited-overs internationals, against Australia at Perth on 4 January 1987.
200th century	West Indian all-rounder Phil Simmons (122) scored the 200th century in limited-overs internationals, against South Africa at Kingston on 7 April 1992.
300th century	Diminutive Indian Sachin Tendulkar (100) scored the 300th century in limited-overs internationals, against Pakistan at Singapore on 5 April 1996.
400th century	Indian opener Sachin Tendulkar (128) scored the 400th century in limited-overs internationals, against Sri Lanka at Colombo (RPS) on 7 July 1998, one of three centuries in the match.
First batsman to score 10 centuries	West Indian Desmond Haynes scored his 10th century (142*) in limited-overs internationals against Pakistan at Port-of-Spain on 18 March 1988.
First batsman to score 20 centuries	India's Sachin Tendulkar scored his 20th century in limited-overs internationals, 118* in 112 balls, in a Champions Trophy match against Zimbabwe in Sharjah on 8 November 1998.

First player to score a century in successive innings	Sri Lanka's Roy Dias was the first player to score centuries in two successive innings: 102 in Delhi on 15 September 1982 and 121 in Bangalore on 26 September 1982. Both matches were against India.
First player to score a century in three successive innings	Pakistan's Zaheer Abbas was the first player to score centuries in three successive innings: against India at Multan (118) on 17 December 1982, at Lahore (105) on 31 December 1982 and at Karachi (113) on 21 January 1983.
First player to bat throughout a completed innings	England's David Lloyd remained 116 not out in England's total of 4 for 244 against Pakistan at Nottingham on 31 August 1974, the first player to bat throughout a completed innings. Despite his efforts England lost the match by seven wickets.
First batsman to carry his bat	Zimbabwe opener Grant Flower was the first player to carry his bat in a limited-overs international, remaining 84* after his team was dismissed for 205 against England at Sydney on 15 December 1994.
First batsman dismissed for 99	England's Geoff Boycott was the first batsman to be dismissed for 99, against Australia at The Oval on 20 August 1980.
First batsman to reach 1000 runs	West Indies' Viv Richards in his 22nd match against England at the Sydney Cricket Ground on 22 January 1980.
First batsman to reach 2000 runs	Australia's Greg Chappell in his 55th match against New Zealand in Auckland on 13 February 1982.
First batsman to reach 3000 runs	West Indies' Viv Richards in his 74th match against England at Manchester on 31 May 1984.
First batsman to reach 4000 runs	West Indies' Viv Richards in his 96th match, against New Zealand at Berbice, Guyana on 14 April 1985.
First batsman to reach 5000 runs	West Indies' Viv Richards in his 126th match, against England in Melbourne on 30 January 1987.
First batsman to reach 6000 runs	West Indies' Viv Richards in his 156th match, against Pakistan in Brisbane on 7 January 1989.
First batsman to reach 7000 runs	West Indies' Desmond Haynes in his 188th match, against India at Sharjah on 22 October 1991.
First batsman to reach 8000 runs	West Indies' Desmond Haynes in his 220th match, against Pakistan at Johannesburg on 27 February 1993.

First century partnership	England's Dennis Amiss and Keith Fletcher added 125 for the second wicket, against Australia at Old Trafford, Manchester on 24 August 1972. The match was only the second one-day international.
First double-century partnership	The second-wicket partnership of 205 between Viv Richards (158*) and Desmond Haynes (80) for the West Indies against Australia at the Melbourne Cricket Ground on 9 December 1979 was the first to reach 200 runs in a one-day international.
First instance of two centuries in a match	Both David Lloyd (116, not out) and Majid Khan (109) recorded centuries in the first Prudential Trophy match between England and Pakistan at Trent Bridge on 31 August 1974.
First instance of three centuries in a match	The Prudential Trophy match between Australia and England at Lord's on 3 June 1985 produced three centuries for the first time in a one-day international. Both Australian opener Graeme Wood (114 not out) and England opener Graham Gooch (117 not out) batted throughout the innings, and Man of the Match David Gower scored 102.
First instance of four centuries in a match	The third one-day international between Pakistan and Australia at Gaddafi Stadium, Lahore on 10 November 1998, is the only occasion when four centuries have been scored in match. The century makers were Pakistan's Ijaz Ahmed (111) and Yousuf Youhana (100), and Australia's Adam Gilchrist (103) and Ricky Ponting (124*). Australia won the match by six wickets.
First instance of two centuries in an innings	Pakistan's Mohsin Khan (117, not out) and Zaheer Abbas (118) recorded the first instance of two centuries in the same innings, against India at Multan on 17 December 1982. It was the first of three successive centuries for Zaheer.

Bowling

First four-wicket haul	England's Geoff Arnold took 4 for 27 off 11 overs against Australia at Edgbaston on 28 August 1972.
First five-wicket haul	Australia's Dennis Lillee took 5 for 34 off 12 overs against Pakistan on the opening day of the inaugural World Cup on 7 June 1975 at Headingley, Leeds. It was Lillee's only five-wicket haul in his one-day international career.
First six-wicket haul	Australia's Gary Gilmour took 6 for 14 against England in the semi-final of the inaugural World Cup at Headingley on 18 June 1975. He then top-scored in Australia's innings with 28 not out.
First seven-wicket haul	West Indian Winston Davis took 7 for 51 in 10.3 overs during a World Cup match against Australia at Headingley, Leeds on 11 June 1983.
First hat-trick	Pakistani fast bowler Jalaluddin took the first hat-trick in a one-day international, dismissing Australia's Rod Marsh, Bruce Yardley and Geoff Lawson in successive balls in the opening match of a three-game series at Hyderabad, Pakistan on 20 September 1982.
First player to take two hat-tricks	Pakistan's Wasim Akram is the only player to take two hat-tricks and every victim was clean-bowled. His first hat-trick was against the West Indies (Jeff Dujon, Malcolm Marshall and Curtly Ambrose) on 14 October 1989 at Sharjah and his second was against Australia on 4 May 1990 (Merv Hughes, Carl Rackemann and Terry Alderman) also at Sharjah.
First bowler to take 100 wickets	Australia's Dennis Lillee took his 100th wicket in his 60th match, on the opening day of the 1983 World Cup against Zimbabwe at Nottingham on 9 June 1983.
First bowler to take 200 wickets	Indian all-rounder Kapil Dev took his 200th wicket in his 167th match against Pakistan at Sharjah on 23 October 1991.
First bowler to take 300 wickets	Pakistan's Wasim Akram took his 300th wicket in his 208th match, against Zimbabwe at Quetta on 30 October 1996.
50th five-wicket haul	West Indian speedster Curtly Ambrose (5-17) took the 50th five-wicket haul in limited-overs internationals, against Australia at Melbourne on 15 December 1988.
100th five-wicket haul	Charlie Lock (5-44) of Zimbabwe took the 100th five-wicket haul in limited-overs internationals against New Zealand at Napier on 3 February 1996.

Fielding

First to hold four catches in an innings	Substitute fieldsman John Bracewell took four catches in a World Series Cup match against Australia in Adelaide on 23 November 1980, the first instance of four catches being taken by a fielder (not including wicket-keepers) in a match.
First to hold five catches in an innings	South Africa's Jonty Rhodes is the only fieldsman (not including wicket-keepers) to bag five catches in a match, against the West Indies at Bombay on 14 November 1993.
First to take 50 catches	West Indies' Viv Richards took his 50th catch in his 107th match, against England at Port-of-Spain, Trinidad on 4 March 1986.
First to take 100 catches	West Indies' Viv Richards took his 100th catch in his 179th match, against England at Georgetown, Guyana on 7 March 1990.
First instance of five run-outs in an innings	Five Australian batsmen were run out in the inaugural World Cup final against the West Indies at Lord's on 21 June 1975.

Wicket-keeping

First to hold five catches in an innings	Australia's Rod Marsh became the first wicket-keeper to hold five catches (or make five dismissals) in a match, against England at Headingley, Leeds on 8 June 1981.
First to make three stumpings in an innings	Pakistan's Salim Yousuf became the first wicket-keeper to stump three batsmen in an innings, against New Zealand at Lahore on 2 November 1990.
First to reach 100 wicket-keeping dismissals	Rod Marsh made his 100th dismissal in his 75th match, the Bushfire Appeal Challenge match against New Zealand at the Sydney Cricket Ground on 17 March 1983.
First to reach 200 wicket-keeping dismissals	West Indies' Jeffrey Dujon in his 166th match, against Pakistan at Sharjah on 17 October 1991.

All-round Performances

First to take four wickets and score a half-century	Zimbabwe's Duncan Fletcher scored 69 not out and took 4 for 42 against Australia in a World Cup match at Trent Bridge, Nottingham on 9 June 1983.
First to take five wickets and score a half-century	India's Kris Srikkanth was the first player to take five wickets (5 for 27) and score a half-century (70) in a match, against New Zealand at Vishakhapatnam on 10 December 1988.
First to take five wickets and score a century	West Indies' Viv Richards is the only player to score a century and take five wickets in a match. Richards achieved the feat against New Zealand in Dunedin on 18 March 1987, scoring 119 and taking 5 for 41.
First to reach 1000 runs and take 100 wickets	England's Ian Botham in his 75th match against Australia at Lord's on 3 June 1985.
First to reach 2000 runs and 200 wickets	Indian all-rounder Kapil Dev achieved this milestone in his 167th match against Pakistan at Sharjah on 23 October 1991.
First to reach 5000 runs and take 50 wickets	West Indies' Viv Richards in his 126th match against England in Melbourne on 30 January 1987.

Umpires

First umpires	Umpires Tom Brooks and Lou Rowan stood in the first one-day international, played between Australia and England in Melbourne on 5 January 1971.
First neutral umpires	Harold 'Dickie' Bird (England) and Shakoor Rana (Pakistan) stood in the second Asia Cup match in Sharjah between India and Sri Lanka on 8 April 1984.
First umpire to make 50 appearances	Australian umpire Dick French stood in his 50th one-day international on 20 January 1987, a World Series Cup match between Australia and the West Indies at the Melbourne Cricket Ground.
First umpire to have also played in one-day internationals	English umpire John Hampshire when he stood in the tied match between England and Australia at Trent Bridge on 27 May 1989. He played three matches for England in 1971 and 1972.

Grounds

First ground	The Melbourne Cricket Ground hosted the first one-day international between Australia and England on 5 January 1971.
50th ground	Lal Bahadur Stadium in Hyderabad, India, became the 50th ground to host a one-day international when India played Pakistan on 11 September 1983.
100th ground	Newlands, Cape Town, became the 100th ground to host a one-day international when South Africa played India on 7 December 1992. It was the first match in South Africa.
First ground under lights	Australia played the West Indies at the Sydney Cricket Ground on 27 November 1979, the first official game under lights.
First ground to stage 50 matches	The Melbourne Cricket Ground staged its 50th match on 20 January 1987, between Australia and the West Indies.
First ground to stage 100 matches	The Sharjah Cricket Association Stadium staged its 100th match on 14 April 1996, a Sharjah Cup game between India and South Africa.
First city to host matches at two grounds	London became the first city with two grounds when The Oval hosted its first match on 7 September 1973. Lord's had previously hosted a match on 26 August 1972.
First city to host matches at three grounds	Colombo became the first city with three venues when Khettarama (later R. Premadasa) Stadium hosted its first match on 5 April 1986. The Sinhalese Sports Club and P. Saravanamuttu Stadium had previously hosted matches.

One-day Curiosities and Controversies

Occasions when the weather has produced some unexpected outcomes

Long may she rain

Australia was chasing an England total of 242 in the third one-day international at The Oval on 6 June 1977 when rain began falling during the twenty-third over, forcing the players from the field. However, match officials knew there could be no television coverage the following day because it was Jubilee Day, celebrating the 25th anniversary of the Queen Elizabeth II reign. They were able to persuade the players to return to the field to complete the game, this time in torrential rain. Greg Chappell spearheaded Australia to victory by two wickets, remaining unbeaten on 125.

The long wait

The combined forces of a fire engine, a squeegee roller, an army of ground staff and a Channel Nine helicopter hovering above a waterlogged pitch eventually got play underway four hours late in the World Series Cup match between New Zealand and England at the WACA in Perth on 5 February 1983. The match was reduced to 23 overs a side and New Zealand reached England's total of 7 for 88 with 15 balls to spare.

Haynes stands his ground

Queen's Park Oval, Trinidad was rocked by an earth tremor during a one-day match between the West Indies and India on 9 March 1983. The tremors shook the ground midway through the West Indian innings, but opening batsman Desmond Haynes stood firm and scored 97 to help his side to a 52-run victory.

Curator storms onto the ground

To the bewilderment of the umpires and players, Gabba curator Kevin Mitchell ran onto the ground during the World Series Cup qualifying match between Australia and New Zealand on 17 January 1988 shouting, 'Get off, get off!' and tore the stumps out of the ground. Years of experience had told him that the heavens were about to open up and dump a colossal amount of water on the ground. The reluctant players were officially timed off the ground at 12.57 pm and exactly one minute later the heavens opened up. The ground was soon saturated, however the storm passed and only 37 minutes of play was lost.

South Africa requires one almighty hit!

South Africa, needing 253 off 45 overs to win their World Cup semi-final against England at the Sydney Cricket Ground on 22 March 1992, had scored all but 22 of them when persistent rain set in with 13 balls remaining. England captain Graham Gooch exercised his option to leave the field, a decision that was met by another storm, this time of booing from the crowd. However, within minutes the rain stopped and the umpires declared that one over had been deducted for the time lost, but that according to an absurdity in the rules, the run target remained the same. The electronic scoreboard flashed 'South Africa requires 22 runs off seven balls'. When Gooch led his players back on to the field he was met by the umpires who told him that after a recalculation, in fact two overs had been lost, there was time left for only one ball and South Africa had to score 21 from it. The scoreboard then flashed 'South Africa requires one almighty hit'.

Dust-up stops play

A dust storm delayed play in the match between Australia and India at Sharjah on 22 April 1998.

Good light stops play

The start of the first one-day international between New Zealand and Pakistan at Gujranwala on 6 December 1996 was delayed because of *good* light. The rising sun was shining straight into the batsmen's eyes at the scheduled start time and the match was reduced to 46 overs per side.

Washout

Heavy rain for over a week left the Galle International Stadium in Sri Lanka saturated, leading to an unprecedented three one-day internationals on 25, 27 and 29 June 1998 being abandoned without a ball being bowled. The stadium would have been the 121st ground to host a one-day international, having become the 79th Test venue three weeks earlier when Sri Lanka played New Zealand.

Matches delayed or abandoned for unusual reasons

Political lie-in

After four overs of the Australian innings in the 1975 World Cup final, a group of about 20 Sri Lankan political protesters raced onto the field and lay across the wicket. A second group appeared after police had cleared the ground, but Rick McCosker and Alan Turner appeared unfazed, going on to record an opening stand of 25.

Indians walk off in protest at Pakistani bowling

Cricketing relations between India and Pakistan were strained following a walk-off by the Indians during the third match of the inaugural series between the two countries at Zafar Ali Stadium in Sahiwal, Pakistan on 3 November 1978. The Indian captain, Bishen Bedi, called his players off in protest against short-pitched bowling by medium quick Sarfraz Nawaz. The Indians also refused to attend the official post-match function because of the incident.

What a riot (1)

A crowd riot spilled onto the field during a match between Pakistan and Sri Lanka in Karachi on 12 March 1982, forcing players to flee to the pavilion. After several attempts to break up the disturbance, police fired tear gas which restored order and Pakistan went on to win the game by eight wickets.

Pelted off

The second one-day match between Australia and Pakistan in Karachi on 22 October 1982 was abandoned after the Australian players walked off the field. The Australians had been pelted with stones and fruit and one spectator hurled a battery, narrowly missing Greg Ritchie. After 12 overs captain Kim Hughes ordered his team off the field, later saying, 'If one of our players had been seriously injured, I doubt whether Australia would have played there again. The rocks (and I am not kidding) were twice as big as golf balls.'

Farce on grass

Play between Australia and India in the third one-day international in a five-match series to commemorate the Golden Jubilee of the Ranji Trophy in 1984 started three hours behind schedule because a truck carrying the Australian and Indian players' clothing and equipment got lost on the way from the airport to the ground at Jamshedpur. The game finally got underway but was washed out by unseasonal rain after just five overs, with India 2 for 21.

Cancellation times two

The second one-day international between India and Pakistan at the Jinnah Stadium in Sialkot on 31 October 1984 was abandoned as soon as news of the death that day of Indian Prime Minister Indira Gandhi came through. India had scored 3 for 210 with Dilip Vengsarkar on 94 not out when the game was called off. The third and final match in the series, scheduled to be played at Peshawar three days later, was also cancelled.

And bless us all...

A match between Pakistan and Sri Lanka in Lahore on 25 October 1985 was shortened by two overs a side from the original 40 overs so that the Sri Lankan innings could end in time for Muslim Friday prayer meetings.

No marks for WACA groundsman

The World Series Cup match between Australia and Sri Lanka on 30 December 1989 was reduced by two overs per side because the groundsman at the WACA in Perth forgot to mark the fielding circles.

Dressed late, bowled slow

A match between India and the West Indies on 7 November 1984 at Vishakhapatnam had to be reduced to 44 overs a side because the West Indies kit arrived late. To rub salt into the wound, the West Indies also had an over cut from their batting quota by match referee Raman Subba Row because they bowled through their overs too slowly.

What a riot (2)

The 1996 World Cup semi-final between Sri Lanka and India at Eden Gardens, Calcutta was abandoned after a partisan Indian crowd began rioting when it became apparent India was about to lose the match. India was struggling at 8 for 120 after 34.1 overs in reply to Sri Lanka's 251 when match referee Clive Lloyd strode onto the field and ordered the players to the pavilion.

Pitched battle

The second one-day international between Sri Lanka and India on 25 December 1997 was abandoned after only 18 balls when officials ruled the pitch at the Nehru Stadium in Indore was too dangerous for play. The ball had begun breaking through the dusty surface from the very first delivery and the game was called off after only 15 minutes with Sri Lanka 1 for 17. A disgruntled Indian fan commenced legal proceedings against the two captains, the match officials and the groundsmen in April 1998.

Helicopter ride, anyone?

Australia and the West Indies forfeited their World Cup matches against Sri Lanka in Colombo on 17 and 25 February 1996 after a bombing in the capital in late January killed over 100 people. The Australian Cricket Board declined the offer of a helicopter gunship flight into Premadasa Stadium in Colombo on the morning of the match from a port in India and an immediate flight back again after the game.

Eight-minute sound check

A World Series Cup match between Australia and Sri Lanka in Perth on 30 December, 1989 was delayed for eight minutes while Channel Nine replaced their TV microphone in one of the stumps.

Lights go out for India

The inaugural one-day international at Owen Delany Park, Taupo between New Zealand and India on 9 January, 1999 was delayed for 50 minutes when a lighting tower blew a fuse. Drinks were taken upon stoppage of play and New Zealand later reached the revised target of 200 with an over to spare.

More runs than bargained for

The first one-day international between South Africa and the West Indies in Johannesburg on 22 January 1999, required the South Africans to chase a target six runs *higher* than their opponents with one less over. After two rain delays, the match was reduced to 28 overs a side and the West Indies innings finished at 4/154. However, for taking longer than allowed to complete their overs, the South Africans were allowed one over fewer to chase 160, a target revised under the mystifying Duckworth-Lewis system for rain-affected innings. The South Africans smashed 111 runs off the final 13 overs and reached the target off the last ball of the match.

Fire and rain

After the devastating Ash Wednesday bushfires swept Victoria and South Australia New Zealand agreed to fly over to Sydney for a one-off match on 17 March, 1983 to help raise funds for an appeal. In an coincidental twist, the match was shortened because of rain, with New Zealand victorious by 14 runs.

Unusual Dismissals

How's that? And that!

During a Prudential Cup trophy match between the West Indies and England at Scarborough on 26 August 1976, a throw from Michael Holding broke the wicket at one end with Graham Barlow safely home, however it ricocheted to the stumps at the other end, where tardy England wicket-keeper Alan Knott was yet to make his ground. The dumbfounded umpires rejected the run out appeal.

Six and out (1)

England's David Bairstow lost his wicket in extraordinary circumstances during the third match of the International Cup against Australia on 7 February 1979 at the Melbourne Cricket Ground. After Mike Brearley hit Gary Cosier deep into the vacant mid-wicket area of the vast arena, the batsmen ran five. As they completed their fifth run, Geoff Dymock's return went past the bowler and was backed up by Kim Hughes fielding in the gully. Brearley called for a sixth run, but Hughes made a smart return to the bowler's end and Cosier found Bairstow short of his ground.

Six and out (2)

Dennis Lillee gave Australia a vital break in an unusual incident from the last ball of his second over in the World Cup final against the West Indies at Lord's on 21 June 1975. Opener Roy Fredericks hooked a bouncer high to fine leg and the ball sailed over the boundary for six. But Fredericks had stood on his wicket, and the result was every boy's backyard cricket nightmare — six and out.

While the crowd was still cheering, he disappointedly walked back to the pavilion.

How's hat?

Two batsmen have been dismissed in one-day cricket when their helmets fell onto their stumps: Sri Lankan Roy Dias against England in Colombo on 14 February 1982 off the bowling of John Lever; and Australian opener Bruce Laird, after a fiery ball from West Indian express bowler Michael Holding during a World Series Cup game at the Melbourne Cricket Ground on 10 January 1982.

Mankaded!

After repeated warnings by the bowler, Greg Chappell, England's Brian Luckhurst was run out in his debut match for backing up too far at the non-striker's end at the Melbourne Cricket Ground on 1 January 1975. Zimbabwe's Grant Flower and South Africa's Peter Kirsten are the only other players to suffer the same fate in a one-day international.

Nine down, none to go

Pakistan were forced to end their innings with only nine wickets down in a World Series Cup qualifying match against Australia in Sydney on 14 January 1982 when last man in Wasim Bari (9) retired hurt and had to be helped from the ground with a torn hamstring.

Obstructing the field

Two batsmen have been given out for obstructing the field in one-day internationals. Merely out of mischief, Pakistan's Ramiz Raja, on 99, saved himself from being run out off the last ball of the match against England in Karachi on 20 October 1987 by intercepting a roll down the pitch by wicket-keeper Bruce French with his bat. India's Mohinder Armanath was given out by the Pakistani umpire on the appeal of Arjuna Ranatunga after he kicked the ball out of the Sri Lankan bowler's reach to avoid being run out in a Nehru Cup match in Ahmedabad on 22 October 1989.

Can't handle it

India's Mohinder Armanath and South Africa's Daryll Cullinan are the only two batsmen to be given out handled the ball in a one-day international. Armanath was given out in the second final of the World Series Cup against Australia in Melbourne on 9 February 1986 while Cullinan fell the same way against the West Indies in the third one-day international at Kingsmead, Durban on 27 January, 1999.

Forgotten runner

England captain David Gower succeeded in having Australia's Dean Jones, who was acting as a runner for the injured Ian Healy, dismissed from the field of play after Healy forgot Jones' presence and inadvertently set off for two runs. The Texaco Trophy match at Nottingham on 27 May 1989 ended in a thrilling tie.

Dream Debuts

Fletcher fleeces Aussie lambs

Zimbabwean captain Duncan Fletcher had a stunning debut against Australia on the opening day of the 1983 World Cup on 9 June at Trent Bridge, Nottingham. After scoring 69 not out Fletcher took 4 for 42, including the prize scalps of Graeme Wood, Kim Hughes, David Hookes and Graham Yallop, to become the first player to take four wickets and score a half-century in a one-day international. The match gave Zimbabwe a win in their first one-day international.

Pollock plunders Poms

South Africa's Sean Pollock scored 66 not out and took 4 for 34 off 9.5 overs in his one-day international debut against England on 9 January 1996 in Cape Town, helping South Africa to their first victory over England in a one-day international.

There's nothing Amiss about Dennis

England opener Dennis Amiss scored a century on debut against Australia at Manchester on 24 August, 1972, in only the second ever limited-overs international ever played. Three other players have also scored a century on debut: West Indies Desmond Haynes (v Australia at St John's on 22 February, 1978), Zimbabwe's Andy Flower (v Sri Lanka at New Plymouth on 23 February, 1992) and Pakistan's Salim Elahi (v Sri Lanka at Gujranwala on 29 September, 1995).

Bunch of fives (1)

Three players have taken five wickets on debut: Australia's Tony Dodemaide took 5 for 21 off 7.2 overs against Sri Lanka in Perth on 2 January 1988; Sri Lanka's Shaul Karnain took 5 for 26 off eight overs against New Zealand at Moratuwa, on 31 March 1984; and South African Allan Donald took 5 for 29 against India in South Africa's inaugural match, against India at Eden Gardens, Calcutta on 10 November 1991. Donald was the only player to achieve the feat on a losing team.

Rundle's bundle

South Africa's Dave Rundle took 4 for 42 on debut, against Australia in Brisbane, on 9 January 1994. Despite his effort, which included the prize wickets of Dean Jones for 98, Damien Martyn, Allan Border and Ian Healy, Rundle only appeared in one other one-day international in his career.

4 for 44

England's Peter Martin took 4 for 44 on his international debut against the West Indies in the Texaco Trophy match at The Oval on 26 May 1995, including a wicket with his fifth ball.

Andy Flowers

In his one-day international debut at the 1992 World Cup, Zimbabwe opener Andy Flower batted throughout the innings and made a century against Sri Lanka at New Plymouth on 23 February, 1992.

Fleming's nervous nineties

New Zealand left-hander Stephen Fleming is the only player to be dismissed in the nineties on both his Test and limited-overs debut. The young Kiwi made 92 in the second innings of his Test debut against India in Hamilton, three days before being run out for 90 in his first limited-overs international against the same opponents at Napier on 25 March 1994.

Dropped and debuted

New Zealand bowler Roydon Hayes made his one-day international debut against the West Indies in Wellington on 28 January 1995, just two days after being dropped by his provincial team Northern Districts. Hayes returned figures of 0 for 31 off his seven overs.

Inglorious Debuts

Stormin' Norman

When England decided not to send a full-strength team to Sharjah for the Four Nations Trophy in 1984/85, they resurrected the career of 44-year-old Norman Gifford, who had played 15 Tests between 1964-73. Gifford captained England in their two games, losing to Australia by two wickets and Pakistan by 43 runs. They were Gifford's only appearances in one-day internationals.

Batsmen tear apart son of Sam

In an embarrassingly undistinguished international debut with the ball at the WACA Ground in Perth on 19 January 1986, Glenn Trimble, son of Queensland cricket legend Sam Trimble, presented New Zealanders Jeff Crowe and Jeremy Coney with four overs of diabolical wides, beamers and full tosses which cost an alarming 32 runs. Trimble did, however, come desperately close to netting a wicket or two from lofted shots — particularly when Craig McDermott made a terrible hash of a skied shot by Coney at deep square leg. Trimble also turfed a catch, dropping Coney at backward point.

Sobering debut

West Indian legend and all-rounder Garfield Sobers made a duck in his first and only one-day international. Sobers was bowled by England paceman Chris Old, but turned the tables on Old by bowling him for four during England's innings, his only wicket.

First ball hit for six

Australian off-spinner Gavin Robertson suffered the indignity of having his first ball in one-day international cricket hit for six, by Sri Lanka's Arjuna Ranatunga at P.S. Saravanamuttu Stadium in Colombo on 13 September 1994. And in a remarkable replay, Englishman Graeme Hick obliged with an effortless six over the square leg fence off Robertson's first ball on his debut on home soil, at the Melbourne Cricket Ground four months later. And just to keep his record of first ball boundaries intact, when Robertson made his Test debut against India in Chennai in March 1998, Nayan Mongia dispatched his first ball one bounce over the fence and into the crowd for four (well, it was almost a six!). Robertson is yet to make his Test debut on Australian soil.

Golden Glenn

Australian fast bowler and no.11 specialist batsman Glenn McGrath was dismissed first ball in both his one-day debut (against South Africa in Melbourne on 9 December 1993) and Test debut (against New Zealand in Perth on 13 November 1993).

One-off birthday appearance

India's Gusharan Singh celebrated his 27th birthday on 8 March 1990 by appearing in his one and only one-day international. In a Rothmans Trophy match against Australia at Hamilton, Gusharan batted at no. 6 and scored four runs, then caught opener Geoff Marsh for 86 in the Australian innings.

Team Curiosities

Team of the Match

The Man of the Match in the fourth one-day international between the West Indies and New Zealand in Georgetown on 3 April 1996 was awarded to the entire New Zealand team for a 'sterling' team effort. After being dismissed for 158 off 35.5 overs, the New Zealanders skittled the home side for 154 off 49.1 overs, levelling the best-of-five series 2-2.

Sixteen in a row

The West Indies reigned supreme at home in the five years from 1986-91, winning 16 successive matches. Between losses to England on 4 March 1986 in Port-of-Spain and Australia on 26 February 1991 in Kingston, the West Indies had 5-0 series victories over both Pakistan in 1987/88 and India in 1988/89, and a 3-0 series victory over England in 1989/90. Their 1-4 loss to Australia in 1990/91 was their first and only one-day series loss on home soil.

Most tournament wins

There have been 78 limited-overs international tournaments involving three or more nations, including the World Cup. Australia heads the list with 17 wins, followed by India (15), West Indies (14), Pakistan (12), Sri Lanka (8), South Africa (7), England (4) and Zimbabwe (1). New Zealand, Kenya and Bangladesh have never won a tournament involving three or more nations, whilst only the West Indies and Zimbabwe have never hosted one.

Bangladesh break the drought

Bangladesh won their first one-day international on 17 May 1998 after a 12-year, 22-game losing streak, the longest of any nation. Bangladesh bowled out Kenya for 236 and scored 4 for 237 in reply in a Coca-Cola Cup triangular series match in Hyderabad, India. Only the Netherlands (five games at the 1995/96 World Cup), Canada (three games at the 1979 World Cup) and East Africa (three games in the 1975 World Cup) have never won a game.

One-day interruption

For the first and only time in history, a Test match was interrupted by a one-day international game, played between Zimbabwe and New Zealand in Harare on Sunday, 8 November 1992 and won by New Zealand by four wickets. The second Test in the inaugural series between the two nations had begun the previous day and resumed the following day, which New Zealand also went on to win, this time by 177 runs.

Once bitten twice shy

A Sri Lankan newspaper columnist claimed his team failed to make the final of the three-nation 1997/98 Standard Bank International series in South Africa because fieldsmen were reluctant to chase the ball all the way to the boundary rope for fear of being bitten by the police guard dogs patrolling the ground inside the fence.

Same teams, same score

The first two matches between Australia and England in Australia produced the same innings totals. In the first match on 5 January, 1971, England were dismissed for 190 and Australia scored 5/191 in reply. In the second match, on 1 January, 1975, Australia scored 190 and England 7/191. Both matches were played at the Melbourne Cricket Ground.

Player Curiosities

Ground guru

During his 225-match career from 1978-94, India's Kapil Dev played at 80 different grounds, three more than the next player Mohammed Azharuddin.

No Khan do

Pakistani batsman Mohsin Khan was so distressed by his poor performance in the World Series Cup match against Australia in Adelaide (out LBW for 19) on 30 January 1984 that he announced his immediate retirement from cricket. Four days later he was back in action in Perth against the West Indies and went on to play 18 more Tests and 37 one-day internationals.

Pay for no play

New Zealand selectors took the unusual step of paying young spinner Daniel Vettori for not playing in the 1997/ 98 Coca Cola Cup in Sharjah, a three-nation tournament also involving Australia and India. Vettori had declared his willingness to play but selectors decided he should rest before the tour of Sri Lanka the following month.

Arise Sir...

Three players who have appeared in limited-overs internationals have been knighted: Colin Cowdrey (England), Garfield Sobers (West Indies) and Richard Hadlee (New Zealand).

Some players who have represented their countries in other sports

Badminton: Phil Horne, New Zealand

Baseball: Ian Chappell, Australia

Hockey: Jonty Rhodes, South Africa

Rugby: Jeff Wilson, New Zealand; Brian McKechnie, New Zealand

Soccer: Mark Burgess, New Zealand; Viv Richards, West Indies (Antigua); Richie Richardson, West Indies (Antigua)

And you are?

Sri Lanka's Warnakulasuriya Patabendige Ushantha Chaminda Joseph Vaas has the longest name of any player in one-day international cricket. Vaas made his debut against India at Rajkot on 15 February 1994.

Half-century roll

New Zealand's Andrew Jones scored a half-century in every match of the five-match series against Pakistan in 1988/89. Jones opened his account with 55 not out at Dunedin, then scored 62 not out at Christchurch, 67 at Wellington, 82 at Auckland and 63 not out at Hamilton for an average of 65.8 for the series.

First and final

Desmond Haynes scored a century in both his debut (148 v Australia at St John's on 22 February 1978) and final match (115 v England at Port-of-Spain on 5 March 1994).

Birthday booty

Vinod Kambli scored an even hundred not out on his 21st birthday, in a match against England at Jaipur on 18 January 1983.

Run of run-outs

New Zealand captain Jeremy Coney was run-out in five consecutive innings in 1986; in the final three Rothmans Cup matches against Australia in New Zealand in March and both Texaco Trophy matches in England in July.

Can't touch it

In a World Series Cup match against New Zealand in Hobart on 18 December 1990, Australia only required two runs to win off the final over of the match, however no. 11 Bruce Reid failed to make any contact with the first five balls of Chris Pringle's over and was run out off the sixth and final ball.

Low scoring come-back

When Terry Alderman was recalled to the Australian team on 11 December 1988 after an absence of three and a half years, it certainly wasn't for his batting. From that match against Pakistan in Adelaide until his final game againt New Zealand in Melbourne on 15 January 1991, Alderman played 42 matches and failed to score in eight of the nine innings in which he was required to bat. His five runs all came in one innings against New Zealand in Hobart on 18 December 1990.

Peace lap follows LBW

After being given out LBW by umpire S.K. Bansal in a Titan Cup match against Australia at Bangalore on 21 October 1996, Indian skipper Mohammed Azharuddin stormed off the field, triggering a riot by the crowd. Appeals for calm by match officials had all fallen on deaf ears when Azharuddin decided on a one-man peace mission to appease the crowd. Waving the match officials and security men away, he ran back onto the field and did a lap of the ground in a conciliatory gesture which paved the way for the match to continue. The extraordinary incident boosted an already exciting match, with Australian captain Mark Taylor hitting his maiden one-day century, and a ninth-wicket stand between Javagal Srinath and Anil Kumble enabling India to snatch a narrow win.

On-field marketing

When Steve Waugh left the field to have an injury attended to by the team physiotherapist during a match between Australia and the West Indies in Sydney on 12 January, 1989 and 12th man Terry Alderman was not able to field because of a shoulder injury, the Fijian-born Marketing Manager of the NSW Cricket Association, Neil Maxwell, borrowed a uniform and acted as a substitute fieldsman for one over.

Hurricane hitch

West Indian quick Curtly Ambrose withdrew from the mini World Cup held in Dhaka, Bangladesh in October/November 1998, to repair damage to his home caused by Hurricane Mitch.

A long wait

Pakistan's Shahid Afridi made his Test debut in the third Test against Australia in Karachi in 1998/99 after playing 67 limited-overs internationals for his country.

Related Players

Father and son

M.C. Cowdrey and C.S. Cowdrey, England

R.A.G. Headley, West Indies and D.W. Headley, England

D. Lloyd and G.D. Lloyd, England

D.J. Pringle, East Africa and D.R. Pringle, England

B.C. Cairns and C.L. Cairns, New Zealand

Four brothers

A. Ranatunga, D. Ranatunga, N. Ranatunga and S. Ranatunga, Sri Lanka

Three brothers

I.M. Chappell, G.S. Chappell and T.M. Chappell, Australia

D.R. Hadlee, R.J. Hadlee and B.G. Hadlee, New Zealand

M. de S Wettimuny, S.R.D. Wettimuny and S. Wettimuny, Sri Lanka

Two Brothers

S.R. Waugh and ME Waugh, Australia

A.J. Hollioake and BC Hollioake, England

C.L. Smith and R.A. Smith, England

C.M. Wells and A.P. Wells, England

M. Armanath and S. Armanath, India

B.P. Bracewell and J.G. Bracewell, New Zealand

P.A. Horne and M.J. Horne, New Zealand

H.J. Howarth and G.P. Howarth, New Zealand

J.M. Parker and N.M. Parker, New Zealand

Manzoor Elahi and Salim Elahi, Pakistan

Moin Khan and Nadeem Khan, Pakistan

Wasim Raja and Ramiz Raja, Pakistan

Mushtaq Mohammed and Sadiq Mohammed, Pakistan

P.N. Kirsten and G. Kirsten, South Africa

M.A.R. Samarasekera, Sri Lanka and J.A. Samarasekara, United Arab Emirates

A. Flower and G.W. Flower, Zimbabwe

P.A. Strang and B.C. Strang, Zimbabwe

E.O. Odumbe and M.O. Odumbe, Kenya

M. Suji and A. Suji, Kenya

L.O. Tikolo and S.O. Tikolo, Kenya

G.J. and J.A. Rennie, Zimbabwe

Twin brothers

S.R. Waugh and M.E. Waugh, Australia

Brother and sister

Nathan and Lisa Astle, New Zealand

Terry Alderman and Denise Emerson (nee Alderman), Australia. Denise is also the wife of umpire Ross Emerson.

Husband and wife

Richard and Karen Hadlee, New Zealand

Batting Curiosities

India goes on run strike

The opening match between England and India at the inaugural World Cup at Lord's on 7 June 1975 was reduced to a farce after India, chasing a target of 334, decided the task was beyond them and made no attempt to win. Opener Sunil Gavaskar batted through the entire 60 overs, scoring only 36 off 174 balls and it was 7.30 pm by the time India's batting fast had ended with the score at 3 for 132. England's winning margin of 202 runs remains a World Cup record. Some unkind observers suggested they were simply playing for a draw!

Squad-dropped

Despite scoring an unbeaten century in a match against the West Indies at Kanpur on 30 October 1994, India's Manoj Prabhakar and wicket-keeper Nayan Mongia were dropped from the squad after the pair scored only 16 runs from the last 43 balls of the innings, ensuring a 46-run defeat. The match referee deducted two points from the Indian team after it was suspected the pair deliberately threw the game, however, the International Cricket Council later reversed the decision.

Low act

The West Indies dismissed Pakistan for 43 runs, the lowest-ever total by any team in a one-day international, at Newlands in Cape Town, South Africa on 25 February 1993. Sent in to bat after losing the toss, Pakistan's innings was also the shortest in terms of balls faced, lasting only 19.5 overs.

Kandy run feast

Batting first, Sri Lanka reached 5 for 398 off 50 overs in their final World Cup preliminary match against Kenya in Kandy on 6 March 1996, the highest score by any team in a one-day international. The Kenyans put up a brave effort in reply, reaching 7 for 254 off 50 overs, with

Steve Tikolo top-scoring on 96, the highest individual innings by a player from an ICC associate member nation at that time. The match also produced a World Cup record aggregate of 652 runs.

Crease lightning

Pakistani batsman Saeed Anwar's 194 is the highest individual innings in a one-day international, scored against India at Chennai on 21 May 1997.

Man of the 20th century

Sachin Tendulkar's 20th century in limited-overs internationals, against Zimbabwe at Sharjah on 8 November, 1998, elevated him to the top of the list for the most centuries in both Test and Limited-overs international cricket (36), one ahead of three other players; Desmond Haynes, Viv Richards and Sunil Gavaskar.

Be Afridi, be very Afridi

On the way to 102 against Sri Lanka at Nairobi's Gymkhana Ground on 4 October 1996, Pakistan's Shahid Afridi reached his century off 37 balls, the fastest in a one-day international. In a touch of irony, Shahid hammered 43 runs off two overs bowled by the previous recordholder, Sanath Jayasuriya.

What a WACA

Twenty batsmen have scored centuries in successive one-day internationals, however only three players have done so on successive days. During the four-nation America's Cup Challenge tournament held at the WACA Ground in Perth in 1987, Australia's Dean Jones hit 104 against England on 1 January and 121 against Pakistan the following day; Pakistan's Saeed Anwar scored 131 against the West Indies and 111 against Sri Lanka at Sharjah on 1 and 2 November 1993; and England's Nick Knight scored 113 at Birmingham and 125 not out at Nottingham against Pakistan on 31 August and 1 September 1996.

Two tons, no wins

Three players have scored centuries in successive innings only to end up on the losing side in both matches. Sri Lankan right-hander Roy Dias scored 102 and 121 against India at Delhi on 15 September 1982 and Bangalore on 26 September 1982; Australia's Dean Jones scored 104 against England on January 1 1987 followed by 121 against Pakistan on January 2 at the WACA; and Englishman Graeme Hick scored 126* against Sri Lanka, and 109 against Australia, on the 23rd and 26th of January 1998, respectively, at the Adelaide Oval.

His innings knows no boundaries

New Zealand's Adam Parore's innings of 96 against India at Baroda on 28 October 1994 did not include a single boundary.

100 and out

Pakastani middle-order batsmen Salim Malik has scored five centuries in one-day internationals, but has failed to pass 102 on each occasion. Malik has been dismissed on 100, 101 and twice on 102 and remained not out 100 on one occasion.

Calypso collapso

After being set the modest target of 167 runs to win, ICC associate member Kenya dismissed the West Indies for a paltry 93, their lowest total in a World Cup match, at Pune on 29 February 1996. Only two players, Shivnarine Chanderpaul (19) and Roger Harper (17), reached double figures.

Last-ball miracle (1)

Trailing Australia by 92 runs with 10 overs to go, then 46 with four overs remaining, Pakistan's Asif Mujtaba hit the final ball of the innings by Australian medium-pacer Steve Waugh over the leg side fence and into the Bellerive Oval crowd. The six resulted in a remarkable tie in the World Series match Cup in Hobart on 10 December 1992.

Last ball miracle (2)

With nine wickets down, one ball remaining and four runs required for victory, Australia's Michael Bevan struck a boundary off Roger Harper's last ball of the innings, ensuring a nail-biting victory over the West Indies in the World Series match at the Sydney Cricket Ground on New Year's Day, 1996.

Sharma Charmer (1)

With four runs required for victory off the last ball and nine wickets down in reply to India's 7 for 245, Pakistan's Javed Miandad hit Chetan Sharma over the fence to win the final of the inaugural five-nation Austral-Asia Cup at Sharjah on 18 April 1986. The Pakistani sponsors later awarded a special prize to Sharma for conceding the six.

Corne on the lob

South African Hansie Cronje's 69 in 65 balls against Australia at Springbok Park, Bloemfontein on 13 April 1997, included one six that hit seven-year-old Corne Van Zyl on the chest while sitting on the hill behind the long-on boundary fence. Young Corne was temporarily knocked unconscious by the blow and taken to hospital.

Smash hits (1)

Sri Lankan opening batsman Sanath Jayasuriya embarked on an electrifying hitting spree off Pakistan bowler Aamir Sohail, smashing 29 runs (no ball, 6, 4, 6, 6, 6, 1) off one over in the inaugural match in Singapore on 2 April 1996.

Smash hits (2)

Pakistani all-rounder Wasim Akram hit consecutive sixes off the last two balls required to win the game against Bangladesh in Sharjah on 8 April 1995.

Smash hits (3)

Moin Khan hit the last three balls of Pakistan's innings (batting first) for six, in a match against the West Indies at Sharjah on 13 October 1995.

Smash hits (4)

Pakistan's Ramiz Raja and Moin Khan equalled the (then) record of 27 runs off a single over in a match against the West Indies in Sharjah on 13 October 1995. In the final over of the innings, Ramiz struck a boundary and a single, before Moin dispatched the last four balls for six, four, six and six.

Smash hits (5)

Pakastani all-rounder Wasim Akram hit a six of the only ball he faced to win the Nehru Cup against the West Indies at Calcutta on 1 November 1989. Pakistan won by four runs with only one ball remaining.

Smash hits (6)

West Indian opener Philo Wallace got his team off to a flying start in their Wills International Cup semi-final against India on 1 November 1998. Chasing 243 for victory, Wallace clubbed the first ball of the innings from Javigal Srinath for six over long-off. He is the only player to have done this in one-day internationals.

Smash hits (7)

When India set the West Indies are target of 283 to win the one-day international at Berbice on 29 March 1983, the home-side batsmen decided to take the long handle to the Indian bowlers. There were seven sixes hit by seven different batsmen with Gordon Greenidge, Viv Richards, Clive Lloyd, Faoud Bacchus, Larry Gomes, Jeff Dujon and Andy Roberts all clearing the boundary. The colossus hitting did not prevent the West Indies from losing by 27 runs.

Six appeal

Richard Hadlee had a splendid match against India in Brisbane on 18 January 1981, the last qualifying game before the World Series Cup finals. He not only thumped two huge sixes in a quick-fire innings of 32 and took 1 for 15 off 9.1 overs with the ball, but an affectionate blonde in a green bikini ran onto the field, lent him her cap and planted a kiss on his cheek when he was fielding in the outfield. New Zealand won the match by 22 runs.

Extra! Extra!

The World Series Cup match between the West Indies and Pakistan in Brisbane on 7 January 1989 produced 90 extras, a record for a one-day international. Fifty-nine were conceded by the West Indies in Pakistan's total of 7 for 258, and 21 were conceded by Pakistan in the West Indies reply of 203.

Bowling Curiosities

A bunch of fives (2)

In 1991 Waqar Younis became the only bowler to take five wickets in three successive one-day internationals. Waqar took 5 for 11 against New Zealand at Peshawar on 4 November, 5 for 16 against New Zealand at Sialkot on 6 November and 5 for 52 against the West Indies at Lahore on 11 November.

I.Khan do

With his last delivery in international cricket at the Melbourne Cricket Ground on 25 March 1992, Pakistan's Imran Khan took the wicket of England's Richard Illingworth and with it came victory in the World Cup.

Bowled 'em - finally

It took Bangladesh 11 matches before they were able to bowl out their opposition for the first time. The team dismissed Sri Lanka for 233 in Sharjah on 6 April 1995, but lost the match by 107 runs.

A bunch of fives (3)

Greg Chappell (5 for 20) and Gary Cosier (5 for 18) recorded the only instance of two bowlers taking five wickets in the same innings in the second Prudential Cup match against England at Edgbaston on 4 June 1977. Although England was dismissed for a modest 171, the efforts of Chappell and Cosier were in vain as Australia collapsed to be all out for 70, their lowest score in a one-day international.

C'mon aussie come off it!

Australian captain Greg Chappell drew howls of protest when he ordered his brother Trevor to bowl the final ball underarm in order to prevent New Zealand from winning the game at the Melbourne Cricket Ground on 1 February 1981, the third final of the season's World Series Cup. Striding to the wicket requiring a six to tie and seven to win, tail-ender Brian McKechnie instead tapped the ball and threw his bat away in disgust, as New Zealand captain Geoff Howarth ran onto the field to debate its legality with the umpires. The incident caused a storm of controversy on both sides of the Tasman, with New Zealand Prime Minister Robert Muldoon saying it was appropriate the Australians should have been dressed in yellow and his Australian counterpart Malcolm Fraser saying the incident was contrary to the good and decent traditions of cricket. The game had already soured when Martin Snedden caught Greg Chappell on 58 in the out-field during the Australian innings, but was given not out because the umpires were unsighted. Chappell was severely reprimanded by the Australian Cricket Board but later carried off the Man of the Series, Australia winning the best-of-five finals series 3-1.

Blinded by the light

Pakistani medium-pace bowler Sarfraz Narwaz insisted that his eyesight was not good enough to play under lights in the World Series Cup qualifying match against the West Indies at the Sydney Cricket Ground on 12 January 1982. 'It was very hard. My eyes are not very good at night. The light reflected in my eyes,' said Sarfraz.

Howzat for openers (1)

Australia's Terry Alderman bowled Pakistan's Ramiz Raja and Aamir Malik off the first two deliveries of their World Series Cup match at the Brisbane Cricket Ground on 8 January 1989.

Let's see that again on the replay

An off-cutter by Australian quick Greg Campbell not only clean-bowled Pakistani Aamir Malik during a World Series Cup match at the Sydney Cricket Ground on 20 February 1990, it blew up the television camera snugly installed inside the middle stump.

Desert storm

Pakistan's Aaqib Javed's bowling figures of 7 for 37 against India at Sharjah on 25 October 1991 included a hat-trick of LBW dismissals — the scalps of opener Ravi Shastri, Mohammed Azharuddin and Sachin Tendulkar.

Howzat for openers (2)

The first ball of each innings produced a wicket in the match between Pakistan and West Indies at Newlands, Cape Town on 25 February 1993. Patrick Patterson had Pakistani opener Ramiz Raja caught off the first ball of the match and West Indian opener Desmond Haynes was out LBW to Waqar Younis.

No-ball! Again

Sri Lanka's Mutiah Muralitharan was no-balled for throw-ing seven times in three overs by umpire Ross Emerson, and once by umpire Tony McQuillan, in a match against the West Indies in Brisbane on 5 January 1996.

Just over three years later, Mutiah Muralitharan was no-balled again by umpire Ross Emerson at the Adelaide Oval on 23 January 1999. The incident nearly led to a walk-off by the Sri Lankans and their captain Arjuna Ranatunga was subsequently charged by match referee Peter van der Merwe and received a six-match suspended sentence.

Wicket drought

Only two wickets fell in the World Cup preliminary match between the West Indies and Pakistan at the Melbourne Cricket Ground on 23 February 1992. Batting first, Pakistan scored 2 for 220 off their 50 overs, including an unbeaten century to Ramiz Raja. The West Indies didn't lose a wicket in reaching the target after 46.5 overs, though Brian Lara retired hurt on 88.

No 'arm in that

On his arrival at the wicket in the first game of the World Series finals between Australia and the West Indies in Sydney on 16 January 1993, Dean Jones demanded that umpire Terry Prue order Curtly Ambrose to remove a white wristband from his bowling arm. But the psychological ploy backfired as a fuming Ambrose produced a fiery spell to finish with 5 for 32, steering the West Indies to victory.

Don't get mad, get even

A competition organised by a New Zealand fast food chain offered entrants the chance to hit a six off an over of underarm deliveries bowled by Trevor Chappell during the lunch time break of the final limited-overs international against Australia at Eden Park on 14 February, 1998. However the winner failed to clear the boundary and claim the $100,000 prize.

Fielding Curiosities

Boundary riders

Chasing 199 runs in 47 overs in a World Series Cup match against England in Sydney on 28 November 1979, the West Indies began strongly, but a steady loss of wickets left no. 11 Colin Croft needing a boundary off Ian Botham's final delivery to win the match. With no fielding restrictions in force, England captain Mike Brearley was able to put every man on the boundary, including the wicket-keeper David Bairstow, who removed his gloves. Botham then bowled, Croft swung and missed and the ball clipped his leg stump to end the match.

Over and out

Two days after ordering his brother to bowl underarm, Greg Chappell strode to the wicket at the Sydney Cricket Ground to a decidedly mixed reception — whistles, cheers, boos and hisses. On Chappell's first scoring stroke, a lofted off-drive, a spectator ran onto the field to retrieve the ball inside the boundary. Richard Hadlee, giving chase, kept right on going and bundled the man heavily into and over the pickets. One spectator even threw a punch at Hadlee!

His Cup runneth over

Clive Lloyd ran out three Australian batsmen during a World Series Cup match in Brisbane on 13 January 1985, before going on to score 52 not out in the West Indies' five-wicket win over Australia.

All-round Curiosities

Sri Lanka's best

Sanath Jayasuriya holds the best batting and bowling figures by a Sri Lankan in one-day internationals. Jayasuriya's 151 not out against India in Mumbai on 17 May 1997 is the highest score and his 6 for 29 against England in Colombo on 20 March 1993 are the best bowling figures by a Sri Lankan.

You can keep your pads on

All three teams in the 1998/99 Carlton & United series featured wicket-keepers who also opened the batting. Australia's Adam Gilchrist, England's Alec Stewart and Sri Lanka's Romesh Kaluwitharana all had the onerous task of keeping wickets and facing the new ball.

Wicket-keeping Curiosities

Struck-down streaker

Two straightforward dropped catches off England's Mike Gatting had Australian wicket-keeper Rod Marsh seething in a Prudential Cup clash at Edgbaston, Birmingham on 6 June 1981, so he was in no mood for frivolity when a streaker ran onto the ground shortly afterwards. Marsh crash-tackled the streaker and pinned him down to the ground in the most painful manner possible until the police arrived, prompting one television commentator to remark, 'It's the first one he's got in his gloves all day.'

Umpiring Curiosities

Wrong end

Umpires J.R. Collins and L.J. Stevens failed to notice English opening batsman Geoff Boycott resuming at the wrong end after the drinks break during the World Series Cup match against Australia in Sydney on 11 December 1979. Boycott scored 105 off 124 balls and was Man of the Match, England winning by 72 runs.

Fielding help

After Doug Walters played a pull shot that headed for the boundary in front of the Ladies' Stand during a World Series Cup match against New Zealand at the Sydney Cricket Ground on 13 January 1981, an enthusiastic youngster jumped the fence and fielded the ball. Umpires Mel Johnson and Don Weser ruled that it was not a four and Walters would receive only what the players had run, which was three. This decision became crucial because by the last ball of the match Walters, still at the crease, required three for victory and two for a tie. Walters dug out Martin Snedden's yorker to mid-on, where Hadlee's throw to the bowler's end beat the other batsman, Shaun Graf, home by half a metre and New Zealand won by one run.

Sorry, I'm tied up tomorrow

After the second game between Australia and the West Indies on 11 February 1984 ended in a tie, and despite the fact that the West Indies could not lose the series, the Australian Cricket Board ruled the third final in the best-of-three series must be played. Incensed at not being awarded the series after a victory and a tie, Clive Lloyd and Viv Richards reported injured the next day and Michael Holding captained the West Indies for the first time in a one-day international.

Bowl it again, Walsh

Although a maximum of nine overs was allotted to each bowler, an umpiring oversight allowed West Indian quick Courtney Walsh to bowl a tenth over against Pakistan at Sharjah in a match on 28 November 1986, during which he terminated the Pakistani innings on 143 by taking the wicket of Salim Jaffar. The West Indies won the match by nine wickets.

Bird takes a bath

Local umpire Fareed Malik deputised at square leg for a dehydrated Harold 'Dickie' Bird after he fainted on the field and had to be stretchered off during a Champions Trophy match between West Indies and Pakistan at Sharjah on 22 October 1988. The other umpire, David Shepherd, stood at both ends for the rest of the match.

Good sport (1)

West Indian opener Desmond Haynes was on 85 in the third match against Pakistan at Port of Spain, Trinidad on 18 March 1988 when the umpire, Mohammed Hosein gave him out LBW to Salim Jaffar. Haynes indicated he had hit the ball with the bat and Imran Khan asked the umpire to rescind his decision. Haynes went on to bat throughout the innings, scoring a brilliant 142 not out.

Good sport (2)

Leading New Zealand's reply to a formidable Australian total of 4 for 258 at Carisbrook in Dunedin on 19 March 1993, captain Martin Crowe walked after being given not out by a New Zealand umpire Chris King. Crowe got a thick edge off Tony Dodemaide and was caught behind by wicket-keeper Ian Healy for one.

Crowded

Despite Ian Bishop scoring the required two runs off the last ball, the deciding match between the West Indies and Pakistan at Georgetown, Guyana on 3 April 1983 was declared a tie, after match referee Raman Subba Row ruled the Pakistani fielders were sufficiently distracted by an invasion of the ground by the jubilant crowd.

What does this button do?

South African wicket-keeper Dave Richardson was given out by the 'third' umpire, who had been called upon to adjudicate on a tight run out decision during a match against Pakistan in Karachi on 16 October 1994. Umpire Atiq Khan later apologised to Richardson for his downfall, admitting he may have pressed the wrong button after reviewing the TV video replay.

Caught Out

After thumping 47 from 46 balls in the fourth one-day international against England at Centurion on 14 January 1996, South African captain Hansie Cronje holed out to Graham Thorpe on the long-on boundary. However Thorpe's appeal for a catch was initially turned down by umpire Wilf Diedricks, who instead signalled six after interpreting Thorpe's nervous glance at his feet as evidence that he had stepped over the boundary. But the bowler, Richard Illingworth, asked him to consult the third umpire, following which he reversed his decision and gave Cronje out.

French Cut

Pakistan's Ramiz Raja was erroneously given run out by umpire Dick French at square leg after Raja failed to hear the other umpire's no-ball call and left the wicket. The incident occurred in a match against England in Perth on 5 January 1987.

Hair today, gone tomorrow

Darrell Hair, at that time the only Australian umpire on the ICC's international panel, voluntarily stood down from all Sri Lanka's matches in the 1998/99 Carlton United Series, after describing spinner Mutiah Muralitharan's bowling action as diabolical in his book *Decision Maker*. Hair had no-balled the Sri Lankan for throwing in the Boxing Day Test in 1995 and said he could have easily "called him" 27 times. His book led to the ICC charging him in January 1999 for breaching its code of conduct.

Stressed out

Three days after no-balling Mutiah Muralitharan in 1999, umpire Ross Emerson was stood down by the Australian Cricket Board when it was revealed that he was on stress leave from his regular job in the Western Australian public service.

Ground Curiosities

Most matches

India has hosted 192 one-day internationals at more grounds (34) and in more cities (30) than any other country. Only five grounds have hosted 10 or more matches.

One player, one run, one game

The moment of glory in the international cricket spotlight for the Queensland city of Mackay was briefer than expected when the World Cup match between India and Sri Lanka at Harrup Park was abandoned because of rain after only two balls on 28 February 1992. Indian opener Kris Srikkanth faced both deliveries, scoring a single off the second ball, becoming the only player to score all the runs in a one-day international.

Bright idea

Local authorities were forced to use smoke bombs to clear vast swarms of insects attracted by the lights during the first one-day international under lights at Eden Gardens, Calcutta on 24 November 1993 between India and South Africa.

Greig unlocks pitch secrets

The pitch prepared for a World Series match between South Africa and Australia at the WACA Ground, Perth on 16 January 1994 sported a lateral crack so deep that when Channel Nine television commentator Tony Greig accidentally dropped South African manager Mike Proctor's hotel key into the crack, he was unable to retrieve it. The key remained there throughout the game.

Cities that have hosted matches at three grounds

Two cities have hosted matches at three grounds: Colombo, Sri Lanka has hosted matches at the Sinhalese Sports Club, P. Saravanamuttu Stadium and the R. Premadasa (formerly Khettarama) Stadium. Nairobi, Kenya has hosted matches at the Gymkhana Ground, the Aga Khan Ground and the Nairobi Club Ground.

Cities that have hosted matches at two grounds

Eight cities have hosted matches at two grounds: London (Lord's and The Oval), Hobart (TCA Ground and Bellerive Oval), Quetta (Ayub National Stadium and Bughti Stadium), Rawalpindi (Pindi Club Ground and Rawalpindi

Cricket Stadium), Ahmedabad (Sardar Patel Stadium and Gujarat Stadium), Vadodara (IPCL Sports Complex and Moti Bagh Stadium), Mumbai (Wankhede and Brabourne Stadiums) and Bulawayo (Queen's Sports Club and Bulawayo Athletic Club).

Around the grounds

One-hundred-and-twenty-three grounds in 106 cities in 14 countries have hosted 1406 one-day internationals from the first match at the Melbourne Cricket Ground on 5 January 1971 until 10 February 1998. Kenya was the latest nation to host its first match, and the Owen Delaney Park in Taupo, New Zealand, the most recent new ground. Non-Test playing nations to have hosted and played in matches are Bangladesh, Canada, Kenya and United Arab Emirates. Singapore and Wales are the only nations to host but never play in a one-day international. The Netherlands is the only nation to play in but never host a match, however South Africa and Kenya are scheduled to play their World Cup qualifying game in Amsterdam on 26 May 1999.

First ball dismissal

The first ball ever bowled at three grounds resulted in a dismissal: West Indian Andy Roberts was responsible for dismissing two Englishmen, Barry Wood at Scarborough on 26 August 1976 and Derek Randall in Brisbane on 23 December 1979; and India's Sunil Gavaskar was dismissed by New Zealand's Richard Hadlee in Perth on 9 December 1980.

Stop, or I'll shoot!

Bangladesh cricket officials successfully discouraged pitch invasions by the crowd during the mini World Cup in Dhaka in October/November 1998, by placing armed security guards around the perimeter fence and announcing over the public address system that anyone entering the field of play would be shot.

Desert Oasis

One of cricket's outposts is Sharjah, part of the United Arab Emirates in the Middle East. Competitions, usually involving three or four teams, are held twice yearly (in March/April and October/November) and it has now hosted more limited-overs internationals (139) than any other ground. The stadium was the brainchild of Abdul Rahman Bukhatir, who realised who a dream of bringing the game to a large expatriate population from the sub-continent in 1984 when India, Pakistan and Sri Lanka played in the inaugural Asia Cup. The 1994 Austral-Asia Cup featured the only appearance of the home team, the United Arab Emirates.

Lunch break all day 'n' night

In the opening day/night clash in the 1998/99 Carlton United Series between Australia and England, two English fans took advantage of the construction upgrade at the 'Gabba for the 2000 Olympic Games' soccer fixtures. With the ground at a reduced capacity, and tickets hard to come by, the two tourists wandered onto to the construction site, complete with hard hats and lunch boxes, and enjoyed an undisturbed view of the entire game from high in the empty stand.

Bad Conduct

Cop that Kapil

During an unsavoury match between South Africa and India at Port Elizabeth on 9 December 1992, the Indians alleged that Kepler Wessels struck Kapil Dev with his bat as he turned to complete a run. The clash between Wessels and Kapil followed the run-out of South African vice-captain Peter Kirsten by Kapil for backing up prematurely at the non-striker's end. Kirsten was later fined half his match fee for protesting, while Kapil was treated for bruises on both shins.

Language, please!

Pakistani fast bowler Aaqib Javed became the first player to be suspended under the ICC's code of conduct, after he called the umpire 'a f***ing cheat' during a game against New Zealand in Napier on 28 December 1992. The trouble flared when Andrew Jones was given not out by umpire Brian Aldridge after a ball lifted sharply and lobbed off Jones' gloves to be caught at slip. Aldridge indicated the delivery was a no ball, above the height permitted in the rules. Aaqib was banned for one match by match referee Peter Burge and New Zealand went on to win the match and level the series 1-all.

Misbehaving captains

Both captains were fined part of their match fee for separate incidents during a Mandela Trophy match between New Zealand and Sri Lanka at Buffalo Park, East London on 18 December 1994. New Zealand captain Ken Rutherford was docked 50% of his match fee for trying to intimidate the umpire into making a favourable decision, whilst Sri Lankan captain Arjuna Ranatunga was fined 25% for showing obvious dissent at being dismissed LBW. Sri Lanka won the match by five wickets.

Black and blue

Gordon Greenidge was reprimanded by the West Indies Cricket Board for physically attacking England's Gladstone Small at the presentation ceremony after the final game of the series at Georgetown, Guyana on 3 April 1990. Greenidge was plainly still upset by something Small said to him as he left the crease after being dismissed for six.

Bat and Brawl

Officials stopped play and ordered the players to the dressing rooms during the second match of the Sahara Cup between India and Pakistan at the Toronto Cricket, Skating and Curling Club on 14 September 1997 following an ugly clash between Inzamam-Ul-Haq and a spectator. The megaphone-wielding heckler was berating the Pakistani star batsman with cries of 'fat' and 'potato' in Punjabi, and told him to stop feeling himself in between balls. Having had enough, Inzamam grabbed a bat from the twelfth man and marched into the stand, threatening to knock his detractor's head off, sending a section of the 4000 strong crowd into a frenzy. Cricket fan Shiv Kumar Thind later said, 'I was calling him a potato in Punjabi because he is a little fat for a player. I had no idea he would come into the stands.'

Pranks

It's just not cricket

During Australia's first game in New Zealand after the underarm incident, in Auckland on 13 February 1982, a member of the crowd rolled a lawn bowl across the outfield as Greg Chappell took guard. Chappell went on to score a superb 108, his century coming off only 82 balls.

Hold the phone!

During a bowling spell against Pakistan in the third Texaco Trophy match against Pakistan on 25 May 1987 at Edgbaston, Ian Botham handed his mobile phone to umpire Harold 'Dickie' Bird to mind. Whilst in his care, it rang no less than three times — first it was Botham's business manager, then his wife, and finally an acquaintance trying to finalise the details of a weekend angling trip.

Cricket buff

The appearance of a 19-year-old athletic female streaker who performed a spectacular cartwheel over the stumps did little to upset the concentration of Australian opener Geoff Marsh in the Texaco Trophy match against England at Lord's on 29 May 1989. Marsh went on to score 111 not out and help Australia to a six-wicket victory in the final match of the series.

Porcine messengers

A pig wandered onto the Brisbane Cricket Ground during a World Series match between Australia and England on 16 January 1983 draped in the Australian flag with the words 'Botham' painted on one side and 'Eddie' (Hemmings) on the other. The pig was taken off by police to the Brisbane watch-house and put safely under lock and key. A piglet labelled 'Gatting' also made an appearance at the Melbourne Cricket Ground on 1 February 1987 during a match between Australia and England.

That's very Fanie

South African 12th man Fanie de Villiers put a toy buggy he had purchased during a late night shopping spree in Perth to good use — De Villiers sent the buggy out to the field carrying a can of soft drink for batsman Gary Kirsten in the World Series match against New Zealand on the following day, 14 January 1994. The buggy stopped right at Kirsten's feet, did a few laps of the stumps, then returned to the pavilion.

That's not so Fanie

In the second match against Zimbabwe in Harare on 22 October 1995, South Africa's Fanie de Villiers began the 42nd over (which turned out to be the final over), by bowling not a cricket ball, but a paper cup at the batsman, H.K. Olonga

Quickie no-balled

One of two streakers who appeared before a Napier court after streaking during a match between New Zealand and Zimbabwe on 3 February 1996 was let off and fined $NZ200 after explaining that two women had offered him and his friend sex if they did a nude lap of honour in front of the players and fans.

Camera misses crash-tackle

Channel Nine has led the way in television coverage of cricket over the last twenty years, but the producer missed some brilliant pictures on their innovative stump cam when a pitch invader crash-tackled the stumps at the Randwick end during a game between Australia and Pakistan at the Sydney Cricket Ground on New Year's Day 1997.

Stop that macareena in the name of the law!

Two female police officers who spontaneously performed the macareena during the dinner break in a game between Australia and Pakistan on New Year's Day 1997 were later lectured for inappropriate behaviour by their superior officer. The performance was captured on the scoreboard's big screen and brought a huge roar from the 40,000 crowd. Their superintendent said the officers would be admonished and instructed to smarten up their act.

Finger lickin' good

Sri Lankan captain Arjuna Ranatunga earned the wrath of the International Cricket Council when he appeared in the first match of the Emirates Triangular Tournament against South Africa at Trent Bridge on 14 August 1998 with a bat emblazoned with a sponsor, "Sam's Chicken and Ribs". It eventuated that Sam was an old friend of Ranatunga's, who said afterwards "A lot of people from London started buying his chickens. I should have charged him much more than I did."

World Cup Curiosities

A dry spell

Not one minute of play was lost to rain during the 15 matches of the inaugural World Cup in England in 1975.

A long day

The first World Cup final between Australia and West Indies at Lord's on 21 June 1975 was the longest one-day international ever played, lasting 8 hours and 42 minutes. The match began at noon and ended at 8.42 pm.

Just for fun

After West Indies reached the target set by Sri Lanka of a mere 87 runs in 21 overs, in their opening World Cup match on 7 June 1975, the players put on a 20-over exhibition match for the disappointed Old Trafford crowd.

Escorted off

When East African batsman Zulfiqar Ali hit a boundary during their first World Cup game against New Zealand at Edgbaston on 7 June 1975 two small boys ran onto the field to congratulate him. Unfortunately, they addressed themselves to the wrong batsman (Qaraishy), but before they could rectify the error, they were escorted from the scene by three large policemen.

Best bowling (1)

Australia's Gary Gilmour was the leading wicket-taker at the 1975 World Cup, despite only playing in two games. Gilmour took 6 for 14 against England in the semi-final at Headingley (then top-scored with 28 not out) on 18 June then took 5 for 48 against the West Indies in the final at Lord's three days later. Spin bowler Ashley Mallett had been preferred to Gilmour in the earlier games.

Minnow's victory

Sri Lanka recorded the first victory by an associate member of the ICC over a full member when they defeated India by 47 runs in a preliminary World Cup game on 16 June and 18 June 1979.

Opening centuries

The opening match in all six World Cups held to date have produced at least one century. The first was when England's Dennis Amiss made 137 in the opening match of the 1975 tournament against India at Lord's; the second in 1979 when Gordon Greenidge scored an unbeaten 106 in their nine-wicket demolition of India at Edgbaston; the third in 1983 when England's Allan Lamb made a century on his World Cup debut against New Zealand at The Oval; the fourth in 1987 when Pakistan's Javed Miandad scored 103 against Sri Lanka; the fifth when both New Zealand captain Martin Crowe and Australia's David Boon scored round hundreds in the opening match between the joint host nations in Auckland in 1992; and finally, when in 1996 New Zealand's Nathan Astle made a century on his World Cup debut against England at Ahmedabad.

It all depends on the referendum

Despite having already qualified for the semi-finals of the 1992 World Cup, the South Africa team was told their place may be in jeopardy if a snap referendum for whites only on the dismantling of apartheid was not passed and international sanctions were reimposed on the Republic.

Ramadan rules

In the early matches of the 1995/96 World Cup, players were requested to leave the field during drink breaks in order to avoid offending spectators who were observing Ramadan.

Triple century?

Australia's Mark Waugh is the only player to score three centuries in a World Cup tournament. During the 1995/96 World Cup, Waugh scored two successive centuries (130 against Kenya at Vishakhapatnam and 126 against India in Bombay) and was well on the way to a third (76 not out) when Australia overhauled Zimbabwe's total in the next match at Nagpur. Waugh scored his third century (110) of the tournament in the quarter-final against New Zealand at Madras.

You again?

Pakistan's Javed Miandad is the only player to have appeared in all six World Cup tournaments. Miandad has also made the most appearances (33) in World Cup matches.

Best bowling (2)

Australia's Graeme Porter headed the bowling averages at the 1979 World Cup in England. In his only two appearances in one-day internationals, Porter took three wickets for 33 runs, at an average of 11.00.

Long wait between wins

After winning their first game against Australia in Nottingham at the 1983 World Cup, Zimbabwe lost their next 18 matches before their next victory, against England at the 1992 World Cup in Albury.

Double opener, thrice

New Zealand seam bowler Martin Snedden opened both the bowling and the batting in three World Cup matches in India in 1987, against Zimbabwe at Hyderabad, India at Bangalore and Australia at Chandigarh.

Four half-centuries

During the 1987 World Cup, Indian batsman Navjot Sidhu scored four consecutive half-centuries in his first four innings in one-day international cricket. Sidhu scored 73 on debut against Australia in Madras on 9 October, 75 against New Zealand in Bangalore on 14 October, 51 against Australia in Delhi on 22 October, and 55 against Zimbabwe in Ahmedabad on 26 October.

Charma sharmer (2)

India's Chetan Sharma is the only bowler to take a hat-trick in a World Cup match. Chetan performed the feat against New Zealand at Nagpur on 31 October 1987, dismissing Ken Rutherford, Ian Smith and Ewen Chatfield in successive balls.

Follow that cable!

South Africa's Andrew Hudson celebrated his team's victory over the West Indies during a World Cup preliminary game at Lancaster Park, Christchurch on 5 March 1992, by souveniring the middle stump and charging off towards the pavilion. It wasn't until he reached the gate that he realised he'd taken the stump that houses the mini television camera and was trailing 10 metres of cable behind him!

World Cup debut

Despite playing more one-day internationals than any other ICC associate member, Bangladesh (25 matches) remains the only limited-overs-playing country not to have played in a World Cup. This will change on 17 May 1999 when they're scheduled to meet New Zealand in their World Cup debut at Chelmsford.

Sultan assassin

During their opening World Cup match against South Africa at Rawalpindi on 16 February 1996, the UAE's captain Sultan Zarawani came to the crease with his side struggling at 6-68. Despite the fact that "White Lightning" Allan Donald was bowling a fiery spell, Zarawani declined to wear a helmet prefering a sun hat instead. In what was an almost predictable consequence, Donald rose to the bait and duly struck Zarawani on the head first ball. Zarawani bravely batted on (without a helmet), but was dismissed next over for a duck by Brian McMillan.

Sri Lanka in song

In a musical tribute to their World Cup victory in 1996, Herb Fernando, the father figure of north-London based Sri Lankan baila band "Family Affair" released a single titled "Sri Lanka Champions of 1996". Sung by Herb's wife Carmen and son Glenn, the song mentions every member of the team and philosophises about the excitement of one-day cricket.

A multi-national side

The UAE's 14-man squad for the 1996 World Cup contained only two players, Sultan Zarawani and Saeed-al-Saffar, who born in the Persian Gulf state. Of the 12 remaining players, eight were born in Pakistan, two in Sri Lanka, one in India and one in the United States.

Dutch Aussie

When Australian-born Peter Cantrell made his one-day international debut for The Netherlands against New Zealand at Vadodara on 17 February 1996, he joined a unique group of players to have played international cricket for two teams. Cantrell had previously acted as a substitute fielder for Australia during the second innings of the opening Ashes Test in 1990/91 at Brisbane. Cantrell took two scorching catches in the gully to dismiss Alec Stewart and Angus Fraser off Terry Alderman's bowling.

Scandals

C'mon Dollar C'mon

After Australia won a rain-shortened World Series Cup final qualifying match against the West Indies on 19 January, 1982, an article appeared in the Melbourne *Age* newspaper alleging the West Indies threw the match for financial reasons to ensure a West Indies v Australia final. Captain Clive Lloyd brought a libel action against the newspaper and on April 15, 1983 the court found in his favour, awarding damages of $100,000 plus costs against the newspaper.

Salim pickings

Fans and administrators alike were shocked when an interim report to the Pakistan Cricket Board in September 1998 alleged that Wasim Akram, Salim Malik and Ijaz Ahmed took bribes from illegal bookmakers to influence the outcomes of at least one Test match and four limited-overs internationals in 1994. The accusations first surfaced when Australian bowlers Tim May and Shane Warne alleged that the captain, Salim Malik, had offered them US$250,000 to bowl badly on the final day of the First Test in Karachi, where Pakistan's last pair snatched a miracle victory. Mark Waugh also alleged that Malik tried to bribe him to bat poorly in a subsequent one-day game on 22 October 1994, where he scored a century.

"It's just not Cricket"

Controversy erupted during the 1998/99 Australian summer when it was revealed that the Australian Cricket Board had kept confidential for four years, disciplinary action taken against Mark Waugh and Shane Warne. Both players were fined in February, 1995 for selling pitch and weather information about matches involving Australia to an illegal Indian bookmaker named "John" over a period of five months from September, 1994 to February, 1995. Waugh had previously given evidence to a Pakistani match-fixing inquiry without mentioning the arrangement.

Tragedies

Stadium tragedy mars win for New Zealand

Eight spectators were killed and more than 70 injured when part of the back wall of a grandstand collapsed as spectators were making their way back after the lunch interval during the fifth one-day international between India and New Zealand at Vidarbha Stadium, Nagpur on 26 November, 1995. Despite the tragedy, New Zealand scored 8-348, their highest ever score in a one-day international and won the match by 99 runs.

Boy 15 falls to his death

A 15-year-old boy died after falling through a roof while trying to get a better view of the Australia-West Indies match at the Sydney Cricket Ground on 19 January 1982. The boy fell 20 metres after apparently trying to jump between two buildings in the neighbouring Sydney Showground.

Women's Cricket Curiosities

Wash out

The first women's limited-overs international was scheduled to be held on 20 June 1973 at Kew in England between Jamaica and New Zealand, the first match of the inaugural World Cup. However the game was washed out and it wasn't until three days later that the first matches were completed between Australia and Young England at Hove, England; England versus International XI at Hove; and New Zealand versus Trinidad and Tobago at St Albans.

Back to nature

On 25 July 1987 Australia played England at Canterbury Ground in Kent, the only international ground which has a tree inside the boundary. The game was the only limited-overs international to be played on a synthetic suface, as rain had ruined the turf area.

The World Cup

The first women's cricket World Cup was held in England in 1973, preceding the first men's World Cup by two years and featuring five teams in 60-overs per side matches. England won the title after finishing top of the table following a round-robin series. The sixth women's World Cup was held in 1997 in India, with 11 nations taking part. Australia will host the seventh Word Cup in 2000.

Players who have represented their countries in other sports

Basketball:	Judy Doull, New Zealand
	Vi Farrell, New Zealand
Hockey:	Lynne Thomas, England (Wales)
	Jean Cummins, England
	Judy Doull, New Zealand
	Rachel Heyhoe-Flint, England
	Janette Brittin, England
	Ina Lamason, New Zealand
	Maia Lewis, New Zealand
	Lesley Murdoch, New Zealand
	Carol Oyler, New Zealand
	Ann McKenna, New Zealand
	Peg Batty, New Zealand
	Betty Thorner, New Zealand
Netball:	Lyn Fullston, Australia
Soccer:	Clare Taylor, England
	Rebecca Rolls, New Zealand
Table tennis:	Lisa Astle, New Zealand

Best One-day Elevens

We asked a group of famous cricketers and followers of the game to choose their best one-day elevens of all time. The team could comprise players of any nationality who have played one-day cricket at international level, however they may not have played together in the same team or against each other.

Tony Greig

South African-born Tony Greig qualified for England through residency and played 22 one-day internationals between 1972 and 1977. Greig joined World Series Cricket for two seasons and has been an integral member of the commentary team on Channel Nine's cricket coverage since his retirement from the game.

1 Sanath Jayasuriya, Sri Lanka
2 Sachin Tendulkar, India
3 Viv Richards, West Indies
4 Javed Miandad, Pakistan
5 Aravinda de Silva, Sri Lanka
6 Gary Sobers, West Indies
7 Alan Knott, England
8 Wasim Akram, Pakistan
9 Shane Warne, Australia
10 Curtly Ambrose, West Indies
11 Andy Roberts, West Indies
12th Man Imran Khan, Pakistan

Greg Chappell

Greg Chappell played in the inaugural one-day match in Melbourne in 1971 and went on to play 74 games for Australia before he retired from international cricket after the 1983/84 Test series against Pakistan. Chappell was the first Australian to score a century in a one-day international and also captained Australia in 49 games.

1 Gordon Greenidge, West Indies
2 Sanath Jayasuriya, Sri Lanka
3 Viv Richards, West Indies
4 Dean Jones, Australia
5 Clive Lloyd, West Indies (capt.)
6 Ian Botham, England
7 Ian Healy, Australia
8 Andy Roberts, West Indies
9 Michael Holding, West Indies
10 Joel Garner, West Indies
11 Shane Warne, Australia
12th Man Derek Underwood, England

Bryce Courtenay

Bryce Courtenay had a 35-year career in advertising before turning to writing full time. His best-selling books include *The Power of One, Yowies, Tandia* and *April Fool's Day* as well as the first two books in a trilogy: *The Potato Factory* and *Tommo and Hawk*. His most recent book is *Jessica* released in 1998.

1 Desmond Haynes, West Indies
2 Sachin Tendulkar, India
3 Viv Richards, West Indies
4 Greg Chappell, Australia
5 Clive Lloyd, West Indies (capt.)
6 Steve Waugh, Australia
7 Ian Botham, England
8 Rod Marsh, Australia
9 Malcolm Marshall, West Indies
10 Shane Warne, Australia
11 Dennis Lillee, Australia
12th Man Richard Hadlee, New Zealand

Sir Richard Hadlee

Richard Hadlee played 115 games for New Zealand between 1973-90 and took 158 wickets, including five wickets in an innings five times. He is one of the three cricketers who have played one-day internationals to be knighted. Surprisingly no New Zealanders make his best one-day side.

1 Graham Gooch, England
2 Desmond Haynes, West Indies
3 Viv Richards, West Indies
4 Greg Chappell, Australia
5 Javed Miandad, Pakistan
6 Ian Botham, England
7 Imran Khan, Pakistan
8 Rodney Marsh, Australia
9 Wasim Akram, Pakistan
10 Shane Warne, Australia
11 Joel Garner, West Indies
12th Man Allan Border, Australia

Kim Hughes

At the time of his last game in 1985, former Australian captain Kim Hughes had played more one-day internationals (97) than any other player. Hughes chose nine West Indians in his side and says about one of the exceptions, Zaheer Abbas: 'Abbas had an average of 46 and an unbelievable strike rate of 106 in 65 games. Dean Jones is unlucky to miss out and no wonder we had trouble beating the West Indies.'

1 Gordon Greenidge, West Indies
2 Desmond Haynes, West Indies
3 Viv Richards, West Indies
4 Javed Miandad, Pakistan
5 Zaheer Abbas, Pakistan
6 Clive Lloyd, West Indies (capt.)
7 Jeff Dujon, West Indies
8 Imran Khan, Pakistan
9 Malcolm Marshall, West Indies
10 Curtly Ambrose, West Indies
11 Joel Garner, West Indies
12th Man Roger Harper, West Indies

Peter Roebuck

The former Somerset captain has listed his best one-day eleven from the current pool of players. Roebuck is a widely respected journalist in both Australia and England writing for such broadsheets as *The Daily Telegraph* in London, *The Sydney Morning Herald* and *The Age* in Melbourne. Since retiring from first-class cricket in 1991, he's led Devon to several titles in the Minor Counties championship.

1 Adam Gilchrist, Australia
2 Mark Waugh, Australia
3 Sachin Tendulkar, India
4 Brian Lara, West Indies
5 Aravinda de Silva, Sri Lanka
6 Hansie Cronje, South Africa
7 Chris Harris, New Zealand
8 Shaun Pollock, South Africa
9 Mutiah Muralitharan, Sri Lanka
10 Glenn McGrath, Australia
11 Alan Mullally, England
12th Man Ricky Ponting, Australia

Clive Rice

Clive Rice never played Test cricket but was a member of the Rest of the World XI during a season of World Series Cricket in 1978/79. Rice captained South Africa in their historic return to official international cricket in the three-game one-day international series against India in November 1991.

1 Barry Richards, South Africa
2 Sachin Tendulkar, India
3 Viv Richards, West Indies
4 Graeme Pollock, South Africa
5 Javed Miandad, Pakistan
6 Gary Sobers, West Indies
7 Richard Hadlee, New Zealand
8 Ian Healy, Australia
9 Shane Warne, Australia
10 Malcolm Marshall, West Indies
11 Joel Garner, West Indies
12th Man Jonty Rhodes, South Africa

Zaheer Abbas

Former Pakistani captain Zaheer Abbas has the second highest average (47.62) of all batsmen who have scored more than 1000 runs in limited-overs internationals. He was the first player to score three consecutive centuries and his 2572 runs came from 62 games, including seven centuries and 13 half-centuries.

1 Brian Lara, West Indies
2 Sachin Tendulkar, India
3 Mark Waugh, Australia
4 Viv Richards, West Indies
5 Gary Sobers, West Indies
6 Kapil Dev, India
7 Ian Botham, England
8 Imran Khan, Pakistan
9 Ian Healy, Australia
10 Saqlain Mushtaq, Pakistan
11 Shane Warne, Australia
12th Man Mohammed Azharuddin, India

Dickie Bird

Harold 'Dickie' Bird is the most famous cricket umpire of them all. A household name, an eccentric and one of the most loved and respected characters in world cricket, he retired in 1997 after standing in 66 Tests and 92 one-day internationals (including women's matches). He also released his best-selling autobiography in 1997.

1 Graham Gooch, England
2 Sunil Gavaskar, India
3 Viv Richards, West Indies (capt.)
4 Sachin Tendulkar, India
5 Brian Lara, West Indies
6 Garfield Sobers, West Indies
7 Alan Knott, England
8 Derek Underwood, England
9 Richard Hadlee, New Zealand
10 Dennis Lillee, Australia
11 Andy Roberts, West Indies
12th Man Allan Border, Australia

Jeffrey Archer

Jeffrey Archer is one of the world's leading storytellers. He is a former Member of the British Parliament and former Deputy Chairman of the Conservative Party. His books include *Cain and Abel*, *As the Crow Flies*, *A Quiver Full of Arrows*, and *Shall We Tell the President*? His latest thriller is *The Eleventh Commandment*.

1 Graham Gooch, England
2 Viv Richards, West Indies
3 Sachin Tendulkar, India
4 Brian Lara, West Indies
5 Sanath Jayasuriya, Sri Lanka
6 Gary Sobers, West Indies
7 Ian Botham, England
8 Alan Knott, England
9 Shane Warne, Australia
10 Malcolm Marshall, West Indies
11 Michael Holding, West Indies
12th Man Jonty Rhodes, South Africa

The Authors' One-Day Team

Selected on batting and bowling strike-rates, together with a batsman wicket-keeper and an all-rounder, this team would be hard to beat in any era. At least a dozen players are unlucky to not make the team, the most notable being Sanath Jayasuriya, Desmond Haynes, Brian Lara, Shane Warne, Waqar Younis and Kapil Dev.

1 Sachin Tendulkar, India
2 Gordon Greenidge, West Indies
3 Zaheer Abbas, Pakistan
4 Viv Richards, West Indies (capt.)
5 Michael Bevan, Australia
6 Adam Gilchrist, Australia
7 Imran Khan, Pakistan
8 Wasim Akram, Pakistan
9 Saqlain Mushtaq, Pakistan
10 Curtly Ambrose, West Indies
11 Joel Garner, West Indies
12th Man Roger Harper, West Indies.

Jan Brittin

Jan Brittin is widely regarded as one of England's greatest players and is the most capped, having appeared in 24 Test and 52 one-day internationals between 1979 and 1996. She is the only player to score 1000 runs in World Cup matches and her five centuries is a record for women's one-day internationals. She's also played hockey for England.

Men's team

1 Desmond Haynes, West Indies
2 Gordon Greenidge, West Indies
3 Viv Richards, West Indies
4 Sachin Tendulkar, India
5 Steve Waugh, Australia
6 Garfield Sobers, West Indies
7 Michael Bevan, Australia
8 Richard Hadlee, New Zealand
9 Ian Healy, Australia
10 Shaun Pollock, South Africa
11 Derek Underwood, England
12th Man Jonty Rhodes, South Africa

Women's team

1 Lyn Larsen, Australia
2 Belinda Clark, Australia
3 Lyndsay Reeler, Australia
4 Debbie Hockley, New Zealand
5 Jan Brittin, England
6 Carole Hodges, England
7 Jo Chamberlain, England
8 Bronwyn Calver, Australia
9 Catherine Fitzpatrick, Australia
10 Christina Matthews, Australia
11 Enid Bakewell, England
12th Emily Drumm, New Zealand

Belinda Clark

Belinda Clark made her Test debut for Australia in 1991 and has been captain since 1994. At the 1997 Women's Cricket World Cup held in India, Clark became the first player, male or female, to score a double century in a one-day international, scoring 229 not out against Denmark in Mumbai. She chose both a best men's and best women's one-day team. In 1998 she was named the inaugural Player of the Year by Australian *Wisden*.

Men's team

1 Desmond Haynes, West Indies
2 David Gower, England
3 Viv Richards, West Indies
4 Sachin Tendulkar, India
5 Steve Waugh, Australia
6 Ian Botham, England
7 Richard Hadlee, New Zealand
8 Ian Healy, Australia
9 Malcolm Marshall, West Indies
10 Michael Holding, West Indies
11 Shane Warne, Australia
12th Man Michael Bevan, Australia

Women's team

1 Lyn Larsen, Australia
2 Lindsay Reeler, Australia
3 Betty Wilson, Australia
4 Catherine Fitzpatrick, Australia
5 Jan Brittin, England
6 Jo Chamberlain, England
7 Debbie Hockley, New Zealand
8 Zoe Goss, Australia
9 Christina Matthews, Australia
10 Emily Drumm, New Zealand
11 Bronwyn Calver, Australia
12th Pormina Ram, India

PricewaterhouseCoopers One-Day Cricket Ratings

PricewaterhouseCoopers, the global professional services firm, has produced the World Ratings of Test cricketers since 1987 and in August 1998 introduced ratings for players in limited-overs internationals.

Players considered must not be retired, and must have appeared in an official limited-overs international in the last 12 months. Batsmen are rated on factors including runs scored, the rate at which they are scored, the overall run-rate for the match, the ratings of opposing bowlers and the result of the match. Bowlers are rated on runs conceded per over, wickets taken and runs conceded for the match, the overall ratings of the opposing batsmen and the result of the match. The maximum number of points a player can achieve is 1000 and players typically move up or down 15 points after a single match. World Cup matches carry more weighting.

Listed below is the top 30 batsmen and bowlers as of 13 February 1999.

Batsmen				Bowlers		
Rank	Player	Rating		Rank	Player	Rating
1	S.R. Tendulkar, India	862		1	Saqlain Mushtaq, Pakistan	820
2	M.G. Bevan, Australia	793		2	S.M. Pollock, South Africa	784
3	B.C. Lara, West Indies	766		3	G.D. McGrath, Australia	755
4	Saeed Anwar, Pakistan	761		4	M. Muralitharan, Sri Lanka	750
5	A.C. Gilchrist, Australia	754		5	D. Gough, England	749
6	W.J. Cronje, South Africa	740		6	A.A. Donald, South Africa	736
7	R.T. Ponting, Australia	717		7	C.L. Ambrose, West Indies	724
8	Ijaz Ahmed snr, Pakistan	710		8	C.Z. Harris, New Zealand	717
9	S.C. Ganguly, India	709		8	A. Kumble, India	717
10	M.E. Waugh, Australia	690		10	A.R. Whittall, Zimbabwe	709
11	S. Chanderpaul, West Indies	687		11	J. Srinath, India	700
12	N.J. Astle, New Zealand	684		12	G.R. Larsen, New Zealand	697
13	S.T. Jayasuriya, Sri Lanka	680		12	Wasim Akram, Pakistan	697
14	G.A. Hick, England	671		14	D.W. Fleming, Australia	695
15	P.A. de Silva, Sri Lanka	668		15	A.C. Dale, Australia	693
15	C.L. Hooper, West Indies	668		16	P.A. Strang, Zimbabwe	692
17	N.V. Knight, England	663		17	R.D.B. Croft, England	688
18	L. Klusener, South Africa	655		18	C.L. Hooper, West Indies	676
19	A.D. Jadeja, India	649		18	P.L. Symcox, South Africa	676
20	M.A. Azharuddin, India	647		20	S.K. Warne, Australia	671
20	C.L. Cairns, New Zealand	647		21	H.H. Streak, Zimbabwe	667
22	D.S. Lehmann, Australia	638		22	W.P.U.C.J. Vaas, Sri Lanka	650
23	J.H. Kallis, South Africa	635		23	Azhar Mahmood, Pakistan	639
24	Inzamam-ul-Haq, Pakistan	629		24	H.D.P.K. Dharmasena, Sri Lanka	632
25	G.W. Flower, Zimbabwe	625		25	L. Klusener, South Africa	631
26	A. Flower, Zimbabwe	623		26	M.A. Ealham, England	615
27	S.P. Fleming, New Zealand	622		27	A.R.C. Fraser, England	614
28	Shahid Afridi, Pakistan	620		28	A.B. Agarkar, India	607
29	J.N. Rhodes, South Africa	616		29	C.L. Cairns, New Zealand	606
30	C.Z. Harris, New Zealand	604		29	A.D. Mullally, England	606

Highest ranked batsmen from other countries				Highest ranked bowlers from other countries		
52	S.O. Tikolo, Kenya	492		41	Aasif Karim, Kenya	525
64	Amin-ul-Islam, Bangladesh	432		70	Mohammad Rafiq, Bangladesh	341

PART 2

STATISTICS AND RECORDS

THE MATCHES

Captains are listed in the order in which the teams are presented in the match column.
†Indicates a revised target.

MATCH	VENUE	SCORES	CAPTAIN	CAPTAIN
1970/71 – Australia v England				
5 Jan 71 Australia v England – Aus won by 5 wickets	Melbourne	Eng 190 – Aus 5/191	W.M. Lawry	R. Illingworth
Series winner: Australia 1-0				
1972 – Prudential Trophy				
24 Aug 72 England v Australia – Eng won by 6 wickets	Manchester	Aus 8/222 – Eng 4/226	D.B. Close	I.M. Chappell
26 Aug 72 England v Australia – Aus won by 5 wickets	Lord's	Eng 9/236 – Aus 5/240	D.B. Close	I.M. Chappell
28 Aug 72 England v Australia – Eng won by 2 wickets	Birmingham	Aus 9/179 – Eng 8/180	D.B. Close	I.M. Chappell
Series winner: England 2-1				
1972/73 – New Zealand v Pakistan				
11 Feb 73 New Zealand v Pakistan – NZ won by 22 runs	Christchurch	NZ 187 – Pak 165	B.E. Congdon	Intikhab Alam
Series winner: New Zealand 1-0				
1973 – Prudential Trophy				
18 Jul 73 England v New Zealand – Eng won by 7 wickets	Swansea	NZ 158 – Eng 3/159	R. Illingworth	B.E. Congdon
20 Jul 73 England v New Zealand – No result	Manchester	Eng 8/167 – NZ DNB	R. Illingworth	B.E. Congdon
Series winner: England 1-0				
1973 – Prudential Trophy				
5 Sep 73 England v West Indies – Eng won by 1 wicket	Leeds	WI 181 – Eng 9/182	M.H. Denness	R.B. Kanhai
7 Sep 73 England v West Indies – WI won by 8 wickets	The Oval	Eng 9/189 – WI 2/190	M.H. Denness	R.B. Kanhai
Series winner: West Indies, due to superior run-rate				
1973/74 – New Zealand v Australia				
30 Mar 74 New Zealand v Australia – Aus won by 7 wickets	Dunedin	NZ 9/194 – Aus 3/195	B.E. Congdon	I.M. Chappell
31 Mar 74 New Zealand v Australia – Aus won by 31 runs	Christchurch	Aus 5/265 – NZ 6/234	B.E. Congdon	I.M. Chappell
Series winner: Australia 2-0				
1974 – Prudential Trophy				
13 Jul 74 England v India – Eng won by 4 wickets	Leeds	Ind 265 – Eng 6/266	M.H. Denness	A.L. Wadekar
15/16 Jul 74 England v India – Eng won by 6 wickets	The Oval	Ind 171 – Eng 4/172	M.H. Denness	A.L. Wadekar
Series winner: England 2-0				

MATCH

MATCH	VENUE	SCORES	CAPTAIN	CAPTAIN
1974 – Prudential Trophy				
31 Aug 74 England v Pakistan – Pak won by 7 wickets	Nottingham	Eng 4/244 – Pak 3/246	M.H. Denness	Intikhab Alam
3 Sep 74 England v Pakistan – Pak won by 8 wickets	Birmingham	Eng 9/81 – Pak 2/84	M.H. Denness	Intikhab Alam
Series winner: Pakistan 2-0				
1974/75 – Australia v England				
1 Jan 75 Australia v England – Eng won by 3 wickets	Melbourne	Aus 190 – Eng 7/191	I.M. Chappell	M.H. Denness
Series winner: England 1-0				
1974/75 – New Zealand v England				
8 Mar 75 New Zealand v England – No result	Dunedin	Eng 136 – NZ 0/15	B.E. Congdon	J.H. Edrich
9 Mar 75 New Zealand v England – No result	Wellington	NZ 227 – Eng 1/35	G.M. Turner	M.H. Denness
1975 – Prudential World Cup				
Group A qualifying matches				
7 Jun 75 England v India – Eng won by 202 runs	Lord's	Eng 4/334 – Ind 3/132	M.H. Denness	S. Venkataraghavan
7 Jun 75 East Africa v New Zealand – NZ won by 181 runs	Birmingham	NZ 5/309 – EAF 8/128	Harilal Shah	G.M. Turner
11 Jun 75 England v New Zealand – Eng won by 80 runs	Nottingham	Eng 6/226 – NZ 186	M.H. Denness	G.M. Turner
11 Jun 75 East Africa v India – Ind won by 10 wickets	Leeds	EAF 120 – Ind 0/123	Harilal Shah	S. Venkataraghavan
14 Jun 75 England v East Africa – Eng won by 196 runs	Birmingham	Eng 5/290 – EAF 94	M.H. Denness	Harilal Shah
14 Jun 75 India v New Zealand – NZ won by 4 wickets	Manchester	Ind 230 – NZ 6/233	S. Venkataraghavan	G.M. Turner
Group B qualifying matches				
7 Jun 75 Australia v Pakistan – Aus won by 73 runs	Leeds	Aus 7/278 – Pak 205	I.M. Chappell	Asif Iqbal
7 Jun 75 Sri Lanka v West Indies – WI won by 9 wickets	Manchester	SL 86 – WI 1/87	A.P.B. Tennekoon	C.H. Lloyd
11 Jun 75 Australia v Sri Lanka – Aus won by 52 runs	The Oval	Aus 5/328 – SL 4/276	I.M. Chappell	A.P.B. Tennekoon
11 Jun 75 Pakistan v West Indies – WI won by 1 wicket	Birmingham	Pak 7/266 – WI 9/267	Majid Khan	C.H. Lloyd
14 Jun 75 Australia v West Indies – WI won by 7 wickets	The Oval	Aus 192 – WI 3/195	I.M. Chappell	C.H. Lloyd
14 Jun 75 Pakistan v Sri Lanka – Pak won by 192 runs	Nottingham	Pak 6/330 – SL 138	Majid Khan	A.P.B. Tennekoon
Semi-finals				
18 Jun 75 England v Australia – Aus won by 4 wickets	Leeds	Eng 93 – Aus 6/94	M.H. Denness	I.M. Chappell
18 Jun 75 New Zealand v West Indies – WI won by 5 wickets	The Oval	NZ 158 – WI 5/159	G.M. Turner	C.H. Lloyd
Final				
21 Jun 75 Australia v West Indies – WI won by 17 runs	Lord's	WI 8/291 – Aus 274	I.M. Chappell	C.H. Lloyd
World Champions: West Indies				
1975/76 – Australia v West Indies				
20 Dec 75 Australia v West Indies - Aus won by 5 wickets	Adelaide	WI 224 – Aus 5/225	G.S. Chappell	C.H. Lloyd
Series winner: Australia 1-0				

108 — One-day International Cricket

MATCH	VENUE	SCORES	CAPTAIN	CAPTAIN
1975/76 – New Zealand v India				
21 Feb 76 New Zealand v India - NZ won by 9 wickets	Christchurch	Ind 154 – NZ 1/155	G.M. Turner	B.S. Bedi
22 Feb 76 New Zealand v India - NZ won by 80 runs	Auckland	NZ 8/236 – Ind 156	G.M. Turner	S. Venkataraghavan
Series winner: New Zealand 2-0				
1976 – Prudential Trophy				
26 Aug 76 England v West Indies – WI won by 6 wickets	Scarborough	Eng 8/202 – WI 4/207	A.P.E. Knott	C.H. Lloyd
28/29 Aug 76 England v West Indies – WI won by 36 runs	Lord's	WI 221 – Eng 185	A.W. Greig	C.H. Lloyd
31 Aug 76 England v West Indies – WI won by 50 runs	Birmingham	WI 9/223 – Eng 173	A.W. Greig	C.H. Lloyd
Series winner: West Indies 3-0				
1976/77 – Pakistan v New Zealand				
16 Oct 76 Pakistan v New Zealand – NZ won by 1 run	Sialkot	NZ 8/198 – Pak 9/197	Mushtaq Mohammed	G.M. Turner
Series winner: New Zealand 1-0				
1976/77 – Guinness Trophy				
16 Mar 77 West Indies v Pakistan – WI won by 4 wickets	Berbice	Pak 7/176 – WI 6/182	C.H. Lloyd	Asif Iqbal
Series winner: West Indies 1-0				
1977 – Prudential Trophy				
2 Jun 77 England v Australia – Eng won by 2 wickets	Manchester	Aus 9/169 – Eng 8/173	J.M. Brearley	G.S. Chappell
4 Jun 77 England v Australia – Eng won by 101 runs	Birmingham	Eng 171 – Aus 70	J.M. Brearley	G.S. Chappell
6 Jun 77 England v Australia – Aus won by 2 wickets	The Oval	Eng 242 – Aus 8/246	J.M. Brearley	G.S. Chappell
Series winner: England 2-1				
1977/78 – Pakistan v England				
23 Dec 77 Pakistan v England – Eng won by 3 wickets	Sahiwal	Pak 6/208 – Eng 7/212	Wasim Bari	J.M. Brearley
30 Dec 77 Pakistan v England – Eng won by 6 wickets	Sialkot	Pak 151 – Eng 4/152	Wasim Bari	G. Boycott
13 Jan 78 Pakistan v England – Pak won by 36 runs	Lahore	Pak 6/158 – Eng 122	Wasim Bari	J.M. Brearley
Series winner: England 2-1				
1977/78 Guinness Trophy				
22 Feb 78 West Indies v Australia – WI won on run-rate	St John's	WI 9/313 – Aus 7/181	D.L. Murray	R.B. Simpson
12 Apr 78 West Indies v Australia – Aus won by 2 wickets	Castries	WI 139 – Aus 8/140	A.I. Kallicharran	R.B. Simpson
Series drawn 1-1				
1978 – Prudential Trophy				
24/25 May 78 England v Pakistan – Eng won by 132 runs	Manchester	Eng 7/217 – Pak 85	G. Boycott	Wasim Bari
26 May 78 England v Pakistan – Eng won by 94 runs	The Oval	Eng 6/248 – Pak 8/154	R.G.D. Willis	Wasim Bari
Series winner: England 2-0				

MATCH	VENUE	SCORES	CAPTAIN	CAPTAIN
1978 – Prudential Trophy				
15 Jul 78 England v New Zealand – Eng won by 19 runs	Scarborough	Eng 8/206 – NZ 8/187	J.M. Brearley	M.G. Burgess
17 Jul 78 England v New Zealand – Eng won by 126 runs	Manchester	Eng 5/278 – NZ 152	J.M. Brearley	M.G. Burgess
Series winner: England 2-0				
1978/79 – Pakistan v India				
1 Oct 78 Pakistan v India – Ind won by 4 runs	Quetta (AN)	Ind 7/170 – Pak 8/166	Mushtaq Mohammed	B.S. Bedi
13 Oct 78 Pakistan v India – Pak won by 8 wickets	Sialkot	Ind 79 – Pak 2/83	Mushtaq Mohammed	B.S. Bedi
3 Nov 78 Pakistan v India – Pak won (conceded by India)	Sahiwal	Pak 7/205 – Ind 2/183	Mushtaq Mohammed	B.S. Bedi
Series winner: Pakistan 2-1				
1978/79 – Benson & Hedges Cup				
13 Jan 79 Australia v England – No result	Sydney	Aus 1/17 – Eng DNB	G.N. Yallop	J.M. Brearley
24 Jan 79 Australia v England – Eng won by 7 wickets	Melbourne	Aus 101 – Eng 3/102	G.N. Yallop	J.M. Brearley
4 Feb 79 Australia v England – Aus won by 4 wickets	Melbourne	Eng 6/212 – Aus 6/215	G.N. Yallop	J.M. Brearley
7 Feb 79 Australia v England – Aus won by 6 wickets	Melbourne	Eng 94 – Aus 4/95	G.N. Yallop	J.M. Brearley
Series winner: Australia 2-1				
1979 – Prudential World Cup				
Group A qualifying matches				
9 Jun 79 England v Australia – Eng won by 6 wickets	Lord's	Aus 9/159 – Eng 4/160	J.M. Brearley	K.J. Hughes
9 Jun 79 Canada v Pakistan – Pak won by 8 wickets	Leeds	Can 9/139 – Pak 2/140	B.M. Mauricette	Asif Iqbal
13/14 Jun 79 Australia v Pakistan – Pak won by 89 runs	Nottingham	Pak 7/286 – Aus 197	K.J. Hughes	Asif Iqbal
14 Jun 79 England v Canada – Eng won by 8 wickets	Manchester	Can 45 – Eng 2/46	J.M. Brearley	B.M. Mauricette
16 Jun 79 Australia v Canada – Aus won by 7 wickets	Birmingham	Can 105 – Aus 3/106	K.J. Hughes	B.M. Mauricette
16 Jun 79 England v Pakistan – Eng won by 14 runs	Leeds	Eng 9/165 – Pak 151	J.M. Brearley	Asif Iqbal
Group B qualifying matches				
9 Jun 79 India v West Indies – WI won by 9 wickets	Birmingham	Ind 190 – WI 1/194	S. Venkataraghavan	C.H. Lloyd
9 Jun 79 New Zealand v Sri Lanka – NZ won by 9 wickets	Nottingham	SL 189 – NZ 1/190	M.G. Burgess	A.P.B. Tennekoon
13 Jun 79 India v New Zealand – NZ won by 8 wickets	Leeds	Ind 182 – NZ 2/183	S. Venkataraghavan	M.G. Burgess
16/18 Jun 79 India v Sri Lanka – SL won by 47 runs	Manchester	SL 5/238 – Ind 191	S. Venkataraghavan	B. Warnapura
16 Jun 79 New Zealand v West Indies – WI won by 32 runs	Nottingham	WI 7/244 – NZ 9/212	M.G. Burgess	C.H. Lloyd
Semi-finals				
20 Jun 79 England v New Zealand – Eng won by 9 runs	Manchester	Eng 8/221 – NZ 9/212	J.M. Brearley	M.G. Burgess
20 Jun 79 Pakistan v West Indies – WI won by 43 runs	The Oval	WI 6/293 – Pak 250	Asif Iqbal	C.H. Lloyd
Final				
23 Jun 79 England v West Indies – WI won by 92 runs	Lord's	WI 9/286 – Eng 194	J.M. Brearley	C.H. Lloyd
World champions: West Indies				

MATCH	VENUE	SCORES	CAPTAIN	CAPTAIN
1979/80 – Benson & Hedges World Series Cup				
Qualifying matches				
27 Nov 79 Australia v West Indies – Aus won by 5 wickets	Sydney	WI 193 – Aus 5/196	G.S. Chappell	C.H. Lloyd
28 Nov 79 England v West Indies – Eng won by 2 runs+	Sydney	Eng 8/211 – WI 196	J.M. Brearley	C.H. Lloyd
8 Dec 79 Australia v England – Eng won by 3 wickets	Melbourne	Aus 9/207 – Eng 7/209	G.S. Chappell	J.M. Brearley
9 Dec 79 Australia v West Indies – WI won by 80 runs	Melbourne	WI 2/271 – Aus 8/191	G.S. Chappell	D.L. Murray
11 Dec 79 Australia v England – Eng won by 72 runs	Sydney	Eng 7/264 – Aus 192	G.S. Chappell	J.M. Brearley
21 Dec 79 Australia v West Indies – Aus won by 7 runs	Sydney	Aus 6/176 – WI 169	G.S. Chappell	C.H. Lloyd
23 Dec 79 England v West Indies – WI won by 9 wickets	Brisbane	Eng 8/217 – WI 1/218	J.M. Brearley	C.H. Lloyd
26 Dec 79 Australia v England – Eng won by 4 wickets	Sydney	Aus 6/194 – Eng 6/195	G.S. Chappell	J.M. Brearley
14 Jan 80 Australia v England – Eng won by 2 wickets	Sydney	Aus 163 – Eng 8/164	G.S. Chappell	J.M. Brearley
16 Jan 80 England v West Indies – WI won by 107 runs	Adelaide	WI 5/246 – Eng 139	J.M. Brearley	C.H. Lloyd
18 Jan 80 Australia v West Indies – Aus won by 9 runs	Sydney	Aus 190 – WI 181	G.S. Chappell	C.H. Lloyd
Finals				
20 Jan 80 England v West Indies – WI won by 2 runs	Melbourne	WI 8/215 – Eng 7/213	J.M. Brearley	C.H. Lloyd
22 Jan 80 England v West Indies – WI won by 8 wickets	Sydney	Eng 8/208 – WI 2/209	J.M. Brearley	C.H. Lloyd
Series winner: West Indies				
1979/80 - New Zealand v West Indies				
6 Feb 80 New Zealand v West Indies – NZ won by 1 wicket	Christchurch	WI 7/203 – NZ 9/207	G.P. Howarth	C.H. Lloyd
Series winner: New Zealand 1-0				
1980 – Prudential Trophy				
28/29 May 80 England v West Indies – WI won by 24 runs	Leeds	WI 198 – Eng 174	I.T. Botham	C.H. Lloyd
30 May 80 England v West Indies – Eng won by 3 wickets	Lord's	WI 9/235 – Eng 7/236	I.T. Botham	I.V.A. Richards
Series winner: West Indies, due to superior run-rate				
1980 – Prudential Trophy				
20 Aug 80 England v Australia – Eng won by 23 runs	The Oval	Eng 6/248 – Aus 8/225	I.T. Botham	G.S. Chappell
22 Aug 80 England v Australia – Eng won by 47 runs	Birmingham	Eng 8/320 – Aus 5/273	I.T. Botham	G.S. Chappell
Series winner: England 2-0				
1980/81 – Wills Series				
1 Nov 80 Pakistan v West Indies – WI won by 4 wickets	Karachi	Pak 9/127 – WI 6/128	Javed Miandad	C.H. Lloyd
5 Dec 80 Pakistan v West Indies – WI won by 7 wickets	Sialkot	Pak 4/200 – WI 3/201	Javed Miandad	C.H. Lloyd
19 Dec 80 Pakistan v West Indies – WI won by 7 runs	Lahore	WI 8/170 – Pak 6/163	Javed Miandad	C.H. Lloyd
Series winner: West Indies 3-0				

1980/81 – Benson & Hedges World Series Cup

Qualifying matches

MATCH	VENUE	SCORES	CAPTAIN	CAPTAIN
23 Nov 80 Australia v New Zealand – NZ won by 3 wickets	Adelaide	Aus 9/217 – NZ 7/219	G.S. Chappell	G.P. Howarth
25 Nov 80 Australia v New Zealand – Aus won by 94 runs	Sydney	Aus 3/289 – NZ 195	G.S. Chappell	G.P. Howarth
6 Dec 80 Australia v India – Ind won by 66 runs	Melbourne	Ind 9/208 – Aus 142	G.S. Chappell	S.M. Gavaskar
7 Dec 80 Australia v New Zealand – Aus won by 4 wickets	Melbourne	NZ 156 – Aus 6/159	G.S. Chappell	M.G. Burgess
9 Dec 80 India v New Zealand – Ind won by 5 runs	Perth	Ind 162 – NZ 157	S.M. Gavaskar	M.G. Burgess
18 Dec 80 Australia v India – Aus won by 9 wickets	Sydney	Ind 9/180 – Aus 1/183	G.S. Chappell	S.M. Gavaskar
21 Dec 80 India v New Zealand – NZ won by 3 wickets	Brisbane	Ind 204 – NZ 7/205	S.M. Gavaskar	G.P. Howarth
23 Dec 80 India v New Zealand – Ind won by 6 runs	Adelaide	Ind 7/230 – NZ 224	S.M. Gavaskar	G.P. Howarth
8 Jan 81 Australia v India – Aus won by 9 wickets	Sydney	Ind 63 – Aus 1/64	G.S. Chappell	S.M. Gavaskar
10 Jan 81 India v New Zealand – NZ won by 10 wickets	Melbourne	Ind 9/112 – NZ 0/113	S.M. Gavaskar	G.P. Howarth
11 Jan 81 Australia v India – Aus won by 7 wickets	Melbourne	Ind 5/192 – Aus 3/193	G.S. Chappell	S.M. Gavaskar
13 Jan 81 Australia v New Zealand – NZ won by 1 run	Sydney	NZ 8/220 – Aus 7/219	G.S. Chappell	G.P. Howarth
15 Jan 81 Australia v India – Aus won by 27 runs	Sydney	Aus 8/242 – Ind 8/215	G.S. Chappell	S.M. Gavaskar
18 Jan 81 India v New Zealand – NZ won by 22 runs	Brisbane	NZ 9/242 – Ind 220	S.M. Gavaskar	G.P. Howarth
21 Jan 81 Australia v New Zealand – No result	Sydney	Aus 180 – NZ 1/23	G.S. Chappell	G.P. Howarth

Series winner: Australia

Finals

MATCH	VENUE	SCORES	CAPTAIN	CAPTAIN
29 Jan 81 Australia v New Zealand – NZ won by 78 runs	Sydney	NZ 6/233 – Aus 155	G.S. Chappell	G.P. Howarth
31 Jan 81 Australia v New Zealand – Aus won by 7 wickets	Melbourne	NZ 126 – Aus 3/130	G.S. Chappell	G.P. Howarth
1 Feb 81 Australia v New Zealand – Aus won by 6 runs	Melbourne	Aus 4/235 – NZ 8/229	G.S. Chappell	G.P. Howarth
3 Feb 81 Australia v New Zealand – Aus won by 6 wickets	Sydney	NZ 8/215 – Aus 4/218	G.S. Chappell	G.P. Howarth

Series winner: Australia

1980/81 – West Indies v England

MATCH	VENUE	SCORES	CAPTAIN	CAPTAIN
4 Feb 81 West Indies v England – WI won by 2 runs	Kingstown	WI 127 – Eng 125	C.H. Lloyd	I.T. Botham
26 Feb 81 West Indies v England – WI won by 6 wickets	Berbice	Eng 137 – WI 4/138	C.H. Lloyd	I.T. Botham

Series winner: West Indies 2-0

1980/81 – New Zealand v India

MATCH	VENUE	SCORES	CAPTAIN	CAPTAIN
14 Feb 81 New Zealand v India – NZ won by 78 runs	Auckland	NZ 6/218 – Ind 9/140	G.P. Howarth	S.M. Gavaskar
15 Feb 81 New Zealand v India – NZ won by 57 runs	Hamilton	NZ 8/210 – Ind 153	G.P. Howarth	G.R. Viswanath

Series winner: New Zealand 2-0

1981 – Prudential Trophy

MATCH	VENUE	SCORES	CAPTAIN	CAPTAIN
4 Jun 81 England v Australia – Eng by 6 wickets	Lord's	Aus 7/210 – Eng 4/212	I.T. Botham	K.J. Hughes
6 Jun 81 England v Australia – Aus won by 2 runs	Birmingham	Aus 8/249 – Eng 247	I.T. Botham	K.J. Hughes
8 Jun 81 England v Australia – Aus won by 71 runs	Leeds	Aus 8/236 – Eng 165	I.T. Botham	K.J. Hughes

Series winner: Australia 2-1

1981/82 – Benson & Hedges World Series Cup

Qualifying matches

MATCH	VENUE	SCORES	CAPTAIN	CAPTAIN
21 Nov 81 Pakistan v West Indies – WI won by 18 runs	Melbourne	WI 8/245 – Pak 6/227	Javed Miandad	C.H. Lloyd
22 Nov 81 Australia v Pakistan – Pak won by 4 wickets	Melbourne	Aus 9/209 – Pak 6/210	G.S. Chappell	Javed Miandad
24 Nov 81 Australia v West Indies – Aus won by 7 wickets	Sydney	WI 8/236 – Aus 3/237	G.S. Chappell	C.H. Lloyd
5 Dec 81 Pakistan v West Indies – Pak won by 8 runs	Adelaide	Pak 140 – WI 132	Javed Miandad	C.H. Lloyd
6 Dec 81 Australia v Pakistan – Aus won by 38 runs	Adelaide	Aus 208 – Pak 8/170	G.S. Chappell	Javed Miandad
17 Dec 81 Australia v Pakistan – Pak won by 6 wickets	Sydney	Aus 6/222 – Pak 4/223	G.S. Chappell	Javed Miandad
19 Dec 81 Pakistan v West Indies – WI won by 7 wickets	Perth	Pak 160 – WI 3/161	Javed Miandad	C.H. Lloyd
20 Dec 81 Australia v West Indies – WI won by 8 wickets	Perth	Aus 9/188 – WI 2/190	G.S. Chappell	C.H. Lloyd
9 Jan 82 Australia v Pakistan – Pak won by 25 runs	Melbourne	Pak 6/218 – Aus 193	G.S. Chappell	Javed Miandad
10 Jan 82 Australia v West Indies – WI won by 5 wickets	Melbourne	Aus 146 – WI 5/147	G.S. Chappell	C.H. Lloyd
12 Jan 82 Pakistan v West Indies – WI won by 7 wickets	Sydney	Pak 7/191 – WI 3/192	Javed Miandad	C.H. Lloyd
14 Jan 82 Australia v Pakistan – Aus won by 76 runs	Sydney	Aus 5/230 – Pak 154	G.S. Chappell	Javed Miandad
16 Jan 82 Pakistan v West Indies – WI won by 1 wicket	Brisbane	Pak 177 – WI 9/107	Javed Miandad	C.H. Lloyd
17 Jan 82 Australia v West Indies – WI won by 5 wickets	Brisbane	Aus 9/185 – WI 5/186	G.S. Chappell	I.V.A. Richards
19 Jan 82 Australia v West Indies – Aus won on run-rate	Sydney	WI 189 – Aus 7/168	G.S. Chappell	I.V.A. Richards

Finals

MATCH	VENUE	SCORES	CAPTAIN	CAPTAIN
23 Jan 82 Australia v West Indies – WI won by 86 runs	Melbourne	WI 8/216 – Aus 130	G.S. Chappell	C.H. Lloyd
24 Jan 82 Australia v West Indies – WI won by 128 runs	Melbourne	WI 9/235 – Aus 107	G.S. Chappell	C.H. Lloyd
26 Jan 82 Australia v West Indies – Aus won by 46 runs	Sydney	Aus 8/214 – WI 168	G.S. Chappell	C.H. Lloyd
27 Jan 82 Australia v West Indies – WI won by 18 runs	Sydney	WI 6/234 – Aus 9/216	G.S. Chappell	C.H. Lloyd

Series winner: West Indies

1981/82 – Wills Series

MATCH	VENUE	SCORES	CAPTAIN	CAPTAIN
25 Nov 81 India v England – Eng won by 5 wickets	Ahmedabad (SP)	Ind 7/156 – Eng 5/160	S.M. Gavaskar	K.W.R. Fletcher
20 Dec 81 India v England – Ind won b 6 wickets	Jullundur	Eng 7/161 – Ind 4/164	S.M. Gavaskar	K.W.R. Fletcher
27 Jan 82 India v England – Ind won by 5 wickets	Cuttack	Eng 6/230 – Ind 5/231	S.M. Gavaskar	K.W.R. Fletcher

Series winner: India 2-1

1981/82 – Sri Lanka v England

MATCH	VENUE	SCORES	CAPTAIN	CAPTAIN
13 Feb 82 Sri Lanka v England – Eng won by 5 runs	Colombo (SSC)	Eng 211 – SL 8/206	B. Warnapura	K.W.R. Fletcher
14 Feb 82 Sri Lanka v England – SL won by 3 runs	Colombo (SSC)	SL 7/215 – Eng 212	B. Warnapura	K.W.R. Fletcher

Series drawn 1-1

1981/82 – Rothmans Cup

MATCH	VENUE	SCORES	CAPTAIN	CAPTAIN
13 Feb 82 New Zealand v Australia – NZ won by 46 runs	Auckland	NZ 6/240 – Aus 194	G.P. Howarth	G.S. Chappell
17 Feb 82 New Zealand v Australia – Aus won by 6 wickets	Dunedin	NZ 9/159 – Aus 4/160	G.P. Howarth	G.S. Chappell
20 Feb 82 New Zealand v Australia – Aus won by 8 wickets	Wellington	NZ 74 – Aus 2/75	G.P. Howarth	G.S. Chappell

Series winner: Australia 2-1

MATCH	VENUE	SCORES	CAPTAIN	CAPTAIN
1981/82 – Wills Series				
12 Mar 82 Pakistan v Sri Lanka – Pak won by 8 wickets	Karachi	SL 3/171 – Pak 2/174	Javed Miandad	B. Warnapura
29 Mar 82 Pakistan v Sri Lanka – SL won on run-rate	Lahore	Pak 4/239 – SL 4/227	Javed Miandad	B. Warnapura
31 Mar 82 Pakistan v Sri Lanka – Pak won by 5 wickets	Karachi	SL 218 – Pak 5/222	Zaheer Abbas	L.R.D. Mendis
Series winner: Pakistan 2-1				
1982 – Prudential Trophy				
2 Jun 82 England v India – Eng won by 9 wickets	Leeds	Ind 193 – Eng 1/194	R.G.D. Willis	S.M. Gavaskar
4 Jun 82 England v India – Eng won by 114 runs	The Oval	Eng 9/276 – Ind 8/162	R.G.D. Willis	S.M. Gavaskar
Series winner: England 2-0				
1982 – Prudential Trophy				
17 Jul 82 England v Pakistan – Eng won by 7 wickets	Nottingham	Pak 6/250 – Eng 3/252	R.G.D. Willis	Imran Khan
19 Jul 82 England v Pakistan – Eng won by 73 runs	Manchester	Eng 8/295 – Pak 222	R.G.D. Willis	Imran Khan
Series winner: England 2-0				
1982/83 – India v Sri Lanka				
12 Sep 82 India v Sri Lanka – Ind won by 78 runs	Amritsar	Ind 7/269 – SL 8/191	Kapil Dev	B. Warnapura
15 Sep 82 India v Sri Lanka – Ind won by 6 wickets	Delhi	SL 8/277 – Ind 4/281	Kapil Dev	B. Warnapura
26 Sep 82 India v Sri Lanka – Ind won by 6 wickets	Bangalore	SL 8/233 – Ind 4/234	Kapil Dev	B. Warnapura
Series winner: India 3-0				
1982/83 – Wills Series				
20 Sep 82 Pakistan v Australia – Pak won by 59 runs	Hyderabad (P)	Pak 6/239 – Aus 9/170	Zaheer Abbas	K.J. Hughes
8 Oct 82 Pakistan v Australia – Pak won by 28 runs	Lahore	Pak 3/234 – Aus 4/206	Imran Khan	K.J. Hughes
22 Oct 82 Pakistan v Australia – No result	Karachi	Pak 1/44 – Aus DNB	Imran Khan	K.J. Hughes
Series winner: Pakistan 2-0				
1982/83 – Wills Series				
3 Dec 82 Pakistan v India – Pak won by 14 runs	Gujranwala	Pak 4/224 – Ind 6/210	Imran Khan	S.M. Gavaskar
17 Dec 82 Pakistan v India – Pak won by 37 runs	Multan	Pak 2/263 – Ind 7/226	Imran Khan	Kapil Dev
31 Dec 82 Pakistan v India – Ind won on run-rate	Lahore	Pak 3/252 – Ind 4/193	Imran Khan	S.M. Gavaskar
21 Jan 83 Pakistan v India – Pak won by 8 wickets	Karachi	Ind 6/197 – Pak 2/198	Imran Khan	S.M. Gavaskar
Series winner: Pakistan 3-1				
1982/83 – Benson & Hedges World Series Cup				
Qualifying matches				
9 Jan 83 Australia v New Zealand – Aus won by 8 wickets	Melbourne	NZ 181 – Aus 2/182	K.J. Hughes	G.P. Howarth
11 Jan 83 Australia v England – Aus won by 31 runs	Sydney	Aus 180 – Eng 149	K.J. Hughes	R.G.D. Willis
13 Jan 83 England v New Zealand – NZ won by 2 runs	Melbourne	NZ 8/239 – Eng 8/237	R.G.D. Willis	G.P. Howarth
15 Jan 83 England v New Zealand – Eng won by 54 runs	Brisbane	Eng 6/267 – NZ 213	R.G.D. Willis	G.P. Howarth
16 Jan 83 Australia v England – Aus won by 7 wickets	Brisbane	Eng 182 – Aus 3/184	K.J. Hughes	R.G.D. Willis

MATCH	VENUE	SCORES	CAPTAIN	CAPTAIN
18 Jan 83 Australia v New Zealand – NZ won by 47 runs	Sydney	NZ 8/226 – Aus 179	K.J. Hughes	G.P. Howarth
20 Jan 83 England v New Zealand – Eng won by 8 wickets	Sydney	NZ 199 – Eng 2/200	R.G.D. Willis	G.P. Howarth
22 Jan 83 Australia v New Zealand – NZ won by 58 runs	Melbourne	NZ 6/246 – Aus 188	K.J. Hughes	G.P. Howarth
23 Jan 83 Australia v England – Aus won by 5 wickets	Melbourne	Eng 5/213 – Aus 5/217	K.J. Hughes	R.G.D. Willis
26 Jan 83 Australia v England – Eng won by 98 runs	Sydney	Eng 207 – Aus 109	K.J. Hughes	R.G.D. Willis
29 Jan 83 England v New Zealand – NZ won by 4 wickets	Adelaide	Eng 5/296 – NZ 6/297	R.G.D. Willis	G.P. Howarth
30 Jan 83 Australia v England – Eng won by 14 runs	Adelaide	Eng 6/228 – Aus 7/214	K.J. Hughes	R.G.D. Willis
31 Jan 83 Australia v New Zealand – NZ won by 47 runs	Adelaide	NZ 9/200 – Aus 153	K.J. Hughes	G.P. Howarth
5 Feb 83 England v New Zealand – NZ won by 7 wickets	Perth	Eng 7/88 – NZ 3/89	R.G.D. Willis	G.P. Howarth
6 Feb 83 Australia v New Zealand – Aus won by 27 runs	Perth	Aus 9/191 – NZ 164	K.J. Hughes	G.P. Howarth

Finals

MATCH	VENUE	SCORES	CAPTAIN	CAPTAIN
9 Feb 83 Australia v New Zealand – Aus won on run-rate	Sydney	NZ 7/193 – Aus 4/155	K.J. Hughes	G.P. Howarth
13 Feb 83 Australia v New Zealand – Aus won by 149 runs	Melbourne	Aus 8/302 – NZ 153	K.J. Hughes	G.P. Howarth

Series winner: Australia

1982/83 – Rothmans Cup

MATCH	VENUE	SCORES	CAPTAIN	CAPTAIN
19 Feb 83 New Zealand v England – NZ won by 6 wickets	Auckland	Eng 9/184 – NZ 4/187	G.P. Howarth	R.G.D. Willis
23 Feb 83 New Zealand v England – NZ won by 103 runs	Wellington	NZ 6/295 – Eng 192	G.P. Howarth	R.G.D. Willis
26 Feb 83 New Zealand v England – NZ won by 84 runs	Christchurch	NZ 8/211 – Eng 127	G.P. Howarth	R.G.D. Willis

Series winner: New Zealand 3-0

1982/83 – Rothmans Cup

MATCH	VENUE	SCORES	CAPTAIN	CAPTAIN
2 Mar 83 New Zealand v Sri Lanka – NZ won by 65 runs	Dunedin	NZ 81/183 – SL 9/118	G.P. Howarth	D.S. de Silva
19 Mar 83 New Zealand v Sri Lanka – NZ won by 7 wickets	Napier	SL 8/167 – NZ 3/168	J.G. Wright	L.R.D. Mendis
20 Mar 83 New Zealand v Sri Lanka – NZ won by 116 runs	Auckland	NZ 5/304 – SL 6/188	G.P. Howarth	L.R.D. Mendis

Series winner: New Zealand 3-0

1982/83 – West Indies v India

MATCH	VENUE	SCORES	CAPTAIN	CAPTAIN
9 Mar 83 West Indies v India – WI won by 52 runs	Port-of-Spain	WI 4/215 – Ind 7/163	C.H. Lloyd	Kapil Dev
29 Mar 83 West Indies v India – Ind won by 27 runs	Berbice	Ind 5/282 – WI 9/255	C.H. Lloyd	Kapil Dev
7 Apr 83 West Indies v India – WI won by 7 wickets	St George's	Ind 166 – WI 3/167	C.H. Lloyd	Kapil Dev

Series winner: West Indies 2-1

1982/83 – Bushfire Appeal Challenge Match

MATCH	VENUE	SCORES	CAPTAIN	CAPTAIN
17 Mar 83 Australia v New Zealand – NZ won by 14 runs	Sydney	NZ 8/138 – Aus 124	K.J. Hughes	G.P. Howarth

Series winner: New Zealand 1-0

1982/83 – Sri Lanka v Australia

MATCH	VENUE	SCORES	CAPTAIN	CAPTAIN
13 Apr 83 Sri Lanka v Australia – SL won by 2 wickets	Colombo (PSS)	Aus 9/168 – SL 8/169	L.R.D. Mendis	G.S. Chappell
16 Apr 83 Sri Lanka v Australia – SL won by 4 wickets	Colombo (PSS)	Aus 5/207 – SL 6/213	L.R.D. Mendis	G.S. Chappell
29 Apr 83 Sri Lanka v Australia – No result	Colombo (SSC)	Aus 5/194 – SL DNB	L.R.D. Mendis	G.S. Chappell
30 Apr 83 Sri Lanka v Australia – No result	Colombo (SSC)	Aus 3/124 – SL DNB	L.R.D. Mendis	G.S. Chappell

Series winner: Sri Lanka 2-0

1983 – Prudential World Cup

Group A Qualifying matches

MATCH	VENUE	SCORES	CAPTAIN	CAPTAIN
9 Jun 83 England v New Zealand – Eng won by 106 runs	The Oval	Eng 6/322 – NZ 216	R.G.D. Willis	G.P. Howarth
9 Jun 83 Pakistan v Sri Lanka – Pak won by 50 runs	Swansea	Pak 5/338 – SL 9/288	Imran Khan	L.R.D. Mendis
11 Jun 83 England v Sri Lanka – Eng won by 47 runs	Taunton	Eng 9/333 – SL 286	R.G.D. Willis	L.R.D. Mendis
11/12 Jun 83 New Zealand v Pakistan – NZ won by 52 runs	Birmingham	NZ 9/238 – Pak 186	G.P. Howarth	Imran Khan
13 Jun 83 England v Pakistan – Eng won by 8 wickets	Lord's	Pak 8/193 – Eng 2/199	R.G.D. Willis	Imran Khan
13 Jun 83 New Zealand v Sri Lanka – NZ won by 5 wickets	Bristol	SL 206 – NZ 5/209	G.P. Howarth	L.R.D. Mendis
15 Jun 83 England v New Zealand – NZ won by 2 wickets	Birmingham	Eng 234 – NZ 8/238	R.G.D. Willis	G.P. Howarth
16 Jun 83 Pakistan v Sri Lanka – Pak won by 11 runs	Leeds	Pak 7/235 – SL 224	Imran Khan	L.R.D. Mendis
18 Jun 83 England v Pakistan – Eng won by 7 wickets	Manchester	Pak 8/232 – Eng 3/233	R.G.D. Willis	Imran Khan
18 Jun 83 New Zealand v Sri Lanka – SL won by 3 wickets	Derby	NZ 181 – SL 7/184	G.P. Howarth	L.R.D. Mendis
20 Jun 83 England v Sri Lanka – Eng won by 9 wickets	Leeds	SL 136 – Eng 1/137	R.G.D. Willis	L.R.D. Mendis
20 Jun 83 New Zealand v Pakistan – Pak won by 11 runs	Nottingham	Pak 3/261 – NZ 250	G.P. Howarth	Imran Khan

Group B Qualifying matches

MATCH	VENUE	SCORES	CAPTAIN	CAPTAIN
9 Jun 83 Australia v Zimbabwe – Zim won by 13 runs	Nottingham	Zim 6/239 – Aus 7/226	K.J. Hughes	D.A.G. Fletcher
9/10 Jun 83 India v West Indies – Ind won by 34 runs	Manchester	Ind 8/262 – WI 228	Kapil Dev	C.H. Lloyd
11/12 Jun 83 Australia v West Indies – WI won by 101 runs	Leeds	WI 9/252 – Aus 151	K.J. Hughes	C.H. Lloyd
11 Jun 83 India v Zimbabwe – Ind won by 5 wickets	Leicester	Zim 155 – Ind 5/157	Kapil Dev	D.A.G. Fletcher
13 Jun 83 Australia v India – Aus won by 162 runs	Nottingham	Aus 9/320 – Ind 158	K.J. Hughes	Kapil Dev
13 Jun 83 West Indies v Zimbabwe – WI won by 8 wickets	Worcester	Zim 7/217 – WI 2/218	C.H. Lloyd	D.A.G. Fletcher
15 Jun 83 India v West Indies – WI won by 66 runs	The Oval	WI 9/282 – Ind 216	Kapil Dev	C.H. Lloyd
16 Jun 83 Australia v Zimbabwe – Aus won by 32 runs	Southampton	Aus 7/272 – Zim 240	K.J. Hughes	D.A.G. Fletcher
18 Jun 83 Australia v West Indies – WI won by 7 wickets	Lord's	Aus 6/273 – WI 3/276	K.J. Hughes	C.H. Lloyd
18 Jun 83 India v Zimbabwe – Ind won by 31 runs	Tunbridge Wells	Ind 8/266 – Zim 235	Kapil Dev	D.A.G. Fletcher
20 Jun 83 Australia v India – Ind won by 118 runs	Chelmsford	Ind 247 – Aus 129	D.W. Hookes	Kapil Dev
20 Jun 83 West Indies v Zimbabwe – WI won by 10 wickets	Birmingham	Zim 171 – WI 0/172	C.H. Lloyd	D.A.G. Fletcher

Semi-finals

MATCH	VENUE	SCORES	CAPTAIN	CAPTAIN
22 Jun 83 England v India – Ind won by 6 wickets	Manchester	Eng 213 – Ind 4/217	R.G.D. Willis	Kapil Dev
22 Jun 83 Pakistan v West Indies – WI won by 8 wickets	The Oval	Pak 8/184 – WI 2/188	Imran Khan	C.H. Lloyd

Final

MATCH	VENUE	SCORES	CAPTAIN	CAPTAIN
25 Jun 83 India v West Indies – Ind won by 43 runs	Lord's	Ind 183 – WI 140	Kapil Dev	C.H. Lloyd

World champions: India

1983/84 – India v Pakistan

MATCH	VENUE	SCORES	CAPTAIN	CAPTAIN
11 Sep 83 India v Pakistan – Ind won by 4 wickets	Hyderabad (I)	Pak 8/151 – Ind 6/152	Kapil Dev	Zaheer Abbas
2 Oct 83 India v Pakistan – Ind won by 4 wickets	Jaipur	Pak 9/166 – Ind 6/169	Kapil Dev	Zaheer Abbas

Series winner: India 2-0

1983/84 – Charminar Challenge Cup

MATCH	VENUE	SCORES	CAPTAIN	CAPTAIN
13 Oct 83 India v West Indies – WI won on run-rate	Srinagar	Ind 176 – WI 0/108	Kapil Dev	C.H. Lloyd
9 Nov 83 India v West Indies – WI won by 4 wickets	Vadodara (MB)	Ind 6/214 – WI 6/217	Kapil Dev	C.H. Lloyd
1 Dec 83 India v West Indies – WI won by 8 wickets	Indore	Ind 7/240 – WI 2/241	Kapil Dev	C.H. Lloyd
7 Dec 83 India v West Indies – WI won by 104 runs	Jamshedpur	WI 8/333 – Ind 5/229	Kapil Dev	C.H. Lloyd
17 Dec 83 India v West Indies – WI won by 6 wickets	Gauhati	Ind 7/178 – WI 4/182	S.M.H. Kirmani	I.V.A. Richards

Series winner: West Indies 5-0

1983/84 – Benson & Hedges World Series Cup

Qualifying matches

MATCH	VENUE	SCORES	CAPTAIN	CAPTAIN
8 Jan 84 Australia v West Indies – WI won by 27 runs	Melbourne	WI 7/221 – Aus 194	K.J. Hughes	C.H. Lloyd
10 Jan 84 Australia v Pakistan – Aus won by 34 runs	Sydney	Aus 8/264 – Pak 9/230	K.J. Hughes	Imran Khan
12 Jan 84 Pakistan v West Indies – Pak won by 97 runs	Melbourne	Pak 8/208 – WI 111	Imran Khan	C.H. Lloyd
14 Jan 84 Pakistan v West Indies – WI won by 5 wickets	Brisbane	Pak 9/174 – WI 5/175	Imran Khan	C.H. Lloyd
15 Jan 84 Australia v Pakistan – No result	Brisbane	Pak 6/184 – Aus 0/15	K.J. Hughes	Imran Khan
17 Jan 84 Australia v West Indies – WI won by 28 runs	Sydney	WI 7/223 – Aus 9/195	K.J. Hughes	C.H. Lloyd
19 Jan 84 Pakistan v West Indies – WI won by 5 wickets	Sydney	Pak 8/184 – WI 5/185	Imran Khan	C.H. Lloyd
21 Jan 84 Australia v Pakistan – Aus won by 43 runs	Melbourne	Aus 8/209 – Pak 166	K.J. Hughes	Imran Khan
22 Jan 84 Australia v West Indies – WI won by 26 runs	Melbourne	WI 6/252 – Aus 226	K.J. Hughes	C.H. Lloyd
25 Jan 84 Australia v West Indies – Aus won by 87 runs	Sydney	Aus 8/244 – Pak 157	K.J. Hughes	Imran Khan
28 Jan 84 Pakistan v West Indies – WI won by 1 wicket	Adelaide	Pak 8/177 – WI 9/180	Javed Miandad	C.H. Lloyd
29 Jan 84 Australia v West Indies – WI won by 6 wickets	Adelaide	Aus 7/165 – WI 4/169	K.J. Hughes	C.H. Lloyd
30 Jan 84 Australia v Pakistan – Aus won by 70 runs	Adelaide	Aus 8/210 – Pak 140	K.J. Hughes	Javed Miandad
4 Feb 84 Pakistan v West Indies – WI won by 7 wickets	Perth	Pak 7/182 – WI 3/183	Javed Miandad	I.V.A. Richards
5 Feb 84 Australia v West Indies – Aus won by 14 runs	Perth	Aus 8/211 – WI 197	K.J. Hughes	C.H. Lloyd

Finals

MATCH	VENUE	SCORES	CAPTAIN	CAPTAIN
8 Feb 84 Australia v West Indies – WI won by 9 wickets	Sydney	Aus 160 – WI 1/161	K.J. Hughes	C.H. Lloyd
11 Feb 84 Australia v West Indies – Match tied	Melbourne	WI 5/222 – Aus 9/222	K.J. Hughes	C.H. Lloyd
12 Feb 84 Australia v West Indies – WI won by 6 wickets	Melbourne	Aus 8/212 – WI 4/213	K.J. Hughes	M.A. Holding

Series winner: West Indies

1983/84 – Rothmans Cup

MATCH	VENUE	SCORES	CAPTAIN	CAPTAIN
18 Feb 84 New Zealand v England – Eng won by 54 runs	Christchurch	Eng 9/188 – NZ 134	G.P. Howarth	R.G.D. Willis
22 Feb 84 New Zealand v England – Eng won by 6 wickets	Wellington	NZ 135 – Eng 4/139	G.P. Howarth	R.G.D. Willis
25 Feb 84 New Zealand v England – NZ won by 7 wickets	Auckland	Eng 9/209 – NZ 3/210	G.P. Howarth	R.G.D. Willis

Series winner: England 2-1

MATCH	VENUE	SCORES	CAPTAIN	CAPTAIN
1983/84 – West Indies v Australia				
29 Feb 84 West Indies v Australia – WI won by 8 wickets	Berbice	Aus 5/231 – WI 2/233	I.V.A. Richards	K.J. Hughes
14 Mar 84 West Indies v Australia – Aus won by 4 wickets	Port-of-Spain	WI 6/190 – Aus 6/194	C.H. Lloyd	K.J. Hughes
19 Apr 84 West Indies v Australia – WI won by 7 wickets	Castries	Aus 9/206 – WI 3/208	M.A. Holding	K.J. Hughes
26 Apr 84 West Indies v Australia – WI won by 9 wickets	Kingston	Aus 7/209 – WI 1/211	I.V.A. Richards	K.J. Hughes
Series winner: West Indies 3-1				
1983/84 – Sri Lanka v New Zealand				
3 Mar 84 Sri Lanka v New Zealand – NZ won by 104 runs	Colombo (SSC)	NZ 6/234 – SL 130	L.R.D. Mendis	G.P. Howarth
31 Mar 84 Sri Lanka v New Zealand – SL won by 41 runs	Moratuwa	SL 8/157 – NZ 116	L.R.D. Mendis	G.P. Howarth
1 Apr 84 Sri Lanka v New Zealand – NZ won by 86 runs	Colombo (PSS)	NZ 8/201 – SL 115	L.R.D. Mendis	J.G. Wright
Series winner: New Zealand 2-1				
1983/84 – Wills Series				
9 Mar 84 Pakistan v England – Pak won by 6 wickets	Lahore	Eng 8/184 – Pak 4/187	Zaheer Abbas	R.G.D. Willis
26 Mar 84 Pakistan v England – Eng won by 6 wickets	Karachi	Pak 8/163 – Eng 4/164	Sarfraz Nawaz	D.I. Gower
Series drawn 1-1				
1983/84 – Asia Cup				
6 Apr 84 Pakistan v Sri Lanka – SL won by 5 wickets	Sharjah	Pak 9/187 – SL 5/190	Zaheer Abbas	L.R.D. Mendis
8 Apr 84 India v Sri Lanka – Ind won by 10 wickets	Sharjah	SL 96 – Ind 0/97	S.M. Gavaskar	L.R.D. Mendis
13 Apr 84 India v Pakistan – Ind won by 54 runs	Sharjah	Ind 4/188 – Pak 134	S.M. Gavaskar	Zaheer Abbas
Series winner: India				
1984 – Texaco Trophy				
31 May 84 England v West Indies – WI won by 104 runs	Manchester	WI 9/272 – Eng 168	D.I. Gower	C.H. Lloyd
2 Jun 84 England v West Indies – Eng won by 3 wickets	Nottingham	WI 179 – Eng 7/180	D.I. Gower	C.H. Lloyd
4 Jun 84 England v West Indies – WI won by 8 wickets	Lord's	Eng 9/196 – WI 2/197	D.I. Gower	C.H. Lloyd
Series winner: West Indies 2-1				
1984/85 – Ranji Trophy Golden Jubilee Series				
28 Sep 84 India v Australia – Aus won by 48 runs	New Delhi	Aus 9/220 – Ind 172	S.M. Gavaskar	K.J. Hughes
1 Oct 84 India v Australia – No result	Trivandrum	Ind 175 – Aus 1/29	S.M. Gavaskar	K.J. Hughes
3 Oct 84 India v Australia – No result	Jamshedpur	Ind 2/21 – Aus DNB	S.M. Gavaskar	K.J. Hughes
5 Oct 84 India v Australia – Aus won by 7 wickets	Ahmedabad (SP)	Ind 6/206 – Aus 3/210	S.M. Gavaskar	K.J. Hughes
6 Oct 84 India v Australia – Aus won by 6 wickets	Indore	Ind 5/235 – Aus 4/236	S.M. Gavaskar	K.J. Hughes
Series winner: Australia 3-0				
1984/85 – Wills Series				
12 Oct 84 Pakistan v India – Pak by 46 runs	Quetta (AN)	Pak 7/199 – Ind 153	Zaheer Abbas	S.M. Gavaskar
31 Oct 84 Pakistan v India – No result	Sialkot	Ind 3/210 – Pak DNB	Zaheer Abbas	M. Amarnath
Series winner: Pakistan 1-0				

MATCH	VENUE	SCORES	CAPTAIN	CAPTAIN
1984/85 – Sri Lanka v New Zealand				
3 Nov 84 Sri Lanka v New Zealand – SL won by 4 wickets	Colombo (PSS)	NZ 6/171 – SL 6/174	L.R.D. Mendis	J.V. Coney
4 Nov 84 Sri Lanka v New Zealand - NZ won by 7 wickets	Moratuwa	SL 9/114 – NZ 3/118	L.R.D. Mendis	J.V. Coney
Series drawn 1-1				
1984/85 – Wills Series				
12 Nov 84 Pakistan v New Zealand – Pak won by 46 runs	Peshawar	Pak 5/191 – NZ 145	Zaheer Abbas	J.V. Coney
23 Nov 84 Pakistan v New Zealand – Pak won by 5 runs	Faisalabad	Pak 5/157 – NZ 7/152	Zaheer Abbas	J.V. Coney
2 Dec 84 Pakistan v New Zealand – NZ won by 34 runs	Sialkot	NZ 9/187 – Pak 8/153	Zaheer Abbas	J.V. Coney
7 Dec 84 Pakistan v New Zealand – Pak won by 1 wicket	Multan	NZ 8/213 – Pak 9/214	Zaheer Abbas	J.V. Coney
Series winner: Pakistan 3-1				
1984/85 – Charminar Challenge Cup				
5 Dec 84 India v England – Eng won by 4 wickets	Pune	Ind 6/214 – Eng 6/215	S.M. Gavaskar	D.I. Gower
27 Dec 84 India v England – Eng won on faster run-rate	Cuttack	Ind 5/252 – Eng 6/241	S.M. Gavaskar	D.I. Gower
20 Jan 85 India v England – Eng won by 3 wickets	Bangalore	Ind 6/205 – Eng 7/206	S.M. Gavaskar	D.I. Gower
23 Jan 85 India v England – Ind won by 3 wickets	Nagpur	Eng 7/240 – Ind 7/241	S.M. Gavaskar	D.I. Gower
27 Jan 85 India v England – Eng won by 7 runs	Chandigarh	Eng 6/121 – Ind 5/114	S.M. Gavaskar	D.I. Gower
Series winner: England 4-1				
1984/85 – Benson & Hedges World Series Cup				
Qualifying matches				
6 Jan 85 Australia v West Indies – WI won by 7 wickets	Melbourne	Aus 6/240 – WI 3/241	A.R. Border	C.H. Lloyd
8 Jan 85 Australia v Sri Lanka – Aus won by 6 wickets	Sydney	SL 7/239 – Aus 4/240	A.R. Border	L.R.D. Mendis
10 Jan 85 Sri Lanka v West Indies – WI won by 8 wickets	Hobart (TCA)	SL 7/197 – WI 2/198	L.R.D. Mendis	I.V.A. Richards
12 Jan 85 Sri Lanka v West Indies – WI won by 90 runs	Brisbane	WI 6/270 – SL 180	L.R.D. Mendis	I.V.A. Richards
13 Jan 85 Australia v West Indies – WI won by 5 wickets	Brisbane	Aus 191 – WI 5/195	A.R. Border	C.H. Lloyd
15 Jan 85 Australia v West Indies – WI won by 5 wickets	Sydney	Aus 5/200 – WI 5/201	A.R. Border	C.H. Lloyd
17 Jan 85 Sri Lanka v West Indies – WI won by 65 runs	Sydney	WI 3/267 – SL 5/202	L.R.D. Mendis	I.V.A. Richards
19 Jan 85 Australia v Sri Lanka – SL won by 4 wickets	Melbourne	Aus 9/226 – SL 6/230	A.R. Border	L.R.D. Mendis
20 Jan 85 Australia v West Indies – WI won by 65 runs	Melbourne	WI 7/271 – Aus 9/206	A.R. Border	C.H. Lloyd
23 Jan 85 Australia v Sri Lanka – Aus won by 3 wickets	Sydney	SL 6/240 – Aus 7/242	A.R. Border	L.R.D. Mendis
26 Jan 85 Sri Lanka v West Indies – WI won by 8 wickets	Adelaide	SL 6/204 – WI 2/205	L.R.D. Mendis	C.H. Lloyd
27 Jan 85 Australia v West Indies – WI won by 6 wickets	Adelaide	Aus 9/200 – WI 4/201	A.R. Border	C.H. Lloyd
28 Jan 85 Australia v Sri Lanka – Aus won by 232 runs	Adelaide	Aus 2/323 – SL 91	A.R. Border	L.R.D. Mendis
2 Feb 85 Sri Lanka v West Indies – WI won by 82 runs	Perth	WI 6/309 – SL 6/227	L.R.D. Mendis	C.H. Lloyd
3 Feb 85 Australia v Sri Lanka – Aus won by 9 wickets	Perth	SL 171 – Aus 1/172	A.R. Border	L.R.D. Mendis

MATCH	VENUE	SCORES	CAPTAIN	CAPTAIN
Finals				
6 Feb 85 Australia v West Indies — Aus won by 26 runs	Sydney	Aus 6/247 — WI 221	A.R. Border	C.H. Lloyd
10 Feb 85 Australia v West Indies — WI won by 4 wickets	Melbourne	Aus 3/271 — WI 6/273	A.R. Border	C.H. Lloyd
12 Feb 85 Australia v West Indies — WI won by 7 wickets	Sydney	Aus 178 — WI 3/179	A.R. Border	C.H. Lloyd
Series winner: West Indies				

1984/85 – Rothmans Cup

MATCH	VENUE	SCORES	CAPTAIN	CAPTAIN
12 Jan 85 New Zealand v Pakistan — NZ won by 110 runs	Napier	NZ 6/277 — Pak 9/167	G.P. Howarth	Javed Miandad
15 Jan 85 New Zealand v Pakistan — NZ won by 4 wickets	Hamilton	Pak 4/221 — NZ 6/222	G.P. Howarth	Javed Miandad
6 Feb 85 New Zealand v Pakistan — NZ won by 13 runs	Christchurch	NZ 8/264 — Pak 251	G.P. Howarth	Javed Miandad
17 Feb 85 New Zealand v Pakistan — No result	Auckland	Pak 189 — NZ DNB	G.P. Howarth	Javed Miandad
Series winner: New Zealand 3-0				

1984/85 – Benson & Hedges World Championship of Cricket

MATCH	VENUE	SCORES	CAPTAIN	CAPTAIN
Group A Qualifying matches				
17 Feb 85 Australia v England — Aus won by 7 wickets	Melbourne	Eng 8/214 — Aus 3/215	A.R. Border	D.I. Gower
20 Feb 85 India v Pakistan — Ind won by 6 wickets	Melbourne	Pak 183 — Ind 4/184	S.M. Gavaskar	Javed Miandad
24 Feb 85 Australia v Pakistan — Pak won by 62 runs	Melbourne	Pak 6/262 — Aus 200	A.R. Border	Zaheer Abbas
26 Feb 85 England v India — Ind won by 86 runs	Sydney	Ind 9/235 — Eng 149	D.I. Gower	S.M. Gavaskar
2 Mar 85 England v Pakistan — Pak won by 67 runs	Melbourne	Pak 8/213 — Eng 146	D.I. Gower	Javed Miandad
3 Mar 85 Australia v India — Ind won by 8 wickets	Melbourne	Aus 163 — Ind 2/165	A.R. Border	S.M. Gavaskar
Group B Qualifying matches				
21 Feb 85 New Zealand v West Indies — No result	Sydney	NZ 2/57 — WI DNB	G.P. Howarth	C.H. Lloyd
23 Feb 85 New Zealand v Sri Lanka — NZ won by 51 runs	Melbourne	NZ 223 — SL 172	G.P. Howarth	L.R.D. Mendis
27 Feb 85 Sri Lanka v West Indies — WI won by 8 wickets	Melbourne	SL 7/135 — WI 2/136	L.R.D. Mendis	C.H. Lloyd
Semi-finals				
5 Mar 85 India v New Zealand — Ind won by 7 wickets	Sydney	NZ 206 — Ind 3/207	S.M. Gavaskar	G.P. Howarth
6 Mar 85 Pakistan v West Indies — Pak won by 7 wickets	Melbourne	WI 159 — Pak 3/160	Javed Miandad	C.H. Lloyd
Third place play-off				
9 Mar 85 New Zealand v West Indies — WI won by 6 wickets	Sydney	NZ 9/138 — WI 4/139	G.P. Howarth	I.V.A. Richards
Final				
10 Mar 85 India v Pakistan — Ind won by 8 wickets	Melbourne	Pak 9/176 — Ind 2/177	S.M. Gavaskar	Javed Miandad
Series winner: India				

1984/85 – West Indies v New Zealand

MATCH	VENUE	SCORES	CAPTAIN	CAPTAIN
20 Mar 85 West Indies v New Zealand — WI won by 23 runs	St John's	WI 8/231 — NZ 8/208	I.V.A. Richards	G.P. Howarth
27 Mar 85 West Indies v New Zealand — WI won by 6 wickets	Port-of-Spain	NZ 3/51 — WI 4/55	I.V.A. Richards	G.P. Howarth
14 Apr 85 West Indies v New Zealand — WI won by 130 runs	Berbice	WI 5/259 — NZ 129	I.V.A. Richards	G.P. Howarth
17 Apr 85 West Indies v New Zealand — WI won by 10 wickets	Port-of-Spain	NZ 116 — WI 0/117	I.V.A. Richards	G.P. Howarth
23 Apr 85 West Indies v New Zealand — WI won by 112 runs	Bridgetown	WI 3/265 — NZ 8/153	I.V.A. Richards	G.P. Howarth
Series winner: West Indies 5-0				

MATCH	VENUE	SCORES	CAPTAIN	CAPTAIN
1984/85 – Rothmans Four Nations Trophy				
Qualifying matches				
22 Mar 85 India v Pakistan – Ind won by 38 runs	Sharjah	Ind 125 – Pak 87	S.M. Gavaskar	Javed Miandad
24 Mar 85 Australia v England – Aus won by 2 wickets	Sharjah	Eng 8/177 – Aus 8/178	A.R. Border	N. Gifford
Third place play-off				
26 Mar 85 England v Pakistan – Pak won by 43 runs	Sharjah	Pak 7/175 – Eng 132	N. Gifford	Javed Miandad
Final				
29 Mar 85 Australia v India – Ind won by 3 wickets	Sharjah	Aus 139 – Ind 7/140	A.R. Border	Kapil Dev
Series winner: India				
1985 – Texaco Trophy				
30 May 85 England v Australia – Aus won by 3 wickets	Manchester	Eng 219 – Aus 7/220	D.I. Gower	A.R. Border
1 Jun 85 England v Australia – Aus won by 4 wickets	Birmingham	Eng 7/231 – Aus 6/233	D.I. Gower	A.R. Border
3 Jun 85 England v Australia – Eng won by 8 wickets	Lord's	Aus 5/254 – Eng 2/257	D.I. Gower	A.R. Border
Series winner: Australia 2-1				
1985/86 – Sri Lanka v India				
25 Aug 85 Sri Lanka v India – Ind won by 2 wickets	Colombo (SSC)	SL 6/241 – Ind 8/242	L.R.D. Mendis	Kapil Dev
21 Sep 85 Sri Lanka v India – SL won by 14 runs	Colombo (PSS)	SL 5/171 – Ind 4/157	L.R.D. Mendis	Kapil Dev
22 Sep 85 Sri Lanka v India – No result	Colombo (PSS)	Ind 6/194 – SL 4/32	L.R.D. Mendis	Kapil Dev
Series drawn 1-1				
1985/86 – Wills Series				
13 Oct 85 Pakistan v Sri Lanka – Pak won by 8 wickets	Peshawar	SL 145 – Pak 2/147	Javed Miandad	L.R.D. Mendis
23 Oct 85 Pakistan v Sri Lanka – Pak won by 15 runs	Gujranwala	Pak 5/224 – SL 7/209	Javed Miandad	L.R.D. Mendis
25 Oct 85 Pakistan v Sri Lanka – Pak won by 5 wickets	Lahore	SL 7/228 – Pak 5/231	Javed Miandad	L.R.D. Mendis
3 Nov 85 Pakistan v Sri Lanka – Pak won by 89 runs	Hyderabad (P)	Pak 7/216 – SL 127	Javed Miandad	L.R.D. Mendis
Series winner: Pakistan 4-0				
1985/86 – Rothmans Three Nations Trophy				
15 Nov 85 Pakistan v West Indies – WI won by 7 wickets	Sharjah	Pak 4/196 – WI 3/199	Imran Khan	I.V.A. Richards
17 Nov 85 India v Pakistan – Pak won by 48 runs	Sharjah	Pak 4/203 – Ind 155	Kapil Dev	Imran Khan
22 Nov 85 India v West Indies – WI won by 8 wickets	Sharjah	Ind 4/180 – WI 2/186	S.M. Gavaskar	I.V.A. Richards
Series winner: West Indies				
1985/86 – Wills Series				
27 Nov 85 Pakistan v West Indies – WI won by 8 wickets	Gujranwala	Pak 5/218 – WI 2/224	Imran Khan	I.V.A. Richards
29 Nov 85 Pakistan v West Indies – Pak won by 6 wickets	Lahore	WI 173 – Pak 4/175	Imran Khan	I.V.A. Richards
2 Dec 85 Pakistan v West Indies – WI won by 40 runs	Peshawar	WI 5/201 – Pak 161	Imran Khan	I.V.A. Richards
4 Dec 85 Pakistan v West Indies – Pak won by 5 wickets	Rawalpindi (PC)	WI 8/199 – Pak 5/203	Imran Khan	I.V.A. Richards
6 Dec 85 Pakistan v West Indies – WI won by 8 wickets	Karachi	Pak 7/127 – WI 2/128	Imran Khan	I.V.A. Richards
Series winner: West Indies 3-2				

MATCH	VENUE	SCORES	CAPTAIN	CAPTAIN
1985/86 – Benson & Hedges World Series Cup				
Qualifying matches				
9 Jan 86 Australia v New Zealand – No result	Melbourne	NZ 7/161 – Aus DNB	A.R. Border	J.V. Coney
11 Jan 86 India v New Zealand – Ind won by 5 wickets	Brisbane	NZ 9/259 – Ind 5/263	Kapil Dev	J.V. Coney
12 Jan 86 Australia v India – Aus won by 4 wickets	Brisbane	Ind 161 – Aus 6/164	A.R. Border	Kapil Dev
14 Jan 86 Australia v New Zealand – Aus won by 3 wickets	Sydney	NZ 152 – Aus 6/153	A.R. Border	J.V. Coney
16 Jan 86 Australia v India – Ind won by 8 wickets	Melbourne	Aus 161 – Ind 2/162	A.R. Border	Kapil Dev
18 Jan 86 India v New Zealand – NZ won by 3 wickets	Perth	Ind 113 – NZ 7/115	Kapil Dev	J.V. Coney
19 Jan 86 Australia v New Zealand – Aus won by 4 wickets	Perth	NZ 6/159 – Aus 6/161	A.R. Border	J.V. Coney
21 Jan 86 Australia v India – Aus won by 100 runs	Sydney	Aus 6/292 – Ind 4/192	A.R. Border	Kapil Dev
23 Jan 86 India v New Zealand – NZ won by 5 wickets	Melbourne	Ind 8/238 – NZ 5/239	Kapil Dev	J.V. Coney
25 Jan 86 India v New Zealand – Ind won by 5 wickets	Adelaide	NZ 172 – Ind 5/174	Kapil Dev	J.V. Coney
26 Jan 86 Australia v India – Aus won by 36 runs	Adelaide	Aus 8/262 – Ind 226	A.R. Border	Kapil Dev
27 Jan 86 Australia v New Zealand – NZ won by 206 runs	Adelaide	NZ 7/276 – Aus 70	A.R. Border	J.V. Coney
29 Jan 86 Australia v New Zealand – Aus won by 99 runs	Sydney	Aus 7/239 – NZ 140	A.R. Border	J.V. Coney
31 Jan 86 Australia v India – Ind won by 6 wickets	Melbourne	Aus 7/235 – Ind 4/238	A.R. Border	Kapil Dev
2 Feb 86 India v New Zealand – Ind won by 21 runs	Launceston	Ind 9/202 – NZ 9/168	Kapil Dev	J.V. Coney
Finals				
5 Feb 86 Australia v India – Aus won by 11 runs	Sydney	Aus 8/170 – Ind 159	A.R. Border	Kapil Dev
9 Feb 86 Australia v India – Aus won by 7 wickets	Melbourne	Ind 187 – Aus 3/188	A.R. Border	Kapil Dev
Series winner: Australia				
1985/86 – West Indies v England				
18 Feb 86 West Indies v England – WI won by 6 wickets	Kingston	Eng 8/145 – WI 4/146	I.V.A. Richards	D.I. Gower
4 Mar 86 West Indies v England – Eng won by 5 wickets	Port-of-Spain	WI 3/229 – Eng 5/230	I.V.A. Richards	D.I. Gower
19 Mar 86 West Indies v England – WI won by 135 runs	Bridgetown	WI 7/249 – Eng 114	I.V.A. Richards	D.I. Gower
31 Mar 86 West Indies v England – WI won by 8 wickets	Port-of-Spain	Eng 9/165 – WI 2/166	I.V.A. Richards	D.I. Gower
Series winner: West Indies 3-1				
1985/86 – Sri Lanka v Pakistan				
2 Mar 86 Sri Lanka v Pakistan – Pak won by 8 wickets	Kandy	SL 6/124 – Pak 2/125	L.R.D. Mendis	Imran Khan
8 Mar 86 Sri Lanka v Pakistan – No result	Moratuwa	Pak 8/125 – SL DNB	L.R.D. Mendis	Imran Khan
11 Mar 86 Sri Lanka v Pakistan – Pak won by 8 wickets	Colombo (SSC)	SL 8/160 – Pak 2/103	L.R.D. Mendis	Imran Khan
Series winner: Pakistan 2-0				
1985/86 – Rothmans Cup				
19 Mar 86 New Zealand v Australia – NZ won by 30 runs	Dunedin	NZ 6/186 – Aus 156	J.V. Coney	A.R. Border
22 Mar 86 New Zealand v Australia – NZ won by 53 runs	Christchurch	NZ 7/258 – Aus 205	J.V. Coney	A.R. Border
26 Mar 86 New Zealand v Australia – Aus won by 3 wickets	Wellington	NZ 9/229 – Aus 7/232	J.V. Coney	A.R. Border
29 Mar 86 New Zealand v Australia – Aus won by 44 runs	Auckland	Aus 231 – NZ 9/187	J.V. Coney	A.R. Border
Series drawn 2-2				

1985/86 – Asia Cup and John Player Tournament

New Zealand were not eligible to compete in the Asia Cup, so the triangular John Player Tournament between New Zealand, Pakistan and Sri Lanka was played concurrently.

MATCH	VENUE	SCORES	CAPTAIN	CAPTAIN
30 Mar 86 Sri Lanka v Pakistan – Pak won by 81 runs	Colombo (PSS)	Pak 197 – SL 116	L.R.D. Mendis	Imran Khan
31 Mar 86 Bangladesh v Pakistan – Pak won by 7 wickets	Moratuwa	Ban 94 – Pak 3/98	Gazi Ashraf	Imran Khan
2 Apr 86 Sri Lanka v Bangladesh – SL won by 7 wickets	Kandy	Ban 8/131 – SL 3/132	L.R.D. Mendis	Gazi Ashraf
5 Apr 86 Sri Lanka v New Zealand[1] – NZ won by 6 wickets	Colombo (RPS)	SL 9/137 – NZ 4/140	L.R.D. Mendis	J.G. Wright
6 Apr 86 Sri Lanka v Pakistan[1,2] – Sri Lanka won by 5 wickets	Colombo (SSC)	Pak 9/191 – SL 5/195	L.R.D. Mendis	Imran Khan
7 Apr 86 New Zealand v Pakistan[1] – Pak won by 4 wickets	Colombo (SSC)	NZ 8/214 – Pak 6/217	J.G. Wright	Javed Miandad

[1] *John Player Tournament matches.*
[2] *Asia Cup Final*
Asia Cup winner: Sri Lanka
John Player Tournament winner: Pakistan due to superior run-rate

1985/86 – Austral-Asia Cup

Qualifying matches

MATCH	VENUE	SCORES	CAPTAIN	CAPTAIN
10 Apr 86 India v New Zealand – Ind won by 3 wickets	Sharjah	NZ 8/132 – Ind 7/134	Kapil Dev	J.J. Crowe
11 Apr 86 Australia v Pakistan – Pak won by 8 wickets	Sharjah	Aus 7/202 – Pak 2/206	J.J. Bright	Javed Miandad

Semi-finals

MATCH	VENUE	SCORES	CAPTAIN	CAPTAIN
13 Apr 86 India v Sri Lanka – Ind won by 3 wickets	Sharjah	SL 9/205 – Ind 7/206	Kapil Dev	L.R.D. Mendis
15 Apr 86 New Zealand v Pakistan – Pak won by 10 wickets	Sharjah	NZ 64 – Pak 0/66	J.J. Crowe	Imran Khan

Note: As the Asia Cup champions Sri Lanka automatically qualified for the semi-finals. New Zealand qualified because they were the narrowest losers in the qualifying matches.

Final

MATCH	VENUE	SCORES	CAPTAIN	CAPTAIN
18 Apr 86 India v Pakistan – Pak won by 1 wicket	Sharjah	Ind 7/245 – Pak 9/248	Kapil Dev	Imran Khan

Series winner: Pakistan

1986 – Texaco Trophy

MATCH	VENUE	SCORES	CAPTAIN	CAPTAIN
24 May 86 England v India – Ind won by 9 wickets	The Oval	Eng 162 – Ind 1/163	D.I. Gower	Kapil Dev
26 May 86 England v India – Eng won by 5 wickets	Manchester	Ind 6/254 – Eng 5/256	D.I. Gower	Kapil Dev

Series winner: India due to a faster run-rate

1986 – Texaco Trophy

MATCH	VENUE	SCORES	CAPTAIN	CAPTAIN
16 Jul 86 England v New Zealand – NZ won by 47 runs	Leeds	NZ 8/217 – Eng 170	M.W. Gatting	J.V. Coney
18 Jul 86 England v New Zealand – Eng won by 6 wickets	Manchester	NZ 5/284 – Eng 4/286	M.W. Gatting	J.V. Coney

Series winner: New Zealand due to a faster run-rate

1986/87 – Charminar Challenge Cup

MATCH	VENUE	SCORES	CAPTAIN	CAPTAIN
7 Sep 86 India v Australia – Ind won by 7 wickets	Jaipur	Aus 3/250 – Ind 3/251	Kapil Dev	A.R. Border
9 Sep 86 India v Australia – Aus won by 3 wickets	Srinagar	Ind 8/222 – Aus 7/226	Kapil Dev	A.R. Border
24 Sep 86 India v Australia – No result	Hyderabad (I)	Aus 6/242 – Ind 1/41	Kapil Dev	A.R. Border

MATCH	VENUE	SCORES	CAPTAIN	CAPTAIN
2 Oct 86 India v Australia – Ind won by 3 wickets	Delhi	Aus 6/238 – Ind 7/242	Kapil Dev	A.R. Border
5 Oct 86 India v Australia – Ind won by 52 runs	Ahmedabad (GS)	Ind 193 – Aus 141	Kapil Dev	A.R. Border
7 Oct 86 India v Australia – Aus won by 7 wickets	Rajkot	Ind 6/260 – Aus 3/263	Kapil Dev	A.R. Border

Series winner: India 3-2

1986/87 – Wills Series

MATCH	VENUE	SCORES	CAPTAIN	CAPTAIN
17 Oct 86 Pakistan v West Indies – WI won by 4 wickets	Peshawar	Pak 7/164 – WI 6/165	Imran Khan	I.V.A. Richards
4 Nov 86 Pakistan v West Indies – WI won on faster run-rate	Gujranwala	WI 7/196 – Pak 6/155	Javed Miandad	I.V.A. Richards
14 Nov 86 Pakistan v West Indies – WI won by 4 wickets	Sialkot	Pak 7/148 – WI 6/151	Imran Khan	I.V.A. Richards
17 Nov 86 Pakistan v West Indies – WI won by 89 runs	Multan	WI 5/202 – Pak 113	Imran Khan	I.V.A. Richards
18 Nov 86 Pakistan v West Indies – Pak won by 11 runs	Hyderabad (P)	Pak 6/202 – WI 7/191	Imran Khan	I.V.A. Richards

Series winner: West Indies 4-1

1986/87 – Champions Trophy

MATCH	VENUE	SCORES	CAPTAIN	CAPTAIN
27 Nov 86 India v Sri Lanka – Ind won by 7 wickets	Sharjah	SL 9/214 – Ind 3/215	Kapil Dev	L.R.D. Mendis
28 Nov 86 Pakistan v West Indies – WI won by 9 wickets	Sharjah	Pak 143 – WI 1/145	Imran Khan	I.V.A. Richards
30 Nov 86 India v West Indies – WI won by 33 runs	Sharjah	WI 8/198 – Ind 8/165	Kapil Dev	I.V.A. Richards
2 Dec 86 Pakistan v Sri Lanka – Pak won by 4 wickets	Sharjah	SL 7/164 – Pak 6/165	Imran Khan	L.R.D. Mendis
3 Dec 86 Sri Lanka v West Indies – WI won by 193 runs	Sharjah	WI 5/248 – SL 55	L.R.D. Mendis	I.V.A. Richards
5 Dec 86 India v Pakistan – Pak won by 3 wickets	Sharjah	Ind 144 – Pak 7/145	Kapil Dev	Imran Khan

Series winner: West Indies

1986/87 – India v Sri Lanka

MATCH	VENUE	SCORES	CAPTAIN	CAPTAIN
24 Dec 86 India v Sri Lanka – SL won by 117 runs	Kanpur	SL 8/195 – Ind 8/195	Kapil Dev	L.R.D. Mendis
11 Jan 87 India v Sri Lanka – Ind won by 8 wickets	Gauhati	SL 8/145 – Ind 2/146	Kapil Dev	L.R.D. Mendis
13 Jan 87 India v Sri Lanka – Ind won by 6 wickets	Delhi	SL 6/208 – Ind 4/209	Kapil Dev	L.R.D. Mendis
15 Jan 87 India v Sri Lanka – Ind won by 94 runs	Vadodara (MB)	Ind 8/235 – SL 141	Kapil Dev	L.R.D. Mendis
17 Jan 87 India v Sri Lanka – Ind won by 10 runs	Mumbai (WS)	Ind 4/299 – SL 7/289	Kapil Dev	L.R.D. Mendis

Series winner: India 4-1

1986/87 – Benson & Hedges America's Cup Challenge

Qualifying matches

MATCH	VENUE	SCORES	CAPTAIN	CAPTAIN
30 Dec 86 Pakistan v West Indies – Pak won by 34 runs	Perth	Pak 8/199 – WI 165	Imran Khan	I.V.A. Richards
1 Jan 87 Australia v England – Eng won by 37 runs	Perth	Eng 6/272 – Aus 235	A.R. Border	M.W. Gatting
2 Jan 87 Australia v Pakistan – Pak won by 1 wicket	Perth	Aus 6/273 – Pak 9/274	A.R. Border	Imran Khan
3 Jan 87 England v West Indies – Eng won by 19 runs	Perth	Eng 9/228 – WI 209	M.W. Gatting	I.V.A. Richards
4 Jan 87 Australia v West Indies – WI won by 164 runs	Perth	WI 8/255 – Aus 91	A.R. Border	I.V.A. Richards
5 Jan 87 England v Pakistan – Eng won by 3 wickets	Perth	Pak 5/229 – Eng 7/232	M.W. Gatting	Imran Khan

Final

MATCH	VENUE	SCORES	CAPTAIN	CAPTAIN
7 Jan 87 England v Pakistan – Eng won by 5 wickets	Perth	Pak 9/166 – Eng 5/167	M.W. Gatting	Imran Khan

Series winner: England

MATCH	VENUE	SCORES	CAPTAIN	CAPTAIN

1986/87 – Benson & Hedges World Series Cup

Qualifying matches

MATCH	VENUE	SCORES	CAPTAIN	CAPTAIN
17 Jan 87 England v West Indies – Eng won by 6 wickets	Brisbane	WI 154 – Eng 4/156	M.W. Gatting	I.V.A. Richards
18 Jan 87 Australia v England – Aus won by 11 runs	Brisbane	Aus 4/261 – Eng 9/250	A.R. Border	M.W. Gatting
20 Jan 87 Australia v West Indies – WI won by 7 wickets	Melbourne	Aus 6/181 – WI 3/182	A.R. Border	I.V.A. Richards
22 Jan 87 Australia v England – Eng won by 3 wickets	Sydney	Aus 8/233 – Eng 7/234	A.R. Border	M.W. Gatting
24 Jan 87 England v West Indies – Eng won by 89 runs	Adelaide	Eng 6/252 – WI 163	M.W. Gatting	I.V.A. Richards
25 Jan 87 Australia v West Indies – WI won by 16 runs	Adelaide	WI 5/237 – Aus 9/221	A.R. Border	I.V.A. Richards
26 Jan 87 Australia v England – Aus won by 33 runs	Adelaide	Aus 6/225 – Eng 192	A.R. Border	M.W. Gatting
28 Jan 87 Australia v West Indies – Aus won by 36 runs	Sydney	Aus 194 – WI 158	A.R. Border	I.V.A. Richards
30 Jan 87 England v West Indies – WI won by 6 wickets	Melbourne	Eng 147 – WI 4/148	M.W. Gatting	I.V.A. Richards
1 Feb 87 Australia v West Indies – Aus won by 109 runs	Melbourne	Aus 5/248 – WI 139	A.R. Border	I.V.A. Richards
3 Feb 87 England v West Indies – Eng won by 29 runs	Devonport	Eng 9/177 – WI 148	M.W. Gatting	I.V.A. Richards
6 Feb 87 Australia v West Indies – Aus won by 2 wickets	Sydney	WI 192 – Aus 8/195	A.R. Border	I.V.A. Richards

Finals

MATCH	VENUE	SCORES	CAPTAIN	CAPTAIN
8 Feb 87 Australia v England – Eng won by 6 wickets	Melbourne	Aus 8/171 – Eng 8/172	A.R. Border	M.W. Gatting
11 Feb 87 Australia v England – Eng won by 8 runs	Sydney	Eng 9/187 – Aus 8/179	A.R. Border	M.W. Gatting

Series winner: England

1986/87 – Charminar Challenge

MATCH	VENUE	SCORES	CAPTAIN	CAPTAIN
27 Jan 87 India v Pakistan – Pak won by 3 wickets	Indore	Ind 7/196 – Pak 7/200	R.J. Shastri	Imran Khan
18 Feb 87 India v Pakistan – Pak won by 2 wickets	Calcutta	Ind 6/238 – Pak 8/241	Kapil Dev	Imran Khan
20 Mar 87 India v Pakistan – Match tied	Hyderabad (I)	Ind 6/212 – Pak 7/212	Kapil Dev	Imran Khan
22 Mar 87 India v Pakistan – Pak won by 6 wickets	Pune	Ind 9/120 – Pak 4/121	Kapil Dev	Imran Khan
24 Mar 87 India v Pakistan – Pak won by 41 runs	Nagpur	Pak 6/286 – Ind 9/245	Kapil Dev	Imran Khan
26 Mar 87 India v Pakistan – Pak won by 5 wickets	Jamshedpur	Ind 3/265 – Pak 5/266	Kapil Dev	Imran Khan

Series winner: Pakistan 5-0

1986/87 – Rothmans Cup

MATCH	VENUE	SCORES	CAPTAIN	CAPTAIN
18 Mar 87 New Zealand v West Indies – WI won by 95 runs	Dunedin	WI 9/237 – NZ 142	J.V. Coney	I.V.A. Richards
21 Mar 87 New Zealand v West Indies – WI won by 6 wickets	Auckland	NZ 213 – WI 4/217	J.V. Coney	I.V.A. Richards
28 Mar 87 New Zealand v West Indies – WI won by 10 wickets	Christchurch	NZ 9/191 – WI 192	J.V. Coney	I.V.A. Richards

Series winner: West Indies 3-0

1986/87 – Sharjah Cup

MATCH	VENUE	SCORES	CAPTAIN	CAPTAIN
2 Apr 87 England v India – Ind won by 3 wickets	Sharjah	Eng 7/211 – Ind 7/214	J.E. Emburey	Kapil Dev
3 Apr 87 Australia v Pakistan – Pak won by 6 wickets	Sharjah	Aus 9/176 – Pak 4/180	A.R. Border	Javed Miandad
5 Apr 87 Australia v India – Ind won by 7 wickets	Sharjah	Aus 6/176 – Ind 3/177	G.R. Marsh	Kapil Dev
7 Apr 87 England v Pakistan – Eng won by 5 wickets	Sharjah	Pak 9/217 – Eng 5/220	J.E. Emburey	Imran Khan
9 Apr 87 Australia v England – Eng won by 11 runs	Sharjah	Eng 6/230 – Aus 9/219	A.R. Border	J.E. Emburey
10 Apr 87 India v Pakistan – Pak won by 8 wickets	Sharjah	Ind 8/183 – Pak 2/184	Kapil Dev	Imran Khan

Series winner: England, due to a faster run-rate

MATCH	VENUE	SCORES	CAPTAIN	CAPTAIN
1987 – Texaco Trophy				
21 May 87 England v Pakistan – Eng won by 7 wickets	The Oval	Pak 6/232 – Eng 3/233	M.W. Gatting	Imran Khan
23 May 87 England v Pakistan – Pak won by 6 wickets	Nottingham	Eng 157 – Pak 4/158	J.E. Emburey	Imran Khan
25 May 87 England v Pakistan – Eng won by 1 wicket	Birmingham	Pak 9/213 – Eng 9/217	M.W. Gatting	Imran Khan
Series winner: England 2-1				
1987/88 – Reliance World Cup				
Group A qualifying matches				
9 Oct 87 India v Australia – Aus won by 1 run	Chennai	Aus 6/270 – Ind 269	Kapil Dev	A.R. Border
10 Oct 87 New Zealand v Zimbabwe – NZ won by 3 runs	Hyderabad (I)	NZ 7/242 – Zim 239	J.J. Crowe	A.J. Traicos
13 Oct 87 Australia v Zimbabwe – Aus won by 96 runs	Chennai	Aus 9/235 – Zim 139	A.R. Border	A.J. Traicos
14 Oct 87 India v New Zealand – Ind won by 16 runs	Bangalore	Ind 7/252 – NZ 8/236	Kapil Dev	J.J. Crowe
17 Oct 87 India v Zimbabwe – Ind won by 8 wickets	Mumbai (WS)	Zim 135 – Ind 2/136	Kapil Dev	A.J. Traicos
19 Oct 87 Australia v New Zealand – Aus won by 3 runs	Indore	Aus 4/199 – NZ 9/196	A.R. Border	J.J. Crowe
22 Oct 87 India v Australia – Ind won by 56 runs	Delhi	Ind 6/289 – Aus 233	Kapil Dev	A.R. Border
23 Oct 87 New Zealand v Zimbabwe – NZ won by 4 wickets	Calcutta	Zim 5/227 – NZ 6/228	J.J. Crowe	A.J. Traicos
26 Oct 87 India v Zimbabwe – Ind won by 7 wickets	Ahmedabad (GS)	Zim 7/191 – Ind 3/194	Kapil Dev	A.J. Traicos
27 Oct 87 Australia v New Zealand – Aus won by 17 runs	Chandigarh	Aus 8/251 – NZ 234	A.R. Border	J.J. Crowe
30 Oct 87 Australia v Zimbabwe – Aus won by 70 runs	Cuttack	Aus 5/266 – Zim 6/196	A.R. Border	A.J. Traicos
31 Oct 87 India v New Zealand – Ind won by 9 wickets	Nagpur	NZ 9/221 – Ind 1/224	Kapil Dev	J.J. Crowe
Group B qualifying matches				
8 Oct 87 Pakistan v Sri Lanka – Pak won by 15 runs	Hyderabad (P)	Pak 6/267 – SL 252	Imran Khan	L.R.D. Mendis
9 Oct 87 England v West Indies – Eng won by 2 wickets	Gujranwala	WI 7/243 – Eng 8/246	M.W. Gatting	I.V.A. Richards
13 Oct 87 Pakistan v England – Pak won by 18 runs	Rawalpindi (PC)	Pak 7/239 – Eng 221	Imran Khan	M.W. Gatting
13 Oct 87 Sri Lanka v West Indies – WI won by 191 runs	Karachi	WI 4/360 – SL 4/169	L.R.D. Mendis	I.V.A. Richards
16 Oct 87 Pakistan v West Indies – Pak won by 1 wicket	Lahore	WI 216 – Pak 9/217	Imran Khan	I.V.A. Richards
17 Oct 87 England v Sri Lanka – Eng won by 109 runs†	Peshawar	Eng 4/296 – SL 8/158	M.W. Gatting	L.R.D. Mendis
20 Oct 87 Pakistan v England – Pak won by 7 wickets	Karachi	Eng 9/244 – Pak 3/247	Imran Khan	M.W. Gatting
21 Oct 87 Sri Lanka v West Indies – WI won by 25 runs	Kanpur	WI 8/236 – SL 8/211	L.R.D. Mendis	I.V.A. Richards
25 Oct 87 Pakistan v Sri Lanka – Pak won by 113 runs	Faisalabad	Pak 7/297 – SL 8/184	Imran Khan	L.R.D. Mendis
26 Oct 87 England v West Indies – Eng won by 34 runs	Jaipur	Eng 5/269 – WI 235	M.W. Gatting	I.V.A. Richards
30 Oct 87 England v Sri Lanka – Eng won by 8 wickets	Pune	SL 7/218 – Eng 2/219	M.W. Gatting	L.R.D. Mendis
30 Oct 87 Pakistan v West Indies – WI won by 28 runs	Karachi	WI 7/258 – Pak 9/230	Imran Khan	I.V.A. Richards
Semi-finals				
4 Nov 87 Pakistan v Australia – Aus won by 18 runs	Lahore	Aus 8/267 – Pak 249	Imran Khan	A.R. Border
5 Nov 87 India v England – Eng won by 35 runs	Mumbai (WS)	Eng 6/254 – Ind 219	Kapil Dev	M.W. Gatting
Final				
8 Nov 87 Australia v England – Aus won by 7 runs	Calcutta	Aus 5/253 – Eng 8/246	A.R. Border	M.W. Gatting
World Champions: Australia				

MATCH	VENUE	SCORES	CAPTAIN	CAPTAIN
1987/88 – Pakistan v England				
18 Nov 87 Pakistan v England – Eng won by 2 wickets	Lahore	Pak 166 – Eng 8/167	Abdul Qadir	M.W. Gatting
20 Nov 87 Pakistan v England – Eng won by 23 runs	Karachi	Eng 6/263 – Pak 8/240	Abdul Qadir	M.W. Gatting
22 Nov 87 Pakistan v England – Eng won by 98 runs	Peshawar	Eng 8/236 – Pak 138	Abdul Qadir	M.W. Gatting
Series winner: England 3-0				
1987/88 – Charminar Challenge Cup				
8 Dec 87 India v West Indies – WI won by 10 runs	Nagpur	WI 8/203 – Ind 193	D.B. Vengsarkar	I.V.A. Richards
23 Dec 87 India v West Indies – WI won by 52 runs	Gauhati	WI 7/187 – Ind 135	D.B. Vengsarkar	I.V.A. Richards
2 Jan 88 India v West Indies – Ind won by 56 runs	Calcutta	Ind 7/222 – WI 166	R.J. Shastri	I.V.A. Richards
5 Jan 88 India v West Indies – WI won by 6 wickets	Rajkot	Ind 7/221 – WI 4/225	R.J. Shastri	I.V.A. Richards
19 Jan 88 India v West Indies – WI won by 4 wickets	Faridabad	Ind 6/230 – WI 6/231	R.J. Shastri	I.V.A. Richards
22 Jan 88 India v West Indies – WI won by 73 runs	Gwalior	WI 6/278 – Ind 205	R.J. Shastri	I.V.A. Richards
25 Jan 88 India v West Indies – WI won by 9 wickets	Trivandrum	Ind 8/239 – WI 1/241	R.J. Shastri	I.V.A. Richards
Series winner: West Indies 6-1				
1987/88 – Indian Board Benevolent Fund Match				
7 Jan 88 India v West Indies – WI won by 2 runs	Ahmedabad (GS)	WI 196 – Ind 9/194	R.J. Shastri	I.V.A. Richards
Series winner: West Indies 1-0				
1987/88 – Benson & Hedges World Series Cup				
Qualifying matches				
2 Jan 88 Australia v Sri Lanka – Aus won by 81 runs	Perth	Aus 7/249 – SL 168	A.R. Border	R.S. Madugalle
3 Jan 88 Australia v New Zealand – NZ won by 1 run	Perth	NZ 9/232 – Aus 231	A.R. Border	J.J. Crowe
5 Jan 88 New Zealand v Sri Lanka – NZ won by 6 wickets	Sydney	SL 174 – NZ 4/178	J.J. Crowe	R.S. Madugalle
7 Jan 88 Australia v New Zealand – Aus won by 6 runs	Melbourne	Aus 216 – NZ 9/210	A.R. Border	J.J. Crowe
9 Jan 88 New Zealand v Sri Lanka – NZ won by 4 wickets	Adelaide	SL 241 – NZ 6/242	J.G. Wright	R.S. Madugalle
10 Jan 88 Australia v Sri Lanka – Aus won by 81 runs	Adelaide	Aus 6/289 – SL 8/208	A.R. Border	R.S. Madugalle
12 Jan 88 New Zealand v Sri Lanka – SL won by 4 wickets	Hobart	NZ 7/199 – SL 6/200	J.J. Crowe	R.S. Madugalle
14 Jan 88 Australia v Sri Lanka – Aus won by 38 runs	Melbourne	Aus 8/243 – SL 205	A.R. Border	R.S. Madugalle
16 Jan 88 New Zealand v Sri Lanka – NZ won by 4 wickets	Brisbane	SL 8/164 – NZ 6/167	J.G. Wright	R.S. Madugalle
17 Jan 88 Australia v New Zealand – Aus won by 5 wickets	Brisbane	NZ 5/176 – Aus 5/177	A.R. Border	J.J. Crowe
19 Jan 88 Australia v Sri Lanka – Aus won by 3 wickets	Sydney	SL 9/188 – Aus 7/189	A.R. Border	R.S. Madugalle
20 Jan 88 Australia v New Zealand – Aus won by 78 runs	Sydney	Aus 8/221 – NZ 143	A.R. Border	J.J. Crowe
Finals				
22 Jan 88 Australia v New Zealand – Aus won by 8 wickets	Melbourne	NZ 177 – Aus 2/180	A.R. Border	J.J. Crowe
24 Jan 88 Australia v New Zealand – Aus won by 6 wickets	Sydney	NZ 5/168 – Aus 4/169	A.R. Border	J.J. Crowe
Series winner: Australia				

MATCH	VENUE	SCORES	CAPTAIN	CAPTAIN
1987/88 – Bicentennial One-Day International				
4 Feb 88 Australia v England – Aus won by 22 runs	Melbourne	Aus 6/235 – Eng 8/213	A.R. Border	M.W. Gatting
Series winner: Australia 1-0				
1987/88 – Rothmans Cup				
9 Mar 88 New Zealand v England – Eng won by 5 wickets	Dunedin	NZ 204 – Eng 5/207	J.G. Wright	M.W. Gatting
12 Mar 88 New Zealand v England – Eng won by 6 wickets	Christchurch	NZ 8/186 – Eng 4/188	J.G. Wright	M.W. Gatting
16 Mar 88 New Zealand v England – NZ won by 7 wickets	Napier	Eng 219 – NZ 3/223	J.G. Wright	M.W. Gatting
19 Mar 88 New Zealand v England – NZ won by 4 wickets	Auckland	Eng 208 – NZ 6/211	J.G. Wright	M.W. Gatting
Series drawn 2-2				
1987/88 – Cable & Wireless Series				
12 Mar 88 West Indies v Pakistan – WI won by 47 runs	Kingston	WI 4/241 – Pak 7/194	I.V.A. Richards	Imran Khan
15 Mar 88 West Indies v Pakistan – WI won by 5 wickets	St John's	Pak 9/166 – WI 5/167	C.G. Greenidge	Imran Khan
18 Mar 88 West Indies v Pakistan – WI won by 50 runs	Port-of-Spain	WI 4/315 – Pak 265	C.G. Greenidge	Imran Khan
20 Mar 88 West Indies v Pakistan – WI won by 7 wickets	Port-of-Spain	Pak 6/271 – WI 3/272	C.G. Greenidge	Imran Khan
30 Mar 88 West Indies v Pakistan – WI won by 7 wickets	Georgetown	Pak 7/221 – WI 3/225	C.G. Greenidge	Imran Khan
Series winner: West Indies 5-0				
1987/88 – Sharjah Cup				
Qualifying matches				
25 Mar 88 India v Sri Lanka – Ind won by 18 runs	Sharjah	Ind 8/219 – SL 201	R.J. Shastri	R.S. Madugalle
27 Mar 88 India v New Zealand – Ind won by 73 runs	Sharjah	Ind 6/267 – NZ 8/194	R.J. Shastri	J.G. Wright
29 Mar 88 New Zealand v Sri Lanka – NZ won by 99 runs	Sharjah	NZ 8/258 – SL 159	J.G. Wright	R.S. Madugalle
31 Mar 88 New Zealand v Sri Lanka – NZ won by 43 runs	Sharjah	NZ 7/249 – SL 9/206	J.G. Wright	R.S. Madugalle
Final				
1 Apr 88 India v New Zealand – Ind won by 52 runs	Sharjah	Ind 7/250 – NZ 198	R.J. Shastri	J.G. Wright
Series winner: India				
1988 – Texaco Trophy				
19 May 88 England v West Indies – Eng won by 6 wickets	Birmingham	WI 217 – Eng 4/219	M.W. Gatting	I.V.A. Richards
21 May 88 England v West Indies – Eng won by 47 runs	Leeds	Eng 8/186 – WI 139	M.W. Gatting	I.V.A. Richards
23/24 May 88 England v West Indies – Eng won by 7 wickets	Lord's	WI 7/178 – Eng 3/180	M.W. Gatting	I.V.A. Richards
Series winner: England 3-0				
1988 – Texaco Trophy				
4 Sep 88 England v Sri Lanka – Eng won by 5 wickets	The Oval	SL 7/242 – Eng 5/245	G.A. Gooch	R.S. Madugalle
Series winner: England 1-0				
1988/89 – Wills Challenge				
14 Oct 88 Pakistan v Australia – Match tied	Lahore	Aus 8/229 – Pak 7/229	Javed Miandad	A.R. Border
Series winner: Pakistan, as they lost fewer wickets				

MATCH	VENUE	SCORES	CAPTAIN	CAPTAIN
1988/89 – Champions Trophy				
Qualifying matches				
16 Oct 88 India v West Indies – Ind won by 23 runs	Sharjah	Ind 5/238 – WI 215	D.B. Vengsarkar	C.G. Greenidge
18 Oct 88 Pakistan v West Indies – Pak won by 84 runs	Sharjah	Pak 6/294 – WI 5/210	Javed Miandad	C.G. Greenidge
19 Oct 88 India v Pakistan – Pak won by 34 runs	Sharjah	Pak 246 – Ind 8/212	D.B. Vengsarkar	Javed Miandad
21 Oct 88 India v West Indies – WI won by 8 wickets	Sharjah	Ind 7/169 – WI 2/175	D.B. Vengsarkar	C.G. Greenidge
Final				
22 Oct 88 Pakistan v West Indies – WI won by 11 runs	Sharjah	WI 6/235 – Pak 224	Javed Miandad	C.G. Greenidge
Series winner: West Indies				
1988/89 – Asia Cup				
Qualifying matches				
27 Oct 88 Pakistan v Sri Lanka – SL won by 5 wickets	Dhaka	Pak 7/194 – SL 5/195	Javed Miandad	R.S. Madugalle
27 Oct 88 Bangladesh v India – Ind won by 9 wickets	Chittagong	Ban 8/99 – Ind 1/100	Gazi Ashraf	D.B. Vengsarkar
29 Oct 88 India v Sri Lanka – SL won by 17 runs	Dhaka	SL 6/271 – Ind 254	D.B. Vengsarkar	A. Ranatunga
29 Oct 88 Bangladesh v Pakistan – Pak won by 173 runs	Chittagong	Pak 3/284 – Ban 6/111	Gazi Ashraf	Abdul Qadir
31 Oct 88 India v Pakistan – Ind won by 4 wickets	Dhaka	Pak 142 – Ind 6/143	D.B. Vengsarkar	Abdul Qadir
2 Nov 88 Bangladesh v Sri Lanka – SL won by 9 wickets	Dhaka	Ban 8/118 – SL 1/120	Gazi Ashraf	J.R. Ratnayeke
Final				
4 Nov 88 India v Sri Lanka – Ind won by 6 wickets	Dhaka	SL 176 – Ind 4/180	D.B. Vengsarkar	A. Ranatunga
Series winner: India				
1988/89 – India v New Zealand				
10 Dec 88 India v New Zealand – Ind won by 4 wickets	Visag	NZ 9/196 – Ind 6/197	D.B. Vengsarkar	J.G. Wright
12 Dec 88 India v New Zealand – Ind won by 5 wickets	Cuttack	NZ 7/160 – Ind 5/161	D.B. Vengsarkar	J.G. Wright
15 Dec 88 India v New Zealand – Ind won by 53 runs	Indore	Ind 6/222 – NZ 9/169	D.B. Vengsarkar	J.G. Wright
17 Dec 88 India v New Zealand – Ind won by 2 wickets	Vadodara (MB)	NZ 3/278 – Ind 8/282	D.B. Vengsarkar	J.G. Wright
Series winner: India 4-0				
1988/89 – Benson & Hedges World Series Cup				
Qualifying matches				
10 Dec 88 Pakistan v West Indies – WI won by 89 runs	Adelaide	WI 9/269 – Pak 7/180	Imran Khan	I.V.A. Richards
11 Dec 88 Australia v Pakistan – Aus won by 9 wickets	Adelaide	Pak 177 – Aus 1/178	A.R. Border	Imran Khan
13 Dec 88 Australia v West Indies – WI won by 1 run	Sydney	WI 220 – Aus 8/219	A.R. Border	I.V.A. Richards
15 Dec 88 Australia v West Indies – WI won by 34 runs	Melbourne	WI 236 – Aus 202	A.R. Border	I.V.A. Richards
17 Dec 88 Pakistan v West Indies – WI won by 17 runs	Hobart (B)	WI 4/244 – Pak 8/227	Imran Khan	I.V.A. Richards
1 Jan 89 Pakistan v West Indies – WI won by 7 wickets	Perth	Pak 9/140 – WI 3/142	Imran Khan	I.V.A. Richards
2 Jan 89 Australia v Pakistan – Pak won by 38 runs	Perth	Pak 7/216 – Aus 178	A.R. Border	Imran Khan
5 Jan 89 Australia v West Indies – Aus won by 8 runs	Melbourne	Aus 226 – WI 8/218	A.R. Border	I.V.A. Richards

MATCH

MATCH	VENUE	SCORES	CAPTAIN	CAPTAIN
7 Jan 89 Pakistan v West Indies – Pak won by 55 runs	Brisbane	Pak 7/258 – WI 203	Imran Khan	I.V.A. Richards
8 Jan 89 Australia v Pakistan – Aus won by 5 wickets	Brisbane	Pak 9/203 – Aus 5/204	A.R. Border	Imran Khan
10 Jan 89 Australia v Pakistan – Aus won by 6 runs†	Melbourne	Aus 4/258 – Pak 7/108	A.R. Border	Imran Khan
12 Jan 89 Australia v West Indies – Aus won by 61 runs	Sydney	Aus 5/215 – WI 8/154	A.R. Border	I.V.A. Richards

Finals

14 Jan 89 Australia v West Indies – Aus won by 2 runs	Melbourne	Aus 9/204 – WI 9/202	A.R. Border	I.V.A. Richards
16 Jan 89 Australia v West Indies – WI won by 92 runs	Sydney	WI 9/277 – Aus 185	A.R. Border	I.V.A. Richards
18 Jan 89 Australia v West Indies – WI won on run-rate	Sydney	Aus 4/226 – WI 2/111	A.R. Border	I.V.A. Richards

Series winner: West Indies

1988/89 – New Zealand v Pakistan

6 Feb 89 New Zealand v Pakistan – NZ won by 8 wickets	Dunedin	Pak 9/170 – NZ 2/174	J.G. Wright	Imran Khan

Series winner: New Zealand 1-0

1988/89 – Rothmans Cup

4 Mar 89 New Zealand v Pakistan – NZ won by 7 wickets	Christchurch	Pak 7/170 – NZ 3/171	J.G. Wright	Imran Khan
8 Mar 89 New Zealand v Pakistan – NZ won by 6 wickets	Wellington	Pak 6/253 – NZ 4/254	J.G. Wright	Imran Khan
11 Mar 89 New Zealand v Pakistan – Pak won by 7 wickets	Auckland	NZ 249 – Pak 3/251	J.G. Wright	Imran Khan
14 Mar 89 New Zealand v Pakistan – NZ won by 7 wickets	Hamilton	Pak 9/138 – 3/139	J.G. Wright	Imran Khan

Series winner: New Zealand 3-1

1988/89 – Cable & Wireless Series

7 Mar 89 West Indies v India – WI won by 50 runs	Bridgetown	WI 4/248 – Ind 8/198	I.V.A. Richards	D.B. Vengsarkar
9 Mar 89 West Indies v India – WI won by 6 wickets	Port-of-Spain	Ind 148 – WI 4/151	I.V.A. Richards	D.B. Vengsarkar
11 Mar 89 West Indies v India – WI won by 6 wickets	Port-of-Spain	Ind 192 – WI 4/193	I.V.A. Richards	D.B. Vengsarkar
18 Mar 89 West Indies v India – WI won by 8 wickets	St John's	Ind 8/237 – WI 2/240	I.V.A. Richards	D.B. Vengsarkar
21 Mar 89 West Indies v India – WI won by 101 runs	Georgetown	WI 2/289 – Ind 8/188	I.V.A. Richards	D.B. Vengsarkar

Series winner: West Indies 5-0

1988/89 – Sharjah Cup

23 Mar 89 Pakistan v Sri Lanka – Pak won by 30 runs	Sharjah	Pak 8/237 – SL 207	Imran Khan	A. Ranatunga
24 Mar 89 Pakistan v Sri Lanka – Pak won by 7 wickets	Sharjah	SL 8/244 – Pak 3/248	Imran Khan	A. Ranatunga

Series winner: Pakistan 2-0

1989 – Texaco Trophy

25 May 89 England v Australia – Eng won by 95 runs	Manchester	Eng 9/231 – Aus 136	D.I. Gower	A.R. Border
27 May 89 England v Australia – Match tied	Nottingham	Eng 5/226 – Aus 8/226	D.I. Gower	A.R. Border
29 May 89 England v Australia – Aus won by 6 wickets	Lord's	Eng 7/278 – Aus 4/279	D.I. Gower	A.R. Border

Series winner: England, because they lost fewer wickets in the tied match

MATCH	VENUE	SCORES	CAPTAIN	CAPTAIN
1989/90 – Champions Trophy				
13 Oct 89 India v West Indies – WI won by 5 wickets	Sharjah	Ind 169 – WI 5/173	K. Srikkanth	I.V.A. Richards
14 Oct 89 Pakistan v West Indies – Pak won by 11 runs	Sharjah	Pak 8/250 – WI 239	Imran Khan	I.V.A. Richards
15 Oct 89 India v Pakistan – Pak won by 6 wickets	Sharjah	Ind 4/273 – Pak 4/274	K. Srikkanth	Imran Khan
16 Oct 89 India v West Indies – Ind won by 37 runs	Sharjah	Ind 9/211 – WI 174	K. Srikkanth	I.V.A. Richards
17 Oct 89 Pakistan v West Indies – Pak won by 57 runs	Sharjah	Pak 7/237 – WI 180	Imran Khan	D.L. Haynes
20 Oct 89 India v Pakistan – Pak won by 38 runs	Sharjah	Pak 4/252 – Ind 9/214	K. Srikkanth	Javed Miandad
Series winner: Pakistan				
1989/90 – Nehru Cup				
Qualifying matches				
15 Oct 89 England v Sri Lanka – Eng won by 5 wickets	Delhi	SL 193 – Eng 5/196	G.A. Gooch	A. Ranatunga
19 Oct 89 Australia v England – Eng won by 7 wickets	Hyderabad (I)	Aus 3/242 – Eng 3/243	A.R. Border	G.A. Gooch
19 Oct 89 Sri Lanka v West Indies – SL won by 4 wickets	Rajkot	WI 9/176 – SL 6/180	A. Ranatunga	I.V.A. Richards
21 Oct 89 Australia v West Indies – Aus won by 99 runs	Chennai	Aus 6/241 – WI 142	A.R. Border	I.V.A. Richards
22 Oct 89 England v Pakistan – Eng won by 4 wickets	Cuttack	Pak 9/148 – Eng 6/149	G.A. Gooch	Imran Khan
22 Oct 89 India v Sri Lanka – Ind won by 6 runs	Ahmedabad (GS)	Ind 8/227 – SL 221	K. Srikkanth	A. Ranatunga
23 Oct 89 Australia v Pakistan – Pak won by 66 runs	Mumbai (BS)	Pak 8/205 – Aus 139	A.R. Border	Imran Khan
23 Oct 89 India v West Indies – WI won by 20 runs	Delhi	WI 9/196 – Ind 176	K. Srikkanth	I.V.A. Richards
25 Oct 89 India v England – Ind won by 6 wickets	Kanpur	Eng 7/255 – Ind 4/259	K. Srikkanth	G.A. Gooch
25 Oct 89 Pakistan v West Indies – WI won by 6 wickets	Jullundur	Pak 5/223 – WI 4/226	Imran Khan	I.V.A. Richards
25 Oct 89 Australia v Sri Lanka – Aus won by 28 runs	Margao	Aus 7/222 – SL 194	A.R. Border	A. Ranatunga
27 Oct 89 England v West Indies – WI won by 26 runs	Gwalior	WI 5/265 – Eng 8/239	G.A. Gooch	I.V.A. Richards
27 Oct 89 India v Australia – Ind won by 3 wickets	Bangalore	Aus 8/247 – Ind 7/249	K. Srikkanth	A.R. Border
27 Oct 89 Pakistan v Sri Lanka – Pak won by 6 runs	Lucknow	Pak 6/219 – SL 213	Imran Khan	A. Ranatunga
28 Oct 89 India v Pakistan – Pak won by 77 runs	Calcutta	Pak 7/279 – Ind 202	K. Srikkanth	Imran Khan
Semi-finals				
30 Oct 89 England v Pakistan – Pak won by 6 wickets	Nagpur	Eng 7/194 – Pak 4/195	G.A. Gooch	Imran Khan
30 Oct 89 India v West Indies – WI won by 8 wickets	Mumbai (WS)	Ind 165 – WI 2/166	K. Srikkanth	I.V.A. Richards
Final				
1 Nov 89 Pakistan v West Indies – Pak won by 4 wickets	Calcutta	WI 5/273 – Pak 6/277	Imran Khan	I.V.A. Richards
Series winner: Pakistan				
1989/90 – Wills Challenge				
18 Dec 89 Pakistan v India – Pak won by 7 runs	Gujranwala	Pak 9/87 – Ind 9/80	Imran Khan	K. Srikkanth
20 Dec 89 Pakistan v India – No result	Karachi	Pak 3/28 – Ind DNB	Imran Khan	K. Srikkanth
22 Dec 89 Pakistan v India – Pak won by 38 runs	Lahore	Pak 8/150 – Ind 112	Imran Khan	K. Srikkanth
Series winner: Pakistan 2-0				

MATCH	VENUE	SCORES	CAPTAIN	CAPTAIN
1989/90 – Benson & Hedges World Series				
Qualifying matches				
26 Dec 89 Australia v Sri Lanka – Aus won by 30 runs	Melbourne	Aus 5/228 – SL 198	A.R. Border	A. Ranatunga
30 Dec 89 Australia v Sri Lanka – Aus won by 9 wickets	Perth	SL 9/203 – Aus 1/204	A.R. Border	A. Ranatunga
31 Dec 89 Pakistan v Sri Lanka – SL won by 3 wickets	Perth	Pak 7/222 – SL 7/223	Imran Khan	A. Ranatunga
3 Jan 90 Australia v Pakistan – Aus won by 7 wickets	Melbourne	Pak 161 – Aus 3/162	A.R. Border	Imran Khan
4 Jan 90 Australia v Sri Lanka – Aus won by 73 runs	Melbourne	Aus 7/202 – SL 129	A.R. Border	A. Ranatunga
10 Feb 90 Pakistan v Sri Lanka – Pak won by 5 wickets	Brisbane	SL 5/253 – Pak 5/254	Imran Khan	A. Ranatunga
11 Feb 90 Australia v Pakistan – Aus won by 67 runs	Brisbane	Aus 5/300 – Pak 233	A.R. Border	Imran Khan
13 Feb 90 Australia v Pakistan – Pak won by 5 wickets	Sydney	Aus 8/165 – Pak 5/167	A.R. Border	Imran Khan
15 Feb 90 Pakistan v Sri Lanka – Pak won by 6 wickets	Hobart (B)	SL 195 – Pak 4/198	Imran Khan	A. Ranatunga
17 Feb 90 Pakistan v Sri Lanka – Pak won by 27 runs	Adelaide	Pak 3/315 – SL 8/288	Imran Khan	A. Ranatunga
18 Feb 90 Australia v Sri Lanka – Aus won by 7 wickets	Adelaide	SL 158 – Aus 3/159	A.R. Border	A. Ranatunga
20 Feb 90 Australia v Pakistan – Pak won by 2 runs	Sydney	Pak 8/220 – Aus 9/218	A.R. Border	Imran Khan
Finals				
23 Feb 90 Australia v Pakistan – Aus won by 7 wickets	Melbourne	Pak 162 – Aus 3/163	A.R. Border	Imran Khan
25 Feb 90 Australia v Pakistan – Aus won by 69 runs	Sydney	Aus 6/255 – Pak 186	A.R. Border	Imran Khan
Series winner: Australia				
1989/90 – Cable & Wireless Series				
14 Feb 90 West Indies v England – No result	Port-of-Spain	WI 8/208 – Eng 1/26	I.V.A. Richards	G.A. Gooch
17 Feb 90 West Indies v England – No result	Port-of-Spain	WI 0/13 – Eng DNB	I.V.A. Richards	G.A. Gooch
3 Mar 90 West Indies v England – WI won by 3 wickets	Kingston	Eng 8/214 – WI 7/216	I.V.A. Richards	G.A. Gooch
7 Mar 90 West Indies v England – WI won by 6 wickets	Georgetown	Eng 8/188 – WI 4/191	I.V.A. Richards	G.A. Gooch
3 Apr 90 West Indies v England – WI won by 4 wickets	Bridgetown	Eng 3/214 – WI 6/217	D.L. Haynes	A.J. Lamb
Series winner: West Indies 3-0				
1989/90 – West Indies v England				
15 Mar 90 West Indies v England – WI won by 7 wickets	Georgetown	Eng 9/166 – WI 3/167	P.J.L. Dujon	G.A. Gooch
Series winner: West Indies 1-0				
1989/90 – Rothmans Cup				
Qualifying matches				
1 Mar 90 India v New Zealand – NZ won by 108 runs	Dunedin	NZ 6/246 – Ind 138	M. Azharuddin	J.G. Wright
3 Mar 90 Australia v India – Aus won by 18 runs	Christchurch	Aus 9/187 – Ind 169	A.R. Border	M. Azharuddin
4 Mar 90 New Zealand v Australia – Aus won by 150 runs	Christchurch	Aus 8/244 – NZ 94	M.D. Crowe	A.R. Border
6 Mar 90 India v New Zealand – Ind won by 1 run	Wellington	Ind 221 – NZ 220	M. Azharuddin	M.D. Crowe
8 Mar 90 Australia v India – Aus won by 7 wickets	Hamilton	Ind 8/211 – Aus 3/212	A.R. Border	M. Azharuddin
10 Mar 90 New Zealand v Australia – Aus won on run-rate	Auckland	Aus 6/239 – NZ 2/167	J.G. Wright	G.R. Marsh

MATCH	VENUE	SCORES	CAPTAIN	CAPTAIN
Final				
11 Mar 90 New Zealand v Australia – Aus won by 8 wickets	Auckland	NZ 162 – Aus 2/164	J.G. Wright	A.R. Border
Series winner: Australia				
1989/90 – Austral-Asia Cup				
Qualifying matches				
25 Apr 90 India v Sri Lanka – SL won by 3 wickets	Sharjah	Ind 8/241 – SL 7/242	M. Azharuddin	A. Ranatunga
26 Apr 90 Australia v New Zealand – Aus won by 63 runs	Sharjah	Aus 5/258 – NZ 7/195	A.R. Border	J.G. Wright
27 Apr 90 India v Pakistan – Pak won by 26 runs	Sharjah	Pak 9/235 – Ind 209	M. Azharuddin	Imran Khan
28 Apr 90 Bangladesh v New Zealand – NZ won by 161 runs	Sharjah	NZ 4/338 – Ban 5/177	Gazi Ashraf	J.G. Wright
29 Apr 90 Pakistan v Sri Lanka – Pak won by 90 runs	Sharjah	Pak 8/311 – SL 221	Imran Khan	A. Ranatunga
30 Apr 90 Australia v Bangladesh – Aus won by 7 wickets	Sharjah	Ban 8/134 – 3/140	A.R. Border	Gazi Ashraf
Semi-Finals				
1 May 90 New Zealand v Pakistan – Pak won by 8 wickets	Sharjah	NZ 74 – Pak 2/77	J.G. Wright	Imran Khan
2 May 90 Australia v Sri Lanka – Aus won by 114 runs	Sharjah	Aus 3/332 – SL 218	A.R. Border	A. Ranatunga
Final				
4 May 90 Australia v Pakistan – Pak won by 36 runs	Sharjah	Pak 7/266 – Aus 230	A.R. Border	Imran Khan
Series winner: Pakistan				
1990 – Texaco Trophy				
23 May 90 England v New Zealand – NZ won by 4 wickets	Leeds	Eng 6/295 – NZ 6/298	G.A. Gooch	J.G. Wright
25 May 90 England v New Zealand – Eng won by 6 wickets	The Oval	NZ 6/212 – Eng 4/213	G.A. Gooch	J.G. Wright
Series winner: England due to a faster run-rate				
1990 – Texaco Trophy				
18 Jul 90 England v India – Ind won by 6 wickets	Leeds	Eng 229 – Ind 4/233	G.A. Gooch	M. Azharuddin
20 Jul 90 England v India – Ind won by 5 wickets	Nottingham	Eng 281 – Ind 5/282	G.A. Gooch	M. Azharuddin
Series winner: India 2-0				
1990/91 – Pakistan v New Zealand				
2 Nov 90 Pakistan v New Zealand – Pak won by 19 runs	Lahore	Pak 8/196 – NZ 177	Javed Miandad	M.D. Crowe
4 Nov 90 Pakistan v New Zealand – Pak won by 8 wickets	Peshawar	NZ 127 – Pak 2/128	Javed Miandad	M.D. Crowe
6 Nov 90 Pakistan v New Zealand – Pak won by 105 runs	Sialkot	Pak 2/223 – NZ 118	Javed Miandad	M.D. Crowe
Series winner: Pakistan 3-0				
1990/91 – Pakistan v West Indies				
9 Nov 90 Pakistan v West Indies – Pak won by 6 runs	Karachi	Pak 5/211 – WI 7/205	Imran Khan	D.L. Haynes
11 Nov 90 Pakistan v West Indies – Pak won by 5 wickets	Lahore	WI 7/176 – Pak 5/177	Imran Khan	D.L. Haynes
13 Nov 90 Pakistan v West Indies – Pak won by 31 runs	Multan	Pak 9/168 – WI 7/137	Imran Khan	D.L. Haynes
Series winner: Pakistan 3-0				

1990/91 – Benson & Hedges World Series

Qualifying matches

MATCH	VENUE	SCORES	CAPTAIN	CAPTAIN
29 Nov 90 Australia v New Zealand – Aus won by 61 runs†	Sydney	Aus 9/236 – NZ 7/174	A.R. Border	M.D. Crowe
1 Dec 90 England v New Zealand – NZ won by 7 runs	Adelaide	NZ 6/199 – Eng 9/192	A.J. Lamb	M.D. Crowe
2 Dec 90 Australia v New Zealand – Aus won by 6 wickets	Adelaide	NZ 7/208 – Aus 4/210	A.R. Border	M.D. Crowe
7 Dec 90 England v New Zealand – Eng won by 4 wickets	Perth	NZ 158 – Eng 6/161	A.J. Lamb	M.D. Crowe
9 Dec 90 Australia v England – Aus won by 6 wickets	Perth	Eng 9/192 – Aus 4/193	A.R. Border	A.J. Lamb
11 Dec 90 Australia v New Zealand – Aus won by 39 runs	Melbourne	Aus 7/263 – NZ 8/224	A.R. Border	M.D. Crowe
13 Dec 90 England v New Zealand – Eng won by 33 runs	Sydney	Eng 194 – NZ 161	G.A. Gooch	M.D. Crowe
15 Dec 90 England v New Zealand – NZ won by 8 wickets	Brisbane	Eng 6/203 – NZ 2/204	G.A. Gooch	M.D. Crowe
16 Dec 90 Australia v England – Aus won by 37 runs	Brisbane	Aus 5/283 – Eng 7/246	A.R. Border	G.A. Gooch
18 Dec 90 Australia v New Zealand – NZ won by 1 run	Hobart (B)	NZ 6/194 – Aus 193	A.R. Border	M.D. Crowe
1 Jan 91 Australia v England – Aus won by 68 runs	Sydney	Aus 7/221 – Eng 153	A.R. Border	G.A. Gooch
10 Jan 91 Australia v England – Aus won by 3 runs	Melbourne	Aus 6/222 – Eng 9/219	A.R. Border	G.A. Gooch

Finals

MATCH	VENUE	SCORES	CAPTAIN	CAPTAIN
13 Jan 91 Australia v New Zealand – Aus won by 6 wickets	Sydney	NZ 7/199 – Aus 4/202	G.R. Marsh	M.D. Crowe
15 Jan 91 Australia v New Zealand – Aus won by 7 wickets	Melbourne	NZ 6/208 – Aus 3/209	G.R. Marsh	M.D. Crowe

Series winner: Australia

1990/91 – India v Sri Lanka

MATCH	VENUE	SCORES	CAPTAIN	CAPTAIN
1 Dec 90 India v Sri Lanka – Ind won by 19 runs	Nagpur	Ind 5/245 – SL 7/226	M. Azharuddin	A. Ranatunga
5 Dec 90 India v Sri lanka – Ind won by 6 wickets	Pune	SL 8/227 – Ind 4/230	M. Azharuddin	A. Ranatunga
8 Dec 90 India v Sri Lanka – Ind won by 7 wickets	Margao	Ind 136 – SL 3/137	M. Azharuddin	A. Ranatunga

Series winner: India 3-0

1990/91 – Sharjah Cup

MATCH	VENUE	SCORES	CAPTAIN	CAPTAIN
20 Dec 90 Pakistan v Sri Lanka – SL won by 6 wickets	Sharjah	Pak 170 – SL 4/172	Imran Khan	A. Ranatunga
21 Dec 90 Pakistan v Sri Lanka – Pak won by 50 runs	Sharjah	Pak 9/181 – SL 9/131	Imran Khan	A. Ranatunga

Series winner: Pakistan due to a faster run-rate

1990/91 – Asia Cup

Qualifying matches

MATCH	VENUE	SCORES	CAPTAIN	CAPTAIN
25 Dec 90 India v Bangladesh – Ind won by 9 wickets	Chandigarh	Ban 6/170 – Ind 1/171	M. Azharuddin	Minhaz-ul-Abedin
28 Dec 90 India v Sri Lanka – SL won by 36 runs	Cuttack	SL 214 – Ind 178	M. Azharuddin	A. Ranatunga
31 Dec 90 Bangladesh v Sri Lanka – SL won by 71 runs	Calcutta	SL 4/249 – Ban 9/178	Minhaz-ul-Abedin	A. Ranatunga

Final

MATCH	VENUE	SCORES	CAPTAIN	CAPTAIN
4 Jan 91 India v Sri Lanka – Ind won by 7 wickets	Calcutta	SL 9/204 – Ind 3/205	M. Azharuddin	A. Ranatunga

Series winner: India

MATCH	VENUE	SCORES	CAPTAIN	CAPTAIN
1990/91 – Bank of New Zealand Trophy				
26 Jan 91 New Zealand v Sri Lanka – NZ won by 5 wickets	Napier	SL 8/177 – NZ 5/178	M.D. Crowe	A. Ranatunga
28 Jan 91 New Zealand v Sri Lanka – NZ won by 41 runs	Auckland	NZ 5/242 – SL 201	M.D. Crowe	A. Ranatunga
6 Feb 91 New Zealand v Sri Lanka – NZ won by 107 runs	Dunedin	NZ 6/272 – SL 165	M.D. Crowe	A. Ranatunga
Series winner: New Zealand 3-0				
1990/91 – Bank of New Zealand Trophy				
9 Feb 91 New Zealand v England – Eng won by 14 runs	Christchurch	Eng 7/230 – NZ 8/216	M.D. Crowe	G.A. Gooch
13 Feb 91 New Zealand v England – NZ won by 9 runs	Wellington	NZ 8/196 – Eng 187	M.D. Crowe	G.A. Gooch
16 Feb 91 New Zealand v England – NZ won by 7 runs	Auckland	NZ 7/224 – Eng 217	M.D. Crowe	G.A. Gooch
Series winner: New Zealand 2-1				
1990/91 – Cable & Wireless Series				
26 Feb 91 West Indies v Australia – Aus won by 35 runs	Kingston	Aus 4/244 – WI 209	I.V.A. Richards	A.R. Border
9 Mar 91 West Indies v Australia – Aus won by 45 runs	Port-of-Spain	Aus 9/172 – WI 127	I.V.A. Richards	A.R. Border
10 Mar 91 West Indies v Australia – WI won on run-rate	Port-of-Spain	Aus 7/245 – WI 3/181	I.V.A. Richards	A.R. Border
13 Mar 91 West Indies v Australia – Aus won by 37 runs	Bridgetown	Aus 6/283 – WI 246	I.V.A. Richards	A.R. Border
20 Mar 91 West Indies v Australia – Aus won by 6 wickets	Georgetown	WI 251 – Aus 4/252	I.V.A. Richards	A.R. Border
Series winner: Australia 4-1				
1991 – Texaco Trophy				
23/24 May 91 England v West Indies – Eng won by 1 wicket	Birmingham	WI 8/173 – Eng 9/175	G.A. Gooch	I.V.A. Richards
25 May 91 England v West Indies – Eng won by 9 runs	Manchester	Eng 4/270 – WI 8/161	G.A. Gooch	I.V.A. Richards
27 May 91 England v West Indies – Eng won by 7 wickets	Lord's	WI 9/264 – Eng 3/265	G.A. Gooch	I.V.A. Richards
Series winner: England 3-0				
1991/92 – Wills Trophy				
Qualifying matches				
17 Oct 91 Pakistan v West Indies – WI won by 1 wicket	Sharjah	Pak 215 – WI 9/217	Imran Khan	R.B. Richardson
18 Oct 91 India v Pakistan – Ind won by 60 runs	Sharjah	Ind 4/238 – Pak 178	M. Azharuddin	Imran Khan
19 Oct 91 India v West Indies – Ind won by 19 runs	Sharjah	Ind 6/240 – WI 221	M. Azharuddin	R.B. Richardson
21 Oct 91 Pakistan v West Indies – Pak won by 1 run	Sharjah	Pak 7/236 – WI 235	Imran Khan	R.B. Richardson
22 Oct 91 India v West Indies – Ind won by 7 wickets	Sharjah	WI 145 – Ind 3/147	M. Azharuddin	R.B. Richardson
23 Oct 91 India v Pakistan – Pak won by 4 runs	Sharjah	Pak 7/257 – Ind 6/253	M. Azharuddin	Imran Khan
Final				
25 Oct 91 India v Pakistan – Pak won by 72 runs	Sharjah	Pak 6/262 – Ind 190	M. Azharuddin	Imran Khan
Series winner: Pakistan				

MATCH	VENUE	SCORES	CAPTAIN	CAPTAIN
1991/92 – India v South Africa				
10 Nov 91 India v South Africa – Ind won by 3 wickets	Calcutta	SAF 8/177 – Ind 7/178	M. Azharuddin	C.E.B. Rice
12 Nov 91 India v South Africa – Ind won by 38 runs	Gwalior	Ind 6/223 – SAF 8/185	M. Azharuddin	C.E.B. Rice
14 Nov 91 India v South Africa – SAF won by 8 wickets	New Delhi	Ind 4/287 – SAF 2/288	R.J. Shastri	C.E.B. Rice
Series winner: India 2-1				
1991/92 – Pakistan v West Indies				
20 Nov 91 Pakistan v West Indies – WI won by 24 runs	Karachi	WI 6/170 – Pak 146	Imran Khan	R.B. Richardson
22 Nov 91 Pakistan v West Indies – match tied	Lahore	WI 5/186 – Pak 9/186	Imran Khan	R.B. Richardson
24 Nov 91 Pakistan v West Indiess – WI won by 17 runs	Faisalabad	WI 5/204 – Pak 8/187	Imran Khan	R.B. Richardson
Series winner: West Indies 2-0				
1991/92 – Benson & Hedges World Series				
Qualifying matches				
6 Dec 91 India v West Indies – Match tied	Perth	Ind 126 – WI 126	M. Azharuddin	R.B. Richardson
8 Dec 91 Australia v India – Ind won by 107 runs	Perth	Ind 7/208 – Aus 101	A.R. Border	M. Azharuddin
10 Dec 91 Australia v India – Aus won by 8 wickets	Hobart (B)	Ind 8/175 – Aus 2/176	A.R. Border	M. Azharuddin
12 Dec 91 Australia v West Indies – Aus won by 9 runs	Melbourne	Aus 9/173 – WI 164	A.R. Border	R.B. Richardson
14 Dec 91 India v West Indies – Ind won by 10 runs	Adelaide	Ind 4/262 – WI 252	M. Azharuddin	R.B. Richardson
15 Dec 91 Australia v India – Aus won by 6 wickets	Adelaide	Ind 157 – Aus 4/158	A.R. Border	M. Azharuddin
18 Dec 91 Australia v West Indies – Aus won by 51 runs	Sydney	Aus 6/234 – WI 183	A.R. Border	R.B. Richardson
9 Jan 92 Australia v West Indies – No result	Melbourne	WI 7/160 – Aus DNB	A.R. Border	R.B. Richardson
11 Jan 92 India v West Indies – WI won by 6 wickets	Brisbane	Ind 191 – WI 4/192	M. Azharuddin	R.B. Richardson
12 Jan 92 Australia v West Indies – WI won by 12 runs	Brisbane	WI 215 – Aus 203	A.R. Border	R.B. Richardson
14 Jan 92 Australia v India – Aus won by 9 wickets	Sydney	Ind 175 – Aus 1/177	A.R. Border	M. Azharuddin
16 Jan 92 India v West Indies – Ind won by 5 wickets	Melbourne	WI 8/175 – Ind 5/176	M. Azharuddin	R.B. Richardson
Finals				
18 Jan 92 Australia v India – Aus won by 88 runs	Melbourne	Aus 5/233 – Ind 145	A.R. Border	M. Azharuddin
20 Jan 92 Australia v India – Aus won by 6 runs	Sydney	Aus 9/208 – Ind 7/202	A.R. Border	M. Azharuddin
Series winner: Australia				
1991/92 – Pakistan v Sri Lanka				
10 Jan 92 Pakistan v Sri Lanka – Pak won by 8 wickets	Sargodha	SL 6/155 – 2/157	Imran Khan	P.A. de Silva
13 Jan 92 Pakistan v Sri Lanka – Pak won by 29 runs	Karachi	Pak 5/210 – SL 181	Imran Khan	P.A. de Silva
15 Jan 92 Pakistan v Sri Lanka – Pak won by 59 runs	Hyderabad (P)	Pak 3/241 – SL 9/182	Imran Khan	P.A. de Silva
17 Jan 92 Pakistan v Sri Lanka – SL won by 4 wickets	Multan	Pak 5/205 – SL 6/206	Imran Khan	P.A. de Silva
19 Jan 92 Pakistan v Sri Lanka – Pak won by 117 runs	Rawalpindi (RC)	Pak 4/271 – SL 154	Imran Khan	P.A. de Silva
Series winner: Pakistan 4-1				

MATCH	VENUE	SCORES	CAPTAIN	CAPTAIN
1991/92 – Bank of New Zealand Series				
11 Jan 92 New Zealand v England – Eng won by 7 wickets	Auckland	NZ 7/178 – Eng 3/179	M.D. Crowe	G.A. Gooch
12 Feb 92 New Zealand v England – Eng won by 3 wickets	Dunedin	NZ 7/186 – Eng 7/188	M.D. Crowe	G.A. Gooch
15 Feb 92 New Zealand v England – Eng won by 71 runs	Christchurch	Eng 7/255 – NZ 8/184	M.D. Crowe	A.J. Stewart
Series winner: England 3-0				
1991/92 – Benson & Hedges World Cup				
Qualifying matches				
22 Feb 92 New Zealand v Australia – NZ won by 37 runs	Auckland	NZ 6/248 – Aus 211	M.D. Crowe	A.R. Border
22 Feb 92 England v India – Eng won by 9 runs	Perth	Eng 9/236 – Ind 227	G.A. Gooch	M. Azharuddin
23 Feb 92 Sri Lanka v Zimbabwe – SL won by 3 wickets	New Plymouth	Zim 4/312 – SL 7/313	P.A. de Silva	D.L. Houghton
23 Feb 92 Pakistan v West Indies – WI won by 10 wickets	Melbourne	Pak 2/220 – WI 0/221	Javed Miandad	R.B. Richardson
25 Feb 92 New Zealand v Sri Lanka – NZ won by 6 wickets	Hamilton	SL 9/206 – NZ 4/210	M.D. Crowe	P.A. de Silva
26 Feb 92 Australia v South Africa – SAF won by 9 wickets	Sydney	Aus 9/170 – SAF 1/171	A.R. Border	K.C. Wessels
27 Feb 92 Pakistan v Zimbabwe – Pak won by 53 runs	Hobart (B)	Pak 4/252 – Zim 7/201	Imran Khan	D.L. Houghton
27 Feb 92 England v West Indies – Eng won by 6 wickets	Melbourne	WI 157 – Eng 4/160	G.A. Gooch	R.B. Richardson
28 Feb 92 India v Sri Lanka – No result	Mackay	Ind 0/1 – SL DNB	M. Azharuddin	P.A. de Silva
29 Feb 92 New Zealand v South Africa – NZ won by 7 wickets	Auckland	SAF 7/190 – NZ 3/191	M.D. Crowe	K.C. Wessels
29 Feb 92 West Indies v Zimbabwe – WI won by 75 runs	Brisbane	WI 8/264 – Zim 7/189	R.B. Richardson	D.L. Houghton
1 Mar 92 Australia v India – Aus won by 1 run+	Brisbane	Aus 9/237 – Ind 234	A.R. Border	M. Azharuddin
1 Mar 92 England v Pakistan – No result	Adelaide	Pak 74 – Eng 1/24	G.A. Gooch	Javed Miandad
2 Mar 92 South Africa v Sri Lanka – SL won by 3 wickets	Wellington	SAF 195 – SL 7/198	K.C. Wessels	P.A. de Silva
3 Mar 92 New Zealand v Zimbabwe – NZ won by 48 runst	Napier	NZ 3/162 – Zim 7/105	M.D. Crowe	D.L. Houghton
4 Mar 92 India v Pakistan – Ind won by 43 runs	Sydney	Ind 7/216 – Pak 173	M. Azharuddin	Imran Khan
5 Mar 92 South Africa v West Indies – SAF won by 64 runs	Christchurch	SAF 8/200 – WI 136	K.C. Wessels	R.B. Richardson
5 Mar 92 Australia v England – Eng won by 8 wickets	Sydney	Aus 171 – Eng 2/173	A.R. Border	G.A. Gooch
7 Mar 92 India v Zimbabwe – Ind won by 55 runst	Hamilton	Ind 7/203 – Zim 1/104	M. Azharuddin	D.L. Houghton
7 Mar 92 Australia v Sri Lanka – Aus won by 7 wickets	Adelaide	SL 9/189 – Aus 3/190	A.R. Border	P.A. de Silva
8 Mar 92 New Zealand v West Indies – NZ won by 5 wickets	Auckland	WI 7/203 – NZ 5/206	M.D. Crowe	R.B. Richardson
8 Mar 92 Pakistan v South Africa – SAF won by 20 runst	Brisbane	SAF 7/211 – Pak 8/173	Imran Khan	K.C. Wessels
9 Mar 92 England v Sri Lanka – Eng won by 106 runs	Ballarat	Eng 6/280 – SL 174	G.A. Gooch	P.A. de Silva
10 Mar 92 India v West Indies – WI won on run-rate	Wellington	Ind 197 – WI 5/195	M. Azharuddin	R.B. Richardson
10 Mar 92 South Africa v Zimbabwe – SAF won by 7 wickets	Canberra	Zim 163 – SAF 3/164	K.C. Wessels	D.L. Houghton
11 Mar 92 Australia v Pakistan – Pak won by 48 runs	Perth	Pak 9/220 – Aus 172	A.R. Border	Imran Khan
12 Mar 92 New Zealand v India – NZ won by 4 wickets	Dunedin	Ind 6/230 – NZ 6/231	M.D. Crowe	M. Azharuddin
12 Mar 92 England v South Africa – Eng won on run-rate	Melbourne	SAF 4/236 – Eng 7/226	A.J. Stewart	K.C. Wessels
13 Mar 92 Sri Lanka v West Indies – WI won by 91 runs	Berri	WI 8/268 – SL 9/177	P.A. de Silva	R.B. Richardson
14 Mar 92 Australia v Zimbabwe – Aus won by 128 runs	Hobart (B)	Aus 6/265 – Zim 137	A.R. Border	D.L. Houghton
15 Mar 92 New Zealand v England – NZ won by 7 wickets	Wellington	Eng 8/200 – NZ 3/201	M.D. Crowe	A.J. Stewart
15 Mar 92 India v South Africa – SAF won by 6 wickets	Adelaide	Ind 6/180 – SAF 4/181	M. Azharuddin	K.C. Wessels

MATCH	VENUE	SCORES	CAPTAIN	CAPTAIN
15 Mar 92 Pakistan v Sri Lanka – Pak won by 4 wickets	Perth	SL 6/212 – Pak 6/216	Imran Khan	P.A. de Silva
18 Mar 92 New Zealand v Pakistan – Pak won by 7 wickets	Christchurch	NZ 166 – Pak 3/167	M.D. Crowe	Imran Khan
18 Mar 92 England v Zimbabwe – Zim won by 9 runs	Albury	Zim 134 – Eng 125	G.A. Gooch	D.L. Houghton
18 Mar 92 Australia v West Indies – Aus won by 57 runs	Melbourne	Aus 6/216 – WI 159	A.R. Border	R.B. Richardson

Semi-finals

MATCH	VENUE	SCORES	CAPTAIN	CAPTAIN
21 Mar 92 New Zealand v Pakistan – Pak won by 4 wickets	Auckland	NZ 7/262 – Pak 6/264	M.D. Crowe	Imran Khan
22 Mar 92 England v South Africa – Eng won by 19 runs+	Sydney	Eng 6/252 – SAF 6/232	G.A. Gooch	K.C. Wessels

Final

MATCH	VENUE	SCORES	CAPTAIN	CAPTAIN
25 Mar 92 England v Pakistan – Pak won by 22 runs	Melbourne	Pak 6/249 – Eng 227	G.A. Gooch	Imran Khan

World Champions: Pakistan

1991/92 – West Indies v South Africa

MATCH	VENUE	SCORES	CAPTAIN	CAPTAIN
7 Apr 92 West Indies v South Africa – WI won by 107 runs	Kingston	WI 6/287 – SAF 180	R.B. Richardson	K.C. Wessels
11 Apr 92 West Indies v South Africa – WI won by 10 wickets	Port-of-Spain	SAF 152 – WI 0/154	R.B. Richardson	K.C. Wessels
12 Apr 92 West Indies v South Africa – WI won by 7 wickets	Port-of-Spain	SAF 6/189 – WI 3/190	R.B. Richardson	K.C. Wessels

Series winner: West Indies 3-0

1992 – Texaco Trophy

MATCH	VENUE	SCORES	CAPTAIN	CAPTAIN
20 May 92 England v Pakistan – Eng won by 79 runs	Lord's	Eng 6/278 – Pak 199	G.A. Gooch	Javed Miandad
22 May 92 England v Pakistan – Eng won by 39 runs	The Oval	Eng 5/302 – Pak 263	G.A. Gooch	Javed Miandad
20 Aug 92 England v Pakistan – Eng won by 198 runs	Nottingham	Eng 7/363 – Pak 165	G.A. Gooch	Salim Malik
22/23 Aug 92 England v Pakistan – Pak won by 3 runs	Lord's	Pak 5/204 – Eng 201	A.J. Stewart	Javed Miandad
24 Aug 92 England v Pakistan – Eng won by 6 wickets	Manchester	Pak 5/254 – Eng 4/255	G.A. Gooch	Ramiz Raja

Series winner: England 4-1

1992/93 – Sri Lanka v Australia

MATCH	VENUE	SCORES	CAPTAIN	CAPTAIN
15 Aug 92 Sri Lanka v Australia – SL won by 4 wickets	Colombo (PSS)	Aus 5/247 – SL 6/251	A. Ranatunga	A.R. Border
4 Sep 92 Sri Lanka v Australia – SL won on faster run-rate	Colombo (RPS)	Aus 7/216 – SL 5/194	A. Ranatunga	A.R. Border
5 Sep 92 Sri Lanka v Australia – Aus won by 5 wickets	Colombo (RPS)	SL 6/207 – Aus 5/208	A. Ranatunga	A.R. Border

Series winner: Sri Lanka 2-1

1992/93 – Zimbabwe v India

MATCH	VENUE	SCORES	CAPTAIN	CAPTAIN
25 Oct 92 Zimbabwe v India – Ind won by 30 runs	Harare	Ind 239 – Zim 209	D.L. Houghton	M. Azharuddin

Series winner: India 1-0

1992/93 – Zimbabwe v New Zealand

MATCH	VENUE	SCORES	CAPTAIN	CAPTAIN
31 Oct 92 Zimbabwe v New Zealand – NZ won by 22 runs	Bulawayo (AC)	NZ 7/244 – Zim 9/222	D.L. Houghton	M.D. Crowe
8 Nov 92 Zimbabwe v New Zealand – NZ won by 4 wickets	Harare	Zim 6/271 – NZ 6/272	D.L. Houghton	M.D. Crowe

Series winner: New Zealand 2-0

MATCH	VENUE	SCORES	CAPTAIN	CAPTAIN
1992/93 – Sri Lanka v New Zealand				
4 Dec 92 Sri Lanka v New Zealand – No result	Colombo (RPS)	NZ 9/166 – SL 2/41	A. Ranatunga	M.D. Crowe
12 Dec 92 Sri Lanka v New Zealand – SL won by 8 wickets	Colombo (PSS)	NZ 7/190 – SL 2/192	A. Ranatunga	A.H. Jones
13 Dec 92 Sri Lanka v New Zealand – SL won by 31 runs	Colombo (RPS)	SL 6/262 – NZ 231	A. Ranatunga	A.H. Jones
Series winner: Sri Lanka 2-0				
1992/93 – Benson & Hedges World Series				
Qualifying matches				
4 Dec 92 Pakistan v West Indies – Pak won by 5 wickets	Perth	WI 9/197 – Pak 5/199	Javed Miandad	R.B. Richardson
6 Dec 92 Australia v West Indies – WI won by 9 wickets	Perth	Aus 7/160 – WI 1/164	A.R. Border	R.B. Richardson
8 Dec 92 Australia v West Indies – Aus won by 14 runs	Sydney	Aus 9/101 – WI 87	M.A. Taylor	R.B. Richardson
10 Dec 92 Australia v Pakistan – Match tied	Hobart (B)	Aus 7/228 – Pak 9/228	M.A. Taylor	Javed Miandad
12 Dec 92 Pakistan v West Indies – WI won by 4 runs	Adelaide	WI 7/177 – Pak 173	Javed Miandad	R.B. Richardson
13 Dec 92 Australia v Pakistan – Aus won by 8 wickets	Adelaide	Pak 6/195 – Aus 2/196	M.A. Taylor	Javed Miandad
15 Dec 92 Australia v West Indies – Aus won by 4 runs	Melbourne	Aus 8/198 – WI 194	A.R. Border	R.B. Richardson
17 Dec 92 Pakistan v West Indies – WI won by 133 runs	Sydney	WI 9/214 – Pak 81	Javed Miandad	R.B. Richardson
9 Jan 93 Pakistan v West Indies – WI won by 9 wickets	Brisbane	Pak 71 – WI 1/72	Javed Miandad	R.B. Richardson
10 Jan 92 Australia v West Indies – WI won by 7 runs	Brisbane	WI 9/197 – Aus 190	A.R. Border	R.B. Richardson
12 Jan 93 Australia v Pakistan – Aus won by 32 runs	Melbourne	Aus 6/212 – Pak 7/180	A.R. Border	Javed Miandad
14 Jan 93 Australia v Pakistan – Aus won by 23 runs	Sydney	Aus 8/260 – Pak 6/237	A.R. Border	Javed Miandad
Finals				
16 Jan 93 Australia v West Indies – WI won by 25 runs	Sydney	WI 8/239 – Aus 214	A.R. Border	R.B. Richardson
18 Jan 93 Australia v West Indies – WI won by 4 wickets	Melbourne	Aus 147 – WI 4/148	A.R. Border	R.B. Richardson
Series winner: West Indies				
1992/93 – South Africa v India				
7 Dec 92 South Africa v India – SAF won by 6 wickets	Cape Town	Ind 184 – Saf 4/185	K.C. Wessels	M. Azharuddin
9 Dec 92 South Africa v India – SAF won by 6 wickets	Port Elizabeth	Ind 147 – SAF 4/148	K.C. Wessels	M. Azharuddin
11 Dec 92 South Africa v India – Ind won by 4 wickets	Centurion	SAF 5/214 – Ind 6/215	K.C. Wessels	M. Azharuddin
13 Dec 92 South Africa v India – SAF won by 6 wickets	Johannesburg	Ind 9/161 – SAF 4/165	K.C. Wessels	M. Azharuddin
15 Dec 92 South Africa v India – SAF won by 8 wickets	Bloemfontein	Ind 4/207 – SAF 2/208	K.C. Wessels	M. Azharuddin
17 Dec 92 South Africa v India – SAF won by 39 runs	Durban	SAF 8/216 – Ind 177	K.C. Wessels	M. Azharuddin
19 Dec 92 South Africa v India – Ind won by 5 wickets	East London	SAF 8/203 – Ind 5/204	K.C. Wessels	M. Azharuddin
Series winner: South Africa 5-2				
1992/93 – New Zealand v Pakistan				
26 Dec 92 New Zealand v Pakistan – Pak won by 50 runs	Wellington	Pak 8/158 – NZ 108	M.D. Crowe	Javed Miandad
28 Dec 92 New Zealand v Pakistan – NZ won by 6 wickets	Napier	Pak 8/136 – NZ 4/137	M.D. Crowe	Javed Miandad
30 Dec 92 New Zealand v Pakistan – NZ won by 6 wickets	Auckland	Pak 139 – NZ 4/140	M.D. Crowe	Javed Miandad
Series winner: New Zealand 2-1				

MATCH	VENUE	SCORES	CAPTAIN	CAPTAIN
1992/93 – Charms Cup				
18 Jan 93 India v England – Eng won by 4 wickets	Jaipur	Ind 3/223 – Eng 6/224	M. Azharuddin	G.A. Gooch
21 Jan 93 India v England – Ind won by 5 wickets	Chandigarh	Eng 6/198 – Ind 5/201	M. Azharuddin	G.A. Gooch
26 Feb 93 India v England – Eng won by 48 runs	Bangalore	Eng 9/218 – Ind 170	M. Azharuddin	G.A. Gooch
1 Mar 93 India v England – Eng won by 6 wickets	Jamshedpur	Ind 7/137 – Eng 4/141	M. Azharuddin	G.A. Gooch
4 Mar 93 India v England – Ind won by 3 wickets	Gwalior	Eng 256 – Ind 7/257	M. Azharuddin	G.A. Gooch
5 Mar 93 India v England – Ind won by 4 wickets	Gwalior	Eng 4/265 – Ind 6/267	M. Azharuddin	G.A. Gooch
Series drawn 3-3				
1992/93 – Wills Trophy				
Qualifying matches				
1 Feb 93 Pakistan v Zimbabwe – Pak won by 49 runs	Sharjah	Pak 8/262 – Zim 6/213	Wasim Akram	D.L. Houghton
2 Feb 93 Pakistan v Sri Lanka – Pak won by 8 wickets	Sharjah	SL 9/180 – Pak 2/181	Wasim Akram	A. Ranatunga
3 Feb 93 Sri Lanka v Zimbabwe – SL won by 30 runs	Sharjah	SL 5/266 – Zim 9/236	A. Ranatunga	D.L. Houghton
Final				
4 Feb 93 Pakistan v Sri Lanka – Pak won by 114 runs	Sharjah	Pak 3/281 – SL 7/167	Wasim Akram	A. Ranatunga
Series winner: Pakistan				
1992/93 – Total Triangular Series				
Qualifying matches				
9 Feb 93 Pakistan v South Africa – Pak won by 10 runs	Durban	Pak 6/208 – SAF 198	K.C. Wessels	Wasim Akram
11 Feb 93 South Africa v West Indies – SAF won by 6 wickets	Port Elizabeth	WI 149 –SAF 4/150	K.C. Wessels	R.B. Richardson
13 Feb 93 Pakistan v West Indies – WI won on run-rate	Johannesburg	Pak 150 – WI 2/109	Wasim Akram	R.B. Richardson
15 Feb 93 Pakistan v South Africa – Pak won by 9 runst	East London	Pak 6/214 – SAF 162	K.C. Wessels	Wasim Akram
17 Feb 93 South Africa v West Indies – SAF won by 4 runs	Cape Town	SAF 9/140 – WI 136	K.C. Wessels	R.B. Richardson
19 Feb 93 Pakistan v West Indies – WI won by 124 runs	Durban	WI 5/268 – Pak 144	Wasim Akram	R.B. Richardson
21 Feb 93 South Africa v West Indies – Pak won by 22 runs	Centurion	Pak 8/220 – SAF 9/198	K.C. Wessels	Wasim Akram
23 Feb 93 South Africa v West Indies – WI won by 9 wickets	Bloemfontein	SAF 6/185 – WI 1/188	K.C. Wessels	R.B. Richardson
25 Feb 93 Pakistan v West Indies – WI won by 7 wickets	Cape Town	Pak 43 – WI 3/45	Wasim Akram	R.B. Richardson
Final				
27 Feb 93 Pakistan v West Indies – WI won by 5 wickets	Johannesburg	Pak 187 – WI 5/190	Wasim Akram	R.B. Richardson
Series winner: West Indies				
1992/93 – Zimbabwe v Pakistan				
2 Mar 93 Zimbabwe v Pakistan – Pak won by 7 wickets	Harare	Zim 164 – Pak 3/165	D.L. Houghton	Wasim Akram
Series winner: Pakistan 1-0				
1992/93 – Sri Lanka v England				
10 Mar 93 Sri Lanka v England – SL won by 32 runst	Colombo (RPS)	SL 5/250 – Eng 170	A.J. Stewart	A. Ranatunga
20 Mar 93 Sri Lanka v England – SL won by 8 wickets	Moratuwa	Eng 180 – SL 2/183	A.J. Stewart	A. Ranatunga
Series winner: Sri Lanka 2-0				

MATCH	VENUE	SCORES	CAPTAIN	CAPTAIN
1992/93 – Bank of New Zealand Trophy				
19 Mar 93 New Zealand v Australia – Aus won by 129 runs	Dunedin	Aus 4/258 – NZ 129	M.D. Crowe	A.R. Border
21/22 Mar 93 New Zealand v Australia – Aus won by 1 wicket	Christchurch	NZ 8/196 – Aus 9/197	M.D. Crowe	M.A. Taylor
24 Mar 93 New Zealand v Australia – NZ won by 88 runs	Wellington	NZ 214 – Aus 126	M.D. Crowe	A.R. Border
27 Mar 93 New Zealand v Australia – NZ won by 3 wickets	Hamilton	Aus 7/247 – NZ 7/250	M.D. Crowe	M.A. Taylor
28 Mar 93 New Zealand v Australia – Aus won by 3 runs	Auckland	Aus 8/232 – NZ 8/229	M.D. Crowe	A.R. Border
Series winner: Australia 3-2				
1992/93 – Charms Cup				
19 Mar 93 India v Zimbabwe – Ind won by 67 runs	Faridabad	Ind 7/249 – Zim 182	M. Azharuddin	D.L. Houghton
22 Mar 93 India v Zimbabwe – Ind won by 7 wickets	Gauhati	Zim 6/149 – Ind 3/150	M. Azharuddin	D.L. Houghton
25 Mar 93 India v Zimbabwe – Ind won by 8 wickets	Pune	Zim 234 – Ind 2/238	M. Azharuddin	D.L. Houghton
Series winner: India 3-0				
1992/93 – Cable & Wireless Series				
23 Mar 93 West Indies v Pakistan – WI won by 4 wickets	Kingston	Pak 6/223 – WI 6/224	R.B. Richardson	Wasim Akram
26 Mar 93 West Indies v Pakistan – WI won by 5 wickets	Port-of-Spain	Pak 7/194 – WI 5/196	R.B. Richardson	Wasim Akram
27 Mar 93 West Indies v Pakistan – Pak won by 7 wickets	Port-of-Spain	WI 4/259 – Pak 3/261	R.B. Richardson	Wasim Akram
30 Mar 93 West Indies v Pakistan – Pak won by 38 runs	Kingstown	Pak 9/189 – WI 148	R.B. Richardson	Wasim Akram
3 Apr 93 West Indies v Pakistan – Match tied	Georgetown	Pak 6/244 – WI 5/244	R.B. Richardson	Wasim Akram
Series drawn 2-2				
1993 – Texaco Trophy				
19 May 93 England v Australia – Aus won by 4 runs	Manchester	Aus 9/258 – Eng 254	G.A. Gooch	A.R. Border
21 May 93 England v Australia – Aus won by 6 wickets	Birmingham	Eng 5/277 – Aus 4/280	G.A. Gooch	A.R. Border
23 May 93 England v Australia – Aus won by 19 runs	Lord's	Aus 5/230 – Eng 211	G.A. Gooch	M.A. Taylor
Series winner: Australia 3-0				
1993/94 – Sri Lanka v India				
25 Jul 93 Sri Lanka v India – Ind won by 1 run	Colombo (RPS)	Ind 8/212 – SL 211	A. Ranatunga	M. Azharuddin
11 Aug 93 Sri Lanka v India – SL won by 8 runs	Colombo (RPS)	SL 7/204 – Ind 196	A. Ranatunga	M. Azharuddin
14 Aug 93 Sri Lanka v India – SL won by 4 wickets	Moratuwa	Ind 9/227 – SL 6/231	A. Ranatunga	M. Azharuddin
Series winner: Sri Lanka 2-1				
1993/94 – Sri Lanka v South Africa				
22 Aug 93 Sri Lanka v South Africa – No result	Kandy	SL 5/179 – SAF 4/52	A. Ranatunga	K.C. Wessels
2 Sep 93 Sri Lanka v South Africa – SAF won by 124 runs	Colombo (RPS)	SAF 7/222 – SL 98	A. Ranatunga	K.C. Wessels
4 Sep 93 Sri Lanka v South Africa – SL won by 44 runs	Colombo (RPS)	SL 9/198 – SAF 154	A. Ranatunga	K.C. Wessels
Series drawn 1-1				

1993/94 – Pepsi Champions Trophy

Qualifying matches

MATCH	VENUE	SCORES	CAPTAIN	CAPTAIN
28 Oct 93 Sri Lanka v West Indies – WI won by 8 wickets	Sharjah	SL 172 – WI 2/173	R.B. Richardson	A. Ranatunga
29 Oct 93 Pakistan v West Indies – WI won by 39 runs	Sharjah	WI 7/267 – Pak 9/228	R.B. Richardson	Wasim Akram
30 Oct 93 Pakistan v Sri Lanka – Pak won by 114 runs	Sharjah	Pak 3/313 – SL 7/199	A. Ranatunga	Wasim Akram
1 Nov 93 Pakistan v West Indies – Pak won by 5 wickets	Sharjah	WI 9/260 – Pak 5/261	R.B. Richardson	Wasim Akram
2 Nov 93 Pakistan v Sri Lanka – Pak won by 2 wickets	Sharjah	SL 6/270 – Pak 8/271	A. Ranatunga	Wasim Akram
3 Nov 93 Sri Lanka v West Indies – WI won by 8 wickets	Sharjah	SL 9/182 – WI 2/183	D.L. Haynes	A. Ranatunga

Final

MATCH	VENUE	SCORES	CAPTAIN	CAPTAIN
5 Nov 93 Pakistan v West Indies – WI won by 6 wickets	Sharjah	Pak 4/284 – WI 4/285	R.B. Richardson	Waqar Younis

Series winner: West Indies

1993/94 – Hero Cup

Qualifying matches

MATCH	VENUE	SCORES	CAPTAIN	CAPTAIN
7 Nov 93 India v Sri Lanka – Ind won by 7 wickets	Kanpur	SL 203 - Ind 3/205	M. Azharuddin	A. Ranatunga
9 Nov 93 Sri Lanka v West Indies – WI won by 46 runs	Mumbai (WS)	WI 8/268 - SL 8/222	A. Ranatunga	D.L. Haynes
10 Nov 93 South Africa v Zimbabwe – No result	Bangalore	SAF 1/22 – Zim DNB	K.C. Wessels	A. Flower
14 Nov 93 South Africa v West Indies – SAF won by 41 runs	Mumbai (BS)	SAF 5/180 – WI 139	K.C. Wessels	R.B. Richardson
15 Nov 93 Sri Lanka v Zimbabwe – SL won by 55 runs	Patna	SL 6/263 - Zim 10/208	A. Ranatunga	A. Flower
16 Nov 93 India v West Indies – WI won by 69 runs+	Ahmedabad (GS)	WI 7/202 - Ind 100	M. Azharuddin	R.B. Richardson
18 Nov 93 India v Zimbabwe – Match tied	Indore	Ind 5/248 - Zim 248	M. Azharuddin	A. Flower
19 Nov 93 South Africa v Sri Lanka – SAF won by 78 runs	Gauhati	SAF 7/214 - SL 136	K.C. Wessels	A. Ranatunga
21 Nov 93 West Indies v Zimbabwe – WI won by 134 runs	Hyderabad (I)	WI 9/233 - Zim 99	R.B. Richardson	A. Flower
22 Nov 93 India v South Africa – Ind won by 43 runs	Mohali	Ind 221 - SAF 9/178	M. Azharuddin	K.C. Wessels

Semi-finals

MATCH	VENUE	SCORES	CAPTAIN	CAPTAIN
24 Nov 93 India v South Africa – Ind won by 2 runs	Calcutta	Ind 195 – SAF 9/193	M. Azharuddin	K.C. Wessels
25 Nov 93 Sri Lanka v West Indies – WI won by 7 wickets	Calcutta	SL 6/188 – WI 3/190	A. Ranatunga	R.B. Richardson

Final

MATCH	VENUE	SCORES	CAPTAIN	CAPTAIN
27 Nov 93 India v West Indies – Ind won by 102 runs	Calcutta	Ind 7/225 - WI 123	M. Azharuddin	R.B. Richardson

Series winner: India

1993/94 – Sri Lanka v West Indies

MATCH	VENUE	SCORES	CAPTAIN	CAPTAIN
1 Dec 93 Sri Lanka v West Indies – No result	Colombo (PSS)	WI 3/197 - SL 1/35	A. Ranatunga	R.B. Richardson
16 Dec 93 Sri Lanka v West Indies – SL won by 3 wickets	Colombo (RPS)	WI 8/229 - SL 7/230	A. Ranatunga	R.B. Richardson
18 Dec 93 Sri Lanka v West Indies – WI won by 6 wickets	Colombo (SSC)	SL 5/103 - WI 4/107	A. Ranatunga	R.B. Richardson

Series drawn 1-1

1993/94 – Benson & Hedges World Series

Qualifying matches

MATCH	VENUE	SCORES	CAPTAIN	CAPTAIN
9 Dec 93 Australia v South Africa – SAF won by 7 wickets	Melbourne	Aus 189 - SAF 3/190	A.R. Border	K.C. Wessels
12 Dec 93 Australia v New Zealand – Aus won by 8 wickets	Adelaide	NZ 135 - Aus 2/136	A.R. Border	K.R. Rutherford
14 Dec 93 Australia v South Africa – Aus won by 103 runs	Sydney	Aus 9/172 - SAF 69	A.R. Border	K.C. Wessels
16 Dec 93 Australia v New Zealand – Aus won by 3 runs	Melbourne	Aus 5/202 - NZ 9/199	A.R. Border	K.R. Rutherford
18 Dec 93 New Zealand v South Africa –.NZ won by 4 wickets	Hobart (B)	SAF 7/147 - NZ 6/148	K.R. Rutherford	K.C. Wessels
8 Jan 94 New Zealand v South Africa – NZ won by 9 runs†	Brisbane	NZ 7/256 - SAF 8/219	K.R. Rutherford	W.J. Cronje
9 Jan 94 Australia v South Africa – Aus won by 48 runs	Brisbane	Aus 9/230 - SAF 182	A.R. Border	W.J. Cronje
11 Jan 94 Australia v New Zealand – NZ won by 13 runs	Sydney	NZ 9/198 - Aus 185	A.R. Border	K.R. Rutherford
14 Jan 94 New Zealand v South Africa – SAF won by 5 wickets	Perth	NZ 150 - SAF 5/151	K.R. Rutherford	W.J. Cronje
16 Jan 94 Australia v South Africa – SAF won by 82 runs	Perth	SAF 7/208 - Aus 126	M.A. Taylor	W.J. Cronje
19 Jan 94 Australia v New Zealand – Aus won by 51 runs	Melbourne	Aus 3/217 - NZ 166	A.R. Border	K.R. Rutherford

Finals

MATCH	VENUE	SCORES	CAPTAIN	CAPTAIN
21 Jan 94 Australia v South Africa – SAF won by 28 runs	Melbourne	SAF 5/230 - Aus 202	A.R. Border	W.J. Cronje
23 Jan 94 Australia v South Africa – Aus won by 69 runs	Sydney	Aus 6/247 - SAF 178	A.R. Border	W.J. Cronje
25 Jan 94 Australia v South Africa – Aus won by 35 runs	Sydney	Aus 8/223 - SAF 9/188	A.R. Border	W.J. Cronje

Series winner: Australia

1993/94 – Pakistan v Zimbabwe

MATCH	VENUE	SCORES	CAPTAIN	CAPTAIN
24 Dec 93 Pakistan v Zimbabwe – Pak won by 7 wickets	Karachi	Zim 143 - Pak 3/147	Wasim Akram	A. Flower
25 Dec 93 Pakistan v Zimbabwe – Pak won by 6 wickets	Rawalpindi (RC)	Zim 5/195 - Pak 4/196	Wasim Akram	A. Flower
27 Dec 93 Pakistan v Zimbabwe – Pak won by 75 runs	Lahore	Pak 4/216 - Zim 9/141	Wasim Akram	A. Flower

Series winner: Pakistan 3-0

1993/94 – India v Sri Lanka

MATCH	VENUE	SCORES	CAPTAIN	CAPTAIN
15 Feb 94 India v Sri Lanka – Ind won by 8 runs	Rajkot	Ind 5/246 - SL 8/238	M. Azharuddin	A. Ranatunga
18 Feb 94 India v Sri Lanka – Ind won by 7 wickets	Hyderabad (I)	SL 7/226 - Ind 3/227	M. Azharuddin	A. Ranatunga
20 Feb 94 India v Sri Lanka – SL won on run-rate	Jullundur	Ind 9/213 - SL 6/141	M. Azharuddin	A. Ranatunga

Series winner: India 2-1

1993/94 – West Indies v England

MATCH	VENUE	SCORES	CAPTAIN	CAPTAIN
16 Feb 94 West Indies v England – Eng won by 61 runs	Bridgetown	Eng 5/202 - WI 141	R.B. Richardson	M.A. Atherton
26 Feb 94 West Indies v England – WI won on run-rate	Kingston	Eng 8/253 - WI 7/240	R.B. Richardson	M.A. Atherton
2 Mar 94 West Indies v England – WI won by 165 runs	Kingstown	WI 6/313 - Eng 9/148	R.B. Richardson	M.A. Atherton
5 Mar 94 West Indies v England – WI won by 15 runs+	Port-of-Spain	WI 7/265 - Eng 9/193	R.B. Richardson	M.A. Atherton
6 Mar 94 West Indies v England – Eng won on run-rate	Port-of-Spain	WI 9/250 - Eng 5/201	R.B. Richardson	M.A. Atherton

Series winner: West Indies 3-2

1993/94 – South Africa v Australia

MATCH	VENUE	SCORES	CAPTAIN	CAPTAIN
19 Feb 94 South Africa v Australia – SAF won by 5 runs	Johannesburg	SAF 3/232 - Aus 5/227	K.C. Wessels	A.R. Border
20 Feb 94 South Africa v Australia – SAF won by 56 runs	Centurion	SAF 5/265 - Aus 209	K.C. Wessels	A.R. Border
22 Feb 94 South Africa v Australia – Aus won by 88 runs	Port Elizabeth	Aus 6/281 - SAF 193	K.C. Wessels	A.R. Border
24 Feb 94 South Africa v Australia – SAF won by 7 wickets	Durban	Aus 154 - SAF 3/157	K.C. Wessels	A.R. Border
2 Apr 94 South Africa v Australia – Aus won by 7 wickets	East London	SAF 158 - Aus 3/159	K.C. Wessels	A.R. Border
4 Apr 94 South Africa v Australia – SAF won by 26 runs	Port Elizabeth	SAF 6/227 - Aus 201	K.C. Wessels	A.R. Border
6 Apr 94 South Africa v Australia – Aus won by 36 runs	Cape Town	Aus 6/242 - SAF 5/206	K.C. Wessels	A.R. Border
8 Apr 94 South Africa v Australia – Aus won by 1 run	Bloemfontein	Aus 6/203 - SAF 8/202	K.C. Wessels	A.R. Border

Series drawn 4-4

1993/94 – Bank of New Zealand Series

MATCH	VENUE	SCORES	CAPTAIN	CAPTAIN
3 Mar 94 New Zealand v Pakistan – Pak won by 5 wickets	Dunedin	NZ 9/122 - Pak 5/123	K.R. Rutherford	Salim Malik
6 Mar 94 New Zealand v Pakistan – Pak won by 36 runs	Auckland	Pak 146 - NZ 110	K.R. Rutherford	Salim Malik
9 Mar 94 New Zealand v Pakistan – Pak won by 11 runs	Wellington	Pak 6/213 - NZ 8/202	K.R. Rutherford	Salim Malik
13 Mar 94 New Zealand v Pakistan – Match tied	Auckland	Pak 9/161 - NZ 161	K.R. Rutherford	Salim Malik
16 Mar 94 New Zealand v Pakistan – NZ won by 7 wickets	Christchurch	Pak 9/145 - NZ 3/146	K.R. Rutherford	Salim Malik

Series winner: Pakistan 3-1

1993/94 – Bank of New Zealand Series

MATCH	VENUE	SCORES	CAPTAIN	CAPTAIN
25 Mar 94 New Zealand v India – NZ won by 28 runs	Napier	NZ 5/240 - Ind 9/212	K.R. Rutherford	M. Azharuddin
27 Mar 94 New Zealand v India – Ind won by 7 wickets	Auckland	NZ 142 - Ind 3/143	K.R. Rutherford	M. Azharuddin
30 Mar 94 New Zealand v India – Ind won by 12 runs	Wellington	Ind 5/255 - NZ 9/243	K.R. Rutherford	M. Azharuddin
2 Apr 94 New Zealand v India – NZ won by 6 wickets	Christchurch	Ind 6/222 - NZ 4/223	K.R. Rutherford	M. Azharuddin

Series drawn 2-2

1993/94 – Austral-Asia Cup

Qualifying matches

MATCH	VENUE	SCORES	CAPTAIN	CAPTAIN
13 Apr 94 UAE v India – Ind won by 71 runs	Sharjah	Ind 5/273 - UAE 9/202	Sultan M. Zarawani	M. Azharuddin
14 Apr 94 Australia v Sri Lanka – Aus won by 9 wickets	Sharjah	SL 154 - Aus 1/158	M.A. Taylor	R.S. Mahanama
15 Apr 94 India v Pakistan – Pak won by 6 wickets	Sharjah	Ind 219 - Pak 4/223	M. Azharuddin	Salim Malik
16 Apr 94 Australia v New Zealand – Aus won by 7 wickets	Sharjah	NZ 9/207 - Aus 3/208	M.A. Taylor	G.R. Larsen
17 Apr 94 UAE v Pakistan – Pak won by 9 wickets	Sharjah	UAE 145 - Pak 1/146	Sultan M. Zarawani	Salim Malik
18 Apr 94 New Zealand v Sri Lanka – NZ won by 2 runs	Sharjah	NZ 8/217 - SL 9/215	G.R. Larsen	R.S. Mahanama

Semi-finals

MATCH	VENUE	SCORES	CAPTAIN	CAPTAIN
19 Apr 94 Australia v India – Ind won by 7 wickets	Sharjah	Aus 9/244 - Ind 3/245	M.A. Taylor	M. Azharuddin
20 Apr 94 New Zealand v Pakistan – Pak won by 62 runs	Sharjah	Pak 2/328 - NZ 7/266	G.R. Larsen	Salim Malik

Final

MATCH	VENUE	SCORES	CAPTAIN	CAPTAIN
22 Apr 94 India v Pakistan – Pak won by 39 runs	Sharjah	Pak 6/250 - Ind 211	M. Azharuddin	Salim Malik

Series winner: Pakistan

MATCH	VENUE	SCORES	CAPTAIN	CAPTAIN
1994 – Texaco Trophy				
19 May 94 England v New Zealand – Eng won by 42 runs	Birmingham	Eng 8/224 – NZ 182	M.A. Atherton	K.R. Rutherford
Series winner: England 1-0				
1994/95 – Sri Lanka v Pakistan				
3 Aug 94 Sri Lanka v Pakistan – Pak won on run-rate	Colombo (RPS)	SL 6/200 – Pak 1/169	A. Ranatunga	Salim Malik
6 Aug 94 Sri Lanka v Pakistan – SL won by 7 wickets	Colombo (RPS)	Pak 8/180 – SL 3/181	A. Ranatunga	Salim Malik
7 Aug 94 Sri Lanka v Pakistan – Pak won by 19 runs	Colombo (SSC)	Pak 7/237 – SL 218	A. Ranatunga	Salim Malik
22 Aug 94 Sri Lanka v Pakistan – Pak won by 5 wickets	Colombo (SSC)	SL 9/174 – Pak 5/175	A. Ranatunga	Salim Malik
24 Aug 94 Sri Lanka v Pakistan – Pak won by 27 runs	Colombo (RPS)	Pak 187 – SL 160	A. Ranatunga	Salim Malik
Series winner: Pakistan 4-1				
1994 – Texaco Trophy				
25 Aug 94 England v South Africa – Eng won by 6 wickets	Birmingham	SAF 7/215 – Eng 4/219	M.A. Atherton	K.C. Wessels
27/28 Aug 94 England v South Africa – Eng won by 4 wickets	Manchester	SAF 9/181 – Eng 6/182	M.A. Atherton	K.C. Wessels
Series winner: England 2-0				
1994/95 – Singer World Series				
Qualifying matches				
4 Sep 94 Sri Lanka v India – No result	Colombo (RPS)	Ind 0/16 – SL DNB	A. Ranatunga	M. Azharuddin
5 Sep 94 Sri Lanka v India – SL won by 7 wickets	Colombo (SSC)	Ind 5/125 – SL 3/126	A. Ranatunga	M. Azharuddin
7 Sep 94 Australia v Pakistan – Aus won by 28 runs	Colombo (RPS)	Aus 7/179 – Pak 9/151	M.A. Taylor	Salim Malik
9 Sep 94 Australia v India – Ind won by 31 runs	Colombo (SSC)	Ind 8/246 – Aus 215	M.A. Taylor	M. Azharuddin
11 Sep 94 Sri Lanka v Pakistan – SL won by 7 wickets	Colombo (SSC)	Pak 6/210 – SL 3/213	A. Ranatunga	Salim Malik
13 Sep 94 Sri Lanka v Australia – SL won on run-rate	Colombo (PSS)	Aus 6/225 – SL 4/164	A. Ranatunga	M.A. Taylor
Final				
17 Sep 94 Sri Lanka v India – Ind won by 6 wickets	Colombo (SC)	SL 9/98 – Ind 4/99	A. Ranatunga	M. Azharuddin
Series winner: India				
1994/95 – Wills Triangular Tournament				
Qualifying matches				
12 Oct 94 Australia v South Africa – Aus won by 6 runs	Lahore	Aus 6/207 – 8/201	M.A. Taylor	K.C. Wessels
14 Oct 94 Pakistan v Australia – Aus won by 7 wickets	Multan	Pak 8/200 – 3/201	Salim Malik	M.A. Taylor
16 Oct 94 Pakistan v South Africa – Pak won by 8 wickets	Karachi	SAF 9/163 – Pak 2/166	Salim Malik	K.C. Wessels
18 Oct 94 Australia v South Africa – Aus won by 22 runs	Faisalabad	Aus 6/208 – SAF 186	M.A. Taylor	K.C. Wessels
20 Oct 94 Pakistan v South Africa – Pak won by 39 runs	Rawalpindi (RC)	Pak 6/249 – SAF 5/210	Salim Malik	K.C. Wessels
22 Oct 94 Pakistan v Australia – Pak won by 9 wickets	Rawalpindi (RC)	Aus 6/250 – Pak 1/251	Salim Malik	M.A. Taylor
24 Oct 94 Australia v South Africa – Aus won by 3 wickets	Peshawar	SAF 6/251 – Aus 7/252	M.A. Taylor	K.C. Wessels
28 Oct 94 Pakistan v South Africa – Pak won by 6 wickets	Faisalabad	SAF 4/222 – Pak 4/223	Salim Malik	K.C. Wessels

MATCH	VENUE	SCORES	CAPTAIN	CAPTAIN
Final				
30 Oct 94 Pakistan v Australia – Aus won by 64 runs	Lahore	Aus 5/269 – Pak 205	Salim Malik	M.A. Taylor
Series winner: Australia				
1994/95 – Pepsi Series				
17 Oct 94 India v West Indies – WI won by 96 runs	Faridabad	WI 5/273 – Ind 177	M. Azharuddin	C.A. Walsh
20 Oct 94 India v West Indies – Ind won on faster run-rate	Mumbai (WS)	WI 9/192 – Ind 4/135	M. Azharuddin	C.A. Walsh
7 Nov 94 India v West Indies – Ind won by 4 runs	Visag	Ind 4/260 – WI 7/256	M. Azharuddin	C.A. Walsh
9 Nov 94 India v West Indies – Ind won by 8 wickets	Cuttack	WI 9/251 – Ind 2/256	M. Azharuddin	C.A. Walsh
11 Nov 94 India v West Indies – Ind won by 5 runs	Jaipur	Ind 5/259 – WI 254	M. Azharuddin	B.C. Lara
Series winner: India				
1994/95 – Wills World Series				
Qualifying matches				
23 Oct 94 India v West Indies – Ind won by 4 wickets	Chennai	WI 221 – Ind 6/225	M. Azharuddin	C.A. Walsh
26 Oct 94 New Zealand v West Indies – No result	Margao	WI 123 – NZ 1/25	K.R. Rutherford	C.A. Walsh
28 Oct 94 India v New Zealand – Ind won by 7 wickets	Vadodara (IPCL)	NZ 4/269 – Ind 3/271	M. Azharuddin	K.R. Rutherford
30 Oct 94 India v West Indies – WI won by 46 runs	Kanpur	WI 6/257 – Ind 5/211	M. Azharuddin	C.A. Walsh
1 Nov 94 New Zealand v West Indies – WI won by 135 runs	Gauhati	WI 6/306 – NZ 9/171	K.R. Rutherford	C.A. Walsh
3 Nov 94 India v New Zealand – Ind won by 107 runs	Delhi	Ind 3/289 – NZ 182	M. Azharuddin	K.R. Rutherford
Final				
5 Nov 94 India v West Indies – Ind won by 72 runs	Calcutta	Ind 6/274 – WI 202	M. Azharuddin	C.A. Walsh
Series winner: India				
1994/95 – Zimbabwe v Sri Lanka				
3 Nov 94 Zimbabwe v Sri Lanka – SL won by 56 runs	Harare	SAF 5/256 – Zim 200	A. Flower	A. Ranatunga
5 Nov 94 Zimbabwe v Sri Lanka – Zim won by 2 runs	Harare	Zim 5/290 – SL 8/288	A. Flower	A. Ranatunga
6 Nov 94 Zimbabwe v Sri Lanka – SL won by 191 runs	Harare	SL 4/296 – Zim 105	A. Flower	A. Ranatunga
Series winner: Sri Lanka 2-1				
1994/95 – Benson & Hedges World Series				
Qualifying matches				
2 Dec 94 Australia v Zimbabwe – Aus won by 2 wickets	Perth	Zim 9/166 – Aus 8/167	M.A. Taylor	A. Flower
6 Dec 94 Australia v England – Aus won by 28 runs	Sydney	Aus 4/224 – Eng 196	M.A. Taylor	M.A. Atherton
8 Dec 94 Australia v Zimbabwe – Aus won by 84 runs	Hobart (B)	Aus 3/254 – Zim 8/170	M.A. Taylor	A. Flower
15 Dec 94 England v Zimbabwe – Zim won by 13 runs	Sydney	Zim 205 – Eng 192	M.A. Atherton	A. Flower
7 Jan 95 England v Zimbabwe – Eng won by 26 runs	Brisbane	Eng 8/200 – Zim 174	M.A. Atherton	A. Flower
10 Jan 95 Australia v England – Eng won by 37 runs	Melbourne	Eng 8/225 – Aus 188	M.A. Taylor	M.A. Atherton
Series winner: Australia				

This series also included an Australia A side which was beaten in the finals by Australia.

1994/95 – Mandela Trophy

Qualifying matches

MATCH	VENUE	SCORES	CAPTAIN	CAPTAIN
2 Dec 94 Pakistan v Sri Lanka – Pak won by 6 wickets	Durban	SL 5/228 – Pak 42/39	Salim Malik	A. Ranatunga
4 Dec 94 Pakistan v Sri Lanka – Pak won by 12 runs	Centurion	Pak 9/245 – SL 9/233	Salim Malik	A. Ranatunga
6 Dec 94 South Africa v New Zealand – SAF won by 69 runs	Cape Town	SAF 8/203 – NZ 134	W.J. Cronje	K.R. Rutherford
8 Dec 94 New Zealand v Sri Lanka – No result	Bloemfontein	SL 4/288 – NZ 1/66	K.R. Rutherford	A. Ranatunga
10 Dec 94 South Africa v Pakistan – SAF won by 7 wickets	Johannesburg	Pak 214 – SAF 3/215	W.J. Cronje	Salim Malik
11 Dec 94 South Africa v New Zealand – SAF won by 81 runs	Centurion	SAF 7/314 – NZ 233	W.J. Cronje	K.R. Rutherford
13 Dec 94 New Zealand v Pakistan – Pak won by 5 wickets	Port Elizabeth	NZ 201 – Pak 5/206	K.R. Rutherford	Salim Malik
15 Dec 94 South Africa v Sri Lanka – SL won by 35 runs	Bloemfontein	SL 8/226 – SAF 191	W.J. Cronje	A. Ranatunga
17 Dec 94 South Africa v Pakistan – Pak won by 8 wickets	Durban	SAF 8/206 – Pak 2/208	W.J. Cronje	Salim Malik
18 Dec 94 New Zealand v Sri Lanka – SL won by 5 wickets	East London	NZ 4/255 – SL 5/257	K.R. Rutherford	A. Ranatunga
19 Dec 94 South Africa v Pakistan – Pak won by 5 wickets	East London	NZ 172 – Pak 5/175	K.R. Rutherford	Salim Malik
21 Dec 94 South Africa v Sri Lanka – SAF won by 44 runs+	Port Elizabeth	SAF 8/237 – SL 6/139	W.J. Cronje	A. Ranatunga

Finals

MATCH	VENUE	SCORES	CAPTAIN	CAPTAIN
10 Jan 95 South Africa v Pakistan – SAF won by 37 runs	Cape Town	SAF 215 – Pak 178	W.J. Cronje	Salim Malik
12 Jan 95 South Africa v Pakistan – SAF won by 157 runs	Johannesburg	SAF 5/266 – Pak 109	W.J. Cronje	Salim Malik

Series winner: South Africa

1994/95 – New Zealand v West Indies

MATCH	VENUE	SCORES	CAPTAIN	CAPTAIN
22 Jan 95 New Zealand v West Indies – WI won on run-rate	Auckland	NZ 6/167 – WI 1/149	K.R. Rutherford	C.A. Walsh
25 Jan 95 New Zealand v West Indies – WI won by 41 runs	Wellington	WI 7/246 – NZ 205	K.R. Rutherford	C.A. Walsh
28 Jan 95 New Zealand v West Indies – WI won by 9 wickets	Christchurch	NZ 146 – WI 1/149	K.R. Rutherford	B.C. Lara

Series winner: West Indies 3-0

1994/95 – Bank of New Zealand Centenary Series

Qualifying matches

MATCH	VENUE	SCORES	CAPTAIN	CAPTAIN
15 Feb 95 Australia v South Africa – Aus won by 3 wickets	Wellington	SAF 123 – Aus 7/124	M.A. Taylor	W.J. Cronje
16 Feb 95 India v New Zealand – NZ won by 4 wickets	Napier	Ind 160 – NZ 6/162	K.R. Rutherford	M. Azharuddin
18 Feb 95 India v South Africa – SAF won by 14 runs	Hamilton	SAF 6/223 – Ind 9/209	M. Azharuddin	W.J. Cronje
19 Feb 95 Australia v New Zealand – Aus won by 27 runs	Auckland	Aus 5/254 – NZ 9/227	K.R. Rutherford	M.A. Taylor
22 Feb 95 Australia v India – Ind won by 5 wickets	Dunedin	Aus 6/250 – Ind 5/252	M.A. Taylor	M. Azharuddin
24 Feb 95 New Zealand v South Africa – NZ won by 46 runs	Christchurch	NZ 7/249 – SAF 203	K.R. Rutherford	W.J. Cronje

Final

MATCH	VENUE	SCORES	CAPTAIN	CAPTAIN
26 Feb 95 Australia v New Zealand – Aus won by 6 wickets	Auckland	NZ 9/137 – Aus 4/138	K.R. Rutherford	M.A. Taylor

Series winner: Australia

MATCH	VENUE	SCORES	CAPTAIN	CAPTAIN
1994/95 – Zimbabwe v Pakistan				
22 Feb 95 Zimbabwe v Pakistan – Match tied	Harare	Zim 9/219 – Pak 219	A. Flower	Salim Malik
25 Feb 95 Zimbabwe v Pakistan – Pak won by 4 wickets	Harare	Zim 5/209 – Pak 6/210	A. Flower	Salim Malik
26 Feb 95 Zimbabwe v Pakistan – Zim won by 74 runs	Harare	Zim 9/222 – Pak 148	A. Flower	Salim Malik
Series drawn 1-1				
1994/95 – West Indies v Australia				
8 Mar 95 West Indies v Australia – WI won by 6 runs	Bridgetown	WI 257 – Aus 6/251	M.A. Taylor	R.B. Richardson
11 Mar 95 West Indies v Australia – Aus won by 26 runs	Port-of-Spain	Aus 8/260 – WI 234	M.A. Taylor	C.A. Walsh
12 Mar 95 West Indies v Australia – WI won by 133 runs	Port-of-Spain	WI 5/282 – Aus 149	M.A. Taylor	C.A. Walsh
15 Mar 95 West Indies v Australia – WI won on run-rate	Kingstown	Aus 9/210 – WI 3/208	M.A. Taylor	C.A. Walsh
18 Mar 95 West Indies v Australia – WI won by 5 wickets	Georgetown	Aus 9/286 – WI 5/287	M.A. Taylor	C.A. Walsh
Series winner: West Indies 4-1				
1994/95 – New Zealand v Sri Lanka				
26 Mar 95 New Zealand v Sri Lanka – NZ won by 33 runs	Christchurch	NZ 6/271 – SL 238	K.R. Rutherford	A. Ranatunga
29 Mar 95 New Zealand v Sri Lanka – NZ won on run-rate	Hamilton	NZ 6/280 – SL 6/117	K.R. Rutherford	A. Ranatunga
1 Apr 95 New Zealand v Sri Lanka – SL won by 51 runs	Auckland	SL 6/250 – NZ 199	K.R. Rutherford	A. Ranatunga
Series winner: New Zealand 2-1				
1994/95 – Asia Cup				
Qualifying matches				
5 Apr 95 Bangladesh v India – Ind won by 9 wickets	Sharjah	Ban 163 – Ind 1/164	Akram Khan	M. Azharuddin
6 Apr 95 Bangladesh v Sri Lanka – SL won by 107 runs	Sharjah	SL 233 – Ban 126	Akram Khan	A. Ranatunga
7 Apr 95 India v Pakistan – Pak won by 97 runs	Sharjah	Pak 9/266 – Ind 169	M. Azharuddin	Moin Khan
8 Apr 95 Bangladesh v Pakistan – Pak won by 6 wickets	Sharjah	Ban 8/151 – Pak 4/152	Akram Khan	Moin Khan
9 Apr 95 India v Sri Lanka – Ind won by 8 wickets	Sharjah	SL 9/202 – Ind 2/206	M. Azharuddin	A. Ranatunga
11 Apr 95 Pakistan v Sri Lanka – SL won by 5 wickets	Sharjah	Pak 9/178 – SL 5/180	Saeed Anwar	A. Ranatunga
Final				
14 Apr 95 India v Sri Lanka – Ind won by 8 wickets	Sharjah	SL 7/230 – Ind 2/233	M. Azharuddin	A. Ranatunga
Series winner: India				
1995 – Texaco Trophy				
24/25 May 95 England v West Indies – WI won by 5 wickets	Nottingham	Eng 9/199 – WI 5/201	M.A. Atherton	R.B. Richardson
26 May 95 England v West Indies – Eng won by 25 runs	The Oval	Eng 5/306 – WI 281	M.A. Atherton	R.B. Richardson
28 May 95 England v West Indies – Eng won by 73 runs	Lord's	Eng 7/276 – WI 203	M.A. Atherton	R.B. Richardson
Series winner: England 2-1				

MATCH	VENUE	SCORES	CAPTAIN	CAPTAIN
1995/96 – Pakistan v Sri Lanka				
29 Sep 95 Pakistan v Sri Lanka – Pak won by 9 wickets	Gujranwala	SL 5/233 – Pak 1/234	Ramiz Raja	A. Ranatunga
1 Oct 95 Pakistan v Sri Lanka – SL won by 49 runs	Faisalabad	SL 7/257 – Pak 8/208	Ramiz Raja	A. Ranatunga
3 Oct 95 Pakistan v Sri Lanka – SL won by 4 wickets	Rawalpindi (RC)	Pak 9/183 – SL 6/184	Ramiz Raja	A. Ranatunga
Series winner: Sri Lanka 2-1				
1995/96 – Singer Champions Trophy				
Qualifying matches				
11 Oct 95 Sri Lanka v West Indies – SL won by 6 runs	Sharjah	SL 7/234 – WI 9/228	A. Ranatunga	R.B. Richardson
12 Oct 95 Pakistan v Sri Lanka – Pak won by 82 runs	Sharjah	Pak 7/264 – SL 8/182	Ramiz Raja	A. Ranatunga
13 Oct 95 Pakistan v West Indies – Pak won by 15 runs	Sharjah	Pak 4/242 – WI 227	Ramiz Raja	R.B. Richardson
15 Oct 95 Pakistan v West Indies – WI won by 4 wickets	Sharjah	Pak 9/194 – WI 6/195	Ramiz Raja	R.B. Richardson
16 Oct 95 Sri Lanka v West Indies – WI won by 4 runs	Sharjah	WI 7/333 – SL 329	A. Ranatunga	R.B. Richardson
17 Oct 95 Pakistan v Sri Lanka – SL won by 8 wickets	Sharjah	Pak 143 – SL 2/149	Ramiz Raja	A. Ranatunga
Final				
20 Oct 95 Sri Lanka v West Indies – SL won by 50 runs	Sharjah	SL 273 – WI 223	A. Ranatunga	R.B. Richardson
Series winner: Sri Lanka				
1995/96 – Zimbabwe v South Africa				
21 Oct 95 Zimbabwe v South Africa – SAF won by 134 runs	Harare	SAF 5/303 – Zim 7/169	W.J. Cronje	A. Flower
22 Oct 95 Zimbabwe v South Africa – SAF won by 112 runs	Harare	SAF 239 – Zim 127	W.J. Cronje	A. Flower
Series winner: South Africa 2-0				
1995/96 – India v New Zealand				
15 Nov 95 India v New Zealand – NZ won by 8 wickets	Jamshedpur	Ind 236 – NZ 2/237	M. Azharuddin	L.K. Germon
18 Nov 95 India v New Zealand – Ind won by 6 wickets	Amritsar	NZ 145 – Ind 4/146	M. Azharuddin	L.K. Germon
24 Nov 95 India v New Zealand – Ind won by 5 wickets	Pune	NZ 6/235 – Ind 5/236	M. Azharuddin	L.K. Germon
26 Nov 95 India v New Zealand – NZ won by 99 runs	Nagpur	NZ 8/348 – Ind 249	M. Azharuddin	L.K. Germon
29 Nov 95 India v New Zealand – Ind won by 6 wickets	Mumbai (BS)	NZ 126 – Ind 4/128	M. Azharuddin	L.K. Germon
Series winner: India 3-2				
1995/96 – New Zealand v Pakistan				
15 Dec 95 New Zealand v Pakistan – Pak won by 20 runs	Dunedin	Pak 9/189 – NZ 169	L.K. Germon	Wasim Akram
17 Dec 95 New Zealand v Pakistan – NZ won by 1 wicket	Christchurch	Pak 9/232 – NZ 9/236	L.K. Germon	Wasim Akram
20 Dec 95 New Zealand v Pakistan – Pak won by 54 runs	Wellington	Pak 4/261 – NZ 207	L.K. Germon	Wasim Akram
23 Dec 95 New Zealand v Pakistan – NZ won by 32 runs	Auckland	NZ 8/244 – Pak 212	L.K. Germon	Wasim Akram
Series drawn 2-2				

MATCH	VENUE	SCORES	CAPTAIN	CAPTAIN
1995/96 – Benson & Hedges World Series				
Qualifying matches				
15 Dec 95 Sri Lanka v West Indies – SL won by 4 wickets	Adelaide	WI 8/160 – SL 6/161	A. Ranatunga	R.B. Richardson
17 Dec 95 Australia v West Indies – Aus won by 121 runs	Adelaide	Aus 6/242 – WI 6/121	M.A. Taylor	R.B. Richardson
19 Dec 95 Australia v West Indies – Aus won by 24 runs	Melbourne	Aus 6/249 – WI 225	M.A. Taylor	R.B. Richardson
21 Dec 95 Australia v Sri Lanka – Aus won by 5 wickets	Sydney	SL 9/255 – Aus 5/257	M.A. Taylor	A. Ranatunga
1 Jan 96 Australia v West Indies – Aus won by 1 wicket	Sydney	WI 9/172 – Aus 9/173	M.A. Taylor	C.A. Walsh
3 Jan 96 Sri Lanka v West Indies – WI won by 70 runs	Hobart (B)	WI 194 – SL 124	P.A. de Silva	R.B. Richardson
5 Jan 96 Sri Lanka v West Indies – WI won by 7 wickets	Brisbane	SL 102 – WI 3/104	P.A. de Silva	R.B. Richardson
7 Jan 96 Australia v West Indies – WI won by 14 runs	Brisbane	WI 231 – Aus 217	M.A. Taylor	R.B. Richardson
9 Jan 96 Australia v Sri Lanka – SL won by 3 wickets	Melbourne	Aus 5/213 – SL 7/214	M.A. Taylor	P.A. de Silva
12 Jan 96 Australia v Sri Lanka – Aus won by 83 runs	Perth	Aus 6/266 – SL 9/183	M.A. Taylor	P.A. de Silva
14 Jan 96 Sri Lanka v West Indies – SL won by 16 runs	Perth	SL 202 – WI 9/186	P.A. de Silva	R.B. Richardson
16 Jan 96 Australia v Sri Lanka – SL won by 3 wickets	Melbourne	Aus 4/242 – SL 7/246	M.A. Taylor	A. Ranatunga
Finals				
18 Jan 96 Australia v Sri Lanka – Aus won by 18 runs	Melbourne	Aus 7/201 – SL 183	M.A. Taylor	A. Ranatunga
20 Jan 96 Australia v Sri Lanka – Aus won by 8 runs+	Sydney	Aus 5/273 – SL 8/159	M.A. Taylor	A. Ranatunga
Series winner: Australia				
1995/96 – South Africa v England				
9 Jan 96 South Africa v England – SAF won by 6 runs	Cape Town	SAF 8/211 – Eng 205	W.J. Cronje	M.A. Atherton
11 Jan 96 South Africa v England – Eng won by 5 wickets	Bloemfontein	SAF 8/262 – Eng 5/265	W.J. Cronje	M.A. Atherton
13 Jan 96 South Africa v England – SAF won by 3 wickets	Johannesburg	Eng 8/198 – SAF 7/199	W.J. Cronje	M.A. Atherton
14 Jan 96 South Africa v England – SAF won by 7 wickets	Centurion	Eng 8/272 – SAF 3/276	W.J. Cronje	A.J. Stewart
17 Jan 96 South Africa v England – SAF won by 5 wickets	Durban	Eng 184 – SAF 5/185	W.J. Cronje	M.A. Atherton
19 Jan 96 South Africa v England – SAF won by 14 runs	East London	SAF 129 – Eng 115	W.J. Cronje	M.A. Atherton
21 Jan 96 South Africa v England – SAF won by 64 runs	Port Elizabeth	SAF 9/218 – Eng 154	W.J. Cronje	M.A. Atherton
Series winner: South Africa 6-1				
1995/96 – New Zealand v Zimbabwe				
28 Jan 96 New Zealand v Zimbabwe – NZ won by 74 runs	Auckland	NZ 5/278 – Zim 204	L.K. Germon	A. Flower
31 Jan 96 New Zealand v Zimbabwe – NZ won by 6 wickets	Wellington	Zim 9/181 – NZ 4/184	L.K. Germon	A. Flower
3 Feb 96 New Zealand v Zimbabwe – Zim won by 21 runs	Napier	Zim 7/267 – NZ 246	L.K. Germon	A. Flower
Series winner: New Zealand 2-1				
1995/96 – Wills World Cup				
Group A qualifying matches				
16 Feb 96 West Indies v Zimbabwe – WI won by 6 wickets	Hyderabad (I)	Zim 9/151 – WI 4/155	R.B. Richardson	A. Flower
18 Feb 96 India v Kenya – Ind won by 7 wickets	Cuttack	Ken 6/199 – Ind 3/203	M. Azharuddin	M. Odumbe
21 Feb 96 Sri Lanka v Zimbabwe – SL won by 6 wickets	Colombo (SSC)	Zim 6/228 – SL 4/229	A. Ranatunga	A. Flower

MATCH	VENUE	SCORES	CAPTAIN	CAPTAIN
21 Feb 96 India v West Indies – Ind won by 5 wickets	Gwalior	WI 173 – Ind 5/174	M. Azaruddin	R.B. Richardson
23 Feb 96 Australia v Kenya – Aus won by 97 runs	Visag	Aus 7/304 – Ken 7/207	M.A. Taylor	M. Odumbe
26 Feb 96 Kenya v Zimbabwe – No result	Patna	Zim 3/45 – Ken DNB	M. Odumbe	A. Flower
27 Feb 96 Kenya v Zimbabwe – Zim won by 5 wickets	Patna	Ken 134 – Zim 5/137	M. Odumbe	A. Flower
27 Feb 96 India v Australia – Aus won by 16 runs	Mumbai (WS)	Aus 258 – Ind 242	M. Azaruddin	M.A. Taylor
29 Feb 96 Kenya v West Indies – Ken won by 73 runs	Pune	Ken 166 – WI 93	M. Odumbe	R.B. Richardson
1 Mar 96 Australia v Zimbabwe – Aus won by 8 wickets	Nagpur	Zim 154 – Aus 2/158	M.A. Taylor	A. Flower
2 Mar 96 India v Sri Lanka – SL won by 6 wickets	Delhi	Ind 3/271 – SL 4/272	M. Azaruddin	A. Ranatunga
4 Mar 96 Australia v West Indies – WI won by 4 wickets	Jaipur	Aus 6/229 – WI 6/232	M.A. Taylor	R.B. Richardson
6 Mar 96 India v Zimbabwe – Ind won by 40 runs	Kanpur	Ind 5/247 – Zim 207	M. Azaruddin	A. Flower
6 Mar 96 Sri Lanka v Kenya – SL won by 144 runs	Kandy	SL 5/398 – Ken 7/254	A. Ranatunga	M. Odumbe

Group B qualifying matches

MATCH	VENUE	SCORES	CAPTAIN	CAPTAIN
14 Feb 96 England v New Zealand – NZ won by 11 runs	Ahmedabad (GS)	NZ 6/239 – Eng 9/228	M.A. Atherton	L.K. Germon
16 Feb 96 South Africa v UAE – SAF won by 169 runs	Rawalpindi (RC)	SAF 2/321 – UA 8/152	W.J. Cronje	Sultan M. Zarawani
17 Feb 96 Netherlands v New Zealand – NZ won by 119 runs	Vadodara (IPCL)	NZ 8/307 – Neth 7/188	S.W. Lubbers	L.K. Germon
18 Feb 96 England v UAE – Eng won by 8 wickets	Peshawar	UAE 136 – Eng 2/140	M.A. Atherton	Sultan M. Zarawani
20 Feb 96 New Zealand v South Africa – SAF won by 5 wickets	Faisalabad	NZ 9/177 – SAF 5/178	L.K. Germon	W.J. Cronje
22 Feb 96 England v Netherlands – Eng won by 49 runs	Peshawar	Eng 4/179 – Neth 6/230	M.A. Atherton	S.W. Lubbers
24 Feb 96 Pakistan v UAE – Pak won by 9 wickets	Gujranwala	UAE 9/109 – Pak 1/112	Wasim Akram	Sultan M. Zarawani
25 Feb 96 England v South Africa – SAF won by 78 runs	Rawalpindi (RC)	SAF 230 – Eng 152	M.A. Atherton	W.J. Cronje
26 Feb 96 Pakistan v Netherlands – Pak won by 8 wickets	Lahore	Neth 7/145 – Pak 2./151	Wasim Akram	R.P. Lefebvre
27 Feb 96 New Zealand v UAE – NZ won by 109 runs	Faisalabad	NZ 8/276 – UAE 9/167	L.K. Germon	Sultan M. Zarawani
29 Feb 96 Pakistan v South Africa – SAF won by 5 wickets	Karachi	Pak 6/242 – SAF 5/243	Wasim Akram	W.J. Cronje
1 Mar 96 Netherlands v UAE – UAE won by 7 wickets	Lahore	Neth 9/216 – UAE 3/220	S.W. Lubbers	Sultan M. Zarawani
3 Mar 96 Pakistan v England – Pak won by 7 wickets	Karachi	Eng 9/249 – Pak 3/250	Wasim Akram	M.A. Atherton
5 Mar 96 Netherlands v South Africa – SAF won by 160 runs	Rawalpindi (RC)	SAF 3/328 – Neth 8/168	S.W. Lubbers	W.J. Cronje
6 Mar 96 Pakistan v New Zealand – Pak won by 46 runs	Lahore	Pak 5/281 – NZ 235	Wasim Akram	L.K. Germon

Quarter-finals

MATCH	VENUE	SCORES	CAPTAIN	CAPTAIN
9 Mar 96 England v Sri Lanka – SL won by 5 wickets	Faisalabad	Eng 8/235 – SL 5/236	M.A. Atherton	A. Ranatunga
9 Mar 96 India v Pakistan – Ind won by 39 runs	Bangalore	Ind 8/287 – Pak 9/248	M. Azaruddin	Aamir Sohail
11 Mar 96 South Africa v West Indies – WI won by 19 runs	Karachi	WI 8/264 – SAF 245	W.J. Cronje	R.B. Richardson
11 Mar 96 Australia v New Zealand – Aus won by 6 wickets	Chennai	NZ 9/286 – Aus 4/289	M.A. Taylor	L.K. Germon

Semi-finals

MATCH	VENUE	SCORES	CAPTAIN	CAPTAIN
13 Mar 96 India v Sri Lanka – SL won by default	Calcutta	SL 8/251 – Ind 8/120	M. Azaruddin	A. Ranatunga
14 Mar 96 Australia v West Indies – Aus won by 5 runs	Mohali	Aus 8/207 – WI 202	M.A. Taylor	R.B. Richardson

Final

MATCH	VENUE	SCORES	CAPTAIN	CAPTAIN
17 Mar 96 Australia v Sri Lanka – SL won by 7 wickets	Lahore	Aus 7/241 – SL 3/245	M.A. Taylor	A. Ranatunga

World Champions: Sri Lanka

MATCH	VENUE	SCORES	CAPTAIN	CAPTAIN
1995/96 – West Indies v New Zealand				
26 Mar 96 West Indies v New Zealand – WI won by 1 wicket	Kingston	NZ 243 – WI 9/244	C.A. Walsh	L.K. Germon
29 Mar 96 West Indies v New Zealand – NZ won by 4 wickets	Port-of-Spain	WI 7/238 – NZ 6/239	C.A. Walsh	L.K. Germon
30 Mar 96 West Indies v New Zealand – WI won by 7 wickets	Port-of-Spain	NZ 8/219 – WI 3/225	C.A. Walsh	L.K. Germon
3 Apr 96 West Indies v New Zealand – NZ won by 4 runs	Georgetown	NZ 158 – WI 154	C.A. Walsh	L.K. Germon
6 Apr 96 West Indies v New Zealand – WI won by 7 wickets	Kingstown	NZ 8/241 – WI 3/242	C.A. Walsh	L.K. Germon
Series winner: West Indies 3-2				
1995/96 – Singer Cup				
Qualifying matches				
1 Apr 96 Pakistan v Sri Lanka – No result	Singapore	Pak 3/54 – SL DNB	Aamir Sohail	A. Ranatunga
2 Apr 96 Pakistan v Sri Lanka – SL won by 34 runs	Singapore	SL 9/349 – Pak 315	Aamir Sohail	A. Ranatunga
3 Apr 96 India v Sri Lanka – Ind won by 12 runs	Singapore	Ind 199 – SL 187	M. Azharuddin	A. Ranatunga
5 Apr 96 India v Pakistan – Pak won on run-rate	Singapore	Ind 8/226 – Pak 2/190	M. Azharuddin	Aamir Sohail
Final				
7 Apr 96 Pakistan v Sri Lanka – Pak won by 43 runs	Singapore	Pak 215 – SL 172	Aamir Sohail	A. Ranatunga
Series winner: Pakistan				
1995/96 – Pepsi Sharjah Cup				
Qualifying matches				
12 Apr 96 India v Pakistan – Pak won by 38 runs	Sharjah	Pak 5/172 – Ind 233	M. Azharuddin	Aamir Sohail
13 Apr 96 Pakistan v South Africa – SAF won by 143 runs	Sharjah	SAF 3/314 – Pak 7/171	Aamir Sohail	W.J. Cronje
14 Apr 96 India v South Africa – SAF won by 80 runs	Sharjah	SAF 6/288 – Ind 8/208	M. Azharuddin	W.J. Cronje
15 Apr 96 India v Pakistan – Ind won by 28 runs	Sharjah	Ind 5/305 – Pak 277	M. Azharuddin	Aamir Sohail
16 Apr 96 Pakistan v South Africa – SAF won by 8 wickets	Sharjah	Pak 188 – SAF 2/189	Aamir Sohail	W.J. Cronje
17 Apr 96 India v South Africa – SAF won by 5 wickets	Sharjah	Ind 8/215 – SAF 5/216	M. Azharuddin	W.J. Cronje
Final				
19 Apr 96 India v South Africa – SAF won by 38 runs	Sharjah	SAF 5/287 – Ind 9/249	M. Azharuddin	W.J. Cronje
Series winner: South Africa				
1995/96 – Queen's Park Oval Centenary				
13 Apr 96 West Indies v Sri Lanka – SL won by 35 runs	Port-of-Spain	SL 251 – WI 9/216	C.A. Walsh	A. Ranatunga
Series winner: Sri Lanka 1-0				
1996 – Texaco Trophy				
23 May 96 England v India – No result	The Oval	Eng 8/291 – Ind 5/96	M.A. Atherton	M. Azharuddin
25 May 96 England v India – Eng won by 6 wickets	Leeds	Ind 158 – Eng 4/162	M.A. Atherton	M. Azharuddin
26/27 May 96 England v India – Eng won by 4 wickets	Manchester	Ind 4/236 – Eng 6/239	M.A. Atherton	M. Azharuddin
Series winner: England 2-0				

MATCH	VENUE	SCORES	CAPTAIN	CAPTAIN
1996/97 – Singer World Series				
Qualifying matches				
26 Aug 96 Australia v Zimbabwe – Aus won by 125 runs	Colombo (RPS)	Aus 7/263 – Zim 138	I.A. Healy	A.D.R. Campbell
28 Aug 96 Sri Lanka v India – SL won by 9 wickets	Colombo (RPS)	Ind 5/226 – SL 1/230	A. Ranatunga	S.R. Tendulkar
30 Aug 96 Sri Lanka v Australia – SL won by 4 wickets	Colombo (RPS)	Aus 9/228 – SL 6/232	A. Ranatunga	I.A. Healy
1 Sep 96 India v Zimbabwe – Ind won by 7 wickets	Colombo (SSC)	Zim 226 – Ind 3/229	S.R. Tendulkar	A.D.R. Campbell
3 Sep 96 Sri Lanka v Zimbabwe – SL won by 6 wickets	Colombo (SSC)	Zim 5/227 – SL 4/228	A. Ranatunga	A.D.R. Campbell
6 Sep 96 Australia v India – Aus won by 3 wickets	Colombo (SSC)	Ind 201 – Aus 7/202	I.A. Healy	S.R. Tendulkar
Final				
7 Sep 96 Sri Lanka v Australia – SL won by 50 runs	Colombo (RPS)	SL 3/234 – Aus 184	A. Ranatunga	I.A. Healy
Series winner: Sri Lanka				
1996 – Texaco Trophy				
29 Aug 96 England v Pakistan – Eng won by 5 wickets	Manchester	Pak 5/225 – Eng 5/226	M.A. Atherton	Wasim Akram
31 Aug 96 England v Pakistan – Eng won by 107 runs	Birmingham	Eng 8/292 – Pak 185	M.A. Atherton	Wasim Akram
1 Sep 96 England v Pakistan – Pak won by 2 wickets	Nottingham	Eng 246 – Pak 8/247	M.A. Atherton	Wasim Akram
Series winner: England 2-1				
1996 – Sahara Cup				
16 Sep 96 India v Pakistan – Ind won by 8 wickets	Toronto	Pak 9/170 – Ind 2/173	S.R. Tendulkar	Wasim Akram
17 Sep 96 India v Pakistan – Pak won by 2 wickets	Toronto	Ind 6/264 – Pak 8/266	S.R. Tendulkar	Wasim Akram
18 Sep 96 India v Pakistan – Ind won by 55 runs	Toronto	Ind 191 – Pak 136	S.R. Tendulkar	Wasim Akram
21 Sep 96 India v Pakistan – Pak won by 97 runs	Toronto	Pak 8/258 – Ind 161	S.R. Tendulkar	Wasim Akram
23 Sep 96 India v Pakistan – Pak won by 52 runs	Toronto	Pak 9/213 – Ind 161	S.R. Tendulkar	Wasim Akram
Series winner: Pakistan 3-2				
1996/97 – KCA Centenary Tournament				
Qualifying matches				
28 Sep 96 Kenya v Sri Lanka – SL won by 7 wickets	Nairobi (NG)	Ken 9/188 – SL 3/190	M. Odumbe	A. Ranatunga
29 Sep 96 Pakistan v South Africa – SAF won by 62 runs	Nairobi (NG)	SAF 8/321 – Pak 259	Wasim Akram	W.J. Cronje
1 Oct 96 South Africa v Sri Lanka – SL won by 2 wickets	Nairobi (NC)	SAF 169 – SL 8/170	W.J. Cronje	A. Ranatunga
2 Oct 96 Kenya v Pakistan – Pak won by 4 wickets	Nairobi (AG)	Ken 148 – Pak 6/149	M. Odumbe	Saeed Anwar
3 Oct 96 Kenya v South Africa – SAF won by 202 runs	Nairobi (NG)	SAF 8/305 – Ken 103	M. Odumbe	W.J. Cronje
4 Oct 96 Pakistan v Sri Lanka – Pak won by 82 runs	Nairobi (NG)	Pak 9/371 – SL 289	Saeed Anwar	A. Ranatunga
Final				
6 Oct 96 Pakistan v South Africa – SAF won by 7 wickets	Nairobi (NG)	Pak 203 – SAF 3/204	Saeed Anwar	W.J. Cronje
Series winner: South Africa				

MATCH

1996/97 – Titan Cup
Qualifying matches

MATCH	VENUE	SCORES	CAPTAIN	CAPTAIN
17 Oct 96 India v South Africa – SAF won by 47 runs	Hyderabad (I)	SAF 7/261 – Ind 214	S.R. Tendulkar	W.J. Cronje
19 Oct 96 Australia v South Africa – SAF won by 7 wickets	Indore	Aus 7/219 – SAF 3/220	M.A. Taylor	W.J. Cronje
21 Oct 96 India v Australia – Ind won by 2 wickets	Bangalore	Aus 7/215 – Ind 8/216	S.R. Tendulkar	M.A. Taylor
23 Oct 96 India v South Africa – SAF won by 27 runs	Jaipur	SAF 6/249 – Ind 7/222	S.R. Tendulkar	W.J. Cronje
25 Oct 96 Australia v South Africa – SAF won by 2 wickets	Faridabad	Aus 215 – SAF 8/218	M.A. Taylor	W.J. Cronje
29 Oct 96 India v South Africa – SAF won by 5 wickets	Rajkot	Ind 185 – SAF 5/188	S.R. Tendulkar	W.J. Cronje
1 Nov 96 Australia v South Africa – SAF won by 8 wickets	Gauhati	Aus 6/238 – SAF 2/239	M.A. Taylor	W.J. Cronje
3 Nov 96 India v Australia – Ind won by 5 runs	Mohali	Ind 6/289 – Aus 284	S.R. Tendulkar	M.A. Taylor

Final

MATCH	VENUE	SCORES	CAPTAIN	CAPTAIN
6 Nov 96 India v South Africa – Ind won by 35 runs	Mumbai (WS)	Ind 7/220 – SAF 185	S.R. Tendulkar	W.J. Cronje

Series winner: India

1996/97 – Pakistan v Zimbabwe

MATCH	VENUE	SCORES	CAPTAIN	CAPTAIN
30 Oct 96 Pakistan v Zimbabwe – Pak won by 3 wickets	Quetta (BS)	Zim 9/237 – Pak 7/239	Wasim Akram	A.D.R. Campbell
1 Nov 96 Pakistan v Zimbabwe – Pak won by 9 wickets	Lahore	Zim 195 – Pak 1/196	Wasim Akram	A.D.R. Campbell
3 Nov 96 Pakistan v Zimbabwe – Pak won by 78 runst	Peshawar	Pak 9/264 – Zim 147	Wasim Akram	A.D.R. Campbell

Series winner: Pakistan 3-0

1996/97 – Singer Champions Trophy
Qualifying matches

MATCH	VENUE	SCORES	CAPTAIN	CAPTAIN
7 Nov 96 New Zealand v Sri Lanka – NZ won by 29 runs	Sharjah	NZ 8/206 – SL 177	L.K. Germon	A. Ranatunga
8 Nov 96 Pakistan v Sri Lanka – SL won by 75 runs	Sharjah	SL 206 – Pak 131	Wasim Akram	A. Ranatunga
10 Nov 96 New Zealand v Pakistan – Pak won by 4 wickets	Sharjah	NZ 197 – Pak 6/198	L.K. Germon	Wasim Akram
11 Nov 96 New Zealand v Sri Lanka – Match tied	Sharjah	NZ 8/169 – SL 169	L.K. Germon	A. Ranatunga
12 Nov 96 Pakistan v Sri Lanka – Pak won by 8 wickets	Sharjah	SL 189 – Pak 2/193	Wasim Akram	A. Ranatunga
13 Nov 96 New Zealand v Pakistan – Pak won by 4 wickets	Sharjah	NZ 192 – Pak 6/196	L.K. Germon	Saeed Anwar

Final

MATCH	VENUE	SCORES	CAPTAIN	CAPTAIN
15 Nov 96 New Zealand v Pakistan – Pak won by 41 runs	Sharjah	Pak 160 – NZ 119	L.K. Germon	Wasim Akram

Series winner: Pakistan

1996/97 – Pakistan v New Zealand

MATCH	VENUE	SCORES	CAPTAIN	CAPTAIN
4 Dec 96 Pakistan v New Zealand – Pak won by 11 runs	Gujranwala	Pak 8/228 – NZ 217	Wasim Akram	L.K. Germon
6 Dec 96 Pakistan v New Zealand – Pak won by 46 runs	Sialkot	Pak 9/277 – NZ 231	Wasim Akram	L.K. Germon
8 Dec 96 Pakistan v New Zealand – NZ won by 7 wickets	Karachi	Pak 4/234 – NZ 3/235	Wasim Akram	L.K. Germon

Series winner: Pakistan 2-1

1996/97 – Carlton & United Series

Qualifying matches

MATCH	VENUE	SCORES	CAPTAIN	CAPTAIN
6 Dec 96 Australia v West Indies – Aus won by 5 wickets	Melbourne	WI 172 – Aus 5/173	M.A. Taylor	C.A. Walsh
8 Dec 96 Australia v West Indies – Aus won by 8 wickets	Sydney	WI 161 – Aus 2/162	M.A. Taylor	C.A. Walsh
15 Dec 96 Australia v Pakistan – Pak won by 12 runs	Adelaide	Pak 223 – Aus 211	M.A. Taylor	Wasim Akram
17 Dec 96 Pakistan v West Indies – WI won by 7 wickets	Adelaide	Pak 176 – WI 3/177	Wasim Akram	C.A. Walsh
1 Jan 97 Australia v Pakistan – Pak won by 4 wickets	Sydney	Aus 199 – Pak 6/203	M.A. Taylor	Wasim Akram
3 Jan 97 Pakistan v West Indies – WI won by 6 wickets	Brisbane	Pak 197 – WI 4/198	Wasim Akram	C.A. Walsh
5 Jan 97 Australia v West Indies – WI won by 7 wickets	Brisbane	Aus 4/281 – WI 3/284	M.A. Taylor	C.A. Walsh
7 Jan 97 Australia v Pakistan – Pak won by 29 runs	Hobart (B)	Pak 149 – Aus 120	M.A. Taylor	Wasim Akram
10 Jan 97 Pakistan v West Indies – WI won by 5 wickets	Perth	Pak 7/257 – WI 5/258	Wasim Akram	C.A. Walsh
12 Jan 97 Pakistan v West Indies – WI won by 4 wickets	Perth	Aus 7/267 – WI 6/269	Wasim Akram	C.A. Walsh
14 Jan 97 Pakistan v West Indies – Pak won by 8 wickets	Sydney	WI 181 – Pak 2/183	Wasim Akram	C.L. Hooper
16 Jan 97 Australia v Pakistan – Aus won by 3 wickets	Melbourne	Pak 9/181 – Aus 7/182	M.A. Taylor	Wasim Akram

Final

MATCH	VENUE	SCORES	CAPTAIN	CAPTAIN
18 Jan 97 Pakistan v West Indies – Pak won by 4 wickets	Sydney	WI 9/179 – Pak 6/185	Wasim Akram	C.A. Walsh
20 Jan 97 Pakistan v West Indies – Pak won by 62 runs	Melbourne	Pak 165 – WI 103	Wasim Akram	C.A. Walsh

Series winner: Pakistan

1996/97 – Mohinder Armanath Benefit Match

MATCH	VENUE	SCORES	CAPTAIN	CAPTAIN
14 Dec 96 India v South Africa – Ind won by 74 runs	Mumbai (WS)	Ind 6/267 – SAF 193	S.R. Tendulkar	W.J. Cronje

Series winner: India 1-0

1996/97 – Zimbabwe v England

MATCH	VENUE	SCORES	CAPTAIN	CAPTAIN
15 Dec 96 Zimbabwe v England – Zim won by 2 wickets	Bulawayo (QS)	Eng 152 – Zim 8/153	A.D.R. Campbell	M. Atherton
1 Jan 97 Zimbabwe v England – Zim won by 6 runs+	Harare	Zim 200 – Eng 7/179	A.D.R. Campbell	M. Atherton
3 Jan 97 Zimbabwe v England – Zim won by 131 runs	Harare	Zim 7/249 – Eng 118	A.D.R. Campbell	M. Atherton

Series winner: Zimbabwe 3-0

1996/97 – Standard Bank International Series

Qualifying matches

MATCH	VENUE	SCORES	CAPTAIN	CAPTAIN
23 Jan 97 South Africa v India – SAF won by 39 runs	Bloemfontein	SAF 4/230 – Ind 231	W.J. Cronje	S.R. Tendulkar
25 Jan 97 South Africa v Zimbabwe – SAF won b 5 wickets	Centurion	Zim 211 – SAF 5/212	W.J. Cronje	A.D.R. Campbell
27 Jan 97 India v Zimbabwe – Match tied	Paarl	Zim 8/236 – Ind 236	S.R. Tendulkar	A.D.R. Campbell
29 Jan 97 South Africa v Zimbabwe – SAF won by 5 wickets	Cape Town	Zim 6/226 – SAF 5/229	W.J. Cronje	A.D.R. Campbell
31 Jan 97 South Africa v Zimbabwe – SAF won by 4 wickets	Johannesburg	Zim 8/256 – SAF 6/259	W.J. Cronje	A.D.R. Campbell
2 Feb 97 South Africa v India – SAF won by 6 wickets	Port Elizabeth	Ind 9/179 – SAF 4/180	W.J. Cronje	S.R. Tendulkar
4 Feb 97 South Africa v India – SAF won by 6 wickets	East London	Ind 5/232 – SAF 4/236	W.J. Cronje	S.R. Tendulkar
7 Feb 97 India v Zimbabwe – Zim won on run-rate	Centurion	Ind 216 – Zim 7/171	S.R. Tendulkar	A.D.R. Campbell
9 Feb 97 India v Zimbabwe – Ind won by 6 wickets	Benoni	Zim 8/240 – Ind 4/241	S.R. Tendulkar	A.D.R. Campbell

MATCH	VENUE	SCORES	CAPTAIN	CAPTAIN
Finals				
12 Feb 97 South Africa v India – No result	Durban	Ind 9/191 – SAF 1/42	W.J. Cronje	S.R. Tendulkar
13 Feb 97 South Africa v India – SAF won by 17 runs†	Durban	SAF 8/278 – Ind 234	W.J. Cronje	S.R. Tendulkar
Series winner: South Africa				
1996/97 – Zimbabwe v India				
15 Feb 97 Zimbabwe v India – Zim won on run-rate	Bulawayo (QS)	Ind 168 – Zim 2/139	A.D.R. Campbell	S.R. Tendulkar
Series winner: Zimbabwe 1-0				
1996/97 – New Zealand v England				
20 Feb 97 New Zealand v England – Eng won by 4 wickets	Christchurch	NZ 6/222 – Eng 6/226	L.K. Germon	M. Atherton
23 Feb 97 New Zealand v England – Eng won on run-rate	Auckland	NZ 8/253 – Eng 4/134	L.K. Germon	N. Hussain
26 Feb 97 New Zealand v England – Match tied	Napier	NZ 237 – Eng 8/237	L.K. Germon	M. Atherton
2 Mar 97 New Zealand v England – NZ won by 9 runs	Auckland	NZ 153 – Eng 144	L.K. Germon	M. Atherton
4 Mar 97 New Zealand v England – NZ won by 28 runs	Wellington	NZ 8/228 – Eng 200	L.K. Germon	M. Atherton
Series drawn 2-2				
1996/97 – New Zealand v Sri Lanka				
25 Mar 97 New Zealand v Sri Lanka – SL won by 6 wickets	Christchurch	NZ 9/201 – SL 4/202	S.P. Fleming	A. Ranatunga
27 Mar 97 New Zealand v Sri Lanka – NZ won by 69 runs	Wellington	NZ 201 – SI 132	S.P. Fleming	A. Ranatunga
Series drawn 1-1				
1996/97 – South Africa v Australia				
29 Mar 97 South Africa v Australia – SAF won by 6 wickets	East London	Aus 9/223 – SAF 4/227	W.J. Cronje	M.A. Taylor
31 Mar 97 South Africa v Australia – Aus won by 7 wickets	Port Elizabeth	SAF 8/221 – Aus 3/222	W.J. Cronje	M.A. Taylor
2 Apr 97 South Africa v Australia – SAF won by 64 runs	Cape Town	SAF 8/245 – Aus 9/199	W.J. Cronje	I.A. Healy
5 Apr 97 South Africa v Australia – Aus won by 15 runs	Durban	Aus 9/211 – SAF 196	W.J. Cronje	I.A. Healy
8 Apr 97 South Africa v Australia – Aus won by 8 runs	Johannesburg	Aus 7/258 – SAF 8/250	W.J. Cronje	I.A. Healy
10 Apr 97 South Africa v Australia – Aus won by 5 wickets	Centurion	SAF 7/284 – Aus 5/287	W.J. Cronje	I.A. Healy
13 Apr 97 South Africa v Australia – SAF won by 109 runs	Bloemfontein	SAF 6/310 – Aus 201	W.J. Cronje	S.R. Waugh
Series winner: Australia 4-3				
1996/97 – Singer-Akai Cup				
Qualifying matches				
3 Apr 97 Sri Lanka v Zimbabwe – SL won by 7 wickets	Sharjah	Zim 9/187 – SL 3/188	A. Ranatunga	A.D.R. Campbell
4 Apr 97 Pakistan v Sri Lanka – SL won by 19 runs	Sharjah	SL 8/243 – Pak 9/224	Wasim Akram	A. Ranatunga
6 Apr 97 Pakistan v Zimbabwe – Pak won by 93 runs	Sharjah	Pak 187 – Zim 94	Wasim Akram	A.D.R. Campbell
7 Apr 97 Pakistan v Sri Lanka – SL won by 51 runs	Sharjah	SL 7/251 – Pak 200	Wasim Akram	A. Ranatunga
8 Apr 97 Sri Lanka v Zimbabwe – Zim won by 50 runs	Sharjah	Zim 203 – SL 153	A. Ranatunga	A.D.R. Campbell
9 Apr 97 Pakistan v Zimbabwe – Pak won by 32 runs	Sharjah	Pak 9/151 – Zim 119	Wasim Akram	A.D.R. Campbell

MATCH	VENUE	SCORES	CAPTAIN	CAPTAIN
Final				
11 Apr 97 Pakistan v Sri Lanka – SL won by 4 wickets	Sharjah	Pak 214 – SL 6/215	Wasim Akram	A. Ranatunga
Series winner: Sri Lanka				
1996/97 – West Indies v India				
26 Apr 97 West Indies v India – WI won on run-rate	Port-of-Spain	Ind 179 – WI 2/149	C.A. Walsh	S.R. Tendulkar
27 Apr 97 West Indies v India – Ind won on run-rate	Port-of-Spain	WI 121 – Ind 0/116	C.A. Walsh	S.R. Tendulkar
30 Apr 97 West Indies v India – WI won by 18 runs	Kingstown	WI 9/249 – Ind 231	C.A. Walsh	S.R. Tendulkar
3 May 97 West Indies v India – WI won by 10 wickets	Bridgetown	Ind 7/199 – WI 0/200	C.A. Walsh	S.R. Tendulkar
Series winner: West Indies 3-1				
1996/97 – Pepsi Independence Cup				
Qualifying matches				
9 May 97 New Zealand v Pakistan – NZ won by 22 runs	Mohali	NZ 7/285 – Pak 9/263	S.P. Fleming	Ramiz Raja
12 May 97 Pakistan v Sri Lanka – Pak won by 30 runs	Gwalior	Pak 6/289 – SL 259	Ramiz Raja	A. Ranatunga
14 May 97 India v New Zealand – Ind won by 8 wickets	Bangalore	NZ 9/220 – Ind 2/221	S.R. Tendulkar	S.P. Fleming
17 May 97 India v Sri Lanka – SL won by 5 wickets	Mumbai (WS)	Ind 7/225 – SL 5/229	S.R. Tendulkar	A. Ranatunga
20 May 97 New Zealand v Sri Lanka – SL won by 52 runs	Hyderabad (I)	SL 214 – NZ 162	S.P. Fleming	A. Ranatunga
21 May 97 India v Pakistan – Pak won by 35 runs	Chennai	Pak 5/327 – Ind 292	S.R. Tendulkar	Ramiz Raja
Finals				
24 May 97 Pakistan v Sri Lanka – SL won by 115 runs	Mohali	SL 4/339 – Pak 224	Ramiz Raja	A. Ranatunga
27 May 97 Pakistan v Sri Lanka – SL won by 85 runs	Calcutta	SL 309 – Pak 224	Ramiz Raja	A. Ranatunga
Series winner: Sri Lanka				
1997 – Texaco Trophy				
22 May 97 England v Australia – Eng won by 6 wickets	Leeds	Aus 8/170 – Eng 4/175	M.A. Atherton	M.A. Taylor
24 May 97 England v Australia – Eng won by 6 wickets	The Oval	Aus 6/249 – Eng 4/253	M.A. Atherton	M.A. Taylor
25 May 97 England v Australia – Eng won by 6 wickets	Lord's	Aus 269 – Eng 4/270	M.A. Atherton	S.R. Waugh
Series winner: England 3-0				
1996/97 – West Indies v Sri Lanka				
6 Jun 97 West Indies v Sri Lanka – WI won by 35 runs	Port-of-Spain	WI 7/283 – SL 8/248	C.A. Walsh	A. Ranatunga
Series winner: West Indies 1-0				
1997/98 – Pepsi Asia Cup				
Qualifying matches				
14 Jul 97 Sri Lanka v Pakistan – SL won by 15 runs	Colombo (RPS)	SL 239 – Pak 224	Ramiz Raja	A. Ranatunga
16 Jul 97 Bangladesh v Pakistan – Pak won by 109 runs	Colombo (RPS)	Pak 5/319 – Ban 210	Ramiz Raja	Akram Khan
18 Jul 97 Sri Lanka v India – SL won by 6 wickets	Colombo (RPS)	Ind 6/227 – SL 4/231	S.R. Tendulkar	A. Ranatunga
20 Jul 97 India v Pakistan – No result	Colombo (SSC)	Pak 5/30 – Ind DNB	Ramiz Raja	S.R. Tendulkar
22 Jul 97 Sri Lanka v Bangladesh – SL won by 103 runs	Colombo (SSC)	SL 4/196 – Ban 8/193	A. Ranatunga	Akram Khan
24 Jul 97 Bangladesh v India – Ind won by 9 wickets	Colombo (SSC)	Ban 8/130 – Ind 1/132	Akram Khan	S.R. Tendulkar

MATCH	VENUE	SCORES	CAPTAIN	CAPTAIN
Final				
26 Jul 97 Sri Lanka v India – SL won by 8 wickets	Colombo (RPS)	Ind 7/239 – SL 2/240	A. Ranatunga	S.R. Tendulkar
Series winner: Sri Lanka				
1997/98 – Sri Lanka v India				
17 Aug 97 Sri Lanka v India – SL won by 2 runs	Colombo (RPS)	SL 4/302 – Ind 7/300	A. Ranatunga	S.R. Tendulkar
20 Aug 97 Sri Lanka v India – SL won by 7 wickets	Colombo (RPS)	Ind 238 – SL 3/241	A. Ranatunga	S.R. Tendulkar
23 Aug 97 Sri Lanka v India – No result	Colombo (SSC)	Ind 9/291 – SL 6/132	A. Ranatunga	S.R. Tendulkar
24 Aug 97 Sri Lanka v India – SL by 9 runs	Colombo (SSC)	SL 264 – Ind 8/255	A. Ranatunga	S.R. Tendulkar
Series winner: Sri Lanka 3-0				
1997 – Sahara Cup				
13 Sep 97 India v Pakistan – Ind won by 20 runs	Toronto	Ind 208 – Pak 188	S.R. Tendulkar	Ramiz Raja
14 Sep 97 India v Pakistan – Ind won by 7 wickets	Toronto	Pak 116 – Ind 3/117	S.R. Tendulkar	Ramiz Raja
17 Sep 97 India v Pakistan – No result	Toronto	Pak 3/169 – Ind DNB	S.R. Tendulkar	Ramiz Raja
18 Sep 97 India v Pakistan – Ind won by 34 runs	Toronto	Ind 6/182 – Pak 148	S.R. Tendulkar	Ramiz Raja
20 Sep 97 India v Pakistan – Ind won by 7 wickets	Toronto	Pak 6/159 – Ind 3/162	S.R. Tendulkar	Ramiz Raja
21 Sep 97 India v Pakistan – Pak won by 5 wickets	Toronto	Ind 5/250 – Pak 5/251	S.R. Tendulkar	Ramiz Raja
Series winner: India 4-1				
1997/98 – Pakistan v India				
28 Sep 97 Pakistan v India – Pak won by 5 wickets	Hyderabad (P)	Ind 170 – Pak 5/171	Saeed Anwar	S.R. Tendulkar
30 Sep 97 Pakistan v India – Ind won by 4 wickets	Karachi	Pak 4/265 – Ind 6/266	Saeed Anwar	S.R. Tendulkar
2 Oct 97 Pakistan v India – Pak won by 9 wickets	Lahore	Ind 216 – Pak 1/219	Saeed Anwar	S.R. Tendulkar
Series winner: Pakistan 2-1				
1997/98 – Zimbabwe v New Zealand				
1 Oct 97 Zimbabwe v New Zealand – Match tied	Bulawayo (QS)	Zim 8/233 – NZ 9/233	A.D.R. Campbell	S.P. Fleming
4 Oct 97 Zimbabwe v New Zealand – Zim won by 3 wickets	Harare	NZ 7/185 – Zim 7/188	A.D.R. Campbell	S.P. Fleming
5 Oct 97 Zimbabwe v New Zealand – NZ won by 83 runs	Harare	NZ 7/294 – Zim 211	A.D.R. Campbell	S.P. Fleming
Series drawn 1-1				
1997/98 – President's Cup				
Qualifying matches				
10 Oct 97 Kenya v Bangladesh – Ken won by 150 runs	Nairobi (NG)	Ken 3/347 – Ban 197	Aasif Karim	Akram Khan
11 Oct 97 Bangladesh v Zimbabwe – Zim won by 48 runs	Nairobi (NG)	Zim 4/305 – Ban 257	Akram Khan	A.D.R. Campbell
12 Oct 97 Kenya v Zimbabwe – Zim won on run-rate	Nairobi (NG)	Ken 8/249 – Zim 4/244	Aasif Karim	A.D.R. Campbell
14 Oct 97 Bangladesh v Zimbabwe – Zim won by 192 runs	Nairobi (AK)	Zim 284 – Ban 92	Akram Khan	A.D.R. Campbell
15 Oct 97 Kenya v Bangladesh – Ken won by 8 wickets	Nairobi (AK)	Ban 100 – Ken 2/102	Aasif Karim	Akram Khan
16 Oct 97 Kenya v Zimbabwe – Zim won by 7 wickets	Nairobi (AK)	Ken 9/207 – Zim 3/210	Aasif Karim	A.D.R. Campbell

MATCH	VENUE	SCORES	CAPTAIN	CAPTAIN
Finals				
18 Oct 97 Kenya v Zimbabwe – Zim won by 73 runs†	Nairobi (NG)	Zim 8/281 – Ken 7/172	Aasif Karim	A.D.R. Campbell
19 Oct 97 Kenya v Zimbabwe – Zim won by 82 runs	Nairobi (NG)	Zim 6/272 – Ken 190	Aasif Karim	A.D.R. Campbell
Series winner: Zimbabwe				
1997/98 – Wills Quadrangular Tournament				
Qualifying matches				
1 Nov 97 Sri Lanka v West Indies – SL won by 7 wickets	Lahore	WI 8/237 – SL 3/240	A. Ranatunga	C.A. Walsh
2 Nov 97 Pakistan v South Africa – SAF won by 9 runs	Lahore	SAF 271 – Pak 9/262	Wasim Akram	W.J. Cronje
3 Nov 97 South Africa v West Indies – SAF won by 5 wickets	Lahore	WI 8/293 – SAF 5/297	W.J. Cronje	C.A. Walsh
4 Nov 97 Pakistan v West Indies – Pak won by 8 wickets	Lahore	WI 7/215 – Pak 2/219	Wasim Akram	C.A. Walsh
5 Nov 97 Pakistan v Sri Lanka – SL won by 8 wickets	Lahore	Pak 280 – SL 2/281	Wasim Akram	A. Ranatunga
6 Nov 97 South Africa v Sri Lanka – SL won by 66 runs	Lahore	SAF 9/311 – SL 9/245	W.J. Cronje	A. Ranatunga
Final				
8 Nov 97 South Africa v Sri Lanka – SAF won by 4 wickets	Lahore	SL 7/209 – SAF 6/201	W.J. Cronje	A. Ranatunga
Series winner: South Africa				
1997/98 – Carlton & United Series				
Qualifying matches				
4 Dec 97 Australia v South Africa – SAF won by 67 runs	Sydney	SAF 200 – Aus 133	S.R. Waugh	W.J. Cronje
6 Dec 97 New Zealand v South Africa – NZ won by 47 runs	Adelaide	NZ 6/224 – SAF 177	S.P. Fleming	W.J. Cronje
7 Dec 97 Australia v New Zealand – Aus won by 3 wickets	Adelaide	NZ 7/260 – Aus 7/263	S.R. Waugh	S.P. Fleming
9 Dec 97 Australia v South Africa – SAF won by 45 runs	Melbourne	SAF 8/170 – Aus 125	S.R. Waugh	W.J. Cronje
11 Dec 97 New Zealand v South Africa – SAF won by 1 run	Hobart (B)	SAF 9/174 – NZ 7/173	S.P. Fleming	W.J. Cronje
17 Dec 97 Australia v New Zealand – Aus won by 6 wickets	Melbourne	NZ 141 – Aus 4/142	S.R. Waugh	S.P. Fleming
9 Jan 98 New Zealand v South Africa – SAF won by 2 runs	Brisbane	SAF 6/300 – NZ 9/298	S.P. Fleming	W.J. Cronje
11 Jan 98 Australia v South Africa – SAF won by 5 wickets	Brisbane	Aus 8/235 – SAF 5/236	S.R. Waugh	W.J. Cronje
14 Jan 98 Australia v New Zealand – Aus won by 131 runs	Sydney	Aus 250 – NZ 119	S.K. Warne	S.P. Fleming
16 Jan 98 New Zealand v South Africa – SAF won by 67 runs	Perth	SAF 7/233 – NZ 166	S.P. Fleming	W.J. Cronje
18 Jan 98 Australia v South Africa – SAF won by 7 wickets	Perth	Aus 165 – SAF 3/170	S.R. Waugh	W.J. Cronje
21 Jan 98 Australia v New Zealand – NZ won by 4 wickets	Melbourne	Aus 4/251 – NZ 6/253	S.R. Waugh	S.P. Fleming
Finals				
23 Jan 98 Australia v South Africa – SAF won by 6 runs	Melbourne	SAF 9/241 – Aus 235	S.R. Waugh	W.J. Cronje
26 Jan 98 Australia v South Africa – Aus won by 7 wickets	Sydney	SAF 6/228 – Aus 3/229	S.R. Waugh	W.J. Cronje
27 Jan 98 Australia v South Africa – Aus won by 14 runs	Sydney	Aus 7/247 – SAF 233	S.R. Waugh	W.J. Cronje
Series winner: Australia				

MATCH	VENUE	SCORES	CAPTAIN	CAPTAIN
1997/98 – Akai-Singer Champions Trophy				
Qualifying matches				
11 Dec 97 England v India – Eng won by 7 runs	Sharjah	Eng 250 – Ind 243	A.J. Hollioake	S.R. Tendulkar
12 Dec 97 Pakistan v West Indies – WI won by 43 runs	Sharjah	WI 7/275 – Pak 232	Wasim Akram	C.A. Walsh
13 Dec 97 England v West Indies – Eng won by 4 wickets	Sharjah	WI 7/197 – Eng 6/198	A.J. Hollioake	C.A. Walsh
14 Dec 97 India v Pakistan – Pak won by 4 wickets	Sharjah	Ind 7/239 – Pak 6/243	S.R. Tendulkar	Wasim Akram
15 Dec 97 England v Pakistan – Eng won by 8 runs	Sharjah	Eng 9/215 – Pak 207	A.J. Hollioake	Wasim Akram
16 Dec 97 India v West Indies – WI won by 41 runs	Sharjah	WI 6/229 – Ind 188	S.R. Tendulkar	C.A. Walsh
Final				
19 Dec 97 England v West Indies – Eng won by 3 wickets	Sharjah	WI 7/235 – Eng 7/239	A.J. Hollioake	C.A. Walsh
Series winner: England				
1997/98 – India v Sri Lanka				
22 Dec 97 India v Sri Lanka – Ind won by 7 wickets	Gauhati	SL 9/172 – Ind 3/173	S.R. Tendulkar	A. Ranatunga
25 Dec 97 India v Sri Lanka – No result	Indore	SL 1/17 – Ind DNB	S.R. Tendulkar	A. Ranatunga
28 Dec 97 India v Sri Lanka – Sri Lanka won by 5 wickets	Margao	Ind 6/228 – SL 5/229	S.R. Tendulkar	A. Ranatunga
Series drawn 1-1				
1997/98 – Silver Jubilee Independence Cup				
Qualifying matches				
10 Jan 98 Bangladesh v India – Ind won by 4 wickets	Dhaka	Ban 190 – Ind 6/191	Akram Khan	M.A. Azharuddin
11 Jan 98 India v Pakistan – Ind won by 18 runs	Dhaka	Ind 7/245 – Pak 9/227	M.A. Azharuddin	Rashid Latif
12 Jan 98 Bangladesh v Pakistan – Pak won by 9 wickets	Dhaka	Ban 134 – Pak 1/136	Akram Khan	Rashid Latif
Finals				
14 Jan 98 India v Pakistan – Ind won by 8 wickets	Dhaka	Pak 8/212 – Ind 2/213	M.A. Azharuddin	Rashid Latif
16 Jan 98 India v Pakistan – Pak won by 6 wickets	Dhaka	Ind 189 – Pak 4/193	M.A. Azharuddin	Rashid Latif
18 Jan 98 India v Pakistan – Ind won by 3 wickets	Dhaka	Pak 5/314 – Ind 7/316	M.A. Azharuddin	Rashid Latif
Series winner: India				
1997/98 – Sri Lanka v Zimbabwe				
22 Jan 98 Sri Lanka v Zimbabwe – SL won by 5 wickets	Colombo (SSC)	Zim 207 – SL 5/210	A. Ranatunga	A.D.R. Campbell
24 Jan 98 Sri Lanka v Zimbabwe – SL won by 5 wickets	Colombo (PSS)	Zim 8/212 – SL 5/213	A. Ranatunga	A.D.R. Campbell
26 Jan 98 Sri Lanka v Zimbabwe – SL won by 4 wickets	Colombo (SSC)	Zim 6/281 – SL 6/286	S.T. Jayasuriya	A.D.R. Campbell
Series winner: Sri Lanka 3-0				
1997/98 – New Zealand v Zimbabwe				
4 Feb 98 New Zealand v Zimbabwe – NZ won by 40 runs	Hamilton	NZ 7/248 – Zim 208	S.P. Fleming	A.D.R. Campbell
6 Feb 98 New Zealand v Zimbabwe – NZ won by 8 wickets	Wellington	Zim 138 – NZ 2/139	S.P. Fleming	A.D.R. Campbell
4 Mar 98 New Zealand v Zimbabwe – Zim won by 1 run	Christchurch	Zim 7/228 – NZ 9/227	S.P. Fleming	A.D.R. Campbell
6 Mar 98 New Zealand v Zimbabwe – NZ won by 9 wickets	Napier	Zim 8/207 – NZ 1/211	S.P. Fleming	A.D.R. Campbell

MATCH	VENUE	SCORES	CAPTAIN	CAPTAIN
8 Mar 98 New Zealand v Zimbabwe – NZ won by 2 runs	Auckland	NZ 9/231 – Zim 9/229	S.P. Fleming	A.D.R. Campbell
Series winner: New Zealand 4-1				
1997/98 – New Zealand v Australia				
8 Feb 98 New Zealand v Australia – Aus won by 7 wickets	Christchurch	NZ 7/212 – Aus 3/215	S.P. Fleming	S.R. Waugh
10 Feb 98 New Zealand v Australia – Aus won by 66 runs	Wellington	Aus 6/297 – NZ 231	S.P. Fleming	S.R. Waugh
12 Feb 98 New Zealand v Australia – NZ won by 7 wickets	Napier	Aus 236 – NZ 3/240	S.P. Fleming	S.R. Waugh
14 Feb 98 New Zealand v Australia – NZ won by 30 runs	Auckland	NZ 7/223 – Aus 193	S.P. Fleming	S.R. Waugh
Series drawn 2-2				
1997/98 – Zimbabwe v Pakistan				
28 Mar 98 Zimbabwe v Pakistan – Pak won by 4 wickets	Harare	Zim 6/236 – Pak 6/237	A.D.R. Campbell	Rashid Latif
29 Mar 98 Zimabwe v Pakistan – Pak won by 4 wickets	Harare	Zim 4/272 – Pak 6/276	A.D.R. Campbell	Rashid Latif
Series winner: Pakistan 2-0				
1997/98 – West Indies v England				
29 Mar 98 West Indies v England – Eng won by 16 runs	Bridgetown	Eng 5/293 – WI 277	B.C. Lara	A.J. Hollioake
1 Apr 98 West Indies v England – WI won by 1 wicket	Bridgetown	Eng 266 – WI 9/267	B.C. Lara	A.J. Hollioake
4 Apr 98 West Indies v England – WI won by 5 wickets	Kingstown	Eng 8/209 – WI 5/213	B.C. Lara	A.J. Hollioake
5 Apr 98 West Indies v England – WI won by 4 wickets	Kingstown	Eng 149 – WI 6/150	B.C. Lara	A.J. Hollioake
8 Apr 98 West Indies v England – WI won by 57 runs	Port-of-Spain	WI 5/302 – Eng 245	B.C. Lara	A.J. Hollioake
Series winner: West Indies 4-1				
1997/98 – Pepsi Triangular Tournament				
Qualifying matches				
1 Apr 98 India v Australia – Ind won by 41 runs	Kochi	Ind 5/309 – Aus 268	M.A. Azharuddin	S.R. Waugh
3 Apr 98 Australia v Zimbabwe – Aus won by 13 runs	Ahmedabad (SP)	Aus 7/252 – Zim 239	S.R. Waugh	A.D.R. Campbell
5 Apr 98 India v Zimbabwe – Ind won by 13 runs	Vadodara (IPCL)	Ind 5/274 – Zim 261	M.A. Azharuddin	A.D.R. Campbell
7 Apr 98 India v Australia – Ind won by 6 wickets	Kanpur	Aus 9/222 – Ind 4/223	M.A. Azharuddin	S.R. Waugh
9 Apr 98 India v Zimbabwe – Ind won by 32 runs	Cuttack	Ind 3/301 – Zim 269	M.A. Azharuddin	A.D.R. Campbell
11 Apr 98 Australia v Zimbabwe – Aus won by 16 runs	Delhi	Aus 3/294 – Zim 9/278	S.R. Waugh	A.D.R. Campbell
Final				
14 Apr 98 India v Australia – Aus won by 4 wickets	Delhi	Ind 227 – Aus 6/231	M.A. Azharuddin	S.R. Waugh
Series winner: Australia				
1997/98 – Standard Bank International Series				
Qualifying matches				
3 Apr 98 South Africa v Pakistan – SAF won by 52 runs	Durban	SAF 4/280 – Pak 228	W.J. Cronje	Aamer Sohail
5 Apr 98 South Africa v Sri Lanka – SAF won by 57 runs	Johannesburg	SAF 8/266 – SL 209	W.J. Cronje	A. Ranatunga
7 Apr 98 Pakistan v Sri Lanka – Pak won by 4 wickets	Kimberley	SL 7/295 – Pak 6/300	Rashid Latif	A. Ranatunga

MATCH	VENUE	SCORES	CAPTAIN	CAPTAIN
9 Apr 98 Pakistan v Sri Lanka – Pak won by 110 runs	Paarl	Pak 249 – SL 139	Rashid Latif	A. Ranatunga
11 Apr 98 South Africa v Pakistan – SAF won by 3 wickets	East London	Pak 8/250 – SAF 7/254	W.J. Cronje	Rashid Latif
13 Apr 98 South Africa v Sri Lanka – SL won by 6 wickets	Port Elizabeth	SAF 231 – SL 4/232	W.J. Cronje	A. Ranatunga
15 Apr 98 Pakistan v Sri Lanka – SL won by 115 runs	Benoni	SL 288 – Pak 173	Rashid Latif	A. Ranatunga
17 Apr 98 South Africa v Pakistan – SAF won by 7 wickets	Centurion	Pak 145 – SAF 3/149	W.J. Cronje	Rashid Latif
19 Apr 98 South Africa v Sri Lanka – SAF won by 5 wickets	Bloemfontein	SL 105 – SAF 5/106	W.J. Cronje	A. Ranatunga

Final

MATCH	VENUE	SCORES	CAPTAIN	CAPTAIN
22 Apr 98 South Africa v Pakistan – SAF won by 9 wickets	Cape Town	Pak 114 – SAF 1/115	W.J. Cronje	Rashid Latif

Series winner: South Africa

1997/98 – Sharjah Cup

Qualifying matches

MATCH	VENUE	SCORES	CAPTAIN	CAPTAIN
17 Apr 98 India v New Zealand – Ind won by 15 runs	Sharjah	Ind 9/220 – NZ 205	M.A. Azharuddin	S.P. Fleming
18 Apr 98 Australia v New Zealand – Aus won by 6 wickets	Sharjah	NZ 159 – Aus 4/160	S.R. Waugh	S.P. Fleming
19 Apr 98 Australia v India – Aus won by 58 runs	Sharjah	Aus 9/264 – Ind 206	S.R. Waugh	M.A. Azharuddin
20 Apr 98 India v New Zealand – NZ won by 4 wickets	Sharjah	Ind 181 – NZ 6/183	M.A. Azharuddin	S.P. Fleming
21 Apr 98 Australia v New Zealand – NZ won by 5 wickets	Sharjah	NZ 5/259 – Aus 5/261	S.R. Waugh	S.P. Fleming
22 Apr 98 Australia v India – Aus won by 26 runs+	Sharjah	Aus 7/284 – Ind 5/250	S.R. Waugh	M.A. Azharuddin

Final

MATCH	VENUE	SCORES	CAPTAIN	CAPTAIN
24 Apr 98 Australia v India – Ind won by 6 wickets	Sharjah	Aus 9/272 – Ind 4/275	S.R. Waugh	M.A. Azharuddin

Series winner: India

1997/98 Coca-Cola Triangular Tournament

Qualifying matches

MATCH	VENUE	SCORES	CAPTAIN	CAPTAIN
14 May 98 India v Bangladesh – Ind won by 5 wickets	Mohali	Ban 9/184 – Ind 5/185	M.A. Azharuddin	Amin-ul Islam
17 May 98 Bangladesh v Kenya – Ban won by 6 wickets	Hyderabad (I)	Ken 235 – Ban 4/236	Akram Khan	Asif Karim
20 May 98 India v Kenya – Ind won by 4 wickets	Bangalore	Ken 9/223 – Ind 6/224	A.D. Jadeja	Asif Karim
23 May 98 Bangladesh v Kenya – Ken won by 28 runs	Chennai	Ken 8/226 – Ban 198	Akram Khan	Asif Karim
25 May 98 India v Bangladesh – Ind won by 5 wickets	Mumbai (WS)	Ban 115-Ind 5/116	A.D. Jadeja	Akram Khan
28 May 98 India v Kenya – Ken won by 69 runs	Gwalior	Ken 5/265 – Ind 196	M.A. Azharuddin	Asif Karim

Final

MATCH	VENUE	SCORES	CAPTAIN	CAPTAIN
31 May 98 India v Kenya-Ind won by 9 wickets	Calcutta	Ken 196-Ind 1-197	M.A. Azharuddin	Asif Karim

Series winner: India

1998 – Texaco Trophy

Qualifying matches

MATCH	VENUE	SCORES	CAPTAIN	CAPTAIN
21 May 98 England v South Africa – SAF won by 3 wickets	The Oval	Eng 9/223 – SAF 7/224	A.J. Hollioake	W.J. Cronje
23 May 98 England v South Africa – SAF won by 30 runs	Manchester	SAF 9/226 – Eng 194	A.J. Hollioake	W.J. Cronje
24 May 98 England v South Africa – Eng won by 7 wickets	Leeds	SAF 5/208 – Eng 3/206	A.J. Hollioake	W.J. Cronje

Series winner: South Africa 2-1

MATCH	VENUE	SCORES	CAPTAIN	CAPTAIN
1997/98 Nidahas (Independence) Cup				
Qualifying matches				
19 Jun 98 Sri Lanka v India – Ind won by 8 wickets	Colombo (RPS)	SL 6/243 – Ind 2/246	A. Ranatunga	M.A. Azaruddin
21 Jun 98 Sri Lanka v New Zealand – SL won by 7 wickets	Colombo (RPS)	NZ 9/200 – SL 3/201	A. Ranatunga	S.P. Fleming
23 Jun 98 India v New Zealand – No result	Colombo (RPS)	NZ 8/219 – Ind 2/131	M.A. Azaruddin	S.P. Fleming
1 Jul 98 Sri Lanka v India – SL won by 8 runs	Colombo (SSC)	SL 8/171 – Ind 163	A. Ranatunga	M.A. Azaruddin
3 Jul 98 India v New Zealand – No result	Colombo (SSC)	NZ 5/128 – Ind DNB	M.A. Azaruddin	S.P. Fleming
5 Jul 98 Sri Lanka v New Zealand – SL won by 87 runs	Colombo (SSC)	SL 4/293 – NZ 206	A. Ranatunga	S.P. Fleming
Final				
7 Jul 98 Sri Lanka v India — Ind won by 6 runs	Colombo (RPS)	Ind 6/307 SL 301	A. Ranatunga	M.A. Azaruddin
Series winner: India				
1998 Emirates Triangular Tournament				
Qualifying matches				
14 Aug 98 South Africa v Sri Lanka – SL won by 57 runs	Nottingham	SL 258 – SAF 201	W.J. Cronje	A. Ranatunga
16 Aug 98 England v Sri Lanka – Eng won by 36 runs	The Oval	Eng 247 – SL 211	A.J. Stewart	A. Ranatunga
18 Aug 98 England v South Africa – SAF won by 14 runs	Birmingham	SAF 7/244 – Eng 230	A.J. Stewart	W.J. Cronje
Final				
20 Aug 98 England v Sri Lanka – SL won by 5 wickets	Lord's	Eng 8/256 – SL 5/260	A.J. Stewart	A. Ranatunga
Series winner: Sri Lanka				
1998– Sahara Cup				
12 Sep 98 India v Pakistan – Ind won by 6 wickets	Toronto	Pak 9/189 – Ind 4/193	M.A. Azaruddin	Aamir Sohail
13 Sep 98 India v Pakistan – Pak won by 51 runs	Toronto	Pak 9/246 – Ind 195	M.A. Azaruddin	Aamir Sohail
16 Sep 98 India v Pakistan – Pak won by 77 runs	Toronto	Pak 5/257 – Ind 180	M.A. Azaruddin	Aamir Sohail
19 Sep 98 India v Pakistan – Pak won by 134 runs	Toronto	Pak 6/316 – Ind 182	M.A. Azaruddin	Aamir Sohail
20 Sep 98 India v Pakistan – Pak won by 5 wickets	Toronto	Ind 9/256 – Pak 5/258	M.A. Azaruddin	Aamir Sohail
Series winner: Pakistan 4-1				
1998/99 – Hero Honda Series				
26 Sep 98 Zimbabwe v India – Ind won by 8 wickets	Bulawayo (QS)	Zim 213 – Ind 2/216	A.D.R. Campbell	M.A. Azaruddin
27 Sep 98 Zimbabwe v India – Ind won by 8 wickets	Bulawayo (QS)	Zim 7/235 – Ind 2/236	A.D.R. Campbell	M.A. Azaruddin
30 Sep 98 Zimbabwe v India – Zim won by 37 runs	Harare	Zim 5/259 – Ind 222	A.D.R. Campbell	M.A. Azaruddin
Series winner: India 2-1				
1998/99 – Wills International Cup				
Preliminary Quarter-final				
24 Oct 98 New Zealand v Zimbabwe – NZ won by 5 wickets	Dhaka	Zim 7/258 – NZ 5/260	S.P. Fleming	A.D.R. Campbell

MATCH	VENUE	SCORES	CAPTAIN	CAPTAIN
Quarter-finals				
25 Oct 98 England v South Africa – SAF won by 6 wickets	Dhaka	Eng 7/281 – SAF 4/283	A.J. Hollioake	W.J. Cronje
26 Oct 98 New Zealand v Sri Lanka – SL won by 5 wickets	Dhaka	NZ 188 – SL 5/191	S.P. Fleming	A. Ranatunga
28 Oct 98 Australia v India – Ind won by 44 runs	Dhaka	Ind 8/307 – Aus 263	S.R. Waugh	M.A. Azharuddin
29 Oct 98 Pakistan v West Indies – WI won by 30 runs	Dhaka	WI 9/289 – Pak 9/259	Aamir Sohail	B.C. Lara
Semi-finals				
30 Oct 98 South Africa v Sri Lanka – SAF won by 92 runs+	Dhaka	SAF 7-240 – SL 132	W.J. Cronje	A. Ranatunga
31 Oct 98 India v West Indies – WI won by 6 wickets	Dhaka	Ind 6/242 – WI 4/245	M.A. Azharuddin	B.C. Lara
Final				
1 Nov 98 South Africa v West Indies – SAF by 4 wickets	Dhaka	WI 245 – SAF 6/248	W.J. Cronje	B.C. Lara
Series winner: South Africa				
1998/99 – Pakistan v Australia				
6 Nov 98 Pakistan v Australia – Aus won by 86 runs	Karachi	Aus 8/324 – Pak 238	Aamir Sohail	S.R. Waugh
8 Nov 98 Pakistan v Australia – Aus won by 5 wickets	Peshawar	Pak 7/217 – Aus 5/220	Aamir Sohail	S.R. Waugh
10 Nov 98 Pakistan v Australia – Aus won by 6 wickets	Lahore	Pak 8/315 – Aus 4/316	Aamir Sohail	S.R. Waugh
Series winner: Australia 3-0				
1998/99 – Coca-Cola Champions Trophy				
Qualifying matches				
6 Nov 98 India v Sri Lanka – Ind won by 3 wickets	Sharjah	SL 7/245 – Ind 7/248	M.A. Azharuddin	A. Ranatunga
7 Nov 98 Sri Lanka v Zimbabwe – Zim won by 7 wickets	Sharjah	SL 196 – Zim 3/197	A. Ranatunga	A.D.R. Campbell
8 Nov 98 India v Zimbabwe – Ind won by 7 wickets	Sharjah	Zim 196 – Ind 3/197	M.A. Azharuddin	A.D.R. Campbell
9 Nov 98 India v Sri Lanka – Ind won by 81 runs	Sharjah	Ind 179 – SL 98	M.A. Azharuddin	A. Ranatunga
10 Nov 98 Sri Lanka v Zimbabwe – Zim won by 24 runs	Sharjah	Zim 7/259 – SL 235	A. Ranatunga	A.D.R. Campbell
11 Nov 98 India v Zimbabwe – Zim won by 13 runs	Sharjah	Zim 7/205 – Ind 192	A.D. Jadeja	A.D.R. Campbell
Final				
13 Nov 98 India v Zimbabwe – Ind won by 10 wickets	Sharjah	Zim 9/196 – Ind 3/197	M.A. Azharuddin	A.D.R. Campbell
Series winner: India				
1998/99 – Pakistan v Zimbabwe				
20 Nov 98 Pakistan v Zimbabwe – Pak won by 4 wickets	Gujranwala	Zim 237 – Pak 6/241	Aamir Sohail	A.D.R. Campbell
22 Nov 98 Pakistan v Zimbabwe – Zim won by 6 wickets	Sheikupura	Pak 211 – Zim 4/212	Aamir Sohail	A.D.R. Campbell
24 Nov 98 Pakistan v Zimbabwe – Pak won by 111 runs	Rawalpindi (RC)	Pak 6/302 – Zim 191	Aamir Sohail	A.D.R. Campbell
Series winner: Pakistan 2-1				

MATCH

1998/99 — New Zealand v India

MATCH	VENUE	SCORES	CAPTAIN	CAPTAIN
9 Jan 99 New Zealand v India – NZ won on run-rate	Taupo	Ind 5/257 – NZ 5/200	S.P. Fleming	M.A. Azharuddin
12 Jan 99 New Zealand v India – Ind won by 2 wickets	Napier	NZ 213 – Ind 8/214	D.J. Nash	M.A. Azharuddin
14 Jan 99 New Zealand v India – No result	Wellington	Ind 4/208 – NZ 2/89	D.J. Nash	M.A. Azharuddin
16 Jan 99 New Zealand v India – Ind won by 5 wickets	Auckland	NZ 7/207 – Ind 5/208	D.J. Nash	M.A. Azharuddin
19 Jan 99 New Zealand v India – NZ won by 70 runs	Christchurch	NZ 8/300 – Ind 230	D.J. Nash	M.A. Azharuddin

Series drawn 2-2

1998/99 — Carlton & United Series

Qualifying matches

MATCH	VENUE	SCORES	CAPTAIN	CAPTAIN
10 Jan 99 Australia v England – Eng won by 7 runs+	Brisbane	Eng 8/178 – Aus 9/145	S.K. Warne	A.J. Stewart
11 Jan 99 England v Sri Lanka – Eng won by 4 wickets	Brisbane	SL 7/207 – Eng 6/208	A.J. Stewart	A. Ranatunga
13 Jan 99 Australia v Sri Lanka – Aus won by 8 wickets	Sydney	SL 9/259 – Aus 2/260	S.K. Warne	A. Ranatunga
15 Jan 99 Australia v England – Aus won by 9 wickets	Melbourne	Eng 178 – Aus 1/182	S.K. Warne	A.J. Stewart
17 Jan 99 Australia v England – Eng won by 7 runs	Sydney	Eng 4/282 – Aus 6/275	S.R. Waugh	A.J. Stewart
19 Jan 99 England v Sri Lanka – Eng won by 7 wickets	Melbourne	SL 186 – Eng 3/189	A.J. Stewart	A. Ranatunga
21 Jan 99 Australia v Sri Lanka – SL won by 3 wickets	Hobart (B)	Aus 9/210 – SL 7/211	S.R. Waugh	A. Ranatunga
23 Jan 99 England v Sri Lanka – SL won by 1 wicket	Adelaide	Eng 3/302 – SL 9/303	A.J. Stewart	A. Ranatunga
24 Jan 99 Australia v Sri Lanka – Aus won by 80 runs	Adelaide	Aus 270 – SL 190	S.K. Warne	A. Ranatunga
26 Jan 99 Australia v England – Aus won by 16 runs	Adelaide	Aus 8/239 – Eng 223	S.K. Warne	A.J. Stewart
29 Jan 99 England v Sri Lanka – Eng won by 128 runs	Perth	Eng 7/227 – SL 99	A.J. Stewart	A. Ranatunga
31 Jan 99 Australia v Sri Lanka – Aus won by 45 runs	Perth	Aus 7/274 – SL 229	S.K. Warne	A. Ranatunga
3 Feb 99 England v Sri Lanka – SL won by 11 runs	Sydney	SL 7/181 – Eng 9/170	A.J. Hollioake	A. Ranatunga
5 Feb 99 Australia v England – Aus won by 4 wickets	Sydney	Eng 8/210 – Aus 6/211	S.K. Warne	A.J. Stewart
7 Feb 99 Australia v Sri Lanka – Aus won by 43 runs	Melbourne	Aus 8/310 – SL 267	S.K. Warne	A. Ranatunga

Finals

MATCH	VENUE	SCORES	CAPTAIN	CAPTAIN
10 Feb 99 Australia v England – Aus won by 10 runs	Sydney	Aus 8/232 – Eng 222	S.K. Warne	A.J. Stewart
13 Feb 99 Australia v England – Aus won by 162 runs	Melbourne	Aus 5/272 – Eng 110	S.K. Warne	A.J. Stewart

Series winner: Australia

1998/99 — South Africa v West Indies

MATCH	VENUE	SCORES	CAPTAIN	CAPTAIN
22 Jan 99 South Africa v West Indies – SAF won on run-rate	Johannesburg	WI 4/154 – SAF 8/160	W.J. Cronje	B.C. Lara
24 Jan 99 South Africa v West Indies – WI won by 43 runs	East London	WI 9/292 – SAF 249	W.J. Cronje	B.C. Lara
27 Jan 99 South Africa v West Indies – SAF won by 55 runs	Durban	SAF 9/274 – WI 219	W.J. Cronje	B.C. Lara
30 Jan 99 South Africa v West Indies – SAF won by 99 runs	Port Elizabeth	SAF 6/278 – WI 179	W.J. Cronje	C.L. Hooper
2 Feb 99 South Africa v West Indies – SAF won by 89 runs	Cape Town	SAF 8/221 – WI 132	W.J. Cronje	C.L. Hooper
5 Feb 99 South Africa v West Indies – SAF won by 114 runs	Bloemfontein	SAF 273 – WI 159	W.J. Cronje	C.L. Hooper
7 Feb 99 South Africa v West Indies – SAF won by 50 runs	Centurion	SAF 8/226 – WI 176	W.J. Cronje	B.C. Lara

Series winner: South Africa 6-1

The Teams

SUMMARY OF LIMITED-OVERS INTERNATIONALS

Country	First Match	M	Won	Lost	NR	Tied	Win%
Australia	5 Jan 1971, Melbourne	418	229	174	11	4	56
Bangladesh	31 Mar 1986, Moratuwa	25	1	24	0	0	4
Canada	9 Jun 1979, Leeds	3	0	3	0	0	-
East Africa	7 Jun 1975, Birmingham	3	0	3	0	0	-
England	5 Jan 1971, Melbourne	292	147	135	8	2	52
India	13 Jul 1974, Leeds	387	173	193	17	4	47
Kenya	18 Feb 1996, Cuttack	20	5	14	1	0	26
Netherlands	17 Feb 1996, Vadodara (IPCL)	5	0	5	0	0	-
New Zealand	11 Feb 1973, Christchurch	316	129	170	13	4	43
Pakistan	11 Feb 1973, Christchurch	414	209	188	10	7	52
South Africa	10 Nov 1991, Calcutta	157	98	56	3	0	64
Sri Lanka	7 Jun 1975, Manchester	293	109	170	13	1	39
UAE	13 Apr 1994, Sharjah	7	1	6	0	0	14
West Indies	5 Sep 1973, Leeds	360	222	128	6	4	63
Zimbabwe	9 Jun 1983, Nottingham	112	26	80	2	4	24
Total		**1406**	**1349**	**1349**	**42**	**15**	**96**

Note: Win % exclude no result matches (NR).

SUMMARY OF LIMITED-OVERS INTERNATIONALS BY COUNTRY

Australia

Versus	First Match	M	Won	Lost	NR	Tied	Win%
Bangladesh	30 Apr 1990, Sharjah	1	1	0	0	0	100
Canada	16 Jun 1979, Birmingham	1	1	0	0	0	100
England	5 Jan 1971, Melbourne	67	34	31	1	1	52
India	6 Dec 1980, Melbourne	54	29	22	3	0	57
Kenya	23 Feb 1996, Visag	1	1	0	0	0	100
New Zealand	30 Mar 1974, Dunedin	73	51	20	2	0	72
Pakistan	7 Jun 1975, Leeds	49	25	20	2	2	53
South Africa	26 Feb 1992, Sydney	37	18	19	0	0	49
Sri Lanka	11 Jun 1975, The Oval	40	26	12	2	0	68
West Indies	14 Jun 1975, The Oval	84	33	49	1	1	40
Zimbabwe	9 Jun 1983, Nottingham	11	10	1	0	0	91
Total		**418**	**229**	**174**	**11**	**4**	**56**

Bangladesh

Versus	First Match	M	Won	Lost	NR	Tied	Win%
Australia	30 Apr 1990, Sharjah	1	0	1	0	0	-
India	27 Oct 1988, Chittagong	7	0	7	0	0	-
Kenya	10 Oct 1997, Nairobi (NG)	4	1	3	0	0	25
New Zealand	28 Apr 1990, Sharjah	1	0	1	0	0	-
Pakistan	31 Mar 1986, Moratuwa	5	0	5	0	0	-
Sri Lanka	2 April 1986, Kandy	5	0	5	0	0	-
Zimbabwe	11 Oct 1997, Nairobi (NG)	2	0	2	0	0	-
Total		**25**	**1**	**24**	**0**	**0**	**4**

Canada

Versus	First Match	M	Won	Lost	NR	Tied	Win%
Australia	16 Jun 1979, Birmingham	1	0	1	0	0	-
England	13 Jun 1979, Manchester	1	0	1	0	0	-
Pakistan	9 Jun 1979, Leeds	1	0	1	0	0	-
Total		**3**	**0**	**3**	**0**	**0**	**-**

East Africa

Versus	First Match	M	Won	Lost	NR	Tied	Win%
England	14 Jun 1975, Birmingham	1	0	1	0	0	-
India	11 Jun 1975, Leeds	1	0	1	0	0	-
New Zealand	7 Jun 1975, Birmingham	1	0	1	0	0	-
Total		3	0	3	0	0	-

England

Versus	First Match	M	Won	Lost	NR	Tied	Win%
Australia	5 Jan 1971, Melbourne	67	31	34	1	1	47
Canada	13 Jun 1979, Manchester	1	1	0	0	0	100
East Africa	14 Jun 1975, Birmingham	1	1	0	0	0	100
India	13 Jul 1974, Leeds	33	19	13	1	0	59
Netherlands	22 Feb 1996, Peshawar	1	1	0	0	0	100
New Zealand	18 Jul 1973, Swansea	47	23	20	3	1	52
Pakistan	31 Aug 1974, Nottingham	41	26	14	1	0	65
South Africa	12 Mar 1992, Melbourne	17	6	11	0	0	35
Sri Lanka	13 Feb 1982, Colombo (SSC)	19	12	7	0	0	63
UAE	18 Feb 1996, Peshawar	1	1	0	0	0	100
West Indies	5 Sep 1973, Leeds	58	25	31	2	0	45
Zimbabwe	18 Mar 1992, Albury	6	1	5	0	0	17
Total		292	147	135	8	2	52

India

Versus	First Match	M	Won	Lost	NR	Tied	Win%
Australia	6 Dec 1980, Melbourne	54	22	29	3	0	43
Bangladesh	27 Oct 1988, Chittagong	7	7	0	0	0	100
East Africa	11 Jun 1975, Leeds	1	1	0	0	0	100
England	13 Jul 1974, Leeds	33	13	19	1	0	41
Kenya	18 Feb 1996, Cuttack	4	3	1	0	0	75
New Zealand	14 Jun 1975, Manchester	51	27	21	3	0	56
Pakistan	1 Oct 1978, Quetta (AN)	71	24	42	4	1	36
South Africa	10 Nov 1991, Calcutta	27	8	18	1	0	31
Sri Lanka	16 Jun 1979, Manchester	57	30	22	5	0	58
UAE	13 Apr 1994, Sharjah	1	1	0	0	0	100
West Indies	9 Jun 1979, Birmingham	57	19	37	0	1	33
Zimbabwe	11 Jun 1983, Leicester	24	18	4	0	2	75
Total		387	173	193	17	4	47

Kenya

Versus	First Match	M	Won	Lost	NR	Tied	Win%
Australia	23 Feb 1996, Visag	1	0	1	0	0	-
Bangladesh	10 Oct 1997, Nairobi (NG)	4	3	1	0	0	75
India	18 Feb 1996, Cuttack	4	1	3	0	0	25
Pakistan	2 Oct 1996, Nairobi (AG)	1	0	1	0	0	-
South Africa	3 Oct 1996, Nairobi (NG)	1	0	1	0	0	-
Sri Lanka	6 Mar 1996, Kandy	2	0	2	0	0	-
West Indies	29 Feb 1996, Pune	1	1	0	0	0	100
Zimbabwe	26 Feb 1996, Patna	6	0	5	1	0	-
Total		20	5	14	1	0	26

SUMMARY OF LIMITED-OVERS INTERNATIONALS BY COUNTRY - CONT

Netherlands

Versus	First Match	M	Won	Lost	NR	Tied	Win%
England	22 Feb 1996, Peshawar	1	0	1	0	0	-
New Zealand	17 Feb 1996, Vadodara (IPCL)	1	0	1	0	0	-
Pakistan	26 Feb 1996, Lahore	1	0	1	0	0	-
South Africa	5 Mar 1996, Rawalpindi (RC)	1	0	1	0	0	-
UAE	1 Mar 1996, Lahore	1	0	1	0	0	-
Total		**5**	**0**	**5**	**0**	**0**	**-**

New Zealand

Versus	First Match	M	Won	Lost	NR	Tied	Win%
Australia	30 Mar 1974, Dunedin	73	20	51	2	0	28
Bangladesh	28 Apr 1990, Sharjah	1	1	0	0	0	100
East Africa	7 Jun 1975, Birmingham	1	1	0	0	0	100
England	18 Jul 1973, Swansea	47	20	23	3	1	45
India	14 Jun 1975, Manchester	51	21	27	3	0	44
Netherlands	17 Feb 1996, Vadodara (IPCL)	1	1	0	0	0	100
Pakistan	11 Feb 1973, Christchurch	48	18	28	1	1	38
South Africa	29 Feb 1992, Auckland	12	5	7	0	0	42
Sri Lanka	9 Jun 1979, Nottingham	40	24	13	2	1	63
United Arab Emirates	27 Feb 1996, Faisalabad	1	1	0	0	0	100
West Indies	18 Jun 1975, The Oval	24	4	18	2	0	18
Zimbabwe	10 Oct 1987, Hyderabad (I)	17	13	3	0	1	76
Total		**316**	**129**	**170**	**13**	**4**	**43**

Pakistan

Versus	First Match	M	Won	Lost	NR	Tied	Win%
Australia	7 Jun 1975, Leeds	49	20	25	2	2	43
Bangladesh	31 Mar 1986, Moratuwa	5	5	0	0	0	100
Canada	9 Jun 1979, Leeds	1	1	0	0	0	100
England	31 Aug 1974, Nottingham	41	14	26	1	0	35
India	1 Oct 1978, Quetta (AN)	71	42	24	4	1	63
Kenya	2 Oct 1996, Nairobi (AG)	1	1	0	0	0	100
Netherlands	26 Feb 1996, Lahore	1	1	0	0	0	100
New Zealand	11 Feb 1973, Christchurch	48	28	18	1	1	60
South Africa	8 Mar 1992, Brisbane	21	7	14	0	0	33
Sri Lanka	14 Jun 1975, Nottingham	71	46	23	2	0	67
UAE	17 Apr 1994, Sharjah	2	2	0	0	0	100
West Indies	11 Jun 1975, Birmingham	84	26	56	0	2	31
Zimbabwe	27 Feb 1992, Hobart (B)	19	16	2	0	1	84
Total		**414**	**209**	**188**	**10**	**7**	**52**

South Africa

Versus	First Match	M	Won	Lost	NR	Tied	Win%
Australia	26 Feb 1992, Sydney	37	19	18	0	0	51
England	12 Mar 1992, Melbourne	17	11	6	0	0	65
India	10 Nov 1991, Calcutta	27	18	8	1	0	69
Kenya	3 Oct 1996, Nairobi (NG)	1	1	0	0	0	100
Netherlands	5 Mar 1996, Rawalpindi (RC)	1	1	0	0	0	100
New Zealand	29 Feb 1992, Auckland	12	7	5	0	0	58
Pakistan	8 Mar 1992, Brisbane	21	14	7	0	0	67
Sri Lanka	2 Mar 1992, Wellington	15	8	6	1	0	57
UAE	16 Feb 1996, Rawalpindi (RC)	1	1	0	0	0	100
West Indies	5 Mar 1992, Christchurch	18	12	6	0	0	67
Zimbabwe	10 Mar 1992, Canberra	7	6	0	1	0	100
Total		**157**	**98**	**56**	**3**	**0**	**64**

Sri Lanka

Versus	First Match	M	Won	Lost	NR	Tied	Win%
Australia	11 Jun 1975, The Oval	40	12	26	2	0	32
Bangladesh	2 April 1986, Kandy	5	5	0	0	0	100
England	13 Feb 1982, Colombo (SSC)	19	7	12	0	0	37
India	16 Jun 1979, Manchester	57	22	30	5	0	42
Kenya	6 Mar 1996, Kandy	2	2	0	0	0	100
New Zealand	9 Jun 1979, Nottingham	40	13	24	2	1	34
Pakistan	14 Jun 1975, Nottingham	71	23	46	2	0	33
South Africa	2 Mar 1992, Wellington	15	6	8	1	0	43
West Indies	7 Jun 1975, Manchester	29	8	20	1	0	29
Zimbabwe	23 Feb 1992, New Plymouth	15	11	4	0	0	73
Total		293	109	170	13	1	39

United Arab Emirates

Versus	First Match	M	Won	Lost	NR	Tied	Win%
England	18 Feb 1996, Peshawar	1	0	1	0	0	-
India	13 Apr 1994, Sharjah	1	0	1	0	0	-
Netherlands	1 Mar 1996, Lahore	1	1	0	0	0	100
New Zealand	27 Feb 1996, Faisalabad	1	0	1	0	0	-
Pakistan	17 Apr 1994, Sharjah	2	0	2	0	0	-
South Africa	16 Feb 1996, Rawalpindi (RC)	1	0	1	0	0	-
Total		7	1	6	0	0	14

West Indies

Versus	First Match	M	Won	Lost	NR	Tied	Win%
Australia	14 Jun 1975, The Oval	84	49	33	1	1	59
England	5 Sep 1973, Leeds	58	31	25	2	0	55
India	9 Jun 1979, Birmingham	57	37	19	0	1	65
Kenya	29 Feb 1996, Pune	1	0	1	0	0	-
New Zealand	18 Jun 1975, The Oval	24	18	4	2	0	82
Pakistan	11 Jun 1975, Birmingham	84	56	26	0	2	67
South Africa	5 Mar 1992, Christchurch	18	6	12	0	0	33
Sri Lanka	7 Jun 1975, Manchester	29	20	8	1	0	71
Zimbabwe	13 Jun 1983, Worcester	5	5	0	0	0	100
Total		360	222	128	6	4	63

Zimbabwe

Versus	First Match	M	Won	Lost	NR	Tied	Win%
Australia	9 Jun 1983, Nottingham	11	1	10	0	0	9
Bangladesh	11 Oct 1997, Nairobi (NG)	2	2	0	0	0	100
England	18 Mar 1992, Albury	6	5	1	0	0	83
India	11 Jun 1983, Leicester	24	4	18	0	2	17
Kenya	26 Feb 1996, Patna	6	5	0	1	0	100
New Zealand	10 Oct 1987, Hyderabad (I)	17	3	13	0	1	18
Pakistan	27 Feb 1992, Hobart (B)	19	2	16	0	1	11
South Africa	10 Mar 1992, Canberra	7	0	6	1	0	-
Sri Lanka	23 Feb 1992, New Plymouth	15	4	11	0	0	27
West Indies	13 Jun 1983, Worcester	5	0	5	0	0	-
Total		112	26	80	2	4	24

SUMMARY OF MATCHES PLAYED IN EACH COUNTRY

Country	First Match	No. of games
Australia	Australia v England, 5 Jan 1971, Melbourne	354
Bangladesh	{ Pakistan v Sri Lanka 27 Oct 1988, Dhaka { Bangladesh v India, 27 Oct 1988, Chittagong }	21
Canada	India v Pakistan, 16 Sep 1996, Toronto	16
England	England v Australia, 24 Aug 1972, Manchester	143
India	India v England, 25 Nov 1981, Ahmedabad (SP)	192
Kenya	Kenya v Sri Lanka, 28 Sep 1996, Nairobi (NG)	15
New Zealand	New Zealand v Pakistan, 11 Feb 1973, Christchurch	130
Pakistan	Pakistan v New Zealand, 16 Oct 1976, Sialkot	126
Singapore	Pakistan v Sri Lanka, 1 Apr 1996, Singapore	5
South Africa	South Africa v India, 7 Dec 1992, Cape Town	81
Sri Lanka	Sri Lanka v England, 13 Feb 1982, Colombo (SSC)	82
UAE	Pakistan v Sri Lanka, 6 Apr 1984, Sharjah	139
Wales	England v New Zealand, 18 Jul 1973, Swansea	2
West Indies	West Indies v Pakistan, 16 Mar 1977, Berbice	76
Zimbabwe	Zimbabwe v India, 25 Oct 1992, Harare	24
Total		**1406**

SUMMARY OF LIMITED-OVERS INTERNATIONALS BY CALENDAR YEAR

Year	Aus	Ban	Can	EAF	Eng	Ind	Ken	Neth	NZ	Pak	SAF	SL	UAE	WI	Zim	Total
1971	1	-	-	-	1	-	-	-	-	-	-	-	-	-	-	1
1972	3	-	-	-	3	-	-	-	-	-	-	-	-	-	-	3
1973	-	-	-	-	4	-	-	-	3	1	-	-	-	2	-	5
1974	2	-	-	-	4	2	-	-	2	2	-	-	-	-	-	6
1975	7	-	-	3	7	3	-	-	6	3	-	3	-	6	-	19
1976	-	-	-	-	3	2	-	-	3	1	-	-	-	3	-	6
1977	3	-	-	-	5	-	-	-	-	3	-	-	-	1	-	6
1978	2	-	-	-	5	3	-	-	2	6	-	-	-	2	-	10
1979	13	-	3	-	14	3	-	-	4	4	-	2	-	9	-	26
1980	9	-	-	-	8	5	-	-	7	3	-	-	-	10	-	21
1981	17	-	-	-	7	9	-	-	10	6	-	-	-	7	-	28
1982	15	-	-	-	7	9	-	-	3	15	-	8	-	9	-	33
1983	23	-	-	-	20	19	-	-	25	10	-	13	-	16	6	66
1984	22	-	-	-	10	11	-	-	12	20	-	7	-	20	-	51
1985	21	-	-	-	11	15	-	-	13	22	-	19	-	29	-	65
1986	23	2	-	-	8	27	-	-	20	19	-	12	-	13	-	62
1987	24	-	-	-	31	22	-	-	9	25	-	10	-	21	6	74
1988	15	3	-	-	9	20	-	-	22	15	-	16	-	22	-	61
1989	18	-	-	-	9	18	-	-	5	27	-	10	-	23	-	55
1990	23	4	-	-	16	13	-	-	21	21	-	15	-	9	-	61
1991	14	-	-	-	8	14	-	-	8	8	3	4	-	19	-	39
1992	21	-	-	-	18	21	-	-	20	28	19	19	-	21	11	89
1993	17	-	-	-	11	18	-	-	8	27	17	23	-	30	13	82
1994	30	-	-	-	10	25	-	-	27	28	29	24	2	15	6	98
1995	13	3	-	-	5	12	-	-	19	19	7	17	-	19	6	60
1996	26	-	-	-	20	32	9	5	22	39	30	30	5	20	16	127
1997	19	7	-	-	14	39	6	-	17	36	23	28	-	19	22	115
1998	25	6	-	-	12	40	5	-	23	26	22	23	-	8	26	108
1999†	12	-	-	-	12	5	-	-	5	-	7	10	-	7	-	29
Total	418	25	3	3	292	387	20	5	316	414	157	293	7	360	112	1406

†As at 13 February 1999

HIGHEST INNINGS TOTALS

Total/Overs	Team	Versus	Venue	Date
5-398 (50 overs)	Sri Lanka	Kenya	Kandy	6 Mar 1996
9-371 (50 overs)	Pakistan	Sri Lanka	Nairobi (NG)	4 Oct 1996
7-363 (55 overs)	England	Pakistan	Nottingham	20 Aug 1992
4-360 (50 overs)	West Indies	Sri Lanka	Karachi	13 Oct 1987
9-349 (50 overs)	Sri Lanka	Pakistan	Singapore	2 Apr 1996
8-348 (50 overs)	New Zealand	India	Nagpur	26 Nov 1995
3-347 (50 overs)	Kenya	Bangladesh	Nairobi (NG)	10 Oct 1997
4-339 (50 overs)	Sri Lanka	Pakistan	Mohali	24 May 1997
4-338 (50 overs)	New Zealand	Bangladesh	Sharjah	28 Apr 1990
5-338 (60 overs)	Pakistan	Sri Lanka	Swansea	9 Jun 1983
4-334 (60 overs)	England	India	Lord's	7 Jun 1975
7-333 (50 overs)	West Indies	Sri Lanka	Sharjah	16 Oct 1995
8-333 (45 overs)	West Indies	India	Jamshedpur	7 Dec 1983
9-333 (60 overs)	England	Sri Lanka	Taunton	11 Jun 1983
3-332 (50 overs)	Australia	Sri Lanka	Sharjah	2 May 1990
6-330 (60 overs)	Pakistan	Sri Lanka	Nottingham	14 Jun 1975
10-329 (49.3 overs)	Sri Lanka	West Indies	Sharjah	16 Oct 1995
2-328 (50 overs)	Pakistan	New Zealand	Sharjah	20 Apr 1994
3-328 (50 overs)	South Africa	Netherlands	Rawalpindi (RC)	5 Mar 1996
5-328 (60 overs)	Australia	Sri Lanka	The Oval	11 Jun 1975
5-327 (50 overs)	Pakistan	India	Chennai	21 May 1997
8-324 (50 overs)	Australia	Pakistan	Karachi	6 Nov 1998
2-323 (50 overs)	Australia	Sri Lanka	Adelaide	28 Jan 1985
6-322 (60 overs)	England	New Zealand	The Oval	9 Jun 1983
2-321 (50 overs)	South Africa	UAE	Rawalpindi (RC)	16 Feb 1996
8-321 (50 overs)	South Africa	Pakistan	Nairobi (NG)	29 Sep 1996
8-320 (55 overs)	England	Australia	Birmingham	22 Aug 1980
9-320 (60 overs)	Australia	India	Nottingham	13 Jun 1983
5-319 (50 overs)	Pakistan	Bangladesh	Colombo (RPS)	16 Jul 1997
4-316 (48.5 overs)	Australia	Pakistan	Lahore	10 Nov 1998
6-316 (50 overs)	Pakistan	India	Toronto	19 Sep 1998
7-316 (47.5 overs)	India	Pakistan	Dhaka	18 Jan 1998
3-315 (50 overs)	Pakistan	Sri Lanka	Adelaide	17 Feb 1990
4-315 (47 overs)	West Indies	Pakistan	Port-of-Spain	18 Mar 1988
8-315 (50 overs)	Pakistan	Australia	Lahore	10 Nov 1998
10-315 (49.4 overs)	Pakistan	Sri Lanka	Singapore	2 Apr 1996
3-314 (50 overs)	South Africa	Pakistan	Sharjah	13 Apr 1996
5-314 (48 overs)	Pakistan	India	Dhaka	18 Dec 1998
7-314 (50 overs)	South Africa	New Zealand	Pretoria	11 Dec 1994
3-313 (50 overs)	Pakistan	Sri Lanka	Sharjah	30 Oct 1993
6-313 (50 overs)	West Indies	England	Kingstown	2 Mar 1994
7-313 (49.2 overs)	Sri Lanka	Zimbabwe	New Plymouth	23 Feb 1992
9-313 (50 overs)	West Indies	Australia	St John's	22 Feb 1978
4-312 (50 overs)	Zimbabwe	Sri Lanka	New Plymouth	23 Feb 1992
8-311 (50 overs)	Pakistan	Sri Lanka	Sharjah	29 Apr 1990
9-311 (50 overs)	South Africa	Sri Lanka	Lahore	6 Nov 1997
6-310 (50 overs)	South Africa	Australia	Bloemfontein	13 Apr 1997
8-310 (50 overs)	Australia	Sri Lanka	Melbourne	7 Feb 1999
5-309 (50 overs)	India	Australia	Kochi	1 April 1998
5-309 (60 overs)	New Zealand	East Africa	Birmingham	7 Jun 1975
6-309 (50 overs)	West Indies	Sri Lanka	Perth	2 Feb 1985
10-309 (49.4 overs)	Sri Lanka	Pakistan	Calcutta	27 May 1997
6-307 (50 overs)	India	Sri Lanka	Colombo (RPS)	7 July 1998
8-307 (50 overs)	New Zealand	Netherlands	Vadodara (IPCL)	17 Feb 1996

Total/Overs	Team	Versus	Venue	Date
8-307 (50 overs)	India	Australia	Dhaka	28 Oct 1998
5-306 (55 overs)	England	West Indies	The Oval	26 May 1995
6-306 (50 overs)	West Indies	New Zealand	Gauhati	1 Nov 1994
4-305 (50 overs)	Zimbabwe	Bangladesh	Nairobi (NG)	11 Oct 1997
5-305 (50 overs	India	Pakistan	Sharjah	15 May 1996
8-305 (50 overs)	South Africa	Kenya	Nairobi (NG)	3 Oct 1996
5-304 (50 overs)	New Zealand	Sri Lanka	Auckland	20 Mar 1983
7-304 (50 overs)	Australia	Kenya	Visag	23 Feb 1996
5-303 (50 overs)	South Africa	Zimbabwe	Harare	21 Oct 1995
9-303 (49.4 overs)	Sri Lanka	England	Adelaide	23 Jan 1999
3-302 (50 overs)	England	Sri Lanka	Adelaide	23 Jan 1999
4-302 (50 overs)	Sri Lanka	India	Colombo (RPS)	17 Aug 1997
5-302 (50 overs)	West Indies	England	Port-of-Spain	8 Apr 1998
5-302 (55 overs)	England	Pakistan	The Oval	22 May 1992
6-302 (50 overs)	Pakistan	Zimbabwe	Rawalpindi (RC)	24 Nov 1998
8-302 (50 overs)	Australia	New Zealand	Melbourne	13 Feb 1983
3-301 (50 overs)	India	Zimbabwe	Cuttack	9 Apr 1998
10-301 (49.3 overs)	Sri Lanka	India	Colombo (RPS)	7 Jul 1998
5-300 (50 overs)	Australia	Pakistan	Brisbane	11 Feb 1990
6-300 (48 overs)	Pakistan	Sri Lanka	Kimberley	7 Apr 1998
6-300 (50 overs)	South Africa	New Zealand	Brisbane	9 Jan 1998
7-300 (50 overs)	India	Sri Lanka	Colombo (RPS)	17 Aug 1997
8-300 (50 overs)	New Zealand	India	Christchurch	19 Jan 1999

HIGHEST INNINGS TOTAL FOR EACH COUNTRY

Team	Total/Overs	Versus	Venue	Date
Australia	3-332 (50 overs)	Sri Lanka	Sharjah	2 May 1990
Bangladesh	10-257 (47.1 overs)	Zimbabwe	Nairobi (NG)	11 Oct 1997
Canada	9-139 (60 overs)	Pakistan	Leeds	9 Jun 1979
East Africa	8-128 (60 overs)	New Zealand	Birmingham	7 Jun 1975
England	7-363 (55 overs)	Pakistan	Nottingham	20 Aug 1992
India	7-316 (47.5 overs)	Pakistan	Dhaka	18 Jan 1998
Kenya	3-347 (50 overs)	Bangladesh	Nairobi (NG)	10 Oct 1997
Netherlands	6-230 (50 overs)	England	Peshawar	22 Feb 1996
New Zealand	8-348 (50 overs)	India	Nagpur	26 Nov 1995
Pakistan	9-371 (50 overs)	Sri Lanka	Nairobi (NG)	4 Oct 1996
South Africa	3-328 (50 overs)	Netherlands	Rawalpindi (RC)	5 Mar 1996
Sri Lanka	5-398 (50 overs)	Kenya	Kandy	6 Mar 1996
UAE	3-220 (44.2 overs)	Netherlands	Lahore	1 Mar 1996
West Indies	4-360 (50 overs)	Sri Lanka	Karachi	13 Oct 1987
Zimbabwe	4-312 (50 overs)	Sri Lanka	New Plymouth	23 Feb 1992

PROGRESSION OF HIGHEST INNINGS TOTALS

Total/Overs	Team	Versus	Venue	Date
10-190 (39.4 overs)	England	Australia	Melbourne	5 Jan 1971
5-191 (34.6 overs)	Australia	England	Melbourne	5 Jan 1971
8-222 (55 overs)	Australia	England	Manchester	24 Aug 1972
4-226 (49.1 overs)	England	Australia	Manchester	24 Aug 1972
9-236 (55 overs)	England	Australia	Lord's	26 Aug 1972
5-240 (51.3 overs)	Australia	England	Lord's	26 Aug 1972
5-265 (35 overs)	Australia	New Zealand	Christchurch	31 Mar 1974
10-265 (53.5 overs)	India	England	Leeds	13 July 1974
6-266 (51.1 overs)	England	India	Leeds	13 July 1974

Total/Overs	Team	Versus	Venue	Date
4-334 (60 overs)	England	India	Lord's	7 June 1975
5-338 (60 overs)	Pakistan	Sri Lanka	Swansea	9 June 1983
4-360 (50 overs)	West Indies	Sri Lanka	Karachi	13 Oct 1987
7-363 (55 overs)	England	Pakistan	Nottingham	28 Aug 1992
5-398 (50 overs)	Sri Lanka	Kenya	Kandy	6 Mar 1996

HIGHEST INNINGS TOTALS BATTING SECOND

Total	Team	Batted 1st	Batted 2nd	Result	Venue	Date
10-329 (49.3 overs)	Sri Lanka	WI 7-333	SL 10-329	WI by 4 runs	Sharjah	16 Oct 1995
4-316 (48.5 overs)	Australia	Pak 8-315	Aus 4-316	Aus by 6 wkts	Lahore	10 Nov 1998
7-316 (47.5 overs)	India	Pak 5-314	Ind 7-316	Ind by 3 wkts	Dhaka	18 Jan 1998
10-315 (49.4 overs)	Pakistan	SL 9-349	Pak 10-315	SL by 34 runs	Singapore	2 Apr 1996
7-313 (49.2 overs)	Sri Lanka	Zim 4-312	SL 7-313	SL by 3 wkts	New Plymouth	23 Feb 1992
9-303 (49.4 overs)	Sri Lanka	Eng 3-302	SL 9-303	SL by 1 wkt	Adelaide	23 Jan 1999
10-301 (49.3 overs)	Sri Lanka	Ind 6-307	SL 10-301	Ind by 6 runs	Colombo (RPS)	7 Jul 1998
6-300 (48 overs)	Pakistan	SL 7-295	Pak 6-300	Pak by 4 wkts	Kimberley	7 Apr 1998
7-300 (50 overs)	India	SL 4-302	Ind 7-300	SL by 2 wkts	Colombo (RPS)	17 Aug 1997
6-298 (54.5 overs)	New Zealand	Eng 6-295	NZ 6-298	NZ by 4 wkts	Leeds	23 May 1990
9-298 (50 overs)	New Zealand	SAF 6-300	NZ 6-298	SAF by 2 runs	Brisbane	9 Jan 1998
5-297 (48.1 overs)	South Africa	WI 8-293	SAF 5-297	SAF by 5 wkts	Lahore	3 Nov 1997
6-297 (48.5 overs)	New Zealand	Eng 5-296	NZ 6-297	NZ by 4 wkts	Adelaide	29 Jan 1983
10-292 (49.2 overs)	India	Pak 5-327	Ind 10-292	Pak by 35 runs	Chennai	21 May 1997
4-289 (47.5 overs)	Australia	NZ 9-286	Aus 4-289	Aus by 6 wkts	Chennai	11 Mar 1996
7-289 (40 overs)	Sri Lanka	Ind 4-299	SL 7-289	Ind by 10 runs	Bombay	17 Jan 1987
10-289 (49.5 overs)	Sri Lanka	Pak 9-371	SL 10-289	Ind by 82 runs	Nairobi (NG)	4 Oct 1996
2-288 (46.4 overs)	South Africa	Ind 4-287	SAF 2-288	SAF by 8 wkts	New Delhi	14 Nov 1991
8-288 (50 overs)	Sri Lanka	Pak 3-315	SL 8-288	Pak by 27 runs	Adelaide	17 Feb 1990
8-288 (50 overs)	Sri Lanka	Zim 5-290	SL 8-288	Zim by 2 wkts	Harare	5 Nov 1994
9-288 (60 overs)	Sri Lanka	Pak 5-338	SL 9-288	Pak by 50 runs	Swansea	9 Jun 1983
5-287 (47.2 overs)	West Indies	Aus 9-286	WI 5-287	WI by 5 wkts	Georgetown	18 Mar 1995
5-287 (49 overs)	Australia	SAF 7-284	Aus 5-287	Aus by 5 wkts	Centurion	10 Apr 1997
4-286 (53.4 overs)	England	NZ 5-284	Eng 4-286	Eng by 6 wkts	Manchester	18 Jul 1986
6-286 (49 overs)	Sri Lanka	Zim 6-281	SL 6-286	SL by 4 wkts	Colombo (SSC)	26 Jan 1998
10-286 (58 overs)	Sri Lanka	Eng 9-333	SL 10-286	Eng by 47 runs	Taunton	11 Jun 1983
4-285 (45.3 overs)	West Indies	Pak 4-284	WI 4-285	WI by 6 wkts	Sharjah	5 Nov 1993
3-284 (48.5 overs)	West Indies	Aus 4-281	WI 3-284	WI by 7 wkts	Brisbane	5 Jan 1997
10-284 (49.1 overs)	Australia	Ind 6-289	Aus 10-284	Ind by 5 runs	Mohali	3 Nov 1996
4-283 (46.4 overs)	South Africa	Eng 7-281	SAF 4-283	SAF by 6 wkts	Dhaka	25 Oct 1998
8-282 (47.1 overs)	India	NZ 3-278	Ind 8-282	Ind by 2 wkts	Vadodara (MB)	17 Dec 1988
5-282 (53 overs)	India	Eng 10-281	Ind 5-282	Ind by 5 wkts	Nottingham	20 Jul 1990
2-281 (40 overs)	Sri Lanka	Pak 10-280	SL 2-281	SL by 8 wkts	Lahore	5 Nov 1997
4-281 (40.5 overs)	India	SL 8-277	Ind 4-281	Ind by 6 wkts	Delhi	15 Sep 1982
10-281 (53 overs)	West Indies	Eng 5-306	WI 10-281	Eng by 25 runs	The Oval	26 May 1995
4-280 (53.3 overs)	Australia	Eng 5-277	Aus 4-280	Aus by 6 wkts	Birmingham	21 May 1993

HIGHEST INNINGS TOTALS UNDER LIGHTS

Total/Overs	Team	Versus	Venue	Date
7-316 (49.3 overs)	India	Pakistan	Dhaka	18 Jan 1998
9-303 (49.4 overs)	Sri Lanka	England	Adelaide	23 Jan 1999
10-301 (49.3 overs)	Sri Lanka	India	Colombo (RPS)	7 Jul 1998
7-300 (50 overs)	India	Sri Lanka	Colombo (RPS)	17 Aug 1997
9-298 (50 overs)	New Zealand	South Africa	Brisbane	9 Jan 1998
5-297 (48.1 overs)	South Africa	West Indies	Lahore	3 Nov 1997
10-292 (49.2 overs)	India	Pakistan	Chennai	21 May 1997
4-289 (47.5 overs)	Australia	New Zealand	Chennai	11 Mar 1996
2-288 (46.4 overs)	South Africa	India	New Delhi	14 Nov 1991
5-287 (49 overs)	Australia	South Africa	Centurion	10 Apr 1997
3-284 (48.5 overs)	West Indies	Australia	Brisbane	5 Jan 1997
10-284 (49.1 overs)	Australia	India	Mohali	3 Nov 1996
4-283 (46.5 overs)	South Africa	England	Dhaka	25 Oct 1998
2-281 (40 overs)	Sri Lanka	Pakistan	Lahore	5 Nov 1997

HIGHEST INNINGS TOTALS AT THE FALL OF EACH WICKET

Total	Team	Versus	Venue	Date
1-252	India	Sri Lanka	Colombo (RPS)	7 Jul 1998
2-320	Pakistan	New Zealand	Sharjah	20 Apr 1994
3-337	Sri Lanka	Pakistan	Mohali	24 May 1997
4-378	Sri Lanka	Kenya	Kandy	6 Mar 1996
5-384	Sri Lanka	Kenya	Kandy	6 Mar 1996
6-353	England	Pakistan	Nottingham	20 Aug 1992
7-357	England	Pakistan	Nottingham	20 Aug 1992
8-343	New Zealand	India	Nagpur	26 Nov 1995
9-364	Pakistan	Sri Lanka	Nairobi (NG)	4 Oct 1996
10-329	Sri Lanka	West Indies	Sharjah	16 Oct 1995

Ross Dundas Cricket Statistics

HIGHEST WINNING TOTALS BATTING SECOND

Total/overs	Team	Batted 1st	Batted 2nd	Result	Venue	Date
4-316 (48.5 overs)	Australia	Pak 8-315	Aus 4-316	Aus by 6 wkts	Lahore	10 Nov 1998
7-316 (47.5 overs)	India	Pak 5-314	Ind 7-316	Ind by 3 wkts	Dhaka	18 Jan 1998
7-313 (49.2 overs)	Sri Lanka	Zim 4-312	SL 7-313	SL by 3 wkts	New Plymouth	23 Feb 1992
9-303 (49.4 overs)	Sri Lanka	Eng 3-302	SL 9-303	SL by 1 wkt	Adelaide	23 Jan 1999
6-300 (48 overs)	Pakistan	SL 7-295	Pak 6-300	Pak by 4 wkts	Kimberley	7 Apr 1998
6-298 (54.5 overs)	New Zealand	Eng 6-295	NZ 6-298	NZ by 4 wkts	Leeds	23 May 1990
5-297 (48.1 overs)	South Africa	WI 8-293	SAF 5-297	SAF by 5 wkts	Lahore	3 Nov 1997
6-297 (48.5 overs)	New Zealand	Eng 5-296	NZ 6-297	NZ by 4 wkts	Adelaide	29 Jan 1983
4-289 (47.5 overs)	Australia	NZ 9-286	Aus 4-289	Aus by 6 wkts	Chennai	11 Mar 1996
2-288 (46.4 overs)	South Africa	Ind 4-287	SAF 2-288	SAF by 8 wkts	New Delhi	14 Nov 1991
5-287 (47.2 overs)	West Indies	Aus 9-286	WI 5-287	WI by 5 wkts	Georgetown	18 Mar 1995
5-287 (49 overs)	Australia	SAF 7-284	Aus 5-287	Aus by 5 wkts	Centurion	10 Apr 1997
4-286 (53.4 overs)	England	NZ 5-284	Eng 4-286	Eng by 6 wkts	Manchester	18 Jul 1986
6-286 (49 overs)	Sri Lanka	Zim 6-281	SL 6-286	SL by 4 wkts	Colombo (SSC)	26 Jan 1998
4-285 (45.3 overs)	West Indies	Pak 4-284	WI 4-285	WI by 6 wkts	Sharjah	5 Nov 1993
3-284 (48.5 overs)	West Indies	Aus 4-281	WI 3-284	WI by 7 wkts	Brisbane	5 Jan 1997
4-283 (46.4 overs)	South Africa	Eng 7-281	SAF 4-283	SAF by 6 wkts	Dhaka	25 Oct 1998
5-282 (53 overs)	India	Eng 10-281	Ind 5-282	Ind by 5 wkts	Nottingham	20 Jul 1990
8-282 (47.1 overs)	India	NZ 3-278	Ind 8-282	Ind by 2 wkts	Vadodara (MB)	17 Dec 1988
2-281 (40 overs)	Sri Lanka	Pak 10-280	SL 2-281	SL by 8 wkts	Lahore	5 Nov 1997
4-281 (40.5 overs)	India	SL 8-277	Ind 4-281	Ind by 6 wkts	Delhi	15 Sep 1982
4-280 (53.3 overs)	Australia	Eng 5-277	Aus 4-280	Aus by 6 wkts	Birmingham	21 May 1993

HIGHEST LOSING TOTALS

Total/overs	Team	Batted 1st	Batted 2nd	Result	Venue	Date
10-329 (49.3 overs)	Sri Lanka	WI 7-333	SL 10-329	WI by 4 runs	Sharjah	16 Oct 1995
8-315 (50 overs)	Pakistan	Pak 8-315	Aus 4-316	Aus by 4 wkts	Lahore	10 Nov 1998
10-315(49.4 overs)	Pakistan	SL 9-349	Pak 10-315	SL by 34 runs	Singapore	2 Apr 1996
5-314 (48 overs)	Pakistan	Pak 5-314	Ind 7-316	Ind by 3 wkts	Dhaka	18 Dec 1998
4-312 (50 overs)	Zimbabwe	Zim 4-312	SL 7-313	SL by 3 wkts	New Plymouth	23 Feb 1992
3-302 (50 overs)	England	Eng 3-302	SL 9-303	SL by 1 wkt	Adelaide	23 Jan 1999
10-301 (49.3 overs)	Sri Lanka	Ind 6-307	SL 10-301	Ind by 6 runs	Colombo (RPS)	7 Jul 1998
7-300 (50 overs)	India	SL 4-302	Ind 7-300	SL by 2 runs	Colombo (RPS)	17 Aug 1997

HIGHEST LOSING TOTALS BATTING SECOND

Total/Overs	Team	Versus	Venue	Date
10-329 (49.3 overs)	Sri Lanka	West Indies	Sharjah	16 Oct 1995
10-315 (49.4 overs)	Pakistan	Sri Lanka	Singapore	2 Apr 1996
10-301 (49.3 overs)	Sri Lanka	India	Colombo (RPS)	7 Jul 1998
7-300 (50 overs)	India	Sri Lanka	Colombo (RPS)	17 Aug 1997
9-298 (50 overs)	New Zealand	South Africa	Brisbane	9 Jan 1998
10-292 (49.2 overs)	India	Pakistan	Chennai	21 May 1997
10-289 (49.5 overs)	Sri Lanka	Pakistan	Nairobi (NG)	4 Oct 1996

HIGHEST % OF EXTRAS IN AN INNINGS TOTAL

%	Extras	Total	Team	Versus	Venue	Date
56.52†	13	1-23	New Zealand	Australia	Sydney	21 Jan 1981
41.67†	10	1-24	England	Pakistan	Adelaide	1 Mar 1992
35.29†	6	1-17	Sri Lanka	India	Indore	25 Dec 1997
33.33†	10	5-30	Pakistan	India	Colombo (SSC)	20 Jul 1997
29.56	34	10-115	Bangladesh	India	Mumbai	25 May 1998
29.27†	12	2-41	Sri Lanka	New Zealand	Colombo (RPS)	4 Dec 1992
26.67†	4	0-15	Australia	Pakistan	Brisbane	15 Jan 1984
25.58	44	4-172	Sri Lanka	Pakistan	Sharjah	20 Dec 1990
25.30	42	166	New Zealand	Pakistan	Christchurch	18 Mar 1992
25.00	16	64	New Zealand	Pakistan	Sharjah	15 Apr 1986
24.57	43	9-175	England	West Indies	Birmingham	23/24 May 1991
24.51	25	102	Sri Lanka	West Indies	Brisbane	5 Jan 1996
24.49	24	98	Sri Lanka	South Africa	Colombo (RPS)	2 Sep 1993

†Match abandoned due to rain

HIGHEST MATCH AGGREGATES

Runs	Match	Batted 1st	Batted 2nd	Result	Venue	Date
664	Pakistan v Sri Lanka	SL 9-349	Pak 10-315	SL by 34 runs	Singapore	2 Apr 1996
662	Sri Lanka v West Indies	WI 7-333	SL 10-329	WI by 4 runs	Sharjah	16 Oct 1995
660	Pakistan v Sri Lanka	Pak 9-371	SL 10-289	Pak by 82 runs	Nairobi (NG)	4 Oct 1996
652	Sri Lanka v Kenya	SL 5-398	Ken 7-254	SL by 144 runs	Kandy	6 Mar 1996
631	Pakistan v Australia	Pak 8-315	Aus 4-316	Aus by 6 wkts	Lahore	10 Nov 1998
630	India v Pakistan	Pak 5-314	Ind 7-316	Ind by 3 wkts	Dhaka	18 Jan 1998
626	Pakistan v Sri Lanka	Pak 5-338	SL 9-288	Pak by 50 runs	Swansea	9 Jun 1983
625	Sri Lanka v Zimbabwe	Zim 4-312	SL 7-313	SL by 3 wkts	New Plymouth	23 Feb 1992
619	India v Pakistan	Pak 5-327	Ind 10-292	Pak by 35 runs	Chennai	21 May 1997
619	England v Sri Lanka	Eng 9-333	SL 10-286	Eng by 47 runs	Taunton	11 Jun 1983
608	Sri Lanka v India	Ind 6-307	SL 10-301	Ind by 6 runs	Colombo (RPS)	7 July 1998
605	England v Sri Lanka	Eng 3-302	SL 9-303	SL by 1 wkt	Adelaide	23 Jan 1998
604	Australia v Sri Lanka	Aus 5-328	SL 4-276	Aus by 52 runs	The Oval	11 Jun 1975
603	Pakistan v Sri Lanka	Pak 3-315	SL 8-288	Pak by 27 runs	Adelaide	17 Feb 1990
602	Sri Lanka v India	SL 4-302	Ind 7-300	SL by 2 runs	Colombo (RPS)	17 Aug 1997

HIGHEST MATCH AGGREGATES WHERE BOTH TEAMS WERE DISMISSED

Runs	Match	Batted 1st	Batted 2nd	Result	Venue	Date
533	Pakistan v Sri Lanka	SL 10-309	Pak 10-224	SL by 85 runs	Calcutta	27 May 1997
500	India v Australia	Aus 10-258	Ind 10-242	Aus by 16 runs	Mumbai	27 Feb 1996
496	Sri Lanka v West Indies	SL 10-273	WI 10-223	SL by 50 runs	Sharjah	20 Oct 1995
493	England v India	Eng 10-250	Ind 10-243	Eng by 7 runs	Sharjah	11 Dec 1997

LOWEST MATCH AGGREGATES

Runs	Match	Batted 1st	Batted 2nd	Result	Venue	Date
88	Pakistan v West Indies	Pak 10-43	WI 3-45	WI by 7 wkts	Cape Town	25 Feb 1993
91	England v Canada	Can 10-45	Eng 2-46	Eng by 8 wkts	Manchester	13 Jun 1979
106	West Indies v New Zealand	NZ 3-51	WI 4-55	WI by 6 wkts	Port of Spain	27 Mar 1985
127	Australia v India	Ind 10-63	Aus 1-64	Aus by 9 wkts	Sydney	8 Jan 1981
130	New Zealand v Pakistan	NZ 10-64	Pak 0-66	Pak by 10 wkts	Sharjah	15 Apr 1986
143	Pakistan v West Indies	Pak 10-71	WI 1-72	WI by 9 wkts	Brisbane	9 Jan 1993
143	New Zealand v Australia	NZ 10-74	Aus 2-75	Aus by 8 wkts	Wellington	20 Feb 1982

LOWEST MATCH AGGREGATES WHERE BOTH TEAMS WERE DISMISSED

Runs	Match	Batted 1st	Batted 2nd	Result	Venue	Date
212	India v Pakistan	Ind 10-125	Pak 10-87	Ind by 38 runs	Sharjah	22 Mar 1985
241	England v Australia	Eng 10-171	Aus 10-70	Eng by 101 runs	Birmingham	4 Jun 1977
244	South Africa v England	SAF 10-129	Eng 10-115	SAF by 14 runs	East London	19 Jan 1996
252	West Indies v England	WI 10-127	Eng 10-125	WI by 2 runs	Kingstown	4 Feb 1981
252	India v West Indies	Ind 10-126	WI 10-126	Match tied	Perth	6 Dec 1991
256	New Zealand v Pakistan	Pak 10-146	NZ 10-110	Pak by 10 runs	Auckland	6 Mar 1994
259	England v Zimbabwe	Zim 10-134	Eng 10-125	Zim by 9 runs	Albury	18 Mar 1992
259	Kenya v West Indies	Ken 10-166	WI 10-93	Ken by 73 runs	Pune	29 Feb 1996
268	Pakistan v West Indies	Pak 10-165	WI 10-103	Pak by 62 runs	Melbourne	20 Jan 1997
269	Australia v Pakistan	Pak 10-149	Aus 10-120	Pak by 29 runs	Hobart (B)	7 Jan 1997
272	Pakistan v West Indies	Pak 10-140	WI 10-132	Pak by 8 runs	Adelaide	5 Dec 1981
279	New Zealand v Pakistan	Pak 10-160	NZ 10-119	Pak by 41 runs	Adelaide	15 Nov 1996
281	Pakistan v Zimbabwe	Pak 10-187	Zim 10-94	Pak by 93 runs	Sharjah	6 Apr 1997
281	New Zealand v England	NZ 10-153	Eng 10-144	NZ by 9 runs	Auckland	2 Mar 199

LOWEST INNINGS TOTALS

Total/Overs	Team	Versus	Venue	Date
10-43 (19.5 overs)	Pakistan	West Indies	Cape Town	25 Feb 1993
10-45 (40.3 overs)	Canada	England	Manchester	13 Jun 1979
10-55 (28.3 overs)	Sri Lanka	West Indies	Sharjah	3 Dec 1986
10-63 (25.5 overs)	India	Australia	Sydney	8 Jan 1981
10-64 (35.5 overs)	New Zealand	Pakistan	Sharjah	15 Apr 1986
10-69 (28 overs)	South Africa	Australia	Sydney	14 Dec 1993
10-70 (25.2 overs)	Australia	England	Birmingham	4 Jun 1977
10-70 (26.3 overs)	Australia	New Zealand	Adelaide	27 Jan 1986
10-71 (23.4 overs)	Pakistan	West Indies	Brisbane	9 Jan 1993
10-74 (29 overs)	New Zealand	Australia	Wellington	20 Feb 1982
10-74 (31.1 overs)	New Zealand	Pakistan	Sharjah	1 May 1990
10-74 (40.2 overs)	Pakistan	England	Adelaide	1 Mar 1992
10-78 (24.1 overs)	India	Sri Lanka	Kanpur	24 Dec 1986
10-79 (34.2 overs)	India	Pakistan	Sialkot	13 Oct 1978
10-81 (48 overs)	Pakistan	West Indies	Sydney	17 Dec 1992
10-85 (47 overs)	Pakistan	England	Manchester	24/25 May 1978
10-86 (37.2 overs)	Sri Lanka	West Indies	Manchester	7 Jun 1975
10-87 (29.3 overs)	West Indies	Australia	Sydney	8 Dec 1992

Total/Overs	Team	Versus	Venue	Date
10-87 (32.5 overs)	Pakistan	India	Sharjah	22 Mar 1985
10-91 (35.4 overs)	Australia	West Indies	Perth	4 Jan 1987
10-91 (35.5 overs)	Sri Lanka	Australia	Adelaide	28 Jan 1985
10-92 (32.3 overs)	Bangladesh	Zimbabwe	Nairobi (AK)	14 Oct 1997
10-93 (36.2 overs)	England	Australia	Leeds	18 Jun 1975
10-93 (35.2 overs)	West Indies	Kenya	Pune	29 Feb 1996
10-94 (35.3 overs)	Bangladesh	Pakistan	Moratuwa	31 Mar 1986
10-94 (31.7 overs)	England	Australia	Melbourne	7 Feb 1979
10-94 (31.4 overs)	Zimbabwe	Pakistan	Sharjah	6 Apr 1997
10-94 (25.2 overs)	New Zealand	Australia	Christchurch	4 Mar 1990
10-94 (52.3 overs)	East Africa	England	Birmingham	14 Jun 1975
10-96 (41 overs)	Sri Lanka	India	Sharjah	8 Apr 1984
10-98 (34 overs)	Sri Lanka	South Africa	Colombo (RPS)	2 Sep 1993
10-98 (39 overs)	Sri Lanka	India	Sharjah	9 Nov 1998
10-99 (36.3 overs)	Zimbabwe	West Indies	Hyderabad (I)	21 Nov 1993
10-99 (33.2 overs)	Sri Lanka	England	Perth	29 Jan 1999

LOWEST INNINGS TOTALS FROM COMPLETED OVERS

Total/Overs	Team	Versus	Venue	Date
9-118 (50 overs)	Sri Lanka	New Zealand	Dunedin	2 Mar 1983
8-128 (60 overs)	East Africa	New Zealand	Birmingham	7 Jun 1975
3-132 (60 overs)	India	England	Lord's	7 Jun 1975
8-134 (50 overs)	Bangladesh	Australia	Sharjah	30 Apr 1990
9-137 (50 overs)	New Zealand	Australia	Auckland	26 Feb 1995
9-138 (50 overs)	New Zealand	West Indies	Sydney	9 Mar 1985
9-138 (50 overs)	Pakistan	New Zealand	Hamilton	14 Mar 1989
9-139 (60 overs)	Canada	Pakistan	Leeds	9 Jun 1979
9-140 (50 overs)	Pakistan	West Indies	Perth	1 Jan 1989
9-140 (50 overs)	South Africa	West Indies	Cape Town	17 Feb 1993
9-145 (50 overs)	Pakistan	New Zealand	Christchurch	16 Mar 1994
7-145 (50 overs)	Netherlands	Pakistan	Lahore	26 Feb 1996
7-147 (50 overs)	South Africa	New Zealand	Hobart (B)	18 Dec 1993
9-148 (50 overs)	Pakistan	England	Cuttack	22 Oct 1989
9-148 (50 overs)	England	West Indies	Kingstown	2 Mar 1994

LOWEST INNINGS TOTALS FOR EACH COUNTRY

Team	Total/Overs	Versus	Venue	Date
Australia	10-70 (25.2 overs)	England	Birmingham	4 Jun 1977
	10-70 (26.3 overs)	New Zealand	Adelaide	27 Jan 1986
Bangladesh	10-92 (32.3 overs)	Zimbabwe	Nairobi (AK)	14 Oct 1997
Canada	10-45 (40.3 overs)	England	Manchester	13 Jun 1979
East Africa	10-94 (52.3 overs)	England	Birmingham	14 Jun 1975
England	10-93 (55 overs)	Australia	Leeds	18 Jun 1975
India	10-63 (25.5 overs)	Australia	Sydney	8 Jan 1981
Kenya	10-103 (25.1 overs)	South Africa	Nairobi (NG)	3 Oct 1996
Netherlands	7-145 (50 overs)	Pakistan	Lahore	26 Feb 1996
New Zealand	10-64 (35.5 overs)	Pakistan	Sharjah	15 Apr 1986
Pakistan	10-43 (19.5 overs)	West Indies	Cape Town	25 Feb 1993
South Africa	10-69 (28 overs)	Australia	Sydney	14 Dec 1993
Sri Lanka	10-55 (28.3 overs)	West Indies	Sharjah	3 Dec 1986
UAE	10-136 (48.3 overs)	England	Peshawar	18 Feb 1996
West Indies	10-93 (35.2 overs)	Kenya	Pune	29 Feb 1996
Zimbabwe	10-94 (31.4 overs)	Pakistan	Sharjah	6 Apr 1997

REGRESSION OF LOWEST INNINGS TOTALS

Total/Overs	Team	Versus	Venue	Date
10-190 (39.4 overs)	England	Australia	Melbourne	5 Jan 1971
9-179 (55 overs)	Australia	England	Birmingham	28 Aug 1972
10-165 (33.3 overs)	Pakistan	New Zealand	Christchurch	11 Feb 1973
10-158 (52.5 overs)	New Zealand	England	Swansea	18 July 1973
10-86 (37.2 overs)	Sri Lanka	West Indies	Manchester	7 Jun 1975
10-70 (25.2 overs)	Australia	England	Birmingham	4 June 1977
10-45 (40.2 overs)	Canada	England	Manchester	14 June 1979
10-43 (19.5 overs)	Pakistan	West Indies	Cape Town	25 Feb 1993

LOWEST INNINGS TOTALS AT THE FALL OF EACH WICKET

Total	Team	Versus	Venue	Date
1-0	*111 instances*			
2-0	Pakistan	New Zealand	Birmingham	11 Jun 1983
2-0	England	Australia	Brisbane	18 Jan 1987
2-0	Pakistan	England	Birmingham	25 May 1987
2-0	Pakistan	Australia	Brisbane	8 Jan 1989
2-0	Pakistan	India	Karachi	20 Dec 1989
2-0	West Indies	India	Perth	6 Dec 1991
2-0	New Zealand	Pakistan	Sharjah	10 Nov 1996
2-0	Sri Lanka	Pakistan	Gwalior	12 May 1997
2-0	Pakistan	South Africa	Lahore	2 Nov 1997
2-0	West Indies	England	Sharjah	13 Dec 1997
3-0	Pakistan	New Zealand	Birmingham	11 Jun 1983
3-0	Pakistan	South Africa	Lahore	2 Nov 1997
4-8	Bangladesh	Sri Lanka	Dhaka	2 Nov 1988
5-12	Pakistan	West Indies	Brisbane	9 Jan 1993
6-14	Pakistan	West Indies	Cape Town	25 Feb 1993
7-25	Pakistan	West Indies	Cape Town	25 Feb 1993
7-25	England	Pakistan	Birmingham	3 Sep 1974
8-25	Pakistan	West Indies	Cape Town	25 Feb 1993
9-26	Pakistan	West Indies	Cape Town	25 Feb 1993
10-43	Pakistan	West Indies	Cape Town	25 Feb 1993

Ross Dundas Cricket Statistics

LOWEST WINNING TOTALS BATTING FIRST

Total/Overs	Team	Batted 1st	Batted 2nd	Result	Venue	Date
9-101(30 overs)	Australia	Aus 9-101	WI 10-87	Aus by 14 runs	Sydney	8 Dec 1992
6-121(15 overs)	England	Eng 6-121	Ind 5-114	Eng by 7 runs	Chandigarh	27 Jan 1985
10-125 (42.4 overs)	India	Ind 10-125	Pak 10-87	Ind by 38 runs	Sharjah	22 Mar 1985
10-127 (47.2 overs)	West Indies	WI 10-127	Eng 10-125	WI by 2 runs	Kingstown	4 Feb 1981
10-129 (41.4 overs)	South Africa	SAF 10-129	Eng 10-115	SAF by 14 runs	East London	19 Jan 1996
10-134 (46.1 overs)	Zimbabwe	Zim 10-134	Eng 10-125	Zim by 9 runs	Albury	18 Mar 1992

BIGGEST WINNING MARGINS (RUNS)

Runs	Team	Versus	Batted 1st	Batted 2nd	Venue	Date
232	Australia	Sri Lanka	Aus 2-323	SL 10-91	Adelaide	28 Jan 1985
206	New Zealand	Australia	NZ 7-276	Aus 10-70	Adelaide	27 Jan 1986
202	England	India	Eng 4-334	Ind 3-132	Lord's	7 Jun 1975
202	South Africa	Kenya	SAF 8-305	Ken 10-103	Nairobi (NG)	3 Oct 1996
198	England	Pakistan	Eng 7-363	Pak 10-165	Nottingham	20 Aug 1992
196	England	East Africa	Eng 5-290	EAF 10-94	Birmingham	14 Jun 1975
193	West Indies	Sri Lanka	WI 5-248	SL 10-55	Sharjah	3 Dec 1986
192	Pakistan	Sri Lanka	Pak 6-330	SL 10-138	Nottingham	14 Jun 1975

Runs	Team	Versus	Batted 1st	Batted 2nd	Venue	Date
192	Zimbabwe	Bangladesh	Zim 10-284	Ban 10-92	Nairobi (AK)	14 Oct 1997
191	West Indies	Sri Lanka	WI 4-360	SL 4-169	Karachi	13 Oct 1987
191	Sri Lanka	Zimbabwe	SL 4-296	Zim 10-105	Harare	6 Nov 1994
181	New Zealand	East Africa	NZ 5-309	EAF 8-128	Birmingham	7 Jun 1975
173	Pakistan	Bangladesh	Pak 3-284	Ban 6-111	Chittagong	29 Oct 1988
169	South Africa	UAE	SAF 2-321	UAE 8-152	Rawalpindi (RC)	16 Feb 1996
165	West Indies	England	WI 6-313	Eng 9-148	Kingstown	2 Mar 1994
164	West Indies	Australia	WI 8-255	Aus 10-91	Perth	4 Jan 1987
162	Australia	India	Aus 9-320	Ind 10-158	Sharjah	13 Jun 1983
162	Australia	England	Aus 5-272	Eng 10-110	Melbourne	13 Feb 1999
161	New Zealand	Bangladesh	NZ 4-338	Ban 5-177	Sharjah	28 Apr 1990
160	South Africa	Netherlands	SAF 3-328	Hol 8-168	Rawalpindi (RC)	5 Mar 1996
157	South Africa	Pakistan	SAF 5-266	Pak 10-109	Johannesburg	12 Jan 1995
150	Kenya	Bangladesh	Ken 3-347	Ban 10-197	Nairobi (NG)	10 Oct 1997
150	Australia	New Zealand	Aus 8-244	NZ 10-94	Christchurch	4 Mar 1990

BIGGEST WINNING MARGINS (10 WICKETS)

Team	Versus	Batted 1st	Batted 2nd	Venue	Date
India	East Africa	EAF 10-120	Ind 0-123	Leeds	11 Jun 1975
New Zealand	India	Ind 9-112	NZ 0-113	Melbourne	10 Jan 1981
West Indies	Zimbabwe	Zim 10-171	WI 0-172	Birmingham	20 Jun 1983
India	Sri Lanka	SL 10-96	Ind 0-97	Sharjah	8 Apr 1984
West Indies	New Zealand	NZ 10-116	WI 0-117	Port-of-Spain	17 Apr 1985
Pakistan	New Zealand	NZ 10-64	Pak 0-66	Sharjah	15 Apr 1986
West Indies	New Zealand	NZ 9-191	WI 0-192	Christchurch	28 Mar 1987
West Indies	Pakistan	Pak 2-220	WI 0-221	Melbourne	23 Feb 1992
West Indies	South Africa	SAF 10-152	WI 0-154	Port-of-Spain	11 Apr 1992
West Indies	India	Ind 7-199	WI 0-200	Bridgetown	3 May 1997
India	Zimbabwe	Zim 9-196	Ind 0-197	Sharjah	13 Nov 1998

NARROWEST WINNING MARGINS (1 RUN)

Team	Versus	Batted 1st	Batted 2nd	Venue	Date
New Zealand	Pakistan	NZ 8-198	Pak 9-197	Sialkot	16 Oct 1976
New Zealand	Australia	NZ 8-220	Aus 7-219	Sydney	13 Jan 1981
Australia	India	Aus 6-270	Ind 10-269	Chennai	9 Oct 1987
New Zealand	Australia	NZ 9-232	Aus 10-231	Perth	3 Jan 1988
India	New Zealand	Ind 10-221	NZ 10-220	Wellington	6 Mar 1990
New Zealand	Australia	NZ 6-194	Aus 10-193	Hobart (B)	18 Dec1990
Pakistan	West Indies	Pak 7-236	WI 10-235	Sharjah	21 Oct 1991
Australia	India	Aus 9-237	Ind 10-234†	Brisbane	1 Mar 1992
India	Sri Lanka	Ind 8-212	SL 10-211	Colombo (RPS)	25 Jul 1993
Australia	South Africa	Aus 6-203	SAF 8-202	Bloemfontein	8 Apr 1994
South Africa	New Zealand	SAF 9-174	NZ 7-173	Hobart (B)	11 Dec 1997
Zimbabwe	New Zealand	Zim 7-228	NZ 9-227	Christchurch	4 Mar 1998

†*revised target*

NARROWEST WINNING MARGINS (1 WICKET)

Team	Versus	Batted 1st	Batted 2nd	Venue	Date
England	West Indies	WI 10-181	Eng 9-182	Leeds	5 Sep 1973
West Indies	Pakistan	Pak 7-266	WI 9-267	Birmingham	11 Jun 1975
New Zealand	West Indies	WI 7-203	NZ 9-207	Christchurch	6 Feb 1980
West Indies	Pakistan	Pak 10-177	WI 9-107†	Brisbane	16 Jan 1982
West Indies	Pakistan	Pak 8-177	WI 9-180	Adelaide	28 Jan 1984
Pakistan	New Zealand	NZ 8-213	Pak 9-214	Multan	7 Dec 1984

Team	Versus	Batted 1st	Batted 2nd	Venue	Date
Pakistan	India	NZ 7-245	Pak 9-248	Sharjah	18 Apr 1986
Pakistan	Australia	Aus 6-273	Pak 9-274	Perth	2 Jan 1987
England	Pakistan	Pak 9-213	Eng 9-217	Birmingham	25 May 1987
Pakistan	West Indies	WI 10-216	Pak 9-217	Lahore	16 Oct 1987
England	West Indies	WI 8-173	Eng 9-175	Birmingham	23/24 May 1987
West Indies	Pakistan	Pak 10-215	WI 9-217	Sharjah	17 Oct 1991
Australia	New Zealand	NZ 8-196	Aus 9-197	Christchurch	21/22 Mar 1993
New Zealand	Pakistan	Pak 9-232	NZ 9-236	Christchurch	17 Dec1995
Australia	West Indies	WI 9-172	Aus 9-173	Sydney	1 Jan 1996
West Indies	New Zealand	NZ 10-243	WI 9-247	Kingston	26 Mar 1996
West Indies	England	Eng 10-266	WI 9-267	Bridgetown	1 Apr 1998
Sri Lanka	England	Eng 3-302	SL 9-303	Adelaide	23 Jan 1999

†revised target

VICTORY WITH ONE BALL TO SPARE*

Team	Versus	Batted 1st	Batted 2nd	Venue	Date
New Zealand	England	Eng 234	NZ 8-238	Birmingham	15 Jun 1983
New Zealand	India	Ind 8-238	NZ 5-239	Melbourne	23 Jan 1986
England	Australia	Aus 8-233	Eng 7-234	Sydney	22 Jan 1987
Pakistan	Australia	Aus 6-273	Pak 9-274	Perth	2 Jan 1987
New Zealand	Sri Lanka	SL 241	NZ 6-242	Adelaide	9 Jan 1988
Pakistan	West Indies	WI 5-273	Pak 6-277	Calcutta	1 Nov 1989
New Zealand	England	Eng 6-295	NZ 6-298	Leeds	23 May 1990
Sri Lanka	South Africa	SAF 195	SL 7-198	Wellington	2 Mar 1992
New Zealand	India	Ind 6-222	NZ 4-223	Christchurch	2 Apr 1994
New Zealand	Pakistan	Pak 9-232	NZ 9-236	Christchurch	17 Dec 1995
New Zealand	West Indies	WI 7-238	NZ 6-239	Port-of-Spain	29 Mar 1996
Pakistan	India	Ind 6-264	Pak 8-266	Toronto	17 Sep 1996
India	Pakistan	Pak 5-314	Ind 7-316	Dhaka	18 Jan 1998
West Indies	England	Eng 266	WI 9-267	Bridgetown	1 Apr 1998
India	New Zealand	NZ 10-213	Ind 8-214	Napier	12 Jan 1999

*by the team batting second   *Ross Dundas Cricket Statistics*

VICTORY OFF THE LAST BALL OF THE MATCH*

Team	Versus	Batted 1st	Batted 2nd	Venue	Date
England	Pakistan	Pak 6-208	Eng 7-212	Sahiwal	23 Dec 1977
Australia	West Indies	WI 139	Aus 8-140	Castries	12 Apr 1978
West Indies	Pakistan	Pak 9-127	WI 6-128	Karachi	21 Nov 1980
Pakistan	New Zealand	NZ 8-213	Pak 9-214	Multan	7 Dec 1984
Australia	England	Eng 8-177	Aus 8-178	Sharjah	24 Mar 1985
England	West Indies	WI 3-229	Eng 5-230	Port-of-Spain	4 Mar 1986
Pakistan	India	Ind 7-245	Pak 9-248	Sharjah	18 Apr 1986
Pakistan	West Indies	WI 216	Pak 9-217	Lahore	16 Oct 1987
West Indies	England	Eng 8-214	WI 7-216	Kingston	3 Mar 1990
England	India	Ind 3-223	Eng 6-224	Jaipur	18 Jan 1993
Australia	West Indies	WI 9-172	Aus 9-173	Sydney	1 Jan 1996
New Zealand	Zimbabwe	Zim 7-258	NZ 5-260	Dhaka	24 Oct 1998
New Zealand	India	Ind 5-257	NZ 5-200†	Taupo	9 Jan 1999
South Africa	West Indies	WI 4-154	SAF 8-160	Johannesburg	22 Jan 1999

*by the team batting second   *Ross Dundas Cricket Statistics*
†revised target

TIED MATCHES

Match	Batted 1st	Batted 2nd	Venue	Date
Australia v West Indies	WI 5-222	Aus 9-222	Melbourne	11 Feb 1984
India v Pakistan	Ind 6-212†	Pak 7-212	Hyderabad (I)	20 Mar 1987
Pakistan v Australia	Aus 8-229	Pak 7-229†	Lahore	14 Oct 1988
England v Australia	Eng 5-226	Aus 8-226	Nottingham	27 May 1989
Pakistan v West Indies	WI 5-186	Pak 9-186	Lahore	22 Nov 1991
India v West Indies	Ind 10-126	WI 10-126	Perth	6 Dec 1991
Australia v Pakistan	Aus 7-228	Pak 9-228	Hobart (B)	10 Dec 1992
West Indies v Pakistan	Pak 6-244	WI 5-244	Georgetown	3 Apr 1993
India v Zimbabwe	Ind 5-248	Zim 10-248	Indore	18 Nov 1993
New Zealand v Pakistan	Pak 9-161	NZ 10-161	Auckland	13 Mar 1994
Zimbabwe v Pakistan	Zim 9-219	Pak 10-219	Harare	22 Feb 1995
New Zealand v Sri Lanka	NZ 8-169	SL 10-169	Sharjah	11 Nov 1996
India v Zimbabwe	Zim 8-236	Ind 10-236	Paarl	27 Jan 1997
New Zealand v England	NZ 10-237	Eng 8-237	Napier	26 Feb 1997
Zimbabwe v New Zealand	Zim 8-233	NZ 9-233	Bulawayo (QS)	1 Oct 1997

†declared winners as they lost fewer wickets

FORFEITED MATCHES

Forfeiting team	Versus	Venue	Date
Australia	Sri Lanka	Colombo (RPS)	17 Feb 1996
West Indies	Sri Lanka	Colombo (RPS)	25 Feb 1996

MATCHES PLAYED OVER TWO DAYS

Match	Venue	Dates
England v India	The Oval	15/16 Jul 1974
England v West Indies	Lord's	28/29 Aug 1976
England v Pakistan	Manchester	24/25 May 1978
Australia v Pakistan	Nottingham	13/14 Jun 1979
India v Sri Lanka	Manchester	16/18 Jun 1979
England v West Indies	Leeds	28/29 May 1980
India v West Indies	Manchester	9/10 Jun 1983
New Zealand v Pakistan	Birmingham	11/12 Jun 1983
Australia v West Indies	Leeds	11/12 Jun 1983
England v West Indies	Lord's	23/24 May 1988
England v West Indies	Birmingham	23/24 May 1991
England v Pakistan	Lord's	22/23 Aug 1992
Australia v New Zealand	Christchurch	21/22 Mar 1993
England v South Africa	Manchester	27/28 Aug 1994
England v West Indies	Nottingham	24/25 May 1995
England v India	Manchester	26/27 May 1995

VICTORIES BY ICC ASSOCIATE MEMBERS OVER FULL MEMBER COUNTRIES

Team	Versus	Batted 1st	Batted 2nd	Result	Venue	Date
Sri Lanka	India	SL 5-238	Ind 191	SL by 47 runs	Manchester	16/18 Jun 1979
Zimbabwe†	Australia	Zim 6-239	Aus 7-226	Zim by 13 runs	Nottingham	9 Jun 1983
Zimbabwe	England	Zim 134	Eng 125	Zim by 9 runs	Albury	18 Mar 1992
Kenya	West Indies	Ken 166	WI 93	Ken by 73 runs	Pune	29 Feb 1996
Kenya	India	Ken 5-265	Ind 196	Ken by 69 runs	New Delhi	28 May 1998

†Zimbabwe's first limited-overs international

MOST CONSECUTIVE WINS
11 by West Indies

Versus	Result	Venue	Date
England	WI won by 8 wkts	Lord's	4 Jun 1984
Australia	WI won by 7 wkts	Melbourne	6 Jan 1985
Sri Lanka	WI won by 8 wkts	Hobart	10 Jan 1985
Sri Lanka	WI won by 90 runs	Brisbane	12 Jan 1985
Australia	WI won by 5 wkts	Brisbane	13 Jan 1985
Australia	WI won by 5 wkts	Sydney	15 Jan 1985
Sri Lanka	WI won by 65 runs	Sydney	17 Jan 1985
Australia	WI won by 65 runs	Melbourne	20 Jan 1985
Sri Lanka	WI won by 8 wkts	Adelaide	26 Jan 1985
Australia	WI won by 6 wkts	Adelaide	27 Jan 1985
Sri Lanka	WI won by 82 runs	Perth	2 Feb 1985

Note: England went 12 games without defeat between 23 May 1991 and 12 March 1992, including a no result against Pakistan on 1 March in which England dismissed Pakistan for 74 and were 1 for 24 in reply when rain intervened. Australia went 11 games without defeat between 7 January 1988 and 12 December 1988, winning 10 and tieing one.

MOST CONSECUTIVE WINS FOR EACH COUNTRY

Country	Wins	From	To
Australia	10	23 Feb 1990	2 May 1990
Bangladesh	1	17 May 1998	17 May 1998
England	{ 8	23 May 1991	27 Feb 1992
	{ 8	22 May 1997	29 Mar 1998
India	8	20 Feb 1985	25 Aug 1985
Kenya	2	23 May 1998	28 May 1998
New Zealand	{ 7	19 Feb 1983	20 Mar 1983
	{ 7	22 Feb 1992	15 Mar 1992
Pakistan	10	27 Apr 1990	13 Nov 1990
South Africa	10	13 Jan 1996	5 Mar 1996
Sri Lanka	7	13 Apr 1996	1 Oct 1996
UAE	1	1 Mar 1996	1 Mar 1996
West Indies	11	4 Jun 1984	2 Feb 1985
Zimbabwe	6	11 Oct 1997	19 Oct 1997

Note: Canada, East Africa and The Netherlands have never won a match.

MOST CONSECUTIVE LOSSES
22 by Bangladesh

Versus	Result	Venue	Date
Pakistan	Ban lost by 7 wkts	Moratuwa	31 Mar 1986
Sri Lanka	Ban lost by 7 wkts	Kandy	2 Apr 1986
India	Ban lost by 9 wkts	Chittagong	27 Oct 1988
Pakistan	Ban lost by 173 runs	Chittagong	29 Oct 1988
Sri Lanka	Ban lost by 9 wkts	Dhaka	2 Nov 1988
New Zealand	Ban lost by 161 runs	Sharjah	28 Apr 1990
Australia	Ban lost by 7 wkts	Sharjah	30 Apr 1990
India	Ban lost by 9 wkts	Chandigarh	25 Dec 1990
Sri Lanka	Ban lost by 71 runs	Calcutta	31 Dec 1990
India	Ban lost by 9 wkts	Sharjah	5 Apr 1995
Sri Lanka	Ban lost by 107 runs	Sharjah	6 Apr 1995
Pakistan	Ban lost by 6 wkts	Sharjah	8 Apr 1995
Pakistan	Ban lost by 109 runs	Colombo (RPS)	16 Jul 1997
Sri Lanka	Ban lost by 103 runs	Colombo (SSC)	22 Jul 1997
India	Ban lost by 9 wkts	Colombo (SSC)	24 Jul 1997

Versus	Result	Venue	Date
Kenya	Ban lost by 150 runs	Nairobi (NG)	10 Oct 1997
Zimbabwe	Ban lost by 48 runs	Nairobi (NG)	11 Oct 1997
Zimbabwe	Ban lost by 192 runs	Nairobi (AK)	14 Oct 1997
Kenya	Ban lost by 8 wkts	Nairobi (AK)	15 Oct 1997
India	Ban lost by 4 wkts	Dhaka	10 Jan 1998
Pakistan	Ban lost by 9 wkts	Dhaka	12 Jan 1998
India	Ban lost by 9 wkts	Mohali	14 May 1998

MOST CONSECUTIVE LOSSES FOR EACH COUNTRY

Country	Losses	From	To
Australia	6	7 Sep 1996	3 Nov 1996
Bangladesh	22	31 Mar 1986	14 May 1998
Canada	3	9 Jun 1979	16 Jun 1979
East Africa	3	7 Jun 1975	14 Jun 1975
England	7	17 Feb 1985	1 Jan 1985
	7	4 Mar 1993	23 May 1993
India	8	8 Jan 1981	25 Nov 1981
Kenya	5	16 Oct 1997	20 May 1998
Netherlands	5	17 Feb 1996	5 Mar 1996
New Zealand	7	5 Mar 1985	23 Apr 1985
	7	11 Dec 1994	28 Jan 1995
Pakistan	10	30 Oct 1987	30 Mar 1988
South Africa	10	6 Apr 1994	28 Oct 1994
Sri Lanka	14	11 Jan 1987	10 Jan 1988
UAE	6	13 Apr 1994	27 Feb 1996
	5	19 May 1988	18 Oct 1988
	5	14 Oct 1989	21 Oct 1989
	5	9 Nov 1990	9 Mar 1991
West Indies	5	13 Mar 1991	27 May 1991
	5	20 Oct 1995	1 Jan 1996
	5	27 Jan 1999	7 Feb 1999
Zimbabwe	18	11 Jun 1983	14 Mar 1992

Note: New Zealand went 15 games without a win between 20 April 1994 and 26 January 1995 which included 13 losses and two no results.

TWO CENTURIES IN AN INNINGS

Players	Versus	Venue	Date
Moshin Khan 117*, Zaheer Abbas 118, Pakistan	India	Multan	17 Dec 1982
Zaheer Abbas 105, Javed Miandad 119*, Pakistan	India	Lahore	31 Dec 1982
C.G. Greenidge 115, I.V.A. Richards 149, West Indies	India	Jamshedpur	7 Dec 1983
G.A. Gooch 117*, D.I. Gower 102, England	Australia	Lord's	3 Jun 1985
G.R. Marsh 104, D.C. Boon 111, Australia	India	Jaipur	7 Sept 1985
D.L. Haynes 105, I.V.A. Richards 181, West Indies	Sri Lanka	Karachi	13 Oct 1987
Moin-ul-Atiq 105 Ijaz Ahmed 124*, Pakistan	Bangladesh	Chittagong	29 Oct 1988
Ramiz Raja 107*, Saeed Anwar 126, Pakistan	Sri Lanka	Adelaide	17 Feb 1990
R.J. Shastri 109, S.V. Manjrekar 105, India	South Africa	New Delhi	14 Nov 1991
Salim Malik 102, Inzamam-ul-Haq 117, Pakistan	Sri Lanka	Rawalpindi (RC)	19 Jan 1992
Saeed Anwar 110, Ramiz Raja 109*, Pakistan	Sri Lanka	Sharjah	4 Feb 1993
Saeed Anwar 110, Asif Mujtaba 113*, Pakistan	Sri Lanka	Sharjah	30 Oct 1993
Aamir Sohail 134, Inzamam-ul-Haq 137*, Pakistan	New Zealand	Sharjah	20 Apr 1994
B.C. Lara 104, P.V. Simmons 103*, West Indies	New Zealand	Kingstown	6 Apr 1996
S.R. Tendulkar 118, N.S. Sidhu 101, India	Pakistan	Sharjah	15 Apr 1996
D.J. Cullinan 124, J.N. Rhodes 121, South Africa	Pakistan	Nairobi (NG)	29 Sept 1996
Saeed Anwar 115, Shahid Afridi 102, Pakistan	Sri Lanka	Nairobi (NG)	4 Oct 1996
B.C. Lara 102, C.L. Hooper 110*, West Indies	Australia	Brisbane	5 Jan 1997

TWO CENTURIES IN AN INNINGS - CONT

Players	Versus	Venue	Date
M.A. Azharuddin 111*, A.D. Jadeja 119, India	Sri Lanka	Colombo (RPS)	17 Aug 1997
D. Chudasama 122, K. Otieno 144, Kenya	Bangladesh	Nairobi (NG)	10 Oct 1997
S.T. Jayasuriya 134*, P.A. de Silva 102*, Sri Lanka	Pakistan	Lahore	5 Nov 1997
Saeed Anwar 140, Ijaz Ahmed 117, Pakistan	India	Dhaka	18 Jan 1998
M.A. Azharuddin 153*, A.D. Jadeja 116*, India	Zimbabwe	Cuttack	9 Apr 1998
S.C. Ganguly 109, S.R. Tendulkar 128, India	Sri Lanka	Colombo (RPS)	7 Jul 1998
Ijaz Ahmed 111, Yousuf Youhana 100, Pakistan	Australia	Lahore	10 Nov 1998
A.C. Gilchrist 103, R.T. Ponting 124*, Australia	Pakistan	Lahore	10 Nov 1998
S. Chanderpaul 150, C.L. Hooper 108, West Indies	South Africa	East London	24 Jan 1999

FOUR CENTURIES IN A MATCH

Players	Venue	Date
Ijaz Ahmed 111, Yousuf Youhana 100, Pakistan A.C. Gilchrist 103, R.T. Ponting 124*, Australia	Lahore	10 Nov 1998

THREE CENTURIES IN A MATCH

Players	Venue	Date
G.A. Gooch 117*, D.I. Gower 102, England G.M. Wood 114*, Australia	Lord's	3 Jun 1985
G.R. Marsh 104, D.C. Boon 111, Australia K. Srikkanth 102, India	Jaipur	7 Sept 1985
Saeed Anwar 115, Shahid Afridi 102, Pakistan P.A. de Silva 122, Sri Lanka	Nairobi (NG)	4 Oct 1996
B.C. Lara 102, C.L. Hooper 110*, West Indies M.E. Waugh 102, Australia	Brisbane	5 Jan 1997
M.A. Azharuddin 111*, A.D. Jadeja 119, India M. Atapattu 118, Sri Lanka	Colombo (RPS)	17 Aug 1997
Saeed Anwar 140, Ijaz Ahmed 117, Pakistan S.C. Ganguly 124, India	Dhaka	18 Jan 1998
M.A. Azharuddin 153*, A.D. Jadeja 116*, India G.W. Flower 102, Zimbabwe	Cuttack	9 Apr 1998
S.C. Ganguly 109, S.R. Tendulkar 128, India P.A. de Silva 105, Sri Lanka	Colombo (RPS)	7 Jul 1998

FOUR HALF-CENTURIES IN AN INNINGS

Players	Versus	Venue	Date
R.B. McCosker 73, A. Turner 101 G.S. Chappell 50, K.D. Walters 59, Australia	Sri Lanka	The Oval	11 June 1975
G.A. Gooch 108, G. Boycott 78 C.W.J. Athey 51, R.O. Butcher 52, England	Australia	Birmingham	22 Aug 1980
Mohsin Khan 82, Zaheer Abbas 82 Javed Miandad 72, Imran Khan 56*, Pakistan	Sri Lanka	Swansea	9 June 1983

Players	Versus	Venue	Date
A. Flower 56, G.W. Flower 63 D.L. Houghton 50, M.H. Dekker 55, Zimbabwe	New Zealand	Harare	8 Nov 1992
D.L. Haynes 83, P.V. Simmons 63 B.C. Lara 60, R.B. Richardson 52*, West Indies	England	Kingstown	2 Mar 1994
C.M. Spearman 68, S.P. Fleming 66 C.L. Cairns 52, A.C. Parore 55, New Zealand	Netherlands	Vadodara (IPCL)	17 Feb 1996
S.T. Jayasuriya 96, P.A. de Silva 90 M.S. Atapattu 53, A. Ranatunga 80, Sri Lanka	Pakistan	Mohali	24 May 1997
Saeed Anwar 90, Ramiz Raja 52 Inzamam-ul-Haq 77, Salim Malik 62, Pakistan	Bangladesh	Colombo (RPS)	16 July 1997
S.T. Jayasuriya 57, R.S. Kaluwitharana 54 P.A. de Silva 62, A. Ranatunga 86, Sri Lanka	Pakistan	Kimberley	7 Apr 1998

SIX HALF-CENTURIES IN A MATCH

Players	Venue	Date
R.B. McCosker 73, A. Turner 101 G.S. Chappell 50, K.D. Walters 59, Australia S.R. de Wettimuny 53, M.H. Tissera 52, Sri Lanka	The Oval	11 June 1975
G.A. Gooch 108, G. Boycott 78 C.W.J. Athey 51, R.O. Butcher 52, England K.J. Hughes 98, G.N. Yallop 52*, Australia	Birmingham	22 Aug 1980
Mohsin Khan 82, Zaheer Abbas 82 Javed Miandad 72, Imran Khan 56*, Pakistan D.S.B.P. Kuruppu 72, R.G. de Alwis 59*, Sri Lanka	Swansea	9 June 1983
J.G. Wright 70, A.H. Jones 57 M.J. Greatbatch 84*, New Zealand S.V. Manjrekar 52, A.K. Sharma 50 M.A. Azharudin 108*, India	Vadodara (MB)	17 Dec 1988
K. Srikkanth 51, N.S. Sidhu 108, M. Armanath 88, India Shahid Saeed 50, Shoaib Mohammed 65 Salim Malik 68*, Pakistan	Sharjah	15 Oct 1989
M.A. Atherton 59, R.A. Smith 103 R.C. Russell 50, England S.V. Manjrekar 59, D.B. Vengsarkar 54 M.A. Azharuddin 63*, India	Nottingham	20 July 1990
R.J. Shastri 109, K. Srikkanth 53 S.V. Manjrekar 105, India K.C. Wessels 90, P.N. Kirsten 86* A.P. Kuiper 63*, South Africa	New Delhi	14 Nov 1991

SIX HALF-CENTURIES IN A MATCH - CONT

Players	Venue	Date
A. Flower 115*, K.J. Arnott 52 A.C. Waller 83*, Zimbabwe R.S. Mahanama 59, A. Ranatunga 88* M.A.R. Samarasekera 75, Sri Lanka	New Plymouth	23 Feb 1992
A. Flower 56, G.W. Flower 63 D.L. Houghton 50, M.H. Dekker 55, Zimbabwe M.J. Greatbatch 55, M.D. Crowe 94, New Zealand	Harare	8 Nov 1992
R.A. Smith 75, M.A. Atherton 66 G.P. Thorpe 52*, England Saeed Anwar 71, Ijaz Ahmed 70, Inzamam-ul-Haq 53*, Pakistan	Karachi	3 Mar 1996
Saeed Anwar 90, Ramiz Raja 52 Inzamam-ul-Haq 77, Salim Malik 62, Pakistan Athar Ali Khan 82, Akram Khan 59, Bangladesh	Colombo (RPS)	16 July 1997
S.T. Jayasuriya 57, R.S. Kaluwitharana 54 P.A. de Silva 62, A. Ranatunga 86, Sri Lanka Ijaz Ahmed 59, Inzamam-ul-Haq 116, Pakistan	Kimberley	7 Apr 1998

FASTEST RUN-RATES IN AN INNINGS (minimum 25 overs)

Run-rate	Team	Versus	Total/Overs	Venue	Date
8.32	Pakistan	India	1-219 (26.2 overs)	Lahore	2 Oct 1997
7.96	Sri Lanka	Kenya	5-398 (50 overs)	Kandy	6 Mar 1996
7.64	Pakistan	India	3-252 (33 overs)	Lahore	31 Dec 1982
7.48	India	Sri Lanka	4-299 (40 overs)	Bombay	17 Jan 1987
7.42	Pakistan	Sri Lanka	9-371 (50 overs)	Nairobi (NG)	4 Oct 1996
7.40	West Indies	India	8-333 (45 overs)	Jamshedpur	7 Dec 1983
7.23	Sri Lanka	India	7-289 (40 overs)	Bombay	17 Jan 1987
7.20	West Indies	Sri Lanka	4-360 (50 overs)	Karachi	13 Oct 1987
7.15	India	Pakistan	4-193 (27 overs)	Lahore	31 Dec 1982
7.03	Sri Lanka	Pakistan	2-281 (40 overs)	Lahore	5 Nov 1997

FASTEST RUN-RATES IN A MATCH (minimum 50 overs)

R-R	Match	Batted 1st	Batted 2nd	Venue	Date
7.42	Pakistan v India	Pak 3-252 (33 overs)	Ind 4-193 (27 overs)	Lahore	31 Dec 1982
7.35	India v Sri Lanka	Ind 4-299 (40 overs)	SL 7-289 (40 overs)	Bombay	17 Jan 1987
6.67	India v New Zealand	NZ 8-348 (50 overs)	Ind 10-249 (39.3 overs)	Nagpur	26 Nov 1995
6.66	Pakistan v Sri Lanka	SL 9-349 (50 overs)	Pak 10-315 (49.4 overs)	Singapore	2 Apr 1996
6.65	England v Pakistan	Eng 7-194 (30 overs)	Pak 4-195 (28.3 overs)	Nagpur	13 Oct 1989
6.65	Sri Lanka v West Indies	WI 7-333 (50 overs)	SL 10-329 (49.3 overs)	Sharjah	16 Oct 1995
6.61	Pakistan v Sri Lanka	Pak 9-371 (50 overs)	SL 10-289 (49.5 overs)	Nairobi (NG)	4 Oct 1996
6.58	Australia v New Zealand	Aus 4-199 (30 overs)	NZ 9-196 (30 overs)	Indore	19 Oct 1987
6.57	India v Pakistan	Pak 5-314 (48 overs)	Ind 7-316 (47.5 overs)	Dhaka	18 Jan 1998
6.56	Australia v West Indies	Aus 4-226 (38 overs)	WI 2-111 (13.2 overs)	Sydney	18 Jan 1989
6.53	West Indies v Pakistan	Pak 6-271 (43 overs)	WI 3-272 (40.1 overs)	Port-of-Spain	20 Mar 1988
6.52	Sri Lanka v Kenya	SL 5-398 (50 overs)	Ken 7-254 (50 overs)	Kandy	6 Mar 1996

SLOWEST RUN-RATES IN AN INNINGS (minimum 25 overs)

R-R	Team	Versus	Total/Overs	Venue	Date
1.11	Canada	England	10-45 (40.3 overs)	Manchester	13 Jun 1979
1.69	Pakistan	West Indies	10-81 (48 overs)	Sydney	17 Dec 1992
1.79	East Africa	England	10-94 (52.3 overs)	Birmingham	14 Jun 1975
1.79	New Zealand	Pakistan	10-64 (35.5 overs)	Sharjah	15 Apr 1986
1.81	Pakistan	England	10-85 (47 overs)	Manchester	24/25 May 1978
1.83	Pakistan	England	10-74 (40.2 overs)	Adelaide	1 Mar 1992
1.93	Sri Lanka	West Indies	10-55 (28.3 overs)	Sharjah	3 Dec 1986

SLOWEST RUN-RATES IN A MATCH (minimum 50 overs)

R-R	Match	Batted 1st	Batted 2nd	Venue	Date
1.67	England v Canada	Can 10-45 (40.3 overs)	Eng 2-46 (13.5 overs)	Manchester	13 Jun 1979
2.22	New Zealand v Pakistan	NZ 10-64 (35.5 overs)	Pak 0-66 (22.4 overs)	Sharjah	15 Apr 1986
2.49	Australia v England	Aus 10-101 (33.5 overs)	Eng 3-102 (28.2 overs)	Melbourne	24 Jan 1979
2.63	West Indies v England	WI 10-127 (47.2 overs)	Eng 10-125 (48.2 overs)	Kingstown	4 Feb 1981
2.65	Australia v England	Eng 10-94 (31.7 overs)	Aus 4-95 (21.5 overs)	Melbourne	7 Feb 1979
2.70	India v New Zealand	Ind 10-113 (44.2 overs)	NZ 7-115 (40.1 overs)	Perth	18 Jan 1986
2.72	England v Zimbabwe	Zim 10-134 (46.1 overs)	Eng 10-125 (49.1 overs)	Albury	18 Mar 1992
2.72	England v Pakistan	Eng 9-165 (60 overs)	Pak 10-151 (56 overs)	Leeds	16 Jun 1979
2.75	Australia v South Africa	SAF 10-123 (46.2 overs)	Aus 7-124 (43.2 overs)	Wellington	15 Feb1995

Note: The matches between Australia and England consisted of eight-ball overs.

MOST FOURS IN AN INNINGS

No.	Team	Versus	Total	Venue	Date
43	Sri Lanka	Kenya	7-398	Kandy	6 Mar 1996
37	Sri Lanka	Australia	4-276	The Oval	11 Jun 1975
36	New Zealand	India	8-348	Nagpur	26 Nov 1995
35	New Zealand	Sri Lanka	5-209	Bristol	13 Jun 1983
35	West Indies	Pakistan	4-315	Port-of-Spain	18 Mar 1988
35	West Indies	Australia	5-287	Georgetown	18 Mar 1995
35	West Indies	England	5-302	Port-of-Spain	8 Apr 1998
34	Pakistan	Sri Lanka	6-330	Nottingham	14 Jun 1975
34	West Indies	Pakistan	4-285	Sharjah	5 Nov 1993
34	Pakistan	New Zealand	2-328	Sharjah	20 Apr 1994
34	Sri Lanka	Pakistan	4-339	Chandigarh	24 May 1997
34	West Indies	England	10-277	Bridgetown	29 Mar 1998
34	India	Australia	5-309	Kochi	1 Apr 1998

MOST SIXES IN AN INNINGS

No.	Team	Versus	Total	Venue	Date
14	Sri Lanka	Kenya	5-398	Kandy	6 Mar 1996
14	Sri Lanka	Pakistan	9-349	Singapore	2 Apr 1996
14	Pakistan	Sri Lanka	9-371	Nairobi (NG)	4 Oct 1996
12	Pakistan	India	1-219	Lahore	2 Oct 1997
11	Pakistan	Sri Lanka	6-300	Kimberely	7 Apr 1998
10	New Zealand	Zimbabwe	7-294	Harare	5 Oct 1997
9	West Indies	India	1-241	Trivandrum	25 Jan 1988
9	Australia	Sri Lanka	3-332	Sharjah	2 May 1990
9	Australia	New Zealand	4-258	Dunedin	19 Mar 1993
9	New Zealand	Sri Lanka	6-280	Hamilton	29 Mar 1995
9	Pakistan	India	6-316	Toronto	19 Sep 1998
9	India	Zimbabwe	0-197	Sharjah	13 Nov 1998

No.	Team	Versus	Total	Venue	Date
8	West Indies	India	8-333	Jamshedpur	7 Dec 1983
8	West Indies	Sri Lanka	4-360	Karachi	3 Oct 1987
8	West Indies	India	2-240	St. John's	18 Mar 1989
8	Pakistan	Sri Lanka	3-315	Adelaide	17 Feb 1990
8	Pakistan	Sri Lanka	7-237	Colombo (SSC)	7 Aug 1994
8	Sri Lanka	New Zealand	4-288	Bloemfontein	8 Dec 1994
8	West Indies	Sri Lanka	7-333	Sharjah	16 Oct 1995
8	Sri Lanka	Zimbabwe	4-229	Colombo (SSC)	21 Feb 1996
8	India	Pakistan	5-305	Sharjah	15 Apr 1996
8	India	Australia	4-223	Kanpur	7 Apr 1998

HIGHEST % OF BOUNDARIES IN AN INNINGS (minimum 200 overs)

%	Team	Versus	Total	Venue	Date
66.98	New Zealand	Sri Lanka	5-209	Bristol	13 Jun 1983
64.32	Sri Lanka	Kenya	7-398	Kandy	6 Mar 1996

MOST BATSMEN CAUGHT IN AN INNINGS

No.	Team	Versus	Venue	Date
10	Sri Lanka	Pakistan	Colombo (PSS)	30 Mar 1986
10	New Zealand	Australia	Auckland	11 Mar 1990
10	Pakistan	India	Toronto	18 Sep 1997

MOST BATSMEN CAUGHT IN A MATCH

No.	Match	Venue	Date
18	Sri Lanka v Pakistan	Colombo (PSS)	30 Mar 1986
16	India v New Zealand	Perth	9 Dec 1980
16	Zimbabwe v Pakistan	Harare	26 Feb 1995
16	India v Pakistan	Toronto	18 Sep 1997
16	Zimbabwe v South Africa	Harare	22 Oct 1995
16	India v Pakistan	Toronto	13 Sep 1998
15	Sri Lanka v West Indies	Hobart (B)	3 Jan 1996
15	Sri Lanka v West Indies	Port-of-Spain	13 Apr 1996

MOST BATSMEN BOWLED IN AN INNINGS

No.	Team	Versus	Venue	Date
8	New Zealand	West Indles	Berbice	14 Apr 1985
7	East Africa	England	Birmingham	14 Jun 1975
7	Australia	West Indies	Melbourne	22 Jan 1984
7	New Zealand	Pakistan	East London	19 Dec 1994
7	India	Pakistan	Hyderabad(P)	28 Sep 1997

MOST BATSMEN BOWLED IN A MATCH

No.	Match	Venue	Date
10	England v East Africa	Birmingham	14 Jun 1975
10	West Indies v Australia	Melbourne	22 Jan 1984
10	Pakistan v West Indies	Multan	13 Nov 1990

MOST BATSMEN RUN OUT IN AN INNINGS

No.	Team	Versus	Venue	Date
5	Australia	West Indies	Lord's	21 Jun 1975
5	New Zealand	Sri Lanka	Sharjah	29 Mar 1988
5	Pakistan	West Indies	Adelaide	12 Dec 1992
5	Australia	India	Mumbai	27 Feb 1996
5	New Zealand	India	Napier	12 Jan 1999

MOST BATSMEN RUN OUT IN A MATCH

No.	Match	Venue	Date
8	New Zealand v India	Napier	12 Jan 1999
7	Australia v New Zealand	Chandigarh	27 Oct 1987
7	New Zealand v Sri Lanka	Sharjah	29 Mar 1988
7	India v South Africa	Calcutta	24 Nov 1993
7	Sri Lanka v Australia	Sydney	21 Dec 1995

MOST BATSMEN STUMPED IN AN INNINGS

No.	Team	Versus	Venue	Date
3	New Zealand	Pakistan	Lahore	2 Nov 1990
3	South Africa	Australia	East London	2 Apr 1994
3	South Africa	Australia	Faisalabad	18 Oct 1994
3	West Indies	Pakistan	Sharjah	13 Oct 1995

MOST BATSMEN STUMPED IN A MATCH

No.	Match	Venue	Date
4	India v Pakistan	Toronto	18 Sep 1996

MOST BATSMEN LBW IN AN INNINGS

No.	Team	Versus	Venue	Date
5	England	Australia	Leeds	18 Jun 1975
5	West Indies	India	Sharjah	19 Oct 1991
5	Sri Lanka	Pakistan	Sharjah	4 Feb 1993
5	New Zealand	Pakistan	Sharjah	15 Nov 1996
5	Sri Lanka	Zimbabwe	Sharjah	7 Nov 1998

MOST BATSMEN LBW IN A MATCH

No.	Match	Venue	Date
8	England v Australia	Leeds	18 Jun 1975
8	Pakistan v New Zealand	Sharjah	15 Nov 1996
6	Pakistan v India	Dhaka	31 Oct 1988
6	South Africa v Kenya	Nairobi (NG)	3 Oct 1996
6	South Africa v Pakistan	Lahore	2 Nov 1997
6	England v South Africa	Manchester	23 May 1998

UNUSUAL DISMISSALS

Handled The Ball

Batsman	Versus	Venue	Date
M. Amarnath, India	Australia	Melbourne	9 Feb 1986
D.J. Cullinan, South Africa	West Indies	Durban	27 Jan 1999

Obstructing The Field

Batsman	Versus	Venue	Date
Ramiz Raja, Pakistan	England	Karachi	20 Nov 1987
M. Amarnath, India	Sri Lanka	Ahmedabad	22 Oct 1989

Mankaded[†]

Batsman	Bowler	Venue	Date
B. Luckhurst, England	G.S. Chappell, Australia	Melbourne	1 Jan 1975
G. Flower, Zimbabwe	Dipak Patel, New Zealand	Harare	8 Nov 1992
P.N. Kirsten, South Africa	Kapil Dev, India	Port Elizabeth	9 Dec 1992

[†]*Run out while backing up too far at the non-striker's end.*

MOST DUCKS IN AN INNINGS

Ducks	Players	Team	Versus	Venue	Date
6	Mudassar Nazar, Mansoor Aktar Manzoor Elahi, Salim Yousef, Wasim Akram, Tausif Ahmed	Pakistan	England	Birmingham	25 May 1987
6	Ramiz Raja, Asif Mujtaba Wasim Akram, Rashid Latif Waqar Younis, Mushtaq Ahmed	Pakistan	West Indies	Cape Town	25 Feb 1993
5	D.I. Gower, W. Larkins C.M. Old, R.W. Taylor, M. Hendrick	England	West Indies	Lord's	23 Jun 1979
5	J.P. Crawley, N. Hussain R.C. Irani, C. White, C.E.W. Silverwood	England	Zimbabwe	Harare	3 Jan 1997
5	S.L. Campbell, J.R. Murray C.L. Hooper, P.V. Simmons, C.A. Walsh	West Indies	Pakistan	Melbourne	20 Jan 1997

MOST DUCKS IN A MATCH

Ducks	Players	Venue	Date
8	D.I. Gower, W Larkins, C.M. Old R.W. Taylor, M. Hendrick, England A.M.E. Roberts, J Garner M.A. Holding, West Indies	Lord's	23 Jun 1979
7	A.R. Border, R.W. Marsh D.K. Lillee, G. Dymock, Australia P. Willey, D.W. Randall I.T. Botham, England	Sydney	14 Jan 1980
7	Ramiz Raja, Asif Mujtaba Wasim Akram, Mushtaq Ahmed Rashid Latif, Waqar Younis, Pakistan DL Haynes, West Indies	Cape Town	25 Feb 1993
7	S.L. Campbell, J.R. Murray C.L. Hooper, P.V. Simmons, C.A. Walsh, West Indies Shahid Afridi, Zahoor Elahi, Pakistan	Melbourne	20 Jan 1997
6	D.W. Randall, D.L. Underwood A.P.E. Knott, A.W. Greig, England I.C. Davis, M.H.N. Walker, Australia	Birmingham	4 June 1977

Ducks	Players	Venue	Date
6	A.M.E Roberts, M.A. Holding, J. Garner, West Indies K.J. Hughes, D.K. Lillee, L.S. Pascoe, Australia	Melbourne	24 Jan 1982
6	Mudassar Nazar, Mansoor Akhtar Manzoor Elahi, Salim Yousef Wasim Akram, Tausif Ahmed, Pakistan[†]	Birmingham	25 May 1987
6	L. Klusener, D.J. Richardson J.H. Kallis,P.R. Adams, South Africa R.A. Smith, G.P. Thorpe,England	East London	19 Jan 1996

[†]versus England

TEAM BREACHES OF THE ICC CODE OF CONDUCT

Team	Offence	Versus	Venue	Date	Punishment
South Africa	Appalling behaviour	India	Port Elizabeth	9 Dec 1992	Warning
India	Appalling behaviour	South Africa	Port Elizabeth	9 Dec 1992	Warning

Source: International Cricket Council

The Players

MOST APPEARANCES

No.	Player	Career
10	M.A. Azharuddin, India	1985-99
276	Salim Malik, Pakistan	1982-98
273	A.R. Border, Australia	1978-94
260	A. Ranatunga, Sri Lanka	1982-99
254	Wasim Akram, Pakistan	1984-98
251	S.R. Waugh, Australia	1986-99
250	P.A. de Silva, Sri Lanka	1984-99
238	D.L. Haynes, West Indies	1978-94
233	Javed Miandad, Pakistan	1975-96
225	Kapil Dev, India	1978-94
224	R.B. Richardson, West Indies	1983-96
215	Ijaz Ahmed, Pakistan	1986-98
211	S.R. Tendulkar, India	1989-99
208	R.S. Mahanama, Sri Lanka	1986-99
198	Ramiz Raja, Pakistan	1985-97
187	I.V.A. Richards, West Indies	1975-91
185	C.A. Walsh, West Indies	1985-98
181	D.C. Boon, Australia	1984-95
178	S.T. Jayasuriya, Sri Lanka	1989-99
177	C.L. Hooper, West Indies	1987-99
176	H.P. Tillakaratne, Sri Lanka	1986-99
175	Imran Khan, Pakistan	1974-92
174	M.E. Waugh, Australia	1988-99
172	Waqar Younis, Pakistan	1989-98
171	Inzamam-ul-Haq, Pakistan	1991-98
169	P.J.L. Dujon, West Indies	1981-91
168	I.A. Healy, Australia	1988-97
164	D.M. Jones, Australia	1984-94
163	Aqib Javed, Pakistan	1988-98
161	Saeed Anwar, Pakistan	1989-98
158	A. Kumble, India	1990-99
158	A.L. Logie, West Indies	1981-93
157	C.E.L. Ambrose, West Indies	1988-99
154	A.D. Jadeja, India	1992-99
153	J. Srinath, India	1991-99
152	W.J. Cronje, South Africa	1992-99
150	R.J. Shastri, India	1981-92

MOST APPEARANCES FOR EACH COUNTRY

Country	Player	M	Career
Australia	A.R. Border	273	1978-94
Bangladesh	Minhaz-ul-Abedin	23	1986-98
Canada	numerous players	3	1979
East Africa	numerous players	3	1975
England	G.A Gooch	125	1976-95
India	M.A. Azharuddin	310	1985-99
Kenya	numerous players	20	1996-98
Netherlands	numerous players	5	1996
New Zealand	J.G. Wright	149	1978-92
Pakistan	Salim Malik	276	1982-98
South Africa	W.J. Cronje	152	1992-99

Country	Player	M	Career
Sri Lanka	A. Ranatunga	260	1982-99
United Arab Emirates	numerous players	7	1994-96
West Indies	D.L Haynes	238	1978-94
Zimbabwe	A.Flower	100	1992-98

MOST CONSECUTIVE APPEARANCES

No.	Player	From	To
184	S.R. Tendulkar, India	25 Apr 1990	24 Apr 1998
131	R.B. Richardson, West Indies	17 Jan 1987	1 Nov 1993
126	W.J. Cronje, South Africa	4 Sep 1993	7 Feb 1999
125	M.A. Azharuddin, India	6 Dec 1991	3 May 1997
100	A. Flower, Zimbabwe	23 Feb 1992	24 Nov 1998
95	P.A. de Silva, Sri Lanka	3 Aug 1994	24 Jan 1998
95	A.D. Jadeja, India	9 Apr 1995	25 May 1998
95	S.T. Jayasuriya, Sri Lanka	10 Mar 1993	7 Apr 1997
89	A.R. Kumble, India	25 Mar 1994	20 Aug 1997
86	S.R. Waugh, Australia	9 Jan 1986	23 Feb 1990
85	A.D.R. Campbell, Zimbabwe	19 Mar 1993	24 Nov 1998
85	P.A. de Silva, Sri Lanka	8 Oct 1987	7 Nov 1993
82	A.R. Border, Australia	20 Aug 1980	5 Oct 1984

Ross Dundas Cricket Statistics

MOST APPEARANCES AS 12TH MAN

No.	Player	M	Career
31	R.A. Harper, West Indies	105	1983-96
19	J.G. Bracewell, New Zealand	53	1983-90
14	T.B.A. May, Australia	47	1987-95
14	M.A. Taylor, Australia	113	1989-97
13	R.I.C. Holder, West Indies	37	1993-98
13	B.C. Hollioake, England	7	1997-99
13	Mushtaq Ahmed, Pakistan	130	1989-98
11	D.R. Martyn, Australia	31	1992-99
11	Salim Malik, Pakistan	268	1982-97

Ross Dundas Cricket Statistics

LEADING MAN OF THE MATCH AWARDS

Awards	Player	M	Career
32	S.R. Tendulkar, India	211	1989-99
31	I.V.A. Richards, West Indies	187	1975-91
26	D.L. Haynes, West Indies	238	1978-94
26	P.A. de Silva, Sri Lanka	250	1984-99

Ross Dundas Cricket Statistics

YOUNGEST PLAYERS ON DEBUT

Age	Player	Versus	Venue	Date
14 years, 233 days	Hasan Raza, Pakistan	Zimbabwe	Quetta (BS)	30 Oct 1996
16 years, 127 days	Aaqib Javed, Pakistan	West Indies	Adelaide	10 Dec 1988
16 years, 215 days	Shahid Afridi, Pakistan	Kenya	Nairobi (AG)	2 Oct 1996
16 years, 238 days	S.R. Tendulkar, India	Pakistan	Gujranwala	18 Dec 1989
16 years, 334 days	Abdur Razzaq, Pakistan	Zimbabwe	Lahore	1 Nov 1996
16 years, 361 days	Zahid Fazal, Pakistan	New Zealand	Sialkot	6 Nov 1990
17 years, 83 days	Fazl-e-Akbar, Pakistan	India	Dhaka	11 Jan 1998
17 years, 155 days	Maqsood Rana, Pakistan	Australia	Melbourne	3 Jan 1990
17 years, 179 days	M. Nkala, Zimbabwe	India	Bulawayo (QS)	27 Sep 1998
17 years, 222 days	Maninder Singh, India	Pakistan	Karachi	21 Jan 1983
17 years, 251 days	Ata-ur-Rehman, Pakistan	West Indies	Perth	4 Dec 1992

YOUNGEST PLAYERS ON DEBUT FOR EACH COUNTRY

Country	Age	Player	Versus	Venue	Date
Australia	19 years, 260 days	R.J. Bright	New Zealand	Dunedin	30 Mar 1974
Bangladesh	17 years, 307 days	Hasib-ul-Hassan	Sri Lanka	Sharjah	6 Apr 1995
Canada	21 years, 8 days	M.P. Stead	Pakistan	Leeds	9 Jun 1979
East Africa	25 years, 311 days	Frasat Ali	New Zealand	Birmingham	7 Jun 1975
England	19 years, 195 days	B.C. Holliaoke	Australia	Lord's	25 May 1997
India	16 years, 238 days	S.R. Tendulkar	Pakistan	Gujranwala	18 Dec 1989
Kenya	17 years, 282 days	T. Odoyo	India	Cuttack	18 Feb 1996
Netherlands	18 years, 351 days	B. Zuiderent	New Zealand	Vadodara (IPCL)	17 Feb 1996
New Zealand	18 years, 57 days	D.L. Vettori	Sri Lanka	Christchurch	25 Mar 1997
Pakistan	14 years, 233 days	Hasan Raza	Zimbabwe	Quetta (BS)	30 Oct 1996
South Africa	18 years, 354 days	V.P. Mpitsang	West Indies	Bloemfontein	5 Feb 1999
Sri Lanka	17 years, 237 days	S.P. Pasqual	New Zealand	Nottingham	9 Jun 1979
UAE	23 years, 136 days	Arshad Laiq	India	Sharjah	13 Apr 1994
West Indies	20 years, 17 days	M.A. Small	Australia	Berbice	29 Feb 1984
Zimbabwe	17 years, 179 days	M. Nkala	India	Bulawayo (QS)	27 Sep 1998

OLDEST PLAYERS ON DEBUT

Age	Player	Versus	Venue	Date
47 years, 240 days	N.E. Clarke, Netherlands	New Zealand	Vadodara (IPCL)	17 Feb 1996
44 years, 359 days	N. Gifford, England	Australia	Sharjah	24 Mar 1985
43 years, 112 days	G.J.A.F. Aponso, Netherlands	New Zealand	Vadodara (IPCL)	17 Feb 1996
43 years, 42 days	D.J. Pringle, East Africa	India	Leeds	11 Jun 1975
42 years, 330 days	S.W. Lubbers, Netherlands	New Zealand	Vadodara (IPCL)	17 Feb 1996
42 years, 110 days	C.E.B. Rice, South Africa	India	Calcutta	10 Nov 1991
42 years, 104 days	F.J. Titmus, England	New Zealand	Dunedin	8 Mar 1975
42 years, 19 days	R.B. Simpson, Australia	West Indies	St John's	22 Feb 1978
41 years, 181 days	D.B. Close, England	Australia	Manchester	24 Aug 1972

OLDEST PLAYERS ON DEBUT FOR EACH COUNTRY

Country	Age	Player	Versus	Venue	Date
Australia	42 years, 19 days	R.B. Simpson	West Indies	St John's	22 Feb 1978
Bangladesh	28 years, 156 days	Sheik Salahuddin	Pakistan	Colombo (RPS)	16 Jul 1997
Canada	39 years, 269 days	C.A. Marshall	Pakistan	Leeds	9 Jun 1979
East Africa	43 years, 42 days	D.J. Pringle	India	Leeds	9 Jun 1979
England	44 years, 359 days	N. Gifford	Australia	Sharjah	24 Mar 1985
India	36 years, 138 days	F.M. Engineer	England	Leeds	13 Jul 1974
Kenya	32 years, 274 days	D. Chudasama	India	Cuttack	18 Feb 1996
Netherlands	47 years, 240 days	N.E. Clarke	New Zealand	Vadodara (IPCL)	17 Feb 1996
New Zealand	35 years, 0 days	B.E. Congdon	Pakistan	Christchurch	11 Feb 1973
Pakistan	39 years, 121 days	Younis Ahmed	India	Calcutta	18 Feb 1987
South Africa	42 years, 110 days	C.E.B. Rice	India	Calcutta	10 Nov 1991
Sri Lanka	36 years, 83 days	M.H. Tissera	West Indies	Manchester	7 Jun 1975
UAE	38 years, 133 days	Shahzad Altaf	South Africa	Rawalpindi (RC)	16 Feb 1996
West Indies	38 years, 341 days	L.R. Gibbs	England	Leeds	5 Sep 1973
Zimbabwe	36 years, 23 days	A.J. Traicos	Australia	Nottingham	9 Jun 1983

OLDEST PLAYERS (IN THEIR LAST GAME)

Age	Player	Versus	Venue	Date
47 years, 256 days	N.E. Clarke, Netherlands	South Africa	Rawalpindi (RC)	5 Mar 1996
45 years, 312 days	A.J. Traicos, Zimbabwe	India	Pune	25 Mar 1993
44 years, 361 days	N. Gifford, England	Pakistan	Sharjah	26 Mar 1985
43 years, 128 days	G.J.A.F. Aponso, Holland	South Africa	Rawalpindi (RC)	5 Mar 1996
43 years, 45 days	D.J. Pringle, East Africa	England	Birmingham	14 Jun 1975
42 years, 346 days	S.W. Lubbers, Netherlands	South Africa	Rawalpindi (RC)	5 Mar 1996

Age	Player	Versus	Venue	Date
42 years, 261 days	D.S. de Silva, Sri Lanka	West Indies	Melbourne	27 Feb 1985
42 years, 223 days	R.W. Taylor, England	New Zealand	Auckland	25 Feb 1984
42 years, 114 days	C.E.B. Rice, South Africa	India	New Delhi	14 Nov 1991
42 years, 68 days	R.B. Simpson, Australia	West Indies	Castries	12 Apr 1978

OLDEST PLAYERS FOR EACH COUNTRY (IN THEIR LAST GAME)

Country	Age	Player	Versus	Venue	Date
Australia	42 years, 68 days	R.B. Simpson	West Indies	Castries	12 Apr 1978
Bangladesh	36 years, 104 days	Athar Ali Khan	India	Mumbai	25 May 1998
Canada	39 years, 273 days	C.A. Marshall	England	Manchester	14 Jun 1979
East Africa	43 years, 45 days	D.J Pringle	England	Birmingham	14 Jun 1975
England	44 years, 361 days	N. Gifford	Pakistan	Sharjah	26 Mar 1985
India	39 years, 36 days	M. Armanath	West Indies	Mumbai	30 Oct 1989
Kenya	35 years, 11 days	D. Chudasama	India	Calcutta	31 May 1998
Netherlands	47 yearsm 256 days	N.E. Clarke	South Africa	Rawalpindi (RC)	5 Mar 1996
New Zealand	40 years, 156 days	B.E. Congdon	England	Manchester	17 Jul 1978
Pakistan	39 years, 151 days	Younis Ahmed	India	Hyderabad(I)	20 Mar 1987
South Africa	42 years, 114 days	C.E.B. Rice	India	New Delhi	14 Nov 1991
Sri Lanka	42 years, 261 days	D.S de Silva	West Indies	Melbourne	27 Feb 1985
UAE	38 years, 146 days	Shahzad Altaf	Netherlands	Lahore	1 Mar 1996
West Indies	40 years, 251 days	L.R. Gibbs	Sri Lanka	Manchester	7 Jun 1975
Zimbabwe	45 years, 312 days	A.J. Traicos	India	Pune	25 Mar 1993

PLAYERS WHO MADE THEIR DEBUT ON THEIR BIRTHDAY

Player	Date of birth	Versus	Venue	Date
B.C. Congdon, New Zealand	11 Feb 1938	Pakistan	Christchurch	11 Feb 1973
M.C. Snedden, New Zealand	23 Nov 1958	Australia	Adelaide	23 Nov 1980
G.A. Paterson, Zimbabwe	9 Jun 1960	Australia	Nottingham	9 June 1983
Asif Mujtaba, Pakistan	4 Nov 1967	West Indies	Gujranwala	4 Nov 1986
C.C. Lewis, England	1 Feb 1968	West Indies	Port-of-Spain	1 Feb 1990
Gusharan Singh, India	8 Mar 1963	Australia	Hamilton	8 Mar 1990
G.A. Hick, England	23 May 1966	West Indies	Birmingham	23 May 1991
I.D.K. Salisbury, England	21 Jan 1970	India	Chandigarh	21 Jan 1993

LONGEST CAREERS

Career length	Player	First Game	Last Game
20 years, 273 days	Javed Miandad, Pakistan	11 Jun 1975 v West Indies	9 Mar 1996 v India
18 years, 137 days	G.A. Gooch, England	26 Aug 1976 v West Indies	10 Jan 1995 v Australia
17 years, 268 days	Imran Khan, Pakistan	31 Aug 1974 v England	25 Mar 1992 v England
17 years, 103 days	R.J. Hadlee, New Zealand	11 Feb 1973 v Pakistan	25 May 1990 v England
16 years, 358 days	A. Ranatunga, Sri Lanka	14 Feb 1982 v England	7 Feb 1999 v Australia
16 years, 292 days	Salim Malik, Pakistan	12 Jan 1982 v West Indies	10 Nov 1998 v Australia

LONGEST INTERVAL BETWEEN APPEARANCES

Interval	Player	From	To
9 years, 266 days	W. Larkins, England	22 Jan 1980 v West Indies	15 Oct 1989 v Sri Lanka
7 years, 230 days	R.R. Singh, India	18 Mar 1989 v West Indies	3 Nov 1996 v Australia
7 years, 8 days	A.M. de Silva, Sri Lanka	2 Mar 1986 v Pakistan	10 Mar 1993 v England
6 years, 348 days	P.R. Downton, England	23 Dec 1977 v Pakistan	5 Dec 1984 v India
6 years, 282 days	T.J. Zoehrer, Australia	9 Apr 1987 v England	16 Jan 1994 v South Africa

ONLY PLAYER TO REPRESENT TWO COUNTRIES

Player	Country	Matches	Career
K.C. Wessels	Australia	54	1983-85
	South Africa	55	1991-94

PLAYERS WHO HAVE APPEARED IN ONLY ONE MATCH

Australia

Player	Versus	Batting	Bowling	Venue	Date
D.J. Colley	England	DNB	0-72	Lord's	28 Aug 1972
A.N. Connolly	England	DNB	0-62	Melbourne	5 Jan 1971
W.J. Edwards	England	2	0-0	Melbourne	1 Jan 1975
M.T.G. Elliott	England	1	DNB	Lord's	25 May 1997
P.A. Emery	Pakistan	11*	DNB	Lahore	30 Oct 1994
J.R. Hammond	England	15*	1-41	Birmingham	28 Aug 1972
T.J. Jenner	England	12	0-28	Melbourne	1 Jan 1975
W.M. Lawry	England	27	DNB	Melbourne	5 Jan 1971
G.D. McKenzie	England	DNB	2-22	Melbourne	5 Jan 1971
J.K. Moss	Pakistan	7	DNB	Nottingham	13/14 Jun 1979
J.D. Siddons	Pakistan	32	DNB	Lahore	14 Oct 1988
A. Symonds	Pakistan	DNB	0-14	Lahore	10 Nov 1998
A.L. Thomson	England	DNB	1-22	Melbourne	5 Jan 1971
D.F. Whatmore	West Indies	2	DNB	Sydney	18 Jan 1980
A.J. Woodcock	New Zealand	53	DNB	Christchurch	31 Mar 1974

Bangladesh

Player	Versus	Batting	Bowling	Venue	Date
Mehrab Hossein	India	6	DNB	Mohali	14 May 1998
Sharif-ul-Haq	India	0	0-21	Dhaka	10 Jan 1998
Wahid-ul-Ghani	Pakistan	DNB	0-32	Chittagong	29 Oct 1988

Canada

Player	Versus	Batting	Bowling	Venue	Date
S. Baksh	Australia	0	DNB	Birmingham	16 Jun 1979

East Africa

Player	Versus	Batting	Bowling	Venue	Date
J. Nagenda	New Zealand	DNB	1-50	Birmingham	7 Jun 1975
Praful Mehta	India	12	DNB	Leeds	11 Jun 1975
Shiraz Sumar	New Zealand	4	DNB	Birmingham	7 Jun 1975

England

Player	Versus	Batting	Bowling	Venue	Date
K.J. Barnett	Sri Lanka	84	DNB	The Oval	4 Sep 1988
M.R. Benson	New Zealand	24	DNB	Leeds	16 Jul 1986
A.R. Butcher	Australia	14	DNB	The Oval	20 Aug 1980
M.C. Cowdrey	Australia	1	DNB	Melbourne	5 Jan 1971
D.V. Lawrence	West Indies	DNB	4-67	Lord's	27 May 1991
P.I. Pocock	Pakistan	4	0-20	Sharjah	26 Mar 1985
K. Shuttleworth	Australia	7	1-29	Melbourne	5 Jan 1971
D.S. Steele	West Indies	8	0-9	Scarborough	26 Aug 1976
J.P. Taylor	Sri Lanka	1	0-20	Moratuwa	20 Mar 1993
R.W. Tolchard	Australia	DNB	DNB	Sydney	13 Jan 1979
M. Watkinson	South Africa	DNB	0-43	Johannesburg	13 Jan 1996
A.P. Wells	West Indies	15	DNB	Lord's	28 May 1995

India

Player	Versus	Batting	Bowling	Venue	Date
G. Bose	England	13	1-39	The Oval	15/16 Jul 1974
B.S. Chandreseker	New Zealand	11*	3-36	Auckland	22 Feb 1976
P. Dharmani	South Africa	8	DNB	Jaipur	23 Oct 1996
D. Ganesh	Zimbabwe	4	1-20	Harare	15 Feb 1997
Gursharan Singh	Australia	4	DNB	Hamilton	8 Mar 1990

Player	Versus	Batting	Bowling	Venue	Date
P. Krishnamurthy	New Zealand	6	DNB	Auckland	22 Feb 1976
A.V. Mankad	England	44	1-47	The Oval	15/16 Jul 1974
R.G.M. Patel	New Zealand	DNB	0-58	Vadodara (MB)	17 Dec 1988
R. Sudhakar Rao	New Zealand	4	DNB	Auckland	22 Feb 1976
M. Venkatarama	New Zealand	0*	2-36	Vadodara (MB)	17 Dec 1988

Kenya
No instances

New Zealand

Player	Versus	Batting	Bowling	Venue	Date
M.D. Bailey	Zimbabwe	DNB	DNB	Dhaka	24 Oct 1998
B.P. Bracewell	England	0*	1-41	Manchester	17 Jul 1978
C.J. Drum	India	DNB	0-36	Wellington	14 Jan 1999
R.T. Hart	West Indies	3	DNB	St John's	20 Mar 1985
M.J. Haslam	Sri Lanka	9	1-28	Colombo (RPS)	13 Dec 1992
R.L. Hayes	West Indies	13	0-31	Christchurch	28 Jan 1995
D.J. Murray	India	3	DNB	Delhi	3 Nov 1994
M.B. Owens	Sri Lanka	0	0-37	Colombo (RPS)	13 Dec 1992
N.M. Parker	Pakistan	2	DNB	Sialkot	16 Oct 1976
A.D.G. Roberts	Pakistan	16	1-30	Sialkot	16 Oct 1976
L.W. Stott	Sri Lanka	DNB	3-48	Nottingham	9 Jun 1979
G.E. Vivian	Pakistan	14	DNB	Christchurch	11 Feb 1973

Netherlands
No instances

Pakistan

Player	Versus	Batting	Bowling	Venue	Date
Fazl-e-Akbar	India	7	0-19	Dhaka	11 Jan 1998
Ifran Bhatti	Zimbabwe	DNB	2-22	Lahore	27 Dec 1993
Javed Qadir	Sri Lanka	12	DNB	Sharjah	11 Apr 1995
Mahmood Hamid	Sri Lanka	1	DNB	Sharjah	11 Apr 1995
Maqsood Rana	Australia	5	0-11	Melbourne	4 Jan 1990
Masood Iqbal	New Zealand	2	DNB	Multan	7 Dec 1994
Naeem Ahmed	England	0*	0-43	The Oval	16 May 1978
Nasim-ul-Ghani	Pakistan	1	DNB	Christchurch	11 Feb 1973
Salim Pervez	West Indies	18	DNB	Lahore	19 Dec 1980
Shahid Anwar	England	37	DNB	Nottingham	1 Sep 1996
Shakil Khan	Pakistan	0	1-50	Peshawar	22 Nov 1987
Tanvir Mehdi	Pakistan	0	1-72	The Oval	22 May 1992

South Africa

Player	Versus	Batting	Bowling	Venue	Date
A.C. Dawson	England	DNB	1-51	Dhaka	25 Oct 1998
A. Hall	West Indies	9*	0-38	Durban	27 Jan 1999
M. Hayward	England	DNB	0-35	Birmingham	Aug 18 1998
P.V. Mpitsang	West Indies	1*	2-49	Bloemfontein	5 Feb 1999
M. Ntini	New Zealand	DNB	2-31	Perth	16 Jan 1998
B.N. Schultz	India	DNB	1-35	Port Elizabeth	9 Dec 1992
P.J.R. Steyn	Zimbabwe	4	DNB	Harare	22 Oct 1995
H.S. Williams	West Indies	1*	0-55	East London	24 Jan 1999
M. Yachad	India	31	DNB	Gwalior	12 Nov 1991

Sri Lanka

Player	Versus	Batting	Bowling	Venue	Date
F.S. Ahangama	Pakistan	DNB	0-23	Lahore	22 Oct 1985
C.I. Dunusinghe	Bangladesh	1	DNB	Sharjah	6 Apr 1995
T.L. Fernando	Australia	8	1-16	Margao	25 Oct 1989
F.R.M. Goonatilleke	India	DNB	0-34	Manchester	16/18 Jun 1979
A.A.W. Gunawardene	India	2	DNB	Hyderabad (I)	18 Feb 1994
M.C. Mendis	New Zealand	3*	DNB	Auckland	1 Apr 1995
M.N. Nawaz	Zimbabwe	5	DNB	Colombo (SSC)	26 Jan 1998
K.G. Perera	Pakistan	DNB	0-15	Kandy	2 Mar 1986
K.J. Silva	New Zealand	1*	0-55	Christchurch	26 Mar 1995
D.M. Vonaght	Australia	8	DNB	Perth	3 Feb 1985
A.P. Weerakkody	New Zealand	2	0-41	Sharjah	18 Apr 1994
M. de S. Wettimuny	New Zealand	2	DNB	Dunedin	2 Mar 1983

United Arab Emirates

Player	Versus	Batting	Bowling	Venue	Date
Saeed-al-Saffar	Netherlands	DNB	0-25	Lahore	1 Mar 1996

West Indies

Player	Versus	Batting	Bowling	Venue	Date
R.A. Austin	Australia	8	0-13	St John's	22 Feb 1978
A.E. Greenidge	Australia	23	DNB	Castries	12 Apr 1978
R.G.A. Headley	England	19	DNB	The Oval	7 Sep 1973
N. Phillip	Australia	0	DNB	Castries	12 Apr 1978
D. Ramnarine	Sri Lanka	DNB	2-54	Port-of-Spain	6 Jun 1997
S. Shivnarine	Australia	20*	0-16	Castries	12 Apr 1978
G.St A. Sobers	England	0	1-31	Leeds	5 Sep 1973
C.M. Tuckett	England	DNB	2-41	Port-of-Spain	8 Apr 1998

Zimbabwe

Player	Versus	Batting	Bowling	Venue	Date
G.K. Bruk-Jackson	Pakistan	12	DNB	Lahore	27 Dec 1993
E.A. Essop-Adam	New Zealand	14*	DNB	Harare	8 Nov 1992
M.A. Meman	India	19	0-34	Mumbai	17 Oct 1988
M. Nkala	Zimbabwe	DNB	1-32	Bulawayo (QS)	27 Sep 1998

PLAYERS WHO HAVE APPEARED IN MOST LIMITED-OVERS INTERNATIONALS BUT NOT A TEST

Players	Matches	Career
A.C. Gilchrist, Australia	51	1996-99
U. Chandana, Sri Lanka	47	1994-99
D.J. Callaghan, South Africa	27	1992-95
H.H. Kanitikar, India	27	1997-99
S.S. Karim, India	26	1997-98
D.N. Crookes, South Africa	24	1994-98
E.O. Simons, South Africa	23	1994-95
M.J.R. Rindel	22	1994-99

PLAYERS WHO HAVE APPEARED IN MOST LIMITED-OVERS INTERNATIONALS BEFORE FIRST TEST

Players	Matches	ODI debut	Test debut
Shahid Afridi, Pakistan	66	2 Oct 1996, Kenya, Nairobi (NG)	22 Oct 1998, Australia, Karachi
R.R. Singh, India	60	11 Mar 89, West Indies, Port-of-Spain	7 Oct 1998, Zimbabwe, Harare

PLAYERS WHO HAVE APPEARED IN LIMITED-OVERS INTERNATIONALS BUT NOT A TEST

Australia

Players	M	Career
G.A. Bishop	2	1987
M.J. Divenuto	9	1997
A.C. Gilchrist	51	1996-99
S.F. Graf	11	1980-81
I.J. Harvey	11	1997-98
S. Lee	16	1995-99
J.P. Maher	2	1998
R.J. McCurdy	11	1985
K.H. MacLeay	16	1983-87
G.D. Porter	2	1979
J.D. Siddons	1	1988
A.M. Stuart	3	1997
A. Symonds	1	1998
G.S. Trimble	2	1986
B.E. Young	6	1998-99
A.K. Zesers	2	1987

England

Players	M	Career
C.J. Adams	2	1998
M.W. Alleyne	4	1999
I.D. Austin	4	1998
A.D. Brown	13	1996-98
D.R. Brown	9	1997-98
M.V. Fleming	11	1997-98
IJ. Gould	18	1983
G.W. Humpage	3	1981
T.E. Jesty	10	1983
G.D. Lloyd	6	1996-98
J.D. Love	3	1981
M.A. Lynch	3	1988
D.L. Maddy	2	1998
M.J. Smith	5	1973-74
N.M.K. Smith	7	1996
S.D. Udal	10	1994-95
V.J. Wells	7	1999
C.M. Wells	2	1985

India

Players	M	Career
S.V. Bahutule	7	1997-98
A.C. Bedade	13	1994
Bhupinder Singh	2	1994
G. Bose	1	1974
V.B. Chadreskahar	7	1988-90
V. Chatterjee	3	1995
N. Chopra	11	1998-99
N.A. David	4	1997
P. Dharmani	1	1996
R.S. Ghai	6	1984-86
H.H. Kanitkar	27	1997-99
S.S. Karim	26	1997-98
S.C. Khanna	10	1979-84
G.K. Khoda	2	1998
S.P. Mukherjee	3	1990-91
J.V. Paranjpe	4	1998
A.K. Patel	8	1984-85
M.S.K. Prasad	2	1998
Randhir Singh	2	1981-83
S.S. Raul	2	1998
R. Sanghvi	10	1998
R.P. Singh	2	1986
S. Somasunder	2	1996
R. Sudhakar Rao	1	1976
P.S. Vaidya	4	1995-96

New Zealand

Players	M	Career
M.D Bailey	1	1998
B.R. Blair	14	1982-86
P.G. Coman	3	1973-74
M.W. Douglas	6	1994-95
C.J. Drum	1	1999
B.G. Hadlee	2	1975
R.T. Hart	1	1985
R.L. Hayes	1	1995
L.G. Howell	12	1998
B.J. McKechnie	14	1975-81
E.B. McSweeney	16	1986-87
J.P. Millmow	5	1990
A.J. Penn	3	1997
R.G. Petrie	12	1990-91
R.B. Reid	9	1988-91
S.J. Roberts	2	1990
L.W. Stott	1	1979
A.R. Tait	2	1998
R.J. Webb	3	1983
J.W. Wilson	4	1993

Pakistan

Players	M	Career
Aamer Hameed	2	1977-78
Aamer Hanif	5	1993-95
Abdur Razzaq	13	1996-98
Akhtar Sarfraz	4	1997
Arhsad Pervez	2	1978
Asif Mahmood	2	1998
Ghulam Ali	3	1993-95
Haafiz Shahid	3	1988
Hasan Jamil	6	1977-78
Iqbal Sikander	4	1992
Ifran Bhatti	1	1993
Javed Qadir	1	1995
Mahmood Hamid	1	1995
Mansoor Rana	2	1990
Manzoor Akhtar	7	1997-98

Maqsood Rana	1	1990
Masood Iqbal	1	1994
Moin-ul-Atiq	5	1988-89
Mujahid Jamshed	4	1997
Naeem Ahmed	1	1978
Naeem Ashraf	2	1995
Naseer Malik	3	1975
Parvez Mir	3	1975-77
Saadat Ali	8	1984
Saeed Azad	4	1995-96
Sajid Ali	13	1984-97
Sajjad Akbar	2	1990
Salim Pervez	1	1980
Shahid Anwar	1	1996
Shakil Khan	1	1987
Sohail Fazal	2	1989
Tanvir Mehdi	1	1992
Wasim Haider	3	1992
Zafar Iqbal	8	1995
Zahid Ahmed	2	1987

South Africa

Players	M	Career
D.M. Beckenstein	7	1998-99
N. Boje	13	1995-99
R.E. Bryson	7	1997
D.J. Callaghan	27	1992-95
D.N. Crookes	24	1994-98
A.C. Dawson	1	1998
A.J. Hall	1	1999
M. Hayward	1	1998
L.J. Koen	2	1997
P.V. Mpitsang	1	1999
S.J. Palframan	7	1996
C.E.B. Rice	3	1991
M.J.R. Rindel	22	1994-99
D.B. Rundle	2	1994
T.G. Shaw	9	1991-94
E.O. Simons	23	1994-95
E.L.R. Stewart	5	1993-94
R. Telemachus	5	1998
C.J.P.G. Van Zyl	2	1992
H.S. Williams	1	1999
M. Yachad	1	1991

Sri Lanka

Players	M	Career
U. Chandana	47	1994-99
D.L.S. de Silva	2	1979
G.N. de Silva	4	1983-85
E.R. Fernando	3	1975
T.L. Fernando	1	1989
U.N.K. Fernando	2	1994
J. Gamage	4	1995
F.R.M. de S Goonatilleke	1	1979
A.A.W. Gunawardene	1	1994
A. Gunawardene	7	1998-99

P.D. Heyn	2	1975
S.A. Jayasinghe	2	1979
S.H.U. Karnain	19	1984-90
M.C. Mendis	1	1995
A.M. Munasinghe	5	1994-96
M.N. Nawaz	1	1998
A.R.M. Opatha	5	1975-79
S.P. Pasqual	2	1979
K.G. Perera	1	1986
R.L. Perera	2	1999
H.S.M. Pieris	3	1975
S.K. Ranasinghe	4	1986
N. Ranatunga	2	1993
N.L.K. Ratnayake	2	1989-90
T.T. Samaweera	6	1998-99
A.P.B. Tennekoon	4	1975-79
M.H. Tissera	3	1975
K.E.A. Upashanta	3	1995-96
D.M. Vonaght	1	1985
A.P. Weerakkody	1	1994
S.R. de S Wettimuny	3	1975-79
R.P.A.H. Wickremaratne	3	1993

West Indies

Players	M	Career
H.A.G. Anthony	3	1995
B.St.A. Browne	4	1994
V.C. Drakes	5	1995
R.S. Gabriel	11	1984
R.C. Haynes	8	1989-91
N.C. McGarrell	5	1998-99
M.R. Pydanna	3	1980-83
K.F. Semple	7	1999
C.M. Tuckett	1	1998
L.R. Williams	6	1996-98

Zimbabwe

Players	M	Career
G.B. Brent	3	1996-98
R.D. Brown	7	1983-87
K.M. Curran	11	1983-87
S.G. Davies	4	1996
K.G. Duers	6	1992
E.A. Essop-Adams	1	1992
D.A.G. Fletcher	6	1983
J.G. Heron	6	1983
V.R. Hogg	2	1983
G.C. Martin	5	1994-95
M.A. Meman	1	1987
M. Nkala	1	1998
G.A. Paterson	10	1983-87
G.E. Peckover	3	1983
P.W.E. Rawson	10	1983-87

PLAYER BREACHES OF THE ICC CODE OF CONDUCT

Player	Offence	V	Venue	Date	Punishment
N.R. Mongia India (3)	Dissent and attempt to intimidate umpire into making favourable decision	SL	Sharjah	14 Apr 1995	Fined 10% of match fee
	Charged umpire when appealing	SL	Mumbai	17 May 1997	Severe reprimand
	Showed dissent to umpire for catch not given	Aus	Sharjah	19 Apr 1994	Fined and suspended for 1 match
Aaqib Javed Pakistan (2)	Abusive language to umpire	NZ	Napier	28 Dec 1992	Suspended for 1 match
	Offensive gestures to dismissed batsmen	NZ	Wellington	20 Dec 1995	Fined 50% of match fee
R.T. Ponting Australia (2)	Breach of logo policy	Ind	Dunedin	22 Feb 1995	Fined 10% of match fee
	Made offensive gesture to bowler after being given out	Ind	Sharjah	22 Apr 1998	Fined 20% of match fee
Inzamam-ul-Haq Pakistan (2)	Conduct unbecoming to an international player (charged into stand with a bat to remonstrate with heckler)	Ind	Toronto	14 Sept 1997	Suspended for 2 matches
	Showed dissent to umpire	SAF	Cape Town	23 Apr 1998	Fined 50% of match fee
P.N. Kirsten South Africa	Showed dissent after being run out (Mankad). Also used offensive language.	Ind	Port Elizabeth	9 Dec 1992	Fined 50% of match fee
D.L. Haynes West Indies	Showed dissent to an umpire	Aus	Brisbane	10 Jan 1993	Fined 50% of match fee
D.J. Nash New Zealand	Showed dissent to umpire and abusive language to another player	Pak	Sharjah	20 Apr 1994	Fined
B.C. Lara West Indies	Showed dissent after being given out	NZ	Goa	26 Oct 1994	Fined 50% of match fee
A. Ranatunga Sri Lanka	Showed dissent after being given out	NZ	East London	18 Dec 1994	Fined 25% of match fee
K.R. Rutherford New Zealand	Attempted to intimidate umpire into making favourable decision	SL	East London	18 Dec 1994	Fined 50% of match fee
D.J. Richardson South Africa	Hit stump out of ground after being run out.	Pak	Cape Town	19 Jan 1995	Fined 20% of match fee
G.S. Blewett Australia	Breach of logo policy	Ind	Dunedin	22 Feb 1995	Fined 15% of match fee
S.K. Warne Australia	Breach of logo policy	Aus	Dunedin	22 Feb 1995	Fined 25% of match fee

Player	Offence	V	Venue	Date	Punishment
B.C. Strang Zimbabwe	Pointed batsman in direction of pavilion	Pak	Harare	25 Feb 1995	Caution
Aamir Nazir Pakistan	Offensive gesture after dismissing batsman	SL	Sharjah	11 Apr 1995	Severe reprimand
A.D. Jadeja India	Made umpire's signal for TV replay	NZ	Pune	24 Nov 1995	Fined 10% of match fee
R.G. Twose New Zealand	Verbal abuse of fielder after claiming a catch	Ind	Nagpur	26 Nov 1995	Fined 50% of match fee
Mushtaq Ahmed Pakistan	Asked umpire to consult TV replay	NZ	Wellington	20 Dec 1995	Fined 10% of match fee
A.Gurusinha Sri Lanka	Comments made to opposing player on field	Aus	Perth	12 Jan 1996	Reprimand
P.V. Simmons West Indies	Attempted to intimidate umpire into making favourable decision.	NZ	Georgetown	3 Apr 1996	Fined 10% of match fee
S.R. Waugh Australia	Showed dissent to umpire for calling wides	Ind	Colombo	6 Sep 1996	Suspended fine (3 months) of 30% of match fee
G. Kirsten South Africa	Wore coloured bandana during his innings	Pak	Nairobi	6 Oct 1996	Fined 10% of match fee
Aamir Sohail Pakistan	Remained at crease after being given out. Asked umpire to consult TV replay	Aus	Malbourne	16 Jan 1997	Suspended for 1 match
P.A. de Silva Sri Lanka	Remained at crease after being given out. Showed dissent to umpire	NZ	Wellington	27 Mar 1997	Severe reprimand
N.S. Sidhu India	Breach of logo policy	SL	Colombo	26 Jul 1997	Fined 20% of match fee
A.C. Parore New Zealand	Showed dissent to umpire after appeal turned down	Zim	Napier	6 Mar 1998	Fined 50% of match fee
S.P Fleming New Zealand	Showed dissent to umpire after appeal turned down	Zim	Napier	6 Mar 1998	Severe reprimand
M.J.R Rindel South Africa	Breach of logo policy	Pak	Durban	3 Apr 1998	Fined 10% of match fee
S.C. Ganguly India	Breach of logo policy	Zim	Vadodara	5 Apr 1998	Fined 35% of match fee
H. Singh India	Pointed batsman in direction of pavilion.	Aus	Sharjah	22 Apr 1998	Fined 50% of match fee.
A. Ranatunga Sri Lanka	Did not maintain spirit or laws of the game.	Eng	Adelaide	23 Jan 1999	Fined 75% of match fee and a suspended six-match sentence.

Batting

LEADING RUN-SCORERS

Runs	Batsman	M	Career
8868	M.A. Azharuddin, India	310	1985-99
8648	D.L. Haynes, West Indies	238	1978-94
7863	P.A. de Silva, Sri Lanka	250	1984-99
7800	S.R. Tendulkar, India	211	1989-99
7381	Javed Miandad, Pakistan	233	1975-96
7248	A. Ranatunga, Sri Lanka	260	1982-99
7053	Salim Malik, Pakistan	276	1982-98
6721	I.V.A. Richards, West Indies	187	1975-91
6524	A.R. Border, Australia	273	1979-94
6248	R.B. Richardson, West Indies	224	1983-96
6068	D.M. Jones, Australia	164	1984-94
6044	M.E. Waugh, Australia	174	1988-99
5964	D.C. Boon, Australia	181	1984-95
5852	Saeed Anwar, Pakistan	161	1989-98
5841	Ramiz Raja, Pakistan	198	1985-97
5706	S.R. Waugh, Australia	251	1986-99
5580	B.C. Lara, West Indies	137	1990-99
5577	Ijaz Ahmed, Pakistan	215	1986-98
5369	Inzamam-ul-Haq, Pakistan	171	1991-98
5134	C.G. Greenidge, West Indies	128	1975-91
5027	R.S. Mahanama, Sri Lanka	208	1986-99
4704	M.D. Crowe, New Zealand	143	1982-95
4695	W.J. Cronje, South Africa	152	1992-99
4672	S.T. Jayasuriya, Sri Lanka	178	1989-99
4651	Aamir Sohail, Pakistan	149	1990-98
4500	C.L. Hooper, West Indies	167	1987-98
4414	N.S. Sidhu, India	136	1987-98
4357	G.R. Marsh, Australia	117	1986-92
4290	G.A. Gooch, England	125	1976-95
4092	K. Srikkanth, India	146	1981-92
4020	A.D. Jadeja, India	154	1992-99
4010	A.J. Lamb, England	122	1982-92

LEADING RUN-SCORERS FOR EACH COUNTRY

Country	Batsman	Runs	M	Career
Australia	A.R. Border	6524	273	1979-94
Bangladesh	Athar Ali Khan	532	19	1988-98
Canada	G.R. Sealy	73	3	1979
East Africa	Frasat Ali	57	3	1975
England	G.A. Gooch	4290	125	1976-95
India	M.A. Azharuddin	8868	310	1985-99
Kenya	K. Otieno	592	20	1996-98
Netherlands	K.J. van Noortwijk	168	5	1996
New Zealand	M.D. Crowe	4704	143	1982-95
Pakistan	Javed Miandad	7381	233	1975-96
South Africa	W.J. Cronje	4695	152	1992-99
Sri Lanka	P.A. de Silva	7863	250	1984-99
United Arab Emirates	Mazhar Hussein	179	7	1994-96
West Indies	D.L. Haynes	8648	238	1978-94
Zimbabwe	A. Flower	2940	100	1992-98

MOST RUNS IN A CALENDAR YEAR

Batsman	Year	M	Inn	NO	Runs	HS	50s	100s	Ave.	Stk Rt
S.R. Tendulkar, India	1998	34	33	4	1894	142	7	9	65.31	102.16
S.R. Tendulkar, India	1996	32	32	2	1611	137	9	6	53.70	82.62
Saeed Anwar, Pakistan	1996	36	36	5	1595	115	10	3	51.45	91.76
G. Kirsten, South Africa	1996	29	29	4	1442	188*	4	6	57.68	83.69
B.C. Lara, West Indies	1993	30	30	3	1349	153	7	4	49.96	72.33
S.C. Ganguly, India	1997	38	35	3	1338	113	10	1	41.81	69.65
S.C. Ganguly, India	1998	36	35	3	1328	124	7	4	41.50	69.82
Ijaz Ahmed, Pakistan	1996	38	36	5	1283	117	9	1	41.39	78.63
M.A. Azharuddin, India	1998	37	33	4	1268	153*	8	3	43.72	76.72
D.L. Haynes, West Indies	1985	28	27	5	1233	146*	7	3	56.05	72.92
I.V.A. Richards, West Indies	1985	29	25	5	1231	103*	12	1	61.55	92.91
P.A. de Silva, Sri Lanka	1997	28	27	4	1212	134	8	3	52.70	86.26
P.A. de Silva, Sri Lanka	1996	30	29	5	1188	145	5	4	49.50	91.17
S.T. Jayasuriya, Sri Lanka	1997	26	26	3	1178	151*	9	3	51.22	113.60
D.M. Jones, Australia	1990	22	22	5	1174	145	7	4	69.06	78.74
R.T. Ponting, Australia	1998	24	24	2	1166	145	6	3	53.00	76.91
W.J. Cronje, South Africa	1994	29	29	3	1133	112	7	2	43.58	69.55
Ijaz Ahmed, Pakistan	1997	31	31	2	1104	139*	8	1	38.07	76.19
M.A. Azharuddin, India	1997	36	32	5	1104	111*	9	1	40.89	71.27
Aamir Sohail, Pakistan	1996	30	30	1	1090	111	7	2	37.59	65.47
S.R. Tendulkar, India	1994	25	25	2	1089	115	9	3	47.35	86.70
D.I. Gower, England	1983	20	20	3	1086	158	4	4	63.88	86.53
Javed Miandad, Pakistan	1987	22	22	6	1084	113	10	2	67.75	70.39
D.C. Boon, Australia	1994	26	26	3	1073	98*	9	-	46.65	61.63
M.E. Waugh, Australia	1996	25	25	2	1059	130	5	4	46.04	76.30
Aamir Sohail, Pakistan	1994	28	28	1	1053	134	6	2	39.00	73.23
B.C. Broad, England	1987	26	26	-	1047	99	10	-	40.27	55.05
D.J. Cullinan, South Africa	1996	24	24	6	1033	124	5	3	57.39	75.90
S.R. Tendulkar, India	1997	39	36	3	1011	117	5	2	30.64	85.03
D.L. Haynes, West Indies	1989	23	23	5	1007	152*	4	4	55.94	73.13
A.D. Jadeja, India	1998	36	34	13	1004	116*	6	2	47.81	72.02

Ross Dundas Cricket Statistics

MOST RUNS IN EACH CALENDAR YEAR

Year	Batsman	M	Inn	NO	Runs	HS	50s	100s	Ave.	Stk Rt
1971	J.H. Edrich, England	1	1	-	82	82	1	-	82.00	68.91
1972	D.L. Amiss, England	3	3	-	168	103	-	1	56.00	65.12
1973	D.L. Amiss, England	2	2	-	134	100	-	1	67.00	72.43
1974	D. Lloyd, England	4	4	1	193	116*	-	1	64.33	60.31
1975	G.M. Turner, New Zealand	6	6	3	359	171*	-	2	119.67	67.71
1976	I.V.A. Richards, West Indies	3	3	1	216	119*	1	1	108.00	94.32
1977	G.S. Chappell, Australia	3	3	1	174	125*	-	1	87.00	78.03
1978	C.T. Radley, England	4	4	1	250	117*	1	1	83.33	68.12
1979	I.V.A. Richards, West Indies	8	8	4	526	153*	2	2	131.50	92.93
1980	C.G. Greenidge, West Indies	7	7	2	469	103	4	1	93.80	61.63
1981	G.M. Wood, Australia	17	16	2	658	108	4	1	47.00	61.04
1982	Zaheer Abbas, Pakistan	14	14	1	677	123	2	4	52.08	98.41
1983	D.I. Gower, England	20	20	3	1086	158	4	4	63.88	86.53
1984	D.L. Haynes, West Indies	20	20	5	813	133*	4	4	54.20	57.95
1985	D.L. Haynes, West Indies	28	27	5	1233	146*	7	3	56.05	72.92
1986	S.M. Gavaskar, India	23	23	2	805	92*	9	-	38.33	61.64
1987	Javed Miandad, Pakistan	22	22	6	1084	113	10	2	67.75	70.39
1988	A.H. Jones, New Zealand	19	19	1	806	90	9	-	44.78	60.15

Year	Batsman	M	Inn	NO	Runs	HS	50s	100s	Ave.	Stk Rt
1989	D.L. Haynes, West Indies	23	23	5	1007	152*	4	4	55.94	73.13
1990	D.M. Jones, Australia	22	22	5	1174	145	7	4	69.06	78.74
1991	R.B. Richardson, West Indies	19	19	1	658	122	3	2	36.56	73.52
1992	Javed Miandad, Pakistan	25	24	6	942	115*	8	1	52.33	62.93
1993	B.C. Lara, West Indies	30	30	3	1349	153	7	4	49.96	72.33
1994	W.J. Cronje, South Africa	29	29	3	1133	112	7	2	43.58	69.55
1995	B.C. Lara, West Indies	15	14	2	806	169	6	2	67.17	95.72
1996	S.R. Tendulkar, India	32	32	2	1611	137	9	6	53.70	82.62
1997	S.C. Ganguly, India	38	35	3	1338	113	10	1	41.81	69.65
1998	S.R. Tendulkar, India	34	33	4	1894	142	9	7	65.31	102.16

Ross Dundas Cricket Statistics

LEADING RUN-SCORER AT THE END OF EACH CALENDAR YEAR

Year	Batsman	M	Inn	NO	Runs	HS	50s	100s	Ave.	Stk Rt
1971	J.H. Edrich, England	1	1	-	82	82	1	-	82.00	68.91
1972	D.L. Amiss, England	3	3	-	168	103	-	1	56.00	65.12
1973	D.L. Amiss, England	5	5	-	302	103	-	2	60.40	68.17
1974	K.W.R. Fletcher, England	12	11	2	340	63	3	-	37.78	64.27
1975	D.L. Amiss, England	12	12	-	615	137	1	3	51.25	74.63
1976	D.L. Amiss, England	15	15	-	708	137	1	3	47.20	74.21
1977	D.L. Amiss, England	18	18	-	859	137	1	4	47.72	73.22
1978	D.L. Amiss, England	18	18	-	859	137	1	4	47.72	73.22
1979	G.S. Chappell, Australia	22	22	5	919	125*	6	1	54.06	73.93
1980	G.S. Chappell, Australia	31	30	7	1265	138*	7	2	55.00	74.63
1981	G.S. Chappell, Australia	45	44	9	1719	138*	11	2	49.11	74.64
1982	G.S. Chappell, Australia	57	56	10	2057	138*	13	3	44.72	74.85
1983	I.V.A. Richards, West Indies	58	55	10	2480	153*	15	5	55.11	88.06
1984	I.V.A. Richards, West Indies	76	71	13	3175	189*	19	7	54.74	90.68
1985	I.V.A. Richards, West Indies	105	96	18	4406	189*	31	8	56.49	91.29
1986	I.V.A. Richards, West Indies	118	107	19	4739	189*	35	8	53.85	91.70
1987	I.V.A. Richards, West Indies	139	126	20	5629	189*	41	10	53.10	91.72
1988	I.V.A. Richards, West Indies	153	139	21	5950	189*	42	11	50.42	91.85
1989	I.V.A. Richards, West Indies	175	157	24	6442	189*	44	11	48.44	92.19
1990	D.L. Haynes, West Indies	177	176	23	6622	152*	38	16	43.28	64.25
1991	D.L. Haynes, West Indies	189	188	23	7062	152*	42	16	42.80	64.39
1992	D.L. Haynes, West Indies	209	208	26	7707	152*	48	16	42.35	63.38
1993	D.L. Haynes, West Indies	234	233	28	8381	152*	55	16	40.88	62.92
1994	D.L. Haynes, West Indies	238	237	28	8648	152*	57	17	41.38	63.38
1995	D.L. Haynes, West Indies	238	237	28	8648	152*	57	17	41.38	63.38
1996	D.L. Haynes, West Indies	238	237	28	8648	152*	57	17	41.38	63.38
1997	D.L. Haynes, West Indies	238	237	28	8648	152*	57	17	41.38	63.38
1998	M.A. Azharuddin, India	305	280	51	8703	153*	53	7	38.00	73.45

Ross Dundas Cricket Statistics

HIGHEST INDIVIDUAL INNINGS

Score	Batsman	Versus	Venue	Date
194	Saeed Anwar, Pakistan	India	Chennai	21 May 1997
189*	I.V.A. Richards, West Indies	England	Manchester	31 May 1984
188*	G. Kirsten, South Africa	UAE	Rawalpindi (RC)	16 Feb 1996
181	I.V.A. Richards, West Indies	Sri Lanka	Karachi	13 Oct 1987
175*	Kapil Dev, India	Zimbabwe	Tunbridge Wells	18 Jun 1983
171*	G.M. Turner, New Zealand	East Africa	Birmingham	7 Jun 1975
169*	D.J. Callaghan, South Africa	New Zealand	Centurion	11 Dec 1994
169	B.C. Lara, West Indies	Sri Lanka	Sharjah	16 Oct 1995

Score	Batsman	Versus	Venue	Date
167*	R.A. Smith, England	Australia	Birmingham	21 May 1993
161	A.C. Hudson, South Africa	Netherlands	Rawalpindi (RC)	5 Mar 1996
158	D.I. Gower, England	New Zealand	Brisbane	15 Jan 1983
154	A.C. Gilchrist, Australia	Sri Lanka	Melbourne	7 Feb 1999
153*	I.V.A. Richards, West Indies	Australia	Melbourne	9 Dec 1979
153	B.C. Lara, West Indies	Pakistan	Sharjah	5 Nov 1993
153	M.A. Azharuddin, India	Zimbabwe	Cuttack	9 Apr 1998
152*	D.L. Haynes, West Indies	India	Georgetown	21 Mar 1989
151*	S.T. Jayasuriya, Sri Lanka	India	Mumbai	17 May 1997
150	S. Chanderpaul, West Indies	South Africa	East London	24 Jan 1999
149	I.V.A. Richards, West Indies	India	Jamshedpur	7 Dec 1983
148	D.L. Haynes, West Indies	Australia	St John's	22 Feb 1978
146*	B.C. Lara, West Indies	New Zealand	Port-of-Spain	30 Mar 1996
145*	D.L. Haynes, West Indies	New Zealand	Berbice	14 Apr 1985
145	D.M. Jones, Australia	England	Brisbane	16 Dec 1990
145	P.A. de Silva, Sri Lanka	Kenya	Kandy	6 Mar 1996
145	R.T. Ponting, Australia	Zimbabwe	Delhi	11 Apr 1998
144	K. Otieno, Kenya	Bangladesh	Nairobi (NG)	10 Oct 1997
142*	C.W.J. Athey, England	New Zealand	Manchester	18 Jul 1986
142*	D.L. Haynes, West Indies	Pakistan	Port-of-Spain	18 Mar 1988
142	D.L. Houghton, Zimbabwe	New Zealand	Hyderabad (I)	10 Oct 1987
142	G.A. Gooch, England	Pakistan	Karachi	20 Nov 1987
142	S.R. Tendulkar, India	Australia	Sharjah	22 Apr 1998
141	S.R. Tendulkar, India	Australia	Dhaka	28 Oct 1998
140	G.M. Turner, New Zealand	Sri Lanka	Auckland	20 Mar 1983
140	S.T. Jayasuriya, Sri Lanka	New Zealand	Bloemfontein	8 Dec 1994
140	Saeed Anwar, Pakistan	India	Dhaka	19 Jan 1998
139*	Ijaz Ahmed, Pakistan	India	Lahore	2 Oct 1997
139	B.C. Lara, West Indies	Australia	Port-of-Spain	12 Mar 1995
138*	I.V.A. Richards, West Indies	England	Lord's	23 Jun 1979
138*	G.S. Chappell, Australia	New Zealand	Sydney	25 Nov 1980
138*	D.L. Haynes, West Indies	England	Gwalior	27 Oct 1989
137*	Inzamam-ul-Haq, Pakistan	New Zealand	Sharjah	20 Apr 1994
137	D.L. Amiss, England	India	Lord's	7 Jun 1975
137	S.R. Tendulkar, India	Sri Lanka	Delhi	2 Mar 1996
136	G.A. Gooch, England	Australia	Lord's	29 May 1989
134*	N.S. Sidhu, India	England	Gwalior	4 Mar 1993
134*	S.T. Jayasuriya, Sri Lanka	Pakistan	Singapore	2 Apr 1996
134	P.A. de Silva, Sri Lanka	Pakistan	Sharjah	7 Apr 1997
134	S.R. Tendulkar, India	Australia	Sharjah	24 Apr 1998
133*	D.L. Haynes, West Indies	Australia	Berbice	29 Feb 1984
133*	C.G. Greenidge, West Indies	New Zealand	Christchurch	28 Mar 1987
132*	M.S. Atapattu, Sri Lanka	England	Lord's	20 Aug 1998
132	Ijaz Ahmed, Pakistan	Zimbabwe	Rawalpindi (RC)	24 Nov 1998
131*	A.D.R. Campbell, Zimbabwe	Sri Lanka	Harare	5 Nov 1994
131*	A. Ranatunga, Sri Lanka	India	Colombo (RPS)	18 Jul 1997
131	K.W.R. Fletcher, England	New Zealand	Nottingham	11 Jun 1975
131	Saeed Anwar, Pakistan	West Indies	Sharjah	1 Nov 1993
131	A.C. Gilchrist, Australia	Sri Lanka	Sydney	13 Jan 1999
130	D.I. Gower, England	Sri Lanka	Taunton	11 Jun 1983
130	M.E. Waugh, Australia	Sri Lanka	Perth	12 Jan 1996
130	M.E. Waugh, Australia	Kenya	Vishakhapatnam	23 Feb 1996
130	C.Z. Harris, New Zealand	Australia	Madras	11 Mar 1996

PROGRESSION OF HIGHEST INDIVIDUAL INNINGS

Score	Batsman	Versus	Venue	Date
82	J.H. Edrich, England	Australia	Melbourne	5 Jan 1971
103	D.L. Amiss, England	Australia	Manchester	24 Aug 1972
105	R.C. Fredericks, West Indies	England	The Oval	7 Sep 1973
116*	D. Lloyd, England	India	Nottingham	31 Aug 1974
171*	G.M. Turner, New Zealand	East Africa	Birmingham	7 June 1975
175*	Kapil Dev, India	Zimbabwe	Tunbridge Wells	18 June 1983
189*	I.V.A. Richards, West Indies	England	Manchester	31 May 1984
194	Saeed Anwar, Pakistan	India	Chennai	21 May 1997

HIGHEST INDIVIDUAL INNINGS FOR EACH COUNTRY

Country	Batsman	Score	Versus	Venue	Date
Australia	A.C. Gilchrist	154	Sri Lanka	Melbourne	7 Feb 1999
Bangladesh	Athar Ali Khan	82	Pakistan	Colombo (RPS)	16 Jul 1997
Canada	G.R. Sealy	45	Pakistan	Leeds	9 June 1979
East Africa	Frasat Ali	45	New Zealand	Birmingham	7 June 1975
England	R.A. Smith	167*	Australia	Birmingham	21 May 1993
India	Kapil Dev	175*	Zimbabwe	Tunbridge Wells	18 June 1983
Kenya	K. Otieno	144	Bangladesh	Nairobi (NG)	10 Oct 1997
Netherlands	K.J. van Noorwijk	64	England	Peshawar	22 Feb 1996
New Zealand	G.M. Turner	171*	East Africa	Birmingham	7 June 1975
Pakistan	Saeed Anwar	194	India	Chennai	21 May 1997
South Africa	G. Kirsten	188*	UAE	Rawalpindi (RC)	16 Feb 1996
Sri Lanka	S.T. Jayasuriya	151*	India	Mumbai	17 May 1997
UAE	Salim Razar	84	Netherlands	Lahore	1 Mar 1996
West Indies	I.V.A. Richards	189*	England	Manchester	31 May 1984
Zimbabwe	D.L. Houghton	142	New Zealand	Hyderabad (I)	10 Oct 1987

HIGHEST INDIVIDUAL AGAINST EACH COUNTRY

Country	Batsman	Score	Venue	Date
Australia	R.A. Smith, England	167*	Birmingham	21 May 1993
Bangladesh	K. Otieno, Kenya	144	Nairobi (NG)	10 Oct 1997
Canada	Sadiq Mohammed, Pakistan	57*	Leeds	9 Jun 1979
East Africa	G.M. Turner, New Zealand	171*	Birmingham	7 Jun 1975
England	I.V.A. Richards, West Indies	189*	Manchester	31 May 1984
India	Saeed Anwar, Pakistan	194	Chennai	21 May 1997
Kenya	P.A. de Silva, Sri Lanka	145	Kandy	6 Mar 1996
Netherlands	A.C. Hudson, South Africa	161	Rawalpindi (RC)	5 Mar 1996
New Zealand	D.J. Callaghan, South Africa	188*	Centurian	11 Dec 1993
Pakistan	B.C. Lara, West Indies	153	Sharjah	5 Nov 1993
South Africa	S. Chanderpaul, West Indies	150	East London	24 Jan 1999
Sri Lanka	I.V.A. Richards, West Indies	181	Karachi	13 Oct 1987
UAE	G. Kirsten, South Africa	188*	Rawalpindi (RC)	16 Feb 1996
West Indies	Saeed Anwar, Pakistan	131	Sharjah	1 Nov 1993
Zimbabwe	Kapil Dev, India	175*	Tunbridge Wells	18 Jun 1983

HIGHEST INDIVIDUAL INNINGS FOR EACH BATTING POSITION

Pos.	Score	Batsman	Versus	Venue	Date
1	194	Saeed Anwar, Pakistan	India	Chennai	21 May 1997
2	188*	G. Kirsten, South Africa	UAE	Rawalpindi (RC)	16 Feb 1996
3	169	B.C. Lara, West Indies	Sri Lanka	Sharjah	16 Oct 1995
4	189*	I.V.A. Richards, West Indies	England	Manchester	31 May 1984
5	130	C.Z. Harris, New Zealand	Australia	Madras	11 Mar 1996
6	175*	Kapil Dev, India	Zimbabwe	Tunbridge Wells	18 Jun 1983
7	100	H.P. Tillekeratne, Sri Lanka	West Indies	Sharjah	16 Oct 1995
8	77*	C.Z. Harris, New Zealand	Zimbabwe	Bulawayo (QS)	1 Oct 1997
9	64	M.A. Holding, West Indies	Australia	Perth	5 Feb 1984
10	46*	Abdul Razzaq, Pakistan	South Africa	Durban	3 Apr 1998
11	37	J. Garner, West Indies	India	Manchester	9/10 Jun 1983

MOST RUNS SCORED OFF ONE OVER

Runs	Batsmen	Bowler	Venue	Date
30 (+6,4,6,6,6,1)	S.T. Jayasuriya, Sri Lanka	Aamir Sohail, Pakistan	Singapore	2 Apr 1996
28 (6,6,2,6,4,4)	Shahid Afridi, Pakistan	S.T. Jayasuriya, Sri Lanka	Nairobi (NG)	4 Oct 1996
27 (4,1)	A. Mujtaba			
(6,4,6,6)	Salim Malik, Pakistan	M. Muralitharan, Sri Lanka	Colombo (SSC)	7 Aug 1994
27 (4,1)	Ramiz Raja			
(4,6,6,6)	Moin Khan, Pakistan	I.R. Bishop, West Indies	Sharjah	13 Oct 1995
26 (6,4,6,4,6+)	R.W. Marsh, Australia	B.L. Cairns, New Zealand	Adelaide	23 Nov 1980
26 (6,2,6,6,6)	M.W. Gatting, England	R.J. Shastri, India	Jullundur	20 Dec 1981
26 (4,6,4,6,6)	B.L. Cairns, New Zealand	V.B. John, Sri Lanka	Colombo (PSS)	1 Apr 1984
26 (4,4,2,4,6,6)	I.T. Botham, England	S.P. Davis, Australia	Perth	1 Jan 1987
26 (2,4,2,6,6,6)	A.P. Kuiper, South Africa	C.J. McDermott, Australia	Centurion	20 Feb 1994
26 (2,2,6,6,6,4)	Saeed Anwar, Pakistan	A.R. Kumble, India	Chennai	21 May 1997
25 (2,6,6,6,4,1)	Wasim Akram, Pakistan	C. Sharma, India	Nagpur	24 Mar 1987
24	I.V.A. Richards, West Indies	Tauseef Ahmed, Pakistan	Gujranwala	27 Nov 1985
24 (4,6,6,6)	Kapil Dev, India	C.J. McDermott, Australia	Rajkot	7 Oct 1986
24 (1,6,1,1)	Imran Khan			
(4,2,4w,4w,1,1)	Javed Miandad, Pakistan	W.K.M Benjamin, West Indies	Brisbane	7 Jan 1989
24 (4,2,2,6,6,4)	M.A. Azharuddin, India	Ata-ur-Rehman, Pakistan	Sharjah	15 Apr 1996
24 (4,6,6,4,4)	S.T. Jayasuriya, Sri Lanka	S.B. Doull, New Zealand	Christchurch	25 Mar 1997
23 (1)	Javed Miandad			
(4,4,4,4,6)	Imran Khan, Pakistan	V.B. John, Sri Lanka	Swansea	9 Jun 1983
23 (4,4,6,1)	A.J. Lamb			
(4,4)	M.W. Gatting, England	M.D. Crowe, New Zealand	The Oval	9 Jun 1983
23	I.V.A. Richards, West Indies	I.T. Botham, England	Port-of-Spain	4 Mar 1986
23 (1)	A.L. Logie			
(6,6,6,4)	I.V.A. Richards, West Indies	J.R. Ratnayeke, Sri Lanka	Karachi	13 Oct 1987
23 (4,4,4,4,4)	S.P. Fleming			
(3)	A.C. Parore, New Zealand	C. Sharma, India	Delhi	3 Nov 1994
23 (6,2,4,6,4,1)	S.R. Tendulkar, India	R.K. Pushpakumara, Sri Lanka	Delhi	2 Mar 1996

Ross Dundas Cricket Statistics

HIGHEST CAREER STRIKE-RATES (minimum 20 innings)

Batsman	M	Inn	NO	Runs	HS	50s	100s	Ave.	Stk Rt
Shahid Afridi, Pakistan	71	68	2	1604	109	8	2	24.30	110.62
B.L. Cairns, New Zealand	78	65	6	987	60	2	-	16.73	106.64
I.D.S. Smith, New Zealand	98	77	16	1054	62*	3	-	17.28	100.67
V.S. Yadav, India	19	12	2	118	34*	-	-	11.80	100.00
R.P. Snell, South Africa	42	28	8	322	63	2	-	16.10	98.47
L. Klusener, South Africa	47	39	7	1121	99	8	-	35.03	94.44
Kapil Dev, India	225	198	39	3781	175*	14	1	23.78	92.90
I.V.A. Richards, West Indies	187	167	24	6721	189*	45	11	47.00	91.28
C. Sharma, India	65	35	15	456	101*	-	1	22.80	90.84
S.T. Jayasuriya, Sri Lanka	178	170	7	4672	151*	29	7	28.66	90.11
Wasim Akram, Pakistan	254	200	36	2508	86	5	-	15.29	89.44
A.C. Gilchrist, Australia	51	49	4	1660	154	5	5	36.89	89.34
S.B. Doull, New Zealand	38	25	12	166	22	-	-	12.77	89.25
Manzoor Elahi, Pakistan	54	46	13	741	50*	1	-	22.45	88.26
C.J. McDermott, Australia	138	78	17	432	37	-	-	7.08	87.80
RS Kaluwitharana, Sri Lanka	112	108	6	1930	100*	12	1	18.92	87.45
Tahir Naqqash, Pakistan	40	23	9	210	61	1	-	15.00	86.78
S.R. Tendulkar, India	211	204	20	7800	142	43	21	42.40	86.49
J. Srinath, India	153	79	24	644	53	1	-	11.71	86.44
E.A. Brandes, Zimbabwe	54	38	9	328	55	1	-	11.31	86.09
A.K. Sharma, India	31	27	6	424	59*	3	-	20.19	86.06

Ross Dundas Cricket Statistics

HIGHEST CAREER BATTING AVERAGES (minimum 20 innings)

Batsman	M	Inn	NO	Runs	HS	50s	100s	Ave.	Stk Rt
M.G. Bevan, Australia	97	86	33	3244	108*	22	3	61.21	77.07
Zaheer Abbas, Pakistan	62	60	6	2572	123	13	7	47.63	82.08
I.V.A. Richards, West Indies	187	167	24	6721	189*	45	11	47.00	91.28
G.M. Turner, New Zealand	41	40	6	1598	171*	9	3	47.00	72.48
B.C. Lara, West Indies	137	135	13	5580	169	37	12	45.74	78.18
C.G. Greenidge, West Indies	128	127	13	5134	133*	31	11	45.04	66.07
D.M. Jones, Australia	164	161	25	6068	145	46	7	44.62	72.49
S.R. Tendulkar, India	211	204	20	7800	142	43	21	42.39	86.49
Javed Miandad, Pakistan	233	218	41	7381	119*	50	8	41.70	67.08
R.T. Ponting, Australia	68	68	8	2492	145	14	5	41.53	72.55
D.L. Haynes, West Indies	238	237	28	8649	152*	57	17	41.38	63.38
G. Kirsten, South Africa	96	96	9	3600	188*	20	8	41.38	71.44
N.H. Fairbrother, England	66	64	17	1918	113	15	1	40.81	73.57
N.V. Knight, England	40	40	3	1497	125*	8	3	40.46	71.32
Saeed Anwar, Pakistan	161	159	14	5852	194	27	15	40.36	84.05
S.C. Ganguly, India	90	85	7	3146	124	22	5	40.33	69.14
G.S. Chappell, Australia	74	72	14	2331	138*	14	3	40.19	74.62
G.P. Thorpe, England	44	44	7	1482	89	14	-	40.05	71.80
B.C. Broad, England	34	34	-	1361	106	11	1	40.03	55.64

CARRIED THE BAT

Batsman	Score	Total/Overs	Versus	Venue	Date
G.W. Flower, Zimbabwe	84*	(205/49.3 overs)	England	Sydney	15 Dec 1994
Saeed Anwar, Pakistan	103*	(219/49.5 overs)	Zimbabwe	Harare	22 Feb 1995
N.V. Knight, England	125*	(246/50 overs)	Pakistan	Nottingham	1 Sept 1996

BATTED THROUGHOUT AN INNINGS (minimum 50 overs)

Batsman	Score	Total/Overs	Versus	Venue	Date
D. Lloyd, England	116*	(4-244/50 overs)	Pakistan	Nottingham	31 Aug1974
S.M. Gavaskar, India	36*	(3-132/60 overs)	England	Lord's	7 June 1975
G.M. Turner, New Zealand	171*	(5-309/60 overs)	East Africa	Birmingham	7 June 1975
G.M. Turner, New Zealand	114*	(6-233/58.5 overs)	India	Manchester	14 June 1975
C.G. Greenidge, West Indies	106*	(1-194/51.3 overs)	India	Birmingham	9 June 1979
B.A. Edgar, New Zealand	84*	(2-183/57 overs)	India	Leeds	13 June 1979
B.A. Edgar, New Zealand	102*	(8-229/ 50 overs)	Australia	Melbourne	1 Feb 1981
G. Boycott, England	75*	(4-212/51.4 overs)	Australia	Lord's	4 June 1981
G. Fowler, England	78*	(2-199/50.4 overs)	Pakistan	Lord's	13 June 1983
G.M. Wood, Australia	104*	(9-200/50 overs)	West Indies	Adelaide	27 Jan 1985
D.L. Haynes, West Indies	145*	(5-259/50 overs)	New Zealand	Berbice	14 Apr 1985
G.M. Wood, Australia	114*	(5-254/55 overs)	England	Lord's	3 June 1985
S.M. Gavaskar, India	92*	(4-192/50 overs)	Australia	Sydney	21 Jan 1986
C.W.J. Athey, England	142*	(4-286/53.4 overs)	New Zealand	Manchester	18 July 1986
G.R. Marsh, Australia	126*	(8-251/50 overs)	New Zealand	Chandigarh	27 Oct 1987
C.G. Greenidge, West Indies	102*	(5-210/50 overs)	Pakistan	Sharjah	18 Oct 1988
Shoaib Mohammed, Pakistan	126*	(6-253/50 overs)	New Zealand	Wellington	8 Mar 1989
D.L. Haynes, West Indies	138*	(5-264/50 overs)	England	Gwalior	27 Oct 1989
D.L. Haynes, West Indies	107*	(5-273/50 overs)	Pakistan	Calcutta	1 Nov 1989
Ramiz Raja, Pakistan	107*	(3-315/50 overs)	Sri Lanka	Adelaide	17 Feb 1990
Ramiz Raja, Pakistan	102*	(2-220/50 overs)	West Indies	Melbourne	23 Feb 1992
A. Flower, Zimbabwe	115*	(4-312/50 overs)	Sri Lanka	New Plymouth	23 Feb 1992
Asif Mujtaba, Pakistan	113*	(3-313/50 overs)	Sri Lanka	Sharjah	30 Oct 1993
M. Prabhakar, India	102*	(5-211/50 overs)	West Indies	Kanpur	30 Oct 1994
R.S. Mahanama, Sri Lanka	119*	(5-256/50 overs)	Zimbabwe	Harare	3 Nov 1994
D.J. Callaghan, South Africa	169*	(7-314/50 overs)	New Zealand	Centurion	11 Dec 1994
G. Kirsten, South Africa	188*	(2-321/50 overs)	UAE	Rawalpindi (RC)	16 Feb 1996
G. Kirsten, South Africa	115*	(5-287/50 overs)	India	Sharjah	19 Apr 1996
N.V. Knight, England	125*	(10-246/50 overs)	Pakistan	Nottingham	1 Sep 1996
S.C. Williams, West Indies	105*	(6-229/50 overs)	India	Sharjah	16 Dec 1997

BATSMEN SCORING OVER 60% OF THE INNINGS TOTAL

%	Batsman	Score	Total	Versus	Venue	Date
100.00	K. Srikkanth, India	1*	0-1	Sri Lanka	Mackay	28 Feb 1992
72.65	D.L. Haynes, West Indies	85*	0-117	New Zealand	Port-of-Spain	17 Apr 1985
71.26	Ramiz Raja, Pakistan	119*	3-167	New Zealand	Christchurch	18 Mar 1992
69.49	I.V.A. Richards, West Indies	189*	9-272	England	Manchester	31 May 1985
69.27	C.G. Greenidge, West Indies	133*	0-192	New Zealand	Christchurch	28 Mar 1987
68.75	S.R. Tendulkar, India	11*	0-16	Sri Lanka	Colombo (RPS)	4 Sep 1994
67.86	Zaheer Abbas, Pakistan	57*	2-84	England	Birmingham	3 Sep 1974
65.94	S.T. Jayasuriya, Sri Lanka	151*	5-229	India	Mumbai	17 May 1997
65.79	Kapil Dev, India	175*	8-266	Zimbabwe	Tunbridge Wells	18 Jun 1983
64.89	B.C. Lara, West Indies	146*	3-225	New Zealand	Port-of-Spain	30 Mar 1996
63.51	A.H. Jones, New Zealand	47	74	Pakistan	Sharjah	1 May 1990
63.47	Ijaz Ahmed, Pakistan	139*	1-219	India	Lahore	2 Oct 1997
62.94	S.R. Tendulkar, India	124*	0-197	Zimbabwe	Sharjah	13 Nov 1998
62.89	D.L. Amiss, England	100	3-159	New Zealand	Swansea	18 Jul 1973
62.69	N.V. Knight, England	84*	4-134	New Zealand	Auckland	23 Feb 1997
62.56	S.R. Tendulkar, India	127*	3-203	Kenya	Cuttack	18 Feb 1996
62.20	D.M. Jones, Australia	102*	2-164	New Zealand	Auckland	11 Mar 1990
61.54	C.G. Greenidge, West Indies	8*	0-13	England	Port-of-Spain	17 Feb 1990
60.82	N.S. Sidhu, India	104*	1-171	Bangladesh	Chandigarh	25 Dec 1990
60.29	R.A. Smith, England	167*	5-277	Australia	Birmingham	21 May 1993

Ross Dundas Cricket Statistics

MOST CENTURIES

No.	Batsman	M	Inn	Career
21	S.R. Tendulkar, India	211	204	1989-99
17	D.L. Haynes, West Indies	238	237	1978-94
15	Saeed Anwar, Pakistan	161	159	1989-98
12	B.C. Lara, West Indies	137	135	1990-99
11	P.A. de Silva, Sri Lanka	250	243	1984-99
11	C.G. Greenidge, West Indies	128	127	1975-91
11	I.V.A. Richards, West Indies	187	167	1975-91
11	M.E. Waugh, Australia	174	169	1988-99
9	Ijaz Ahmed, Pakistan	215	198	1986-98
9	G.R. Marsh, Australia	117	115	1986-92
9	Ramiz Raja, Pakistan	198	197	1985-97
8	G.A. Gooch, England	125	122	1976-95
8	Javed Miandad, Pakistan	233	218	1975-96
8	G. Kirsten, South Africa	96	96	1993-99
7	M.A. Azharuddin, India	310	285	1985-99
7	D.I. Gower, England	114	111	1978-91
7	S.T. Jayasuriya, Sri Lanka	178	170	1989-99
7	D.M. Jones, Australia	164	161	1984-94
7	Zaheer Abass, Pakistan	62	60	1974-85

CONSECUTIVE CENTURIES

Batsman	Scores	Versus	Venue	Date
Zaheer Abbas, Pakistan (3)	118	India	Multan	17 Dec 1982
	105	India	Lahore	31 Dec 1982
	113	India	Karachi	21 Jan 1983
Saeed Anwar, Pakistan (3)	107	Sri Lanka	Sharjah	30 Oct 1993
	131	West Indies	Sharjah	1 Nov 1993
	111	Sri Lanka	Sharjah	2 Nov 1993
R.L. Dias, Sri Lanka (2)	102	India	Delhi	15 Sep 1982
	121	India	Bangalore	26 Sep 1982
D.I. Gower, England (2)	122	New Zealand	Melbourne	13 Jan 1983
	158	New Zealand	Brisbane	15 Jan 1983
D.L. Haynes, West Indies (2)	102*	Australia	Castries	19 Apr 1984
	104*	Australia	Kingston	26 Apr 1984
A.R. Border, Australia (2)	118*	Sri Lanka	Adelaide	28 Jan 1985
	127*	West Indies	Sydney	6 Feb 1985
G.A. Gooch, England (2)	115	Australia	Birmingham	1 Jun 1985
	115	Australia	Lord's	3 Jun 1985
D.M. Jones, Australia (2)	104	England	Perth	1 Jan 1987
	121	Pakistan	Perth	2 Jan 1987
C.G. Greenidge, West Indies (2)	104	New Zealand	Auckland	21 Mar 1987
	133*	New Zealand	Christchurch	28 Mar 1987
Ramiz Raja, Sri Lanka (2)	116*	Sri Lanka	Hobart (B)	15 Feb 1990
	107*	Sri Lanka	Adelaide	17 Feb 1990
M.J. Greatbatch, New Zealand (2)	102*	England	Leeds	23 May 1990
	111	England	Lord's	25 May 1990
G.R. Marsh, Australia (2)	113	West Indies	Bridgetown	13 Mar 1991
	106*	West Indies	Georgetown	20 Mar 1991
Inzamam-ul-Haq, Pakistan (2)	101	Sri Lanka	Multan	17 Jan 1992
	117	Sri Lanka	Rawalpindi (RC)	19 Jan 1992
P.V. Simmons, West Indies (2)	122	South Africa	Kingston	7 Apr 1992
	104	South Africa	Port-of-Spain	12 Apr 1992

Batsman	Scores	Versus	Venue	Date
B.C. Lara, West Indies (2)	128	Pakistan	Durban	19 Feb 1993
	111*	South Africa	Bloemfontein	23 Feb 1993
R.S. Mahanama, Sri Lanka (2)	119*	Zimbabwe	Harare	3 Nov 1994
	108	Zimbabwe	Harare	5 Nov 1994
M.E. Waugh, Australia (2)	130	Kenya	Visag	23 Feb 1996
	126	India	Mumbai	27 Feb 1996
N.V. Knight, England (2)	113	Pakistan	Birmingham	31 Aug 1996
	125*	Pakistan	Nottingham	1 Sep 1996
Saeed Anwar, Pakistan (2)	104*	New Zealand	Sharjah	10 Nov 1996
	112*	Sri Lanka	Sharjah	12 Nov 1996
B.C. Lara, West Indies (2)	102	Australia	Brisbane	5 Jan 1997
	103*	Pakistan	Perth	10 Jan 1997
S.R. Tendulkar, India (2)	142	Australia	Sharjah	22 Apr 1998
	134	Australia	Sharjah	24 Apr 1998
G.A. Hick, England (2)	126*	Sri Lanka	Adelaide	23 Jan 1999
	109	Australia	Adelaide	26 Jan 1999

CENTURY ON DEBUT

Batsman	Score	Versus	Venue	Date
D.L. Amiss, England	103	Australia	Manchester	24 Aug 1972
D.L. Haynes, West Indies	148	Australia	St John's	22 Feb 1978
A. Flower, Zimbabwe	115*	Sri Lanka	New Plymouth	23 Feb 1992
Salim Elahi, Pakistan	102*	Sri Lanka	Gujranwala	29 Sep 1995

Note: A. Flower batted throughout the innings.

CENTURY IN DEBUT INNINGS[†]

Batsman	Score	Versus	Venue	Date
Shahid Afridi, Pakistan	102	Sri Lanka	Nairobi (NG)	4 Oct 1996

†*Not required to bat in debut match.*

FASTEST CENTURIES

Balls	Batsman	Versus	Venue	Date
37	Shahid Afridi, Pakistan	Sri Lanka	Nairobi (NG)	4 Oct 1996
48	S.T. Jayasuriya, Sri Lanka	Pakistan	Singapore	7 Apr 1996
62	M.A. Azharuddin, India	New Zealand	Vadodara (MB)	17 Dec 1988
67	Basit Ali, Pakistan	West Indies	Sharjah	5 Nov 1993
69	Javed Miandad, Pakistan	India	Lahore	31 Dec 1982
71	S.R. Tendulkar, India	Zimbabwe	Sharjah	13 Nov 1998
72	Zaheer Abbas, Pakistan	India	Multan	17 Dec 1982
72	Kapil Dev, India	Zimbabwe	Tunbridge Wells	18 Jun 1983
72	I.V.A. Richards, West Indies	India	Jamshedpur	7 Dec 1983
75	I.V.A. Richards, West Indies	India	Rajkot	5 Jan 1988
75	C.L. Cairns, New Zealand	India	Christchurch	19 Jan 1999
78	A..R. Border, Australia	Sri Lanka	Adelaide	28 Jan 1985
79	Zaheer Abbas, Pakistan	India	Lahore	31 Dec 1982
80	Zaheer Abbas, Pakistan	Sri Lanka	Lahore	29 Mar 1982
82	C.H. Lloyd, West Indies	Australia	Lord's	21 Jun 1975
82	G.S. Chappell, Australia	New Zealand	Auckland	13 Feb 1982
82	D.I. Gower, England	New Zealand	Adelaide	29 Jan 1983
82	S.V. Manjrekar, India	South Africa	Delhi	14 Nov 1991
83	B.C. Lara, West Indies	South Africa	Karachi	11 Mar 1996
84	C.L. Cairns, New Zealand	India	Pune	24 Nov 1995
85	D.I. Gower, England	New Zealand	Brisbane	15 Jan 1983
85	S.M. Gavaskar, India	New Zealand	Nagpur	31 Oct 1987

85	A.C. Gilchrist, Australia	Sri Lanka	Melbourne	7 Feb 1999
86	Ijaz Ahmed, Pakistan	Zimbabwe	Rawalpindi (RC)	24 Nov 1998
87	Ijaz Ahmed, Pakistan	Bangladesh	Chittagong	29 Oct 1988
87	Saeed Anwar, Pakistan	Sri Lanka	Adelaide	17 Feb 1990
87	A.C. Parore, New Zealand	South Africa	Centurion	11 Dec 1994
88	Majid Khan, Pakistan	England	Nottingham	31 Aug 1974
88	S.R. Tendulkar, India	Zimbabwe	Benoni	9 Feb 1997
88	Shahid Afridi, Pakistan	India	Toronto	19 Sep 1998
89	H.A. Gomes, West Indies	Sri Lanka	Perth	2 Feb 1985
89	K. Srikkanth, India	Pakistan	Calcutta	18 Feb 1987
89	R.S. Kaluwitharana, Sri Lanka	Kenya	Nairobi (NG)	28 Sep 1996

Ross Dundas Cricket Statistics

CENTURIES BY PINCH HITTERS[†]

Batsman	Score	Versus	Venue	Date
C. Sharma, India	101*	England	Kanpur	25 Oct 1989

†Pinch hitters are players promoted up the batting order to lift the run-rate.

CENTURY IN A LIMITED-OVERS INTERNATIONAL BUT NOT A TEST

Batsman	Score	Versus	Venue	Date	HS	Tests
Asif Mujtaba, Pakistan	113*	Sri Lanka	Sharjah	30 Oct 1993	65*	25
M.G. Bevan, Australia (3)	103	South Africa	Centurion	10 Apr 1997	91	18
	108*	England	Lord's	24 May 1997	-	-
	101*	India	Sharjah	22 Apr 1998	-	-
A.D.R. Campbell, Zimbabwe (3)	131*	Sri Lanka	Harare	5 Nov 1994	99	33
	103	Australia	Ahmedabad	3 Apr 1998	-	-
	100	New Zealand	Dhaka	24 Oct 1998	-	-
T.M. Chappell, Australia	110	India	Nottingham	13 Jun 1983	27	3
N.H. Fairbrother, England	113	West Indies	Lord's	27 May 1991	83	10
H.H. Gibbs, South Africa	125	West Indies	Port Elizabeth	30 Jan 1999	54	11
C.Z. Harris, New Zealand	130	Australia	Chennai	11 Mar 1996	71	14
A.D. Jadeja, India (4)	104	West Indies	Cuttack	9 Nov 1994	96	13
	119	Sri Lanka	Colombo (RPS)	17 Aug 1997	-	-
	105*	Australia	Kochi	1 Apr 1998	-	-
	116*	Zimbabwe	Cuttack	9 Apr 1998	-	-
R. Lamba, India	102	Australia	Rajkot	7 Oct 1986	53	4
W. Larkins, England	124	Australia	Hyderabad (I)	19 Oct 1989	64	13
S.G. Law, Australia	110	Zimbabwe	Hobart (B)	8 Dec 1994	54*	1
D.S. Lehmann, Australia	103	Pakistan	Karachi	6 Nov 1998	98	5
W.V. Raman, India	114	South Africa	Centurion	11 Dec 1992	96	11
Salim Elahi, Pakistan	102*	Sri Lanka	Gujranwala	29 Sep 1995	17	4
C. Sharma, India	101*	England	Kanpur	25 Oct 1989	54	23
R.R. Singh, India	100	Sri Lanka	Colombo	23 Aug 1997	15	1
S.B. Smith, Australia (2)	117	New Zealand	Melbourne	17 Feb 1983	12	3
	106	Pakistan	Sydney	25 Jan 1984	-	-
K.J. Wadsworth, New Zealand	104	New Zealand	Christchurch	31 Mar 1974	80	33
P.A. Wallace, West Indies	103	India	Dhaka	31 Oct 1998	92	7
C.B. Wishart, Zimbabwe	102	India	Harare	30 Sep 1998	63	11

CENTURY SCORERS IN LIMITED-OVERS INTERNATIONALS WHO HAVE NOT APPEARED IN A TEST

Batsman	Score	Versus	Venue	Date
A.D. Brown, England	118	India	Manchester	26/27 May 1996
D.J. Callaghan, South Africa	169*	New Zealand	Centurion	11 Dec 1994
D.Chudasama, Kenya	122	Bangladesh	Nairobi	10 Oct 1997
A.C. Gilchrist, Australia (5)	100	South Africa	Sydney	26 Jan 1998
	118	New Zealand	Christchurch	8 Feb 1998
	103	Pakistan	Lahore	10 Nov 1998
	131	Sri Lanka	Sydney	13 Jan 1999
	154	Sri Lanka	Melbourne	7 Feb 1999
M.J.R. Rindel, South Africa	106	Pakistan	Johannesburg	12 Jan 1995
Moin-ul-Atiq, Pakistan	105	Bangladesh	Sydney	26 Jan 1998
K. Otieno, Kenya	144	Bangladesh	Nairobi	10 Oct 1997

YOUNGEST CENTURY-MAKERS

Age	Batsman	Score	Versus	Venue	Date
16 years, 217 days	Shahid Afridi, Pakistan	102	Sri Lanka	Nairobi (NG)	4 Oct 1996
18 years, 202 days	Shahid Afridi, Pakistan	109	India	Toronto	19 Sep 1998
18 years, 312 days	Salim Elahi, Pakistan	102*	Sri Lanka	Gujranwala	29 Sep 1995
20 years, 39 days	Ijaz Ahmed, Pakistan	124*	Bangladesh	Chittagong	29 Oct 1988
21 years, 0 days	Vinod Kambli, India	100*	England	Jaipur	18 Jan 1993
21 years, 21 days	R.T. Ponting, Australia	123	Sri Lanka	Melbourne	9 Jan 1996

YOUNGEST CENTURY-MAKER FOR EACH COUNTRY

Country	Age	Batsman	Score	Versus	Venue	Date
Australia	21 years, 21 days	R.T.Ponting	123	Sri Lanka	Melbourne	9 Jan 1996
England	21 years, 55 days	D.I.Gower	114*	Pakistan	The Oval	26 May 1978
India	21 years, 0 days	Vinod Kambli	100*	England	Jaipur	18 Jan 1993
Kenya	25 years, 214 days	K. Otieno	144	Banglandesh	Nairobi (NG)	10 Oct 1997
New Zealand	21 years, 156 days	M.D. Crowe	105*	England	Auckland	25 Feb 1984
Pakistan	16 years, 217 days	Shahid Afridi	012	Sri Lanka	Nairobi (NG)	4 Oct 1996
South Africa	22 years, 92 days	J.H. Kallis	111	New Zealand	Perth	16 Jan 1998
Sri Lanka	21 years, 88 days	D.P.M. Jayawardene	120	England	Adelaide	23 Jan 1999
West Indies	21 years, 38 days	C.L. Hooper	113*	India	Gwalior	22 Jan 1988
Zimbabwe	22 years, 43 days	A.D.R. Campbell	131*	Sri Lanka	Harare	5 Nov 1994

Note: No player from Bangladesh, Canada, East Africa, Netherlands, or United Arab Emirates has scored a century.

OLDEST CENTURY-MAKERS

Age	Batsman	Score	Versus	Venue	Date
39 years, 51 days	G. Boycott, England	105	Australia	Sydney	11 Dec 1979
38 years, 113 days	S.M. Gavaskar, India	103*	New Zealand	Nagpur	31 Oct 1987
38 years, 18 days	D.L. Haynes, West Indies	115	England	Port-of-Spain	5 Mar 1994
37 years, 321 days	C.G. Greenidge, West Indies	117	India	St John's	18 Mar 1989
37 years, 184 days	M. Armanath, India	102*	New Zealand	Sharjah	27 Mar 1988
37 years, 26 days	B.E. Congdon, New Zealand	101	England	Wellington	9 Mar 1975
36 years, 306 days	G.A. Gooch, England	112*	New Zealand	The Oval	25 May 1990

MOST HALF-CENTURIES

No.	Batsman	100s	50s	Inn	M	Career
74	D.L. Haynes, West Indies	17	57	237	238	1978-94
64	P.A. de Silva, Sri Lanka	11	53	243	250	1984-99
64	S.R. Tendulkar, India	21	43	204	211	1989-99
62	M.A. Azharuddin, India	7	55	291	310	1985-99
58	Javed Miandad, Pakistan	8	50	218	233	1975-96
56	I.V.A. Richards, West Indies	11	45	167	187	1975-91
53	D.M. Jones, Australia	7	46	161	164	1984-94
52	A. Ranatunga, Sri Lanka	4	48	246	260	1982-99
51	Salim Malik, Pakistan	5	46	250	276	1982-98
50	M.E. Waugh, Australia	11	39	169	173	1988-99
49	B.C. Lara, West Indies	12	37	135	137	1990-99
49	R.B. Richardson, West Indies	5	44	217	224	1983-96
42	D.C. Boon, Australia	5	37	177	181	1984-95
42	A.R. Border, Australia	3	39	252	273	1979-94
42	C.G. Greenidge, West Indies	11	31	127	128	1975-91
42	Inzamam-ul-Haq, Pakistan	5	37	161	171	1991-98
42	Saeed Anwar, Pakistan	15	27	159	161	1989-98
40	Ramiz Raja, Pakistan	9	31	197	198	1985-97
39	Ijaz Ahmed, Pakistan	9	30	198	215	1986-98
39	R.S. Mahanama, Sri Lanka	4	5H	193	208	1986-99
39	N.S. Sidhu, India	6	33	127	136	1987-98
38	M.D. Crowe, New Zealand	4	34	141	143	1982-95
36	Aamir Sohail, Pakistan	5	31	148	149	1990-98
36	S.T. Jayasuriya, Sri Lanka	7	29	170	178	1989-99
35	W.J. Cronje, South Africa	2	33	142	152	1992-99
35	S.R. Waugh, Australia	1	34	228	251	1986-99
31	G.A. Gooch, England	8	23	122	125	1976-95
31	C.L. Hooper, West Indies	6	25	161	177	1987-99
31	G.R. Marsh, Australia	9	22	115	117	1986-92
31	K.S. Srikkanth, India	4	27	145	146	1981-92
30	A.J. Lamb, England	4	26	118	122	1982-92

MOST CONSECUTIVE HALF-CENTURIES

No.	Batsman	Score	Versus	Venue	Date
9	Javed Miandad, Pakistan	78	India	Nagpur	24 Mar 1987
		78*	India	Jamshedpur	26 Mar 1987
		74*	Australia	Sharjah	3 Apr 1987
		60	England	Sharjah	7 Apr 1987
		52*	India	Sharjah	10 Apr 1987
		113	England	The Oval	21 May 1987
		71*	England	Nottingham	23 May 1987
		68	England	Birmingham	25 May 1987
		103	Sri Lanka	Hyderabad (P)	8 Oct 1987
6	C.G. Greenidge, West Indies	85*	England	Brisbane	23 Dec 1979
		50	England	Adelaide	16 Jan 1980
		80	England	Melbourne	20 Jan 1980
		98*	England	Sydney	22 Jan 1980
		103	New Zealand	Christchurch	6 Feb 1980
		78	England	Leeds	28 May 1980
6	A.H. Jones, New Zealand	57	India	Vadodara (MB)	17 Dec 1988
		55*	Pakistan	Dunedin	6 Feb 1989
		62*	Pakistan	Christchurch	4 Mar 1989
		67	Pakistan	Wellington	8 Mar 1989
		82	Pakistan	Auckland	11 Mar 1989
		63*	Pakistan	Hamilton	14 Mar 1989

No.	Batsman	Score	Versus	Venue	Date
6	M.E Waugh, Australia	64	Sri Lanka	Sydney	13 Jan 1999
		83*	England	Melbourne	15 Jan 1999
		85	England	Sydney	17 Jan 1999
		65	Sri Lanka	Hobart (B)	21 Jan 1999
		57	Sri Lanka	Adelaide	24 Jan 1999
		65	England	Adelaide	26 Jan 1999

HALF-CENTURY ON DEBUT

Batsman	Score	Versus	Venue	Date
J.H. Edrich, England	82	Australia	Melbourne	5 Jan 1971
I.M. Chappell, Australia	60	England	Melbourne	5 Jan 1971
D.L. Amiss, England	103	Australia	Manchester	24 Aug 1972
R. Edwards, Australia	57	England	Manchester	24 Aug 1972
V. Pollard, New Zealand	55	England	Swansea	18 Jul 1973
R.B. Kanhai, West Indies	55	England	Leeds	5 Sep 1973
M.H. Denness, England	66	West Indies	Leeds	5 Sep 1973
A.J. Woodcock, Australia	53	New Zealand	Christchurch	31 Mar 1974
A.L. Wadekar, India	67	England	Leeds	13 Jul 1974
B.P. Patel, India	82	England	Leeds	13 Jul 1974
S.R. de S.Wettimuny, Sri Lanka	53*	Australia	The Oval	11 Jun 1975
G.D. Barlow, England	80*	West Indies	Scarborough	26 Aug 1976
D.W. Randall, England	88	West Indies	Lord's	28/29 Aug 1976
B.C. Rose, England	54	Pakistan	Sahiwal	23 Dec 1977
D.L. Haynes, West Indies	148	Australia	St John's	22 Feb 1978
C.T. Radley, England	79	Pakistan	Manchester	24 May 1978
C.J. Tavare, England	82*	West Indies	Leeds	28/29 May 1980
R.O. Butcher, England	52	Australia	Birmingham	22 Aug 1980
S.M. Patil, India	64	Australia	Melbourne	6 Dec 1980
K.C. Wessels, Australia†	79	New Zealand	Melbourne	9 Jan 1983
D.A.G. Fletcher, Zimbabwe	69*	Australia	Nottingham	9 Jun 1983
M.D. Moxon, England	70	India	Nagpur	23 Jan 1985
Ramiz Raja, Pakistan	75	New Zealand	Christchurch	6 Feb 1985
R. Lamba, India	64	Australia	Jaipur	7 Sep 1986
B.C. Broad, England	76	Australia	Perth	1 Jan 1987
Younis Ahmed, Pakistan	58	India	Calcutta	18 Feb 1987
N.S. Sidhu, India	73	Australia	Madras	9 Oct 1987
P.V. Simmons, West Indies	50	Pakistan	Lahore	16 Oct 1987
K.J. Barnett, England	84	Sri Lanka	The Oval	4 Sep 1988
J.E. Morris, England	63*	New Zealand	Adelaide	1 Dec 1990
P.K. Amre, India	55	South Africa	Calcutta	10 Nov 1991
A. Flower, Zimbabwe	115*	Sri Lanka	New Plymouth	23 Feb 1992
G.J. Crocker, Zimbabwe	50	India	Harare	25 Oct 1992
M.H. Dekker, Zimbabwe	79	New Zealand	Bulawayo (AC)	31 Oct 1992
M.J. Slater, Australia	73	South Africa	Melbourne	9 Dec 1993
S.P. Fleming, New Zealand	90	India	Napier	25 Mar 1994
Mazhar Hussain, UAE	70	India	Sharjah	13 Apr 1994
S.C. Williams, West Indies	61	India	Faridabad	17 Oct 1994
Salim Elahi, Pakistan	102*	Sri Lanka	Gujranwala	29 Sep 1995
S.M. Pollock, South Africa	66*	England	Cape Town	9 Jan 1996
S.O. Tikolo, Kenya	65	India	Cuttack	18 Feb 1996
S.S. Karim, India	55	South Africa	Bloemfontein	23 Jan 1997
Yousuf Youhana, Pakistan	59*	Zimbabwe	Harare	28 Mar 1998
Ravindu Shah, Kenya	52	Bangladesh	Hyderabad (I)	17 May 1998

†*K.C. Wessels also scored 50 in his first match for South Africa, against India at Calcutta on 10 November 1991.*

HALF-CENTURY IN DEBUT INNINGS†

Batsman	Score	Versus	Venue	Date
D.S.B. Kuruppu, Sri Lanka	72	Pakistan	Swansea	9 Jun 1983
Shahid Afridi, Pakistan	102	Sri Lanka	Nairobi (NG)	4 Oct 1996
Azam Khan, Pakistan	72	Zimbabwe	Peshawar	3 Nov 1996
A. Suji, Kenya	67	Zimbabwe	Nairobi (AK)	16 Oct 1997

†Not required to bat in debut match.

FASTEST HALF-CENTURIES

Balls	Batsman	Versus	Venue	Date
17	S.T. Jayasuriya, Sri Lanka	Pakistan	Singapore	7 Apr 1996
18	S.P. O'Donnell, Australia	Sri Lanka	Sharjah	2 May 1990
18	Shahid Afridi, Pakistan	Sri Lanka	Nairobi (NG)	4 Oct 1996
21	B.L. Cairns, New Zealand	Australia	Melbourne	13 Feb 1983
22	Kapil Dev, India	West Indies	Berbice	29 Mar 1983
23	Salim Malik, Pakistan	India	Calcutta	18 Feb 1987
25	I.V.A. Richards, West Indies	England	Port-of-Spain	4 Mar 1986
25	R.B. Richardson, West Indies	England	Kingstown	2 Mar 1994
26	W.B. Phillips, Australia	New Zealand	Wellington	26 Mar 1986
26	Kapil Dev, India	Australia	Rajkot	7 Oct 1986
27	S.M. Patil, India	Pakistan	Jaipur	2 Oct 1983
27	S.T. Jayasuriya, Sri Lanka	Pakistan	Sharjah	2 Nov 1993
28	C.H. Lloyd, West Indies	Sri Lanka	Perth	2 Feb 1985
28	Shahid Afridi, Pakistan	Sri Lanka	Gwalior	12 May 1997
28	S.R. Tendulkar, India	Zimbabwe	Sharjah	13 Nov 1998
29	I.V.A. Richards, West Indies	India	Berbice	29 Mar 1983
29	I.V.A. Richards, West Indies	Pakistan	Gujranwala	27 Nov 1985
29	S.P. Fleming, New Zealand	India	Nagpur	26 Nov 1995
29	A. Ranatunga, Sri Lanka	Kenya	Kandy	6 Mar 1996
29	S.T. Jayasuriya, Sri Lanka	New Zealand	Christchurch	25 Mar 1997

Ross Dundas Cricket Statistics

NINETY-NINES

Batsman	Versus	Venue	Date
G. Boycott, England	Australia	The Oval	20 Aug 1980
B.A. Edgar, New Zealand*	India	Auckland	14 Feb 1981
A.J. Lamb, England	India	The Oval	4 June 1982
K. Srikkanth, India	England	Cuttack	27 Dec 1984
D.M. Jones, Australia*	Sri Lanka	Adelaide	28 Jan 1985
R.B. Richardson, West Indies*	Pakistan	Sharjah	15 Nov 1985
B.C. Broad, England	Pakistan	The Oval	21 May 1987
Ramiz Raja, Pakistan	England	Karachi	20 Nov 1987
L. Klusener, South Africa	Sri Lanka	Lahore	8 Nov 1997

* not out

MOST NINETIES

No.	Batsman	M	Career
7	M.A. Azharuddin, India	310	1985-99
7	P.A. de Silva, Sri Lanka	250	1984-99
6	R.B. Richardson, West Indies	224	1983-96
6	D.M. Jones, Australia	164	1984-94
6	M.D. Crowe, New Zealand	143	1982-95

MOST FOURS OFF AN OVER

4s	Batsman	Bowler	Venue	Date
5	S. Wettimuny (2) R.L. Dias (3), Sri Lanka	Tahir Naqqash, Pakistan	Lahore	29 Mar 1982
5	Salim Malik (1) Imran Khan (4), Pakistan	V.B. John, Sri Lanka	Faisalabad	25 Oct 1987
5	S.P. Fleming, New Zealand	C. Sharma, India	Delhi	3 Nov 1994
5	B.C. Lara, West Indies	P.L. Symcox, South Africa	Karachi	11 Mar 1996
4	G.R. Sealy, Canada	R.M. Hogg, Australia	Birmingham	16 Jun 1979
4	D.W. Hookes, Australia	R.G.D. Willis, England	Brisbane	16 Jan 1983
4	G.S. Chappell, Australia	I.T. Botham, England	Melbourne	23 Jan 1983
4	Imran Khan, Pakistan	V.B. John, Sri Lanka	Swansea	9 Jun 1983
4	A.J. Lamb (2) MW Gatting (2), England	M.D. Crowe, New Zealand	The Oval	9 Jun 1983
4	S.T. Jayasuriya, Sri Lanka	M. Prabhakar, India	Delhi	2 Mar 1996

Ross Dundas Cricket Statistics

MOST FOURS IN AN INNINGS

No.	Batsman	Score	Versus	Venue	Date
22	Saeed Anwar, Pakistan	194	India	Chennai	21 May 1997
21	I.V.A. Richards, West Indies	189*	England	Manchester	31 May 1994
21	B.C. Lara, West Indies	153	Pakistan	Sharjah	5 Nov 1993
20	I.V.A. Richards, West Indies	119*	England	Scarborough	26 Aug 1976
20	I.V.A. Richards, West Indies	149	India	Jamshedpur	7 Dec 1983
20	B.C. Lara, West Indies	128	Pakistan	Durban	19 Feb 1993
20	S. Chanderpaul, West Indies	150	South Africa	East London	24 Jan 1999

MOST SIXES OFF AN OVER

6s	Batsman	Bowler	Venue	Date
4	M.W. Gatting, England	R.J. Shastri, India	Jullundur	20 Dec 1981
4	S.T. Jayasuriya, Sri Lanka	Aamir Sohail, Pakistan	Singapore	2 Apr 1996
3	R.W. Marsh, Australia	B.L. Cairns, New Zealand	Adelaide	23 Nov 1980
3	B.L. Cairns, New Zealand	V.B. John, Sri Lanka	Colombo	1 Apr 1984
3	Kapil Dev, India	C.J. McDermott, Australia	Rajkot	7 Oct 1986
3	Wasim Akram, Pakistan	C. Sharma, India	Nagpur	24 Mar 1987
3	I.V.A. Richards, West Indies	J.R. Ratnayeke, Sri Lanka	Karachi	13 Oct 1987
3	K. Srikkanth, India	R.A. Harper, West Indies	Sharjah	16 Oct 1988
3	A.R. Border, Australia	G.C. Small, England	Hyderabad (I)	19 Oct 1989
3	A.P. Kuiper, South Africa	C.J. McDermott, Australia	Centurion	20 Feb 1994

Ross Dundas Cricket Statistics

MOST SIXES IN AN INNINGS

No.	Batsman	Score	Versus	Venue	Date
11	S.T. Jayasuriya, Sri Lanka	134	Pakistan	Singapore	2 Apr 1996
11	Shahid Afridi, Pakistan	102	Sri Lanka	Nairobi (NG)	4 Oct 1996
9	Ijaz Ahmed, Pakistan	139*	India	Lahore	2 Oct 1997
8	C.G. Greenidge, West Indies	117	India	St John's	18 Mar 1989
7	I.V.A. Richards, West Indies	181	Sri Lanka	Karachi	13 Oct 1987
7	I.V.A. Richards, West Indies	110	India	Rajkot	5 Jan 1988
7	S.R. Tendulkar, India	117	Australia	Kanpur	7 Apr 1998
7	C.L. Cairns, New Zealand	115	India	Christchurch	19 Jan 1999

MOST SIXES IN A CAREER

No.	Batsman	M	Career
122	I.V.A. Richards, West Indies	187	1975-91
102	S.T. Jayasuriya, Sri Lanka	178	1989-99
97	S.R. Tendulkar, India	211	1989-99
88	P.A. de Silva, Sri Lanka	250	1984-99
83	C.G. Greenidge, West Indies	128	1975-91
80	Saeed Anwar, Pakistan	161	1989-98
77	Ijaz Ahmed, Pakistan	215	1986-98
77	Wasim Akram, Pakistan	254	1984-98
74	W.J. Cronje, South Africa	152	1992-99
73	M.A. Azharuddin, India	310	1985-99
67	Inzamam-ul-Haq, Pakistan	171	1991-98
65	C.L. Cairns, New Zealand	100	1991-99
65	Kapil Dev, India	225	1978-94
61	A. Ranatunga, Sri Lanka	260	1982-99

Ross Dundas Cricket Statistics

MOST CONSECUTIVE BOUNDARIES

Total	Batsman	Versus	Venue	Date
5 (4,4,4,4,6)	Imran Khan, Pakistan	Sri Lanka	Swansea	9 Jun 1983
5 (4,6,4,6,6)	B.L. Cairns, New Zealand	Sri Lanka	Colombo (PSS)	1 Apr 1984
5 (6,4,6,6,6)	S.T. Jayasuriya, Sri Lanka	Pakistan	Singapore	7 Apr 1996
5 (4,4,4,4,4)	S.P. Fleming, New Zealand	India	Delhi	3 Nov 1994
4 (4,4,6,4)	D.W. Hookes, Australia	England	Brisbane	16 Jan 1983
4 (4,4,4,4)	Imran Khan, Pakistan	Sri Lanka	Swansea	9 Jun 1983
4 (6,6,6,4)	Wasim Akram, Pakistan	India	Nagpur	24 Mar 1987
4 (6,6,6,4)	I.V.A. Richards, West Indies	Sri Lanka	Karachi	13 Oct 1987
4 (6,6,4,4)	S.M. Gavaskar, India	New Zealand	Nagpur	31 Oct 1987
4 (6,4,4,4)	A.R. Border, Australia	England	Hyderabad (I)	19 Oct 1989
4 (4,6,6,6)	Moin Khan, Pakistan	West Indies	Sharjah	13 Oct 1995
4 (4,4,4,4)	B.C. Lara, West Indies	South Africa	Karachi	11 Mar 1996
4 (6,6,4,4)	S.T. Jayasuriya, Sri Lanka	New Zealand	Christchurch	25 Mar 1997

Ross Dundas Cricket Statistics

HIGHEST % OF AN INDIVIDUAL INNINGS SCORED BY BOUNDARIES

(minimum 25 runs)

%	4s	6s	R	Batsman	Versus	Venue	Date
96.77	3	3	31	W.K.M. Benjamin, West Indies	India	Nagpur	8 Dec 1987
96.00	6	0	25	D.I. Gower, England	India	Nottingham	20 July 1990
96.00	6	0	25	B.A. Young, New Zealand	South Africa	Cape Town	6 Dec 1994
96.00	3	2	25	Aamir Sohail, Pakistan	India	Toronto	13 Sep 1998
94.12	8	0	34	D.L. Haynes, West Indies	England	Arnos Vale	4 Feb 1981
92.31	3	2	26	Kapil Dev, India	Australia	Jaipur	7 Sep 1986
92.31	6	0	26	R.S. Kaluwitharana, Sri Lanka	India	Delhi	2 Mar 1996
92.31	9	2	52	Shahid Afridi, Pakistan	Sri Lanka	Gwalior	12 May 1997
90.91	6	1	33	W.B. Phillips, Australa	India	Indore	6 Oct 1984
89.47	7	1	38	K. Srikkanth, India	West Indies	Lord's	25 Jun 1983
88.24	6	11	102	Shahid Afridi, Pakistan	Sri Lanka	Nairobi (NG)	4 Oct 1996
88.00	4	1	25	Zaheer Abbas, Pakistan	New Zealand	Faisalabad	23 Nov 1984
88.00	4	1	25	Saeed Anwar, Pakistan	Zimbabwe	Harare	29 Mar 1998
87.80	15	2	82	S.R. Tendulkar, India	New Zealand	Auckland	27 Mar 1994
87.50	7	0	32	D.L. Haynes, West Indies	Sri Lanka	Hobart (TCA)	10 Jan 1985
87.50	9	1	48	S.R. Tendulkar, India	Bangladesh	Sharjah	5 Apr 1995

%	4s	6s	R	Batsman	Versus	Venue	Date
87.50	4	2	32	N.E. Clarke, Netherlands	South Africa	Rawalpindi (RC)	5 Mar 1996
86.67	5	1	30	S.R. Tendulkar, India	England	The Oval	23 May 1996
86.49	8	0	37	P.V. Simmons, West Indies	Australia	Bridgetown	8 Mar 1995
86.36	5	3	44	S.T. Jayasuriya, Sri Lanka	Kenya	Kandy	6 Mar 1996
86.36	8	1	44	S.T. Jayasuriya, Sri Lanka	Australia	Colombo (RPS)	30 Aug 1996

Ross Dundas Cricket Statistics

HIGHEST INDIVIDUAL INNINGS WITHOUT SCORING A BOUNDARY

Score	Batsman	Versus	Venue	Date
96	A.C. Parore, New Zealand	India	Vadodara (IPCL)	28 Oct 1994
84	Zaheer Abbas, Pakistan	Australia	Melbourne	9 Jan 1982
64	D.C. Boon, Australia	Pakistan	Melbourne	12 Jan 1993
59	Javed Miandad, Pakistan	West Indies	Perth	4 Dec 1992
58	M.G. Bevan, Australia	India	Sharjah	19 Apr 1998
54	R.S. Kaluwitharana, Sri Lanka	Pakistan	Kimberley	7 Apr 1998
53	R.T. Ponting, Australia	Zimbabwe	Colombo (RPS)	26 Aug 1996
50	K.C. Wessels, Australia	West Indies	Perth	5 Feb 1984
50	R.S. Mahanama, Sri Lanka	India	Colombo (SSC)	5 Sep 1994
50	I.A. Healy, Australia	Sri Lanka	Melbourne	18 Jan 1996

Ross Dundas Cricket Statistics

CAUGHT MOST TIMES IN A CAREER

No.	M	Inn	Batsman	Career
140	310	285	M.A. Azharuddin, India	1985-99
140	250	243	P.A. de Silva, Sri Lanka	1984-99
130	276	250	Salim Malik, Pakistan	1982-98
125	224	217	R.B. Richardson, West Indies	1983-96
121	260	246	A. Ranatunga, Sri Lanka	1982-99
120	211	204	S.R. Tendulkar, India	1989-99
114	273	252	A.R. Border, Australia	1979-94
114	238	237	D.L. Haynes, West Indies	1978-94
112	178	170	S.T. Jayasuriya, Sri Lanka	1989-99
110	215	198	Ijaz Ahmed, Pakistan	1986-98

Ross Dundas Cricket Statistics

CAUGHT MOST OFTEN IN A CAREER (minimum 10 innings)

%	Inn	Ct	Batsman	Career
80.65	31	25	C.M. Spearman, New Zealand	1995-98
75.00	20	15	J.M. Parker, New Zealand	1974-81
75.00	12	9	Sajid Ali, Pakistan	1984-97
70.00	10	7	S.C. Khanna, India	1979-84
69.23	13	9	C. White, England	1994-97
67.47	83	56	M.J. Greatbatch, New Zealand	1988-96
66.89	148	99	Aamir Sohail, Pakistan	1990-98
66.67	21	14	Akram Khan, Bangladesh	1988-98
66.67	12	8	L.G. Howell, New Zealand	1998
66.67	51	34	S.G. Law, Australia	1994-99
66.67	24	16	P. Willey, England	1977-86
66.67	18	12	Zahid Fazal, Pakistan	1990-94

Ross Dundas Cricket Statistics

BOWLED MOST TIMES IN A CAREER

No.	M	Inn	Batsman	Career
57	253	252	A.R. Border, Australia	1979-94
54	238	237	D.L. Haynes, West Indies	1978-94
49	251	228	S.R. Waugh, Australia	1986-99
47	254	200	Wasim Akram, Pakistan	1984-98
38	310	285	M.A. Azharuddin, India	1985-99
38	276	250	Salim Malik, Pakistan	1982-98
36	125	122	G.A. Gooch, England	1976-95
36	174	169	M.E. Waugh, Australia	1988-99
35	181	177	D.C. Boon, Australia	1984-95
35	187	167	I.V.A. Richards, West Indies	1975-91

Ross Dundas Cricket Statistics

BOWLED MOST OFTEN IN A CAREER (minimum 10 innings)

%	Inns	Bwld	Batsman	Career
58.33	12	7	B. Wood, England	1972-82
50.00	18	9	T.M. Alderman, Australia	1981-91
50.00	12	6	B.P. Julien, Australia	1993-99
50.00	10	5	Shahid Saeed, Pakistan	1989-92
45.83	24	11	V.J. Marks, England	1980-88
44.44	18	8	D.L. Amiss, England	1972-77
43.33	30	13	J.R. Thomson, Australia	1975-85
41.18	17	7	D. Chudasama, Kenya	1996-98
40.74	27	11	A.A. Donald, South Africa	1991-99
40.48	42	17	S.M. Patil, India	1980-96

Ross Dundas Cricket Statistics

LBW MOST TIMES IN A CAREER

No	M	Inn	Batsman	Career
33	208	193	R.S. Mahanama, Sri Lanka	1986-99
29	233	218	Javed Miandad, Pakistan	1975-96
25	238	237	D.L. Haynes, West Indies	1978-94
20	89	88	A.C. Hudson, South Africa	1991-97
20	225	198	Kapil Dev, India	1978-94
19	250	243	P.A. de Silva, Sri Lanka	1984-99
19	133	130	P.V. Simmons, West Indies	1987-98
18	178	170	S.T. Jayasuriya, Sri Lanka	1989-99
18	276	250	Salim Malik, Pakistan	1982-98
17	310	285	M.A. Azharuddin, India	1985-99

Ross Dundas Cricket Statistics

LBW MOST OFTEN IN A CAREER (minimum 10 innings)

%	Inns	LBW	Batsman	Career
33.33	12	4	J.P. Crawley, England	1994-99
30.00	10	3	G.A. Paterson, Zimbabwe	1983-87
30.00	10	3	K.J. Wadsworth, New Zealand	1973-76
26.09	23	6	B.M. Laird, Australia	1979-82
23.08	26	6	R.T. Robinson, England	1984-88
22.73	88	20	A.C. Hudson, South Africa	1991-97
21.43	14	3	C.L. King, West Indies	1976-80
21.43	14	3	R.B. McCosker, Australia	1975-82
20.00	30	6	C.W.J. Athey, England	1980-88
20.00	15	3	D.G. Cork, England	1992-97
20.00	15	3	T.J. Zoehrer, Australia	1986-94

Ross Dundas Cricket Statistics

STUMPED MOST TIMES IN A CAREER

No.	M	Inn	Batsman	Career
13	254	200	Wasim Akram, Pakistan	1984-98
9	310	285	M.A. Azharuddin, India	1985-99
9	174	169	M.E. Waugh, Australia	1988-99
8	211	204	S.R. Tendulkar, India	1989-99
8	251	228	S.R. Waugh, Australia	1986-99
7	273	252	A.R. Border, Australia	1979-94
7	250	243	P.A. de Silva, Sri Lanka	1984-99
7	149	148	J.G. Wright, New Zealand	1978-92
6	92	89	A.D.R. Campbell, Zimbabwe	1992-98
6	108	105	D.J. Cullinan, South Africa	1993-99
6	169	120	P.J.L. Dujon, West Indies	1981-91
6	198	197	Ramiz, Raja, Pakistan	1985-97
6	150	128	R.J. Shastri, India	1981-92
6	146	145	K. Srikkanth, India	1981-92

Ross Dundas Cricket Statistics

STUMPED MOST OFTEN IN A CAREER (minimum 10 innings)

%	Inn	St	Batsman	Career
17.65	17	3	T. Odoyo, Kenya	1996-98
16.67	12	2	Naved Anjum, Pakistan	1984-92
15.38	13	2	Aasif Karim, Kenya	1996-98
14.29	28	4	M.J. Horne, New Zealand	1997-99
14.29	28	4	N. Hussain, England	1989-99
12.50	16	2	B.R. Hartland, New Zealand	1992-94
12.00	25	3	S.B. Doull, New Zealand	1992-99
11.11	18	2	C.O. Browne, West Indies	1995-97
11.11	18	2	M.O. Odumbe, Kenya	1996-98
11.11	18	2	E.O. Simons, South Africa	1994-95

Ross Dundas Cricket Statistics

RUN OUT MOST TIMES IN A CAREER

No.	M	Inn	Batsman	Career
30	310	285	M.A. Azharuddin, India	1985-99
29	254	200	Wasim Akram, Pakistan	1984-98
28	273	252	A.R. Border, Australia	1979-94
28	260	246	A. Ranatunga, Sri Lanka	1982-99
27	147	143	A.P. Gurusinha, Sri Lanka	1985-96
26	171	161	Inzamam-ul-Haq, Pakistan	1991-98
24	233	218	Javed Miandad, Pakistan	1975-96
24	276	250	Salim Malik, Pakistan	1982-98
24	251	228	S.R. Waugh, Australia	1986-99
23	198	197	Ramiz Raja, Pakistan	1985-97
23	174	169	M.E. Waugh, Australia	1988-99

Ross Dundas Cricket Statistics

RUN OUT MOST OFTEN IN A CAREER (minimum 10 innings)

%	Inn	RO	Batsman	Career
36.36	11	4	S. Ranatunga, Sri Lanka	1994-96
35.29	17	6	R.W. Taylor, England	1973-84
31.25	16	5	S.L.V. Raju, India	1990-96
30.77	13	4	Aasif Karim, Kenya	1996-98
30.43	23	7	Aamir Malik, Pakistan	1988-94

%	Inn	RO	Batsman	Career
30.00	10	3	P.B. Dassanayake, Sri Lanka	1993-94
27.78	18	5	Salim Elahi, Pakistan	1995-98
27.27	11	3	S.P. Davis, Australia	1986-88
27.27	11	3	R.K. Illingworth, England	1991-96
27.27	11	3	A. Kuruvilla, India	1997
27.27	22	6	M.J.R. Rindel, South Africa	1994-99
27.27	11	3	F.A. Rose, West Indies	1997-98
27.27	11	3	M.H.N. Walker, Australia	1974-81
27.27	11	3	Yousuf Youhana, Pakistan	1998

Ross Dundas Cricket Statistics

MOST CONSECUTIVE RUN-OUTS

No.	Batsman	From	To
5	J.V. Coney, New Zealand	22 Mar 1986	18 Jul 1986
4	S.R. Waugh, Australia	4 Feb 1988	15 Dec 1988
4	I.R. Bishop, West Indies	3 Jan 1996	21 Feb 1996
4	M.J.R. Rindel, South Africa	15 Dec 1994	12 Jan 1995

Ross Dundas Cricket Statistics

MOST NOT OUTS IN A CAREER

No.	Batsman	Inn	M	Career
51	M.A. Azharuddin, India	285	310	1985-99
47	A. Ranatunga, Sri Lanka	246	260	1982-99
44	S.R. Waugh, Australia	228	251	1986-99
41	Javed Miandad, Pakistan	218	233	1975-96
40	Imran Khan, Pakistan	151	175	1974-92
39	A.R. Border, Australia	252	273	1979-94
39	Kapil Dev, India	198	225	1978-94
37	E.J. Chatfield, New Zealand	48	114	1979-89
37	Salim Malik, Pakistan	250	276	1982-98
36	P.J.L. Dujon, West Indies	120	169	1981-91
36	I.A. Healy, Australia	120	168	1988-97
36	C.L. Hooper, West Indies	161	177	1987-99
36	A.L. Logie, West Indies	133	158	1981-93
36	H.P. Tillakaratne, Sri Lanka	149	176	1986-99
36	Wasim Akram, Pakistan	200	254	1984-98
34	C.L. Ambrose, West Indies	86	157	1988-99
34	C.Z. Harris, New Zealand	106	120	1990-99
33	M.G. Bevan, Australia	86	97	1994-99
33	D.J. Richardson, South Africa	77	122	1991-98
31	Mustaq Ahmed, Pakistan	69	130	1989-98
31	Waqar Younis, Pakistan	85	72	1989-98
30	R.B. Richardson, West Indies	217	224	1983-96

NOT OUT MOST OFTEN IN A CAREER (minimum 10 innings)

%	Inns	NO	Batsman	Career
90.00	10	9	P.C.R. Tufnell, England	1990-97
84.62	13	1l	Salim Jaffar, Pakistan	1986-90
77.78	18	14	Maninder Singh, India	1983-93
77.08	48	37	E.J. Chatfield, New Zealand	1979-89
75.00	20	15	B.P. Patterson, West Indies	1986-93
70.00	10	7	Azeem Hafeez, Pakistan	1983-85
66.67	18	12	S.D. Anurasiri, Sri Lanka	1986-94

66.67	12	8	T.B.A. May, Australia	1987-95
66.67	12	8	G.B. Troup, New Zealand	1976-85
64.29	14	9	D.W. Fleming, Australia	1994-99
64.29	14	9	M.A. Suji, Kenya	1996-98

Ross Dundas Cricket Statistics

MOST DUCKS IN A CAREER

No.	Batsman	Inn	M	Career
21	Wasim Akram, Pakistan	200	254	1984-98
18	Salim Malik, Pakistan	250	276	1982-98
17	R.S. Kaluwitharana, Sri Lanka	108	112	1990-99
17	A. Ranatunga, Sri Lanka	246	260	1982-99
15	R.S. Mahanama, Sri Lanka	193	208	1986-99
15	C.J. McDermott, Australia	78	138	1984-96
15	Ramiz Raja, Pakistan	197	198	1985-97
14	P.V. Simmons, West Indies	130	133	1987-98
13	D.L. Haynes, West Indies	237	238	1978-94
13	Kapil Dev, India	198	225	1978-94
13	A.L. Logie, West Indies	133	158	1981-93
13	S.R. Waugh, Australia	228	251	1986-99
12	C.L. Ambrose, West Indies	86	157	1988-99
12	K.J. Hughes, Australia	88	97	1977-85
12	A. Kumble, India	77	158	1990-99
12	Waqar Younis, Pakistan	85	172	1989-98
11	K.L.T. Arthurton, West Indies	88	98	1988-99
11	A.R. Border, Australia	252	273	1979-94
11	K. Srikkanth, India	145	146	1981-92
10	Aamir Sohail, Pakistan	148	149	1990-98
10	W.K.M. Benjamin, West Indies	52	85	1986-95
10	Saeed Anwar, Pakistan	159	161	1989-98
10	J. Srinath, India	79	153	1991-99
10	C.A. Walsh, West Indies	68	185	1985-98
10	M.E. Waugh, Australia	169	174	1988-98

MOST CONSECUTIVE DUCKS

No.	Batsman	From	To
4	A.L. Logie, West Indies	2 Dec 1985	4 Nov 1986
4	G.P. Wickramasinghe, Sri Lanka	7 Apr 1996	19 Apr 1998

Ross Dundas Cricket Statistics

LONGEST CAREER WITHOUT A DUCK

Player	M	Inn	Runs	Career
K.C. Wessels, Australia & South Africa	109	105	3367	1983-94
H.D.P.K. Dharmasena, Sri Lanka	94	57	849	1994-98
Yashpal Sharma, India	42	40	883	1978-85
D.S. de Silva, Sri Lanka	41	29	371	1975-85
P.N. Kirsten, South Africa	40	40	1293	1991-94
R.C. Russell, England	40	31	423	1987-98
D.S. Lehmann, Australia	38	36	1102	1996-99
C.D. McMillan, New Zealand	38	36	898	1997-99

DISMISSED FIRST BALL OF THE MATCH

Batsman	Bowler	Venue	Date
B. Wood, England	A.M.E. Roberts, West Indies	Scarborough	26 Aug 1976
D.W. Randall, England	A.M.E. Roberts, West Indies	Brisbane	23 Dec 1979
S.M. Gavaskar, India	R.J. Hadlee, New Zealand	Perth	9 Dec 1980
J.G. Wright, New Zealand	J.R. Thomson, Australia	Wellington	20 Feb 1982
G.M. Wood, Australia	J. Garner, West Indies	Melbourne	6 Jan 1985
R.J. Shastri, India	Imran Khan, Pakistan	Sharjah	22 Mar 1985
J.G. Bracewell, New Zealand	C.J. McDermott, Australia	Adelaide	27 Jan 1986
Mudassar Nazar, Pakistan	J.G. Thomas, England	Birmingham	25 May 1987
Ramiz Raja, Pakistan	T.M. Alderman, Australia	Brisbane	8 Jan 1989
J.G. Wright, New Zealand	C.J. McDermott, Australia	Auckland	22 Feb 1992
R.S. Mahanama, Sri Lanka	C.J. McDermott, Australia	Colombo (RPS)	5 Sep 1992
Ramiz Raja, Pakistan	B.P. Patterson, West Indies	Cape Town	25 Feb 1993
A. Flower, Zimbabwe	Wasim Akram, Pakistan	Karachi	24 Dec 1993
A.P. Gurusinghe, Sri Lanka	Saif-ul-Islam, Bangladesh	Sharjah	6 Apr 1995
Shahid Afridi, Pakistan	NŒ Matambanadzo, Zimbabwe	Peshawar	3 Nov 1996
S.C. Ganguly, India	W.P.U.C.J. Vaas, Sri Lanka	Mumbai	17 May 1997
P.A. Wallace, West Indies	D.R. Brown, England	Sharjah	13 Dec 1997
P.A. Wallace, West Indies	S.M. Pollock, South Africa	East London	24 Jan 1999

Ross Dundas Cricket Statistics

DISMISSED FIRST BALL OF THE INNINGS (TEAM BATTING SECOND)

Batsman	Bowler	Venue	Date
G.R. Marsh, Australia	P.A.J. De Freitas, England	Sharjah	9 Apr 1987
D.L. Haynes, West Indies	Kapil Dev, India	Perth	6 Dec 1991
Aamir Sohail, Pakistan	D.K. Morrison, New Zealand	Christchurch	18 Mar 1992
G.A. Gooch, England	E.A. Brandes, Zimbabwe	Albury	18 Mar 1992
D.L. Haynes, West Indies	M.W. Pringle, South Africa	Port-of-Spain	12 Apr 1992
D.L. Haynes, West Indies	Waqar Younis, Pakistan	Cape Town	25 Feb 1993
M. Prabhakar, India	C.A. Walsh, West Indies	Mumbai	20 Oct 1994
R.S. Mahanama, Sri Lanka	C.E.L. Ambrose, West Indies	Adelaide	15 Dec 1995
A.C. Hudson, South Africa	E.A. Brandes, Zimbabwe	Centurion	25 Jan 1997
S.T. Jayasuriya, Sri Lanka	Aaqib Javed, Pakistan	Gwalior	12 May 1997
S.T. Jayasuriya, Sri Lanka	B.K.V. Prasad, India	Colombo (RPS)	18 July 1997
Saeed Anwar, Pakistan	S.M. Pollock, South Africa	Lahore	2 Nov 1997
S.T. Jayasuriya, India	S.B. Doull, New Zealand	Dhaka	26 Oct 1998

Ross Dundas Cricket Statistics

Batting Partnerships

HIGHEST PARTNERSHIPS

Runs	Wkt	Batsmen	Versus	Venue	Date
275*	4th	M.A. Azharuddin 153*, A.D. Jadeja 116*, India	Zimbabwe	Cuttack	9 Apr 1998
263	2nd	Aamir Sohail 134, Inzamam-ul-Haq 137*, Pakistan	New Zealand	Sharjah	20 Apr 1994
252	1st	S.C. Ganguly 109, S.R. Tendulkar 128, India	Sri Lanka	Colombo (RPS)	7 Jul 1998
232	4th	D.J. Cullinan 124, J.N. Rhodes 121, South Africa	Pakistan	Nairobi (NG)	29 Sept 1996
231	2nd	S.R. Tendulkar 118, N.S. Sidhu 101, India	Pakistan	Sharjah	15 Apr 1996
230	3rd	Saeed Anwar 140, Ijaz Ahmed 117, Pakistan	India	Dhaka	18 Jan 1998
226	4th	S. Chanderpaul 150, C.L. Hooper 108, West Indies	South Africa	East London	24 Jan 1999
225	1st	D. Chudasama 122, K. Otieno 144, Kenya	Bangladesh	Nairobi (NG)	10 Oct 1997
224*	3rd	D.M. Jones 99*, A.R. Border 118*, Australia	Sri Lanka	Adelaide	28 Jan 1985
223	5th	M.A. Azharuddin 111*, A.D. Jadeja 119, India	Sri Lanka	Colombo (RPS)	17 Aug 1997
221	2nd	C.G. Greenidge 115, I.V.A. Richards 149, West Indies	India	Jamshedpur	7 Dec 1983
219	2nd	M.E. Waugh 87, R.T. Ponting 145, Australia	Zimbabwe	Delhi	11 Apr 1998
213	3rd	G.A. Hick 86*, N.H. Fairbrother 113, England	West Indies	Lord's	27 May 1991
213*	3rd	S.T. Jayasuriya 134*, P.A. de Silva 102*, Sri Lanka	Pakistan	Lahore	5 Nov 1997
212	1st	D.C. Boon 111, G.R. Marsh 104, Australia	India	Jaipur	7 Sept 1986
207	3rd	M.E. Waugh 130, S.R. Waugh 82, Australia	Kenya	Visag	23 Feb 1996
205	3rd	Moin-ul-Atiq 105, Ijaz Ahmed 124*, Pakistan	Bangladesh	Chittagong	29 Oct 1988
205	2nd	D.L. Haynes 80, I.V.A. Richards 153*, West Indies	Australia	Melbourne	9 Dec 1979
205	2nd	Mohsin Khan 117*, Zaheer Abbas 118, Pakistan	India	Multan	17 Dec 1982
204	2nd	Inzamam-ul-Haq 117, Salim Malik 102, Pakistan	Sri Lanka	Rawalpindi (RC)	19 Jan1992
204	1st	Saeed Anwar 110, Ramiz Raja 109*, Pakistan	Sri Lanka	Sharjah	4 Feb 1993
202	1st	Saeed Anwar 126, Ramiz Raja 107*, Pakistan	Sri Lanka	Adelaide	17 Feb 1990
202	2nd	G.A. Gooch 117*, D.I. Gower 102, England	Australia	Lord's	3 June 1985
200*	1st	S.C. Williams 78*, S. Chanderpaul 109*, West Indies	India	Bridgetown	3 May 1997

Ross Dundas Cricket Statistics

HIGHEST PARTNERSHIPS FOR EACH COUNTRY

Australia

Wkt	Ttl	Batsmen	Versus	Venue	Date
3rd	224*	D.M. Jones 99*, A.R. Border 118*	Sri Lanka	Adelaide	28 Jan 1985
2nd	219	M.E. Waugh 87, R.T. Ponting 145	Zimbabwe	Delhi	11 Apr 1998
1st	212	G.R. Marsh 104, D.C. Boon 111	India	Jaipur	7 Sept 1986
3rd	207	M.E. Waugh 130, S.R. Waugh 82	Kenya	Visag	23 Feb 1996
2nd	193	A.C. Gilchrist 103, R.T. Ponting 124*	Pakistan	Lahore	10 Nov 1998

Ross Dundas Cricket Statistics

Bangladesh

Wkt	Ttl	Batsmen	Versus	Venue	Date
1st	137	Athar Ali Khan 47, Mohammad Rafiq 77	Kenya	Hyderabad (I)	17 May 1998
4th	110	Akram Khan 59, Athar Ali Khan 82	Pakistan	Colombo (RPS)	16 Jul 1997
5th	109	Amin-Ul-Islam 69*, Khaled Mahmud 47	India	Dhaka	10 Jan 1998
3rd	108	Farooq Ahmed 57, Athar Ali Khan 44	India	Chandigarh	25 Dec 1990
4th	87	Habib-Ul-Bashar 70, Akram Khan 59	Zimbabwe	Nairobi (NG)	11 Oct 1997

Ross Dundas Cricket Statistics

Canada

Wkt	Ttl	Batsmen	Versus	Venue	Date
1st	54	C.J.D. Chappell 14, G.R. Sealy 45	Pakistan	Leeds	9 Jun 1979
1st	44	C.J.D. Chappell 19, G.R. Sealy 25	Australia	Birmingham	16 Jun 1979
2nd	31	G.R. Sealy 45, F.A. Dennis 25	Pakistan	Leeds	9 Jun 1979
5th	27	C.J.D. Chappell 19, J.C.B. Vaughan 29	Australia	Birmingham	16 Jun 1979
6th	19	C.A. Marshall 8, B.M. Mauricette 15	Pakistan	Leeds	9 Jun 1979
6th	19	J.C.B. Vaughan 29, B.M. Mauricette 5	Australia	Birmingham	16 Jun 1979

Ross Dundas Cricket Statistics

East Africa

Wkt	Ttl	Batsmen	Versus	Venue	Date
6th	42	Jawahir Shah 37, R.K. Sethi 23	India	Leeds	11 Jun 1975
7th	37	Mehmood Quaraishy 16*, Zulfaqir Ali 30	New Zealand	Birmingham	7 Jun 1975
1st	30	Frasat Ali 45, S. Walusimba 15	New Zealand	Birmingham	7 Jun 1975
6th	30	R.K. Sethi 30, Mehmood Quaraishy 19	England	Birmingham	14 Jun 1975
1st	26	Frasat Ali 12, S. Walusimba 16	India	Leeds	11 Jun 1975

Ross Dundas Cricket Statistics

England

Wkt	Ttl	Batsmen	Versus	Venue	Date
3rd	213	G.A. Hick 86*, N.H. Fairbrother 113	West Indies	Lord's	27 May 1991
2nd	202	G.A. Gooch 117*, D.I. Gower 102	Australia	Lord's	3 Jun 1985
1st	193	C.W.J. Athey 142*, G.A. Gooch 91	New Zealand	Manchester	18 July 1986
3rd	190*	C.J. Tavare 83*, A.J. Lamb 108*	New Zealand	Sydney	20 Jan 1983
3rd	190	G.A. Hick 108, N. Hussain 93	Australia	Sydney	17 Jan 1999

Ross Dundas Cricket Statistics

India

Wkt	Ttl	Batsmen	Versus	Venue	Date
4th	275*	M.A. Azharuddin 153*, A.D. Jadeja 116*	Zimbabwe	Cuttack	9 Apr 1998
1st	252	S.C. Ganguly 109, S.R. Tendular 128	Sri Lanka	Colombo (RPS)	7 Jul 1998
2nd	231	S.R. Tendulkar 118, N.S. Sidhu 101	Pakistan	Sharjah	15 Apr 1996
5th	223	M.A. Azharuddin 111*, A.D. Jadeja 119	Sri Lanka	Colombo (RPS)	17 Aug 1997
1st	197*	S.R. Tendulkar 124*, S.C. Ganguly 63*	Zimbabwe	Sharjah	13 Nov 1998

Ross Dundas Cricket Statistics

Kenya

Wkt	Ttl	Batsmen	Versus	Venue	Date
1st	225	D. Chudasama 122, K. Otieno 144	Bangladesh	Nairobi (NG)	10 Oct 1997
4th	137	S.O. Tikolo 96, H.S. Modi 41	Sri Lanka	Kandy	6 Mar 1996
7th	119	T. Odoyo 41, A. Suji 67	Zimbabwe	Nairobi (AK)	16 Oct 1997
3rd	102	K. Otieno 85, M. Odumbe 50	Australia	Visag	23 Feb 1996
8th	100	H.S. Modi 57, Asif Karim 53	Zimbabwe	Nairobi (NG)	19 Oct 1997
4th	100	M. Odombe 83, H.S. Modi 51	India	Gwalior	28 May 1998

Ross Dundas Cricket Statistics

Netherlands

Wkt	Ttl	Batsmen	Versus	Venue	Date
5th	111	K.J. Van Noortwijk 64, B. Zuiderent 54	England	Peshawar	22 Feb 1996
2nd	74	P.E. Cantrell 47, G.J.A.F. Aponso 45	UAE	Lahore	1 Mar 1996
4th	73	K.J. Van Noortwijk 33, G.J.A.F. Aponso 58	Pakistan	Lahore	26 Feb 1996
3rd	71	P.E. Cantrell 47, T.B.M. de Leede 36	UAE	Lahore	1 Mar 1996
1st	56	N.E. Clarke 32, P.E. Cantrell 23	South Africa	Rawalpindi (RC)	5 Mar 1996

Ross Dundas Cricket Statistics

New Zealand

Wkt	Ttl	Batsmen	Versus	Venue	Date
3rd	181	A.C. Parore 96, K.R. Rutherford 108	India	Vadodara (IPCL)	28 Oct 1994
3rd	171*	M.D. Crowe 107*, S.P. Fleming 78*	India	Jamshedpur	15 Nov 1995
4th	168	L.K. Germon 89, C.Z. Harris 130	Australia	Chennai	11 Mar 1996
3rd	160	G.P. Howarth 72, M.D. Crowe 105*	England	Auckland	25 Feb 1984
1st	158	M.D. Crowe 69, J.G. Wright 93	Bangladesh	Sharjah	28 Apr 1990

Ross Dundas Cricket Statistics

Pakistan

Wkt	Ttl	Batsmen	Versus	Venue	Date
2nd	263	Aamir Sohail 134, Inzamam-ul-Haq 137*	New Zealand	Sharjah	20 Apr 1994
3rd	230	Saeed Anwar 140, Ijaz Ahmed 117	India	Dhaka	18 Jan 1998
2nd	205	Mohsin Khan 117*, Zaheer Abbas 118	India	Multan	17 Dec 1982
3rd	205	Moin-Ul-Atiq 105, Ijaz Ahmed 124*	Bangladesh	Chittagong	29 Oct 1988
2nd	204	Inzamam-ul-Haq 117, Salim Malik 102	Sri Lanka	Rawalpindi (RC)	19 Jan 1992
1st	204	Saeed Anwar 110, Ramiz Raja 109*	Sri Lanka	Sharjah	4 Feb 1993

Ross Dundas Cricket Statistics

South Africa

Wkt	Ttl	Batsmen	Versus	Venue	Date
4th	232	D.J. Cullinan 124, J.N. Rhodes 121	Pakistan	Nairobi (NG)	29 Sept 1996
1st	190	G. Kirsten 87, M.J.R. Rindel 106	Pakistan	Johannesburg	12 Jan 1995
1st	186	G. Kirsten 83, A.C. Hudson 161	Netherlands	Rawalpindi (RC)	5 Mar 1996
4th	183*	J.H. Kallis 109*, J.N. Rhodes 94*	Pakistan	Durban	3 Apr 1998
3rd	160	H.H. Gibbs 125, W.J. Cronje 72	West Indies	Port Elizabeth	30 Jan 1999

Ross Dundas Cricket Statistics

Sri Lanka

Wkt	Ttl	Batsmen	Versus	Venue	Date
3rd	213*	S.T. Jayasuriya 134*, P.A de Silva 102*	Pakistan	Lahore	5 Nov 1997
3rd	184	M.S. Atapattu 94, P.A. de Silva 97	Pakistan	Sharjah	4 Apr 1997
3rd	184	A.P. Gurusinha 84, P.A. de Silva 145	Kenya	Kandy	6 Mar 1996
3rd	172	A.P. Gurusinha 87, P.A. de Silva 91	Zimbabwe	Colombo (SSC)	21 Feb 1996
4th	171*	R.S Mahanama 94*, A. Ranatunga 87*	West Indies	Lahore	1 Nov 1997
1st	171	M.S. Atapattu 60, S.T. Jayasuriya 108	Bangladesh	Colombo (SSC)	22 Jul 1997

Ross Dundas Cricket Statistics

United Arab Emirates

Wkt	Ttl	Batsmen	Versus	Venue	Date
1st	117	Azhar Saeed 32, Salim Raza 84	Netherlands	Lahore	1 Mar 1996
3rd	94	Mazhar Hussain 70, V Mehra 43	India	Sharjah	13 Apr 1994
4th	82*	V. Mehra 29*, Mohammad Ishaq 51*	Netherlands	Lahore	1 Mar 1996
9th	80*	Arshad Laiq 43*, S.F. Dukanwala 40*	South Africa	Rawalpindi (RC)	16 Feb 1996
7th	57	J.A. Samarasekara 31*, Arshad Laiq 31	Pakistan	Sharjah	17 Apr 1994

Ross Dundas Cricket Statistics

West Indies

Wkt	Ttl	Batsmen	Versus	Venue	Date
4th	226	S. Chanderpaul 150, C.L. Hooper 108	South Africa	East London	24 Jan 1999
2nd	221	C.G. Greenidge 115, I.V.A.Richards 149	India	Jamshedpur	7 Dec 1983
2nd	205	D.L. Haynes 80, I.V.A. Richards 153*	Australia	Melbourne	9 Dec 1979
1st	200*	S.C Williams 78*, S. Chanderpaul 109*	India	Bridgetown	3 May 1997
2nd	197	B.C. Lara 128, P.V. Simmons 70	Pakistan	Durban	19 Feb 1993

Ross Dundas Cricket Statistics

Zimbabwe

Wkt	Ttl	Batsmen	Versus	Venue	Date
1st	161	G.W. Flower 79, A. Flower 81	Bangladesh	Nairobi (NG)	11 Oct 1997
4th	158	N.C. Johnson 72, A. Flower 95	Sri Lanka	Sharjah	10 Nov 1998
1st	154	G.W. Flower 69, A. Flower 79	Kenya	Nairobi (NG)	18 Oct 1997
2nd	150	G.W. Flower 78, G.J. Rennie 76	Kenya	Nairobi (NG)	19 Oct 1997
5th	145*	A. Flower 115*, A.C. Waller 83*	Sri Lanka	New Plymouth	23 Feb 1992

Ross Dundas Cricket Statistics

RECORD WICKET PARTNERSHIPS

Wkt	Runs	Batsmen	Versus	Venue	Date
1st	252	S.C. Ganguly 109, S.R. Tendulkar 128, India	Sri Lanka	Colombo	7 Jul 1998
2nd	263	Aamir Sohail 134, Inzamam-ul-Haq 137*, Pakistan	New Zealand	Sharjah	20 Apr 1994
3rd	230	Saeed Anwar 140, Ijaz Ahmed 117, Pakistan	India	Dhaka	18 Jan 1998
4th	275*	M.A. Azharuddin 153*, A.D. Jadeja 116*, India	Zimbabwe	Cuttack	9 Apr 1998
5th	223	M.A. Azharuddin 111*, A.D Jadeja 119, India	Sri Lanka	Colombo	17 Aug 1997
6th	154	R.B. Richardson 122, P.J.L. Dujon 53, West Indies	Pakistan	Sharjah	21 Oct 1991
7th	119	T. Odoyo 67, T. Suji 41, Kenya	Zimbabwe	Nairobi (AK)	16 Oct 1997
8th	109	P.R. Reiffel 58, S.K. Warne 55, Australia	South Africa	Port Elizabeth	4 April 1994
9th	126*	Kapil Dev 175*, S.M.H. Kirmani 24*, India	Zimbabwe	Tunbridge Wells	18 June1983
10th	106*	I.V.A. Richards 189*, M.A. Holding 12*, West Indies	England	Manchester	31 May 1984

Ross Dundas Cricket Statistics

RECORD WICKET PARTNERSHIPS FOR EACH COUNTRY

Australia

Wkt	Ttl	Batsmen	Versus	Venue	Date
1st	212	D.C. Boon 111, G.R. Marsh 104	India	Jaipur	7 Sept 1986
2nd	219	M.E. Waugh 87, R.T. Ponting 145	Zimbabwe	Delhi	11 Apr 1998
3rd	224*	D.M. Jones 99*, A.R. Border 118*	Sri Lanka	Adelaide	28 Jan 1985
4th	189	S.R. Waugh 89, M.G. Bevan 103	South Africa	Centurion	10 Apr 1997
5th	159	R.T. Ponting 123, M.G. Bevan 65*	Sri Lanka	Melbourne	9 Jan 1996
6th	112	M.E. Waugh 62, S.P. O'Donnell 71*	England	Sydney	1 Jan 1991
7th	102*	S.R. Waugh 57*, G.C. Dyer 45*	India	Delhi	2 Oct 1986
8th	119	P.R. Reiffel 58, S.K. Warne 55	South Africa	Port Elizabeth	4 Apr 1994
9th	57	I.J. Harvey 43, A.J. Bichel 27*	South Africa	Perth	18 Jan 1998
10th	45	T.J. Laughlin 74, M.H.N. Walker 9*	England	Sydney	11 Dec 1979
10th	45*	M.G. Bevan 51*, A.C. Dale 15*	South Africa	East London	29 Mar 1997

Ross Dundas Cricket Statistics

Bangladesh

Wkt	Ttl	Batsmen	Versus	Venue	Date
1st	137	Athar Ali Khan 47, Mohammad Rafiq 77	Kenya	Hyderabad (I)	17 May 1998
2nd	57	Mojhammad Rafiq 23, Minhaj-ul-Abedin 45	Kenya	Chennai	23 May 1998
3rd	108	Farooq Ahmed 57, Athar Ali Khan 44	India	Chandigarh	25 Dec 1990
4th	110	Akram Khan 59, Athar Ali Khan 82	Pakistan	Colombo (RPS)	16 July 1997
5th	109	Amin-Ul-Islam 69*, Khaled Mashud 47	India	Dhaka	10 Jan 1998
6th	56	Naim-ur-Rahman 41, Khaled Mashud 5	Kenya	Chennai	23 May 1998
7th	48	Amin-Ul-Islam 41*, Enam-Ul-Haq 18	Australia	Sharjah	30 Apr 1990
8th	46	Amin-Ul-Islam 27, Golam Faruq 23*	Sri Lanka	Dhaka	2 Nov 1988
9th	44	Khaled Mashud 15*, Hasib-ul-Hussain 21	India	Mumbai	25 May 1998
10th	25	Saif-Ul-Islam 22*, Anis-Ur-Rehman 2	India	Sharjah	5 Apr 1995

Ross Dundas Cricket Statistics

Canada

Wkt	Ttl	Batsmen	Versus	Venue	Date
1st	54	C.J.D. Chappell 14, G.R. Sealy 45	Pakistan	Leeds	9 Jun 1979
2nd	31	G.R. Sealy 45, F.A. Dennis 25	Pakistan	Leeds	9 Jun 1979
3rd	18	G.R. Sealy 45, M.P. Stead 10	Pakistan	Leeds	9 Jun 1979
4th	7	M.P. Stead 10, C.A. Marshall 8	Pakistan	Leeds	9 Jun 1979
5th	27	C.J.D. Chappell 19, J.C.B. Vaughan 29	Australia	Birmingham	16 Jun 1979
6th	19	C.A. Marshall 8, B.M. Mauricette 15	Pakistan	Leeds	9 June1979
6th	19	J.C.B. Vaughan 29, B.M. Mauricette 5	Australia	Birmingham	16 Jun 1979
7th	5	B.M. Mauricette 15, J.C.B. Vaughan 0	Pakistan	Leeds	9 Jun 1979
8th	4	B.M. Mauricette 15, Tariq Javed 3	Pakistan	Leeds	9 Jun 1979
9th	6	R.G. Callender 0, C.C. Henry 5	Australia	Birmingham	16 Jun 1979
10th	3	R.G. Callender 0, J.N. Valentine 3*	England	Manchester	14 Jun 1979

Ross Dundas Cricket Statistics

East Africa

Wkt	Ttl	Batsmen	Versus	Venue	Date
1st	30	Frasat Ali 45, S. Walusimba 15	New Zealand	Birmingham	7 Jun 1975
2nd	10	S. Walusimba 16, P.S. Mehta 12	India	Leeds	11 Jun 1975
3rd	8	S. Walusimba 7, Jawahir Shah 4	England	Birmingham	14 Jun 1975
4th	23	Frasat Ali 45, S. Sumar 4	India	Leeds	11 Jun 1975
5th	21	R.K. Sethi 30, Mehmood Quaraishy 19	England	Birmingham	14 Jun 1975
6th	42	Jawahir Shah 37, R.K. Sethi 23	India	Leeds	11 Jun 1975
7th	37	Mehmood Quaraishy 16*, Zulfiqar Ali 30	New Zealand	Birmingham	7 Jun 1975
8th	5	Zulfiqar Ali 30, H. McLeod 5	New Zealand	Birmingham	7 Jun 1975
9th	9	Mehmood Quaraishy 19, P.G. Nana 8*	England	Birmingham	14 Jun 1975
10th	6	P.G. Nana 8*, D.J. Pringle 3	England	Birmingham	14 Jun 1975

Ross Dundas Cricket Statistics

England

Wkt	Ttl	Batsmen	Versus	Venue	Date
1st	193	C.W.J. Athey 142*, G.A. Gooch 91	New Zealand	Manchester	18 Jul 1986
2nd	202	G.A. Gooch 117*, D.I. Gower 102	Australia	Lord's	3 Jun 1985
3rd	213	G.A. Hick 86*, N.H. Fairbrother 113	West Indies	Lord's	27 May 1991
4th	154*	G.A. Hick 126*, N.H. Fairbrother 78*	Sri Lanka	Adelaide	23 Jan 1999
5th	142	R.A. Smith 167*, G.P. Thorpe 36	Australia	Birmingham	21 May 1993
6th	112	N.H. Fairbrother 56, A.J. Hollioake 83*	South Africa	Dhaka	25 Oct 1998
7th	86*	M.W. Gatting 115*, P.R. Downton 27*	India	Pune	5 Dec 1984
8th	62	D.A. Reeve 35, D. Gough 26*	Sri Lanka	Faisalabad	9 Mar 1996
9th	47	A.J. Lamb 75, N.A. Foster 24	West Indies	Manchester	31 May 1984
10th	44	R.D.B. Croft 13*, A.R.C. Fraser 30	West Indies	Port-of-Spain	8 Apr 1998

Ross Dundas Cricket Statistics

India

Wkt	Ttl	Batsmen	Versus	Venue	Date
1st	252	S.C. Ganguly 109, S.R. Tendular 128	Sri Lanka	Colombo (RPS)	7 Jul 1998
2nd	231	N.S. Sidhu 101, S.R. Tendulkar 118	Pakistan	Sharjah	15 Apr 1996
3rd	175*	N.S. Sidhu 84*, M.A. Azharuddin 90*	Sri Lanka	Sharjah	14 Apr 1995
3rd	175	S.R. Tendulkar 137, M.A. Azharuddin 72*	Sri Lanka	Delhi	2 Mar 1996
4th	275*	M.A. Azharuddin 153*, A.D. Jadeja 116*	Zimbabwe	Cuttack	9 Apr 1998
5th	223	M.A. Azharuddin 111*, A.D. Jadeja 119	Sri Lanka	Colombo (RPS)	17 Aug 1997
6th	127	M.A. Azharuddin 108*, A.K. Sharma 50	New Zealand	Vadodara (MB)	17 Dec 1988
7th	100	S.C. Ganguly 59, S.B. Joshi 48	Australia	Colombo (SSC)	6 Sept 1996
8th	82*	Kapil Dev 72*, K.S. More 42*	New Zealand	Bangalore	14 Oct 1987
9th	126*	Kapil Dev 175*, S.M.H. Kirmani 24*	Zimbabwe	Tunbridge Wells	18 Jun 1983
10th	53	R.J. Shastri 73*, N.D. Hirwani 2	West Indies	Gwalior	22 Jan 1988

Ross Dundas Cricket Statistics

Kenya

Wkt	Ttl	Batsmen	Versus	Venue	Date
1st	225	D. Chudasama 122, K. Otieno 144	Bangladesh	Nairobi (NG)	10 Oct 1997
2nd	84	K. Otieno 144, S.O. Tikolo 32	Bangladesh	Nairobi (NG)	10 Oct 1997
3rd	102	K. Otieno 85, M. Odumbe 50	Australia	Visag	23 Feb 1996
4th	137	S.O. Tikolo 96, H.S. Modi 41	Sri Lanka	Kandy	6 Mar 1996
5th	82	H.S. Modi 71, K. Otieno 28	India	Calcutta	31 May 1998
6th	42	M. Odumbe 30, E.T. Odumbe 20	Zimbabwe	Patna	27 Feb 1996
7th	119	T. Odoyo 67, A. Suji 41	Zimbabwe	Nairobi (AK)	16 Oct 1997
8th	100	H.S. Modi 57, Asif Karim 53	Zimbabwe	Nairobi (NG)	19 Oct 1997
9th	89	Asif Karim 24, H.S. Modi 78*	Sri Lanka	Nairobi (NG)	28 Sep 1996
10th	15	H.S. Modi 57, J. Angara 3*	Zimbabwe	Nairobi (NG)	19 Oct 1997

Ross Dundas Cricket Statistics

Netherlands

Wkt	Ttl	Batsmen	Versus	Venue	Date
1st	56	N.E. Clarke 32, P.E. Cantrell 23	South Africa	Rawalpindi (RC)	5 Mar 1996
2nd	74	P.E. Cantrell 47, G.J.A.F. Aponso 45	UAE	Lahore	1 Mar 1996
3rd	71	G.J.A.F. Aponso 45, T.B.M. de Leede 36	UAE	Lahore	1 Mar 1996
4th	73	K.J. Van Noortwijk 33, G.J.A.F. Aponso 58	Pakistan	Lahore	26 Feb 1996
5th	111	K.J. Van Noortwijk 64, B Zuiderent 54	England	Peshawar	22 Feb 1996
6th	45	R.P. Lefebvre 45, K.J. Van Noortwijk 36*	New Zealand	Vadodara (IPCL)	17 Feb 1996
7th	35	K.J. Van Noortwijk 36*, M.M.C. Schewe 12	New Zealand	Vadodara (IPCL)	17 Feb 1996
8th	9	R.P. Lefebvre 12, M.M.C. Schewe 6	UAE	Lahore	1 Mar 1996
9th	5*	R.F. Van Oosterom 5*, S.W. Lubbers 2*	South Africa	Rawalpindi (RC)	5 Mar 1996
10th	6*	R.F. Van Oosterom 2*, P.J. Bakker 0*	UAE	Lahore	1 Mar 1996

Ross Dundas Cricket Statistics

New Zealand

Wkt	Ttl	Batsmen	Versus	Venue	Date
1st	158	M.D. Crowe 69, J.G. Wright 93	Bangladesh	Sharjah	28 Apr 1990
2nd	130	B.A. Edgar 75, M.D. Crowe 76	India	Brisbane	11 Jan 1986
3rd	181	A.C. Parore 96, K.R. Rutherford 108	India	Vadodara (IPCL)	28 Oct 1994
4th	168	L.K. Germon 89, C.Z. Harris 130	Australia	Chennai	11 Mar 1996
5th	147	R.G. Twose 46, C.L. Cairns 103	India	Pune	24 Nov 1995
6th	130	K.J. Wadsworth 104, B.E. Congdon 49*	Australia	Christchurch	31 Mar 1974
7th	115	A.C. Parore 78, L.K. Germon 52	Pakistan	Sharjah	13 Nov 1996
8th	69	A.C. Parore 67, D.J. Nash 38	South Africa	Brisbane	9 Jan 1998
9th	63	R.J. Hadlee 21, G.B. Troup 39	England	Brisbane	15 Jan 1983
10th	65	M.C. Snedden 40, E.J. Chatfield 19*	Sri Lanka	Derby	18 Jun 1983

Ross Dundas Cricket Statistics

Pakistan

Wkt	Ttl	Batsmen	Versus	Venue	Date
1st	204	Saeed Anwar 110, Ramiz Raja 109*	Sri Lanka	Sharjah	4 Feb 1993
2nd	263	Aamir Sohail 134, Inzamam-ul-Haq 137*	New Zealand	Sharjah	20 Apr 1994
3rd	230	Saeed Anwar 140, Ijaz Ahmed 117	India	Dhaka	18 Jan 1998
4th	172	Salim Malik 84, Basit Ali 127*	West Indies	Sharjah	5 Nov 1993
5th	152	Inzamam-ul-Haq 116*, Ijaz Ahmed 54	Zimbabwe	Harare	25 Feb 1995
6th	144	Imran Khan 102*, Shahid Mahboob 77	Sri Lanka	Leeds	16 Jun 1983
7th	108	Ramiz Raja 75, Anil Dalpat 37	New Zealand	Christchurch	6 Feb 1985
8th	92	Yousuf Youhana 92, Shoaib Akhtar 36	Australia	Karachi	6 Nov 1998
9th	57	Hasan Raza 46, Saqlain Mushtaq 29	Zimbabwe	Sheikupura	22 Nov 1998
10th	72	Waqar Younis 33, Abdur Razzaq 46*	South Africa	Durban	3 Apr 1998

Ross Dundas Cricket Statistics

South Africa

Wkt	Ttl	Batsmen	Versus	Venue	Date
1st	190	G. Kirsten 87, M.J.R. Rindel 106	Pakistan	Johannesburg	12 Jan 1995
2nd	149	D.J. Callaghan 169*, W.J. Cronje 68	New Zealand	Centurion	11 Dec 1994
3rd	160	H.H. Gibbs 125, W.J. Cronje 74	West Indies	Port Elizabeth	30 Jan 1999
4th	232	D.J. Cullinan 124, J.N. Rhodes 121	Pakistan	Nairobi (NG)	29 Sept 1996
5th	183*	J.H. Kallis 109*, J.N. Rhodes 94*	Pakistan	Durban	3 Apr 1998
6th	137	W.J. Cronje 70*, S.M. Pollock 75	Zimbabwe	Johannesburg	31 Jan 1997
7th	76	W.J. Cronje 63*, B.M. McMillan 32	India	Hyderabad (I)	17 Oct 1996
8th	91	D.M. Beckenstein 69, L. Klusener 54*	West Indies	Cape Town	2 Feb 1999
9th	36*	L. Klusener 21*, P.L. Symcox 17*	West Indies	Centurion	7 Feb 1999
10th	51	R.P. Snell 51, P.S. de Villiers 12	Sri Lanka	Colombo (RPS)	4 Sept 1993

Ross Dundas Cricket Statistics

Sri Lanka

Wkt	Ttl	Batsmen	Versus	Venue	Date
1st	171	M.S. Atapattu 60, S.T. Jayasuriya 108	Bangladesh	Colombo (SSC)	22 Jul 1997
2nd	170	S. Wettimuny 74, R.L. Dias 102	India	Delhi	15 Sept 1982
3rd	213*	S.T. Jayasuriya 134*, P.A. de Silva 102*	Pakistan	Lahore	5 Nov 1997
4th	171*	R.S. Mahanama 94*, A. Ranatunga 87*	West Indies	Lahore	1 Nov 1997
5th	139	L.R.D. Mendis 80, P.A. de Silva 81	Australia	Sydney	23 Jan 1985
6th	132	A. Ranatunga 98, R.S. Kalpage 51	India	Hyderabad (I)	18 Feb 1994
7th	110	P.A. de Silva 122, H.D.P.K. Dharmasena 51	Pakistan	Nairobi (NG)	4 Oct 1996
8th	91	H.D.P.K. Dharmasena 51*, D.K. Liyanage 43	West Indies	Port-of-Spain	6 Jun 1997
9th	76	R.S. Kalpage 44*, W.P.J.U.C. Vaas 33	Pakistan	Colombo (SSC)	7 Aug 1994
10th	33	R.J. Ratnayake 20*, V.B. John 15	England	Leeds	20 Jun 1983

Ross Dundas Cricket Statistics

United Arab Emirates

Wkt	Ttl	Batsmen	Versus	Venue	Date
1st	117	Azhar Saeed 32, Salim Raza 84	Netherlands	Lahore	1 Mar 1996
2nd	33	R.H. Poonawalla 22, Mazhar Hussain 10	Pakistan	Sharjah	17 Apr 1994
3rd	94	Mazhar Hussain 70, V. Mehra 43	India	Sharjah	13 Apr 1994
4th	82*	V. Mehra 29*, Mohammad Ishaq 51*	Netherlands	Lahore	1 Mar 1996
5th	20	Mazhar Hussain 10, Salim Raza 16	Pakistan	Sharjah	17 Apr 1994
6th	31	Mohammad Aslam 23, J. Samarasekera 29	England	Peshawar	18 Feb 1996
7th	57	J. Samarasekera 31*, Arshad Laiq 31	Pakistan	Sharjah	17 Apr 1994
8th	32	Arshad Laiq 14, J. Samarasekera 47*	New Zealand	Faisalabad	27 Feb 1996
9th	80*	Arshad Laiq 43*, S.F. Dukanwala 40*	South Africa	Rawalpindi (RC)	16 Feb 1996
10th	10*	Imtiaz Abbasi 6*, Sohail Butt 6*	India	Sharjah	13 Apr 1994

Ross Dundas Cricket Statistics

West Indies

Wkt	Ttl	Batsmen	Versus	Venue	Date
1st	200*	S.C. Williams 78*, S. Chanderpaul 109*	India	Bridgetown	3 May 1997
2nd	221	C.G. Greenidge 115, I.V.A. Richards 149	India	Jamshedpur	7 Dec 1983
3rd	195*	C.G. Greenidge 105*, H.A. Gomes 75*	Zimbabwe	Worcester	13 Jun 1983
4th	226	S. Chanderpaul 150, C.L. Hooper 108	South Africa	East London	24 Jan 1999
5th	152	I.V.A. Richards 98, C.H. Lloyd 89*	Sri Lanka	Brisbane	12 Jan 1985
6th	154	R.B. Richardson 122, P.J.L. Dujon 53	Pakistan	Sharjah	21 Oct 1991
7th	115	P.J.L. Dujon 57*, M.D. Marshall 66	Pakistan	Gujranwala	4 Nov 1986
8th	65	C.L. Hooper 57*, W.K.M. Benjamin 31	India	Nagpur	8 Dec 1987
9th	63	M.D. Marshall 43, J. Garner 27	Australia	Sydney	6 Feb 1985
10th	106*	I.V.A. Richards 189*, M.A. Holding 12*	England	Manchester	31 May 1984

Ross Dundas Cricket Statistics

Zimbabwe

Wkt	Ttl	Batsmen	Versus	Venue	Date
1st	161	G.W. Flower 79, A. Flower 81	Bangladesh	Nairobi (NG)	11 Oct 1997
2nd	150	G.W. Flower 78, G.J. Rennie 76	Kenya	Nairobi (NG)	19 Oct 1997
3rd	144	G.W. Flower 112, A. Flower 68	Sri Lanka	Colombo (SSC)	26 Jan 1998
4th	158	N.C. Johnson 72, A. Flower 95	Sri Lanka	Sharjah	10 Nov 1998
5th	145*	A. Flower 115*, A.C. Waller 83*	Sri Lanka	New Plymouth	23 Feb 1992
6th	103	D.L. Houghton 84, K.M. Curran 35	Australia	Southampton	16 Jun 1983
7th	81	A.D.R. Campbell 83*, A.R. Whittall 31	India	Sharjah	11 Nov 1998
8th	117	D.L. Houghton 142, I.P. Butchart 54	New Zealand	Hyderabad (I)	10 Oct 1987
9th	55	K.M. Curran 62, P.W.E. Rawson 19	West Indies	Birmingham	20 Jun 1983
10th	36	M.A. Meman 19, M.P. Jarvis 8*	India	Mumbai	17 Oct 1987

Ross Dundas Cricket Statistics

MOST CENTURY PARTNERSHIPS AS A PAIR

No.	Batsmen
15	C.G. Greenidge, D.L. Haynes, West Indies
9	D.L. Haynes, R.B. Richardson, West Indies
8	D.C. Boon, G.R. Marsh, Australia
8	A. Flower, G.W. Flower, Zimbabwe
8	M.A. Azharuddin, S.R. Tendulkar, India
8	S.C. Ganguly, S.R. Tendulkar, India
8	A.D. Jadeja, S.R. Tendulkar, India
8	P.A. de Silva, A. Ranatunga, Sri Lanka
7	C.G. Greenidge, I.V.A. Richards, West Indies
7	D.L. Haynes, I.V.A. Richards, West Indies
7	A.R. Border, G.R. Marsh, Australia
7	D.M. Jones, G.R. Marsh, Australia

Ross Dundas Cricket Statistics

MOST CENTURY PARTNERSHIPS

No.	Batsmen
46	D.L. Haynes, West Indies
33	M.A. Azharuddin, India
33	S.R. Tendulkar, India
32	P.A. de Silva, Sri Lanka
32	I.V.A. Richards, West Indies
28	D.M. Jones, Australia
26	D.C. Boon, Australia
25	Javed Miandad, Pakistan

MOST DOUBLE CENTURY PARTNERSHIPS AS A PAIR

No.	Batsmen
2	M.A. Azharuddin, A.D. Jadeja, India
2	Saeed Anwar, Ramiz Raja, Pakistan

MOST DOUBLE CENTURY PARTNERSHIPS

No.	Batsmen
3	Saeed Anwar, Pakistan
2	M.A. Azharuddin, India
2	S. Chanderpaul, West Indies
2	Ijaz Ahmed, India
2	A.D. Jadeja, India
2	Ramiz Raja, Pakistan
2	S.R. Tendulkar, India

Bowling

LEADING WICKET-TAKERS

Wkts	Bowler	M	Career
363	Wasim Akram, Pakistan	253	1984-98
283	Waqar Younis, Pakistan	172	1989-98
253	Kapil Dev, India	225	1978-94
212	A. Kumble, India	158	1986-99
212	J. Srinath, India	153	1991-99
210	C.E.L. Ambrose, West Indies	157	1988-99
204	C.A. Walsh, West Indies	185	1985-98
203	C.J. McDermott, Australia	138	1984-96
185	S.R. Waugh, Australia	251	1986-99
182	Aqib Javed, Pakistan	163	1988-98
182	A.A. Donald, South Africa	108	1991-99
182	Imran Khan, Pakistan	175	1974-92
176	Saqlain Mushtaq, Pakistan	88	1995-98
169	S.K. Warne, Australia	108	1993-99
160	C.L. Hooper, West Indies	177	1987-99
158	R.J. Hadlee, New Zealand	115	1973-90
157	M.D. Marshall, West Indies	136	1980-92
157	M. Prabhakar, India	130	1984-96
152	S.T. Jayasuriya, Sri Lanka	178	1989-99
151	M. Muralitharan, Sri Lanka	110	1993-99
146	J. Garner, West Indies	98	1977-87
145	I.T. Botham, England	116	1976-92
144	Mushtaq Ahmed, Pakistan	130	1989-98
142	M.A. Holding, West Indies	102	1976-87
140	E.J. Chatfield, New Zealand	114	1979-89
132	Abdul Qadir, Pakistan	104	1983-93
132	W.P.U.C.J. Vaas, Sri Lanka	105	1994-99
129	R.J. Shastri, India	150	1981-92
126	D.K. Morrison, New Zealand	96	1987-96
122	G.D. McGrath, Australia	85	1993-99
119	B.K.V. Prasad, India	104	1994-99
118	I.R. Bishop, West Indies	84	1988-97
118	I.V.A. Richards, West Indies	187	1975-91
117	C.Z. Harris, New Zealand	120	1990-99
115	P.A.J. DeFreitas, England	103	1987-97
114	M.C. Snedden, New Zealand	93	1980-90
111	Mudassar Nazar, Pakistan	122	1977-89
108	S.P. O'Donnell, Australia	87	1985-91
103	G.R. Larsen, New Zealand	106	1990-99
103	D.K. Lillee, Australia	63	1972-83
103	C. Pringle, New Zealand	64	1990-95
100	W.K.M. Benjamin, West Indies	85	1986-95
100	R.A. Harper, West Indies	105	1983-96

LEADING WICKET-TAKERS FOR EACH COUNTRY

Country	Bowler	Wkts	M	Career
Australia	C.J. McDermott	203	138	1984-96
Bangladesh	Mohammed Rafiq	15	12	1995-98
Canada	J.N. Valentine	3	3	1979
East Africa	Zulfiqar Ali	4	3	1975
England	I.T. Botham	145	116	1976-92
India	Kapil Dev	253	225	1978-94
Kenya	{ Aasif Karim	17	20	1996-98
	{ M.O. Odumbe	17	20	1996-98
Netherlands	S.W. Lubbers	5	4	1996
New Zealand	R.J. Hadlee	158	115	1973-90
Pakistan	Wasim Akram	363	254	1984-98
South Africa	A.A. Donald	182	108	1991-99
Sri Lanka	S.T. Jayasuriya	152	178	1989-99
UAE	{ Azhar Saeed	6	7	1994-96
	{ S.F. Dukanwala	6	5	1996
West Indies	C.E.L. Ambrose	210	157	1988-99
Zimbabwe	H.H. Streak	85	69	1993-98

MOST WICKETS IN A CALENDAR YEAR

Year	Bowler	M	Balls	Mdn	Runs	Wkts	Ave.	5wi	Best	Stk Rt	RPO
1997	Saqlain Mushtaq, Pakistan	36	1886	17	1294	69	18.75	2	5-38	27.33	4.12
1996	Saqlain Mushtaq, Pakistan	33	1734	12	1270	65	19.54	2	5-29	26.68	4.39
1996	A.R. Kumble, India	32	1825	17	1232	61	20.20	-	4-12	29.92	4.05
1996	Waqar Younis, Pakistan	35	1721	18	1348	60	22.47	2	6-44	28.68	4.70
1998	A.B. Agarkar, India	30	1613	13	1378	58	23.76	-	4-35	27.81	5.13
1996	A.A. Donald, South Africa	20	1102	5	787	51	15.43	1	6-23	21.61	4.28
1994	S.K. Warne, Australia	29	1640	13	1045	50	20.90	-	4-34	32.80	3.82
1990	Waqar Younis, Pakistan	19	948	12	594	47	12.64	5	6-26	20.17	3.76
1994	C. Pringle, New Zealand	26	1357	12	1041	46	22.63	1	5-45	29.50	4.60
1996	B.K.V. Prasad, India	30	1642	11	1298	45	28.84	-	4-27	36.49	4.74
1993	Wasim Akram, Pakistan	26	1372	13	850	45	18.89	2	5-15	30.49	3.72
1987	J.E. Emburey, England	31	1741	16	1215	43	28.26	-	4-37	40.49	4.19
1992	Wasim Akram, Pakistan	27	1461	17	930	43	21.63	1	5-19	33.98	3.82
1994	Waqar Younis, Pakistan	24	1303	13	974	42	23.19	1	6-30	31.02	4.49
1987	P.A.J. DeFreitas, England	30	1658	38	989	39	25.36	-	4-35	42.51	3.58
1987	Imran Khan, Pakistan	21	1079	18	741	37	20.03	-	4-27	29.16	4.12
1998	A. Kumble, India	25	1410	16	930	37	25.14	-	3-17	38.11	4.67
1998	J. Srinath, India	19	1049	11	817	37	22.08	1	5-23	28.35	4.67
1996	W.P.U.J.C. Vaas, Sri Lanka	29	1426	29	887	37	23.97	-	4-22	38.54	3.73

Ross Dundas Cricket Statistics

MOST WICKETS IN EACH CALENDAR YEAR

Year	Bowler	M	Balls	Mdn	Runs	Wkts	Ave.	5wi	Best	Stk Rt	RPO
1971	{ R. Illingworth, England	1	64	1	50	3	16.67	-	3-50	21.33	4.69
	{ A.A. Mallett, Australia	1	64	1	34	3	11.33	-	3-34	21.33	3.19
	{ K.R. Stackpole, Australia	1	64	-	40	3	13.33	-	3-40	21.33	3.75
1972	G.G. Arnold, England	3	198	3	112	6	18.67	-	4-27	33.00	3.39
1973	G.G. Arnold, England	3	120	3	52	5	10.40	-	3-28	24.00	2.60
1974	C.M. Old, England	4	212	-	169	6	28.17	-	3-36	35.33	4.78
1975	G.J. Gilmour, Australia	3	208	8	110	13	8.46	2	6-14	16.00	3.17
1976	A.M.E. Roberts, West Indies	3	144	2	68	8	8.50	-	4-27	18.00	2.83
1977	J.K. Lever, England	4	234	4	135	10	13.50	-	4-29	23.40	3.46
1978	{ Sarfraz Nawaz, Pakistan	6	292	13	124	8	15.50	-	3-34	36.50	2.55
	{ Hasan Jamil, India	4	184	3	115	8	14.38	-	3-18	23.00	3.75

Year	Bowler	M	Balls	Mdns	Runs	Wkts	Ave.	5wi	Best	Stk Rt	RPO
1979	I.T. Botham, England	14	732	21	433	16	27.06	-	3-16	45.75	3.55
	R.G.D. Willis, England	12	693	19	321	16	20.06	-	4-11	43.31	2.78
1980	D.K. Lillee, Australia	9	516	17	243	23	10.57	-	4-12	22.43	2.83
1981	G.S. Chappell, Australia	14	721	16	441	25	17.64	1	5-15	28.84	3.67
1982	D.K. Lillee, Australia	12	699	21	403	18	22.39	-	3-14	38.83	3.46
	J. Garner , West Indies	9	438	8	213	18	11.83	-	4-45	24.33	2.92
1983	E.J. Chatfield, New Zealand	25	1472	35	873	36	24.25	-	4-20	40.89	3.56
1984	C.G. Rackemann, Australia	20	1059	27	702	31	22.65	1	5-16	34.16	3.98
1985	M.A. Holding, West Indies	28	1402	22	813	35	23.23	1	5-26	40.06	3.48
	J. Garner, West Indies	26	1308	53	633	35	18.09	-	4-10	37.37	2.90
1986	Kapil Dev, India	27	1434	37	834	32	26.06	-	4-30	44.81	3.49
1987	J.E. Emburey, England	31	1741	16	1215	43	28.26	-	4-37	40.49	4.19
1988	C.E.L. Ambrose, West Indies	13	713	19	426	28	15.21	1	5-17	25.46	3.58
1989	C.E.L Ambrose, West Indies	22	1200	17	744	33	22.55	1	5-26	36.36	3.72
1990	Waqar Younis, Pakistan	19	948	12	594	47	12.64	5	6-26	20.17	3.76
1991	C.E.L. Ambrose, West Indies	18	994	25	571	30	19.03	1	5/53	33.13	3.45
1992	Wasim Akram, Pakistan	27	1461	17	930	43	21.63	1	5-19	33.98	3.82
1993	Wasim Akram, Pakistan	26	1372	13	850	45	18.89	2	5-15	30.49	3.72
1994	S.K. Warne, Australia	29	1640	13	1045	50	20.90	-	4-34	32.80	3.82
1995	Aaqib Javed, Pakistan	18	947	10	664	23	28.87	1	5-19	41.17	4.21
1996	Saqlain Mushtaq, Pakistan	33	1734	12	1270	65	19.54	2	5-29	26.68	4.39
1997	Saqlain Mushtaq, Pakistan	36	1886	17	1294	69	18.75	2	5-38	27.33	4.12
1998	A.B. Agarkar, India	30	1613	13	1378	58	23.76	-	4-35	27.81	5.13

Ross Dundas Cricket Statistics

LEADING WICKET-TAKERS AT THE END OF EACH CALENDAR YEAR

Year	Bowler	M	Balls	Mdns	Runs	Wkts	Ave.	5wi	Best	Stk Rt	RPO
1971	R. Illingworth, England	1	64	1	50	3	16.67	-	3-50	21.33	4.69
	A.A. Mallett, Australia	1	64	1	34	3	11.33	-	3-34	21.33	3.19
	K.R. Stackpole, Australia	1	64	-	40	3	13.33	-	3-40	21.33	3.75
1972	G.G. Arnold, England	3	198	3	112	6	18.67	-	4-27	33.00	3.39
1973	G.G. Arnold, England	6	318	6	164	11	14.91	-	4-27	28.91	3.09
1974	G.G. Arnold, England	9	456	10	233	14	16.64	-	4-27	32.57	3.07
1975	C.M. Old, England	13	645	9	439	21	20.90	-	4-57	30.71	4.08
1976	C.M. Old, England	13	645	9	439	21	20.90	-	4-57	30.71	4.08
1977	C.M. Old, England	17	871	14	589	25	23.56	-	4-57	34.84	4.06
1978	C.M. Old, England	20	1035	19	656	30	21.87	-	4-57	34.50	3.80
1979	C.M. Old, England	27	1473	31	849	41	20.71	-	4-8	35.93	3.46
1980	D.K. Lillee, Australia	24	1425	32	865	50	17.30	1	5-34	28.50	3.64
1981	D.K. Lillee, Australia	39	2198	49	1288	70	18.40	1	5-34	31.40	3.52
1982	D.K. Lillee, Australia	51	2897	70	1691	88	19.22	1	5-34	32.92	3.50
1983	D.K. Lillee, Australia	63	3593	80	2145	103	20.83	1	5-34	34.88	3.58
1984	D.K. Lillee, Australia	63	3593	80	2145	103	20.83	1	5-34	34.88	3.58
1985	M.A. Holding, West Indies	94	5032	93	2811	133	21.14	1	5-26	37.83	3.35
1986	M.A. Holding, West Indies	97	5206	95	2902	135	21.50	1	5-26	38.56	3.34
1987	J. Garner, West Indies	98	5330	141	2752	146	18.85	3	5-31	36.51	3.10
1988	Kapil Dev, India	134	6756	148	4179	158	26.45	1	5-43	42.76	3.71
1989	Kapil Dev, India	149	7502	163	4654	174	26.75	1	5-43	43.11	3.72
1990	Kapil Dev, India	162	8171	172	5119	193	26.52	1	5-43	42.34	3.76
1991	Kapil Dev, India	176	8903	191	5529	216	25.60	1	5-43	41.22	3.73
1992	Kapil Dev, India	197	9948	213	6149	232	26.50	1	5-43	42.88	3.71
1993	Kapil Dev, India	214	10794	230	6674	248	26.91	1	5-43	43.52	3.71
1994	Wasim Akram, Pakistan	181	9345	122	5891	262	22.48	5	5-15	35.67	3.78

Year	Bowler	M	Balls	Mdns	Runs	Wkts	Ave.	5wi	Best	Stk Rt	RPO
1995	Wasim Akram, Pakistan	193	10018	125	6280	282	22.27	5	5-15	35.52	3.76
1996	Wasim Akram, Pakistan	219	11285	143	7166	315	22.75	5	5-15	35.83	3.81
1997	Wasim Akram, Pakistan	238	12254	156	7759	341	22.75	5	5-15	35.94	3.80
1998	Wasim Akram, Pakistan	254	13112	160	8387	363	23.10	5	5-15	36.12	3.84

Ross Dundas Cricket Statistics

BEST INNINGS ANALYSES

Wkts	Bowler	Versus	Venue	Date
7-37	Aaqib Javed, Pakistan	India	Sharjah	25 Oct 1991
7-51	W.W. Davis, West Indies	Australia	Leeds	11 Jun 1983
6-12	A. Kumble, India	West Indies	Calcutta	27 Nov 1993
6-14	G.J. Gilmour, Australia	England	Leeds	18 Jun 1975
6-14	Imran Khan, Pakistan	India	Sharjah	22 Mar 1985
6-15	C.E.H. Croft, West Indies	England	Kingstown	4 Feb 1981
6-20	B.C. Strang, Zimbabwe	Bangladesh	Nairobi	14 Oct 1997
6-23	A.A. Donald, South Africa	Kenya	Nairobi	3 Oct 1996
6-26	Waqar Younis, Pakistan	Sri Lanka	Sharjah	29 Apr 1990
6-29	B.P. Patterson, West Indies	India	Nagpur	8 Dec 1987
6-29	S.T. Jayasuriya, Sri Lanka	England	Moratuwa	20 Mar 1993
6-30	Waqar Younis, Pakistan	New Zealand	Auckland	13 Mar 1994
6-35	S.M. Pollock, South Africa	West Indies	East London	24 Jan 1999
6-39	K.H. Macleay, Australia	India	Nottingham	13 Jun 1983
6-41	I.V.A. Richards, West Indies	India	Delhi	23 Oct 1989
6-44	Waqar Younis, Pakistan	New Zealand	Sharjah	13 Nov 1996
6-49	L. Klusener, South Africa	Sri Lanka	Lahore	6 Nov 1997
6-50	A.H. Gray, West Indies	Australia	Port-of-Spain	9 Mar 1991
5-1	C.A. Walsh, West Indies	Sri Lanka	Sharjah	3 Dec 1986
5-11	Waqar Younis, Pakistan	New Zealand	Peshawar	4 Nov 1990

MOST FIVE WICKETS IN AN INNINGS

Player	No.	M	Balls	Runs	Wkts	Ave.	Stk Rt	Ec Rt	Best
Waqar Younis, Pakistan	9	172	8561	6545	283	23.13	30.25	4.59	6-26
R.J. Hadlee, New Zealand	5	115	6182	3407	158	21.56	39.13	3.31	5-25
Wasim Akram, Pakistan	5	254	13112	8387	363	23.10	36.12	3.84	5-15
C.E.L. Ambrose, West Indies	4	157	8350	4939	210	23.52	39.76	3.55	5-17
Aqib Javed, Pakistan	4	163	8012	5721	182	31.43	44.02	4.28	7-37
L. Klusener, South Africa	4	43	2079	1699	63	26.97	33.00	4.90	6-49
Saqlain Mushtaq, Pakistan	4	88	4609	3294	176	18.72	26.19	4.29	5-29
J. Garner, West Indies	3	98	5330	2752	146	18.85	36.51	3.10	5-31
J. Srinath, India	3	153	7969	5755	212	27.15	37.59	4.33	5-23

MOST FOUR WICKETS IN AN INNINGS

Player	No.	M	Wkts	Ave.	Stk Rt	Ec Rt	4wi	5wi	Best
Waqar Younis, Pakistan	20	172	283	23.13	30.25	4.59	11	9	6-26
Wasim Akram, Pakistan	20	254	363	23.10	36.12	3.84	15	5	5-15
Saqlain Mushtaq, Pakistan	13	88	176	18.72	26.19	4.29	9	4	5-29
C.E.L. Ambrose, West Indies	10	157	210	23.52	39.76	3.55	6	4	5-17
S.K. Warne, Australia	10	108	169	25.06	35.94	4.18	9	1	5-33
I.R. Bishop, West Indies	9	84	118	26.50	36.71	4.33	7	2	5-25
A.A. Donald, South Africa	9	108	182	21.42	31.62	4.06	7	2	6-23
A. Kumble, India	7	158	212	27.55	40.20	4.11	5	2	6-12
G.D. McGrath, Australia	7	85	122	25.28	37.76	4.02	5	2	5-40

Player	No.	M	Wkts	Ave.	Stk Rt	Ec Rt	4wi	5wi	Best
Abdul Qadir, Pakistan	6	104	132	26.16	38.64	4.06	4	2	5-44
Aqib Javed, Pakistan	6	163	182	31.43	44.02	4.28	2	4	7-37
D. Gough, England	6	56	89	24.75	35.01	4.24	4	2	5-44
R.J. Hadlee, New Zealand	6	115	158	21.56	39.13	3.31	1	5	5-25
M.A. Holding, West Indies	6	102	142	21.37	38.54	3.33	5	1	5-26
S.T. Jayasuriya, Sri Lanka	6	178	152	35.20	43.34	4.87	4	2	6-29
D.K. Lillee, Australia	6	63	103	20.83	34.88	3.58	5	1	5-34
M.D. Marshall, West Indies	6	136	157	26.96	45.70	3.54	6	-	4-18
S.P. O'Donnell, Australia	6	87	108	28.72	40.28	4.28	5	1	5-13
M. Prabhakar, India	6	130	157	28.88	40.51	4.28	4	2	5-33
C.A. Walsh, West Indies	6	185	204	30.94	47.90	3.88	5	1	5-1
J. Garner, West Indies	5	98	146	18.85	36.51	3.10	2	3	5-31
R.M. Hogg, Australia	5	71	85	28.45	43.26	3.95	5	-	4-29
C.J. McDermott, Australia	5	138	203	24.72	36.75	4.04	4	1	5-44
M. Muralitharan, Sri Lanka	5	110	151	27.95	39.56	4.24	3	2	5-23
L.S. Pascoe, Australia	5	29	53	20.11	29.58	4.08	4	1	5-30
P.R. Reiffel, Australia	5	83	97	28.42	44.02	3.87	5	-	4-13
J. Srinath, India	5	153	212	27.15	37.57	4.33	2	3	5-23

BEST CAREER AVERAGES (minimum 15 wickets)

Ave.	Bowler	Wkts	M	Career
10.31	G.J. Gilmour, Australia	16	5	1974-75
17.84	G.G. Arnold, England	19	14	1972-75
18.20	D.R. Hadlee, New Zealand	20	11	1973-76
18.26	O.D. Gibson, West Indies	34	15	1995-97
18.12	Saqlain Mushtaq, Pakistan	176	88	1995-98
18.85	J. Garner, West Indies	146	98	1977-87
18.98	A.H. Gray, West Indies	44	25	1985-91
19.46	M. Hendrick, England	35	22	1973-81
20.11	L.S. Pascoe, Australia	53	29	1977-82
20.36	A.M.E. Roberts, West Indies	87	56	1975-83
20.67	C.E.H. Croft, West Indies	30	19	1977-81
20.83	D.K. Lillee, Australia	103	63	1972-83
20.92	A.I.C. Dodemaide, Australia	36	24	1988-93
21.37	M.A. Holding, West Indies	142	102	1976-87
21.42	A.A. Donald, South Africa	182	108	1991-99
21.56	R.J. Hadlee, New Zealand	158	115	1973-90
22.20	C.M. Old, England	45	32	1973-81
22.35	C.G. Rackemann, Australia	82	52	1983-91
22.44	G.D. Campbell, Australia	18	12	1989-90
22.94	D.L. Underwood, England	32	26	1973-82
23.10	Wasim Akram, Pakistan	363	254	1984-98
23.13	Waqar Younis, Pakistan	283	172	1989-98
23.22	Sarfraz Nawaz, Pakistan	63	45	1973-84
23.36	T.M. Alderman, Australia	88	65	1981-91
23.52	C.E.L. Ambrose, West Indies	210	157	1988-99
23.63	Asif Iqbal, Pakistan	16	10	1973-79
23.74	S.M. Pollock, South Africa	92	63	1996-99
23.76	A.B. Agarkar, India	58	30	1998
23.82	D.R. Doshi, India	22	15	1980-82
23.83	C. Pringle, New Zealand	103	64	1990-95
23.85	Harvinder Singh, India	20	13	1997-98
23.89	V.A. Holder, West Indies	19	12	1973-78

Ave.	Bowler	Wkts	M	Career
24.34	D.W. Fleming, Australia	70	44	1994-99
24.51	B.P. Patterson, West Indies	90	59	1986-93
24.55	E.O. Simons, South Africa	33	23	1994-95
24.60	R.W. Willis, England	80	64	1973-84
24.72	C.J. McDermott, Australia	203	138	1984-96
24.72	G.B. Troup, New Zealand	32	22	1976-85
24.75	K.L.T. Arthurton, West Indies	40	90	1988-99
24.75	D. Gough, England	89	56	1994-99
24.81	S. Elworthy, South Africa	16	11	1998-99
24.88	K.S.C. de Silva, Sri Lanka	23	16	1996-98
24.96	T.G. Hogan, Australia	23	16	1983-84

BEST CAREER STRIKE RATES (minimum 100 overs)

Player	Stk Rt	M	Balls	Runs	Wkts	Ave.	Ec Rt	4wi	5wi	Best
O.D. Gibson, West Indies	21.74	15	739	621	34	18.26	5.04	2	2	5-40
Saqlain Mushtaq, Pakistan	26.19	88	4609	3294	176	18.72	4.30	9	4	5-29
A.B. Agarkar, India	27.81	30	1613	1378	58	23.76	5.13	3	-	4-35
K. Srikkanth, India	28.48	146	712	641	25	25.64	5.40	-	2	5-27
A.H. Gray, West Indies	28.86	25	1270	835	44	18.98	3.94	2	1	6-50
L.S. Pascoe, Australia	29.58	29	1568	1066	53	20.11	4.08	4	1	5-30
K.L.T Arthurton, West Indies	29.65	98	1186	990	40	24.75	5.01	-	3	4-31
Waqar Younis, Pakistan	30.25	172	8561	6545	283	23.13	4.59	11	9	6-26
K.S.C. de Silva, Sri Lanka	30.54	33	1466	1194	48	24.88	4.89	-	-	3-18
S.B. O'Connor, New Zealand	31.07	23	901	794	29	27.38	5.29	1	1	5-39
D.R. Hadlee, New Zealand	31.40	11	628	364	20	18.20	3.48	1	-	4-34
A.A. Donald, South Africa	31.62	108	5754	3898	182	21.42	4.06	7	2	6-23
C. Pringle, New Zealand	32.17	64	3314	2455	103	23.83	4.44	2	1	5-45
H.A. Gomes, West Indies	32.80	83	1345	1045	41	25.49	4.66	2	-	4-31
L. Klusener, South Africa	33.00	43	2079	1699	63	26.97	4.90	-	4	6-49
D.W. Fleming, Australia	33.23	44	2326	1704	70	24.34	4.40	3	1	5-36
B.P. Patterson, West Indies	33.89	59	3050	2206	90	24.51	4.34	1	1	6-29
C.G. Rackemann, Australia	34.04	52	2791	1833	82	22.35	3.94	3	1	5-16
G.D. Campbell, Australia	34.06	12	613	404	18	22.44	3.95	-	-	3-17
A.J. Hollioake, England	34.52	31	1070	899	31	29.00	5.04	2	-	4-23
D.K. Lillee, Australia	34.88	63	3593	2145	103	20.83	3.58	5	1	5-34
D. Gough, England	35.01	56	3116	2203	89	24.75	4.24	4	2	5-44
B.C. Strang, Zimbabwe	35.04	18	806	576	23	25.04	4.29	1	1	6-20
M. Hendrick, England	35.66	22	1248	681	35	19.46	3.27	2	1	5-31
C.E.H. Croft, West Indies	35.67	19	1070	620	30	20.67	3.48	-	1	6-15
V.A. Holder, West Indies	35.84	12	681	454	19	23.89	4.00	-	1	5-50
A.M.E. Roberts, West Indies	35.90	56	3123	1771	87	20.36	3.40	2	1	5-22
S.K. Warne, Australia	35.94	108	6074	4235	169	25.06	4.18	9	1	5-33

BEST ECONOMY RATES (minimum 100 overs)

Player	Ec Rt	M	Balls	Runs	Wkts	Ave	Stk Rt	4wi	5wi	Best
G.G. Arnold, England	2.85	14	714	339	19	17.84	37.58	1	-	4-27
G. Dymock, Australia	3.07	15	806	412	15	27.47	53.73	-	-	2-21
M.F. Malone, Australia	3.09	10	612	315	11	28.64	55.64	-	-	2-9
J. Garner, West Indies	3.10	98	5330	2752	146	18.85	36.51	2	3	5-31
M.H.N. Walker, Australia	3.26	17	1006	546	20	27.30	50.30	1	-	4-19
M. Hendrick, England	3.27	22	1248	681	35	19.46	35.66	2	1	5-31
R.W. Willis, England	3.28	64	3595	1968	80	24.60	44.94	4	-	4-11

Player	Ec Rt	M	Balls	Runs	Wkts	Ave	Stk Rt	4wi	5wi	Best
R.J. Hadlee, New Zealand	3.31	115	6182	3407	158	21.56	39.13	1	5	5-25
M.A. Holding, West Indies	3.33	102	5473	3034	142	21.37	38.54	5	1	5-26
R.O. Collinge, New Zealand	3.35	15	859	479	18	26.61	47.72	-	1	5-23
S.P. Davis, Australia	3.38	39	2016	1135	44	25.80	45.82	-	-	3-10
A.I.C. Dodemaide, Australia	3.40	24	1327	753	36	20.92	36.86	1	1	5-21
A.M.E. Roberts, West Indies	3.40	56	3123	1771	87	20.36	35.90	2	1	5-22
Majid Khan, Pakistan	3.41	23	658	374	13	28.77	50.62	-	-	3-27
C.M. Old, England	3.42	32	1755	999	45	22.20	39.00	2	-	4-8
D.L. Underwood, England	3.45	26	1278	734	32	22.94	39.94	1	-	4-44
C.E.H. Croft, West Indies	3.48	19	1070	620	30	20.67	35.67	-	1	6-15
D.R. Hadlee, New Zealand	3.48	11	628	364	20	18.20	31.40	1	-	4-34
M.D. Marshall, West Indies	3.54	136	7175	4233	157	26.96	45.70	6	-	4-18
C.E.L. Ambrose, West Indies	3.55	157	8350	4939	210	23.52	39.76	6	4	5-17
M. Whitney, Australia	3.56	38	2106	1249	46	27.15	45.78	2	-	4-34
A.R.C. Fraser, England	3.57	37	2092	1245	42	29.64	49.81	1	-	4-22
B.D. Julien, West Indies	3.57	12	778	463	18	25.72	43.22	2	-	4-20
E.J. Chatfield, New Zealand	3.58	114	6065	3618	140	25.84	43.32	3	1	5-34
P.S. de Villiers, South Africa	3.58	83	4422	2636	95	27.75	46.55	2	-	4-27
D.K. Lillee, Australia	3.58	63	3593	2145	103	20.83	34.88	5	1	5-34
B.J. McKechnie, New Zealand	3.63	14	818	495	19	26.05	43.05	-	-	3-23
Sarfraz Nawaz, Pakistan	3.64	45	2412	1463	63	23.22	38.29	4	-	4-27
G.F. Lawson, Australia	3.65	79	4259	2592	88	29.45	48.40	1	-	4-26
T.M. Alderman, Australia	3.66	65	3371	2056	88	23.36	38.31	1	2	5-17
J.K. Lever, England	3.71	22	1152	713	24	29.71	48.00	1	-	4-29
V.J. Marks, England	3.71	34	1838	1135	44	25.80	41.77	-	2	5-20
Akram Raza, Pakistan	3.72	49	2601	1611	38	42.39	68.45	-	-	3-18
Kapil Dev, India	3.72	225	11202	6945	253	27.45	44.28	3	1	5-43
S. Venkataraghavan, India	3.75	15	868	542	5	108.40	173.60	-	-	2-34
T.G. Hogan, Australia	3.76	16	917	574	23	24.96	39.87	1	-	4-33
P.H. Edmonds, England	3.77	29	1534	965	26	37.12	59.00	-	-	3-39
G.R. Larsen, New Zealand	3.77	106	5606	3525	103	34.22	54.43	1	-	4-24
G.R. Dilley, England	3.79	36	2043	1291	48	26.90	42.56	3	-	4-23
P. Willey, England	3.84	26	1031	659	13	50.69	79.31	-	-	3-33
Wasim Akram, Pakistan	3.84	254	13112	8387	363	23.10	36.12	15	5	5-15
G. Miller, England	3.85	25	1268	813	25	32.52	50.72	-	-	3-27
A.C. Dale, England	3.87	24	1272	821	27	30.41	47.11	-	-	3-18
P.R. Reiffel, Australia	3.87	83	4270	2757	97	28.42	44.02	5	-	4-13
C.A. Walsh, West Indies	3.88	185	9772	6312	204	30.94	47.90	5	1	5-1
S.M. Pollock, South Africa	3.89	63	3370	2184	92	23.74	36.63	3	1	6-35
A.J. Traicos, Zimbabwe	3.89	27	1524	987	19	51.95	80.21	-	-	3-35
Imran Khan, Pakistan	3.90	175	7461	4845	182	26.62	40.99	3	1	6-14
W. Daniel, West Indies	3.91	18	912	595	23	25.87	39.65	-	-	3-27
Rashid Khan, Pakistan	3.92	29	1414	923	20	46.15	70.70	-	-	3-47
A.H. Gray, West Indies	3.94	25	1270	835	44	18.98	28.86	2	1	6-50
C.G. Rackemann, Australia	3.94	52	2791	1833	82	22.35	34.04	3	1	5-16
G.D. Campbell, Australia	3.95	12	613	404	18	22.44	34.06	-	-	3-17
R.M. Hogg, Australia	3.95	71	3677	2418	85	28.45	43.26	5	-	4-29
C.R. Matthews, South Africa	3.95	56	3003	1975	79	25.00	38.01	3	-	4-10
I.T. Botham, England	3.96	116	6271	4139	145	28.54	43.25	3	-	4-31
Maninder Singh, India	3.96	59	3133	2067	66	31.32	47.47	1	-	4-22
P.J. DeFreitas, England	3.97	103	5712	3775	115	32.83	49.67	1	-	4-35
D.R. Doshi, India	3.97	15	792	524	22	23.82	36.00	2	-	4-30
A.D. Mullally, England	3.97	22	1166	772	28	27.57	41.64	1	-	4-18
R.A. Harper, West Indies	3.98	105	5175	3431	100	34.31	51.75	3	-	4-40
Wasim Raja, Pakistan	3.98	54	1036	687	21	32.71	49.33	1	-	4-25

HAT-TRICKS

Bowler	Batsmen	Venue	Date
Jalaluddin, Pakistan	R.W. Marsh, B. Yardley, G.F. Lawson, Australia	Hyderabad (P)	20 Sep 1982
B.A. Reid, Australia	B.R. Blair, E.B. McSweeney, S.R. Gillespie, NZ	Sydney	29 Jan 1986
Chetan Sharma, India	K.R. Rutherford, I.D.S. Smith, E.J. Chatfield, NZ	Nagpur	31 Oct 1987
Wasim Akram, Pak	P.J.L. Dujon, M.D. Marshall, C.E.L. Ambrose, WI	Sharjah	14 Oct 1989
Wasim Akram, Pak	M.G. Hughes, C.G. Rackemann, T.M. Alderman, Aus	Sharjah	4 May 1990
Kapil Dev, India	R.S. Mahanama, S.T. Jayasuriya, R.J Ratnayake, SL	Calcutta	4 Jan 1991
Aaqib Javed, Pakistan	R.J. Shastri, M.A. Azharuddin, S.R. Tendulkar, India	Sharjah	25 Oct 1991
D.K Morrison, NZ	Kapil Dev, S.A. Ankola, N.R. Mongia, India	Napier	25 Mar 1994
Waqar Younis, Pak	C.Z. Harris, C Pringle, R.P. de Groen, New Zealand	East London	19 Dec 1994
Saqlain Mushtaq, Pak	G.W. Flower, JA Rennie, A.R. Whittall, Zimbabwe	Peshawar	3 Nov 1996
E.A. Brandes, Zim	N.V. Knight, J.P. Crawley, N. Hussain, England	Harare	3 Jan 1997
A.M. Stuart, Australia	Ijaz Ahmed, Mohammad Wasim, Moin Khan, Pakistan	Melbourne	16 Jan 1997

FOUR WICKETS IN FIVE BALLS

Bowler	Batsmen	Venue	Date
Saqlain Mushtaq, Pakistan	G.J. Rennie, G.W. Flower, J.A. Rennie, A.R. Whittall, Zimbabwe	Peshawar	3 Nov 1996

BEST BOWLING ON DEBUT (WICKETS)

Wkts	Bowler	Versus	Venue	Date
5-21	A.I.C. Dodemaide, Australia	Sri Lanka	Perth	2 Jan 1988
5-26	U.S.H. Karnain, Sri Lanka	New Zealand	Moratuwa	31 Mar 1984
5-29	A.A. Donald, South Africa	India	Calcutta	10 Nov 1991

Ross Dundas Cricket Statistics

BEST BOWLING ON DEBUT (RUNS PER 100 BALLS)

Bowler	Wkts	Runs	Balls	R/100 B	Team	Venue	Date
Abdul Qadir, Pakistan	4	21	72	29.17	New Zealand	Birmingham	11/12 Jun 1983
Zakir Khan, Pakistan	4	19	48	39.58	New Zealand	Peshawar	12 Nov 1984
R. Dhanraj, West Indies	4	26	60	43.33	New Zealand	Gauhati	1 Nov 1994
A.I.C. Dodemaide, Australia	5	21	44	47.73	Sri Lanka	Perth	2 Jan 1988
D.R. Hadlee, New Zealand	4	34	64	53.13	Pakistan	Christchurch	11 Feb 1973

Ross Dundas Cricket Statistics

MOST CAUGHT & BOWLED BY A BOWLER

No.	Bowler	M	Career
19	C.Z. Harris, New Zealand	122	1990-99
16	R.A. Harper, West Indies	105	1983-96
15	A.R. Border, Australia	273	1979-94
15	A.R. Kumble, India	158	1986-99
13	C.L. Hooper, West Indies	177	1987-99
13	I.V.A. Richards, West Indies	187	1975-91
12	S.T. Jayasuriya, Sri Lanka	178	1989-99
12	Saqlain Mushtaq, Pakistan	88	1995-98
11	M. Muralitharan, Sri Lanka	110	1993-99
11	Salim Malik, Pakistan	276	1982-98
11	R.J. Shastri, India	150	1981-92
10	P.L. Taylor, Australia	83	1986-92
10	S.R. Tendulkar, India	211	1989-99

Ross Dundas Cricket Statistics

MOST RUNS CONCEDED FROM MAXIMUM ALLOWABLE OVERS

Bowler	O	M	R	W	Versus	Venue	Date
M.C. Snedden, New Zealand	12	1	105	2	England	The Oval	9 Jun 1983
A.L.F. del Mel, Sri Lanka	10	0	97	1	West Indies	Karachi	13 Oct 1987
S.T. Jayasuriya, Sri Lanka	10	0	94	3	Pakistan	Nairobi (NG)	4 Oct 1996
Ata-ur-Rehman, Pakistan	10	0	85	1	India	Sharjah	15 Apr 1996
B.L. Cairns, New Zealand	11	0	84	0	England	Manchester	17 July 1978
D.R. Pringle, England	10	0	83	0	West Indies	Gujranwala	9 Oct 1987
C.P.H. Ramanayake, Sri Lanka	10	0	82	1	Australia	Sharjah	2 May 1990
Sheikh Salahuddin, Bangladesh	10	0	80	0	Kenya	Nairobi (NG)	10 Oct 1997
A. Kuruvilla, India	9.5	0	80	0	Pakistan	Toronto	21 Sept 1997

LEAST RUNS CONCEDED FROM MAXIMUM ALLOWABLE OVERS

Bowler	O	M	R	W	Versus	Venue	Date
P.V. Simmons, West Indies	10	8	3	4	Pakistan	Sydney	17 Dec 1992
B.S. Bedi, India	12	8	6	1	East Africa	Leeds	11 Jun 1975
C.M. Old, England	10	5	8	4	Canada	Manchester	14 Jun 1979
E.J. Chatfield, New Zealand	10	4	8	1	Sri Lanka	Dunedin	2 Mar 1983
M.F. Malone, Australia	10	5	9	2	West Indies	Sydney	10 Jan 1982
Abdul Qadir, Pakistan	10	4	9	4	New Zealand	Sharjah	15 Apr 1986
Maninder Singh, India	9†	6	9	1	Bangladesh	Chittagong	27 Oct 1988
J.N. Maguire, Australia	7†	0	9	2	New Zealand	Sydney	17 Mar 1983

† overs reduced because of rain

MOST WIDES BY A BOWLER IN A CAREER

No.	Bowler	M	Career
378	Wasim Akram, Pakistan	254	1984-98
244	Waqar Younis, Pakistan	172	1989-98
197	J. Srinath, India	153	1991-99
182	C.E.L. Ambrose, West Indies	157	1988-99
153	Aaqib Javed, Pakistan	163	1988-98
149	I.R. Bishop, West Indies	84	1988-97
143	B.K.V. Prasad, India	104	1994-99
141	G.P. Wickramasinghe, Sri Lanka	107	1990-99
134	A.A. Donald, South Africa	110	1991-99
131	H.H. Streak, Zimbabwe	69	1993-98
126	S.R. Tendulkar, India	211	1989-99
118	S.R. Waugh, Australia	251	1986-99
115	S.K. Warne, Australia	108	1993-99
103	D.K. Morrison, New Zealand	96	1987-96
101	S.T. Jayasuriya, Sri Lanka	178	1989-99
100	C.J. McDermott, Australia	138	1984-96
100	Kapil Dev, India	225	1978-94

Ross Dundas Cricket Statistics

MOST WIDES BY A BOWLER IN AN INNINGS

No.	Bowler	Versus	Venue	Date
15	I.R. Bishop, West Indies	Pakistan	Brisbane	7 Jan 1989
13	Azhar Mahmood, Pakistan	India	Toronto	18 Sep 1997
12	R.J. Kennedy, New Zealand	Zimbabwe	Napier	3 Feb 1996
12	H.H. Streak, Zimbabwe	Sri Lanka	Colombo (SSC)	21 Feb 1996
10	S.T. Jayasuriya, Sri Lanka	Pakistan	Sharjah	11 Apr 1995
10	I.R. Bishop, West Indies	Pakistan	Sharjah	15 Oct 1995
10	G.J. Whittall, Zimbabwe	India	Vadodara (IPCL)	5 Apr 1998

Ross Dundas Cricket Statistics

MOST NO-BALLS BY A BOWLER IN A CAREER

No.	Bowler	M	Career
243	Wasim Akram, Pakistan	253	1984-98
140	J. Srinath, India	153	1991-99
137	C.A. Walsh, West Indies	185	1985-98
111	I.R. Bishop, West Indies	84	1988-97
106	C.E.L. Ambrose, West Indies	157	1988-99
105	Aqib Javed, Pakistan	157	1988-98

Ross Dundas Cricket Statistics

MOST NO-BALLS BY A BOWLER IN AN INNINGS

No.	Bowler	Versus	Venue	Date
10	B.P. Patterson, West Indies	South Africa	Port Elizabeth	11 Feb 1993
9	R.L. Perera, Sri Lanka	England	Perth	29 Jan 1999
8	J. Garner, West Indies	England	Perth	3 Jan 1987
8	Aamir Nazir, Pakistan	West Indies	Arnos Vale	30 Mar 1993
8	P.R. Reiffel, Australia	England	Birmingham	21 May 1993
8	D.K. Morrison, New Zealand	West Indies	Christchurch	28 Jan 1995
8	A.C. Dale, Australia	Zimbabwe	Ahmedabad (SP)	3 Apr 1998

Ross Dundas Cricket Statistics

MOST BOWLERS USED IN AN INNINGS

No.	Team	Venue	Date
9	New Zealand v Sri Lanka	Auckland	20 Mar 1983

Bowlers: R.J Hadlee 0-18 (7 overs), M.C. Snedden 0-22 (7 overs), B.L. Cairns 4-23 (10 overs), M.D.Crowe 1-51 (10 overs), E.J. Chatfield 0-47 (10 overs), J.G. Wright 0-2 (2 overs), B.A. Edgar 0-5 (2 overs), J.J. Crowe 0-1 (1 over), G.M. Turner 0-0 (1 over)

No.	Team	Venue	Date
9	England v Sri Lanka	Peshawar	17 Oct 1987

Bowlers: P.J. DeFreitas 1-24 (9 overs), G.C. Small 0-27 (7 overs), D.R. Pringle 1-11 (4 overs), J.E. Emburey 2-26 (10 overs), E.E. Hemmings 2-31 (10 overs), G.A. Gooch 0-9 (2 overs) C.W.J. Athey 0-10 (1 over), B.C. Broad 0-6 (1 over), A.J. Lamb 0-3 (1 over)

No.	Team	Venue	Date	Bowlers
9	New Zealand v Pakistan	Christchurch	18 Mar 1992	

Bowlers: D.K. Morrison 3-42 (10 overs), D.N. Patel 0-25 (10 overs), W. Watson 0-26 (10 overs) C.Z. Harris 0-18 (4 overs), G.R. Larsen 0-16 (3 overs), A.H. Jones 0-10 (3 overs), R.T. Latham 0-13 (2 overs), K.R. Rutherford 0-11 (1.4 overs), M.J. Greatbatch 0-5 (1 over)

No.	Team	Venue	Date
9	Sri Lanka v New Zealand	Colombo (RPS)	13 Dec 1992

Bowlers: G.P. Wickremasinghe 0-13 (6 overs), A.P. Gurusinha 2-29 (7 overs),
U.C. Hathurusinghe 0-16 (2 overs), S.D. Anurasiri 2-45 (10 overs), R.S. Kalpage 3-46 (10 overs),
A. Ranatunga 0-26 (5 overs), P.A. de Silva 0-31 (6 overs), S.T. Jayasuriya 0-8 (2 overs),
H.P. Tillakeratne 1-3 (0.5 over)

MOST BOWLERS USED IN A MATCH

No.	Match	Venue	Date
16	New Zealand v Sri Lanka	Auckland	20 Mar 1983

Sri Lanka: A.L.F. de Mel 1-65 (10 overs), R.J. Ratnayake 2-50 (10 overs), J.R. Ratnayeke 0-41 (5 overs)
D.S. de Silva 0-46 (10 overs), S. Jeganathan 0-49 (10 overs), Y. Goonasekera 1-24 (3 overs)
S. Wettimuny 1-13 (2 overs)
New Zealand: R.J Hadlee 0-18 (7 overs), M.C. Snedden 0-22 (7 overs), B.L. Cairns 4-23 (10 overs),
M.D.Crowe 1-51 (10 overs), E.J. Chatfield 0-47 (10 overs), J.G. Wright 0-2 (2 overs),
B.A. Edgar 0-5 (2 overs), J.J. Crowe 0-1 (1 over), G.M. Turner 0-0 (1 over)

No.	Match	Venue	Date
16	Sri Lanka v New Zealand	Colombo	13 Dec 1992

New Zealand: M.B. Owens 0-37 (8 overs), C. Pringle 3-59 (8 overs), D.J. Nash 0-44 (6 overs),
J.T.C. Vaughan 0-27 (10 overs), C.Z. Harris 1-48 (10 overs), G.E. Bradburn 0-17 (2 overs),
M.J. Haslam 1-28 (5 overs)
Sri Lanka: G.P. Wickremasinghe 0-13 (6 overs), A.P. Gurusinha 2-29 (7 overs),
U.C. Hathurusinghe 0-16 (2 overs), S.D. Anurasiri 2-45 (10 overs),
R.S. Kalpage 3-46 (10 overs), A. Ranatunga 0-26 (5 overs), P.A. de Silva 0-31 (6 overs),
S.T. Jayasuriya 0-8 (2 overs), H.P. Tillakeratne 1-3 (0.5 over)

No.	Match	Venue	Date
16	Zimbabwe v Sri Lanka	Harare	6 Nov 1994

Zimbabwe: H.H. Streak 0-40 (10 overs), D.H. Brain 3-67 (10 overs), J.A. Rennie 0-60 (7 overs),
G.J. Whittall 1-43 (6 overs), S.G. Peall 0-41 (8 overs), G.W. Flower 0-13 (3 overs),
A.D.R. Campbell 0-14 (3 overs), M.H. Dekker 0-12 (2 overs)
Sri Lanka: W.P.U.C. Vaas 2-12 (7 overs), K.R. Pushpakumara 3-25 (9 overs),
G.P. Wrickemasinghe 1-17 (9 overs), M. Muralitharan 1-21 (10 overs),
R.S. Kalpage 0-21 (10 overs), S.T. Jayasuriya 0-2 (2 overs), H.P. Tillakeratne 0-1 (1 over),
R.S. Mahanama 0-3 (0.1 over)

No.	Match	Venue	Date
16	New Zealand v Australia	Auckland	14 Feb 1998

Australia: P. Wilson 0-25 (4 overs), A.C. Dale 0-33 (6 overs), A.J. Bichel 1-33 (7 overs),
G.R. Robertson 3-29 (10 overs), M.E. Waugh 0-11 (2 overs), M.G. Bevan 1-37 (10 overs),
D.S. Lehmann 1-37 (9 overs), S.G. Law 0-18 (2 overs)
New Zealand: S.B. O'Connor 0-21 (2 overs), C.L. Cairns 1-32 (9.1 overs), S.B. Doull 4-25 (8 overs),
D.J. Nash 1-23 (5 overs), M.W. Priest 2-31 (10 overs), C.Z. Harris 1-33 (10 overs),
C.D. McMillan 1-14 (3 overs), N.J. Astle 0-10 (2 overs)

Fielding

MOST CATCHES IN AN INNINGS

No.	Player	Versus	Venue	Date
5	J.N. Rhodes, South Africa	West Indies	Mumbai (BS)	14 Nov 1993
4	Salim Malik, Pakistan	New Zealand	Sialkot	2 Dec 1984
4	S.R. Gavaskar, India	Pakistan	Sharjah	22 Mar 1985
4	R.B. Richardson, West Indies	England	Birmingham	23/24 May 1991
4	K.C. Wessels, South Africa	West Indies	Kingston	7 Apr 1992
4	M.A. Taylor, Australia	West Indies	Sydney	8 Dec 1992
4	C.L. Hooper, West Indies	Pakistan	Durban	19 Feb 1993
4	K.R. Rutherford, New Zealand	India	Napier	16 Feb 1995
4	P.V. Simmons, West Indies	Sri Lanka	Sharjah	11 Oct 1995
4	M.A. Azharuddin, India	Pakistan	Toronto	13 Sep 1997
4	S.R. Tendulkar, India	Pakistan	Dhaka	11 Jan 1998

Note: J.G. Bracewell (New Zealand) took four catches as a substitute fieldsman against Australia in Adelaide on 23 Nov 1980.

MOST CATCHES IN A CAREER

No.	Player	M	Career
146	M.A. Azharuddin, India	310	1985-99
127	A.R. Border, Australia	273	1978-94
107	R.S. Mahanama, Sri Lanka	208	1986-99
101	I.V.A. Richards, West Indies	187	1975-91
86	S.R. Waugh, Australia	251	1986-99
85	C.L. Hooper, West Indies	177	1987-99
80	Salim Malik, Pakistan	276	1982-98
79	Ijaz Ahmed, Pakistan	215	1986-98
76	P.A. de Silva, Sri Lanka	250	1984-99
74	R.B. Richardson, West Indies	224	1983-96
71	Javed Miandad, Pakistan	233	1975-96
71	Kapil Dev, India	225	1978-94
71	S.R. Tendulkar, India	211	1989-99
70	J.N. Rhodes, South Africa	146	1992-99
68	M.E. Waugh, Australia	174	1988-99
66	M.D. Crowe, New Zealand	143	1982-95
63	B.C. Lara, West Indies	137	1990-99
62	Wasim Akram, Pakistan	254	1984-98
61	A.L. Logie, West Indies	158	1981-93
61	A. Ranatunga, Sri Lanka	260	1982-99
60	W.J. Cronje, South Africa	152	1992-99
59	D.L. Haynes, West Indies	238	1978-94
59	S.T. Jayasuriya, Sri Lanka	178	1989-99
58	A. Kumble, India	158	1986-99
56	M.A. Taylor, Australia	113	1989-97
55	R.A. Harper, West Indies	105	1983-96
54	D.M. Jones, Australia	164	1984-94
53	P.V. Simmons, West Indies	133	1987-98
51	J.G. Wright, New Zealand	149	1978-92

Wicket-keeping

MOST DISMISSALS IN AN INNINGS

No.	Player	Versus	Venue	Date
5 (5 ct)	R.W. Marsh, Australia	England	Leeds	8 Jun 1981
5 (5 ct)	R.G. de Alwis, Sri Lanka	Australia	Colombo (PSS)	13 Apr 1983
5 (5 ct)	S.M.H. Kirmani, India	Zimbabwe	Leicester	11 Jun 1983
5 (3 ct, 2 st)	S. Viswanath, India	England	Sydney	26 Feb 1985
5 (3 ct, 2 st)	K.S. More, India	New Zealand	Sharjah	27 Mar 1988
5 (5ct)	H.P. Tillakeratne, Sri Lanka	Pakistan	Sharjah	20 Dec 1990
5 (3 ct, 2 st)	N.R. Mongia, India	New Zealand	Auckland	27 Mar 1994
5 (3 ct, 2 st)	A.C. Parore, New Zealand	West Indies	Margao	26 Oct 1994
5 (5 ct)	D.J. Richardson, South Africa	Pakistan	Johannesburg	12 Jan 1995
5 (5 ct)	Moin Khan, Pakistan	Zimbabwe	Harare	26 Feb 1995
5 (4 ct, 1 st)	R.S. Kaluwitharana, Sri Lanka	Pakistan	Sharjah	11 Apr 1995
5 (5 ct)	D.J. Richardson, South Africa	Zimbabwe	Harare	21 Oct 1995
5 (5 ct)	A. Flower, Zimbabwe	South Africa	Harare	22 Oct 1995
5 (5 ct)	C.O. Browne, West Indies	Sri Lanka	Brisbane	5 Jan 1996
5 (4 ct, 1 st)	J.C. Adams, West Indies	Kenya	Pune	29 Feb 1996
5 (4 ct, 1 st)	Rashid Latif, Pakistan	New Zealand	Lahore	6 Mar 1996
5 (3 ct, 2 st)	N.R. Mongia, India	Pakistan	Toronto	18 Sep 1996
5 (5 ct)	A. Flower, Zimbabwe	England	Harare	3 Jan 1997
5 (4ct, 1 st)	R.D. Jacobs, West Indies	England	Kingstown	5 Apr 1998

MOST DISMISSALS IN A CAREER

No.	Player	M	C	St	Career
234	I.A. Healy, Australia	168	195	34	1988-97
204	P.J. Dujon, West Indies	169	183	21	1982-91
165	D.J. Richardson, South Africa	122	148	17	1991-98
143	Moin Khan, Pakistan	118	104	39	1990-98
135	N.R. Mongia, India	123	96	39	1994-98
124	R.W. Marsh, Australia	92	120	4	1971-84
123	R.S. Kaluwitharana, Sri Lanka	112	76	47	1990-99
122	Rashid Latif, Pakistan	101	94	28	1992-98
112	A.J. Stewart, England	116	101	11	1989-99
103	Salim Yousuf, Pakistan	86	81	22	1982-90
94	A. Flower, Zimbabwe	100	73	21	1992-98
90	K.S. More, India	94	63	27	1984-93
86	I.D.S. Smith, New Zealand	98	81	5	1980-92
81	H.P. Tillakeratne, Sri Lanka	176	76	5	1986-89
76	A.C. Parore, New Zealand	107	61	15	1992-99
73	A.C. Gilchrist, Australia	51	63	10	1996-99
62	Wasim Bari, Pakistan	51	52	10	1973-84
53	J.R. Murray, West Indies	55	46	7	1992-99

Note: H.P. Tillakeratne played 127 matches as a fielder, A.J. Stewart 33, A.C. Parore 28, Moin Khan 9, A. Flower 6, A.C. Gilchrist 6, R.S. Kaluwitharana 5, J.R. Murray 5 and P.J.L. Dujon 3.

MOST CATCHES IN AN INNINGS

No.	Player	Versus	Venue	Date
5	R.W. Marsh, Australia	England	Leeds	8 Jun 1981
5	R.G. de Alwis, Sri Lanka	Australia	Colombo (PSS)	13 Apr 1983
5	S.M.H. Kirmani, Sri Lanka	Zimbabwe	Leicester	11 Jun 1983
5	H.P. Tillakeratne, Sri Lanka	Pakistan	Sharjah	20 Dec 1990
5	D.J. Richardson, South Africa	Pakistan	Johannesburg	12 Jan 1995
5	Moin Khan, Pakistan	Zimbabwe	Harare	26 Feb 1995
5	D.J. Richardson, South Africa	Zimbabwe	Harare	21 Oct 1995
5	A. Flower, Zimbabwe	South Africa	Harare	22 Oct 1995
5	C.O. Browne, West Indies	Sri Lanka	Brisbane	5 Jan 1996
5	A. Flower, Zimbabwe	England	Harare	3 Jan 1997

MOST CATCHES IN A CAREER

No.	Player	M	Career
195	I.A. Healy, Australia	168	1988-97
183	P.J. Dujon, West Indies	169	1982-91
148	D.J. Richardson, South Africa	122	1991-98
120	R.W. Marsh, Australia	92	1971-84
104	Moin Khan, Pakistan	118	1990-98
101	A.J. Stewart, England	116	1989-99
96	N.R. Mongia, India	123	1994-98
94	Rashid Latif, Pakistan	101	1992-98
81	Salim Yousuf, Pakistan	86	1982-90
81	I.D.S. Smith, New Zealand	98	1980-92
76	R.S. Kaluwitharana, Sri Lanka	112	1990-99
76	H.P. Tillakeratne, Sri Lanka	176	1986-89
73	A. Flower, Zimbabwe	100	1992-98
63	A.C. Gilchrist, Australia	51	1996-99
63	K.S. More, India	94	1984-93
61	A.C. Parore, New Zealand	107	1992-99
52	Wasim Bari, Pakistan	51	1973-84

Note: H.P. Tillakeratne played 127 matches as a fielder, A.J. Stewart 33, A.C. Parore 28, Moin Khan 9, A. Flower 6, A.C. Gilchrist 6, R.S. Kaluwitharana 5, and P.J.L. Dujon 3.

MOST STUMPINGS IN AN INNINGS

No.	Player	Versus	Venue	Date
3	Salim Yousuf, Pakistan	New Zealand	Lahore	2 Nov 1990
3	I.A. Healy, Australia	South Africa	East London	2 Apr 1994
3	I.A. Healy, Australia	Pakistan	Faisalabad	18 Oct 1994
3	Moin Khan, Pakistan	West Indies	Sharjah	13 Oct 1995

MOST STUMPINGS IN A CAREER

No.	Player	M	Career
47	R.S. Kaluwitharana, Sri Lanka	112	1990-99
39	I.A. Healy, Australia	168	1988-97
39	Moin Khan, Pakistan	118	1990-98
39	N.R. Mongia, India	123	1994-99
28	Rashid Latif, Pakistan	101	1992-98
27	K.S. More, India	94	1984-93
22	Salim Yousuf, Pakistan	86	1982-90
21	P.J. Dujon, West Indies	169	1982-91
21	A. Flower, Zimbabwe	100	1992-99

No.	Player	M	Career
17	D.J. Richardson, South Africa	122	1991-98
15	C.S. Pandit, India	36	1986-92
15	A.C. Parore, New Zealand	107	1992-99
11	A.J. Stewart, England	116	1989-99
10	A.C. Gilchrist, Australia	51	1996-99
10	Wasim Bari, Pakistan	51	1973-84
10	D. Williams, West Indies	36	1988-97

MOST BYES CONCEDED IN AN INNINGS

No.	Player	Versus	Venue	Date
18	J.M. Parker, New Zealand	Pakistan	Sialkot	16 Oct 1976
18	R.W. Marsh, Australia	New Zealand	Sydney	29 Jan 1981
18	Masood Iqbal, Pakistan	New Zealand	Multan	7 Dec 1984
16	Salim Yousuf, Pakistan	West Indies	Multan	17 Nov 1986
13	Salim Yousuf, Pakistan	England	Lahore	18 Nov 1987
13	Moin Khan, Pakistan	Zimbabwe	Harare	25 Feb 1995

Ross Dundas Cricket Statistics

MOST BYES CONCEDED IN A CAREER

Byes	Player	M	Career
378	P.J.L. Dujon, West Indies	169	1982-91
164	Salim Yousuf, Pakistan	86	1982-90
146	I.A. Healy, Australia	168	1988-98
142	R.W. Marsh, Australia	92	1971-84
124	N.R. Mongia, India	121	1994-98
121	Moin Khan, Pakistan	110	1990-98
118	A. Flower, Zimbabwe	92	1992-98
110	I.D.S. Smith, New Zealand	98	1980-92
101	Rashid Latif, Pakistan	101	1992-98

Ross Dundas Cricket Statistics

LEAST BYES CONCEDED IN A CAREER (AVE. PER 100 RUNS)

Byes/100 runs	Player	M[†]	Career
0.18	C.O. Browne, West Indies	24	1995-97
0.22	S.S. Karim, India	25	1997-98
0.29	D.J. Richardson, South Africa	122	1991-98
0.30	R.S. Kaluwitharana, Sri Lanka	112	1990-99
0.31	D. Williams, West Indies	29	1988-93
0.32	J.R. Murray, West Indies	38	1992-99
0.34	L.K. Germon, New Zealand	37	1994-97
0.34	A.C. Gilchrist, Australia	46	1997-99
0.35	T.E. Blain, New Zealand	38	1986-94
0.36	A.J. Stewart, England	83	1989-99
0.38	A.C. Parore, New Zealand	96	1992-98

[†]*minimum 20 matches as a wicket-keeper*

Ross Dundas Cricket Statistics

All-round Performances

2000 RUNS AND 200 WICKETS IN A CAREER

Runs	Wkts	Player	M	Career
3783	253	Kapil Dev, India	225	1978-94
2508	363	Wasim Akram, Pakistan	254	1984-98

1000 RUNS AND 100 WICKETS IN A CAREER

Runs	Wkts	Player	M	Career
2113	145	I.T. Botham, England	116	1976-92
1751	158	R.J. Hadlee, New Zealand	115	1973-90
2199	117	C.Z. Harris, New Zealand	120	1990-99
4500	160	C.L. Hooper, West Indies	177	1987-99
3709	182	Imran Khan, Pakistan	175	1974-92
4672	152	S.T. Jayasuriya, Sri Lanka	178	1989-99
3783	253	Kapil Dev, India	225	1978-94
2653	111	Mudassar Nazar, Pakistan	122	1977-89
1242	108	S.P. O'Donnell, Australia	87	1985-91
1858	157	M. Prabhakar, India	130	1984-96
6721	118	I.V.A. Richards, West Indies	187	1975-91
3108	129	R.J. Shastri, India	150	1981-92
2508	363	Wasim Akram, Pakistan	254	1984-98
5706	185	S.R. Waugh, Australia	251	1986-99

5000 RUNS AND 50 WICKETS IN A CAREER

Runs	Wkts	Player	M	Career
6524	73	A.R. Border, Australia	273	1979-94
7863	81	P.A. de Silva, Sri Lanka	250	1984-99
7248	79	A. Ranatunga, Sri Lanka	260	1982-99
6721	118	I.V.A. Richards, West Indies	187	1975-91
7053	89	Salim Malik, Pakistan	268	1982-98
7800	78	S.R. Tendulkar, India	211	1989-99
6044	80	M.E. Waugh, Australia	174	1988-99
5706	185	S.R. Waugh, Australia	251	1986-99

CENTURY AND 5 WICKETS IN A MATCH

Player	Batting	Bowling	Versus	Venue	Date
I.V.A. Richards, West Indies	119	5-41	New Zealand	Dunedin	18 Mar 1987

HALF-CENTURY AND 5 WICKETS IN A MATCH

Player	Batting	Bowling	Versus	Venue	Date
K. Srikkanth, India	70	5-27	New Zealand	Visag	10 Dec 1988
M.E. Waugh, Australia	57	5-24	West Indies	Melbourne	15 Dec 1992
L. Klusener, South Africa	54	6-49	Sri Lanka	Lahore	6 Nov 1997

CENTURY AND 4 WICKETS IN A MATCH

Player	Batting	Bowling	Versus	Venue	Date
N. Astle, New Zealand	117	4-43	Pakistan	Mohali	9 May 1997
S.R. Tendulkar, India	141	4-38	Australia	Dhaka	28 Oct 1998

HALF-CENTURY AND 4 WICKETS IN A MATCH

Player	Batting	Bowling	Versus	Venue	Date
D.A.G. Fletcher, Zimbabwe	69	4-42	Australia	Nottingham	9 Jun 1983
S.R. Waugh, Australia	82	4-48	Pakistan	Perth	2 Jan 1987
S.P. O'Donnell, Australia	57	4-36	Sri Lanka	Melbourne	26 Dec 1989
I.T. Botham, England	53	4-31	Australia	Sydney	5 Mar 1992
G.J. Crocker, Zimbabwe	50	4-26	India	Harare	25 Oct 1992
Aamer Sohail, Pakistan	85	4-22	Sri Lanka	Sharjah	12 Oct 1995
S.M. Pollock, South Africa	66	4-34	England	Cape Town	9 Jan 1996

Note: D.A.G. Fletcher, G.J. Crocker and S.M. Pollock all performed the feat on debut.

1000 RUNS AND 100 WICKET-KEEPING DISMISSALS IN A CAREER

Runs	Dismissals	Player	M	Career
1945	204	P.J.L. Dujon, West Indies	169	1981-91
1764	234	I.A. Healy, Australia	168	1988-97
1930	123	R.S. Kaluwitharana, Sri Lanka	112	1990-99
1225	124	R.W. Marsh, Australia	92	1971-84
1684	143	Moin Khan, Pakistan	118	1990-98
1125	135	N.R. Mongia, India	123	1994-99
3211	112	A.J. Stewart, England	116	1989-99

Note: A.J. Stewart has played 33 matches as a fieldsman.

The Captains

SUMMARY OF RESULTS BY CAPTAIN FOR EACH COUNTRY

Australia

Captain	Career	M	Won	Lost	NR	Tie	Win%
W.M. Lawry	1971	1	1	-	-	-	100
I.M. Chappell	1972-75	11	6	5	-	-	55
G.S. Chappell	1975-83	49	21	25	3	-	46
R.B. Simpson	1978	2	1	1	-	-	50
G.N. Yallop	1979	4	2	1	1	-	67
K.J. Hughes	1979-84	49	21	23	4	1	47
D.W. Hookes	1983	1	-	1	-	-	-
A.R. Border	1985-94	178	107	66	3	2	61
R.J. Bright	1986	1	-	1	-	-	-
G.R. Marsh	1987-91	4	3	1	-	-	75
M.A. Taylor	1992-97	67	36	30	-	1	54
I.A. Healy	1995-97	8	5	3	-	-	63
S.R. Waugh	1997-99	32	16	16	-	-	50
S.K. Warne	1998-99	11	10	1	-	-	91

Bangladesh

Captain	Career	M	Won	Lost	NR	Tie	Win%
Gazi Ashraf	1986-90	7	-	7	-	-	-
Minhaz-ul-Abedin	1990	2	-	2	-	-	-
Akram Khan	1995-98	15	1	14	-	-	6
Amin-ul-Islam	1998	1	-	1	-	-	-

Canada

Captain	Career	M	Won	Lost	NR	Tie	Win%
B.M. Mauricette	1979	3	-	3	-	-	-

East Africa

Captain	Career	M	Won	Lost	NR	Tie	Win%
Harilal Shah	1975	3	-	3	-	-	-

England

Captain	Career	M	Won	Lost	NR	Tie	Win%
R. Illingworth	1971-73	3	1	1	1	-	50
D.B. Close	1972	3	2	1	-	-	67
M.H. Denness	1973-75	12	7	4	1	-	64
J.H. Edrich	1975	1	-	-	1	-	-
A.P.E. Knott	1976	1	-	1	-	-	-
A.W. Greig	1976	2	-	2	-	-	-
J.M. Brearley	1977-80	25	15	9	1	-	63
G. Boycott	1977-78	2	2	-	-	-	100
R.G.D. Willis	1978-84	29	16	13	-	-	55
I.T. Botham	1980-81	9	4	5	-	-	44
K.W.R. Fletcher	1981-82	5	2	3	-	-	40
D.I. Gower	1984-89	24	10	13	-	1	42
N. Gifford	1985	2	-	2	-	-	-
M.W. Gatting	1986-88	37	26	11	-	-	70
J.E. Emburey	1987	4	2	2	-	-	50
G.A. Gooch	1988-93	50	24	23	3	-	51
A.J. Lamb	1990	4	1	3	-	-	25

Captain	Career	M	Won	Lost	NR	Tie	Win%
A.J. Stewart	1992-99	21	8	13	-	-	38
M.A. Atherton	1994-97	43	20	21	1	1	48
N. Hussain	1997	1	1	-	-	-	100
A.J. Hollioake	1997-98	14	6	8	-	-	43

India

Captain	Career	M	Won	Lost	NR	Tie	Win%
A.L. Wadekar	1974	2	-	2	-	-	-
S. Venkatraghaven	1975-79	7	1	6	-	-	14
B.S. Bedi	1978	4	1	3	-	-	25
S.M. Gavaskar	1980-85	39	15	22	2	-	41
G.R. Viswanath	1981	1	-	1	-	-	-
Kapil Dev	1982-87	72	37	32	2	1	53
S.M.H. Kirmani	1983	1	-	1	-	-	-
M. Armanath	1984	1	-	-	1	-	-
R.J. Shastri	1987-91	11	4	7	-	-	36
D.B. Vengsarker	1987-89	18	8	10	-	-	44
K. Srikkanth	1989	13	4	8	1	-	33
M.A. Azharuddin	1990-99	161	84	69	6	2	54
S.R. Tendulkar	1996-97	54	17	31	5	1	35
A.D. Jadeja	1998-99	3	2	1	-	-	67

Kenya

Captain	Career	M	Won	Lost	NR	Tie	Win%
M. Odumbe	1996	9	1	7	1	-	13
Aasif Karim	1997-98	11	4	7	-	-	36

Netherlands

Captain	Career	M	Won	Lost	NR	Tie	Win%
S.W. Lubbers	1996	4	-	4	-	-	-
R.P. Lefebvre	1996	1	-	1	-	-	-

New Zealand

Captain	Career	M	Won	Lost	NR	Tie	Win%
B.E. Congdon	1973-75	6	1	3	2	-	25
G.M. Turner	1975-76	8	5	2	1	-	71
M.G. Burgess	1978-80	8	2	6	-	-	25
G.P. Howarth	1980-85	60	31	26	3	-	54
J.G. Wright	1984-90	31	16	15	-	-	52
J.V. Coney	1984-87	25	8	16	1	-	33
J.J. Crowe	1986-88	16	4	12	-	-	25
M.D. Crowe	1990-93	44	21	22	1	-	49
A.H. Jones	1992	2	-	2	-	-	-
K.R. Rutherford	1993-95	37	10	24	2	1	29
G.R. Larsen	1994	3	1	2	-	-	33
L.K. Germon	1995-97	36	15	19	-	2	42
S.P. Fleming	1997-99	36	14	19	2	1	39
D.J. Nash	1999	4	1	2	1	-	33

Pakistan

Captain	Career	M	Won	Lost	NR	Tie	Win%
Intikhab Alam	1973-74	3	2	1	-	-	67
Asif Iqbal	1975-79	6	2	4	-	-	33
Majid Khan	1975	2	1	1	-	-	50
Mushtaq Mohammed	1976-78	4	2	2	-	-	50
Wasim Bari	1977-78	5	1	4	-	-	20
Javed Miandad	1980-93	61	24	33	2	2	41
Zaheer Abbas	1982-85	14	8	5	1	-	62
Imran Khan	1982-92	139	75	58	4	2	56
Sarfraz Nawaz	1984	1	-	1	-	-	-
Abdul Qadir	1987-88	5	1	4	-	-	20
Ramiz Raja	1992-97	22	7	13	2	-	35
Salim Malik	1992-95	34	21	11	-	2	62
Wasim Akram	1993-97	72	43	28	-	1	60
Waqar Younis	1993	1	-	1	-	-	-
Moin Khan	1995	2	2	-	-	-	100
Saeed Anwar	1995-97	8	5	3	-	-	63
Aamir Sohail	1996-98	22	9	12	1	-	43
Rashid Latif	1998	13	6	7	-	-	46

South Africa

Captain	Career	M	Won	Lost	NR	Tie	Win%
C.E.B. Rice	1991	3	1	2	-	-	33
K.C. Wessels	1992-94	52	20	30	2	-	38
W.J. Cronje	1994-99	102	77	24	1	-	76

Sri Lanka

Captain	Career	M	Won	Lost	NR	Tie	Win%
A.P.B. Tennekoon	1975-79	4	-	4	-	-	-
B. Warnapura	1979-82	8	3	5	-	-	38
L.R.D. Mendis	1982-87	61	11	46	4	-	19
D.S. de Silva	1983	1	-	1	-	-	-
R.S. Madugalle	1988	13	2	11	-	-	15
A. Ranatunga	1988-99	184	86	89	8	1	49
J.R. Ratnayeke	1988	1	1	-	-	-	100
P.A. de Silva	1992-96	18	5	12	1	-	29
R.S. Mahanama	1994	2	-	2	-	-	-
S.T. Jayasuriya	1998	1	1	-	-	-	100

United Arab Emirates

Captain	Career	M	Won	Lost	NR	Tie	Win%
Sultan M. Zarawani	1994-96	7	1	7	-	-	14

West Indies

Captain	Career	M	Won	Lost	NR	Tie	Win%
R.B. Kanhai	1973	2	1	1	-	-	50
C.H. Lloyd	1975-85	83	63	18	1	1	76
D.L. Murray	1978-79	2	2	-	-	-	100
A.I. Kallicharran	1978	1	-	1	-	-	-
I.V.A. Richards	1980-91	106	68	36	2	-	65
M.A. Holding	1984	2	2	-	-	-	100
C.G. Greenidge	1988	8	6	2	-	-	75
D.L. Haynes	1989-93	7	3	4	-	-	43
P.J.L. Dujon	1990	1	1	-	-	-	-

Captain	Career	M	Won	Lost	NR	Tie	Win%
R.B. Richardson	1991-96	87	46	36	2	3	54
C.A. Walsh	1994-97	43	22	20	1	-	52
B.C. Lara	1994-99	14	8	6	-	-	57
C.L. Hooper	1997-99	4	-	4	-	-	-

Zimbabwe

Captain	Career	M	Won	Lost	NR	Tie	Win%
D.A.G. Fletcher	1983	6	1	5	-	-	17
A.J. Traicos	1987	6	-	6	-	-	-
D.L. Houghton	1992-93	17	1	16	-	-	6
A. Flower	1993-96	28	5	19	2	2	19
A.D.R. Campbell	1996-98	55	19	34	-	2	35

MOST MATCHES AS CAPTAIN

No.	Captain	Career
184	A. Ranatunga, Sri Lanka	1988-99
178	A.R. Border, Australia	1985-94
161	M.A. Azharuddin, India	1990-99
139	Imran Khan, Pakistan	1982-92
106	I.V.A. Richards, West Indies	1980-91
102	W.J. Cronje, South Africa	1994-98
87	R.B. Richardson, West Indies	1991-96
83	C.H. Lloyd, West Indies	1975-85
72	Kapil Dev, India	1982-87
72	Wasim Akram, Pakistan	1993-97
67	M.A. Taylor, Australia	1992-97
61	Javed Miandad, Pakistan	1980-93
61	L.R.D. Mendis, Sri Lanka	1982-67
60	G.P. Howarth, New Zealand	1980-85
55	A.D.R. Campbell, Zimbabwe	1996-98
54	S.R. Tendulkar, India	1996-97
52	K.C. Wessels, South Africa	1994-98
50	G.A. Gooch, England	1988-93

MOST CONSECUTIVE MATCHES AS CAPTAIN

No.	Captain	From	To
98	M.A. Azharuddin, India	6 Dec 1991	26 May 1996
95	W.J. Cronje, South Africa	6 Dec 1994	7 Feb 1999
60	L.R.D. Mendis, Sri Lanka	19 Mar 1983	30 Oct 1987
55	A.D.R. Campbell, Zimbabwe	26 Aug 1996	24 Nov 1998
55	A. Ranatunga, Sri Lanka	16 Jan 1996	24 Jan 1998
54	I.V.A. Richards, West Indies	9 Mar 1985	12 Mar 1988
54	S.R. Tendulkar, India	26 Aug 1996	28 Dec 1997
53	A.R. Border, Australia	9 Apr 1987	8 Mar 1990
51	R.B. Richardson, West Indies	17 Oct 1991	1 Nov 1993

Note: Both W.J. Cronje's and A.D.R. Campbell's streak remained unbroken at the time of publication.

MOST TOSS WINS

No.	M	% Won	Captain	Career
99	184	53.81	A. Ranatunga, Sri Lanka	1988-99
90	161	55.90	M.A. Azharuddin, India	1990-99
85	178	47.75	A.R. Border, Australia	1985-94
70	139	50.35	Imran Khan, Pakistan	1982-92
55	102	53.92	W.J. Cronje, South Africa	1994-99
44	87	50.57	R.B. Richardson, West Indies	1991-96
43	106	40.57	I.V.A. Richards, West Indies	1980-91
42	83	50.60	C.H. Lloyd, West Indies	1975-85
38	72	52.78	Kapil Dev, India	1982-87
38	72	52.78	Wasim Akram, Pakistan	1993-97
34	67	50.75	M.A. Taylor, Australia	1992-97
31	49	63.27	K.J. Hughes, Australia	1979-84
31	54	57.41	S.R. Tendulkar, India	1996-97

MOST CONSECUTIVE TOSS WINS

No.	Captain	From	To
10	A. Ranatunga, Sri Lanka	9 Nov 1998	31 Jan 1999
9	A.R. Border, Australia	7 Jan 1988	4 Feb 1988
9	M.A. Azharuddin, India	7 Jun 1998	30 Sep 1998
7	M.W. Gatting, England	8 Feb 1987	17 Oct 1987
7	D.B. Vengsarker, India	19 Oct 1988	10 Dec 1988
7	R.B. Richardson, West Indies	1 Nov 1993	27 Nov 1993
7	W.J. Cronje, South Africa	15 Feb 1995	11 Jan 1996
7	I.A. Healy, Australia	20 Aug 1996	8 Apr 1997
6	Kapil Dev, India	9 Nov 1983	21 Sep 1985
6	J.G. Wright, New Zealand	12 Dec 1988	8 Mar 1989
6	Imran Khan, Pakistan	31 Dec 1989	15 Feb 1990
6	J.G. Wright, New Zealand	10 Mar 1990	23 May 1990
6	M.A. Azharuddin, India	8 Dec 1991	14 Jan 1992
6	M.D. Crowe, New Zealand	26 Dec 1992	24 Mar 1993
6	R.B. Richardson, West Indies	25 Feb 1993	30 Mar 1993
6	R.B. Richardson, West Indies	6 Mar 1994	11 Oct 1995
6	A. Flower, Zimbabwe	16 Feb 1996	6 Mar 1996
6	Wasim Akram, Pakistan	14 Jan 1997	6 Apr 1997
6	W.J. Cronje, South Africa	8 Nov 1997	9 Jan 1998

YOUNGEST CAPTAINS

Age	Player	Versus	Venue	Date
23 years, 126 days	S.R. Tendulkar, India	Sri Lanka	Colombo	28 Aug 1996
23 years, 249 days	Kapil Dev, India	Sri Lanka	Amritsar	12 Sep 1982
23 years, 358 days	S.P. Fleming, New Zealand	Sri Lanka	Christchurch	25 Mar 1997
23 years, 354 days	Waqar Younis, Pakistan	West Indies	Sharjah	5 Nov 1993
23 years, 162 days	Javed Miandad, Pakistan	West Indies	Karachi	21 Nov 1980

OLDEST CAPTAINS

Age	Player	Versus	Venue	Date
44 years, 361 days	N. Gifford, England	Pakistan	Sharjah	26 Mar 1985
42 years, 346 days	S.W. Lubbers, Netherlands	South Africa	Rawalpindi	5 Mar 1996
42 years, 114 days	C.E.B. Rice, South Africa	India	New Delhi	14 Nov 1991
42 years, 68 days	R.B. Simpson, Australia	West Indies	Castries	12 Apr 1978
41 years, 187 days	C.H. Lloyd, West Indies	Pakistan	Melbourne	6 Mar 1985

CAPTAINS IN LIMITED-OVER MATCHES BUT NOT IN TESTS

Australia

Captain	Career	M	Won	Lost	NR	Tie	Win%
D.W. Hookes	1983	1	-	1	-	-	-
R.J. Bright	1986	1	-	1	-	-	-
G.R. March	1987-91	4	3	1	-	-	75
I.A. Healy	1995-97	8	5	3	-	-	63
S.R. Waugh	1997-99	32	16	16	-	-	50
S.K. Warne	1998-99	11	10	1	-	-	91

Note: At the time of publication S.R. Waugh had just been selected captain of Australia's four-test tour of the West Indies.

England

Captain	Career	M	Won	Lost	NR	Tie	Win%
A.P.E. Knott	1976	1	-	1	-	-	-
N. Gifford	1985	2	-	2	-	-	-
N. Hussain	1997	1	1	-	-	-	100
A.J. Hollioake	1997-98	14	6	8	-	-	43

India

Captain	Career	M	Won	Lost	NR	Tie	Win%
S.M.H. Kirmani	1983	1	-	1	-	-	-
M. Armanath	1984	1	-	-	1	-	-
A.D. Jadeja	1998-99	3	2	1	-	-	67

New Zealand

Captain	Career	M	Won	Lost	NR	Tie	Win%
A.H. Jones	1992	2	-	2	-	-	-
G.R. Larsen	1994	3	1	2	-	-	33
D.J. Nash	1999	4	1	2	1	-	33

Pakistan

Captain	Career	M	Won	Lost	NR	Tie	Win%
Sarfraz Nawaz	1984	1	-	1	-	-	-
Abdul Qadir	1987-88	5	1	4	-	-	20
Moin Khan	1995	2	2	-	-	-	100

South Africa

Captain	Career	M	Won	Lost	NR	Tie	Win%
C.E.B. Rice	1991	3	1	2	-	-	33

Sri Lanka

Captain	Career	M	Won	Lost	NR	Tie	Win%
A.P.B. Tennekoon	1975-79	4	-	4	-	-	-
J.R. Ratnayeke	1988	1	1	-	-	-	100
R.S. Mahanama	1994	2	-	2	-	-	-

| S.T. Jayasuriya | 1998 | 1 | 1 | - | - | - | 100 |

West Indies

Captain	Career	M	Won	Lost	NR	Tie	Win%
M.A. Holding	1984	2	2	-	-	-	100
C.G. Greenidge	1988	8	6	2	-	-	75
P.J.L. Dujon	1990	1	1	-	-	-	-
C.L. Hooper	1997-99	4	-	4	-	-	-

Zimbabwe

Captain	Career	M	Won	Lost	NR	Tie	Win%
D.A.G. Fletcher	1983	6	1	5	-	-	17
A.J. Traicos	1987	6	-	6	-	-	-

Umpires

MOST APPEARANCES AS UMPIRE

No.	Umpire	Career
88	S.G. Randell, Australia	1984-98
84	A.R. Crafter, Australia	1979-92
75	D.R. Shepherd, England	1983-98
70	H.D. Bird, England	1973-97
68	P.J. McConnell, Australia	1983-92
67	R.S. Dunne, New Zealand	1989-99
58	S.A. Bucknor, West Indies	1989-98
58	C.J. Mitchley, South Africa	1992-99
58	I.D. Robinson, Zimbabwe	1992-98
57	R.A. French, Australia	1979-88
55	Khizer Hayat, Pakistan	1978-96
49	M.W. Johnson, Australia	1979-88
46	R.E. Koertzen, South Africa	1992-99
45	B.L. Aldridge, New Zealand	1986-95
44	K.T. Francis, Sri Lanka	1982-98

Ross Dundas Cricket Statistics

UMPIRES WHO HAVE PLAYED IN LIMITED-OVERS INTERNATIONALS

Player/Umpire	Played	Career	Umpired	Career
J.H. Hampshire, England	3	1971-72	8	1989-98
Mohammad Nazir, Pakistan	4	1980-84	8	1994-98
S. Venkatraghaven, India	15	1974-83	18	1993-98
P. Willey, England	26	1977-86	8	1996-98

UMPIRES WHO HAVE STOOD IN LIMITED-OVERS INTERNATIONALS BUT NOT IN TESTS

Australia

Umpire	M
K.J. Carmody	2
G. Duperouzel	1
R.A. Emerson	10
R.G. Harris	1
L.J. Stevens	1
S.J.A. Taufel	4
I.S. Thomas	8
A.G. Watson	3

England

Umpire	M
J.C. Balderstone	2
A.A. Jones	1
R. Julian	3
B. Leadbeater	4
A.S.M. Oakman	1

India

Umpire	M
S. Asnani	1
A. Bhattacharjee	1
V. Chopra	2
S. Chowdhury	8
S. Dandapani	1
S.K. Das	1
S. Deo	1
R. Desraj	1
Devendra Sharma	1
N. Dutta	1
K.S. Giridharan	5
T. Handu	1
B.A. Jamula	4
Jasbir Singh	2
R.R. Kadam	4
K.R. Karimaniokam	1
B.R. Keshavamurthy	1
J.V. Khurushinkal	1
O. Krishna	1
J. Kurishankel	2

Umpire	M
N. Menon	4
P.R. Mohite	1
R. Mrithyunjayan	2
M.G. Mukherjee	1
K. Murali	3
R. Nagaraja Rao	3
P.G. Pandit	9
K. Parthasarathi	1
S.K. Porel	5
G.A. Pratap Kumar	1
K.N. Raghavan	1
R.S. Rahtore	1
R.T. Ramachandran	4
R.V. Ramani	13
V.K. Ramaswami	15
B.S. Rao	1
R. Ravindram	1
J.D. Roy	1
B.K. Sadashiva	1
S.T. Sambandam	1
C.K. Sathe	5
H.S. Sekhon	1
R. Seth	1
D. Sharma	1
S.K. Sharma	5
M.N. Shekhan	1
I. Shivram	2
M.R. Singh	5
V. Srinivasan	1
Suresh Shastri	4
C.R. Vijayaraghavan	1

New Zealand

Umpire	M
B.F. Bowden	8
G.I.J. Cowan	5
S.C. Cowman	2
E.W. Dempster	3
L.H.G. Harmer	1
A.L. Hill	2
T.A. McCall	2
A.M. Rangi	1
E.G. Wainscott	3
E.A. Watkin	9

Pakistan

Umpire	M
Afzaal Ahmed	1
Agha Saadat	1
Azhar Hussain	1
Feroze Butt	4
Ghafoor Butt	1
Iftikhar Malik	1
Islam Khan	2

Umpire	M
Masroor Ali	1
Mian Muhammed Aslam	1
Rab Nawaz	2
Salim Badar	1
Saqib Qureshi	1
Siddiq Khan	4
B.K. Tahir	1
Taufiq Khan	1

South Africa

Umpire	M
D.F. Becker	11

Sri Lanka

Umpire	M
D.N. Pathirana	7
K.T. Ponnambalam	2
D.N. Pathirana	7

West Indies

Umpire	M
P. Alleyne	1
M. Baksh	1
G.T. Browne	1
W. Docktrove	2
A. Gaynor	6
R. Haynes	1
D. Holder	1
G.T. Johnson	5
Z. Maccum	1
Mohammad Hosein	1
B. Morgan	3
N.G. Nichollss	1
P.C. White	4

Zimbabwe

Umpire	M
K.C. Barbour	2
M. Esat	2
G.R. Evans	4
S.N. Fleming	2

Ross Dundas Cricket Statistics

The Grounds

SUMMARY OF MATCHES AT EACH GROUND

Australia (14 grounds)

Ground	First match	Date	M
Adelaide, Adelaide Oval	Australia v West Indies	20 Dec 1975	46
Albury, Lavington Sports Ground	England v Zimbabwe	18 Mar 1992	1
Ballarat, Eastern Oval	England v Sri Lanka	9 Mar 1992	1
Berri, Berri Oval	Sri Lanka v West Indies	13 Mar 1992	1
Brisbane, Brisbane Cricket Ground	West Indies v England	23 Dec 1979	41
Canberra, Manuka Oval	South Africa v Zimbabwe	10 Mar 1992	1
Devonport, Devonport Oval	England v West Indies	3 Feb 1987	1
Hobart, Bellerive Oval	New Zealand v Sri Lanka	12 Jan 1988	14
Hobart, TCA Ground	Sri Lanka v West Indies	10 Jan 1985	1
Launceston, NTCA Ground	India v New Zealand	2 Feb 1986	1
Mackay, Harrup Park	India v Sri Lanka	28 Feb 1992	1
Melbourne, Melbourne Cricket Ground	Australia v England	5 Jan 1971	100
Perth, WACA Ground	New Zealand v India	9 Dec 1980	44
Sydney, Sydney Cricket Ground	Australia v England	13 Jan 1979	101

Bangladesh (2 grounds)

Ground	First match	Date	M
Chittagong, Chittagong Stadium	Bangladesh v India	27 Oct 1988	2
Dhaka, Bangabandhu National Stadium	Pakistan v Sri Lanka	27 Oct 1988	19

Canada (1 ground)

Ground	First match	Date	M
Toronto Cricket, Skating and Curling Club	India v Pakistan	16 Sept 1996	16

England (15 grounds)

Ground	First match	Date	M
Birmingham, Edgbaston	England v Australia	28 Aug 1972	23
Bristol, County Ground	New Zealand v Sri Lanka	13 Jun 1983	1
Chelmsford, County Ground	Australia v India	20 Jun 1983	1
Derby, County (Racecourse) Ground	New Zealand v Sri Lanka	18 Jun 1983	1
Leeds, Headingley	England v West Indies	5 Sep 1973	21
Leicester, Grace Road	India v Zimbabwe	11 Jun 1983	1
London, Kennington Oval	England v West Indies	7 Sep 1973	22
London, Lord's Cricket Ground	England v Australia	26 Aug 1972	23
Manchester, Old Trafford	England v Australia	24 Aug 1972	26
Nottingham, Trent Bridge	England v Pakistan	31 Aug 1974	18
Scarborough, North Marine Road	England v West Indies	26 Aug 1976	2
Southampton, County Ground	Australia v Zimbabwe	16 Jun 1983	1
Taunton, County Ground	England v Sri Lanka	11 Jun 1983	1
Tunbridge Wells, Nevill Ground	India v Zimbabwe	18 Jun 1983	1
Worcester, New Road	West Indies v Zimbabwe	13 Jun 1983	1

India (34 grounds)

Ground	First match	Date	M
Ahmedabad, Gujarat Motera Stadium	India v Australia	5 Oct 1986	6
Ahmedabad, Sardar Patel Stadium	India v England	25 Nov 1981	3
Amristar, Gandhi Sports Complex	India v Sri Lanka	12 Sep 1982	2

India -cont

Ground	First match	Date	M
Bangalore,Chinnaswamy Stadium	India v Sri Lanka	26 Sep 1982	10
Calcutta, Eden Gardens	India v Pakistan	18 Feb 1987	16
Chandigarh, Sector 16 Stadium	India v England	27 Jan 1985	4
Chennai, MA Chidambaram Stadium	India v Australia	9 Oct 1987	7
Cuttack, Barabatti Stadium	India v England	27 Jan 1982	9
Delhi, Feroz Shah Kotla	India v Sri Lanka	15 Sep 1982	10
Faridabad, Nahar Singh Stadium	India v West Indies	19 Jan 1988	4
Gauhati, Jawaharlal Nehru Stadium	India v West Indies	17 Dec 1983	8
Gwalior, Capt. Roop Singh Stadium	India v West Indies	22 Jan 1988	8
Hyderabad, Lal Bahadur Stadium	India v Pakistan	11 Sep 1983	11
Indore, Jawaharlal Nehru Stadium	India v West Indies	1 Dec 1983	8
Jaipur, Sawai Mansingh Stadium	India v Pakistan	2 Oct 1983	7
Jamshedpur, Keenan Stadium	India v West Indies	7 Dec 1983	5
Jullundur, Burlton Park	India v England	20 Dec 1981	3
Kanpur, Green Park	India v Sri Lanka	24 Dec 1986	7
Kochi, Jawaharlal Nehru Stadium	India v Australia	1 Apr 1998	1
Lucknow, KD 'Babu' Singh Stadium	Pakistan v Sri Lanka	27 Oct 1989	1
Margao, Fatorda Stadium	Australia v Sri Lanka	25 Oct 1989	4
Mohali, Punjab CA Stadium	India v South Africa	22 Nov 1993	6
Mumbai, Brabourne Stadium	Australia v Pakistan	23 Oct 1989	3
Mumbai, Wankhede Stadium	India v Sri Lanka	17 Jan 1987	11
Nagpur, Vidarbha CA Ground	India v England	23 Jan 1985	8
New Delhi, Jawaharlal Nehru Stadium	India v Australia	28 Sep 1984	2
Patna, Moin-ul-Haq Stadium	Sri Lanka v Zimbabwe	15 Nov 1993	3
Pune, Jawaharlal Nehru Stadium	India v England	5 Dec 1984	7
Rajkot, Municipal Ground	India v Australia	7 Oct 1986	5
Srinigar, Sher-i-Kashmir Stadium	India v West Indies	13 Oct 1983	2
Trivandrum, University Stadium	India v Australia	1 Oct 1984	2
Vadodara, IPCL Sports Complex	India v New Zealand	28 Oct 1984	3
Vadodara, Moti Bagh Stadium	India v West Indies	9 Nov 1983	3
Visag, Indira Priyadarshani Stadium	India v New Zealand	10 Dec 1988	3

Kenya (3 grounds)

Ground	First match	Date	M
Nairobi, Aga Khan Sports Club	Kenya v Pakistan	2 Oct 1996	4
Nairobi, Gymkhana Club Ground	Kenya v Sri Lanka	28 Sept 1996	10
Nairobi, Nairobi Sports Club	South Africa v Sri Lanka	1 Oct 1996	1

New Zealand (8 grounds)

Ground	First match	Date	M
Auckland, Eden Park	New Zealand v India	22 Feb 1976	36
Christchurch, Jade Stadium	New Zealand v Pakisitan	11 Feb 1973	29
Dunedin, Carisbrook	New Zealand v Australia	30 Mar 1974	16
Hamilton, Seddon Park	New Zealand v India	15 Feb 1981	10
Napier, McLean Park	New Zealand v Sri Lanka	19 Mar 1983	13
New Plymouth, Pukekura Park	Sri Lanka v Zimbabwe	23 Feb 1992	1
Taupo, Owen Delaney Park	New Zealand v India	9 Jan 1999	1
Wellington, Basin Reserve	New Zealand v England	9 Mar 1975	24

Pakistan (15 grounds)

Ground	First match	Date	M
Faisalabad, Iqbal Stadium	Pakistan v New Zealand	23 Nov 1984	9
Gujranwala, Municipal Stadium	Pakistan v India	3 Dec 1982	10
Hyderabad, Niaz Stadium	Pakistan v Australia	20 Sep 1982	6
Karachi, National Stadium	Pakistan v West Indies	21 Nov 1980	23
Lahore, Gaddafi Stadium	Pakistan v England	13 Jan 1978	33
Multan, Ibn-e-Qasim Stadium	Pakistan v India	17 Dec 1982	6
Peshawar, Arbab Niaz Stadium	Pakistan v New Zealand	12 Nov 1984	12
Quetta, Ayub National Stadium	Pakistan v India	1 Oct 1978	2
Quetta, Bughti Stadium	Pakistan v Zimbabwe	30 Oct 1996	1
Rawalpindi, Pindi Club Ground	Pakistan v West Indies	4 Dec 1985	2
Rawalpindi, Rawalpindi Cricket Stadium	Pakistan v Sri Lanka	19 Jan 1992	9
Sahiwal, Zafar Ali Stadium	Pakistan v England	23 Dec 1977	2
Sargodha, Sargodha Stadium	Pakistan v Sri Lanka	10 Jan 1993	1
Sialkot, Jinnah Stadium	Pakistan v New Zealand	16 Oct 1976	9
Sheikupura, Sheikupura Stadium	Pakistan v Zimbabwe	22 Nov 1998	1

Singapore (1 ground)

Ground	First match	Date	M
Singapore, Padang Ground	Sri Lanka v Pakistan	1/2 Apr 1996	5

South Africa (10 grounds)

Ground	First match	Date	M
Benoni, Willowmoore Park	India v Zimbabwe	9 Feb 1997	2
Bloemfontein, Springbok Park	South Africa v India	15 Dec 1992	10
Cape Town, Newlands	South Africa v India	7 Dec 1992	11
Centurion, Centurion Park	South Africa v India	11 Dec 1992	11
Durban, Kingsmead	South Africa v India	17 Dec 1992	12
East London, Buffalo Park	South Africa v India	19 Dec 1992	10
Johannesburg, The Wanderers	South Africa v India	13 Dec 1992	11
Kimberley, Kimberley Country Club	Pakistan v Sri Lanka	7 Apr 1998	1
Paarl, Boland Park	India v Zimbabwe	27 Jan 1997	2
Port Elizabeth, St George's Park	South Africa v India	9 Dec 1992	11

Sri Lanka (5 grounds)

Ground	First match	Date	M
Colombo, R Premadasa Stadium	Sri Lanka v New Zealand	5 Apr 1986	32
Colombo, P Saravanamuttu Stadium	Sri Lanka v Australia	13 Apr 1983	11
Colombo, Sinhalese Sports Club	Sri Lanka v England	13 Feb 1982	29
Kandy, Asgiriya Stadium	Sri Lanka v Pakistan	2 Mar 1986	4
Tyronne Fernanado Stadium, Moratuwa	Sri Lanka v New Zealand	31 Mar 1984	6

United Arab Emirates (1 ground)

Ground	First match	Date	M
Sharjah Cricket Association Stadium	Pakistan v Sri Lanka	6 Apr 1994	139

Wales (1 ground)

Ground	First match	Date	M
St Helen's, Swansea	England v New Zealand	18 Jul 1973	2

West Indies (9 grounds)

Ground	First match	Date	M
Berbice, Guyana, Albion Sports Complex	West Indies v Pakistan	16 Mar 1977	5
Bridgetown, Barbados, Kensington Oval	West Indies v New Zealand	23 Apr 1985	10
Castries, St Lucia, Mindoo Phillip Park	West Indies v Australia	12 Apr 1978	2

Ground	First match	Date	M
Georgetown, Guyana, Bourda	West Indies v Pakistan	30 Mar 1988	8
Kingston, Jamaica, Sabina Park	West Indies v Australia	26 Apr 1984	9
Kingstown, St Vincent, Arnos Vale	West Indies v England	4 Feb 1981	8
Port-of-Spain, Trinidad, Queen's Park Oval	West Indies v India	9 Mar 1983	29
St George's, Grenada, Queen's Park	West Indies v India	7 Apr 1983	1
St John's, Antigua, Recreation Ground	West Indies v Australia	22 Feb 1978	4

Zimbabwe (3 grounds)

Ground	First match	Date	M
Bulawayo, Bulawayo Athletic Club	Zimbabwe v New Zealand	31 Oct 1992	1
Bulawayo, Queen's Club	Zimbabwe v England	15 Dec 1996	5
Harare Sports Club, Harare	Zimbabwe v India	25 Oct 1992	18

MOST MATCHES

Ground	M
Sharjah, Sharjah Cricket Association Stadium	139
Sydney, Sydney Cricket Ground	101
Melbourne, Melbourne Cricket Ground	100
Adelaide, Adelaide Oval	46
Perth, WACA Ground	44
Brisbane, Brisbane Cricket Ground	41
Auckland, Eden Park	36
Lahore, Gaddafi Stadium	33
Colombo, R Premadasa Stadium	32
Christchurch, Jade Stadium	29
Colombo, Sinhalese Sports Club	29
Port-of-Spain, Trinidad, Queen's Park Oval	29
Manchester, Old Trafford	26

SUMMARY OF LIMITED-OVERS INTERNATIONALS UNDER LIGHTS AT EACH GROUND

Ground	First Match Under Lights	Date	M
Sydney, Sydney Cricket Ground	Australia v West Indies	27 Nov 1979	95
Melbourne, Melbourne Cricket Ground	Australia v England	17 Feb 1985	58
Perth, WACA Ground	Australia v New Zealand	3 Jan 1988	16
Brisbane, Brisbane Cricket Ground	Sri Lanka v West Indies	5 Jan 1996	7
Cape Town, Newlands	South Africa v England	9 Jan 1996	3
Bloemfontein, Springbok Park	South Africa v England	11 Jan 1996	2
Durban, Kingsmead	South Africa v England	17 Jan 1996	4
East London, Buffalo Park	South Africa v England	19 Jan 1996	2
Napier, McLean Park	New Zealand v Zimbabwe	3 Feb 1996	5
Hyderabad (I), Lal Bahadur Stadium	West Indies v Zimbabwe	16 Feb 1996	4
Gwalior, Capt. Roop Singh Stadium	India v West Indies	21 Feb 1996	3
Mumbai, Wankhede Stadium	India v Australia	27 Feb 1996	5
Bangalore, Chinnaswamy Stadium	India v Pakistan	9 Mar 1996	4
Chennai, MA Chidambaram Stadium	Australia v New Zealand	11 Mar 1996	3
Calcutta, Eden Gardens	India v Sri Lanka	13 Mar 1996	3
Mohali, Punjab CA Stadium	Australia v West Indies	14 Mar 1996	5
Lahore, Gaddafi Stadium	Australia v Sri Lanka	17 Mar 1996	9
Colombo, R Premadasa Stadium	Australia v Zimbabwe	26 Aug 1996	12
Johannesburg, The Wanderers	South Africa v Zimbabwe	31 Jan 1997	3
Centurion, Centurion Park	India v Zimbabwe	7 Feb 1997	2
Christchurch, Jade Stadium	New Zealand v England	20 Feb 1997	5

Ground	First Match Under Lights	Date	M
Port Elizabeth, St George's Park	South Africa v Australia	31 Mar 1997	1
Adelaide, Adelaide Oval	South Africa v NewZealand	6 Dec 1997	5
Sharjah, Sharjah Cricket Association Ground	England v India	11 Dec 1997	18
Dhaka, Bangabandhu National Stadium	India v Pakistan	18 Jan 1998	9
Paarl, Boland Park	Pakistan v Sri Lanka	9 April 1998	1
Taupo, Owen Delaney Park	New Zealand v India	9 Jan 1999	1

Ross Dundas Cricket Statistics

SUMMARY OF LIMITED-OVERS INTERNATIONALS UNDER LIGHTS FOR EACH COUNTRY

Country	M	Won	Lost	NR	Tied	Win%
Australia	155	98	54	3	-	64
Bangladesh	4	1	3	-	-	25
England	51	26	24	-	1	51
India	66	30	33	2	1	47
Kenya	5	2	3	-	-	40
New Zealand	63	18	40	4	1	31
Pakistan	47	18	29	-	-	38
Sri Lanka	50	22	28	-	-	44
South Africa	45	28	16	1	-	64
West Indies	70	29	38	2	1	43
Zimbabwe	14	5	9	-	-	36
Total	**285**	**277**	**277**	**12**	**4**	

Ross Dundas Cricket Statistics

Individual Ground Records

AUSTRALIA

Adelaide Oval (46 matches)

Summary of Matches

Team	First Match	Played	Won	Lost	NR	Tie
Australia	20 Dec 1975 v West Indies	26	18	8	-	-
England	16 Jan 1980 v West Indies	9	2	6	1	-
India	23 Dec 1980 v New Zealand	6	3	3	-	-
New Zealand	23 Nov 1980 v Australia	12	7	5	-	-
Pakistan	5 Dec 1981 v West Indies	12	3	8	1	-
South Africa	15 Mar 1992 v India	2	1	1	-	-
Sri Lanka	26 Jan 1985 v West Indies	10	2	8	-	-
West Indies	20 Dec 1975 v Australia	15	9	6	-	-

Highest Innings Total

Runs	Team	Batted 1st	Batted 2nd	Date
323	Australia	Aus 2-323	SL 91	28 Jan 1985
315	Pakistan	Pak 3-315	SL 8-288	17 Feb 1990
303	Sri Lanka	Eng 3-302	SL 9-303	23 Jan 1999

Lowest Completed Innings Total

Runs	Team	Batted 1st	Batted 2nd	Date
70	Australia	NZ 7-276	Aus 70	27 Jan 1986
74	Pakistan	Pak 74	Eng 1-24	1 Mar 1992
91	Sri Lanka	Aus 2-323	SL 91	28 Jan 1985

Leading Run-scorers

Player	M	I	NO	Runs	HS	50	100	Ave.	Stk Rt
D.M. Jones, Australia	12	12	7	563	99*	5	-	112.60	70.46
A.R. Border, Australia	19	16	1	518	118*	3	1	34.53	78.72
G.R. Marsh, Australia	9	9	1	358	94	3	-	44.75	57.65

Highest Individual Innings

Runs	Player	Versus	Date
126*	G.A. Hick, England	Sri Lanka	23 Jan 1999
126	Saeed Anwar, Pakistan	Sri Lanka	17 Feb 1990
122	D.C. Boon, Australia	Sri Lanka	10 Jan 1988

Highest Partnerships

Wkt	Runs	Batsmen	Versus	Date
3rd	224*	A.R. Border 118*, D.M. Jones 99*, Australia	Sri Lanka	28 Jan 1985
1st	202	Saeed Anwar 126, Ramiz Raja 107*, Pakistan	Sri Lanka	17 Feb 1990
1st	169	C.G. Greenidge 70, DL Haynes 111, West Indies	Pakistan	10 Dec 1988

Leading Wicket-takers

Player	M	Wkts	Best	4wi	5wi	Ave.	Stk Rt
C.J. McDermott, Australia	10	18	3-20	-	-	19.17	29.89
G.D. McGrath, Australia	6	16	5-40	1	1	13.94	19.81
M.D. Marshall, West Indies	8	15	4-34	1	-	17.87	30.80

Best Bowling

Total	Player	Versus	Date
5-16	C.G. Rackemann, Australia	Pakistan	30 Jan 1984
5-22	A.M.E. Roberts, West Indies	England	16 Jan 1980
5-29	Saqlain Mushtaq, Pakistan	Australia	15 Dec 1996

Brisbane, Brisbane Cricket Ground (Woolloongabba) (41 matches)

Summary of Matches

Team	First Match	Played	Won	Lost	NR	Tie
Australia	17 Jan 1982 v West Indies	18	9	8	1	-
England	23 Dec 1979 v West Indies	10	5	5	-	-
India	21 Dec 1980 v New Zealand	6	1	5	-	-
New Zealand	21 Dec 1980 v India	9	5	4	-	-
Pakistan	16 Jan 1982 v West Indies	10	2	7	1	-
South Africa	8 Mar 1992 v Pakistan	5	3	2	-	-
Sri Lanka	12 Jan 1985 v West Indies	5	-	5	-	-
West Indies	23 Dec 1979 v England	17	15	2	-	-
Zimbabwe	29 Feb 1992 v West Indies	2	-	2	-	-

Highest Innings Total

Runs	Team	Batted 1st	Batted 2nd	Date
300	Australia	Aus 5-300	Pak 233	11 Feb 1990
300	South Africa	SAF 6-300	NZ 9-298	9 Jan 1998
298	New Zealand	SAF 6-300	NZ 9-298	9 Jan 1998

Lowest Completed Innings Total

Runs	Team	Batted 1st	Batted 2nd	Date
71	Pakistan	Pak 71	WI 1-72	9 Jan 1993
102	Sri Lanka	SL 102	WI 3-104	5 Jan 1996
154	West Indies	WI 154	Eng 4-156	17 Jan 1987

Leading Run-scorers

Player	M	I	NO	Runs	HS	50	100	Ave.	Stk Rt
D.M. Jones, Australia	9	9	-	513	145	2	2	57.00	86.51
R.B. Richardson, WI	12	12	2	375	81	4	-	37.50	62.60
D.L. Haynes, West Indies	11	11	1	362	53	2	-	36.20	52.62
C.L. Hooper, West Indies	10	9	4	362	110*	3	1	72.40	79.91

Highest Individual Innings

Runs	Player	Versus	Date
158	D.I. Gower, England	New Zealand	15 Jan 1983
145	D.M. Jones, Australia	England	16 Dec 1990
111	C.W.J. Athey, England	Australia	18 Jan 1987

Highest Partnerships

Wkt	Runs	Batsmen	Versus	Date
2nd	185	G.R. Marsh 82, D.M. Jones 145, Australia	England	16 Dec 1990
2nd	178	G.R. Marsh 93, D.M. Jones 101, Australia	England	18 Jan 1987
1st	154	M.A. Taylor 66, T.M. Moody 89, Australia	Pakistan	11 Feb 1990

Ross Dundas Cricket Statistics

Leading Wicket-takers

Player	M	Wkts	Best	4wi	5wi	Ave.	Stk Rt
I.R. Bishop, West Indies	6	15	5-25	1	1	14.27	22.20
M.A. Holding, West Indies	7	13	3-38	-	-	19.46	29.54
C.E.L. Ambrose, West Indies	8	12	3-13	-	-	20.75	37.00
S.R. Waugh, Australia	11	12	3-31	-	-	27.42	37.00

Best Bowling

Total	Player	Versus	Date
5-25	I.R. Bishop, West Indies	Pakistan	9 Jan 1993
5-31	A.C. Cummins, West Indies	India	11 Jan 1992
4-18	A.D. Mullally, England	Australia	10 Jan 1999

Hobart, Bellerive Oval (14 matches)

Summary of Matches

Team	First Match	Played	Won	Lost	NR	Tie
Australia	18 Dec 1990 v New Zealand	7	3	3	-	1
India	10 Dec 1991 v Australia	1	-	1	-	-
New Zealand	12 Jan 1988 v Sri Lanka	4	2	2	-	-
Pakistan	17 Dec 1988 v West Indies	5	3	1	-	1
South Africa	18 Dec 1993 v New Zealand	2	1	1	-	-
Sri Lanka	12 Jan 1988 v New Zealand	4	2	2	-	-
West Indies	17 Dec 1988 v Pakistan	2	2	-	-	-
Zimbabwe	27 Feb 1992 v Australia	3	-	3	-	-

Highest Innings Total

Runs	Team	Batted 1st	Batted 2nd	Date
265	Australia	Aus 6-265	Zim 137	14 Mar 1992
254	Pakistan	Pak 4-254	Zim 7-201	27 Feb 1992
254	Australia	Aus 3-254	Zim 8-170	8 Dec 1994

Lowest Completed Innings Total

Runs	Team	Batted 1st	Batted 2nd	Date
120	Australia	Pak 149	Aus 120	7 Jan 1997
124	Sri Lanka	WI 194	SL 124	3 Jan 1996
137	Zimbabwe	Aus 6-265	Zim 137	14 Mar 1992

Leading Run-scorers

Player	M	I	NO	Runs	HS	50	100	Ave.	Stk Rt
D.C. Boon, Australia	5	5	2	264	102*	1	1	88.00	66.00
Javed Miandad, Pakistan	4	4	-	207	89	2	-	51.75	66.35
M.E. Waugh, Australia	6	6	1	188	66*	2	-	37.60	76.11

Highest Individual Innings

Runs	Player	Versus	Date
116*	Ramiz Raja, Pakistan	Sri Lanka	15 Feb 1990
114	Aamir Sohail, Pakistan	Zimbabwe	27 Feb 1992
110	S.G. Law, Australia	Zimbabwe	8 Dec 1994

Highest Partnerships

Wkt	Runs	Batsmen	Versus	Date
3rd	159	S.G. Law 110, D.C. Boon 98*, Australia	Zimbabwe	8 Dec 1994
2nd	145	D.L. Haynes 101, P.J.L. Dujon 63, West Indies	Pakistan	17 Dec 1988
3rd	145	Aamir Sohail 114, Javed Miandad 89, Pakistan	Zimbabwe	27 Feb 1992

Leading Wicket-takers

Player	M	Wkts	Best	4wi	5wi	Ave.	Stk Rt
C.J. McDermott, Australia	3	8	4-42	1	-	10.88	21.00
Wasim Akram, Pakistan	5	8	3-13	-	-	15.75	34.50
W.P.U.J.C. Vaas, Sri Lanka	2	6	3-21	-	-	8.00	19.00
S.K. Warne, Australia	3	6	3-45	-	-	17.17	26.33

Best Bowling

Total	Player	Versus	Date
5-42	O.D. Gibson, West Indies	Sri Lanka	3 Jan 1996
4-38	C.R. Matthews, South Africa	New Zealand	18 Dec 1993
4-39	Waqar Younis, Pakistan	Sri Lanka	15 Feb 1990

Melbourne, Melbourne Cricket Ground (100 matches)

Summary of Matches

Team	First Match	Played	Won	Lost	NR	Tie
Australia	5 Jan 1971 v England	80	43	34	2	1
England	5 Jan 1971 v Australia	23	8	15	-	-
India	6 Dec 1980 v Australia	12	7	5	-	-
New Zealand	7 Dec 1980 v Australia	19	6	12	1	-
Pakistan	21 Nov 1981 v West Indies	18	8	10	-	-
South Africa	12 Mar 1992 v England	5	4	1	-	-
Sri Lanka	19 Jan 1985 v Australia	11	3	8	-	-
West Indies	9 Dec 1979 v Australia	32	18	12	1	1

Highest Innings Total

Runs	Team	Batted 1st	Batted 2nd	Date
310	Australia	Aus 8-310	SL 267	7 Feb 1999
302	Australia	Aus 8-302	NZ 153	13 Feb 1983
273	West Indies	Aus 3-271	WI 6-273	10 Feb 1985

Lowest Completed Innings Total

Runs	Team	Batted 1st	Batted 2nd	Date
94	England	Eng 94	Aus 4-95	7 Feb 1979
101	Australia	Aus 101	Eng 3-102	24 Jan 1979
103	West Indies	Pak 165	WI 103	20 Jan 1997

Leading Run-scorers

Player	M	I	NO	Runs	HS	50	100	Ave.	Stk Rt
A.R. Border, Australia	60	55	8	1516	84*	12	-	32.26	68.85
D.M. Jones, Australia	35	34	6	1287	93	12	-	45.96	67.14
D.C. Boon, Australia	33	31	1	995	100	5	1	33.17	58.98

Highest Individual Innings

Runs	Player	Versus	Date
154	A.C. Gilchrist, Australia	Sri Lanka	7 Feb 1999
153*	I.V.A. Richards, West Indies	Australia	9 Dec 1979
125*	G.R. Marsh, Australia	Pakistan	10 Jan 1989

Highest Partnerships

Wkt	Runs	Batsmen	Versus	Date
1st	221*	B.C. Lara 88[†], D.L. Haynes 93*, R.B Richardson 20, West Indies	Pakistan	23 Feb 1992
2nd	205	D.L. Haynes 80, I.V.A. Richards 153*, West Indies	Australia	9 Dec 1979
1st	182	C.G. Greenidge 103, D.L. Haynes 84, West Indies	Pakistan	21 Nov 1981

[†]B.C. Lara retired hurt

Leading Wicket-takers

Player	M	Wkts	Best	4wi	5wi	Ave.	Stk Rt
C.J. McDermott, Australia	29	43	4-38	1	-	25.51	37.21
S.K. Warne, Australia	18	31	4-19	1	-	21.42	33.13
P.L. Taylor, Australia	21	30	4-38	1	-	23.30	37.00

Best Bowling

Total	Player	Versus	Date
5-17	C.E.L. Ambrose, West Indies	Australia	15 Dec 1988
5-21	Wasim Akram, Pakistan	Australia	24 Feb 1985
5-24	M.E. Waugh, Australia	West Indies	15 Dec 1992
5-24	L. Klusener, South Africa	Australia	9 Dec 1997

Perth, WACA Ground (44 matches)

Summary of Matches

Team	First Match	Played	Won	Lost	NR	Tie
Australia	20 Dec 1981 v West Indies	22	10	12	-	-
England	5 Feb 1983 v New Zealand	9	7	2	-	-
India	9 Dec 1980 v New Zealand	5	2	2	-	1
New Zealand	9 Dec 1980 v India	9	3	6	-	-
Pakistan	19 Dec 1981 v West Indies	13	6	7	-	-
South Africa	14 Jan 1994 v New Zealand	4	4	-	-	-
Sri Lanka	2 Feb 1985 v West Indies	10	2	8	-	-
West Indies	19 Dec 1981 v Pakistan	15	9	5	-	1
Zimbabwe	2 Dec 1994 v Australia	1	-	1	-	-

Highest Innings Total

Runs	Team	Batted 1st	Batted 2nd	Date
309	West Indies	WI 6-309	SL 6-227	2 Feb 1985
274	Pakistan	Aus 6-273	Pak 9-274	2 Jan 1987
274	Australia	Aus 7-274	SL 229	31 Jan 1999

Lowest Completed Innings Total

Runs	Team	Batted 1st	Batted 2nd	Date
91	Australia	WI 8-255	Aus 91	4 Jan 1987
99	Sri Lanka	Eng 7-227	SL 99	29 Jan 1999
101	Australia	Ind 7-208	Aus 101	8 Dec 1991

Leading Run-scorers

Player	M	I	NO	Runs	HS	50	100	Ave.	Stk Rt
D.M. Jones, Australia	14	12	1	545	121	3	2	49.55	76.22
Javed Miandad, Pakistan	12	12	3	542	77*	6	-	60.22	63.10
D.L. Haynes, West Indies	12	12	3	400	82*	4	-	44.44	55.56

Highest Individual Innings

Runs	Player	Versus	Date
130	M.E. Waugh, Australia	Sri Lanka	12 Jan 1996
121	D.M. Jones, Australia	Pakistan	2 Jan 1987
111	J.H. Kallis, South Africa	New Zealand	16 Jan 1998

Highest Partnerships

Wkt	Runs	Batsmen	Versus	Date
1st	189	M.A. Taylor 85, M.E. Waugh 130, Australia	Sri Lanka	12 Jan 1996
4th	173	D.M. Jones 121, S.R. Waugh 82, Australia	Pakistan	2 Jan 1987
2nd	157*	S.B. Smith 73*, W.B. Phillips 75*, Australia	Sri Lanka	3 Feb 1985

Leading Wicket-takers

Player	M	Wkts	Best	4wi	5wi	Ave.	Stk Rt
Wasim Akram, Pakistan	11	23	4-25	2	-	15.87	26.48
S.R. Waugh, Australia	16	22	4-48	1	-	24.00	32.68
R.J. Hadlee, New Zealand	6	16	5-32	-	1	8.75	18.44

Best Bowling

Total	Player	Versus	Date
5-15	R.J. Shastri, India	Australia	8 Dec 1991
5-21	A.C. Dodemaide, Australia	Sri Lanka	2 Jan 1988
5-27	I.R. Bishop, West Indies	Pakistan	1 Jan 1989

Sydney, Sydney Cricket Ground (101 matches)

Summary of Matches

Team	First Match	Played	Won	Lost	NR	Tie
Australia	13 Jan 1979 v England	82	52	28	2	-
England	13 Jan 1979 v Australia	22	12	9	1	-
India	18 Dec 1980 v Australia	10	3	7	-	-
New Zealand	25 Nov 1980 v Australia	22	6	14	2	-
Pakistan	17 Dec 1981 v Australia	14	6	8	-	-
South Africa	26 Feb 1992 v Australia	8	2	6	-	-
Sri Lanka	8 Jan 1985 v Australia	8	1	7	-	-
West Indies	27 Nov 1979 v Australia	34	15	18	1	-
Zimbabwe	15 Dec 1994 v England	1	1	-	-	-

Highest Innings Total

Runs	Team	Batted 1st	Batted 2nd	Date
292	Australia	Aus 6-292	Ind 4-192	21 Jan 1986
289	Australia	Aus 3-289	NZ 195	25 Nov 1980
282	England	Eng 4-282	Aus 6-275	17 Jan 1999

Lowest Completed Innings Total

Runs	Team	Batted 1st	Batted 2nd	Date
63	India	Ind 63	Aus 1-64	8 Jan 1981
69	South Africa	Aus 9-172	SAF 69	14 Dec 1993
81	Pakistan	WI 9-214	Pak 81	17 Dec 1992

Leading Run-scorers

Player	M	I	NO	Runs	HS	50	100	Ave.	Stk Rt
A.R. Border, Australia	65	62	8	1561	127*	7	2	28.91	68.56
M.E Waugh, Australia	30	29	1	1051	107	8	1	37.54	77.11
D.C. Boon, Australia	30	30	3	990	83	10	-	36.67	63.34

Runs	Player	Versus	Date
138*	G.S. Chappell, Australia	New Zealand	25 Nov 1980
131	A.C. Gilchrist, Australia	Sri Lanka	13 Jan 1999
127*	A.R. Border, Australia	West Indies	6 Feb 1985

Highest Partnerships

Wkt	Runs	Batsmen	Versus	Date
3rd	190*	C.J. Tavare 83*, A.J. Lamb 108*, England	New Zealand	20 Jan 1983
3rd	190	G.A. Hick 108, N. Hussain 93, England	Australia	17 Jan 1999
3rd	175	D.M. Jones 79, M.E. Waugh 107, Australia	South Africa	23 Jan 1994

Leading Wicket-takers

Player	M	Wkts	Best	4wi	5wi	Ave.	Stk Rt
D.K. Lillee, Australia	21	42	4-12	4	-	14.10	26.19
C.J. McDermott, Australia	27	36	3-30	-	-	23.50	37.89
G.S. Chappell, Australia	25	32	5-15	-	1	23.16	36.13
L.S. Pascoe, Australia	15	32	5-30	1	1	17.75	25.72
S.K. Warne, Australia	18	32	5-33	1	1	20.63	29.78

Best Bowling

Total	Player	Versus	Date
5-15	G.S. Chappell, Australia	India	8 Jan 1981
5-26	R.J. Hadlee, New Zealand	Australia	29 Jan 1981
5-26	M.A. Holding, West Indies	Australia	12 Feb 1985

Australia - other grounds

Albury, Lavington Sports Ground (1 match)

Match	Batted 1st	Batted 2nd	Result	Date
England v Zimbabwe	Zim 134	Eng 125	Zim by 9 runs	18 Mar 1992

Ballarat, Eastern Oval (1 match)

Match	Batted 1st	Batted 2nd	Result	Date
England v Sri Lanka	Eng 6-280	SL 174	Eng by 106 runs	9 Mar 1992

Berri, Berri Oval (1 match)

Match	Batted 1st	Batted 2nd	Result	Date
Sri Lanka v West Indies	WI 8-268	SL 9-177	WI by 91 runs	13 Mar 1992

Canberra, Manuka Oval (1 match)

Match	Batted 1st	Batted 2nd	Result	Date
South Africa v Zimbabwe	Zim 163	SAF 3-164	SAF by 7 wkts	10 Mar 1992

Devonport, Devonport Oval (1 match)

Match	Batted 1st	Batted 2nd	Result	Date
England v West Indies	Eng 9-177	WI 148	Eng by 29 runs	3 Feb 1987

Hobart, Tasmanian Cricket Association Ground (1 match)

Match	Batted 1st	Batted 2nd	Result	Date
Sri Lanka v West Indies	SL 7-197	WI 2-198	WI by 8 wkts	10 Jan 1985

Launceston, North Tasmania Cricket Association Ground (1 match)

Match	Batted 1st	Batted 2nd	Result	Date
India v New Zealand	Ind 9-202	NZ 9-168	Ind by 21 runs†	2 Feb 1986

†revised target

Mackay, Harrup Park (1 match)

Match	Batted 1st	Batted 2nd	Result	Date
India v Sri Lanka	Ind 0-1	SL DNB	No result	28 Feb 1992

Bangladesh - other grounds

Chittagong, Chittagong Stadium (2 matches)

Match	Batted 1st	Batted 2nd	Result	Date
Bangladesh v India	Ban 8-99	Ind 1-100	Ind by 9 wkts	27 Oct 1988
Bangladesh v Pakistan	Pak 3-284	Ban 6-111	Pak by 173 runs	29 Oct 1988

BANGLADESH

Dhaka, Bangabandhu National Stadium (19 matches)

Summary of Matches

Team	First Match	Played	Won	Lost	NR	Tie
Australia	28 Oct 1998 v India	1	-	1	-	-
Bangladesh	2 Nov 1988 v Sri Lanka	3	-	3	-	-
England	25 Oct 1998 v South Africa	1	-	1	-	-
India	29 Oct 1988 v Sri Lanka	10	7	3	-	-
New Zealand	24 Oct 1998 v Zimbabwe	2	1	1	-	-
Pakistan	27 Oct 1988 v Sri Lanka	8	2	6	-	-
South Africa	25 Oct 1998 v England	3	3	-	-	-
Sri Lanka	27 Oct 1988 v Pakistan	6	4	2	-	-
West Indies	29 Oct 1998 v Pakistan	3	2	1	-	-
Zimbabwe	24 Oct 1998 v England	1	-	1	-	-

Highest Innings Total

Runs	Team	Batted 1st	Batted 2nd	Date
316	India	Pak 5-314	Ind 7-316	18 Jan 1998
314	Pakistan	Pak 5-314	Ind 7-316	18 Jan 1998
307	India	Ind 8-307	Aus 263	28 Oct 1998

Lowest Completed Innings Total

Runs	Team	Batted 1st	Batted 2nd	Date
132	Sri Lanka	SAF 7-240	SL 132	30 Oct 1998
134	Bangladesh	Ban 134	Pak 1-136	12 Jan 1998
142	Pakistan	Pak 142	Ind 6-143	31 Oct 1988

Leading Run-scorers

Player	M	I	NO	Runs	HS	50	100	Ave.	Stk Rt
S.R. Tendulkar	7	7	-	407	141	3	1	58.14	109.41
M.A. Azharuddin, India	10	10	1	334	100	2	1	37.11	75.40
Ijaz Ahmed, Pakistan	8	7	1	328	117	2	1	54.67	85.65

Highest Individual Innings

Runs	Player	Versus	Date
141	S.R. Tendulkar, India	Australia	28 Oct 1998
140	Saeed Anwar, Pakistan	India	18 Jan 1998
124	S.C. Ganguly, India	Pakistan	18 Jan 1998

Highest Partnerships

Wkt	Runs	Batsmen	Versus	Date
3rd	230	Saeed Anwar 140, Ijaz Ahmed 117, Pakistan	India	18 Jan 1998
2nd	179	S.C. Ganguly 124, R.R. Singh 82, India	Pakistan	18 Jan 1998
1st	159	S.C. Ganguly 68, S.R. Tendulkar 95, India	Pakistan	14 Jan 1998

Leading Wicket-takers

Player	M	Wkts	Best	4wi	5wi	Ave.	Stk Rt
J. Srinath, India	7	14	5-23	-	1	21.00	25.71
Saqlain Mushtaq, Pakistan	6	13	4-41	1	-	21.00	24.31
S.R. Tendulkar, India	7	11	4-38	1	-	19.55	23.27

Best Bowling

Total	Player	Versus	Date
5-21	Arshad Ayub, India	Pakistan	31 Oct 1988
5-33	J. Srinath, India	Bangladesh	10 Jan 1998
5-30	J.H. Kallis, South Africa	West Indies	1 Nov 1998

CANADA

Toronto, Toronto Cricket, Skating and Curling Club (16 matches)

Summary of Matches

Team	First Match	Played	Won	Lost	NR	Tie
India	16 Sep 1996 v Pakistan	16	7	8	1	-
Pakistan	16 Sep 1996 v India	16	8	7	1	-

Highest Innings Total

Runs	Team	Batted 1st	Batted 2nd	Date
316	Pakistan	Pak 6-316	Ind 182	19 Sep 1998
266	Pakistan	Ind 6-264	Pak 8-266	17 Sep 1996
264	India	Ind 6-264	Pak 8-266	17 Sep 1996

Lowest Completed Innings Total

Runs	Team	Batted 1st	Batted 2nd	Date
116	Pakistan	Pak 116	Ind 3-117	14 Sep 1997
136	Pakistan	Ind 191	Pak 136	18 Sep 1996
148	Pakistan	Ind 6-182	Pak 148	18 Sep 1997

Leading Run-scorers

Player	M	I	NO	Runs	HS	50	100	Ave.	Stk Rt
M.A. Azharuddin, India	16	15	2	566	101	4	1	43.54	70.84
Saeed Anwar, Pakistan	15	15	1	550	83	4	-	39.29	83.21
Salim Malik, Pakistan	16	16	1	422	70*	2	-	28.13	71.04

Highest Individual Innings

Runs	Player	Versus	Date
109	Shahid Afridi, Pakistan	India	19 Sep 1998
101	M.A. Azharuddin, India	Pakistan	20 Sep 1998
97*	Aamir Sohail, Pakistan	India	20 Sep 1998

Highest Partnerships

Wkt	Runs	Batsmen	Versus	Date
3rd	161	R. Dravid 90, M.A. Azharuddin 88, India	Pakistan	17 Sep 1996
2nd	141	Shahid Afridi 109, Aamir Sohail 78, Pakistan	India	19 Sep 1998
3rd	121	S.R. Tendulkar 77, M.A. Azharuddin 101, India	Pakistan	20 Sep 1998

Leading Wicket-takers

Player	M	Wkts	Best	4wi	5wi	Ave.	Stk Rt
Saqlain Mushtaq, Pakistan	14	25	5-45	1	1	18.64	26.36
S.C. Ganguly, India	13	19	5-16	-	1	17.79	25.21
J. Srinath, India	10	18	3-23	-	-	24.00	31.22

Best Bowling

Total	Player	Versus	Date
5-16	S.C. Ganguly, India	Pakistan	18 Sep 1997
5-36	Mushtaq Ahmed, Pakistan	India	23 Sep 1996
5-45	Saqlain Mushtaq, Pakistan	India	13 Sep 1997

ENGLAND

Birmingham, Edgbaston (23 matches)

Summary of Matches

Team	First Match	Played	Won	Lost	NR	Tie
Australia	28 Aug 1972 v England	7	4	3	-	-
Canada	16 Jun 1979 v Australia	1	-	1	-	-
East Africa	7 Jun 1975 v New Zealand	2	-	2	-	-
England	28 Aug 1972 v Australia	17	10	7	-	-
India	9 Jun 1979 v West Indies	1	-	1	-	-
New Zealand	7 Jun 1975 v East Africa	4	3	1	-	-
Pakistan	3 Sep 1974 v England	5	1	4	-	-
South Africa	25 Aug 1994 v England	2	1	1	-	-
West Indies	11 Jun 1975 v Pakistan	6	4	2	-	-
Zimbabwe	20 Jun 1983 v West Indies	1	-	1	-	-

Highest Innings Total

Runs	Team	Batted 1st	Batted 2nd	Date
320	England	Eng 8-320	Aus 5-273	22 Aug 1980
309	New Zealand	NZ 5-309	EAF 8-128	7 Jun 1975
292	England	Eng 8-292	Pak 185	31 Aug 1996

Lowest Completed Innings Total

Runs	Team	Batted 1st	Batted 2nd	Date
70	Australia	Eng 171	Aus 70	4 Jun 1977
94	East Africa	Eng 5-290	EAF 94	14 Jun 1975
105	Canada	Can 105	Aus 3-106	16 Jun 1979

Leading Run-scorers

Player	M	I	NO	Runs	HS	50	100	Ave.	Stk Rt
G.A. Gooch, England	8	8	-	320	115	-	2	40.00	64.52
A.R. Border, Australia	5	5	2	239	86*	2	-	79.67	75.87
M.W. Gatting, England	6	6	1	228	96	2	-	45.60	68.06

Highest Individual Innings

Runs	Player	Versus	Date
171*	G.M. Turner, New Zealand	East Africa	7 Jun 1975
167*	R.A. Smith, England	Australia	21 May 1993
115	G.A. Gooch, England	Australia	1 Jun 1985

Highest Partnerships

Wkt	Runs	Batsmen	Versus	Date
1st	172*	D.L. Haynes 88*, S.F.A.F. Bacchus 80*, WI	Zimbabwe	20 Jun 1983
4th	168	M.E. Waugh 113, A.R. Border 86*, Australia	England	21 May 1993
1st	158	B. Wood 77, D.L. Amiss 88, England	East Africa	14 Jun 1975

Leading Wicket-takers

Player	M	Wkts	Best	4wi	5wi	Ave.	Stk Rt
I.T. Botham, England	7	10	4-45	1	-	27.70	41.40
C.C. Lewis, England	4	9	3-20	-	-	17.11	26.22
D. Gough, England	4	8	3-39	-	-	19.75	30.00

Best Bowling

Total	Player	Versus	Date
5-18	G.J. Cosier, Australia	England	4 Jun 1977
5-20	G.S. Chappell, Australia	England	4 Jun 1977
5-21	A.G. Hurst, Australia	Canada	16 Jun 1979

Leeds, Headingley (21 matches)

Summary of Matches

Team	First Match	Played	Won	Lost	NR	Tie
Australia	7 Jun 1975 v Pakistan	5	3	2	-	-
Canada	9 Jun 1979 v Pakistan	1	-	1	-	-
East Africa	11 Jun 1975 v India	1	-	1	-	-
England	5 Sep 1973 v West Indies	15	9	6	-	-
India	13 Jul 1974 v England	6	2	4	-	-
New Zealand	13 Jun 1979 v India	3	3	-	-	-
Pakistan	7 Jun 1975 v Australia	4	2	2	-	-
South Africa	24 May 1998 v England	1	-	1	-	-
Sri Lanka	16 Jun 1983 v Pakistan	2	-	2	-	-
West Indies	5 Sep 1973 v England	4	2	2	-	-

Highest Innings Total

Runs	Team	Batted 1st	Batted 2nd	Date
298	New Zealand	Eng 6-295	NZ 6-298	23 May 1990
295	England	Eng 6-295	NZ 6-298	23 May 1990
278	Australia	Aus 7-278	Pak 205	7 Jun 1975

Lowest Completed Innings Total

Runs	Team	Batted 1st	Batted 2nd	Date
93	England	Eng 93	Aus 6-94	18 Jun 1975
120	East Africa	EAF 120	Ind 0-123	11 Jun 1975
136	Sri Lanka	SL 136	Eng 1-137	20 Jun 1983

Leading Run-scorers

Player	M	I	NO	Runs	HS	50	100	Ave.	Stk Rt
G.A. Gooch, England	7	7	-	222	55	1	-	31.71	48.47
S.M. Gavaskar, India	4	4	1	186	65*	2	-	62.00	72.94
C.J. Tavare, England	3	3	1	167	82*	2	-	83.50	56.23

Highest Individual Innings

Runs	Player	Versus	Date
128	R.A. Smith, England	New Zealand	23 May 1990
108	G.M. Wood, Australia	England	8 Jun 1981
102*	Imran Khan, Pakistan	Sri Lanka	16 Jun 1983
102*	M.J. Greatbatch, New Zealand	England	23 May 1990

Highest Partnerships

Wkt	Runs	Batsmen	Versus	Date
6th	144	Imran Khan 102*, Shahid Mahboob 77, Pakistan	Sri Lanka	16 Jun 1983
5th	135*	G.P. Thorpe 75*, A.J. Hollioake 66*, England	Australia	22 May 1997
1st	133	B. Wood 78*, C.J. Tavare 66, England	India	2 Jun 1982

Leading Wicket-takers

Player	M	Wkts	Best	4wi	5wi	Ave.	Stk Rt
C.M. Old, England	5	12	3-29	-	-	12.92	25.92
I.T. Botham, England	5	11	4-56	1	-	17.55	29.45
D.K. Lillee, Australia	4	8	5-34	-	1	19.00	30.00
R.G.D. Willis, England	5	8	2-29	-	-	17.75	39.00

Best Bowling

Total	Player	Versus	Date
7-51	W.W. Davis, West Indies	Australia	12 Jun 1983
6-14	G.J. Gilmour, Australia	England	18 Jun 1975
5-34	D.K. Lillee, Australia	Pakistan	7 Jun 1975

London, Kennington Oval (The Oval) (22 matches)

Summary of Matches

Team	First Match	Played	Won	Lost	NR	Tie
Australia	11 Jun 1975 v Sri Lanka	5	2	3	-	-
England	7 Sep 1973 v West Indies	16	11	4	1	-
India	15 Jul 1974 v England	5	1	3	1	-
New Zealand	18 Jun 1975 v West Indies	3	-	3	-	-
Pakistan	26 May 1978 v England	5	-	5	-	-
South Africa	21 May 1998 v England	1	1	-	-	-
Sri Lanka	11 Jun 1975 v Australia	2	-	2	-	-
West Indies	7 Sep 1973 v England	7	6	1	-	-

Highest Innings Total

Runs	Team	Batted 1st	Batted 2nd	Date
328	Australia	Aus 5-328	SL 4-276	11 Jun 1975
322	England	Eng 6-322	NZ 216	9 Jun 1983
306	England	Eng 5-306	WI 281	26 May 1995

Lowest Completed Innings Total

Runs	Team	Batted 1st	Batted 2nd	Date
154	Pakistan	Eng 6-248	Pak 8-154	26 May 1978
158	New Zealand	NZ 158	WI 5-159	18 Jun 1975
162	India	Eng 9-276	Ind 8-162	4 Jun 1982
162	England	Eng 162	Ind 1-163	24 May 1986

Leading Run-scorers

Player	M	I	NO	Runs	HS	50	100	Ave.	Stk Rt
A.J. Lamb, England	7	7	-	343	102	3	1	49.00	90.74
I.V.A. Richards, West Indies	5	5	2	261	119	1	1	87.00	77.68
D.I. Gower, England	6	6	2	248	114*	1	1	62.00	84.93

Highest Individual Innings

Runs	Player	Versus	Date
125*	G.S. Chappell, Australia	England	6 Jun 1977
119	I.V.A. Richards, West Indies	India	15 Jun 1983
114*	D.I. Gower, England	Pakistan	26 May 1978

Highest Partnerships

Wkt	Runs	Batsmen	Versus	Date
1st	182	R.B. McCosker 73, A.Turner 101, Australia	Sri Lanka	11 Jun 1975
2nd	166	Majid Khan 81, Zaheer Abbas 93, Pakistan	West Indies	20 Jun 1979
2nd	163*	S.M. Gavasker 65*, M. Azharuddin 83*, India	England	24 May 1986

Leading Wicket-takers

Player	M	Wkts	Best	4wi	5wi	Ave.	Stk Rt
A.M.E. Roberts, West Indies	5	11	3-39	-	-	13.82	28.36
C.C. Lewis, England	4	7	4-40	1	-	26.29	30.71
C.M. Old, England	5	7	3-36	-	-	30.43	42.71

Best Bowling

Total	Player	Versus	Date
5-31	M. Hendrick, England	Australia	20 Aug 1980
4-27	B.D. Julien, West Indies	New Zealand	18 Jun 1975
4-35	D.K. Lillee, Australia	England	20 Aug 1980

London, Lord's Cricket Ground (23 matches)

Summary of Matches

Team	First Match	Played	Won	Lost	NR	Tie
Australia	26 Aug 1972 v England	9	3	6	-	-
England	26 Aug 1972 v Australia	20	12	8	-	-
India	7 Jun 1975 v England	2	1	1	-	-
Pakistan	13 Jun 1983 v England	3	1	2	-	-
Sri Lanka	16 Aug 1998 v England	2	1	1	-	-
West Indies	21 Jun 1975 v Australia	10	5	5	-	-

Highest Innings Total

Runs	Team	Batted 1st	Batted 2nd	Date
334	England	Eng 4-334	Ind 3-132	7 Jun 1975
291	West Indies	WI 8-291	Aus 274	21 Jun 1975
286	West Indies	WI 9-286	Eng 194	23 Jun 1979

Lowest Completed Innings Total

Runs	Team	Batted 1st	Batted 2nd	Date
132	India	Eng 4-334	Ind 3-132	7 Jun 1975
140	West Indies	Ind 183	WI 140	25 Jun 1983
159	Australia	Aus 9-159	Eng 4-160	9 Jun 1979

Leading Run-scorers

Player	M	I	NO	Runs	HS	50	100	Ave.	Stk Rt
I.V.A. Richards, West Indies	9	9	3	524	138*	3	1	87.33	90.66
G.A. Gooch, England	11	11	1	498	136	2	2	49.80	62.09
D.I. Gower, England	8	8	1	321	102	1	1	45.86	72.30

Highest Individual Innings

Runs	Player	Versus	Date
138*	I.V.A. Richards, West Indies	England	23 Jun 1979
137	D.L. Amiss, England	India	7 Jun 1975
136	G.A. Gooch, England	Australia	29 May 1989

Highest Partnerships

Wkt	Runs	Batsmen	Versus	Date
3rd	213	G.A. Hick 86*, N.H. Fairbrother 113, England	West Indies	27 May 1991
2nd	202	G.A. Gooch 117*, D.I. Gower 102, England	Australia	3 Jun 1985
2nd	176	D.L. Amiss 137, K.W.R. Fletcher 68, England	India	7 Jun 1975

Leading Wicket-takers

Player	M	Wkts	Best	4wi	5wi	Ave.	Stk Rt
D. Gough, England	4	12	5-44	-	1	14.67	20.00
I.T. Botham, England	10	11	2-36	-	-	35.91	55.64
M.A. Holding, West Indies	6	10	3-28	-	-	18.50	35.80

Best Bowling

Total	Player	Versus	Date
5-34	M. Muralitharan, Sri Lanka	England	20 Aug 1998
5-38	J. Garner, West Indies	England	23 Jun 1979
5-44	D. Gough, England	Australia	25 May 1997

Manchester, Old Trafford (26 matches)

Summary of Matches

Team	First Match	Played	Won	Lost	NR	Tie
Australia	24 Aug 1972 v England	5	2	3	-	-
Canada	13 Jun 1979 v England	1	-	1	-	-
England	24 Aug 1972 v Australia	22	16	5	1	-
India	14 Jun 1975 v New Zealand	6	2	4	-	-
New Zealand	20 Jul 1973 v England	5	1	3	1	-
Pakistan	24 May 1978 v England	5	-	5	-	-
South Africa	27 Aug 1994 v England	2	1	1	-	-
Sri Lanka	7 Jun 1975 v West Indies	2	1	1	-	-
West Indies	7 Jun 1975 v Sri Lanka	4	2	2	-	-

Highest Innings Totals

Runs	Team	Batted 1st	Batted 2nd	Date
295	England	Eng 8-295	Pak 222	19 Jul 1982
286	England	NZ 5-284	Eng 4-286	18 Jul 1986
284	New Zealand	NZ 5-284	Eng 4-286	18 Jul 1986

Lowest Completed Innings Total

Runs	Team	Batted 1st	Batted 2nd	Date
45	Canada	Can 45	Eng 2-46	13 Jun 1979
85	Pakistan	Eng 7-217	Pak 85	24/25 May 1978
86	Sri Lanka	SL 86	WI 1-87	7 Jun 1975

Leading Run-scorers

Player	M	I	NO	Runs	HS	50	100	Ave.	Stk Rt
G.A. Gooch, England	10	10	1	405	91	5	-	45.00	63.68
A.J. Lamb, England	10	10	1	341	75	2	-	37.89	75.61
D.I. Gower, England	12	11	-	309	81	2	-	28.09	69.59

Highest Individual Innings

Runs	Player	Versus	Date
189*	I.V.A. Richards, West Indies	England	31 May 1984
142*	C.W.J. Athey, England	New Zealand	18 Jul 1986
118	A.D. Brown, England	India	29 Aug 1996

Highest Partnerships

Wkt	Runs	Batsmen	Versus	Date
1st	193	G.A. Gooch 91, C.W.J. Athey 142*, England	New Zealand	18 Jul 1986
1st	156	G.A. Gooch 54, M.A. Atherton 74, England	West Indies	25 May 1991
4th	127	G.A. Hick 85, N.H. Fairbrother 59, England	Australia	19 May 1993

Leading Wicket-takers

Player	M	Wkts	Best	4wi	5wi	Ave.	Stk Rt
R.G.D. Willis, England	9	15	4-11	2	-	17.13	36.87
I.T. Botham, England	11	11	2-17	-	-	36.82	60.45
C.M. Old, England	4	8	4-8	1	-	9.63	30.00

Best Bowling

Total	Player	Versus	Date
4-8	C.M. Old, England	Canada	13 Jun 1979
4-11	R.G.D. Willis, England	Canada	13 Jun 1979
4-15	R.G.D. Willis, England	Pakistan	24/25 May 1978

Nottingham, Trent Bridge (18 matches)

Summary of Matches

Team	First Match	Played	Won	Lost	NR	Tie
Australia	13 Jun 1979 v Pakistan	4	1	2	-	1
England	31 Aug 1974 v Pakistan	10	4	5	-	1
India	13 Jun 1983 v Australia	2	1	1	-	-
New Zealand	11 Jun 1975 v England	4	1	3	-	-
Pakistan	31 Aug 1974 v England	8	6	2	-	-
South Africa	14 Aug 1998 v Sri Lanka	1	-	1	-	-
Sri Lanka	14 Jun 1975 v Pakistan	3	1	2	-	-
West Indies	16 Jun 1979 v New Zealand	3	2	1	-	-
Zimbabwe	9 Jun 1983 v Australia	1	1	-	-	-

Highest Innings Total

Runs	Team	Batted 1st	Batted 2nd	Date
363	England	Eng 7-363	Pak 165	20 Aug 1992
330	Pakistan	Pak 6-330	SL 138	14 Jun 1975
320	Australia	Aus 9-320	Ind 158	13 Jun 1983

Lowest Completed Innings Total

Runs	Team	Batted 1st	Batted 2nd	Date
138	Sri Lanka	Pak 6-330	SL 138	14 Jun 1975
157	England	Eng 157	Pak 4-158	23 May 1987
158	India	Aus 9-320	Ind 158	13 Jun 1983

Leading Run-scorers

Player	M	I	NO	Runs	HS	50	100	Ave.	Stk Rt
Zaheer Abbas, Pakistan	5	5	1	300	103*	2	1	75.00	74.09
Majid Khan, Pakistan	4	4	-	277	109	2	1	69.25	87.38
A.J. Lamb, England	6	6	1	274	118	-	2	54.80	78.96

Highest Individual Innings

Runs	Player	Versus	Date
131	K.W.R. Fletcher, England	New Zealand	11 Jun 1975
125*	N.V. Knight, England	Pakistan	1 Sep 1996
118	A.J. Lamb, England	Pakistan	17 Jul 1982

Highest Partnerships

Wkt	Runs	Batsmen	Versus	Date
1st	159	Sadiq Mohammad 74, Majid Khan 84, Pakistan	Sri Lanka	14 Jun 1975
4th	147*	Zaheer Abbas 103*, Imran Khan 79, Pakistan	New Zealand	20 Jun 1983
2nd	144	T.M. Chappell 110, K.J. Hughes 52, Australia	India	13 Jun 1983

Leading Wicket-takers

Player	M	Wkts	Best	4wi	5wi	Ave.	Stk Rt
Imran Khan, Pakistan	6	9	3-15	-	-	16.22	31.56
Kapil Dev, India	2	7	5-43	-	1	11.86	19.71
I.T. Botham, England	5	6	3-57	-	-	34.50	49.00
K.H. Macleay, Australia	1	6	6-39	-	1	6.50	11.83
D.R. Pringle, England	3	6	3-21	-	-	18.17	32.00
Waqar Younis, Pakistan	2	6	4-73	1	-	20.33	21.00
Wasim Akram, Pakistan	3	6	3-45	-	-	19.67	30.17

Best Bowling

Total	Player	Versus	Date
6-39	K.H. Macleay, Australia	India	13 Jun 1983
5-43	Kapil Dev, India	Australia	13 Jun 1983
4-42	D.A.G. Fletcher, Zimbabwe	Australia	9 Jun 1983

England - other grounds

Bristol, County Ground (1 match)

Match	Batted 1st	Batted 2nd	Result	Date
New Zealand v Sri Lanka	SL 206	NZ 5-209	NZ by 5 wkts	13 Jun 1983

Chelmsford, County Ground (1 match)

Match	Batted 1st	Batted 2nd	Result	Date
Australia v India	Ind 247	Aus 129	Ind by 118 runs	20 Jun 1983

Derby, County (Racecourse) Ground (1 match)

Match	Batted 1st	Batted 2nd	Result	Date
New Zealand v Sri Lanka	NZ 181	SL 7-184	SL by 3 wkts	18 Jun 1983

Leicester, Grace Road (1 match)

Match	Batted 1st	Batted 2nd	Result	Date
India v Zimbabwe	Zim155	Ind 5-157	Ind by 5 wkts	11 Jun 1983

Scarborough, North Marine Road (2 matches)

Match	Batted 1st	Batted 2nd	Result	Date
England v West Indies	Eng 8-202	WI 4-207	WI by 6 wkts	26 Aug 1976
England v New Zealand	Eng 8-206	NZ 8-187	Eng by 19 runs	15 Jul 1978

Southampton, County Ground (1 match)

Match	Batted 1st	Batted 2nd	Result	Date
Australia v Zimbabwe	Aus 7-272	Zim 240	Aus by 32 runs	16 Jun 1983

Taunton, County Ground (1 match)

Match	Batted 1st	Batted 2nd	Result	Date
England v Sri Lanka	Eng 9-333	SL 286	Eng by 47 runs	11 Jun 1983

Tunbridge Wells, Nevill Ground (1 match)

Match	Batted 1st	Batted 2nd	Result	Date
India v Zimbabwe	Ind 8-266	Zim 235	Ind by 31 runs	18 Jun 1983

Worcester, New Road (1 match)

Match	Batted 1st	Batted 2nd	Result	Date
West Indies v Zimbabwe	Zim 7-217	WI 2-218	WI by 8 wkts	13 Jun 1983

INDIA

Bangalore, Chinnaswamy Stadium (10 matches)
Formerly Karnataka State Cricket Association Stadium

Summary of Matches

Team	First Match	Played	Won	Lost	NR	Tie
Australia	27 Oct 1989 v India	2	-	2	-	-
England	20 Jan 1985 v India	2	2	-	-	-
India	26 Sep 1982 v Sri Lanka	9	7	2	-	-
Kenya	20 May 1998 v India	1	-	1	-	-
New Zealand	14 Oct 1987 v India	2	-	2	-	-
Pakistan	9 Mar 1996 v India	1	-	-	1	-
South Africa	10 Nov 1993 v Zimbabwe	1	-	-	1	-
Sri Lanka	26 Sep 1982 v India	1	-	1	-	-
Zimbabwe	10 Nov 1993 v South Africa	1	-	-	1	-

Highest Completed Innings Total

Runs	Team	Batted 1st	Batted 2nd	Date
287	India	Ind 8-287	Pak 9-248	9 Mar 1996
252	India	Ind 7-252	NZ 8-236	14 Oct 1987
249	India	Aus 8-247	Ind 7-249	27 Oct 1989

Lowest Completed Innings Total

Runs	Team	Batted 1st	Batted 2nd	Date
170	India	Eng 9-218	Ind 170	26 Feb 1993
205	India	Ind 6-205	Eng 7-206	20 Jan 1985
215	Australia	Aus 7-215	Ind 8-216	21 Oct 1996

Leading Run-scorers

Player	M	I	NO	Runs	HS	50	100	Ave.	Stk Rt
S.R. Tendulkar, India	4	4	-	239	117	1	1	59.75	76.11
N.S. Sidhu, India	3	3	-	208	93	2	-	69.33	83.87
K. Srikkanth, India	4	4	-	188	92	2	-	47.00	90.38

Highest Individual Innings

Runs	Player	Versus	Date
121	R.L. Dias, Sri Lanka	India	26 Sep 1982
117	S.R. Tendulkar, India	New Zealand	14 May 1997
105	M.A. Taylor, Australia	India	21 Oct 1996

Highest Partnerships

Wkt	Runs	Batsmen	Versus	Date
1st	169	S.C.Ganguly 62, S.R. Tendulkar 117, India	New Zealand	14 May 1997
2nd	119	K. Srikkanth 58, R. Lama 57, India	Australia	27 Oct 1989
1st	115	K. Srikkanth 58, R. Lamba 57, India	Australia	27 Oct 1989

Leading Wicket-takers

Player	M	Wkts	Best	4wi	5wi	Ave.	Stk Rt
Kapil Dev, India	5	8	3-38	-	-	26.13	36.00
A. Kumble, India	4	6	3-48	-	-	26.17	40.00
B.K.V. Prasad, India	3	6	3-37	-	-	20.33	30.00
J. Srinath, India	3	6	5-41	-	1	22.83	28.00

Best Bowling

Total	Player	Versus	Date
5-35	P.W. Jarvis, England	India	26 Feb 1993
5-41	J. Srinth, India	England	26 Feb 1993
3-35	V.J. Marks, England	India	20 Jan 1985

Calcutta, Eden Gardens (16 matches)

Summary of Matches

Team	First Match	Played	Won	Lost	NR	Tie
Australia	8 Nov 1987 v England	1	1	-	-	-
Bangladesh	13 Dec 1990 v Sri Lanka	1	-	1	-	-
England	8 Nov 1987 v Australia	1	-	1	-	-
India	18 Feb 1987 v Pakistan	10	7	3	-	-
Kenya	31 May 1998 v India	1	-	1	-	-
New Zealand	23 Oct 1987 v Zimbabwe	1	1	-	-	-
Pakistan	18 Feb 1987 v India	4	3	1	-	-
South Africa	10 Nov 1991 v India	2	-	2	-	-
Sri Lanka	13 Dec 1990 v Bangladesh	5	3	2	-	-
West Indies	2 Jan 1988 v India	5	1	4	-	-
Zimbabwe	23 Oct 1987 v New Zealand	1	-	1	-	-

Highest Innings Total

Runs	Team	Batted 1st	Batted 2nd	Date
309	Sri Lanka	SL 309	Pak 224	27 May 1997
279	Pakistan	Pak 7-279	Ind 202	28 Oct 1989
277	Pakistan	WI 5-273	Pak 6-277	1 Nov 1989

Lowest Completed Innings Total

Runs	Team	Batted 1st	Batted 2nd	Date
123	West Indies	Ind 7-225	WI 123	27 Nov 1993
166	West Indies	Ind 7-222	WI 166	2 Jan 1988
188	Sri Lanka	SL 6-188	WI 3-190	25 Nov 1993

Leading Run-scorers

Player	M	I	NO	Runs	HS	50	100	Ave.	Stk Rt
S.R. Tendulkar, India	7	7	2	389	100*	4	1	77.80	81.72
M.A. Azharuddin, India	9	8	1	332	90	2	-	47.43	86.46
P.A. de Silva, Sri Lanka	5	5	-	306	89	4	-	61.20	112.50

Highest Individual Innings

Runs	Player	Versus	Date
123	K. Srikkanth, India	Pakistan	18 Feb 1987
107*	D.L. Haynes, West Indies	Pakistan	1 Nov 1989
100	S.R. Tendulkar, India	Kenya	31 May 1998

Highest Partnerships

Wkt	Runs	Batsmen	Versus	Date
3rd	163	B.C. Lara 82, K.L.T. Arthurton 72*, West Indies	Sri Lanka	25 Nov 1993
4th	145	K. Srikkanth 123, M. Azharuddin 49, India	Pakistan	18 Feb 1987
4th	139	P.A. de Silva 89, A. Ranatunga 64*, Sri Lanka	Bangladesh	31 Dec 1990

Leading Wicket-takers

Player	M	Wkts	Best	4wi	5wi	Ave.	Stk Rt
Kapil Dev, India	7	14	4-31	1	-	16.86	26.79
A. Kumble, India	5	12	6-12	-	1	12.75	21.58
A.C. Cummins, West Indies	3	6	3-38	-	-	21.00	30.00
S.T. Jayasuriya, Sri Lanka	5	6	3-12	-	-	22.83	30.00
B.K.V. Prasad, India	3	6	4-23	1	-	16.00	25.00
R.J. Shastri, India	4	6	4-38	1	-	16.83	25.00
J. Srinath, India	5	6	3-34	-	-	24.83	38.00

Best Bowling

6-12	A. Kumble, India	West Indies	27 Nov 1993
5-29	A.A. Donald, South Africa	India	10 Nov 1991
4-23	B.K.V. Prasad, India	Kenya	31 May 1998

Delhi, Feroz Shah Kotla (10 matches)

Summary of Matches

Team	First Match	Played	Won	Lost	NR	Tie
Australia	2 Oct 1986 v India	4	2	2	-	-
England	15 Oct 1989 v Sri Lanka	1	1	-	-	-
India	15 Sep 1982 v Sri Lanka	8	5	3	-	-
New Zealand	3 Nov 1994 v India	1	-	1	-	-
Sri Lanka	15 Sep 1982 v India	4	1	3	-	-
West Indies	23 Oct 1989 v India	1	1	-	-	-
Zimbabwe	11 Apr 1998 v Australia	1	-	1	-	-

Highest Innings Total

Runs	Team	Batted 1st	Batted 2nd	Date
294	Australia	Aus 3-294	Zim 9-278	11 Apr 1998
289	India	Ind 3-289	NZ 182	3 Nov 1994
289	India	Ind 6-289	Aus 233	22 Oct 1987

Lowest Completed Innings Total

Runs	Team	Batted 1st	Batted 2nd	Date
176	India	WI 9-196	Ind 176	23 Oct 1989
182	New Zealand	Ind 3-289	NZ 182	3 Nov 1994
193	Sri Lanka	SL 193	Eng 5-196	15 Oct 1989

Leading Run-scorers

Player	M	I	NO	Runs	HS	50	100	Ave.	Stk Rt
M.A. Azharuddin, India	7	7	3	267	72*	3	-	66.75	96.39
S.R. Tendulkar, India	3	3	-	214	137	1	1	71.33	99.53
D.B. Vengsarker, India	4	4	-	209	63	3	-	52.25	70.85

Highest Individual Innings

Runs	Player	Versus	Date
145	R.T. Ponting, Australia	Zimbabwe	11 Apr 1998
137	S.R. Tendulkar, India	Sri Lanka	2 Mar 1996
102	R.L. Dias, Sri Lanka	India	15 Sep 1982

Highest Partnerships

Wkt	Runs	Batsmen	Versus	Date
2nd	219	M.E. Waugh 87, R.T. Ponting 145, Australia	Zimbabwe	11 Apr 1998
3rd	175	S.R. Tendulkar 137, M.A. Azharuddin 72*, India	Sri Lanka	2 Mar 1996
2nd	170	S. Wettimuny 74, R.L. Dias 102, Sri Lanka	India	15 Sep 1982

Leading Wicket-takers

Player	M	Wkts	Best	4wi	5wi	Ave.	Stk Rt
Kapil Dev, India	5	6	2-41	-	-	31.33	44.00
I.V.A. Richards, West Indies	1	6	6-41	-	1	6.83	9.67
S.R. Waugh, Australia	4	6	2-42	-	-	34.00	37.00

Best Bowling

Total	Player	Versus	Date
6-41	I.V.A. Richards, West Indies	India	23 Oct 1989
3-19	M.A. Azharuddin, India	Australia	22 Oct 1987
3-34	Maninder Singh, India	Australia	22 Oct 1987

Hyderabad, Lal Bahadur Stadium (11 matches)

Summary of Matches

Team	First Match	Played	Won	Lost	NR	Tie
Australia	24 Sep 1986 v India	2	-	1	1	-
Bangladesh	17 May 1998 v Kenya	1	1	-	-	-
England	19 Oct 1989 v Australia	1	1	-	-	-
India	11 Sep 1983 v Pakistan	5	2	1	1	1
Kenya	17 May 1998 v Bangladesh	1	-	1	-	-
New Zealand	10 Oct 1987 v Zimbabwe	2	1	1	-	-
Pakistan	11 Sep 1983 v India	2	-	1	-	1
South Africa	17 Oct 1996 v India	1	1	-	-	-
Sri Lanka	18 Feb 1994 v India	2	1	1	-	-
West Indies	21 Nov 1993 v Zimbabwe	2	2	-	-	-
Zimbabwe	10 Oct 1987 v New Zealand	3	-	3	-	-

Highest Innings Total

Runs	Team	Batted 1st	Batted 2nd	Date
261	South Africa	SAF 7-261	Ind 214	17 Oct 1996
243	England	Aus 3-242	Eng 3-243	19 Oct 1989
242	Australia	Aus 3-242	Eng 3-243	19 Oct 1989
242	Australia	Aus 6-242	Ind 1-41	24 Sep 1986
242	New Zealand	NZ 7-242	Zim 239	10 Oct 1987

Lowest Completed Innings Total

Runs	Team	Batted 1st	Batted 2nd	Date
99	Zimbabwe	WI 9-233	Zim 99	21 Nov 1993
151	Zimbabwe	Zim 9-151	WI 4-155	16 Feb 1996
162	New Zealand	SL 214	NZ 162	20 May 1997

Leading Run-scorers

Player	M	I	NO	Runs	HS	50	100	Ave.	Stk Rt
D.L. Houghton, Zimbabwe	2	2	-	164	142	-	1	82.00	88.65
W. Larkins, England	1	1	-	124	124	-	1	124.00	98.41
A. Ranatunga, Sri Lanka	2	2	-	113	98	1	-	56.50	78.47

Highest Individual Innings

Runs	Player	Versus	Date
142	D.L. Houghton, Zimbabwe	New Zealand	10 Oct 1987
124	W. Larkins, England	Australia	19 Oct 1989
98	A. Ranatunga, Sri Lanka	India	18 Feb 1994

Highest Partnerships

Wkt	Runs	Batsmen	Versus	Date
1st	185	G.A. Gooch 56, W. Larkins 124, England	Australia	19 Oct 1989
1st	137	Athar Ali Khan 47, Mohammad Kafia 77, Bangladesh	Kenya	17 May 1998
6th	132	A. Ranatunga 98, R.S. Kalpage 51, Sri Lanka	India	18 Feb 1994

Leading Wicket-takers

Player	M	Wkts	Best	4wi	5wi	Ave.	Stk Rt
M. Prabhakar, India	2	5	5-35	-	1	13.40	21.60
G. Sharma, India	2	4	3-29	-	-	16.75	19.50
P. Strang, Zimbabwe	1	4	4-40	1	-	10.00	11.25

Best Bowling

Total	Player	Versus	Date
5-35	M. Prabhakar, India	Sri Lanka	18 Feb 1994
4-40	P. Strang, Zimbabwe	West Indies	16 Feb 1996
3-17	Muddassar Nazar, Pakistan	India	11 Sep 1983

Mumbai, Wankhede Stadium (10 matches)

Summary of Matches

Team	First Match	Played	Won	Lost	NR	Tie
Australia	27 Feb 1996 v India	1	1	-	-	-
Bangladesh	25 May 1998 v India	1	-	1	-	-
England	5 Nov 1987 v India	1	1	-	-	-
India	17 Jan 1987 v Sri Lanka	10	6	4	-	-
South Africa	6 Nov 1996 v India	2	-	2	-	-
Sri Lanka	17 Jan 1987 v India	3	1	2	-	-
West Indies	30 Oct 1989 v India	3	2	1	-	-
Zimbabwe	17 Oct 1987 v India	1	-	1	-	-

Highest Innings Total

Runs	Team	Batted 1st	Batted 2nd	Date
299	India	Ind 4-299	SL 7-289	17 Jan 1987
289	Sri Lanka	Ind 4-299	SL 7-289	17 Jan 1987
268	West Indies	WI 8-268	SL 8-222	9 Nov 1993

Lowest Completed Innings Total

Runs	Team	Batted 1st	Batted 2nd	Date
115	Bangladesh	Ban 155	Ind 5-116	25 May 1998
135	Zimbabwe	Zim 135	Ind 2-136	17 Oct 1987
165	India	Ind 165	WI 2-166	30 Oct 1989

Leading Run-scorers

Player	M	I	NO	Runs	HS	50	100	Ave.	Stk Rt
S.R. Tendulkar, India	6	6	-	306	114	2	1	51.00	90.27
M.A. Azharuddin, India	8	7	1	302	108*	1	1	50.33	72.77
A.D. Jadeja, India	5	5	3	186	72	2	-	93.00	73.81

Highest Individual Innings

Runs	Player	Versus	Date
151*	S.T. Jayasuriya, Sri Lanka	India	17 May 1997
126	M.E. Waugh, Australia	India	27 Feb 1996
115	G.A.Gooch, England	India	5 Nov 1987

Highest Partnerships

Wkt	Runs	Batsmen	Versus	Date
2nd	138	S.T. Jayasuriya 151*, M.A. Atapattu 38, Sri Lanka	India	17 May 1997
3rd	117	G.A. Gooch 115, M.W. Gatting 56, England	India	5 Nov 1987
2nd	117	D.L. Haynes 64, R.B. Richardson 58, West Indies	India	30 Oct 1989

Leading Wicket-takers

Player	M	Wkts	Best	4wi	5wi	Ave.	Stk Rt
B.K.V. Prasad, India	6	15	4-27	1	-	14.87	22.40
A. Kumble, India	6	12	4-25	1	-	18.17	28.67
W.K.M. Benjamin, West Indies	2	7	5-22	-	1	8.00	16.29

Best Bowling

Wkts	Player	Versus	Date
5-22	W.K.M. Benjamin, West Indies	Sri Lanka	9 Nov 1993
5-36	D.W. Fleming, Australia	India	27 Feb 1996
4-19	M. Prabhakar, India	Zimbabwe	17 Oct 1987

India - other grounds

Ahmedabad, Gujarat Stadium (6 matches)

Team	Batted 1st	Batted 2nd	Result	Date
India v Australia	Ind 193	Aus 141	Ind by 52 runs	5 Oct 1986
India v Zimbabwe	Zim 7-191	Ind 3-194	Ind by 7 wkts	26 Oct 1987
India v West Indies	WI 196	Ind 9-194	WI by 2 runs	7 Jan 1988
India v Sri Lanka	Ind 8-227	SL 221	Ind by 6 runs	22 Oct 1989
India v West Indies	WI 7-202	Ind 100	WI by 69 runs[†]	16 Nov 1993
England v New Zealand	NZ 6-239	Eng 9-228	NZ by 11 runs	14 Feb 1996

†revised target

Ahmedabad, Sardar Patel Stadium (3 matches)

Match	Batted 1st	Batted 2nd	Result	Date
India v England	Ind 7-156	Eng 5-160	Eng by 5 wkts	25 Nov 1981
India v Australia	Ind 6-206	Aus 3-210	Aus by 7 wkts	5 Oct 1984
Australia v Zimbabwe	Aus 7-252	Zim 239	Aus by 13 runs	3 Apr 1998

Amritsar, Gandhi Sports Complex (2 matches)

Match	Batted 1st	Batted 2nd	Result	Date
India v Sri Lanka	Ind 7-269	SL 8-191	Ind by 78 runs	12 Sep 1982
India v New Zealand	NZ 145	Ind 4-146	Ind by 6 wkts	18 Nov 1995

Chandigarh, Sector 16 Stadium (4 matches)

Match	Batted 1st	Batted 2nd	Result	Date
India v England	Eng 6-121	Ind 5-114	Eng by 7 runs	27 Jan 1985
Australia v New Zealand	Aus 8-251	NZ 234	Aus by 17 runs	27 Oct 1987
India v Bangladesh	Ban 6-170	Ind 1-171	Ind by 9 wkts	25 Dec 1990
England v India	Eng 6-198	Ind 5-201	Ind by 5 wkts	21 Jan 1993

Chennai[†], M.A. Chidambaram Stadium (7 matches)

Match	Batted 1st	Batted 2nd	Result	Date
India v Australia	Aus 6-270	Ind 269	Aus by 1 run	9 Oct 1987
Australia v Zimbabwe	Aus 9-235	Zim 139	Aus by 96 runs	13 Oct 1987
Australia v West Indies	Aus 6-241	WI 142	Aus by 99 runs	21 Oct 1989
India v West Indies	WI 221	Ind 6-225	Ind by 4 wkts	23 Oct 1994
Australia v New Zealand	NZ 9-286	Aus 4-289	Aus by 6 wkts	11 Mar 1996
India v Pakistan	Pak 5-327	Ind 292	Pak by 35 runs	21 May 1997
Bangladesh v Kenya	Ken 8-226	Ban 198	Ken by 28 runs	23 May 1998

†formerly Madras

Cuttack, Barabatti Stadium (9 matches)

Match	Batted 1st	Batted 2nd	Result	Date
India v England	Eng 6-230	Ind 5-231	Ind by 5 wkts	27 Jan 1982
India v England	Ind 5-252	Eng 6-241	Eng on run-rate	27 Dec 1984
Australia v Zimbabwe	Aus 5-266	Zim 6-196	Aus by 70 runs	30 Oct 1987
India v New Zealand	NZ 7-160	Ind 5-161	Ind by 5 wkts	12 Dec 1988
England v Pakistan	Pak 9-148	Eng 6-149	Eng by 4 wkts	22 Oct 1989
India v Sri Lanka	SL 214	Ind 178	SL by 36 runs	28 Dec 1990
India v West Indies	WI 9-251	Ind 2-256	Ind by 8 wkts	9 Nov 1994
India v Kenya	Ken 6-199	Ind 3-203	Ind by 7 wkts	18 Feb 1996
India v Zimbabwe	Ind 3-301	Zim 269	Ind by 32 runs	9 Apr 1998

Faridabad, Nahar Singh Stadium (4 matches)

Match	Batted 1st	Batted 2nd	Result	Date
India v West Indies	Ind 6-230	WI 6-231	WI by 4 wkts	19 Jan 1988
India v Zimbabwe	Ind 7-249	Zim 182	Ind by 67 runs	19 Mar 1993
India v West Indies	WI 5-273	Ind 177	WI by 96 runs	17 Oct 1994
Australia v South Africa	Aus 215	SAF 8-218	SAF by 2 wkts	25 Oct 1996

Gauhati, Jawaharlal Nehru Stadium (8 matches)

Match	Batted 1st	Batted 2nd	Result	Date
India v West Indies	Ind 7-178	WI 4-182	WI by 6 wkts	17 Dec 1983
India v Sri Lanka	SL 8-145	Ind 2-146	Ind by 8 wkts	11 Jan 1987
India v West Indies	WI 7-187	Ind 135	WI by 52 runs	23 Dec 1987
India v Zimbabwe	Zim 6-149	Ind 3-150	Ind by 7 wkts	22 Mar 1993
South Africa v Sri Lanka	SAF 7-214	SL 136	SAF by 78 runs	19 Nov 1993
New Zealand v West Indies	WI 6-306	NZ 9-171	WI by 135 runs	1 Nov 1994
Australia v South Africa	Aus 6-238	SAF 2-239	SAF by 8 wkts	1 Nov 1996
India v Sri Lanka	SL 9-172	Ind 3-173	Ind by 7 wkts	22 Dec 1997

Gwalior, Capt. Roop Singh Stadium (8 matches)

Match	Batted 1st	Batted 2nd	Result	Date
India v West Indies	WI 6-278	Ind 205	WI by 73 runs	22 Jan 1988
England v West Indies	WI 5-265	Eng 8-239	WI by 26 runs	27 Oct 1989
India v South Africa	Ind 6-223	SAF 8-185	Ind by 38 runs	12 Nov 1991
India v England	Eng 256	Ind 7-257	Ind by 3 wkts	4 Mar 1993
India v England	Eng 4-265	Ind 6-267	Ind by 4 wkts	5 Mar 1993
India v West Indies	WI 173	Ind 5-174	Ind by 5 wkts	21 Feb 1996
Pakistan v Sri Lanka	Pak 6-289	SL 259	Pak by 30 runs	12 May 1997
India v Kenya	Ken 5-265	Ind 196	Ken by 69 runs	28 May 1998

Indore, Jawarharlal Nehru Stadium (8 matches)

Match	Batted 1st	Batted 2nd	Result	Date
India v West Indies	Ind 7-240	WI 2-241	WI by 8 wkts	1 Dec 1983
India v Australia	Ind 5-235	Aus 4-236	Aus by 6 wkts	6 Oct 1984
India v Pakistan	Ind 7-196	Pak 7-200	Pak by 3 wkts	27 Jan 1987
Australia v New Zealand	Aus 4-199	NZ 9-196	Aus 3 runs	19 Oct 1987
India v New Zealand	Ind 6-222	NZ 9-169	Ind by 53 runs	15 Dec 1988
India v Zimbabwe	Ind 5-248	Zim 248	Match tied	18 Nov 1993
Australia v South Africa	Aus 7-219	SAF 3-220	SAF by 7 wkts	19 Oct 1996
India v Sri Lanka	SL 1-17	Ind DNB	No result	25 Dec 1997

Jaipur, Sawai Mansingh Stadium (7 matches)

Match	Batted 1st	Batted 2nd	Result	Date
India v Pakistan	Pak 9-166	Ind 6-169	Ind by 4 wkts	2 Oct 1983
India v Australia	Aus 3-250	Ind 3-251	Ind 7 by wkts	7 Sep 1986
England v West Indies	Eng 5-269	WI 235	Eng by 34 runs	26 Oct 1987
India v England	Ind 3-223	Eng 6-224	Eng by 4 wkts	18 Jan 1993
India v West Indies	Ind 5-259	WI 254	Ind by 5 runs	11 Nov 1994
Australia v West Indies	Aus 6-229	WI 6-232	WI by 4 wkts	4 Mar 1996
India v South Africa	SAF 6-249	Ind 7-222	SAF by 27 runs	23 Oct 1996

Jamshedpur, Keenan Stadium (5 matches)

Match	Batted 1st	Batted 2nd	Result	Date
India v West Indies	WI 8-333	Ind 5-229	WI by 104 runs	7 Dec 1983
India v Australia	Ind 2-21	Aus DNB	No result	3 Oct 1984
India v Pakistan	Ind 3-265	Pak 5-266	Pak by 5 wkts	26 Mar 1987
India v England	Ind 7-137	Eng 4-141	Eng by 6 wkts	1 Mar 1993
India v New Zealand	Ind 236	NZ 2-237	NZ by 8 wkts	15 Nov 1995

Jullundur, Burlton Park (3 matches)

Match	Batted 1st	Batted 2nd	Result	Date
India v England	Eng 7-161	Ind 4-164	Ind by 6 wkts	20 Dec 1981
Pakistan v West Indies	Pak 5-223	WI 4-226	WI by 6 wkts	25 Oct 1989
India v Sri Lanka	Ind 9-213	SL 6-141	SL by 4 wkts[†]	20 Feb 1994

Kanpur, Green Park (7 matches)

Match	Batted 1st	Batted 2nd	Result	Date
India v Sri Lanka	SL 8-195	Ind 78	SL by 117 runs	24 Dec 1986
Sri Lanka v West Indies	WI 8-236	SL 8-211	WI by 25 runs	21 Oct 1987
India v England	Eng 7-255	Ind 4-259	Ind by 6 wkts	25 Oct 1989
India v Sri Lanka	SL 203	Ind 3-205	Ind by 7 wkts	7 Nov 1993
India v West Indies	WI 6-257	Ind 5-211	WI by 46 runs	30 Oct 1994
India v Zimbabwe	Ind 5-247	Zim 207	Ind by 40 runs	6 Mar 1996
India v Australia	Aus 9-222	Ind 4-233	Ind by 6 wkts	7 Apr 1998

Kochi[†], Jawaharlal Nehru Stadium (1 match)

Match	Batted 1st	Batted 2nd	Result	Date
India v Australia	Ind 5-309	Aus 268	Ind by 41 runs	1 Apr 1998

[†]*formerly Cochin*

Lucknow, K.D. 'Babu' Singh Stadium (1 match)

Match	Batted 1st	Batted 2nd	Result	Date
Pakistan v Sri Lanka	Pak 6-219	SL 213	Pak by 6 runs	27 Oct 1989

Margao[†], Fatorda Stadium (4 matches)

Match	Batted 1st	Batted 2nd	Result	Date
Australia v Sri Lanka	Aus 7-222	SL 194	Aus by 28 runs	25 Oct 1989
India v Sri Lanka	Ind 136	SL 3-137	SL by 7 wkts	8 Dec 1990
New Zealand v West Indies	WI 123	NZ 1-25	No result	26 Oct 1994
India v Sri Lanka	Ind 6-228	SL 5-229	SL by 5 wkts	28 Dec 1997

[†]*formerly Goa*

Mohali, Punjab Cricket Association Stadium (6 matches)

Match	Batted 1st	Batted 2nd	Result	Date
India v South Africa	Ind 221	SAF 9-178	Ind by 43 runs	22 Nov 1993
Australia v West Indies	Aus 8-207	WI 202	Aus by 5 runs	14 Mar 1996
India v Australia	Ind 6-289	Aus 284	Ind by 5 runs	3 Nov 1996
New Zealand v Pakistan	NZ 7-285	Pak 9-263	NZ by 22 runs	9 May 1997
Pakistan v Sri Lanka	SL 4-339	Pak 224	SL by 115 runs	24 May 1997
India v Bangladesh	Ban 9-184	Ind 5-185	Ind by 5 wkts	14 May 1998

Mumbai[†], Brabourne Stadium (3 matches)

Match	Batted 1st	Batted 2nd	Result	Date
Australia v Pakistan	Pak 8-205	Aus 139	Pak by 66 runs	23 Oct 1989
South Africa v West Indies	SAF 5-180	WI 139	SAF by 41 runs	14 Nov 1993
India v New Zealand	NZ 126	Ind 4-128	Ind by 6 wkts	29 Nov 1995

[†]*formerly Bombay*

Nagpur, Vidarbha Cricket Association Ground (8 matches)

Match	Batted 1st	Batted 2nd	Result	Date
India v England	Eng 7-240	Ind 7-241	Ind by 3 wkts	23 Jan 1985
India v Pakistan	Pak 6-286	Ind 9-245	Pak by 41 runs	24 Mar 1987
India v New Zealand	NZ 9-221	Ind 1-224	Ind by 9 wkts	31 Oct 1987
India v West Indies	WI 8-203	Ind 193	WI by 10 runs	8 Dec 1987
England v Pakistan	Eng 7-194	Pak 4-195	Pak by 6 wkts	30 Oct 1989
India v Sri Lanka	Ind 5-245	SL 7-226	Ind by 19 runs	1 Dec 1990
India v New Zealand	NZ 8-348	Ind 249	NZ by 99 runs	26 Nov 1995
Australia v Zimbabwe	Zim 154	Aus 2-158	Aus by 8 wkts	1 Mar 1996

New Delhi, Jawaharlal Nehru Stadium (2 matches)

Match	Batted 1st	Batted 2nd	Result	Date
India v Australia	Aus 9-220	Ind 172	Aus by 48 runs	28 Sep 1984
India v South Africa	Ind 4-287	SAF 2-288	SAF by 8 wkts	14 Nov 1991

Patna, Moin-ul-Haq Stadium (3 matches)

Match	Batted 1st	Batted 2nd	Result	Date
Sri Lanka v Zimbabwe	SL 6-263	Zim 208	SL by 55 runs	15 Nov 1993
Kenya v Zimbabwe	Zim 3-45	Ken DNB	No result	26 Feb 1996
Kenya v Zimbabwe	Ken 134	Zim 5-137	Zim by 5 wkts	27 Feb 1996

Pune, Jawarharlal Nehru Stadium (7 matches)

Match	Batted 1st	Batted 2nd	Result	Date
India v England	Ind 6-214	Eng 6-215	Eng by 4 wkts	5 Dec 1984
India v Pakistan	Ind 9-120	Pak 4-121	Pak by 6 wkts	22 Mar 1987
England v Sri Lanka	SL 7-218	Eng 2-219	Eng by 8 wkts	30 Oct 1987
India v Sri Lanka	SL 8-227	Ind 4-230	Ind by 6 wkts	5 Dec 1990
India v Zimbabwe	Zim 234	Ind 2-238	Ind by 8 wkts	25 Mar 1993
India v New Zealand	NZ 6-235	Ind 5-236	Ind by 5 wkts	24 Nov 1995
Kenya v West Indies	Ken 166	WI 93	Ken by 73 runs	29 Feb 1996

Rajkot, Municipal Ground[†] (5 matches)

Match	Batted 1st	Batted 2nd	Result	Date
India v Australia	Ind 6-260	Aus 3-263	Aus by 7 wkts	7 Oct 1986
India v West Indies	Ind 7-221	WI 4-225	WI by 6 wkts	5 Jan 1988
Sri Lanka v West Indies	WI 9-176	SL 6-180	SL by 4 wkts	19 Oct 1989
India v Sri Lanka	Ind 5-246	SL 8-238	Ind by 8 runs	15 Feb 1994
India v South Africa	Ind 185	SAF 5-188	SAF by 5 wkts	29 Oct 1996

[†]formerly Racecourse Ground

Srinagar, Sher-I-Kashmir Stadium (2 matches)

Match	Batted 1st	Batted 2nd	Result	Date
India v West Indies	Ind 176	WI 0-108	WI on run-rate	13 Oct 1983
India v Australia	Ind 8-222	Aus 7-226	Aus by 3 wkts	9 Sep 1986

Trivandrum, University Stadium (2 matches)

Match	Batted 1st	Batted 2nd	Result	Date
India v Australia	Ind 175	WI 1-29	No result	1 Oct 1984
India v West Indies	Ind 8-239	Ind 1-241	WI by 9 wkts	25 Jan 1988

Vadodara[†], I.P.C.L. Sports Complex (3 matches)

Match	Batted 1st	Batted 2nd	Result	Date
India v New Zealand	NZ 4-269	Ind 3-271	Ind by 7 wkts	28 Oct 1994
Netherlands v New Zealand	NZ 8-307	Neth 7-188	NZ by 119 runs	17 Feb 1996
India v Zimbabwe	Ind 5-274	Zim 261	Ind by 13 runs	5 Apr 1998

[†]formerly Baroda

Vadodara[†], Moti Bagh Stadium (3 matches)

Match	Batted 1st	Batted 2nd	Result	Date
India v West Indies	Ind 6-214	WI 6-217	WI by 4 wkts	9 Nov 1983
India v Sri Lanka	Ind 8-235	SL 141	Ind by 94 runs	15 Jan 1987
India v New Zealand	NZ 3-278	Ind 8-282	Ind by 2 wkts	17 Dec 1988

[†]formerly Baroda

Visag[†], Indira Priyadarshani Stadium (3 matches)

Match	Batted 1st	Batted 2nd	Result	Date
India v New Zealand	NZ 9-196	Ind 6-197	Ind by 4 wkts	10 Dec 1988
India v West Indies	Ind 4-260	WI 7-256	Ind by 4 runs	7 Nov 1994
Australia v Kenya	Aus 7-304	Ken 7-207	Aus by 97 runs	23 Feb 1996

[†]formerly Vishakhapatnam

KENYA-

Nairobi, Nairobi Gymkhana Ground (10 matches)

Summary of Matches

Team	First Match	Played	Won	Lost	NR	Tie
Bangladesh	10 Oct 1997 v Kenya	2	-	2	-	-
Kenya	28 Sep 1996 v Sri Lanka	6	1	5	-	-
Pakistan	29 Sep 1996 v South Africa	3	1	2	-	-
South Africa	29 Sep 1996 v Pakistan	3	3	-	-	-
Sri Lanka	28 Sep 1996 v Kenya	2	1	1	-	-
Zimbabwe	11 Oct 1997 v Bangladesh	4	4	-	-	-

Highest Innings Total

Runs	Team	Batted 1st	Batted 2nd	Date
371	Pakistan	Pak 9-371	SL 289	4 Oct 1996
347	Kenya	Ken 3-347	Ban 197	10 Oct 1997
321	South Africa	SAF 8-321	Pak 259	29 Sep 1996

Lowest Completed Innings Total

Runs	Team	Batted 1st	Batted 2nd	Date
103	Kenya	SAF 8-205	Ken 103	3 Oct 1996
188	Kenya	Ken 9-188	SL 3-190	28 Sep 1996
190	Kenya	Zim 6-272	Ken 190	19 Oct 1997

Leading Run-scorers

Player	M	I	NO	Runs	HS	50	100	Ave.	Stk Rt
K. Otieno, Kenya	6	6	-	282	144	1	1	47.00	81.73
A. Flower, Zimbabwe	4	4	-	239	81	3	-	59.75	85.97
G.W. Flower, Zimbabwe	4	4	-	233	79	3	-	58.25	86.62

Highest Individual Innings

Runs	Player	Versus	Date
144	K. Otieno, Kenya	Bangladesh	10 Oct 1997
124	D.J. Cullinan, South Africa	Pakistan	29 Sep 1996
122	P.A. de Silva, Sri Lanka	Pakistan	4 Oct 1996
122	D. Chudasama, Kenya	Bangladesh	10 Oct 1997

Highest Partnerships

Wkt	Runs	Batsmen	Versus	Date
4th	232	D.J. Cullinan 124, J.N. Rhodes 121, South Africa	Pakistan	29 Sep 1996
1st	225	D. Chudasama 122, K. Otieno 144, Kenya	Bangladesh	10 Oct 1997
1st	161	G.W. Flower 79, A. Flower 81, Zimbabwe	Bangladesh	11 Oct 1997

Leading Wicket-takers

Player	M	Wkts	Best	4wi	5wi	Ave.	Stk Rt
A.A. Donald, South Africa	3	12	6-23	-	1	7.00	12.67
P.A. Strang, Zimbabwe	4	9	3-37	-	-	15.11	24.78
Saqlain Mushtaq, Pakistan	3	7	4-33	1	-	16.71	25.71
Waqar Younis, Pakistan	3	7	5-52	-	1	21.29	23.00
G.W. Flower, Zimbabwe	4	7	2-6	-	-	17.14	21.57
Aasif Karim, Kenya	6	7	5-33	-	1	30.14	36.86

Best Bowling

Total	Player	Versus	Date
6-23	A.A. Donald, South Africa	Kenya	3 Oct 1996
5-33	Aasif Karim, Kenya	Bangladesh	10 Oct 1997
5-52	Waqar Younis, Pakistan	Sri Lanka	4 Oct 1996

Kenya - other grounds

Nairobi, Aga Khan Sports Club (4 matches)

Match	Batted 1st	Batted 2nd	Result	Date
Kenya v Pakistan	Ken 148	Pak 6-149	Pak by 4 wkts	2 Oct 1996
Bangladesh v Zimbabwe	Zim 284	Ban 92	Zim by 192 runs	14 Oct 1997
Kenya v Bangladesh	Ban 100	Ken 2-102	Ken by 8 wkts	15 Oct 1997
Kenya v Zimbabwe	Ken 9-207	Zim 3-210	Zim by 7 wkts	16 Oct 1997

Nairobi, Nairobi Club Ground (1 match)

Match	Batted 1st	Batted 2nd	Result	Date
South Africa v Sri Lanka	SAF 169	SL 8-170	SL by 2 wkts	1 Oct 1996

New Zealand - other grounds

New Plymouth, Pukekura Park (1 match)

Match	Batted 1st	Batted 2nd	Result	Date
Sri Lanka v Zimbabwe	Zim 4-312	SL 7-313	SL by 3 wkts	23 Feb 1992

Taupo, Owen Delaney Park (1 match)

Match	Batted 1st	Batted 2nd	Result	Date
India v New Zealand	Ind 5-257	NZ 5-200	NZ by 5 wkts	9 Jan 1999

NEW ZEALAND

Auckland, Eden Park (36 matches)

Summary of Matches

Team	First Match	Played	Won	Lost	NR	Tie
Australia	13 Feb 1982 v New Zealand	9	6	3	-	-
England	19 Feb 1983 v New Zealand	7	2	5	-	-
India	22 Feb 1976 v New Zealand	4	2	2	-	-
New Zealand	22 Feb 1976 v India	36	18	16	1	1
Pakistan	17 Feb 1985 v New Zealand	7	3	2	1	1
South Africa	29 Feb 1992 v New Zealand	1	-	1	-	-
Sri Lanka	20 Mar 1983 v New Zealand	3	1	2	-	-
West Indies	21 Mar 1987 v New Zealand	3	2	1	-	-
Zimbabwe	28 Mar 1996 v New Zealand	2	-	2	-	-

Highest Innings Total

Runs	Team	Batted 1st	Batted 2nd	Date
304	New Zealand	NZ 5-304	SL 6-188	20 Mar 1983
278	New Zealand	NZ 5-278	Zim 204	28 Jan 1996
264	Pakistan	NZ 7-262	Pak 6-264	21 Mar 1992

Lowest Completed Innings Total

Runs	Team	Batted 1st	Batted 2nd	Date
110	New Zealand	Pak 146	NZ 110	6 Mar 1994
137	New Zealand	NZ 9-137	Aus 4-138	26 Feb 1995
139	Pakistan	Pak 139	NZ 4-140	30 Dec 1992

Leading Run-scorers

Player	M	I	NO	Runs	HS	50	100	Ave.	Stk Rt
M.D. Crowe, New Zealand	17	16	7	719	105*	6	2	79.89	74.20
A.H. Jones, New Zealand	16	16	3	446	90	4	-	34.31	56.67
M.J. Greatbatch, NZ	16	16	-	435	74	4	-	27.19	69.38

Highest Individual Innings

Runs	Player	Versus	Date
140	G.M. Turner, New Zealand	Sri Lanka	20 Mar 1983
120	N.J. Astle, New Zealand	Zimbabwe	28 Jan 1996
108	G.S. Chappell, Australia	New Zealand	13 Feb 1982
108	A.P. Gurusinha, Sri Lanka	New Zealand	1 Apr 1995

Highest Partnerships

Wkt	Runs	Batsmen	Versus	Date
3rd	160	G.P. Howarth 72, M.D. Crowe 105*, New Zealand	England	25 Feb 1984
2nd	147	M.A. Taylor 97, M.E. Waugh 74, Australia	New Zealand	19 Feb 1995
3rd	135	N.J. Astle 120, R.G. Twose 53, New Zealand	Zimbabwe	28 Jan 1996

Leading Wicket-takers

Player	M	Wkts	Best	4wi	5wi	Ave.	Stk Rt
G.R. Larsen, New Zealand	23	25	4-24	1	-	29.76	46.72
C.Z. Harris, New Zealand	15	17	2-32	-	-	28.76	39.94
C.L. Cairns, New Zealand	16	16	4-55	1	-	25.75	33.06
E.J. Chatfield, New Zealand	8	16	3-20	-	-	15.88	28.13

Best Bowling

Total	Player	Versus	Date
6-30	Waqar Younis, Pakistan	New Zealand	13 Mar 1994
5-32	R.T. Latham, New Zealand	Australia	28 Mar 1993
4-23	B.L. Cairns, New Zealand	Sri Lanka	20 Mar 1983
4-23	Wasim Akram, Pakistan	New Zealand	6 Mar 1994

Christchurch, Jade Stadium (29 matches)
formerly Lancaster Park

Summary of Matches

Team	First Match	Played	Won	Lost	NR	Tie
Australia	31 Mar 1974 v New Zealand	6	5	1	-	-
England	26 Feb 1983 v New Zealand	6	5	1	-	-
India	21 Feb 1976 v New Zealand	4	-	4	-	-
New Zealand	11 Feb 1973 v Pakistan	27	13	14	-	-
Pakistan	11 Feb 1973 v New Zealand	6	1	5	-	-
South Africa	5 Mar 1992 v West Indies	2	1	1	-	-
Sri Lanka	26 Mar 1995 v New Zealand	2	1	1	-	-
West Indies	6 Feb 1980 v New Zealand	4	2	2	-	-
Zimbabwe	4 Mar 1998 v New Zealand	1	1	-	-	-

Highest Innings Total

Runs	Team	Batted 1st	Batted 2nd	Date
271	New Zealand	NZ 6-271	SL 238	26 Mar 1995
265	Australia	Aus 5-265	NZ 6-234	31 Mar 1974
264	New Zealand	NZ 8-264	Pak 251	6 Feb 1985

Lowest Completed Innings Total

Runs	Team	Batted 1st	Batted 2nd	Date
94	New Zealand	Aus 8-244	NZ 94	4 Mar 1990
127	England	NZ 8-211	Eng 127	26 Feb 1983
134	New Zealand	Eng 9-188	NZ 134	18 Feb 1984

Leading Run-scorers

Player	M	I	NO	Runs	HS	50	100	Ave.	Stk Rt
K.R. Rutherford, NZ	13	13	-	466	77	5	-	35.85	68.23
C.L. Cairns, New Zealand	10	9	-	339	115	2	1	37.67	86.92
A.C. Parore, New Zealand	11	10	2	266	47*	-	-	33.25	73.89

Highest Individual Innings

Runs	Player	Versus	Date
133*	C.G. Greenidge, West Indies	New Zealand	28 Mar 1987
119*	Ramiz Raja, Pakistan	New Zealand	18 Mar 1992
118	A.C. Gilchrist, Australia	New Zealand	8 Feb 1998

Highest Partnerships

Wkt	Runs	Batsmen	Versus	Date
1st	192*	C.G. Greenidge 133*, D.L. Haynes 53*, West Indies	New Zealand	28 Mar 1987
3rd	170	A.J. Stewart 81, G.P. Thorpe 82, England	New Zealand	20 Feb 1997
1st	146	A.C. Gilchrist 118, M.E. Waugh 65, Australia	New Zealand	8 Feb 1998

Leading Wicket-takers

Player	M	Wkts	Best	4wi	5wi	Ave.	Stk Rt
D.K. Morrison, New Zealand	9	20	5-46	-	1	17.70	25.80
R.J. Hadlee, New Zealand	8	14	5-32	-	1	19.21	30.57
B.L. Cairns, New Zealand	6	12	3-39	-	-	17.33	27.83
G.R. Larsen, New Zealand	14	12	3-39	-	-	38.33	60.00

Best Bowling

Total	Player	Versus	Date
5-13	S.P. O'Donnell, Australia	New Zealand	4 Mar 1990
5-23	R.O. Collinge, New Zealand	India	21 Feb 1976
5-32	R.J. Hadlee, New Zealand	England	18 Feb 1984
5-32	T.M. Alderman, Australia	India	3 Mar 1990

Dunedin, Carisbrook (16 matches)

Summary of Matches

Team	First Match	Played	Won	Lost	NR	Tie
Australia	30 Mar 1974 v New Zealand	5	3	2	-	-
England	8 Mar 1975 v New Zealand	3	2	-	1	-
India	1 Mar 1990 v New Zealand	3	1	2	-	-
New Zealand	30 Mar 1974 v Australia	15	6	8	1	-
Pakistan	6 Feb 1989 v New Zealand	3	2	1	-	-
Sri Lanka	2 Mar 1983 v New Zealand	2	-	2	-	-
West Indies	18 Mar 1987 v New Zealand	1	1	-	-	-

Highest Innings Total

Runs	Team	Batted 1st	Batted 2nd	Date
272	New Zealand	NZ 6-272	SL 165	6 Feb 1991
258	Australia	Aus 6-258	NZ 129	19 Mar 1993
252	India	Aus 6-250	Ind 5-252	22 Feb 1995

Lowest Completed Innings Total

Runs	Team	Batted 1st	Batted 2nd	Date
118	Sri Lanka	NZ 8-183	SL 9-118	2 Mar 1983
129	New Zealand	Aus 6-258	NZ 129	19 Mar 1993
136	England	Eng 136	NZ 0-15	8 Mar 1975

Leading Run-scorers

Player	M	I	NO	Runs	HS	50	100	Ave.	Stk Rt
M.D. Crowe, New Zealand	10	10	1	283	104	-	1	31.44	63.74
K.R. Rutherford, NZ	8	8	1	276	78*	3	-	39.43	67.81
J.G. Wright, New Zealand	7	7	-	218	70	1	-	31.14	55.61

Highest Individual Innings

Runs	Player	Versus	Date
119	I.V.A. Richards, West Indies	New Zealand	18 Mar 1987
104	M.D. Crowe, New Zealand	India	1 Mar 1990
84	S.R. Tendulkar, India	New Zealand	12 Mar 1992

Highest Partnerships

Wkt	Runs	Batsmen	Versus	Date
4th	152	M.D. Crowe 104, K.R. Rutherford 78*, New Zealand	India	1 Mar 1990
2nd	145	M.A. Azharuddin 55, S.R. Tendulkar 84, India	New Zealand	12 Mar 1992
2nd	136	K.R. Stackpole 50, I.M. Chappell 83, Australia	New Zealand	30 Mar 1974

Leading Wicket-takers

Player	M	Wkts	Best	4wi	5wi	Ave.	Stk Rt
R.J. Hadlee, New Zealand	7	18	5-38	1	1	10.44	21.11
D.K. Morrison, New Zealand	6	7	3-43	-	-	22.86	32.00
C.Z. Harris, New Zealand	5	6	3-55	-	-	28.67	37.00
G.R. Larsen, New Zealand	8	6	2-24	-	-	35.67	67.00
M. Prabhakar, India	3	6	3-46	-	-	26.00	30.00
W. Watson, New Zealand	5	6	3-39	-	-	34.67	47.00

Best Bowling

Total	Player	Versus	Date
5-38	R.J. Hadlee, New Zealand	Pakistan	6 Feb 1989
5-41	I.V.A. Richards, West Indies	New Zealand	18 Mar 1987
4-15	R.J. Hadlee, New Zealand	Australia	19 Mar 1986

Hamilton, Seddon Park (10 matches)

Summary of Matches

Team	First Match	Played	Won	Lost	NR	Tie
Australia	8 Mar 1990 v India	2	1	1	-	-
India	15 Feb 1981 v New Zealand	4	1	3	-	-
New Zealand	15 Feb 1981 v India	7	7	-	-	-
Pakistan	15 Jan 1985 v New Zealand	2	-	2	-	-
South Africa	18 Feb 1995 v India	1	1	-	-	-
Sri Lanka	25 Feb 1982 v New Zealand	2	-	2	-	-
Zimbabwe	7 Mar 1992 v India	2	-	2	-	-

Highest Innings Total

Runs	Team	Batted 1st	Batted 2nd	Date
280	New Zealand	NZ 6-280	SL 6-117	29 Mar 1995
250	New Zealand	Aus 7-247	NZ 7-250	27 Mar 1993
248	New Zealand	NZ 7-248	Zim 208	4 Feb 1998

Lowest Completed Innings Total

Runs	Team	Batted 1st	Batted 2nd	Date
138	Pakistan	Pak 9-138	NZ 3-139	14 Mar 1989
153	India	NZ 8-210	Ind 153	15 Feb 1981
206	Sri Lanka	SL 9-206	NZ 4-210	25 Feb 1992

Leading Run-scorers

Player	M	I	NO	Runs	HS	50	100	Ave.	Stk Rt
M.D. Crowe, New Zealand	4	4	-	170	91	2	-	42.50	76.58
N.J. Astle, New Zealand	2	2	-	144	95	1	-	72.00	70.59
J.G. Wright, New Zealand	4	4	-	135	57	1	-	33.75	61.36

Highest Individual Innings

Runs	Player	Versus	Date
108	M.E. Waugh, Australia	New Zealand	27 Mar 1993
95	N.J. Astle, New Zealand	Sri Lanka	29 Mar 1995
91	M.D. Crowe, New Zealand	Australia	27 Mar 1993

Highest Partnerships

Wkt	Runs	Batsmen	Versus	Date
2nd	143	M.E. Waugh 108, D.M. Jones 64, Australia	New Zealand	27 Mar 1993
2nd	120	G. Kirsten 80, D.J. Cullinan 65, South Africa	India	18 Feb 1995
1st	112	G.R. Marsh 86, M.A. Taylor 56, Australia	India	8 Mar 1990

Leading Wicket-takers

Player	M	Wkts	Best	4wi	5wi	Ave.	Stk Rt
D.K. Morrison, New Zealand	3	7	4-33	1	-	14.86	23.14
C.Z. Harris, New Zealand	3	6	3-43	-	-	21.17	27.00
M.G. Hughes, Australia	2	4	3-36	-	-	16.00	25.50
A. Kumble, India	1	4	4-40	1	-	10.00	15.00
M.C. Snedden, New Zealand	2	4	2-14	-	-	12.25	27.00
D.L. Vettori, New Zealand	1	4	4-49	1	-	12.25	15.00
W. Watson, New Zealand	2	4	3-37	-	-	14.25	30.00

Best Bowling

Total	Player	Versus	Date
4-33	D.K. Morrison, New Zealand	Pakistan	14 Mar 1989
4-40	A. Kumble, India	South Africa	18 Feb 1995
4-49	D.L. Vettori, New Zealand	Zimbabwe	4 Feb 1998

Napier, McLean Park (13 matches)

Summary of Matches

Team	First Match	Played	Won	Lost	NR	Tie
Australia	12 Feb 1998 v New Zealand	1	-	1	-	-
England	16 Mar 1988 v New Zealand	2	-	1	-	1
India	25 Mar 1994 v New Zealand	3	1	2	-	-
New Zealand	19 Mar 1983 v Sri Lanka	13	10	2	-	1
Pakistan	12 Jan 1985 v New Zealand	2	-	2	-	-
Sri Lanka	19 Mar 1983 v New Zealand	2	-	2	-	-
Zimbabwe	3 Mar 1992 v New Zealand	3	1	2	-	-

Highest Innings Total

Runs	Team	Batted 1st	Batted 2nd	Date
277	New Zealand	NZ 6-277	Pak 9-167	12 Jan 1985
267	Zimbabwe	Zim 7-267	NZ 246	3 Feb 1996
240	New Zealand	Aus 236	NZ 3-240	12 Feb 1998
240	New Zealand	NZ 5-240	Ind 9-212	25 Mar 1994

Lowest Completed Innings Total

Runs	Team	Batted 1st	Batted 2nd	Date
160	India	Ind 160	NZ 6-162	16 Feb 1995
167	Pakistan	NZ 6-277	Pak 9-167	12 Jan 1985
167	Sri Lanka	SL 8-167	NZ 3-168	19 Mar 1983

Leading Run-scorers

Player	M	I	NO	Runs	HS	50	100	Ave.	Stk Rt
S.P. Fleming, New Zealand	6	6	3	355	111*	3	1	118.33	82.56
N.J. Astle, New Zealand	4	4	1	223	104*	1	1	74.33	74.33
J.G. Wright, New Zealand	4	4	-	220	101	1	1	55.00	68.97

Highest Individual Innings

Runs	Player	Versus	Date
111*	S.P. Fleming, New Zealand	Australia	12 Feb 1998
106	B.C. Broad, England	New Zealand	16 Mar 1988
104*	N.J. Astle, New Zealand	Zimbabwe	6 Mar 1998

Highest Partnerships

Wkt	Runs	Batsmen	Versus	Date
1st	147	L.G. Howell 66, N.J. Astle 104*, New Zealand	Zimbabwe	6 Mar 1998
4th	144	S.P. Fleming 90, S.A. Thomson 83, New Zealand	India	25 Mar 1994
3rd	129	A.H. Jones 57, M.D. Crowe 74*, New Zealand	Zimbabwe	3 Mar 1992

Leading Wicket-takers

Player	M	Wkts	Best	4wi	5wi	Ave.	Stk Rt
C.Z. Harris, New Zealand	9	12	3-15	-	-	21.75	37.50
G.R. Larsen, New Zealand	7	11	3-16	-	-	19.82	33.82
D.K. Morrison, New Zealand	7	11	3-22	-	-	18.36	30.45

Best Bowling

Total	Player	Versus	Date
5-42	C.L. Cairns, New Zealand	Australia	12 Feb 1998
5-44	A.C.I. Lock, Zimbabwe	New Zealand	3 Feb 1996
4-34	M.C. Snedden, New Zealand	England	16 Mar 1988

Wellington, Basin Reserve (24 matches)

Summary of Matches

Team	First Match	Played	Won	Lost	NR	Tie
Australia	20 Feb 1982 v New Zealand	5	4	1	-	-
England	9 Mar 1975 v New Zealand	6	1	4	1	-
India	6 Mar 1990 v New Zealand	4	2	1	1	-
New Zealand	9 Mar 1975 v England	21	9	10	2	-
Pakistan	8 Mar 1989 v New Zealand	4	3	1	-	-
South Africa	2 Mar 1992 v Sri Lanka	2	-	2	-	-
Sri Lanka	2 Mar 1992 v South Africa	2	1	1	-	-
West Indies	10 Mar 1992 v India	2	2	-	-	-
Zimbabwe	31 Jan 1996 v New Zealand	2	-	2	-	-

Highest Innings Total

Runs	Team	Batted 1st	Batted 2nd	Date
297	Australia	Aus 6-297	NZ 231	10 Feb 1998
295	New Zealand	NZ 6-295	Eng 192	23 Feb 1983
261	Pakistan	Pak 4-261	NZ 207	20 Dec 1995

Lowest Completed Innings Total

Runs	Team	Batted 1st	Batted 2nd	Date
74	New Zealand	NZ 74	Aus 2-75	20 Feb 1982
108	New Zealand	Pak 8-158	NZ 108	26 Dec 1992
123	South Africa	SAF 123	Aus 7-124	15 Feb 1995

Leading Run-scorers

Player	M	I	NO	Runs	HS	50	100	Ave.	Stk Rt
M.D. Crowe, New Zealand	9	9	3	345	91*	3	-	57.50	76.16
A.H. Jones, New Zealand	8	8	-	311	78	3	-	38.88	63.60
K.R. Rutherford, NZ	8	8	1	260	79	1	-	37.14	64.20

Highest Individual Innings

Runs	Player	Versus	Date
126*	Shoaib Mohammed, Pakistan	New Zealand	8 Mar 1989
101	B.E. Congdon, New Zealand	England	9 Mar 1975
94	G.M. Turner, New Zealand	England	23 Feb 1983
94	N.J. Astle, New Zealand	England	4 Mar 1997

Highest Partnerships

Wkt	Runs	Batsmen	Versus	Date
1st	152	G.M. Turner 94, B.A. Edgar 60, New Zealand	England	23 Feb 1983
3rd	152	Shoaib Mohammad 126*, Ramiz Raja 72, Pakistan	New Zealand	8 Mar 1989
2nd	142	Aamir Sohail 76, Inzamam-ul-Haq 88, Pakistan	New Zealand	9 Mar 1994

Leading Wicket-takers

Player	M	Wkts	Best	4wi	5wi	Ave.	Stk Rt
D.K. Morrison, New Zealand	9	16	3-32	-	-	22.00	29.25
C.Z. Harris, New Zealand	10	11	3-24	-	-	29.36	44.18
G.R. Larsen, New Zealand	12	11	3-17	-	-	35.73	62.73

Best Bowling

Wkts	Player	Versus	Date
5-17	T.M. Alderman, Australia	New Zealand	20 Feb 1982
5-19	Wasim Akram, Pakistan	New Zealand	26 Dec 1992
5-20	V.J. Marks, England	New Zealand	22 Feb 1982

PAKISTAN

Gujranwala, Municipal Stadium (10 matches)

Summary of Matches

Team	First Match	Played	Won	Lost	NR	Tie
England	9 Oct 1987 v West Indies	1	1	-	-	-
India	3 Dec 1982 v Pakistan	2	-	2	-	-
New Zealand	4 Dec 1996 v Pakistan	1	-	1	-	-
Pakistan	3 Dec 1982 v India	9	7	2	-	-
Sri Lanka	23 Oct 1985 v Pakistan	2	-	2	-	-
West Indies	27 Nov 1985 v Pakistan	3	2	1	-	-
UAE	24 Feb 1996 v Pakistan	1	-	1	-	-
Zimbabwe	20 Nov 1998 v Pakistan	1	-	1	-	-

Highest Innings Total

Runs	Team	Batted 1st	Batted 2nd	Date
246	England	WI 7-243	Eng 8-246	9 Oct 1987
243	West Indies	WI 7-243	Eng 8-246	9 Oct 1987
241	Pakistan	Zim 237	Pak 6-241	20 Nov 1998

Lowest Completed Innings Total

Runs	Team	Batted 1st	Batted 2nd	Date
196	West Indies	WI 7-196	Pak 6-155	4 Nov 1986
217	New Zealand	Pak 8-228	NZ 217	4 Dec 1996
233	Sri Lanka	SL 5-233	Pak 1-234	29 Sep 1995

Leading Run-scorers

Player	M	I	NO	Runs	HS	50	100	Ave.	Stk Rt
Javed Miandad, Pakistan	6	5	2	213	106*	1	1	71.00	69.38
Aamir Sohail, Pakistan	3	3	-	173	91	2	-	57.67	83.57
Salim Malik, Pakistan	5	4	3	156	73*	2	-	156.00	101.96

Highest Individual Innings

Runs	Player	Versus	Date
106*	Javed Miandad, Pakistan	India	3 Dec 1982
102*	Salim Elahi, Pakistan	Sri Lanka	29 Sep 1995
102*	A. Ranatunga, Sri Lanka	Pakistan	29 Sep 1995

Highest Partnerships

Wkt	Runs	Batsmen	Versus	Date
1st	156	Aamir Sohail 77, Salim Elahi 102*, Pakistan	Sri Lanka	29 Sep 1995
4th	137	A.P. Gurusinha 57, A. Ranatunga 102*, Sri Lanka	Pakistan	29 Sep 1995
3rd	119*	A.L. Logie 78*, I.V.A. Richards 80*, West Indies	Pakistan	27 Nov 1985

Leading Wicket-takers

Player	M	Wkts	Best	4wi	5wi	Ave.	Stk Rt
Saqlain Mushtaq, Pakistan	3	9	5-44	1	1	11.78	16.11
Imran Khan, Pakistan	4	6	3-18	-	-	22.83	28.00
Waqar Younis, Pakistan	3	6	3-21	-	-	9.33	16.17

Best Bowling

Total	Player	Versus	Date
5-44	Saqlain Mushtaq, Pakistan	New Zealand	4 Dec 1996
4-35	Saqlain Mushtaq, Pakistan	Zimbabwe	20 Nov 1998
3-16	Mushtaq Ahmed, Pakistan	UAE	24 Feb 1996

Karachi, National Stadium (23 matches)

Summary of Matches

Team	First Match	Played	Won	Lost	NR	Tie
Australia	22 Oct 1982 v Pakistan	2	1	-	1	-
England	26 Mar 1984 v Pakistan	4	2	2	-	-
India	21 Jan 1983 v Pakistan	3	1	1	1	-
New Zealand	8 Dec 1996 v Pakistan	1	1	-	-	-
Pakistan	21 Nov 1980 v West Indies	21	9	10	2	-
South Africa	26 Oct 1994 v Pakistan	3	1	2	-	-
Sri Lanka	12 Mar 1982 v Pakistan	4	-	4	-	-
West Indies	21 Nov 1980 v Pakistan	7	6	1	-	-
Zimbabwe	24 Dec 1993 v Pakistan	1	-	1	-	-

Highest Innings Total

Runs	Team	Batted 1st	Batted 2nd	Date
360	West Indies	WI 4-360	SL 4-169	13 Oct 1987
324	Australia	Aus 8-324	Pak 238	6 Nov 1998
266	India	Pak 4-265	Ind 6-266	30 Sep 1997

Lowest Completed Innings Total

Runs	Team	Batted 1st	Batted 2nd	Date
143	Zimbabwe	Zim 143	Pak 3-147	24 Dec 1993
146	Pakistan	WI 6-170	Pak 146	20 Nov 1991
163	South Africa	SAF 9-163	Pak 2-166	16 Oct 1994

Leading Run-scorers

Player	M	I	NO	Runs	HS	50	100	Ave.	Stk Rt
Salim Malik, Pakistan	14	11	1	367	88	3	-	36.70	78.25
Ramiz Raja, Pakistan	9	9	1	340	113	2	1	42.50	65.89
I.V.A. Richards, West Indies	4	4	1	324	181	1	1	108.00	119.12

Highest Individual Innings

Runs	Player	Versus	Date
181	I.V.A. Richards, West Indies	Sri Lanka	13 Oct 1987
142	G.A. Gooch, England	Pakistan	20 Nov 1987
113	Zaheer Abbas, Pakistan	India	21 Jan 1983
113	Ramiz Raja, Pakistan	England	20 Oct 1987

Highest Partnerships

Wkt	Runs	Batsmen	Versus	Date
3rd	182	D.L. Haynes 105, I.V.A. Richards 181, West Indies	Sri Lanka	13 Oct 1987
2nd	170	Mudassar Nazar 61*, Zaheer Abbas 113, Pakistan	India	21 Jan 1983
2nd	167	Ramiz Raja 113, Salim Malik 88, Pakistan	England	20 Oct 1987

Leading Wicket-takers

Player	M	Wkts	Best	4wi	5wi	Ave.	Stk Rt
Wasim Akram, Pakistan	13	20	5-15	-	1	19.40	28.05
Imran Khan, Pakistan	11	14	4-37	1	-	19.93	30.43
Waqar Younis, Pakistan	9	13	5-52	-	1	25.08	30.00

Best Bowling

Total	Player	Versus	Date
5-15	Wasim Akram, Pakistan	Zimbabwe	24 Dec 1993
5-52	Waqar Younis, Pakistan	West Indies	20 Dec 1989
4-34	C.L. Hooper, West Indies	Pakistan	20 Nov 1991

Lahore, Gaddafi Stadium (33 matches)

Summary of Matches

Team	First Match	Played	Won	Lost	NR	Tie
Australia	8 Oct 1982 v Pakistan	7	4	2	-	1
England	13 Jan 1978 v Pakistan	3	1	2	-	-
Netherlands	26 Feb 1996 v Pakistan	2	-	2	-	-
India	31 Dec 1982 v Pakistan	3	1	2	-	-
New Zealand	2 Nov 1990 v Pakistan	2	-	2	-	-
Pakistan	13 Jan 1978 v England	26	15	9	-	2
South Africa	12 Oct 1994 v Australia	5	4	1	-	-
Sri Lanka	29 Mar 1982 v Pakistan	7	4	3	-	-
UAE	1 Mar 1996 v Netherlands	1	1	-	-	-
West Indies	19 Dec 1980 v Pakistan	8	1	6	-	1
Zimbabwe	27 Dec 1993 v Pakistan	2	-	2	-	-

Highest Innings Total

Runs	Team	Batted 1st	Batted 2nd	Date
316	Australia	Pak 8-315	Aus 4-316	10 Nov 1998
315	Pakistan	Pak 8-315	Aus 4-316	10 Nov 1998
311	South Africa	SAF 9-311	SL 9-245	6 Nov 1997

Lowest Completed Innings Total

Runs	Team	Batted 1st	Batted 2nd	Date
112	India	Pak 8-150	Ind 112	22 Dec 1989
122	England	Pak 6-158	Eng 122	13 Jan 1978
145	Netherlands	Neth 7-145	Pak 2-151	26 Feb 1996

Leading Run-scorers

Player	M	I	NO	Runs	HS	50	100	Ave.	Stk Rt
Javed Miandad, Pakistan	16	15	3	604	119*	4	1	50.33	75.50
Ijaz Ahmed, Pakistan	15	15	2	554	139*	1	2	42.62	87.11
Saeed Anwar, Pakistan	12	11	3	501	108*	3	2	62.63	88.83

Highest Individual Innings

Runs	Player	Versus	Date
139*	Ijaz Ahmed, Pakistan	India	2 Oct 1997
134*	S.T. Jayasuriya, Sri Lanka	Pakistan	5 Nov 1997
124*	R.T. Ponting, Australia	Pakistan	10 Nov 1998

Highest Partnerships

Wkt	Runs	Batsmen	Versus	Date
3rd	213*	S.T. Jayasuriya 134*, P.A. de Silva 102*, Sri Lanka	Pakistan	5 Nov 1997
2nd	193	A.C. Gilchrist 103, R.T. Ponting 124*, Australia	Pakistan	10 Nov 1998
4th	171*	R.S. Mahanama 94*, A. Ranatunga 87*, Sri Lanka	West Indies	1 Nov 1997

Leading Wicket-takers

Player	M	Wkts	Best	4wi	5wi	Ave.	Stk Rt
Wasim Akram, Pakistan	16	20	4-33	1	-	27.65	37.25
Salim Malik, Pakistan	17	15	5-35	-	1	17.40	21.40
Waqar Younis, Pakistan	11	13	4-26	1	-	32.46	42.31

Best Bowling

Total	Player	Versus	Date
6-49	L. Klusener, South Africa	Sri Lanka	6 Nov 1997
5-29	S.F. Dukanwala, UAE	Netherlands	1 Mar 1996
5-35	Salim Malik, Pakistan	New Zealand	2 Nov 1990

Peshawar, Arbab Niaz Stadium (12 matches)
(formerly Shahi Bagh Stadium)

Summary of Matches

Team	First Match	Played	Won	Lost	NR	Tie
Australia	24 Oct 1994 v South Africa	2	2	-	-	-
England	17 Oct 1987 v Sri Lanka	4	4	-	-	-
Netherlands	22 Feb 1996 v England	1	-	-	-	-
New Zealand	12 Nov 1984 v Pakistan	2	-	2	-	-
Pakistan	12 Nov 1984 v New Zealand	8	4	4	-	-
South Africa	24 Oct 1994 v Australia	1	-	1	-	-
Sri Lanka	13 Oct 1985 v Pakistan	2	-	2	-	-
UAE	18 Feb 1996 v England	1	-	1	-	-
West Indies	2 Dec 1985 v Pakistan	2	2	-	-	-
Zimbabwe	3 Nov 1996 v Pakistan	1	-	2	-	-

Highest Innings Total

Runs	Team	Batted 1st	Batted 2nd	Date
296	England	Eng 4-296	SL 8-158	17 Oct 1987
279	England	Eng 4-279	Neth 6-230	22 Feb 1996
264	Pakistan	Pak 9-264	Zim 147	3 Nov 1996

Lowest Completed Innings Total

Runs	Team	Batted 1st	Batted 2nd	Date
127	New Zealand	NZ 127	Pak 2-128	4 Nov 1990
136	UAE	UAE 136	Eng 2-140	18 Feb 1996
138	England	Eng 8-236	Pak 138	22 Nov 1987

Leading Run-scorers

Player	M	I	NO	Runs	HS	50	100	Ave.	Stk Rt
Ijaz Ahmed, Pakistan	4	4	1	144	117	-	1	48.00	87.27
G.A. Gooch, England	2	2	-	141	84	2	-	70.50	79.21
G.P. Thorpe, England	2	2	1	133	89	1	-	133.00	89.86

Highest Individual Innings

Runs	Player	Versus	Date
117	Ijaz Ahmed, Pakistan	Zimbabwe	3 Nov 1996
104*	G.A. Hick, England	Holland	22 Feb 1996
100*	W.J. Cronje, South Africa	Australia	24 Oct 1994

Highest Partnerships

Wkt	Runs	Batsmen	Versus	Date
4th	151	Ijaz Ahmed 117, Azam Khan 72, Pakistan	Zimbabwe	3 Nov 1996
3rd	143	G.A. Hick 104*, G.P. Thorpe 89, England	Netherlands	22 Feb 1996
1st	113	Mudassar Nazar 40, Shoaib Mohammed 72*, Pakistan	Sri Lanka	13 Oct 1985

Leading Wicket-takers

Player	M	Wkts	Best	4wi	5wi	Ave.	Stk Rt
P.J. DeFreitas, England	4	8	3-31	-	-	12.75	26.63
Saqlain Mushtaq, Pakistan	2	7	4-28	1	-	9.00	13.86
Abdul Qadir, Pakistan	4	6	3-49	-	-	28.00	33.00
Imran Khan, Pakistan	3	6	3-39	-	-	13.83	22.50
Mudassar Nazar, Pakistan	5	6	3-34	-	-	20.50	28.33

Best Bowling

Wkts	Player	Versus	Date
5-11	Waqar Younis, Pakistan	New Zealand	4 Nov 1990
4-17	M.A. Holding, West Indies	Pakistan	2 Dec 1985
4-19	Zakir Khan, Pakistan	New Zealand	12 Nov 1984

Pakistan - other grounds

Faisalabad, Iqbal Stadium (9 matches)

Match	Batted 1st	Batted 2nd	Result	Date
Pakistan v New Zealand	Pak 5-157	NZ 7-152	Pak by 5 runs	23 Nov 1984
Pakistan v Sri Lanka	Pak 7-297	SL 8-184	Pak by 113 runs	25 Oct 1987
Pakistan v West Indies	WI 5-204	Pak 8-187	WI by 17 runs	24 Nov 1991
Australia v South Africa	Aus 6-208	SAF 186	Aus by 22 runs	18 Oct 1994
Pakistan v South Africa	SAF 4-222	Pak 4-223	Pak by 6 wkts	28 Oct 1994
Pakistan v Sri Lanka	SL 7-257	Pak 8-208	SL by 49 runs	1 Oct 1995
New Zealand v South Africa	NZ 9-177	SAF 5-178	SAF by 5 wkts	20 Feb 1996
New Zealand v UAE	NZ 8-276	UAE 9-167	NZ by 109 runs	27 Feb 1996
England v Sri Lanka	Eng 8-235	SL 5-236	SL by 5 wkts	9 Mar 1996

Hyderabad, Niaz Stadium (6 matches)

Match	Batted 1st	Batted 2nd	Result	Date
Pakistan v Australia	Pak 6-229	Aus 9-170	Pak by 59 runs	20 Sep 1982
Pakistan v Sri Lanka	Pak 7-216	SL 127	Pak by 89 runs	3 Nov 1985
Pakistan v West Indies	Pak 6-202	WI 7-191	Pak by 11 runs	18 Nov 1986
Pakistan v Sri Lanka	Pak 6-267	SL 252	Pak by 15 runs	8 Oct 1987
Pakistan v Sri Lanka	Pak 3-241	SL 9-182	Pak by 59 runs	15 Jan 1992
Pakistan v India	Ind 170	Pak 5-171	Pak by 5 wkts	28 Sep 1997

Multan, Ibn-e-Qasim Bagh Stadium (6 matches)

Match	Batted 1st	Batted 2nd	Result	Date
Pakistan v India	Pak 2-263	Ind 7-226	Pak by 37 runs	17 Dec 1982
Pakistan v New Zealand	NZ 8-213	Pak 9-214	Pak by 1 wkt	7 Dec 1984
Pakistan v West Indies	WI 5-202	Pak 113	WI by 89 runs	17 Nov 1986
Pakistan v West Indies	Pak 9-168	WI 7-137	Pak by 31 runs	13 Nov 1990
Pakistan v Sri Lanka	Pak 5-205	SL 6-206	SL by 4 wkts	17 Jan 1992
Pakistan v Australia	Pak 8-200	Aus 3-201	Aus by 7 wkts	14 Oct 1994

Quetta, Ayub National Stadium (2 matches)

Match	Batted 1st	Batted 2nd	Result	Date
Pakistan v India	Ind 7-170	Pak 8-166	Ind by 4 runs	1 Oct 1978
Pakistan v India	Pak 7-199	Ind 153	Pak by 46 runs	12 Dec 1984

Quetta, Bughti Stadium (1 match)

Match	Batted 1st	Batted 2nd	Result	Date
Pakistan v Zimbabwe	Zim 9-237	Pak 7-239	Pak by 3 wkts	30 Oct 1996

Rawalpindi, Pindi Club Ground (2 matches)

Match	Batted 1st	Batted 2nd	Result	Date
Pakistan v West Indies	WI 8-199	Pak 5-203	Pak by 5 wkts	4 Dec 1985
Pakistan v England	Pak 7-239	Eng 221	Pak by 18 runs	13 Oct 1987

Rawalpindi, Rawalpindi Cricket Stadium (9 matches)

Match	Batted 1st	Batted 2nd	Result	Date
Pakistan v Sri Lanka	Pak 4-271	SL 154	Pak by 117 runs	19 Jan 1992
Pakistan v Zimbabwe	Zim 5-195	Pak 4-196	Pak by 6 wkts	25 Dec 1993
Pakistan v South Africa	Pak 6-249	SAF 5-210	Pak by 39 runs	20 Oct 1994
Pakistan v Australia	Aus 6-250	Pak 1-251	Pak by 9 wkts	22 Oct 1994
Pakistan v Sri Lanka	Pak 9-183	SL 6-184	SL by 4 wkts	3 Oct 1995
South Africa v UAE	SAF 2-321	UAE 8-152	SAF by 169 runs	16 Feb 1996
England v South Africa	SAF 230	Eng 152	SAF by 78 runs	25 Feb 1996
Netherlands v South Africa	SAF 3-328	Neth 8-168	SAF by 160 runs	5 Mar 1996
Pakistan v Zimbabwe	Pak 6-302	Zim 191	Pak by 111 runs	24 Nov 1998

Sahiwal, Zafar Ali Stadium (2 matches)

Match	Batted 1st	Batted 2nd	Result	Date
Pakistan v England	Pak 6-208	Eng 7-212	Eng by 3 wkts	23 Dec 1977
Pakistan v India	Pak 7-205	Ind 2-183	Pak[1]	3 Nov 1978

[1]*India conceded the match*

Sargodha, Sargodha Stadium (1 match)

Match	Batted 1st	Batted 2nd	Result	Date
Pakistan v Sri Lanka	SL 6-155	Pak 2-157	Pak by 8 wkts	10 Jan 1992

Sialkot, Jinnah Stadium (9 matches)

Match	Batted 1st	Batted 2nd	Result	Date
Pakistan v New Zealand	NZ 8-198	Pak 9-197	NZ by 1 run	16 Oct 1976
Pakistan v England	Pak 151	Eng 4-152	Eng by 6 wkts	30 Dec 1977
Pakistan v India	Ind 79	Pak 2-83	Pak by 8 wkts	13 Oct 1978
Pakistan v West Indies	Pak 4-200	WI 3-201	WI by 7 wkts	5 Dec 1980
Pakistan v India	Ind 3-210	Pak DNB	No result	31 Oct 1984
Pakistan v New Zealand	NZ 9-187	Pak 8-153	NZ by 34 runs	2 Dec 1984
Pakistan v West Indies	Pak 7-148	WI 6-151	WI by 4 wkts	14 Nov 1986
Pakistan v New Zealand	Pak 2-223	NZ 118	Pak by 105 runs	6 Nov 1990
Pakistan v New Zealand	Pak 9-277	NZ 231	Pak by 46 runs	6 Dec 1996

Sheikupura, Sheikupura Stadium (1 match)

Match	Batted 1st	Batted 2nd	Result	Date
Pakistan v Zimbabwe	Pak 211	Zim 4-212	Zim by 6 wkts	22 Nov 1998

SINGAPORE

Padang Ground (5 matches)

Team	Batted 1st	Batted 2nd	Result	Date
Pakistan v Sri Lanka	Pak 3-54	SL DNB	No result	1 Apr 1996
Pakistan v Sri Lanka	SL 9-349	Pak 315	SL by 34 runs	2 Apr 1996
India v Sri Lanka	Ind 199	SL 187	Ind by 12 runs	3 Apr 1996
India v Pakistan	Ind 8-226	Pak 2-190	Pak by 8 wkts[†]	5 Apr 1996
Pakistan v Sri Lanka	Pak 215	SL 172	Pak by 43 runs	7 Apr 1996

[†]*revised target*

SOUTH AFRICA

Bloemfontein, Springbok Park (10 matches)

Summary of Matches

Team	First Match	Played	Won	Lost	NR	Tie
Australia	8 Apr 1994 v South Africa	2	1	1	-	-
England	11 Jan 1996 v South Africa	1	1	-	-	-
India	15 Dec 1992 v South Africa	2	-	2	-	-
New Zealand	8 Dec 1994 v Sri Lanka	1	-	-	1	-
South Africa	15 Dec 1992 v India	9	5	4	-	-
Sri Lanka	8 Dec 1994 v New Zealand	3	1	1	1	-
West Indies	23 Feb 1993 v South Africa	2	1	1	-	-

Highest Innings Total

Runs	Team	Batted 1st	Batted 2nd	Date
310	South Africa	SAF 6-310	Aus 201	13 Apr 1997
288	Sri Lanka	SL 4-288	NZ 1-66	8 Dec 1994
273	South Africa	SAF 273	WI 159	5 Feb 1999

Lowest Completed Innings Total

Runs	Team	Batted 1st	Batted 2nd	Date
105	Sri Lanka	SL 105	SAF 5-106	19 Apr 1998
159	West Indies	SAF 273	WI 159	5 Feb 1999
185	South Africa	SAF 6-185	WI 1-188	23 Feb 1993

Leading Run-scorers

Player	M	I	NO	Runs	HS	50	100	Ave.	Stk Rt
W.J. Cronje, South Africa	9	7	1	251	82	2	-	41.83	92.62
D.J. Cullinan, South Africa	6	6	1	202	57*	2	-	40.40	68.01
S.T. Jayasuriya, Sri Lanka	3	3	-	170	140	-	1	56.67	83.33

Highest Individual Innings

Runs	Player	Versus	Date
140	S.T. Jayasuriya, Sri Lanka	New Zealand	8 Dec 1994
111*	B.C. Lara, West Indies	South Africa	23 Feb 1993
108	A.C. Hudson, South Africa	India	15 Dec 1992

Highest Partnerships

Wkt	Runs	Batsmen	Versus	Date
3rd	123	M.A. Taylor 63, M.E. Waugh 71, Australia	South Africa	6 Apr 1994
3rd	92	W.V. Raman 47, A.D. Jadeja 48, India	South Africa	7 Dec 1992
2nd	72	A.C. Hudson 62, W.J. Cronje 37, South Africa	Australia	6 Apr 1994

Leading Wicket-takers

Player	M	Wkts	Best	4wi	5wi	Ave.	Stk Rt
L. Klusener, South Africa	3	10	5-42	-	1	10.10	13.00
S.M. Pollock, South Africa	5	10	3-21	-	-	16.40	24.90
P.L. Symcox, South Africa	4	6	2-38	-	-	20.00	28.00

Best Bowling

Total	Player	Versus	Date
5-42	L. Klusener, South Africa	India	23 Jan 1997
4-44	K.L.T. Arthurton, West Indies	South Africa	5 Feb 1999
3-21	S.M. Pollock, South Africa	Sri Lanka	19 Apr 1998

Cape Town, Newlands (11 matches)

Summary of Matches

Team	First Match	Played	Won	Lost	NR	Tie
Australia	6 Apr 1994 v South Africa	2	1	1	-	-
England	9 Jan 1996 v South Africa	1	-	1	-	-
India	7 Dec 1992 v South Africa	1	-	1	-	-
New Zealand	6 Dec 1994 v South Africa	1	-	1	-	-
Pakistan	25 Feb 1993 v West Indies	3	-	3	-	-
South Africa	7 Dec 1992 v India	10	9	1	-	-
West Indies	17 Feb 1993 v South Africa	3	1	2	-	-
Zimbabwe	29 Jan 1997 v South Africa	1	-	1	-	-

Highest Innings Total

Runs	Team	Batted 1st	Batted 2nd	Date
245	South Africa	SAF 8-245	Aus 9-199	2 Apr 1997
242	Australia	Aus 6-242	SAF 5-206	6 Apr 1994
229	South Africa	Zim 6-226	SAF 5-229	29 Jan 1997

Lowest Completed Innings Total

Runs	Team	Batted 1st	Batted 2nd	Date
43	Pakistan	Pak 43	WI 3-45	25 Feb 1993
114	Pakistan	Pak 114	SAF 1-115	23 Apr 1998
132	West Indies	SAF 8-221	WI 132	2 Feb 1999

Leading Run-scorers

Player	M	I	NO	Runs	HS	50	100	Ave.	Stk Rt
J.N. Rhodes, South Africa	10	9	2	234	83*	1	-	33.43	77.48
D.J. Cullinan, South Africa	7	6	-	191	64	1	-	31.83	63.04
W.J. Cronje, South Africa	10	9	1	190	38	-	-	23.75	56.89

Highest Individual Innings

Runs	Player	Versus	Date
83*	J.N. Rhodes, South Africa	Australia	2 Apr 1997
82	M.G. Bevan, Australia	South Africa	2 Apr 1997
71	Aamir Sohail, Pakistan	South Africa	10 Jan 1995
71	M.E. Waugh, Australia	South Africa	6 Apr 1994

Highest Partnerships

Wkt	Runs	Batsmen	Versus	Date
3rd	123	M.A. Taylor 63, M.E. Waugh 71, Australia	South Africa	6 Apr 1994
3rd	92	W.V. Raman 47, A.D. Jadeja 48, India	South Africa	7 Dec 1992
8th	91	D.M. Beckenstein 69, L. Klusener 54, South Africa	West Indies	2 Feb 1999

Leading Wicket-takers

Player	M	Wkts	Best	4wi	5wi	Ave.	Stk Rt
W.J. Cronje, South Africa	10	16	5-32	-	1	15.38	25.06
S.M. Pollock, South Africa	5	9	4-34	1	-	16.11	27.89
A.A. Donald, South Africa	6	7	3-38	-	-	26.57	46.14
L. Klusener, South Africa	3	7	5-25	-	1	11.43	21.57
E.O. Simons, South Africa	3	7	4-42	1	-	14.43	23.00

Best Bowling

Total	Player	Versus	Date
5-25	L. Klusener, South Africa	Pakistan	23 Apr 1998
5-32	W.J. Cronje, South Africa	India	7 Dec 1992
4-16	C.A. Walsh, West Indies	Pakistan	25 Feb 1993

Centurion, Centurion Park (11 matches)

Summary of Matches

Team	First Match	Played	Won	Lost	NR	Tie
Australia	20 Feb 1994 v South Africa	2	1	1	-	-
England	14 Jan 1996 v South Africa	1	-	1	-	-
India	11 Dec 1992 v South Africa	2	1	1	-	-
New Zealand	11 Dec 1994 v South Africa	1	-	1	-	-
Pakistan	21 Dec 1993 v South Africa	3	2	1	-	-
South Africa	11 Dec 1992 v India	9	6	3	-	-
Sri Lanka	4 Dec 1994 v Pakistan	1	-	1	-	-
West Indies	7 Feb 1999 v South Africa	1	-	1	-	-
Zimbabwe	25 Jan 1997 v South Africa	2	1	1	-	-

Highest Innings Total

Runs	Team	Batted 1st	Batted 2nd	Date
314	South Africa	SAF 7-314	NZ 233	11 Dec 1994
287	Australia	SAF 7-284	Aus 5-287	10 Apr 1997
284	South Africa	SAF 7-284	Aus 5-287	10 Apr 1997

Lowest Completed Innings Total

Runs	Team	Batted 1st	Batted 2nd	Date
145	Pakistan	Pak 145	SAF 3-149	17 Apr 1998
176	West Indies	SAF 8-226	WI 176	7 Feb 1999
198	South Africa	Pak 8-220	SAF 9-198	21 Feb 1993

Leading Run-scorers

Player	M	I	NO	Runs	HS	50	100	Ave.	Stk Rt
W.J. Cronje, South Africa	9	9	2	414	97	4	-	59.14	83.13
D.J. Cullinan, South Africa	6	6	1	254	89	2	-	50.80	81.15
D.J. Callaghan, South Africa	2	2	2	201	169*	-	1	-	118.93

Highest Individual Innings

Runs	Player	Versus	Date
169*	D.J. Callaghan, South Africa	New Zealand	11 Dec 1994
116	G. Kirsten, South Africa	England	14 Jan 1996
114	W.V. Raman, India	South Africa	11 Dec 1992

Highest Partnerships

Wkt	Runs	Batsmen	Versus	Date
4th	189	S.R. Waugh 89, M.G. Bevan 103, Australia	South Africa	10 Apr 1997
1st	156	A.C. Hudson 72, G. Kirsten 116, South Africa	England	14 Jan 1996
2nd	149	D.J. Callaghan 169*, W.J. Cronje 68, South Africa	New Zealand	11 Dec 1994

Leading Wicket-takers

Player	M	Wkts	Best	4wi	5wi	Ave.	Stk Rt
A.A. Donald, South Africa	7	11	4-37	1	-	29.90	35.36
W.J. Cronje, South Africa	9	9	2-21	-	-	35.22	41.22
C.R. Matthews, South Africa	4	9	3-26	-	-	17.56	22.67

Best Bowling

Total	Player	Versus	Date
4-37	A.A. Donald, South Africa	Zimbabwe	25 Jan 1997
4-59	M.L. Su'a, New Zealand	South Africa	11 Dec 1994
3-26	C.R. Matthews, South Africa	Australia	20 Feb 1994

Durban, Kingsmead (12 matches)

Summary of Matches

Team	First Match	Played	Won	Lost	NR	Tie
Australia	24 Feb 1994 v South Africa	2	1	1	-	-
England	5 Apr 1997 v South Africa	1	-	1	-	-
India	17 Dec 1992 v South Africa	3	-	2	1	-
Pakistan	9 Feb 1993 v South Africa	5	3	2	-	-
South Africa	17 Dec 1992 v India	9	5	3	1	-
Sri Lanka	2 Dec 1994 v Pakistan	1	-	1	-	-
West Indies	19 Feb 1993 v South Africa	1	1	-	-	-

Highest Innings Total

Runs	Team	Batted 1st	Batted 2nd	Date
280	South Africa	SAF 4-280	Pak 228	3 Apr 1998
278	South Africa	SAF 8-278	Ind 234	13 Feb 1997
274	South Africa	SAF 9-274	WI 219	27 Jan 1999

Lowest Completed Innings Total

Runs	Team	Batted 1st	Batted 2nd	Date
144	Pakistan	WI 5-268	Pak 144	19 Feb 1993
154	Australia	Aus 154	SAF 3-157	24 Feb 1994
177	India	SAF 8-216	Ind 177	17 Dec 1992

Leading Run-scorers

Player	M	I	NO	Runs	HS	50	100	Ave.	Stk Rt
W.J. Cronje, South Africa	10	9	1	296	78	3	-	37.00	73.27
J.H. Kallis, South Africa	6	6	2	258	109*	1	1	64.50	76.56
J.N. Rhodes, South Africa	10	9	2	244	94*	2	-	34.86	82.71

Highest Individual Innings

Runs	Player	Versus	Date
128	B.C. Lara, West Indies	Pakistan	19 Feb 1993
114*	Ijaz Ahmed, Pakistan	South Africa	17 Dec 1994
109*	J.H. Kallis, South Africa	Pakistan	3 Apr 1998

Highest Partnerships

Wkt	Runs	Batsmen	Versus	Date
2nd	197	B.C. Lara 128, P.V. Simmons 70, West Indies	Pakistan	19 Feb 1993
5th	183*	J.H. Kallis 109*, J.N. Rhodes 94*, South Africa	Pakistan	3 Apr 1998
3rd	136*	Ijaz Ahmed 114*, Salim Malik 36*, Pakistan	South Africa	17 Dec 1994

Leading Wicket-takers

Player	M	Wkts	Best	4wi	5wi	Ave.	Stk Rt
Waqar Younis, Pakistan	5	14	5-25	1	1	18.07	21.43
A.A. Donald, South Africa	6	12	4-41	1	-	16.58	28.17
W.J. Cronje, South Africa	10	9	3-45	-	-	26.11	38.22
C.R. Matthews, South Africa	5	9	4-10	1	-	21.67	31.33
S.M. Pollock, South Africa	4	9	4-33	1	-	14.89	24.00

Best Bowling

Total	Player	Versus	Date
5-25	Waqar Younis, Pakistan	South Africa	9 Feb 1993
4-10	C.R. Matthews, South Africa	Australia	24 Feb 1994
4-32	I.R. Bishop, West Indies	Pakistan	19 Feb 1993

East London, Buffalo Park (10 matches)

Summary of Matches

Team	First Match	Played	Won	Lost	NR	Tie
Australia	2 Apr 1994 v South Africa	2	1	1	-	-
England	19 Jan 1996 v South Africa	1	-	1	-	-
India	19 Dec 1992 v South Africa	2	1	1	-	-
New Zealand	18 Dec 1994 v Sri Lanka	2	-	2	-	-
Pakistan	15 Feb 1993 v South Africa	3	2	1	-	-
South Africa	19 Dec 1992 v India	8	4	4	-	-
Sri Lanka	18 Dec 1994 v New Zealand	1	1	-	-	-
West Indies	24 Jan 1999 v South Africa	1	1	-	-	-

Highest Innings Total

Runs	Team	Batted 1st	Batted 2nd	Date
292	West Indies	WI 9-292	SAF 249	24 Jan 1999
257	Sri Lanka	NZ 4-255	SL 5-257	18 Dec 1994
255	New Zealand	NZ 4-255	SL 5-257	18 Dec 1994

Lowest Completed Innings Total

Runs	Team	Batted 1st	Batted 2nd	Date
115	England	SAF 129	Eng 115	19 Jan 1996
129	South Africa	SAF 129	Eng 115	19 Jan 1996
158	South Africa	SAF 158	Aus 3-159	2 Apr 1994

Leading Run-scorers

Player	M	I	NO	Runs	HS	50	100	Ave.	Stk Rt
W.J. Cronje, South Africa	8	7	1	266	81	3	-	44.33	85.26
J.N. Rhodes, South Africa	8	8	1	175	37	-	-	25.00	68.36
J.H. Kallis, South Africa	5	5	1	172	63	3	-	43.00	76.79

Highest Individual Innings

Runs	Player	Versus	Date
150	S. Chanderpaul, West Indies	South Africa	24 Jan 1999
108	C.L. Hooper, West Indies	South Africa	24 Jan 1999
107	Javed Miandad, Pakistan	South Africa	15 Feb 1993

Highest Partnerships

Wkt	Runs	Batsmen	Versus	Date
4th	226	S. Chanderpaul 150, C.L. Hooper 108, West Indies	South Africa	24 Jan 1999
4th	165	Javed Miandad 107, Asif Mujtaba 74, Pakistan	South Africa	15 Feb 1993
3rd	136	A.C. Parore 67, K.R. Rutherford 102*, New Zealand	Sri Lanka	18 Dec 1994

Leading Wicket-takers

Player	M	Wkts	Best	4wi	5wi	Ave.	Stk Rt
S.M. Pollock, South Africa	5	9	6-35	-	1	17.67	33.33
Waqar Younis, Pakistan	3	7	4-33	1	-	15.71	21.14
P.S. De Villiers, South Africa	4	6	4-27	1	-	15.67	34.33
L. Klusener, South Africa	5	6	2-29	-	-	21.67	31.33
Wasim Akram, Pakistan	2	6	5-16	-	1	9.33	16.17

Best Bowling

Total	Player	Versus	Date
6-35	S.M. Pollock, South Africa	West Indies	24 Jan 1999
5-16	Wasim Akram, Pakistan	South Africa	15 Feb 1993
4-27	P.S. De Villiers, South Africa	Pakistan	15 Feb 1993

Johannesburg, The Wanderers (11 matches)

Summary of Matches

Team	First Match	Played	Won	Lost	NR	Tie
Australia	19 Feb 1994 v South Africa	2	1	1	-	-
England	13 Jan 1996 v South Africa	1	-	1	-	-
India	13 Dec 1992 v South Africa	1	-	1	-	-
Pakistan	13 Feb 1993 v West Indies	4	-	4	-	-
South Africa	13 Dec 1992 v India	9	8	1	-	-
Sri Lanka	5 Apr 1998 v South Africa	1	-	1	-	-
West Indies	13 Feb 1993 v Pakistan	3	2	1	-	-
Zimbabwe	31 Jan 1997 v South Africa	1	-	1	-	-

Highest Innings Total

Runs	Team	Batted 1st	Batted 2nd	Date
266	South Africa	SAF 5-266	Pak 109	12 Jan 1995
266	South Africa	SAF 8-266	Pak 209	5 Apr 1998
259	South Africa	Zim 8-256	SAF 6-259	31 Jan 1997

Lowest Completed Innings Total

Runs	Team	Batted 1st	Batted 2nd	Date
109	Pakistan	SAF 5-266	Pak 109	12 Jan 1995
150	Pakistan	Pak 150	WI 2-109	13 Feb 1993
161	India	Ind 9-161	SAF 4-165	13 Dec 1992

Leading Run-scorers

Player	M	I	NO	Runs	HS	50	100	Ave.	Stk Rt
W.J. Cronje, South Africa	9	9	3	404	112	2	1	67.33	87.26
J.N. Rhodes, South Africa	9	8	3	256	47*	-	-	51.20	91.10
M.J.R. Rindel, South Africa	3	3	1	178	106	1	1	89.00	79.46

Highest Individual Innings

Runs	Player	Versus	Date
112	W.J. Cronje, South Africa	Australia	19 Feb 1994
106	M.J.R. Rindel, South Africa	Pakistan	12 Jan 1995
89	M.J. Di Venuto, Australia	South Africa	8 Apr 1997

Highest Partnerships

Wkt	Runs	Batsmen	Versus	Date
1st	190	G. Kirsten 87, M.J.R. Rindel 106, South Africa	Pakistan	12 Jan 1995
2nd	145	A.C. Hudson 74, W.J. Cronje 81, South Africa	Pakistan	10 Dec 1994
6th	137	W.J. Cronje 70*, S.M. Pollock 75, South Africa	Zimbabwe	31 Jan 1997

Leading Wicket-takers

Player	M	Wkts	Best	4wi	5wi	Ave.	Stk Rt
A.A. Donald, South Africa	6	15	4-46	1	-	17.60	22.80
W.J. Cronje, South Africa	9	9	2-37	-	-	25.11	34.00
Waqar Younis, Pakistan	4	7	2-19	-	-	25.29	28.57

Best Bowling

Total	Player	Versus	Date
4-25	I.R. Bishop, West Indies	Pakistan	13 Feb 1993
4-37	R.P. Snell, South Africa	Pakistan	10 Dec 1994
4-43	R. Telemachus, South Africa	Sri Lanka	5 Apr 1998

Port Elizabeth, St George's Park (11 matches)

Summary of Matches

Team	First Match	Played	Won	Lost	NR	Tie
Australia	22 Feb 1994 v South Africa	3	2	1	-	-
England	21 Jan 1996 v South Africa	1	-	1	-	-
India	9 Dec 1992 v South Africa	2	-	2	-	-
New Zealand	13 Dec 1994 v Pakistan	1	-	1	-	-
Pakistan	13 Dec 1994 v New Zealand	1	1	-	-	-
South Africa	9 Dec 1992 v India	10	7	3	-	-
Sri Lanka	21 Dec 1994 v South Africa	2	1	1	-	-
West Indies	11 Feb 1993 v South Africa	2	-	2	-	-

Highest Innings Total

Runs	Team	Batted 1st	Batted 2nd	Date
281	Australia	Aus 6-281	SAF 193	22 Feb 1994
278	South Africa	SAF 6-278	WI 179	30 Jan 1999
237	South Africa	SAF 6-237	SL 6-139	21 Dec 1994

Lowest Completed Innings Total

Runs	Team	Batted 1st	Batted 2nd	Date
147	India	Ind 147	SAF 4-148	9 Dec 1992
149	West Indies	WI 149	SAF 4-150	11 Feb 1993
154	England	SAF 8-218	Eng 154	21 Jan 1996

Leading Run-scorers

Player	M	I	NO	Runs	HS	50	100	Ave.	Stk Rt
J.N. Rhodes, South Africa	9	9	2	363	66	3	-	51.86	68.11
W.J. Cronje, South Africa	10	10	2	285	74	2	-	35.63	78.51
M.E. Waugh, Australia	3	3	1	192	115*	1	1	96.00	92.75

Highest Individual Innings

Runs	Player	Versus	Date
115*	M.E. Waugh, Australia	South Africa	31 Mar 1997
93*	A. Ranatunga, Sri Lanka	South Africa	13 Apr 1998
83	M.D. Crowe, New Zealand	Pakistan	13 Dec 1994

Highest Partnerships

Wkt	Runs	Batsmen	Versus	Date
4th	160	H.H. Gibbs 125, W.J. Cronje 74, South Africa	West Indies	30 Jan 1999
2nd	123	D.C. Boon 76, D.M. Jones 67, Australia	South Africa	22 Feb 1994
8th	119	P.R. Reiffel 58, S.K. Warne 55, Australia	South Africa	4 Apr 1994

Leading Wicket-takers

Player	M	Wkts	Best	4wi	5wi	Ave.	Stk Rt
P.S. De Villiers, South Africa	5	10	4-32	1	-	17.40	26.50
B.M. McMillan, South Africa	4	9	4-32	1	-	14.56	23.78
A.A. Donald, South Africa	5	8	3-27	-	-	21.88	36.75

Best Bowling

Total	Player	Versus	Date
4-32	B.M. McMillan, South Africa	India	9 Dec 1992
4-32	P.S. De Villiers, South Africa	England	21 Jan 1996
4-32	Waqar Younis, Pakistan	New Zealand	13 Dec 1994

South Africa - other grounds

Benoni, Willowmoore Park (2 matches)

Match	Batted 1st	Batted 2nd	Result	Date
India v Zimbabwe	Zim 8-240	Ind 4-241	Ind by 6 wkts	9 Feb 1997
Pakistan v Sri Lanka	SL 288	Pak 173	SL by 115 runs	15 Apr 1998

Kimberley, Kimberley Country Club (1 match)

Match	Batted 1st	Batted 2nd	Result	Date
Pakistan v Sri Lanka	SL 7-295	Pak 6-300	Pak by 4 wkts	7 Apr 1998

Paarl, Boland Park (2 matches)

Match	Batted 1st	Batted 2nd	Result	Date
India v Zimbabwe	Zim 8-236	Ind 236	Match tied	27 Jan 1997
Pakistan v Sri Lanka	Pak 249	SL 139	Pak by 110 runs	9 Apr 1998

Sri Lanka - other grounds

Kandy, Asigiriya Stadium (4 matches)

Match	Batted 1st	Batted 2nd	Result	Date
Sri Lanka v Pakistan	SL 6-124	Pak 2-125	Pak by 8 wkts	2 Mar 1986
Sri Lanka v Bangladesh	Ban 8-131	SL 3-132	SL by 7 wkts	2 Apr 1986
Sri Lanka v South Africa	SL 5-179	SAF 4-52	No result	22 Aug 1993
Sri Lanka v Kenya	SL 5-398	Ken 7-254	SL by 144 runs	6 Mar 1996

Moratuwa, Tyronne Fernando Stadium (6 matches)

Match	Batted 1st	Batted 2nd	Result	Date
Sri Lanka v New Zealand	SL 8-157	NZ 116	SL by 41 runs	31 Mar 1984
Sri Lanka v New Zealand	SL 9-114	NZ 3-118	NZ by 7 wkts	4 Nov 1984
Sri Lanka v Pakistan	Pak 8-125	SL DNB	No result	8 Mar 1986
Bangladesh v Pakistan	Ban 94	Pak 3-98	Pak by 7 wkts	31 Mar 1986
Sri Lanka v England	Eng 180	SL 2-183	SL by 8 wkts	20 Mar 1993
Sri Lanka v India	Ind 9-227	SL 6-231	SL by 4 wkts	14 Aug 1993

SRI LANKA

Colombo, P. Saravanamuttu Stadium (11 matches)

Summary of Matches

Team	First Match	Played	Won	Lost	NR	Tie
Australia	13 Apr 1983 v Sri Lanka	4	-	4	-	-
India	29 Sep 1985 v Sri Lanka	2	-	1	1	-
New Zealand	1 Apr 1984 v Sri Lanka	3	1	2	-	-
Pakistan	30 Mar 1986 v Sri Lanka	1	1	-	-	-
Sri Lanka	13 Apr 1983 v Australia	11	7	2	2	-
West Indies	1 Dec 1993 v Sri Lanka	1	-	-	1	-

Highest Innings Total

Runs	Team	Batted 1st	Batted 2nd	Date
251	Sri Lanka	Aus 5-247	SL 6-251	15 Aug 1992
247	Australia	Aus 5-247	SL 6-251	15 Aug 1992
225	Australia	Aus 6-225	SL 4-164	13 Sep 1994

Lowest Completed Innings Total

Runs	Team	Batted 1st	Batted 2nd	Date
115	Sri Lanka	NZ 8-201	SL 115	1 Apr 1984
116	Sri Lanka	Pak 197	SL 116	30 Mar 1986
190	New Zealand	NZ 7-190	SL 2-192	12 Dec 1992

Leading Run-scorers

Player	M	I	NO	Runs	HS	50	100	Ave.	Stk Rt
P.A. de Silva, Sri Lanka	9	9	2	278	105	1	1	39.71	89.10
A. Ranatunga, Sri Lanka	11	10	4	216	59	2	-	36.00	82.44
R.S. Madugalle, Sri Lanka	6	6	1	138	50*	1	-	27.60	67.98

Highest Individual Innings

Runs	Batsman	Versus	Date
105	P.A. de Silva, Sri Lanka	Australia	15 Aug 1992
94	M.A. Taylor, Australia	Sri Lanka	15 Aug 1992
89	B.C. Lara, West Indies	Sri Lanka	1 Dec 1993

Highest Partnerships

Wkt	Runs	Batsmen	Versus	Date
3rd	147	A.P. Gurusinha 53, P.A. de Silva 105, Sri Lanka	Australia	15 Aug 1992
1st	109	T.M. Moody 54, M.A. Taylor 94, Sri Lanka	Sri Lanka	15 Aug 1992
1st	101	S. Wettimuny 56, E.R.N.S. Fernando 34, Sri Lanka	Australia	16 Apr 1983

Leading Wicket-takers

Player	M	Wkts	Best	4wi	5wi	Ave.	Stk Rt
A. Ranatunga, Sri Lanka	11	10	3-49	-	-	28.00	38.40
V.B. John, Sri Lanka	6	9	3-37	-	-	21.56	33.33
Abdul Qadir, Pakistan	2	6	3-15	-	-	6.50	15.33
A.L.F. de Mel, Sri Lanka	6	6	2-35	-	-	31.50	47.00
S.T. Jayasuriya, Sri Lanka	3	6	3-33	-	-	19.17	25.00
R.S. Kalpage, Sri Lanka	4	6	2-34	-	-	27.50	37.00
J.R. Ratnayeke, Sri Lanka	5	6	3-32	-	-	29.33	39.00

Best Bowling

Total	Player	Versus	Date
4-19	Wasim Akram, Pakistan	Bangladesh	31 Mar 1986
3-15	Abdul Qadir, Pakistan	Bangladesh	31 Mar 1993
3-19	R.J. Hadlee, New Zealand	Sri Lanka	1 Apr 1984

Colombo, R. Premadasa Stadium (32 matches)
(formerly Khettarama Stadium)

Summary of Matches

Team	First Match	Played	Won	Lost	NR	Tie
Australia	4 Sep 1992 v Sri Lanka	6	2	4	-	-
Bangladesh	16 Jul 1997 v Pakistan	1	-	1	-	-
England	10 Mar 1993 v Sri Lanka	1	-	1	-	-
India	25 Jul 1993 v Sri Lanka	13	4	7	2	-
New Zealand	5 Apr 1986 v Sri Lanka	5	1	2	2	-
Pakistan	3 Aug 1994 v Sri Lanka	5	3	2	-	-
South Africa	2 Sep 1993 v Sri Lanka	2	1	1	-	-
Sri Lanka	5 Apr 1986 v New Zealand	28	18	8	2	-
West Indies	16 Dec 1993 v Sri Lanka	1	-	1	-	-
Zimbabwe	26 Aug 1996 v Australia	2	-	2	-	-

Highest Innings Total

Runs	Team	Batted 1st	Batted 2nd	Date
319	Pakistan	Pak 5-319	Ban 210	16 July 1997
307	India	Ind 6-307	SL 301	7 Jul 1998
302	Sri Lanka	SL 4-302	Ind 7-300	17 Aug 1997

Lowest Completed Innings Total

Runs	Team	Batted 1st	Batted 2nd	Date
98	Sri Lanka	SAF 7-222	SL 98	2 Sep 1993
138	Zimbabwe	Aus 7-263	Zim 138	26 Aug 1996
154	South Africa	SL 9-198	SAF 154	4 Sep 1993

Leading Run-scorers

Player	M	I	NO	Runs	HS	50	100	Ave.	Stk Rt
P.A. de Silva, Sri Lanka	28	27	5	1014	105	7	1	44.09	83.18
S.T. Jayasuriya, Sri Lanka	26	25	2	833	120*	7	1	34.71	93.49
A. Ranatunga, Sri Lanka	28	24	8	740	131*	3	1	37.50	80.91

Highest Individual Innings

Runs	Player	Versus	Date
131*	A. Ranatunga, Sri Lanka	India	18 Jul 1997
128	S.R. Tendulkar, India	Sri Lanka	7 Jul 1998
120*	S.T. Jayasuriya, Sri Lanka	India	28 Aug 1996

Highest Partnerships

Wkt	Runs	Batsmen	Versus	Date
1st	252	S.C. Ganguly 109, S.R. Tendulkar 128, India	Sri Lanka	7 Jul 1998
5th	223	M. Azharuddin 111*, A.D. Jadeja 119, India	Sri Lanka	17 Aug 1997
2nd	166	R.S. Mahanama 107, A.P. Gurusinha 76, Sri Lanka	New Zealand	13 Dec 1992

Leading Wicket-takers

Player	M	Wkts	Best	4wi	5wi	Ave.	Stk Rt
R.S. Kalpage, Sri Lanka	18	27	4-36	2	-	20.78	30.44
S.T. Jayasuriya, Sri Lanka	26	27	4-49	2	-	32.19	41.22
G.P. Wickramasinghe, Sri Lanka	18	16	3-28	-	-	33.75	45.44
U.D.U. Chandana, Sri Lanka	7	16	4-35	1	-	12.75	16.88
H.D.P.K. Dharmasena, Sri Lanka	15	16	3-40	-	-	39.06	47.88

Best Bowling

Total	Player	Versus	Date
5-38	Saqlain Mushtaq, Pakistan	Bangladesh	16 Jul 1997
4-17	C.P.H. Ramanayake, Sri Lanka	South Africa	4 Sep 1993
4-33	A.C. Cummins, West Indies	Sri Lanka	16 Dec 1993

Colombo, Sinhalese Sports Club (29 matches)

Summary of Matches

Team	First Match	Played	Won	Lost	NR	Tie
Australia	29 Apr 1983 v Sri Lanka	4	2	-	2	-
Bangladesh	22 Jul 1997 v Sri Lanka	2	-	2	-	-
England	13 Feb 1982 v Sri Lanka	2	1	1	-	-
India	25 Aug 1985 v Sri Lanka	10	4	3	3	-
New Zealand	3 Mar 1984 v Sri Lanka	4	1	2	1	-
Pakistan	11 Mar 1986 v Sri Lanka	8	4	3	1	-
Sri Lanka	13 Feb 1982 v England	22	11	8	3	-
West Indies	18 Dec 1993 v Sri Lanka	1	1	-	-	-
Zimbabwe	21 Feb 1996 v Sri Lanka	5	-	5	-	-

Highest Innings Total

Runs	Team	Batted 1st	Batted 2nd	Date
296	Sri Lanka	SL 4-296	Ban 8-193	22 July 1997
293	Sri Lanka	SL 4-293	NZ 206	5 Jul 1998
291	India	Ind 9-291	SL 6-132	23 Aug 1997

Lowest Completed Innings Total

Runs	Team	Batted 1st	Batted 2nd	Date
130	Sri Lanka	NZ 6-234	SL 134	3 Mar 1984
151	Pakistan	Aus 7-179	Pak 9-151	7 Sep 1994
163	India	SL 8-171	Ind 163	1 Jul 1998

Leading Run-scorers

Player	M	I	NO	Runs	HS	50	100	Ave.	Stk Rt
A. Ranatunga, Sri Lanka	20	18	3	706	102*	6	1	47.07	89.79
P.A. de Silva, Sri Lanka	16	16	1	636	127*	4	2	42.40	85.73
S.T. Jayasuriya, Sri Lanka	14	14	-	441	108	2	2	31.71	100.68

Highest Individual Innings

Runs	Player	Versus	Date
127*	P.A. de Silva, Sri Lanka	Zimbabwe	3 Sep 1996
112	G.W. Flower, Zimbabwe	Sri Lanka	26 Jan 1998
108	S.T. Jayasuriya, Sri Lanka	Bangladesh	22 Jul 1997

Highest Partnerships

Wkt	Runs	Batsmen	Versus	Date
3rd	172	A.P. Gurusinha 87, P.A. de Silva 91, Sri Lanka	Zimbabwe	21 Feb 1996
1st	171	M.S. Atapattu 60, S.T. Jayasuriya 108, Sri Lanka	Bangladesh	22 Jul 1997
3rd	162	R.R. Singh 100, R.S. Dravid 78, India	Sri Lanka	23 Aug 1997

Leading Wicket-takers

Player	M	Wkts	Best	4wi	5wi	Ave.	Stk Rt
Wasim Akram, Pakistan	6	14	4-28	1	-	10.86	23.29
S.T. Jayasuriya, Sri Lanka	12	12	2-28	-	-	36.42	45.40
B.K.V. Prasad, India	9	13	4-17	1	-	19.46	30.00
U.D.U. Chandana, Sri Lanka	8	11	4-31	2	-	22.27	28.18
A.L.F. De Mel, Sri Lanka	8	11	4-34	1	-	21.64	34.26

Best Bowling

Wkts	Player	Versus	Date
4-17	B.K.V. Prasad, India	Pakistan	20 Jul 1997
4-18	S.T. Jayasuriya, Sri Lanka	India	1 Jul 1998
4-28	Wasim Akram, Pakistan	Sri Lanka	11 Mar 1986

UNITED ARAB EMIRATES

Sharjah, Sharjah Cricket Association Stadium (139 matches)

Summary of Matches

Team	First Match	Played	Won	Lost	NR	Tie
Australia	24 Mar 1985 v England	18	10	8	-	-
Bangladesh	28 Apr 1990 v New Zealand	5	-	5		
England	24 Mar 1985 v Australia	9	6	3	-	-
India	8 Apr 1984 v Sri Lanka	58	29	29	-	-
New Zealand	10 Apr 1986 v India	21	6	14	-	1
Pakistan	6 Apr 1984 v Sri Lanka	71	47	24	-	-
South Africa	13 Apr 1996 v Pakistan	5	5	-	-	-
Sri Lanka	6 Apr 1984 v Pakistan	47	14	32	-	1
UAE	13 Apr 1994 v India	2	-	2		
West Indies	15 Nov 1985 v Pakistan	31	17	14	-	-
Zimbabwe	1 Feb 1993 v Pakistan	11	4	7	-	-

Highest Innings Total

Runs	Team	Batted 1st	Batted 2nd	Date
338	New Zealand	NZ 4-338	Ban 5-177	28 Apr 1990
333	West Indies	WI 7-333	SL 329	16 Oct 1995
332	Australia	Aus 3-332	SL 218	2 May 1990

Lowest Completed Innings Total

Runs	Team	Batted 1st	Batted 2nd	Date
55	Sri Lanka	WI 5-248	SL 55	3 Dec 1986
64	New Zealand	NZ 64	Pak 0-66	15 Apr 1986
74	New Zealand	NZ 74	Pak 2-77	1 May 1990

Leading Run-scorers

Player	M	I	NO	Runs	HS	50	100	Ave.	Stk Rt
Salim Malik, Pakistan	57	48	7	1617	102	10	3	39.44	76.42
Saeed Anwar, Pakistan	36	36	2	1553	131	4	7	45.68	85.71
S.R. Tendulkar, India	33	33	5	1534	142	6	6	54.79	99.35

Highest Individual Innings

Runs	Player	Versus	Date
169	B.C. Lara, West Indies	Sri Lanka	16 Oct 1995
153	B.C. Lara, West Indies	Pakistan	5 Nov 1993
142	S.R. Tendulkar, India	Australia	22 Apr 1998

Highest Partnerships

Wkt	Runs	Batsmen	Versus	Date
2nd	263	Aamir Sohail 134, Inzamam-ul-Haq 137*, Pakistan	New Zealand	20 Apr 1994
2nd	231	S.R. Tendulkar 118, N.S. Sidhu 101, India	Pakistan	15 Apr 1996
1st	204	Saeed Anwar 110, Ramiz Raja 109*, Pakistan	Sri Lanka	4 Feb 1993

Leading Wicket-takers

Player	M	Wkts	Best	4wi	5wi	Ave.	Stk Rt
Wasim Akram, Pakistan	54	92	5-38	4	1	19.12	31.68
Waqar Younis, Pakistan	38	70	6-26	3	3	19.97	27.03
Mushtaq Ahmed, Pakistan	37	46	4-27	2	-	31.78	43.89

Best Bowling

Total	Player	Versus	Date
7-37	Aaqib Javed, Pakistan	India	25 Oct 1991
6-14	Imran Khan, Pakistan	India	22 Mar 1985
6-26	Waqar Younis, Pakistan	Sri Lanka	29 Apr 1990

WEST INDIES

Bridgetown, Barbados, Kensington Oval (10 matches)

Summary of Matches

Team	First Match	Played	Won	Lost	NR	Tie
Australia	13 Mar 1991 v West Indies	2	1	1	-	-
England	19 Mar 1986 v West Indies	5	2	3	-	-
India	7 Mar 1989 v West Indies	2	-	2	-	-
New Zealand	23 Apr 1985 v West Indies	1	-	1	-	-
West Indies	23 Apr 1985 v New Zealand	10	7	3	-	-

Highest Innings Total

Runs	Team	Batted 1st	Batted 2nd	Date
293	England	Eng 5-293	WI 277	29 Mar 1998
283	Australia	Aus 6-283	WI 246	13 Mar 1991
277	West Indies	Eng 5-293	WI 277	29 Mar 1998

Lowest Completed Innings Total

Runs	Team	Batted 1st	Batted 2nd	Date
114	England	WI 7-249	Eng 114	19 Mar 1986
141	West Indes	Eng 5-202	WI 141	16 Feb 1994
199	India	Ind 7-199	WI 0-200	3 May 1997

Leading Run-scorers

Player	M	I	NO	Runs	HS	50	100	Ave.	Stk Rt
D.L. Haynes, West Indies	6	6	1	345	117*	-	2	69.00	78.77
R.B. Richardson, WI	7	7	-	227	80	2	-	32.43	81.65
C.L. Hooper, West Indies	6	5	-	225	84	2	-	45.00	91.09

Highest Individual Innings

Runs	Player	Versus	Date
122	N.V. Knight, England	West Indies	29 Mar 1998
117*	D.L. Haynes, West Indies	India	7 Mar 1989
116	D.L. Haynes, West Indies	New Zealand	23 Apr 1985

Highest Partnerships

Wkt	Runs	Batsmen	Versus	Date
1st	200*	S.C. Williams 78*, S. Chanderpaul 109*, West Indies	India	3 May 1997
2nd	184	D.L. Haynes 116, H.A. Gomes 78, West Indies	New Zealand	23 Apr 1985
1st	165	N.V. Knight 122, A.J. Stewart 74, England	West Indies	29 Mar 1998

Leading Wicket-takers

Player	M	Wkts	Best	4wi	5wi	Ave.	Stk Rt
C.A. Walsh, West Indies	8	8	2-26	-	-	44.13	57.75
C.E.L. Ambrose, West Indies	8	7	3-38	-	-	44.00	66.00
R.A. Harper, West Indies	3	6	3-38	-	-	18.33	28.00
M.E. Waugh, Australia	2	6	3-34	-	-	12.67	13.67

Best Bowling

Wkts	Player	Versus	Date
3-14	M.D. Marshall, West Indies	England	19 Mar 1986
3-18	C.C. Lewis, England	West Indies	16 Feb 1994
3-25	C.J. McDermott, Australia	West Indies	8 Mar 1995

Port-of-Spain, Trinidad & Tobago, Queen's Park Oval (29 matches)

Summary of Matches

Team	First Match	Played	Won	Lost	NR	Tie
Australia	14 Mar 1984 v West Indies	5	3	2	-	-
England	4 Mar 1986 v West Indies	7	2	3	2	-
India	9 Mar 1983 v West Indies	5	1	4	-	-
New Zealand	27 Mar 1985 v West Indies	4	1	3	-	-
Pakistan	18 Mar 1988 v West Indies	4	1	3	-	-
South Africa	11 Apr 1992 v West Indies	2	-	2	-	-
Sri Lanka	13 Apr 1996 v West Indies	2	1	1	-	-
West Indies	9 Mar 1983 v India	29	18	9	2	-

Highest Innings Total

Runs	Team	Batted 1st	Batted 2nd	Date
315	West Indies	WI 4-315	Pak 265	18 Mar 1988
302	West Indies	WI 5-302	Eng 245	8 Apr 1998
283	West Indies	WI 7-283	SL 8-248	6 Jun 1997

Lowest Completed Innings Total

Runs	Team	Batted 1st	Batted 2nd	Date
116	New Zealand	NZ 116	WI 0-117	17 Apr 1985
121	West Indies	WI 121	Ind 0-116	27 Apr 1997
127	West Indies	Aus 9-172	WI 127	9 Mar 1991

Leading Run-scorers

Player	M	I	NO	Runs	HS	50	100	Ave.	Stk Rt
B.C. Lara, West Indies	15	15	4	870	146*	6	2	79.09	86.57
D.L. Haynes, West Indies	18	18	5	828	142*	6	2	63.69	77.31
R.B. Richardson, WI	19	17	5	652	90	5	-	54.33	75.55

Highest Individual Innings

Runs	Player	Versus	Date
146*	B.C. Lara, West Indies	New Zealand	30 Mar 1996
142*	D.L. Haynes, West Indies	Pakistan	18 Mar 1988
139	B.C. Lara, West Indies	New Zealand	12 Mar 1995

Highest Partnerships

Wkt	Runs	Batsmen	Versus	Date
3rd	185	C.B. Lambert 119, B.C. Lara 93, West Indies	England	8 Apr 1998
1st	154*	D.L. Haynes 59*, B.C. Lara 86*, West Indies	South Africa	11 Apr 1992
2nd	152	D.L. Haynes 142*, R.B. Richardson 78, West Indies	Pakistan	18 Mar 1988

Leading Wicket-takers

Player	M	Wkts	Best	4wi	5wi	Ave.	Stk Rt
C.E.L. Ambrose, West Indies	17	22	4-36	1	-	24.00	40.50
R.A. Harper, West Indies	11	14	4-40	1	-	21.21	34.93
C.A. Walsh, West Indies	19	13	2-25	-	-	49.54	67.38

Best Bowling

Total	Player	Versus	Date
6-50	A.H. Gray, West Indies	Australia	9 Mar 1991
5-58	S.T. Jayasuriya, Sri Lanka	West Indies	6 Jun 1997
4-10	J. Garner, West Indies	New Zealand	17 Apr 1985

WALES

Swansea, St Helen's (2 matches)

Match	Batted 1st	Batted 2nd	Result	Date
England v New Zealand	NZ 158	Eng 3-159	Pak by 50 runs	18 Jul 1973
Pakistan v Sri Lanka	Pak 5-338	SL 9-288	Eng by 7 wkts	9 Jun 1983

West Indies - Other Grounds

Berbice, Guyana, Albion Sports Complex (5 matches)

Match	Batted 1st	Batted 2nd	Result	Date
West Indies v Pakistan	Pak 7-176	WI 6-182	WI by 4 wkts	16 Mar 1977
West Indies v England	Eng 137	WI 4-138	WI by 6 wkts	26 Feb 1981
West Indies v India	Ind 5-282	WI 9-255	Ind by 27 runs	29 Mar 1983
West Indies v Australia	Aus 5-231	WI 2-233	WI by 8 wkts	29 Feb 1984
West Indies v New Zealand	WI 5-259	NZ 129	WI by 130 runs	14 Apr 1985

Castries, St Lucia, Mindoo Phillip Park (2 matches)

Match	Batted 1st	Batted 2nd	Result	Date
West Indies v Australia	WI 139	Aus 8-140	Aus by 2 wkts	12 Apr 1978
West Indies v Australia	Aus 9-206	WI 3-208	WI by 7 wkts	19 Apr 1984

Georgetown, Guyana, Bourda Ground (8 matches)

Match	Batted 1st	Batted 2nd	Result	Date
West Indies v Pakistan	Pak 7-221	WI 3-225	WI by 7 wkts	30 Mar 1988
West Indies v India	WI 2-289	Ind 8-188	WI by 101 runs	21 Mar 1989
West Indies v England	Eng 8-188	WI 4-191	WI by 6 wkts	7 Mar 1990
West Indies v England	Eng 9-166	WI 3-167	WI by 7 wkts	15 Mar 1990
West Indies v Australia	WI 251	Aus 4-252	Aus by 6 wkts	20 Mar 1991
West Indies v Pakistan	Pak 6-244	WI 5-244	Match tied	3 Apr 1993
West Indies v Australia	Aus 9-286	WI 5-287	WI by 5 wkts	18 Mar 1995
West Indies v New Zealand	NZ 158	WI 154	NZ by 4 runs	3 Apr 1996

Kingston, Jamaica, Sabina Park (9 matches)

Match	Batted 1st	Batted 2nd	Result	Date
West Indies v Australia	Aus 7-209	WI 1-211	WI by 9 wkts	26 Apr 1984
West Indies v England	Eng 8-145	WI 4-146	WI by 6 wkts	18 Feb 1986
West Indies v Pakistan	WI 4-241	Pak 7-194	WI by 47 runs	12 Mar 1988
West Indies v England	Eng 8-214	WI 7-216	WI by 3 wkts	3 Mar 1990
West Indies v Australia	Aus 4-244	WI 209	Aus by 35 runs	26 Feb 1991
West Indies v South Africa	WI 6-287	SAF 180	WI by 107 runs	7 Apr 1992
West Indies v Pakistan	Pak 6-223	WI 6-224	WI by 4 wkts	23 Mar 1993
West Indies v England	Eng 8-253	WI 7-240	WI by 3 wkts[1]	26 Feb 1994
West Indies v New Zealand	NZ 243	WI 9-244	WI by 1 wkt	26 Mar 1996

[1]*revised target*

Kingstown, St Vincent, Arnos Vale (8 matches)

Match	Batted 1st	Batted 2nd	Result	Date
West Indies v England	WI 127	Eng 125	WI by 2 runs	4 Feb 1981
West Indies v Pakistan	Pak 9-186	WI 148	Pak by 38 runs	30 Mar 1993
West Indies v England	WI 6-313	Eng 9-148	WI by 165 runs	2 Mar 1994
West Indies v Australia	Aus 9-210	WI 3-208	WI on run-rate	15 Mar 1995
West Indies v New Zealand	NZ 8-241	WI 3-242	WI by 7 wkts	6 Apr 1996
West Indies v India	WI 9-249	Ind 231	WI by 18 runs	30 Apr 1997
West Indies v England	Eng 8-209	WI 5-213	WI by 5 wkts	4 Apr 1998
West Indies v England	Eng 149	WI 6-150	WI by 4 wkts	5 Apr 1998

St George's, Grenada, Queen's Park (1 match)

Match	Batted 1st	Batted 2nd	Result	Date
West Indies v India	Ind 166	WI 3-167	WI by 7 wkts	7 Apr 1983

St John's, Antigua & Barbuda, St John's Recreation Ground (4 matches)

Match	Batted 1st	Batted 2nd	Result	Date
West Indies v Australia	WI 9-313	Aus 7-181	WI on run-rate	22 Feb 1978
West Indies v New Zealand	WI 8-231	NZ 8-208	WI by 23 runs	20 Mar 1985
West Indies v Pakistan	Pak 9-166	WI 5-167	WI by 5 wkts	15 Mar 1988
West Indies v India	Ind 8-237	WI 2-240	WI by 8 wkts	18 Mar 1989

Zimbabwe - other grounds

Bulawayo, Bulawayo Athletic Club (1 match)

Match	Batted 1st	Batted 2nd	Result	Date
Zimbabwe v New Zealand	NZ 7-244	Zim 9-222	NZ by 22 runs	31 Oct 1992

Bulawayo, Queen's Park (5 matches)

Match	Batted 1st	Batted 2nd	Result	Date
Zimbabwe v England	Eng 152	Zim 8-153	Zim by 2 wkts	15 Dec 1996
Zimbabwe v India	Ind 168	Zim 2-139	Zim on run-rate	5 Feb 1997
Zimbabwe v New Zealand	Zim 8-233	NZ 9-233	Match tied	1 Oct 1997
Zimbabwe v India	Zim 213	Ind 2-216	Ind by 8 wkts	26 Sep 1998
Zimbabwe v India	Zim 7-235	Ind 2-236	Ind by 8 wkts	27 Sep 1998

Statistics on highest innings, most runs, partnerships, wicket-takers and bowling analyses for this chapter were supplied by Ross Dundas Cricket Statistics.

ZIMBABWE

Harare, Harare Sports Club (18 matches)

Summary of Matches

Team	First Match	Played	Won	Lost	NR	Tie
England	1 Jan 1997 v Zimbabwe	2	-	2	-	-
India	25 Oct 1992 v Zimbabwe	2	1	1	-	-
New Zealand	8 Nov 1992 v Zimbabwe	3	2	1	-	-
Pakistan	2 Mar 1993 v Zimbabwe	6	4	1	-	1
South Africa	21 Oct 1995 v Zimbabwe	2	2	-	-	-
Sri Lanka	3 Nov 1994 v Zimbabwe	3	2	1	-	-
Zimbabwe	25 Oct 1992 v India	18	6	11	-	1

Highest Innings Total

Runs	Team	Batted 1st	Batted 2nd	Date
303	South Africa	SAF 5-303	Zim 7-169	21 Oct 1995
296	Sri Lanka	SL 4-296	Zim 105	6 Nov 1994
294	New Zeland	NZ 7-294	Zim 211	5 Oct 1997

Lowest Completed Innings Total

Runs	Team	Batted 1st	Batted 2nd	Date
105	Zimbabwe	SL 4-296	Zim 105	6 Nov 1994
118	England	Zim 7-249	Eng 118	3 Jan 1997
127	Zimbabwe	SAF 239	Zim 127	22 Oct 1995

Leading Run-scorers

Player	M	I	NO	Runs	HS	50	100	Ave.	Stk Rt
A. Flower, Zimbabwe	18	18	-	612	76	7	-	34.00	69.23
A.D.R. Campbell, Zim	16	16	4	502	131*	3	1	41.83	69.05
G.W. Flower, Zimbabwe	17	17	-	479	81	3	-	28.18	55.96

Highest Individual Innings

Runs	Player	Versus	Date
131*	A.D.R. Campbell, Zimbabwe	Sri Lanka	5 Nov 1994
127	B.M. McMillan, South Africa	Zimbabwe	21 Oct 1995
119*	R.S. Mahanama, Sri Lanka	Zimbabwe	3 Nov 1994

Highest Partnerships

Wkt	Runs	Batsmen	Versus	Date
5th	152	Inzamam-ul-Haq 116*, Ijaz Ahmed 54, Pakistan	Zimbabwe	25 Feb 1995
4th	144	Mohammad Wasim 76, Yousuf Youhana 66, Pakistan	Zimbabwe	29 Mar 1998
4th	143	P.A. de Silva 107*, A. Ranatunga 85, Sri Lanka	Zimbabwe	6 Nov 1994

Leading Wicket-takers

Player	M	Wkts	Best	4wi	5wi	Ave.	Stk Rt
H.H. Streak, Zimbabwe	12	21	4-25	2	-	22.76	31.14
G.J. Whittall, Zimbabwe	14	21	3-46	-	-	24.29	27.86
E.A. Brandes, Zimbabwe	7	13	5-28	-	1	18.15	23.92

Best Bowling

Total	Player	Versus	Date
5-28	E.A. Brandes, Zimbabwe	England	3 Jan 1997
4-20	W.P.U.C.J. Vaas, Sri Lanka	Zimbabwe	3 Nov 1994
4-25	H.H. Streak, Zimbabwe	South Africa	22 Oct 1995

Individual Player Career Records

AUSTRALIA (139 PLAYERS)

Batting and Fielding Player	M	Inns	NO	Runs	HS	Ave.	100s	50s	Ct	St	Bowling Balls	Runs	Wkts	Ave.	Stk Rt	Ec Rt	4wi	5wi	Best
Alderman, T.M.	65	18	6	32	9*	2.67	-	-	29	-	3371	2056	88	23.36	38.31	3.66	1	2	5-17
Angel, J.	3	1	0	0	0	0.00	-	-	-	-	162	113	4	28.25	40.50	4.19	-	-	2-47
Beard, G.R.	2	-	-	-	-	-	-	-	-	-	112	70	4	17.50	28.00	3.75	-	-	2-20
Bennett, M.J.	8	4	1	9	6*	3.00	-	-	1	-	408	275	4	68.75	102.00	4.04	-	-	2-27
Bevan, M.G.	97	86	33	3244	108*	61.21	3	22	37	-	1532	1265	30	42.17	51.07	4.95	-	-	3-36
Bichel, A.J.	17	11	4	101	29*	14.43	-	-	3	-	890	701	21	33.38	42.38	4.73	-	-	3-17
Bishop, G.A.	2	2	0	13	7	6.50	-	-	-	-	-	-	-	-	-	-	-	-	-
Blewett, G.S.	32	30	3	551	57*	20.41	-	2	7	-	749	646	14	46.14	53.50	5.17	-	-	2-6
Boon, D.C.	181	177	16	5964	122	37.04	5	37	45	-	82	86	0	-	-	6.29	-	-	-
Border, A.R.	273	252	39	6524	127*	30.63	3	39	127	-	2661	2071	73	28.37	36.45	4.67	-	-	3-20
Bright, R.J.	11	8	4	66	19*	16.50	-	-	2	-	462	350	3	116.67	154.00	4.55	-	-	1-28
Callen, I.W.	5	3	2	6	3*	6.00	-	-	2	-	180	148	5	29.60	36.00	4.93	-	-	3-24
Campbell, G.D.	12	3	1	6	4*	3.00	-	-	4	-	613	404	18	22.44	34.06	3.95	-	-	3-17
Carlson, P.H.	4	2	0	11	11	5.50	-	-	-	-	168	70	2	35.00	84.00	2.50	-	-	1-21
Chappell, G.S.	74	72	14	2331	138*	40.19	3	14	23	-	3108	2097	72	29.13	43.17	4.05	-	2	5-15
Chappell, I.M.	16	16	2	673	86	48.07	-	8	5	-	42	23	2	11.50	21.00	3.29	-	-	2-14
Chappell, T.M.	20	13	0	229	110	17.62	1	-	8	-	736	538	19	28.32	38.74	4.39	-	-	3-31
Clark, W.M.	2	-	-	-	-	-	-	-	-	-	100	61	3	20.33	33.33	3.66	-	-	2-39
Colley, D.J.	1	-	-	-	-	-	-	-	-	-	66	72	0	-	-	6.55	-	-	-
Connolly, A.N.	1	-	-	-	-	-	-	-	-	-	64	62	0	-	-	5.81	-	-	-
Cosier, G.J.	9	7	2	154	84	30.80	-	1	4	-	409	248	14	17.71	29.21	3.64	1	-	5-18
Dale, A.C.	24	9	6	56	15*	18.67	-	-	9	-	1272	821	27	30.41	47.11	3.87	-	-	3-18
Darling, W.M.	18	18	1	363	74	21.35	-	1	6	-	-	-	-	-	-	-	-	-	-
Davis, I.C.	3	3	1	12	11*	6.00	-	-	-	-	-	-	-	-	-	-	-	-	-
Davis, S.P.	39	11	7	20	6	5.00	-	-	5	-	2016	1135	44	25.80	45.82	3.38	-	-	3-10
Di Venuto, M.J.	9	9	0	241	89	26.78	-	2	1	-	-	-	-	-	-	-	-	-	-
Dodemaide, A.I.C.	24	16	7	124	30	13.78	-	-	7	-	1327	753	36	20.92	36.86	3.40	1	-	5-21
Dyer, G.C.	23	13	2	174	45*	15.82	-	-	24	4	-	-	-	-	-	-	-	-	-
Dymock, G.	15	7	4	35	14*	11.67	-	-	1	-	806	412	15	27.47	53.73	3.07	-	-	2-21
Dyson, J.	29	27	4	755	79	32.83	-	4	12	-	-	-	-	-	-	-	-	-	-
Edwards, R.	9	8	1	255	80*	36.43	-	3	-	-	-	-	-	-	-	-	-	-	-
Edwards, W.J.	1	1	0	2	2	2.00	-	-	-	-	1	0	0	-	-	0.00	-	-	-
Elliott, M.T.G.	1	1	0	1	1	1.00	-	-	-	-	-	-	-	-	-	-	-	-	-
Emery, P.A.	1	1	1	11	11*	-	-	-	3	-	-	-	-	-	-	-	-	-	-

	Batting and Fielding										Bowling								
Player	M	Inns	NO	Runs	HS	Ave.	100s	50s	Ct	St	Balls	Runs	Wkts	Ave.	Stk Rt	Ec Rt	4wi	5wi	Best
Fleming, D.W.	44	14	9	32	5*	6.40	-	-	6	-	2326	1704	70	24.34	33.23	4.40	3	1	5-36
Gilbert, D.R.	14	8	3	39	8	7.80	-	-	3	-	684	552	18	30.67	38.00	4.84	-	1	5-46
Gilchrist, A.C.	51	49	4	1660	154	36.89	5	5	63	10	-	-	-	-	-	-	-	-	-
Gillespie, J.N.	14	8	2	65	26	10.83	-	-	-	-	757	607	13	46.69	58.23	4.81	-	-	2-39
Gilmour, G.J.	5	2	1	42	28*	42.00	-	-	2	-	320	165	16	10.31	20.00	3.09	-	2	6-14
Graf, S.F.	11	6	0	24	8	4.00	-	-	1	-	522	345	8	43.13	65.25	3.97	-	-	2-23
Hammond, J.R.	1	1	1	15	15*	-	-	-	-	-	54	41	1	41.00	54.00	4.56	-	-	1-41
Harvey, I.J.	11	9	2	101	43	14.43	-	-	6	-	417	325	7	46.43	59.57	4.68	-	-	3-17
Hayden, M.L.	13	12	1	286	67	26.00	-	2	4	-	-	-	-	-	-	-	-	-	-
Healy, I.A.	168	120	36	1764	56	21.00	-	4	195	39	-	-	-	-	-	-	-	-	-
Hilditch, A.M.J.	8	8	0	226	72	28.25	-	1	2	-	-	-	-	-	-	-	-	-	-
Hogan, T.G.	16	12	4	72	27	9.00	-	-	10	-	917	574	23	24.96	39.87	3.76	1	-	4-33
Hogg, G.B.	7	7	4	38	11*	12.67	-	-	2	-	295	218	3	72.67	98.33	4.43	-	-	1-23
Hogg, R.M.	71	35	20	137	22	9.13	-	-	8	-	3677	2418	85	28.45	43.26	3.95	5	-	4-29
Holland, R.G.	2	-	-	-	-	-	-	-	-	-	126	99	2	49.50	63.00	4.71	-	-	2-49
Hookes, D.W.	39	36	2	826	76	24.29	-	5	11	-	29	28	1	28.00	29.00	5.79	-	-	1-2
Hughes, K.J.	97	88	6	1968	98	24.00	-	17	27	-	4	4	0	-	-	24.00	-	-	-
Hughes, M.G.	33	17	8	100	20	11.11	-	-	6	-	1639	1115	38	29.34	43.13	4.08	1	-	4-44
Hurst, A.G.	8	4	4	7	3*	-	-	-	-	-	402	203	12	16.92	33.50	3.03	-	1	5-21
Jenner, T.J.	1	1	0	12	12	12.00	-	-	-	-	64	28	1	28.00	64.00	2.63	-	-	-
Jones, D.M.	164	161	25	6068	145	44.62	7	46	54	-	106	81	3	27.00	35.33	4.58	-	-	2-34
Julien, B.P.	18	12	0	129	25	10.75	-	-	7	-	864	733	21	34.90	41.14	5.09	-	-	3-40
Kasprowicz, M.S.	16	8	6	60	28*	30.00	-	-	3	-	817	709	22	32.23	37.14	5.21	-	-	3-50
Kent, M.F.	5	5	1	78	33	19.50	-	-	4	-	-	-	-	-	-	-	-	-	-
Kerr, R.B.	4	4	1	97	87*	32.33	-	1	1	-	-	-	-	-	-	-	-	-	-
Laird, B.M.	23	23	3	594	117*	29.70	1	2	5	-	-	-	-	-	-	-	-	-	-
Langer, J.L.	8	7	2	160	36	32.00	-	-	2	-	-	-	-	-	-	-	-	-	-
Laughlin, T.J.	6	5	1	105	74	26.25	-	1	2	-	308	224	8	28.00	38.50	4.36	-	-	3-54
Law, S.G.	54	51	5	1237	110	26.89	1	7	12	-	807	635	12	52.92	67.25	4.72	-	-	2-22
Lawry, W.M.	1	1	0	27	27	27.00	-	-	1	-	-	-	-	-	-	-	-	-	-
Lawson, G.F.	79	52	18	378	33*	11.12	-	-	18	-	4259	2592	88	29.45	48.40	3.65	5	-	4-26
Lee, S.	16	14	3	207	41	18.82	-	-	9	-	565	405	12	33.75	47.08	4.30	-	1	5-33
Lehmann, D.S.	38	36	5	1102	103	35.55	1	7	7	-	360	323	7	46.14	51.43	5.38	-	-	2-11
Lillee, D.K.	63	34	8	240	42*	9.23	-	-	10	-	3593	2145	103	20.83	34.88	3.58	-	1	5-34
Maclean, J.A.	2	1	0	11	11	11.00	-	-	2	1	-	-	-	-	-	-	-	-	-
MacLeay, K.H.	16	13	2	139	41	12.64	-	-	2	-	857	626	15	41.73	57.13	4.38	-	1	6-39
Maguire, J.N.	23	11	5	42	14*	7.00	-	-	2	-	1009	769	19	40.47	53.11	4.57	-	-	3-61

Batting and Fielding Player	M	Inns	NO	Runs	HS	Ave.	100s	50s	Ct	St	Bowling Balls	Runs	Wkts	Ave.	Stk Rt	Ec Rt	4wi	5wi	Best
Maher, J.P.	2	2	0	21	13	10.50	-	-	-	-	-	-	-	-	-	-	-	-	-
Mallett, A.A.	9	3	1	14	8	7.00	-	-	4	-	502	341	11	31.00	45.64	4.08	-	-	3-34
Malone, M.F.	10	7	3	36	15*	9.00	-	-	1	-	612	315	11	28.64	55.64	3.09	-	-	2-9
Marsh, G.R.	117	115	6	4357	126*	39.97	9	22	31	-	6	4	0	-	-	4.00	-	-	-
Marsh, R.W.	92	76	15	1225	66	20.08	-	4	120	4	-	-	-	-	-	-	-	-	-
Martyn, D.R.	31	28	6	572	59*	26.00	-	3	7	-	118	107	1	107.00	118.00	5.44	-	-	1-30
Massie, R.A.L.	3	1	0	16	16*	-	-	-	1	-	183	129	3	43.00	61.00	4.23	-	-	2-35
Matthews, G.R.J.	59	50	13	619	54	16.73	-	1	23	-	2808	2004	57	35.16	49.26	4.28	-	-	3-27
May, T.B.A.	47	12	8	39	15	9.75	-	-	3	-	2504	1772	39	45.44	64.21	4.25	-	-	3-19
McCosker, R.B.	14	14	0	320	95	22.86	-	2	3	-	-	-	-	-	-	-	-	-	-
McCurdy, R.J.	11	6	2	33	13*	8.25	-	-	1	-	515	375	12	31.25	42.92	4.37	-	-	3-19
McDermott, C.J.	138	78	17	432	37	7.08	-	-	27	-	7461	5018	203	24.72	36.75	4.04	4	1	5-44
McGrath, G.D.	85	27	15	49	10	4.08	-	-	11	-	4607	3084	122	25.28	37.76	4.02	5	2	5-40
McKenzie, G.D.	1	-	-	-	-	-	-	-	1	-	60	22	2	11.00	30.00	2.20	-	-	2-22
Moody, T.M.	58	52	5	1013	89	21.55	-	8	16	-	2017	1469	37	39.70	54.51	4.37	-	-	3-39
Moss, J.K.	1	1	0	7	7	7.00	-	-	2	-	-	-	-	-	-	-	-	-	-
O'Donnell, S.P.	87	64	15	1242	74*	25.35	-	9	22	-	4350	3102	108	28.72	40.28	4.28	5	1	5-13
O'Keefe, K.J.	2	2	1	16	16*	16.00	-	-	-	-	132	79	2	39.50	66.00	3.59	-	-	1-36
Pascoe, L.S.	29	11	7	39	15*	9.75	-	-	6	-	1568	1066	53	20.11	29.58	4.08	4	1	5-30
Phillips, W.B.	48	41	6	852	75*	24.34	-	6	42	7	84	62	1	62.00	84.00	4.43	-	-	1-41
Ponting, R.T.	68	68	8	2492	145	41.53	5	14	16	-	108	33	3	11.00	36.00	1.83	-	-	2-13
Porter, G.D.	2	1	0	3	3	3.00	-	-	1	-	-	-	-	-	-	-	-	-	-
Rackemann, C.G.	52	18	6	34	9*	2.83	-	-	6	-	2791	1833	82	22.35	34.04	3.94	3	1	5-16
Redpath, I.R.	5	5	0	46	24	9.20	-	-	2	-	-	-	-	-	-	-	-	-	-
Reid, B.A.	61	21	8	49	10	3.77	-	-	6	-	3250	2203	63	34.97	51.59	4.07	5	1	5-53
Reiffel, P.R.	83	54	20	493	58	14.50	-	1	23	-	4270	2757	97	28.42	44.02	3.87	5	-	4-13
Ritchie, G.M.	44	42	7	959	84	27.40	-	6	9	-	-	-	-	-	-	-	-	-	-
Rixon, S.J.	6	6	3	40	20*	13.33	-	-	9	2	-	-	-	-	-	-	-	-	-
Robertson, G.R.	13	7	4	45	15	15.00	-	-	3	-	597	430	8	53.75	74.63	4.32	-	-	3-29
Robinson, R.D.	2	2	0	82	70	41.00	-	1	3	1	-	-	-	-	-	-	-	-	-
Serjeant, C.S.	3	3	0	73	46	24.33	-	-	1	-	-	-	-	-	-	-	-	-	-
Sheahan, A.P.	3	3	0	75	50	25.00	-	1	-	-	-	-	-	-	-	-	-	-	-
Siddons, J.D.	1	1	0	32	32	32.00	-	-	-	-	-	-	-	-	-	-	-	-	-
Simpson, R.B.	2	2	0	36	23	18.00	-	-	4	-	102	95	2	47.50	51.00	5.59	-	-	2-30
Slater, M.J.	42	42	1	987	73	24.07	-	9	9	-	12	11	0	-	-	5.50	-	-	-
Smith, S.B.	28	24	2	861	117	39.14	2	8	8	-	7	5	0	-	-	4.29	-	-	-
Stackpole, K.R.	6	6	0	224	61	37.33	-	3	1	-	77	54	3	18.00	25.67	4.21	-	-	3-40
Stuart, A.M.	3	1	0	1	1	1.00	-	-	2	-	180	109	8	13.63	22.50	3.63	-	1	5-26

Batting and Fielding / Bowling

Player	M	Inns	NO	Runs	HS	Ave.	100s	50s	Ct	St	Balls	Runs	Wkts	Ave.	Stk Rt	Ec Rt	4wi	5wi	Best
Symonds, A.	1	1	1	-	-	-	-	-	-	-	12	14	0	-	-	7.00	-	-	-
Taylor, M.A.	113	110	1	3514	105	32.24	1	28	56	-	-	-	-	-	-	-	-	-	-
Taylor, P.L.	83	47	25	437	54*	19.86	-	1	34	-	3937	2740	97	28.25	40.59	4.18	1	-	4-38
Thomson, A.L.	1	-	-	-	-	-	-	-	-	-	64	22	1	22.00	64.00	2.06	-	-	1-22
Thomson, J.R.	50	30	6	181	21	7.54	-	-	9	-	2696	1942	55	35.31	49.02	4.32	1	-	4-67
Toohey, P.M.	5	4	2	105	54*	52.50	-	1	-	-	-	-	-	-	-	-	-	-	-
Trimble, G.S.	2	2	1	4	4	4.00	-	-	-	-	-	-	-	-	-	-	-	-	-
Turner, A.	6	6	0	247	101	41.17	1	-	3	-	24	32	0	-	-	8.00	-	-	-
Veletta, M.R.J.	20	19	4	484	68*	32.27	-	2	8	-	-	-	-	-	-	-	-	-	-
Walker, M.H.N.	17	11	3	79	20	9.88	-	-	6	-	1006	546	20	27.30	50.30	3.26	1	-	4-19
Walters, K.D.	28	24	6	513	59	28.50	-	2	10	-	314	273	4	68.25	78.50	5.22	-	-	2-24
Warne, S.K.	108	64	19	512	55	11.38	-	1	39	-	6074	4235	169	25.06	35.94	4.18	9	1	5-33
Watson, G.D.	2	2	1	11	11*	11.00	-	-	-	-	48	28	2	14.00	24.00	3.50	-	-	2-28
Waugh, M.E.	174	169	13	6044	130	38.74	11	39	68	-	3123	2500	80	31.25	39.04	4.80	1	1	5-24
Waugh, S.R.	251	228	44	5706	102*	31.01	1	34	86	-	8429	6374	185	34.45	45.56	4.54	3	-	4-33
Wellham, D.M.	17	17	2	379	97	25.27	-	1	8	-	-	-	-	-	-	-	-	-	-
Wessels, K.C.	54	51	3	1740	107	36.25	1	14	19	-	737	655	18	36.39	40.94	5.33	-	-	2-16
Whatmore, D.F.	1	1	0	2	2	2.00	-	-	-	-	-	-	-	-	-	-	-	-	-
Whitney, M.	38	13	7	40	9*	6.67	-	-	11	-	2106	1249	46	27.15	45.78	3.56	2	-	4-34
Wiener, J.M.	7	7	0	140	50	20.00	-	1	2	-	24	34	0	-	-	8.50	-	-	-
Wilson, P.	11	5	2	4	2	1.33	-	-	-	-	562	450	13	34.62	43.23	4.80	-	-	3-39
Wood, G.M.	83	77	11	2219	114*	33.62	3	11	17	-	-	-	-	-	-	-	-	-	-
Woodcock, A.J.	1	1	0	53	53	53.00	-	-	-	-	-	-	-	-	-	-	-	-	-
Woolley, R.D.	4	3	2	31	16	31.00	-	-	1	1	-	-	-	-	-	-	-	-	-
Wright, K.J.	5	2	0	29	23	14.50	-	-	8	1	-	-	-	-	-	-	-	-	-
Yallop, G.N.	30	27	6	823	66*	39.19	-	7	5	-	138	119	3	39.67	46.00	5.17	-	-	2-28
Yardley, B.	7	4	0	58	28	14.50	-	-	1	-	198	130	7	18.57	28.29	3.94	-	-	3-28
Young, B.E.	6	3	1	31	18	15.50	-	-	2	-	234	251	1	251.00	234.00	6.44	-	-	-
Zesers, A.K.	2	2	2	10	8*	-	-	-	1	-	90	74	1	74.00	90.00	4.93	-	-	1-37
Zoehrer, T.J.	22	15	3	130	50	10.83	-	1	21	2	-	-	-	-	-	-	-	-	-

BANGLADESH (42 PLAYERS)

Player	M	Inns	NO	Runs	HS	Ave.	100s	50s	Ct	St	Bowling Balls	Runs	Wkts	Ave.	Stk Rt	Ec Rt	4wi	5wi	Best
Akram Khan	21	21	1	453	59	22.65	-	2	6	-	117	138	0	-	-	7.08	-	-	-
Alam Talukdar	4	3	1	11	7*	5.50	-	-	-	-	42	36	0	-	-	5.14	-	-	-
Amin-ul-Islam	21	21	5	497	70	31.06	-	2	7	-	220	219	3	73.00	73.33	5.97	-	-	3-57
Anis-ur-Rehman	2	2	1	2	2	2.00	-	-	-	-	48	68	0	-	-	8.50	-	-	-
Athar Ali Khan	19	19	1	532	82	29.55	-	3	2	-	420	365	6	60.83	70.00	5.21	-	-	2-33
Azhar Hussain	7	7	0	96	54	13.71	-	1	1	-	263	209	4	52.25	65.75	4.77	-	-	1-20
Farooq Ahmed	5	5	0	89	57	17.80	-	1	1	-	-	-	-	-	-	-	-	-	-
Farooq Chowdury	2	2	1	17	14	17.00	-	-	-	-	87	35	1	35.00	87.00	2.41	-	-	1-22
Gazi Ashraf	7	7	0	59	18	8.43	-	-	1	-	51	33	2	16.50	25.50	3.88	-	-	1-7
Ghulam Farooq	3	2	1	27	23*	27.00	-	-	-	-	99	81	1	81.00	99.00	4.91	-	-	1-28
Ghulam Nousher	9	3	2	8	4	8.00	-	-	-	-	408	314	5	62.80	81.60	4.62	-	-	1-27
Habib-ul-Bashar	8	8	0	113	70	14.13	-	1	3	-	36	26	0	-	-	4.33	-	-	-
Hafiz-ur-Rehman	2	1	0	8	8	8.00	-	-	2	-	-	-	-	-	-	-	-	-	-
Harun-ur-Rashid	2	2	0	0	0	0.00	-	-	-	-	-	-	-	-	-	-	-	-	-
Hasib-ul-Hassan	15	13	2	96	21*	8.72	-	-	3	-	644	636	13	48.92	49.53	5.93	-	-	2-44
Inam-ul-Haq	12	11	2	71	18	7.88	-	-	3	-	402	365	5	73.00	80.40	5.45	-	-	2-46
Jahangir Shah	5	4	2	16	8*	8.00	-	-	1	-	234	172	2	86.00	117.00	4.41	-	-	2-23
Javed Omar	4	4	0	48	18	12.00	-	-	-	-	-	-	-	-	-	-	-	-	-
Khaled Mahmud	6	5	0	132	47	26.40	-	-	-	-	232	162	7	23.14	33.14	4.19	-	-	2-12
Khaled Mashud	16	15	4	117	27*	10.63	-	-	13	2	-	-	-	-	-	-	-	-	-
Mafiz-ur-Rehman	4	4	1	53	16	17.67	-	-	1	-	66	73	0	-	-	6.64	-	-	-
Mehrab Hussain	1	1	0	6	6	6.00	-	-	-	-	-	-	-	-	-	-	-	-	-
Minhaz-ul-Abedin	23	22	0	313	45	14.22	-	-	2	-	426	404	9	44.89	47.33	5.69	-	-	2-39
Mohammad Rafiq	12	12	0	194	77	16.16	-	1	1	-	598	480	15	32.00	39.86	4.82	1	-	3-55
Morshed Ali Khan	3	1	1	2	2*	-	-	-	2	-	138	85	2	42.50	69.00	3.70	-	-	1-26
Naim-ur-Rehman	8	8	1	135	47	19.28	-	-	4	-	250	209	2	104.50	125.00	5.02	-	-	1-29
Nasir Ahmed	7	4	2	25	11	12.50	-	-	1	1	-	-	-	-	-	-	-	-	-
Nur-ul-Abedin	4	4	0	15	13	3.75	-	-	-	-	-	-	-	-	-	-	-	-	-
Rafiq Alam	2	2	0	24	14	12.00	-	-	-	-	-	-	-	-	-	-	-	-	-
Raquib-ul-Hassan	2	2	0	17	12	8.50	-	-	1	-	1	4	0	-	-	24.00	-	-	-
Saif-ul-Islam	7	4	2	37	22*	18.50	-	-	-	-	303	256	6	42.67	50.50	5.07	1	-	4-36
Sajjad Ahmed	2	2	0	15	11	7.50	-	-	-	-	-	-	-	-	-	-	-	-	-
Sami-ur-Rehman	2	2	0	4	4	2.00	-	-	-	-	60	30	0	-	-	3.00	-	-	-
Sanu-ar-Hussain	3	3	0	22	13	7.33	-	-	1	-	-	-	-	-	-	-	-	-	-
Shafuddin Ahmed	5	5	3	27	11	13.50	-	-	-	-	234	192	6	32.00	39.00	4.92	-	-	3-42
Shahid-ur-Rehman	2	2	0	62	37	31.00	-	-	-	-	-	-	-	-	-	-	-	-	-
Shahri-ar-Hussain	5	5	0	41	16	8.20	-	-	2	-	-	-	-	-	-	-	-	-	-
Sharif-ul-Haq	1	1	0	0	0	0.00	-	-	-	-	18	21	0	-	-	7.00	-	-	-

Player	M	Inns	NO	Runs	HS	Ave.	100s	50s	Ct	St	Balls	Runs	Wkts	Ave.	Stk Rt	Ec Rt	4wi	5wi	Best
Sheikh Salahuddin	6	5	3	24	12	12.00	-	-	-	-	246	249	4	62.25	61.50	6.07	-	-	2-48
Wahid-ul-Ghani	1	3	-	14	6	4.67	-	-	-	-	36	32	0	-	-	5.33	-	-	-
Zahid Razzak	3	3	0	0	0	0.00	-	-	-	-	-	-	-	-	-	-	-	-	-
Zakir Hasan	2	1	0	0	0	0.00	-	-	-	-	36	35	0	-	-	5.83	-	-	-

CANADA (13 PLAYERS)

Batting and Fielding / **Bowling**

Player	M	Inns	NO	Runs	HS	Ave.	100s	50s	Ct	St	Balls	Runs	Wkts	Ave.	Stk Rt	Ec Rt	4wi	5wi	Best
Baksh, S.	1	1	0	0	0	0.00	-	-	-	-	-	-	-	-	-	-	-	-	-
Callendar, R.G.	2	2	0	0	0	0.00	-	-	-	-	54	26	1	26.00	54.00	2.89	-	-	1-14
Chappell, C.J.D.	3	3	0	38	19	12.67	-	-	-	-	-	-	-	-	-	-	-	-	-
Dennis, F.A.	3	3	0	47	25	15.67	-	-	-	-	-	-	-	-	-	-	-	-	-
Henry, C.C.	2	2	1	6	5	6.00	-	-	-	-	90	53	2	26.50	45.00	3.53	-	-	2-27
Marshall, C.A.	2	2	0	10	8	5.00	-	-	-	-	-	-	-	-	-	-	-	-	-
Mauricette, B.M.	3	3	0	20	15	6.67	-	-	-	-	-	-	-	-	-	-	-	-	-
Patel, J.M.	3	3	0	3	2	1.00	-	-	-	-	91	47	0	-	-	3.10	-	-	-
Sealy, G.R.	3	3	0	73	45	24.33	-	-	-	-	36	21	0	-	-	3.50	-	-	-
Stead, M.P.	2	2	0	10	10	5.00	-	-	-	-	29	24	0	-	-	4.97	-	-	-
Tariq Javed	3	3	0	15	8	5.00	-	-	-	-	-	-	-	-	-	-	-	-	-
Valentine, J.N.	3	2	2	3	3*	-	-	-	1	-	114	66	3	22.00	38.00	3.47	-	-	1-18
Vaughan, J.C.B.	3	3	0	30	29	10.00	-	-	-	-	66	36	0	-	-	3.27	-	-	-

EAST AFRICA (14 PLAYERS)

Batting and Fielding / **Bowling**

Player	M	Inns	NO	Runs	HS	Ave.	100s	50s	Ct	St	Balls	Runs	Wkts	Ave.	Stk Rt	Ec Rt	4wi	5wi	Best
Frasat Ali	3	3	0	57	45	19.00	-	-	-	-	144	107	0	-	-	4.46	-	-	-
Harilal Shah	3	3	0	6	6	2.00	-	-	-	-	-	-	-	-	-	-	-	-	-
Jawahir Shah	3	3	0	46	37	15.33	-	-	-	-	-	-	-	-	-	-	-	-	-
McLeod, H.	2	2	0	5	5	2.50	-	-	-	-	-	-	-	-	-	-	-	-	-
Mehmood Quaraishy	3	3	1	41	19	20.50	-	-	-	-	108	94	3	31.33	36.00	5.22	-	-	2-55
Nagenda, J.	1	-	-	-	-	-	-	-	-	-	108	94	3	31.33	36.00	5.22	-	-	2-55
Nana, P.G.	3	3	2	9	8*	9.00	-	-	2	-	54	50	1	50.00	54.00	5.56	-	-	1-50
Praful Mehta	1	1	0	12	12	12.00	-	-	-	-	173	116	1	116.00	173.00	4.02	-	-	1-34
Pringle, D.J.	2	2	0	5	3	2.50	-	-	-	-	90	55	0	-	-	3.67	-	-	-
Sethi, R.K.	3	3	0	54	30	18.00	-	-	1	-	120	100	1	100.00	120.00	5.00	-	-	1-51
Sumar, S.	1	1	0	4	4	4.00	-	-	-	-	-	-	-	-	-	-	-	-	-
Walusimba, S.	3	3	0	38	16	12.67	-	-	-	-	-	-	-	-	-	-	-	-	-
Yunus Badat	2	2	0	1	1	0.50	-	-	-	-	-	-	-	-	-	-	-	-	-
Zulfiqar Ali	3	3	1	39	30	19.50	-	-	1	-	210	166	4	41.50	52.50	4.74	-	-	3-63

ENGLAND (153 PLAYERS)

Batting and Fielding

Player	M	Inns	NO	Runs	HS	Ave.	100s	50s	Ct	St	Bowling Balls	Runs	Wkts	Ave.	Stk Rt	Ec Rt	4wi	5wi	Best
Adams, C.J.	2	2	0	28	25	14.00	-	-	2	-	126	120	3	40.00	42.00	5.71	-	-	3-38
Agnew, J.P.	3	1	1	2	2*	-	-	-	1	-	90	58	3	19.33	30.00	3.87	-	-	3-27
Alleyne, M.W.	4	4	1	76	38*	25.23	-	-	-	-	-	-	-	-	-	-	-	-	-
Allott, P.J.W.	13	6	1	15	8	3.00	-	-	2	-	819	552	15	36.80	54.60	4.04	-	-	3-41
Amiss, D.L.	18	18	0	859	137	47.72	4	1	2	-	-	-	-	-	-	-	-	-	-
Arnold, G.G.	14	6	3	48	18*	16.00	-	-	2	-	714	339	19	17.84	37.58	2.85	1	-	4-27
Atherton, M.A.	54	54	3	1791	127	35.12	2	12	15	-	-	-	-	-	-	-	-	-	-
Athey, C.J.	31	30	3	848	142*	31.41	2	4	16	-	6	10	0	-	-	10.00	-	-	-
Austin, I.D.	4	3	1	29	11*	14.50	-	-	1	-	225	179	3	59.67	75.00	4.77	-	-	2-37
Bailey, R.J.	4	4	2	137	43*	68.50	-	1	1	-	36	25	0	-	-	4.17	-	-	-
Bairstow, D.L.	21	20	6	206	23*	14.71	-	-	17	4	-	-	-	-	-	-	-	-	-
Barlow, G.D.	6	6	1	149	80*	29.80	-	1	4	-	-	-	-	-	-	-	-	-	-
Barnett, K.J.	1	1	0	84	84	84.00	-	1	-	-	72	47	1	47.00	72.00	3.92	-	-	1-22
Benjamin, J.E.	2	1	1	0	0*	0.00	-	-	-	-	-	-	-	-	-	-	-	-	-
Benson, M.R.	1	1	0	24	24	24.00	-	-	-	-	-	-	-	-	-	-	-	-	-
Bicknell, M.P.	7	6	2	96	31*	24.00	-	-	2	-	413	347	13	26.69	31.77	5.04	-	-	3-55
Blakey, R.J.	3	2	0	25	25	12.50	-	-	2	1	-	-	-	-	-	-	-	-	-
Botham, I.T.	116	106	15	2113	79	23.22	-	9	36	-	6271	4139	145	28.54	43.25	3.96	3	-	4-31
Boycott, G.	36	34	4	1082	105	36.07	1	9	5	-	168	105	5	21.00	33.60	3.75	-	-	2-14
Brealey, J.M.	25	24	3	510	78	24.29	-	3	12	-	-	-	-	-	-	-	-	-	-
Broad, B.C.	34	34	0	1361	106	40.03	1	11	10	-	6	6	0	-	-	6.00	-	-	-
Brown, A.D.	13	13	0	333	118	25.62	1	1	6	-	6	5	0	-	-	5.00	-	-	-
Brown, D.R.	9	8	4	99	21	24.75	-	-	1	-	324	305	7	43.57	46.29	5.65	-	-	2-28
Butcher, A.R.	1	1	0	14	14	14.00	-	-	-	-	-	-	-	-	-	-	-	-	-
Butcher, R.O.	3	3	0	58	52	19.33	-	1	-	-	-	-	-	-	-	-	-	-	-
Caddick, A.R.	9	5	4	35	20*	35.00	-	-	2	-	522	398	15	26.53	34.80	4.57	-	-	3-35
Capel, D.J.	23	19	2	327	50	19.24	-	1	6	-	1038	805	17	47.35	61.06	4.65	-	-	3-38
Close, D.B.	3	3	0	49	43	16.33	-	-	1	-	18	21	0	-	-	7.00	-	-	-
Cook, G.	6	6	0	106	32	17.67	-	-	2	-	-	-	-	-	-	-	-	-	-
Cook, N.G.B.	3	1	1	1	1*	-	-	-	2	-	144	95	5	19.00	28.80	3.96	-	-	2-18
Cope, G.A.	2	1	1	1	1*	-	-	-	-	-	112	35	2	17.50	56.00	1.88	-	-	1-16
Cork, D.G.	25	15	2	132	31*	10.15	-	-	6	-	1440	1071	35	30.60	41.14	4.46	-	-	3-27
Cowans, N.G.	23	8	3	13	4*	2.60	-	-	5	-	1282	913	23	39.70	55.74	4.27	-	-	3-44
Cowdrey, C.S.	3	3	1	51	46*	25.50	-	-	-	-	52	55	2	27.50	26.00	6.35	-	-	1-3
Cowdrey, M.C.	1	1	0	1	1	1.00	-	-	-	-	-	-	-	-	-	-	-	-	-
Crawley, J.P.	13	12	1	235	73	21.36	-	2	1	1	-	-	-	-	-	-	-	-	-

Batting and Fielding / Bowling

Player	M	Inns	NO	Runs	HS	Ave.	100s	50s	Ct	St	Balls	Runs	Wkts	Ave.	Stk Rt	Ec Rt	4wi	5wi	Best
Croft, R.D.B.	40	28	11	274	32	16.12	-	-	9	-	2106	1464	40	36.60	52.65	4.17	-	-	3-51
DeFreitas, P.A.J.	103	66	23	690	67	16.05	-	1	26	-	5712	3775	115	32.83	49.67	3.97	1	-	4-35
Denness, M.H.	12	11	2	264	66	29.33	-	1	1	-	-	-	-	-	-	-	-	-	-
Dilley, G.R.	36	18	8	114	31*	11.40	-	-	4	-	2043	1291	48	26.90	42.56	3.79	3	-	4-23
D'Oliveira, B.L.	4	4	1	30	17	10.00	-	-	1	-	204	140	3	46.67	68.00	4.12	-	-	1-19
Downton, P.R.	28	20	5	242	44*	16.13	-	-	26	3	-	-	-	-	-	-	-	-	-
Ealham, M.A.	30	22	1	380	45	18.10	-	-	3	-	1472	1047	30	34.90	49.07	4.27	-	1	5-32
Edmonds, P.H.	29	18	7	116	20	10.55	-	-	6	-	1534	965	26	37.12	59.00	3.77	-	-	3-39
Edrich, J.H.	7	6	0	223	90	37.17	-	2	-	-	-	-	-	-	-	-	-	-	-
Ellison, R.M.	14	12	4	86	24	10.75	-	-	2	-	696	510	12	42.50	58.00	4.40	-	-	3-42
Emburey, J.E.	61	45	10	501	34	14.31	-	-	19	-	3425	2346	76	30.87	45.07	4.11	2	-	4-37
Fairbrother, N.H.	66	64	17	1918	113	40.81	1	15	32	-	6	9	0	-	-	9.00	-	-	-
Fleming, M.V.	11	10	1	141	34	15.55	-	-	1	-	523	434	17	25.53	30.76	4.98	1	-	4-45
Fletcher, K.W.	24	22	3	757	131	39.84	1	5	4	-	-	-	-	-	-	-	-	-	-
Foster, N.A.	48	25	12	150	24	11.54	-	-	12	-	2627	1836	59	31.12	44.53	4.19	-	-	3-20
Fowler, G.	26	26	2	744	81*	31.00	-	4	4	2	120	50	4	12.50	30.00	2.50	1	-	4-23
Fraser, A.R.C.	37	16	7	122	38*	13.56	-	-	2	-	2092	1245	42	29.64	49.81	3.57	1	-	4-22
French, B.N.	13	8	3	34	9*	6.80	-	-	13	3	228	197	5	39.40	45.60	5.18	-	-	2-37
Gatting, M.W.	92	88	17	2095	115*	29.51	1	9	22	-	392	336	10	33.60	39.20	5.14	-	-	3-32
Gifford, N.	2	1	0	0	0	0.00	-	-	1	-	108	96	4	24.00	27.00	5.33	1	-	4-23
Giles, A.F	5	3	2	17	10*	17.00	-	-	1	-	246	178	5	35.60	49.20	4.34	-	-	2-37
Gooch, G.A.	125	122	6	4290	142	36.98	8	23	45	-	2066	1516	36	42.11	57.39	4.40	-	-	3-19
Gough, D.	56	37	13	269	45	11.21	-	-	7	-	3116	2203	89	24.75	35.01	4.24	4	2	5-44
Gould, I.J.	18	14	2	155	42	12.92	-	-	15	3	-	-	-	-	-	-	-	-	-
Gower, D.I.	114	111	8	3170	158	30.78	7	12	44	-	5	14	0	-	-	16.80	-	-	-
Greig, A.W.	22	19	3	269	48	16.81	-	-	7	-	916	619	19	32.58	48.21	4.05	1	-	4-45
Hampshire, J.H.	3	3	1	48	25*	24.00	-	-	-	-	-	-	-	-	-	-	-	-	-
Hayes, F.C.	6	6	1	128	52	25.60	-	1	-	-	-	-	-	-	-	-	-	-	-
Headley, D.W.	13	6	4	22	10*	11.00	-	-	3	-	594	520	11	47.27	54.00	5.25	-	-	2-38
Hemmings, E.E.	33	12	6	30	8*	5.00	-	-	5	-	1752	1294	37	34.97	47.35	4.43	2	-	4-52
Hendrick, M.	22	10	5	6	2*	1.20	-	-	5	-	1248	681	35	19.46	35.66	3.27	-	1	5-31
Hick, G.A.	87	86	9	2990	126*	38.83	5	19	40	-	895	741	19	39.00	47.11	4.97	-	-	3-41
Hollioake, A.J.	31	28	6	582	83*	26.45	-	3	12	-	1070	899	31	29.00	34.52	5.04	2	-	4-23
Hollioake, B.C.	7	6	0	122	63	20.33	-	1	1	-	150	122	2	61.00	75.00	4.88	-	-	2-43
Humpage, G.W.	3	2	0	11	6	5.50	-	-	2	-	-	-	-	-	-	-	-	-	-
Hussain, N.	28	28	5	550	93	23.91	-	2	14	-	-	-	-	-	-	-	-	-	-
Igglesden, A.P.	4	3	1	20	18	10.00	-	-	1	-	168	122	2	61.00	84.00	4.36	-	-	2-12
Illingworth, R.	3	2	0	5	4	2.50	-	-	1	-	130	84	4	21.00	32.50	3.88	-	-	3-50

Batting and Fielding

Player	M	Inns	NO	Runs	HS	Ave.	100s	50s	Ct	St	Bowling Balls	Runs	Wkts	Ave.	Stk Rt	Ec Rt	4wi	5wi	Best
Illingworth, R.K.	25	11	5	68	14	11.33	-	-	8	-	1501	1059	30	35.30	50.03	4.23	-	-	3-33
Irani, R.C.	10	10	2	78	45*	9.75	-	-	2	-	329	246	4	61.50	82.25	4.49	-	-	1-23
Jackman, R.D.	15	9	1	54	14	6.75	-	-	4	-	873	598	19	31.47	45.95	4.11	-	-	3-41
Jameson, J.A.	3	3	0	60	28	20.00	-	-	-	-	12	3	0	-	-	1.50	-	-	-
Jarvis, P.W.	16	8	4	31	16*	5.17	-	-	1	-	879	672	24	28.00	36.63	4.59	1	1	5-35
Jesty, T.E.	10	10	4	127	52*	21.17	-	1	5	-	108	93	1	93.00	108.00	5.17	-	-	1-23
Knight, N.V.	40	40	3	1497	125*	40.46	3	8	14	-	-	-	-	-	-	-	-	-	-
Knott, A.P.E.	20	14	4	200	50	20.00	-	1	15	1	-	-	-	-	-	-	-	-	-
Lamb, A.J.	122	118	16	4010	118	39.31	4	26	31	-	6	3	0	-	-	3.00	-	-	-
Larkins, W.	25	24	0	591	124	24.63	1	-	8	-	15	22	0	-	-	8.80	-	-	-
Lawrence, D.V.	1	-	-	-	-	-	-	-	-	-	66	67	4	16.75	16.50	6.09	1	-	4-67
Lever, J.K.	22	11	4	56	27*	8.00	-	-	6	-	1152	713	24	29.71	48.00	3.71	1	-	4-29
Lever, P.	10	10	2	17	8*	17.00	-	-	2	-	440	261	11	23.73	40.00	3.56	1	-	4-35
Lewis, C.C.	53	40	14	374	33	14.38	-	-	20	-	2625	1942	66	29.42	39.77	4.44	4	-	4-30
Lloyd, D.	8	8	1	285	116*	40.71	1	-	3	-	12	3	1	3.00	12.00	1.50	-	-	1-3
Lloyd, G.D.	6	5	1	39	22	9.75	-	-	2	-	-	-	-	-	-	-	-	-	-
Lloyd, T.A.	3	3	0	101	49	33.67	-	-	-	-	-	-	-	-	-	-	-	-	-
Love, J.D.	3	3	0	61	43	20.33	-	-	1	-	-	-	-	-	-	-	-	-	-
Luckhurst, B.W.	3	3	0	15	14	5.00	-	-	-	-	-	-	-	-	-	-	-	-	-
Lynch, M.A.	3	3	0	8	6	2.67	-	-	1	-	-	-	-	-	-	-	-	-	-
Maddy, D.L.	2	1	0	1	1	1.00	-	-	1	-	-	-	-	-	-	-	-	-	-
Malcolm, D.E.	10	5	2	9	4	3.00	-	-	-	-	526	404	16	25.25	32.88	4.61	-	-	3-40
Marks, V.J.	34	24	3	285	44	13.57	-	-	8	-	1838	1135	44	25.80	41.77	3.71	-	2	5-20
Martin, P.J.	20	13	7	38	6	6.33	-	-	-	-	1048	806	27	29.85	38.81	4.61	1	-	4-44
Maynard, M.P.	10	10	1	153	41	17.00	-	-	2	-	-	-	-	-	-	-	-	-	-
Miller, G.	25	18	2	136	46	8.50	-	-	4	-	1268	813	25	32.52	50.72	3.85	-	-	3-27
Morris, J.E.	8	8	1	167	63*	23.86	-	1	2	-	-	-	-	-	-	-	-	-	-
Moxon, M.D.	8	8	0	174	70	21.75	-	1	5	-	-	-	-	-	-	-	-	-	-
Mullally, A.D.	22	9	2	42	20	6.00	-	-	5	-	1166	772	28	27.57	41.64	3.97	1	-	4-18
Old, C.M.	32	25	7	338	51*	18.78	-	1	8	-	1755	999	45	22.20	39.00	3.42	2	-	4-8
Pocock, P.I.	1	1	0	4	4	4.00	-	-	-	-	60	20	0	-	-	2.00	-	-	-
Pringle, D.R.	44	30	12	425	49*	23.61	-	-	11	-	2379	1677	44	38.11	54.07	4.23	1	-	4-42
Radford, N.V.	6	6	2	0	0*	0.00	-	-	2	-	348	230	2	115.00	174.00	3.97	-	-	1-32
Radley, C.T.	4	4	1	250	117*	83.33	1	1	-	-	-	-	-	-	-	-	-	-	-
Ramprakash, M.R.	13	13	3	265	51	26.50	-	1	6	-	12	14	0	-	-	7.00	-	-	-
Randall, D.W.	49	45	5	1067	88	26.68	-	5	25	-	2	2	1	2.00	2.00	6.00	-	-	1-2
Reeve, D.A.	29	21	9	291	35	24.25	-	-	12	-	1147	820	20	41.00	57.35	4.29	-	-	3-20
Rhodes, S.J.	9	8	2	107	56	17.83	-	1	9	2	-	-	-	-	-	-	-	-	-

Batting and Fielding

Player	M	Inns	NO	Runs	HS	Ave.	100s	50s	Ct	St	Bowling Balls	Runs	Wkts	Ave.	Stk Rt	Ec Rt	4wi	5wi	Best
Richards, C.J.	22	16	3	154	50	11.85	-	1	16	1	-	-	-	-	-	-	-	-	-
Robinson, R.T.	26	26	0	597	83	22.96	-	3	6	-	-	-	-	-	-	-	-	-	-
Roope, G.R.J.	8	8	0	173	44	21.63	-	-	2	-	-	-	-	-	-	-	-	-	-
Rose, B.C.	2	2	0	99	54	49.50	-	1	1	-	-	-	-	-	-	-	-	-	-
Russell, R.C.	40	31	7	423	50	17.63	-	1	41	6	-	-	-	-	-	-	-	-	-
Salisbury, I.D.K.	4	2	1	7	5	7.00	-	-	1	-	186	177	5	35.40	37.20	5.71	-	-	3-41
Shuttleworth, K.	1	1	0	7	7	7.00	-	-	1	-	56	29	1	29.00	56.00	3.11	-	-	1-29
Silverwood, C.E.W.	6	4	0	17	12	4.25	-	-	-	-	252	201	3	67.00	84.00	4.79	-	-	2-27
Slack, W.N.	2	2	0	43	34	21.50	-	-	-	-	-	-	-	-	-	-	-	-	-
Small, G.C.	53	24	9	98	18*	6.53	-	-	7	-	2793	1942	58	33.48	48.16	4.17	1	-	4-31
Smith, C.L.	4	4	0	109	70	27.25	-	1	-	-	36	28	2	14.00	18.00	4.67	-	-	2-8
Smith, D.M.	2	2	1	15	10*	15.00	-	-	-	-	-	-	-	-	-	-	-	-	-
Smith, M.J.	5	5	0	70	31	14.00	-	-	1	-	-	-	-	-	-	-	-	-	-
Smith, N.M.K.	7	6	1	100	31	20.00	-	-	1	-	261	190	6	31.67	43.50	4.37	-	-	3-29
Smith, R.A.	71	70	8	2419	167*	39.02	4	15	26	-	-	-	-	-	-	-	-	-	-
Snow, J.A.	9	4	2	9	5*	4.50	-	-	1	-	538	232	14	16.57	38.43	2.59	2	-	4-11
Steele, D.S.	1	1	0	8	8	8.00	-	-	-	-	6	9	0	-	-	9.00	-	-	-
Stevenson, G.B.	4	4	3	43	28*	43.00	-	-	2	-	192	125	7	17.86	27.43	3.91	1	-	4-33
Stewart, A.J.	116	111	8	3211	116	31.17	2	18	101	11	-	-	-	-	-	-	-	-	-
Tavare, C.J.	29	28	2	720	83*	27.69	-	4	7	-	-	-	-	-	-	-	-	-	-
Taylor, J.P.	1	1	0	1	1	1.00	-	-	-	-	12	3	0	-	-	1.50	-	-	-
Taylor, L.B.	2	1	1	1	1*	-	-	-	-	-	18	20	0	-	-	6.67	-	-	-
Taylor, R.W.	27	17	7	130	26*	13.00	-	-	26	6	84	47	0	-	-	3.36	-	-	-
Thomas, J.G.	3	3	2	2	1*	1.00	-	-	-	-	156	144	3	48.00	52.00	5.54	-	-	2-59
Thorpe, G.P.	44	44	7	1482	89	40.05	-	14	24	-	120	97	2	48.50	60.00	4.85	-	-	2-15
Titmus, F.J.	2	1	0	11	11	11.00	-	-	1	-	56	53	3	17.67	18.67	5.68	-	-	3-53
Tolchard, R.W.	1	-	-	-	-	-	-	-	1	-	-	-	-	-	-	-	-	-	-
Tufnell, P.C.R.	20	10	9	15	5*	15.00	-	-	4	-	1020	699	19	36.79	53.68	4.11	1	-	4-22
Udal, S.D.	10	6	4	35	11*	17.50	-	-	1	-	570	371	8	46.38	71.25	3.91	-	-	2-37
Underwood, D.L.	26	13	4	53	17	5.89	-	-	6	-	1278	734	32	22.94	39.94	3.45	1	-	4-44
Watkin, S.L.	4	2	0	4	4	2.00	-	-	-	-	221	193	7	27.57	31.57	5.24	1	-	4-49
Watkinson, M.	1	-	-	-	-	-	-	-	-	-	54	43	0	-	-	4.78	-	-	-
Wells, A.P.	1	1	0	15	15	15.00	-	-	-	-	-	-	-	-	-	-	-	-	-
Wells, C.M.	2	2	0	22	17	11.00	-	-	-	-	-	-	-	-	-	-	-	-	-
Wells, V.J.	7	5	0	131	39	26.20	-	-	3	-	196	153	8	19.13	24.50	4.68	-	-	3-30
Whitaker, J.J.	2	2	1	48	44*	48.00	-	-	1	-	-	-	-	-	-	-	-	-	-
White, C.	15	13	0	187	38	14.38	-	-	2	-	608	445	15	29.67	40.53	4.39	1	-	4-37
Willey, P.	26	24	1	538	64	23.39	-	5	4	-	1031	659	13	50.69	79.31	3.84	-	-	3-33

Batting and Fielding — **Bowling**

Player	M	Inns	NO	Runs	HS	100s	50s	Ct	St	Balls	Runs	Wkts	Ave.	Stk Rt	Ec Rt	4wi	5wi	Best
Willis, R.W.	64	22	14	83	24	-	-	22	-	3595	1968	80	24.60	44.94	3.28	4	-	4-11
Wood, B.	13	12	2	314	78*	-	2	6	-	420	224	9	24.89	46.67	3.20	-	-	2-14
Woolmer, R.A.	6	4	0	21	9	-	-	3	-	321	260	9	28.89	35.67	4.86	-	-	3-33

INDIA (118 PLAYERS)

Batting and Fielding — **Bowling**

Player	M	Inns	NO	Runs	HS	Ave.	100s	50s	Ct	St	Balls	Runs	Wkts	Ave.	Stk Rt	Ec Rt	4wi	5wi	Best
Abid Ali, S.	5	3	0	93	70	31.00	-	1	-	-	336	187	7	26.71	48.00	3.34	-	-	2-22
Agarkar, A.B.	30	13	2	177	30	16.09	-	-	13	-	1613	1378	58	23.76	27.81	5.13	3	-	4-35
Amarnath, M.	85	75	12	1924	102*	30.54	2	13	23	-	2730	1971	46	42.85	59.35	4.33	-	-	3-12
Amarnath, S.	3	3	0	100	62	33.33	-	1	1	-									
Amre, P.K.	37	30	5	513	84*	20.52	-	2	12	-	2	4	0			12.00			
Ankola, S.A.	20	13	4	34	9	3.78	-	-	2	-	807	615	13	47.31	62.08	4.57	-	-	3-33
Arshad Ayub	32	17	7	116	31*	11.60	-	-	5	-	1769	1216	31	39.23	57.06	4.12	-	1	5-21
Arun Lal	13	13	0	122	51	9.38	-	1	4	-									
Arun, B.	4	3	1	21	8	10.50	-	-	-	-	102	103	1	103.00	102.00	6.06	-	-	1-43
Azad, K.	25	21	2	269	39*	14.16	-	-	7	-	390	273	7	39.00	55.71	4.20	-	-	2-48
Azharuddin, M.	310	285	51	8868	153*	37.90	7	55	146	-	552	479	12	39.92	46.00	5.21	-	-	3-19
Bahutule, S.V.	7	3	1	12	11	6.00	-	-	3	-	276	259	2	129.50	138.00	5.63	-	-	1-31
Banerjee, S.T.	6	5	3	49	25*	24.50	-	-	3	-	240	202	5	40.40	48.00	5.05	-	-	3-30
Bedade, A.C.	13	10	3	158	51	22.57	-	1	4	-									
Bedi, B.S.	10	7	2	31	13	6.20	-	-	4	-	590	340	7	48.57	84.29	3.46	-	-	2-44
Bhupinder Singh	2	1	0	6	6	6.00	-	-	-	-	102	78	3	26.00	34.00	4.59	-	-	3-34
Binny, R.M.H.	72	49	10	629	57	16.13	-	1	12	-	2957	2260	77	29.35	38.40	4.59	3	-	4-29
Bose, G.	1	1	0	13	13	13.00	-	-	-	-	66	39	1	39.00	66.00	3.55	-	-	1-39
Chandrasekhar, B.S.	1	1	1	11	11*	-	-	-	1	-	56	36	3	12.00	18.67	3.86	-	-	3-36
Chandrasekhar, V.B.	7	7	0	88	53	12.57	-	1	1	-									
Chatterjee, U.	3	2	1	6	3*	6.00	-	-	-	-	161	117	3	39.00	53.67	4.36	-	-	2-35
Chauhan, C.P.S.	7	7	0	153	46	21.86	-	-	3	-									
Chauhan, R.K.	35	18	5	132	32	10.15	-	-	10	-	1634	1215	29	41.90	56.34	4.46	-	-	3-29
Chopra, N.	11	6	1	77	39	15.40	-	-	2	-	504	322	7	46.00	72.00	3.83	-	-	1-65
David, N.	4	2	2	9	8*	-	-	-	-	-	192	133	4	33.25	48.00	4.16	-	-	3-21
Dharmani, P.	1	1	0	8	8	8.00	-	-	3	-									
Doshi, D.R.	15	5	2	9	5*	3.00	-	-	3	-	792	524	22	23.82	36.00	3.97	2	-	4-30
Dravid, R.S.	70	63	5	2017	123*	34.78	2	14	32	-	84	71	0			5.07			
Engineer, F.M.	5	4	1	114	54*	38.00	-	1	1	1									
Gaekwad, A.D.	15	14	1	269	78*	20.69	-	1	6	-	48	39	1	39.00	48.00	4.88	-	-	1-39

Batting and Fielding / Bowling

Player	M	Inns	NO	Runs	HS	Ave.	100s	50s	Ct	St	Balls	Runs	Wkts	Ave.	Stk Rt	Ec Rt	4wi	5wi	Best
Ganesh, D.	1	1	0	4	4	4.00	-	-	-	-	30	20	1	20.00	30.00	4.00	-	-	1-20
Ganguly, S.C.	90	85	7	3146	124	40.33	5	22	27	-	1291	1014	26	39.00	49.65	4.71	-	1	5-16
Gavaskar, S.M.	108	102	14	3092	103*	35.14	1	27	22	-	20	25	1	25.00	20.00	7.50	-	-	1-10
Ghai, R.S.	6	1	0	1	1	1.00	-	-	-	-	275	260	3	86.67	91.67	5.67	-	-	1-38
Ghavri, K.D.	19	16	6	114	20	11.40	-	-	2	-	1033	708	15	47.20	68.87	4.11	-	-	3-40
Gusharan Singh	1	1	0	4	4	4.00	-	-	1	-									
Harbhajan Singh	13	5	2	9	4	3.00	-	-	3	-	690	491	18	27.28	38.33	4.27	-	-	3-41
Harvinder Singh	13	4	1	5	3*	1.67	-	-	4	-	512	477	20	23.85	25.60	5.59	-	-	3-44
Hirwani, N.D.	18	7	3	8	4	2.00	-	-	2	-	960	719	23	31.26	41.74	4.49	3	-	4-43
Jadeja, A.D.	154	139	27	4020	119	35.89	4	23	45	-	1192	1043	14	74.50	85.14	5.25	-	-	2-16
Joshi, S.B.	34	20	4	181	48	11.31	-	-	12	-	1678	1223	36	33.97	46.61	4.37	-	-	3-17
Kambli, V.G.	86	79	19	2225	106	37.08	2	13	12	-	4	7	1	7.00	4.00	10.50	-	-	1-7
Kanitkar, H.H.	27	21	8	290	57	22.31	-	1	11	-	946	750	17	44.12	55.65	4.76	-	-	2-22
Kapil Dev	225	198	39	3783	175*	23.79	1	14	71	-	11202	6945	253	27.45	44.28	3.72	3	1	5-43
Kapoor, A.R.	15	6	0	43	19	7.17	-	-	1	-	816	547	8	68.38	102.00	4.02	-	-	2-33
Karim, S.S.	26	20	2	295	55	16.38	-	1	23	2									
Khanna, S.C.	10	10	2	176	56	22.00	-	2	4	4									
Khoda, G.K.	2	2	0	115	89	57.50	-	1	-	-									
Kirmani, S.M.H.	49	31	13	373	48*	20.72	-	-	27	9									
Krishnamurthy, P.	1	1	0	6	6	6.00	-	-	2	1									
Kulkarni, N.M.	10	5	3	11	5*	5.50	-	-	2	-	402	357	11	32.45	36.55	5.33	-	-	3-27
Kulkarni, R.R.	10	5	3	33	15	16.50	-	-	2	-	444	345	10	34.50	44.40	4.66	-	-	3-42
Kumble, A.	158	77	26	518	24	10.16	-	-	58	-	8522	5841	212	27.55	40.20	4.11	5	2	6-12
Kuruvilla, A.	25	11	4	26	7	3.71	-	-	4	-	1131	890	25	35.60	45.24	4.72	1	-	4-43
Lamba, R.	32	31	2	782	102	26.97	1	6	10	-	19	20	1	20.00	19.00	6.32	-	-	1-9
Laxman, V.S.	7	6	1	62	23*	12.40	-	-	4	-	36	32	0			5.33	-	-	
Madal Lal	67	35	14	401	53*	19.10	-	1	18	-	3164	2137	73	29.27	43.34	4.05	2	-	4-20
Malhotra, A.	20	19	4	457	65	30.47	-		4	-	6	0	0			0.00	-	-	
Maninder Singh	59	18	14	49	8*	12.25	-	-	18	-	3133	2067	66	31.32	47.47	3.96	2	-	4-22
Manjrekar, S.V.	74	70	10	1994	105	33.23	1	15	23	-	8	10	1	10.00	8.00	7.50	1	-	1-2
Mankad, A.V.	1	1	0	44	44	44.00	-	-	-	-	35	47	1	47.00	35.00	8.06	-	-	1-47
Mhambrey, P.L.	3	1	1	7	7*		-	-	-	-	126	120	3	40.00	42.00	5.71	-	-	2-69
Mohanty, D.S.	20	5	4	9	4*	9.00	-	-	5	-	828	739	20	36.95	41.40	5.36	-	-	3-15
Mongia, N.R.	123	82	25	1125	69	19.74	-	2	96	39									
More, K.S.	94	65	22	563	42*	13.09	-	-	63	27									
Mukherjee, S.P.	3	1	1	2	2*		-	-	1	-	174	98	2	49.00	87.00	3.38	-	-	1-30
Naik, S.S.	2	2	0	38	20	19.00	-	-	-	-									
Nayak, S.V.	4	1	0	3	3	3.00	-	-	-	-	222	161	1	161.00	222.00	4.35	-	-	1-51

Batting and Fielding

Player	M	Inns	NO	Runs	HS	Ave.	100s	50s	Ct	St	Bowling Balls	Runs	Wkts	Ave.	Stk Rt	Ec Rt	4wi	5wi	Best
Pandit, C.S.	36	23	9	290	33*	20.71	-	-	15	15	-	-	-	-	-	-	-	-	-
Paranjpe, J.V.	4	4	1	54	27	18.00	-	-	2	-	-	-	-	-	-	-	-	-	-
Parkar, G.A.	10	10	1	165	42	18.33	-	-	4	-	-	-	-	-	-	-	-	-	-
Patel, A.K.	8	2	0	6	6	3.00	-	-	1	-	360	263	7	37.57	51.43	4.38	-	-	3-43
Patel, B.P.	10	9	1	243	82	30.38	-	1	1	-	60	58	0	-	-	5.80	-	-	-
Patil, R.G.M.	1	-	-	-	-	-	-	-	1	-	-	-	-	-	-	-	-	-	-
Patil, S.M.	45	42	1	1005	84	24.51	-	9	11	-	864	589	15	39.27	57.60	4.09	-	-	2-28
Prabhakar, M.	130	98	21	1858	106	24.13	2	11	27	-	6360	4534	157	28.88	40.51	4.28	4	2	5-33
Prasad, B.K.V.	104	42	20	121	19	5.50	-	-	28	-	5177	4103	119	34.48	43.50	4.76	3	-	4-17
Prasad, M.S.K.	2	1	1	11	11*	-	-	-	1	-	-	-	-	-	-	-	-	-	-
Raiput, L.S.	4	4	1	9	9	3.00	-	-	2	-	42	42	0	-	-	6.00	-	-	-
Raju, S.L.V.	53	16	8	32	8	4.00	-	-	8	-	2770	2014	63	31.97	43.97	4.36	2	-	4-46
Raman, W.V.	27	27	1	617	114	23.73	1	3	2	-	162	170	2	85.00	81.00	6.30	-	-	1-23
Randhir Singh	2	-	-	-	-	-	-	-	-	-	72	48	1	48.00	72.00	4.00	-	-	1-30
Rathour, V.S.	7	7	0	193	54	27.57	-	2	4	-	-	-	-	-	-	-	-	-	-
Raul, S.S.	2	2	0	8	8	4.00	-	-	2	-	36	27	1	27.00	36.00	4.50	-	-	1-13
Razdan, V.	3	3	1	23	18	11.50	-	-	4	-	84	77	1	77.00	84.00	5.50	-	-	1-37
Reddy, B.	3	2	2	11	8*	-	-	-	2	-	-	-	-	-	-	-	-	-	-
Sandhu, B.S.	22	7	3	51	16*	12.75	-	-	5	-	1110	763	16	47.69	69.38	4.12	-	-	3-27
Sanghvi, R.	10	2	0	8	8	4.00	-	-	4	-	498	398	10	39.80	49.80	4.80	-	-	3-29
Sekhar, T.A.	4	-	-	-	-	-	-	-	-	-	156	128	5	25.60	31.20	4.92	-	-	3-23
Sharma, A.K.	31	27	6	424	59*	20.19	-	3	6	-	1140	875	15	58.33	76.00	4.61	-	-	3-41
Sharma, C.	65	35	16	456	101*	24.00	1	-	7	-	2835	2336	67	34.87	42.31	4.94	-	-	3-22
Sharma, G.	11	2	0	11	7	5.50	-	-	2	-	486	361	10	36.10	48.60	4.46	-	-	3-29
Sharma, P.	2	2	0	20	14	10.00	-	-	2	-	-	-	-	-	-	-	-	-	-
Sharma, S.K.	23	12	4	80	28	10.00	-	-	7	-	979	813	22	36.95	44.50	4.98	1	1	5-26
Shastri, R.J.	150	128	21	3108	109	29.05	4	18	40	-	6613	4650	129	36.05	51.26	4.22	2	1	5-15
Sidhu, N.S.	136	127	8	4414	134*	37.09	6	33	20	-	4	3	0	-	-	4.50	-	-	-
Singh, R.P.	2	-	-	-	-	-	-	-	1	-	82	77	1	77.00	82.00	5.63	-	-	1-58
Singh, R.R.	72	56	14	1215	100	28.93	1	5	15	-	2215	1778	44	40.41	50.34	4.82	1	1	5-22
Sivaramakrishnan, L.	16	4	2	5	2*	2.50	-	-	7	-	756	538	15	35.87	50.40	4.27	-	-	3-35
Solkar, E.D.	7	6	0	27	13	4.50	-	-	2	-	252	169	4	42.25	63.00	4.02	-	-	2-31
Somasunder, S.	2	2	0	16	9	8.00	-	-	2	-	-	-	-	-	-	-	-	-	-
Srikkanth, K.	146	145	4	4092	123	29.02	4	27	42	-	712	641	25	25.64	28.48	5.40	2	2	5-27
Srinath, J.	153	79	24	644	53	11.71	-	1	24	-	7969	5755	212	27.15	37.59	4.33	2	3	5-23
Srinivasan, T.E.	2	2	0	10	6	5.00	-	-	1	-	-	-	-	-	-	-	-	-	-
Sudhakar Rao	1	1	0	4	4	4.00	-	-	-	-	-	-	-	-	-	-	-	-	-
Tendulkar, S.R.	211	204	20	7800	142	42.39	21	43	71	-	4464	3645	78	46.73	57.23	4.90	2	1	5-32

Batting and Fielding

Player	M	Inns	NO	Runs	HS	Ave.	100s	50s	Ct	St	Bowling Balls	Runs	Wkts	Ave.	Stk Rt	Ec Rt	4wi	5wi	Best
Vaidya, P.S.	4	2	0	15	12	7.50	-	-	2	-	184	174	4	43.50	46.00	5.67	-	-	2-41
Vengsarker, D.B.	129	120	19	3508	105	34.73	1	23	37	-	6	4	0	-	-	4.00	-	-	-
Venkataraghavan, S.	15	9	4	54	26*	10.80	-	-	4	-	868	542	5	108.40	173.60	3.75	-	-	2-34
Venkataramana, M.	1	1	1	0	0*	-	-	-	-	-	60	36	2	18.00	30.00	3.60	-	-	2-36
Viswanath, G.R.	25	23	1	439	75	19.95	-	2	3	-									-
Viswanath, S.	22	12	4	72	23*	9.00	-	-	17	7									-
Wadekar, A.L.	2	2	0	73	67	36.50	-	1	1	-									-
Wassan, A.S.	9	6	2	33	16	8.25	-	-	2	-	426	283	11	25.73	38.73	3.99	-	-	3-28
Yadav, N.S.	7	2	2	1	1*	-	-	-	1	-	330	228	8	28.50	41.25	4.15	-	-	2-18
Yadav, V.	19	12	2	118	34*	11.80	-	-	12	7									-
Yashpal Sharma	42	40	9	883	89	28.48	-	4	10	-	201	199	1	199.00	201.00	5.94	-	-	1-27
Yograj Singh	6	4	2	1	1	0.50	-	-	2	-	244	186	4	46.50	61.00	4.57	-	-	2-44

KENYA (19 PLAYERS)

Batting and Fielding

Player	M	Inns	NO	Runs	HS	Ave.	100s	50s	Ct	St	Bowling Balls	Runs	Wkts	Ave.	Stk Rt	Ec Rt	4wi	5wi	Best
Aasif Karim	20	13	1	135	53	11.25	-	1	2	-	971	655	17	38.53	57.12	4.05	-	1	5-33
Angara, J.	3	2	1	6	3*	6.00	-	-	-	-	108	90	2	45.00	54.00	5.00	-	-	1-19
Chudasama, D.	19	17	0	431	122	25.41	1	1	2	-									-
Gupta, S.K.	3	3	0	43	41	14.33	-	-	-	-									-
Modi, H.	20	17	1	453	78*	28.31	-	4	5	-	12	14	0	-	-	7.00	-	-	-
Mohammed Sheikh	11	6	3	19	6*	6.33	-	-	5	-	448	337	10	33.70	44.80	4.51	-	-	2-41
Odoyo, T.	19	17	2	217	41	14.47	-	-	5	-	672	584	11	53.09	61.09	5.21	-	-	3-25
Odumbe, E.O.	8	7	1	61	20	10.17	-	-	4	-	137	137	6	22.83	22.83	6.00	-	-	2-8
Odumbe, M.O.	20	18	1	446	83	26.24	-	3	2	-	749	589	17	34.65	44.06	4.72	-	-	3-14
Onyango, L.	3	3	0	29	23	9.67	-	-	1	-	54	96	1	96.00	54.00	10.67	-	-	1-45
Otieno, K.	20	19	1	592	144	32.89	1	2	7	4									-
Rajab Ali	9	3	3	7	6*	-	-	-	1	-	338	255	11	23.18	30.73	4.53	-	-	3-17
Ravindu Shah	5	5	0	213	70	42.60	-	3	3	-	6	5	0	-	-	5.00	-	-	-
Suji, A.	8	7	1	115	67	19.17	-	1	1	-	200	154	3	51.33	66.67	4.62	-	-	1-16
Suji, M.A.	19	14	10	46	15	11.50	-	-	5	-	828	643	14	45.93	59.14	4.66	1	-	4-24
Tariq Iqbal	3	2	0	17	16	8.50	-	-	2	-									-
Tikolo, L.O.	3	2	2	36	25*	-	-	-	2	-	48	55	0	-	-	6.88	-	-	-
Tikolo, S.O.	20	19	0	501	96	26.37	-	4	11	-	538	444	13	34.15	41.38	4.95	-	-	3-41
Vader, A.	8	7	4	93	42*	31.00	-	-	4	-									-

THE NETHERLANDS (13 PLAYERS)

Batting and Fielding

Player	M	Inns	NO	Runs	HS	Ave.	100s	50s	Ct	St
Aponso, G.J.A.F.	5	4	0	120	58	30.00	-	1	0	-
Bakker, P.J.	5	1	1	0	0*	-	-	-	-	-
Cantrell, P.E.	5	5	0	160	47	32.00	-	-	-	-
Clarke, N.E.	5	5	0	50	32	10.00	-	-	3	-
de Leede, T.B.M.	5	5	0	90	41	18.00	-	-	-	-
Gouka, E.	3	2	1	19	19	19.00	-	-	0	-
Jansen, F.	2	-							1	-
Lefebvre, R.P.	4	4	1	78	45	26.00	-	-	1	-
Lubbers, S.W.	4	4	1	24	9	8.00	-	-	1	-
Schewe, M.	5	4	1	49	20	16.33	0	0	2	1
van Noortwijk, K.J.	5	5	1	168	64	42.00	-	1	0	-
van Oosterom, F.R.	2	2	2	7	5*	-	-	-	0	-
Zuiderent, B.	5	5	1	91	54	22.75	-	1	5	-

Bowling

Player	Balls	Runs	Wkts	Ave.	Stk Rt	Ec Rt	4wi	5wi	Best
Aponso, G.J.A.F.	242	257	2	128.50	121.00	6.37	-	-	1-57
Bakker, P.J.	258	215	3	71.67	86.00	5.00	-	-	2-51
Cantrell, P.E.	186	170	3	56.67	62.00	5.48	-	-	1-18
Clarke, N.E.	-	-	-	-	-	-	-	-	-
de Leede, T.B.M.	162	179	0	-	-	6.63	-	-	-
Gouka, E.	22	51	1	51.00	22.00	13.91	-	-	1-32
Jansen, F.	54	62	1	62.00	54.00	6.89	-	-	1-40
Lefebvre, R.P.	210	132	3	44.00	70.00	3.77	-	-	1-20
Lubbers, S.W.	216	187	5	37.40	43.20	5.19	-	-	3-48

NEW ZEALAND (109 PLAYERS)

Batting and Fielding

Player	M	Inns	NO	Runs	HS	Ave.	100s	50s	Ct	St
Allott, G.I.	6	4	2	14	7*	7.00	-	-	3	-
Anderson, R.W.	2	2	1	16	12	16.00	-	-	1	-
Astle, N.J.	75	75	2	2512	120	34.41	5	16	27	-
Bailey, M.D.	1	-								
Bell, M.D.	2	2	0	18	16	9.00	-	-	-	-
Blain, T.	38	38	11	442	49*	16.37	-	-	37	1
Blair, B.R.	14	14	2	174	29*	14.50	-	-	4	-
Boock, S.L.	14	7	4	30	12	10.00	-	-	5	-
Bracewell, B.P.	1	1	1	0	0*	-	-	-	-	-
Bracewell, J.G.	53	43	12	512	43	16.52	-	-	19	-
Bradburn, G.E.	7	7	1	57	30	9.50	-	-	1	-
Brown, V.R.	3	3	0	44	32	14.67	-	-	2	-
Burgess, M.G.	26	20	0	336	47	16.80	-	-	8	-
Cairns, B.L.	78	65	6	987	60	16.73	-	2	19	-
Cairns, C.L.	100	92	6	2335	115	27.15	2	12	32	-
Chatfield, E.J.	114	48	37	118	19*	10.73	-	-	19	-
Collinge, R.O.	15	9	3	34	9	5.67	-	-	1	-
Coman, P.G.	3	3	0	62	38	20.67	-	-	2	-

Bowling

Player	Balls	Runs	Wkts	Ave.	Stk Rt	Ec Rt	4wi	5wi	Best
Allott, G.I.	248	222	9	24.67	27.56	5.37	-	-	3-54
Anderson, R.W.	-	-	-	-	-	-	-	-	-
Astle, N.J.	2254	1666	50	33.32	45.08	4.43	1	-	4-43
Bailey, M.D.	-	-	-	-	-	-	-	-	-
Bell, M.D.	-	-	-	-	-	-	-	-	-
Blain, T.	-	-	-	-	-	-	-	-	-
Blair, B.R.	30	34	1	34.00	30.00	6.80	-	-	1-7
Boock, S.L.	700	513	15	34.20	46.67	4.40	-	-	3-28
Bracewell, B.P.	66	41	1	41.00	66.00	3.73	-	-	1-41
Bracewell, J.G.	2447	1884	33	57.09	74.15	4.62	-	-	2-3
Bradburn, G.E.	234	195	4	48.75	58.50	5.00	-	-	2-18
Brown, V.R.	66	75	1	75.00	66.00	6.82	-	-	1-24
Burgess, M.G.	74	69	1	69.00	74.00	5.59	-	-	1-10
Cairns, B.L.	4015	2717	89	30.53	45.11	4.06	2	1	5-28
Cairns, C.L.	3969	3031	92	32.95	43.14	4.58	2	1	5-42
Chatfield, E.J.	6065	3618	140	25.84	43.32	3.58	3	1	5-34
Collinge, R.O.	859	479	18	26.61	47.72	3.35	-	-	5-23
Coman, P.G.	-	-	-	-	-	-	-	-	-

Batting and Fielding

Player	M	Inns	NO	Runs	HS	Ave.	100s	50s	Ct	St	Bowling Balls	Runs	Wkts	Ave.	Stk Rt	Ec Rt	4wi	5wi	Best
Coney, J.V.	88	80	19	1874	66*	30.72		8	40		2931	2039	54	37.76	54.28	4.17	1		4-46
Congdon, B.E.	11	9	3	338	101	56.33	1	2			437	287	7	41.00	62.43	3.94			2-17
Crowe, J.J.	75	71	12	1518	88*	25.73		7	28		6	1	0			1.00			-
Crowe, M.D.	143	141	19	4704	107*	38.56	4	34	66		1296	954	29	32.90	44.69	4.42			2-9
Davis, H.T.	11	6	4	13	7*	6.50			2		432	436	11	39.64	39.27	6.06	1		4-35
de Groen, R.P.	12	8	3	12	7*	2.40			2		549	477	8	59.63	68.63	5.21			2-34
Douglas, M.W.	6	6	0	55	30	9.17			2		-	-	-	-	-	-			-
Doull, S.B.	38	25	12	166	22	12.77			9		1601	1336	34	39.29	47.09	5.01	1		4-25
Drum, C.J.	1	-	-	-	-	-			1		36	46	0			7.67			-
Edgar, B.A.	64	64	5	1814	102*	30.75	1	10	12		12	5	0			2.50			-
Edwards, G.N.	6	6	0	138	41	23.00			5		6	5	1	5.00	6.00	5.00			1-5
Fleming, S.P.	96	94	9	2799	116*	32.93	3	16	43		29	28	1	28.00	29.00	5.79			1-8
Franklin, T.J.	3	3	0	27	21	9.00			0		-	-	-	-	-	-			-
Germon, L.K.	37	31	5	518	89	19.92		3	21	9	-	-	-	-	-	-			-
Gillespie, S.R.	19	11	5	70	18*	11.67			7		963	736	23	32.00	41.87	4.59	1		4-30
Gray, E.J.	10	7	1	98	38	16.33			3		386	286	8	35.75	48.25	4.45			2-26
Greatbatch, M.J.	84	83	5	2206	111	28.28	2	13	35		6	5	0			5.00			-
Hadlee, B.G.	2	2	1	26	19	26.00			2		-	-	-	-	-	-			-
Hadlee, D.R.	11	7	2	40	20	8.00			2		628	364	20	18.20	31.40	3.48	1		4-34
Hadlee, R.J.	115	98	17	1751	79	21.62		4	27		6182	3407	158	21.56	39.13	3.31	1	5	5-25
Harris, C.Z.	120	106	34	2199	130	30.54	1	9	45		5665	4006	117	34.24	48.42	4.24	1	1	5-42
Hart, M.N.	11	6	0	49	16	8.17			7		548	347	13	26.69	42.15	3.80		1	5-22
Hart, R.T.	1	1	0	3	3	3.00					-	-	-	-	-	-			-
Hartland, B.R.	16	16	1	311	68*	20.73		2	5		-	-	-	-	-	-			-
Haslam, M.J.	9	1	0	9	9	9.00					30	28	1	28.00	30.00	5.60			1-28
Hastings, B.F.	11	9	1	151	37	18.88			4		-	-	-	-	-	-			-
Hayes, R.L.	1	1	0	13	13	13.00					42	31	0			4.43			-
Horne, M.J.	29	28	0	542	61	19.36		3	8		-	-	-	-	-	-			-
Horne, P.A.	4	4	0	50	18	12.50					-	-	-	-	-	-			-
Howarth, G.P.	70	65	5	1384	76	23.07		6	16		90	68	3	22.67	30.00	4.53			1-4
Howarth, H.J.	9	5	2	18	11	6.00			3		492	280	11	25.45	44.73	3.41			3-29
Howell, L.G.	12	12	0	287	68	23.92		1	2		-	-	-	-	-	-			-
Jones, A.H.	87	87	9	2784	93	35.69		25	23		306	216	4	54.00	76.50	4.24			2-42
Kennedy, R.J.	7	4	3	17	8*	17.00			1		312	283	5	56.60	62.40	5.44			2-36
Kuggeleijn, C.M.	16	11	2	142	40	15.78			9		817	604	12	50.33	68.08	4.44			2-31
Larsen, G.R.	106	63	24	572	37	14.68			21		5606	3525	103	34.22	54.43	3.77	1		4-24
Latham, R.T.	33	33	4	583	60	20.10		1	11		450	386	11	35.09	40.91	5.15	1	1	5-32
Lees, W.K.	31	24	5	215	26	11.32			28	2	-	-	-	-	-	-			-

Batting and Fielding Player	M	Inns	NO	Runs	HS	Ave.	100s	50s	Ct	St	Bowling Balls	Runs	Wkts	Ave.	Stk Rt	Ec Rt	4wi	5wi	Best
McEwan, P.E.	17	15	0	204	41	13.60	-	-	1	-	420	353	6	58.83	70.00	5.04	-	-	2-29
McKechnie, B.J.	14	8	4	54	27	13.50	-	-	2	-	818	495	19	26.05	43.05	3.63	-	-	3-23
McMillan, C.D.	36	34	1	883	86	26.76	-	5	11	-	569	462	16	28.88	35.56	4.87	-	-	2-17
McSweeney, E.B.	16	14	5	73	18*	8.11	-	-	14	3	-	-	-	-	-	-	-	-	-
Millmow, J.P.	5	1	1	0	0*	-	-	-	1	-	270	232	4	58.00	67.50	5.16	-	-	2-22
Morrison, D.K.	96	43	24	171	20*	9.00	-	-	19	-	4586	3468	126	27.52	36.40	4.54	1	2	5-34
Morrison, J.F.M.	18	15	3	252	55	21.00	-	1	6	-	283	199	8	24.88	35.38	4.22	-	-	3-24
Murray, D.J.	1	1	0	3	3	3.00	-	-	0	-	-	-	-	-	-	-	-	-	-
Nash, D.J.	51	34	9	382	40*	15.28	-	-	16	-	2219	1735	44	39.43	50.43	4.69	1	-	4-38
O'Connor, S.B.	23	8	4	21	8	5.25	-	-	7	-	901	794	29	27.38	31.07	5.29	1	1	5-39
O'Sullivan, D.R.	3	2	1	2	1*	2.00	-	-	-	-	168	123	2	61.50	84.00	4.39	-	-	1-38
Owens, M.B.	3	2	2	0	0	0.00	-	-	-	-	48	37	0	-	-	4.63	-	-	-
Parker, J.M.	24	20	0	248	66	12.40	-	1	11	1	16	10	1	10.00	16.00	3.75	-	-	1-10
Parker, N.M.	1	1	0	0	0	0.00	-	-	1	-	-	-	-	-	-	-	-	-	-
Parore, A.C.	107	101	17	2500	108	29.76	1	13	61	15	-	-	-	-	-	-	-	-	-
Patel, D.N.	75	63	10	623	71	11.75	-	1	23	-	3251	2260	45	50.22	72.24	4.17	-	-	3-22
Penn, A.J.	3	2	1	8	7*	8.00	-	-	-	-	99	123	1	123.00	99.00	7.45	-	-	1-50
Petrie, R.G.	12	8	3	65	21	13.00	-	-	2	-	660	449	12	37.42	55.00	4.08	-	-	2-25
Pollard, V.	3	2	0	67	55	33.50	-	1	1	-	-	-	-	-	-	-	-	-	-
Priest, M.W.	18	14	4	103	24	10.30	-	-	2	-	752	590	8	73.75	94.00	4.71	-	-	2-27
Pringle, C.	64	41	19	193	34*	8.77	-	-	7	-	3314	2455	103	23.83	32.17	4.44	2	1	5-45
Redmond, R.E.	2	1	0	3	3	3.00	-	-	-	-	-	-	-	-	-	-	-	-	-
Reid, J.F.	25	24	1	633	88	27.52	-	4	5	-	7	13	1	13.00	7.00	11.14	-	-	1-13
Reid, R.B.	9	9	0	248	64	27.56	-	2	3	-	56	30	1	30.00	56.00	3.21	-	-	1-30
Roberts, A.D.G.	1	1	0	16	16	16.00	-	-	1	-	42	47	0	-	-	6.71	-	-	-
Roberts, S.J.	2	1	0	1	1*	-	-	-	-	-	-	-	-	-	-	-	-	-	-
Robertson, G.K.	10	6	0	49	17	8.17	-	-	2	-	498	321	6	53.50	83.00	3.87	-	-	2-29
Rutherford, K.R.	121	115	9	3143	108	29.65	2	18	41	-	389	323	10	32.30	38.90	4.98	-	-	2-39
Smith, I.D.S.	98	77	16	1055	62*	17.30	-	3	81	5	-	-	-	-	-	-	-	-	-
Sneddon, M.C.	93	54	19	535	64	15.29	-	1	19	-	4525	3237	114	28.39	39.69	4.29	1	-	4-34
Spearman, C.M.	31	31	0	532	78	17.16	-	2	8	-	3	6	0	-	-	12.00	-	-	-
Stirling, D.A.	6	5	2	21	13*	7.00	-	-	3	-	234	207	6	34.50	39.00	5.31	-	-	2-29
Stott, L.W.	1	-	-	-	-	-	-	-	1	-	72	48	3	16.00	24.00	4.00	-	-	3-48
Su'a, M.L.	12	7	2	24	12*	4.80	-	-	1	-	463	367	9	40.78	51.44	4.76	1	-	4-59
Tait, A.R.	2	2	1	17	10*	17.00	-	-	-	-	54	46	2	23.00	27.00	5.11	-	-	2-37
Taylor, B.R.	2	1	0	22	22	22.00	-	-	1	-	114	62	4	15.50	28.50	3.26	-	-	3-25
Thomson, S.A.	56	52	10	964	83	22.95	-	5	18	-	2121	1602	42	38.14	50.50	4.53	-	-	3-14
Troup, G.B.	22	12	8	101	39	25.25	-	-	2	-	1180	791	32	24.72	36.88	4.02	3	-	4-19

Batting and Fielding

Player	M	Inns	NO	Runs	HS	Ave.	100s	50s	Ct	St	Balls	Runs	Wkts	Ave.	Stk Rt	Ec Rt	4wi	5wi	Best
Turner, G.M.	41	40	6	1598	171*	47.00	3	9	13	-	6	0	0	-	-	0.00	-	-	-
Twose, R.G.	30	29	1	745	92	26.61	-	5	7	-	272	237	4	59.25	68.00	5.23	-	-	2-31
Vance, R.H.	8	8	0	248	96	31.00	-	1	4	-	-	-	-	-	-	-	-	-	-
Vaughan, J.T.C.	18	16	7	162	33	18.00	-	-	4	-	696	524	16	32.75	43.50	4.52	1	-	4-33
Vettori, D.L.	31	19	8	159	25*	14.45	-	-	10	-	1227	992	25	39.68	49.08	4.85	1	-	4-49
Vivian, G.E.	1	1	0	14	14	14.00	-	-	-	-	-	-	-	-	-	-	-	-	-
Wadsworth, K.J.	13	10	1	258	104	28.67	1	-	13	2	-	-	-	-	-	-	-	-	-
Watson, W.	61	24	13	86	21	7.82	-	-	9	-	3251	2247	74	30.36	43.93	4.15	1	-	4-27
Webb, P.N.	5	5	1	38	10*	9.50	-	-	3	-	-	-	-	-	-	-	-	-	-
Webb, R.J.	3	1	1	6	6*	-	-	-	-	-	161	105	4	26.25	40.25	3.91	-	-	2-28
White, D.J.	3	3	0	37	15	12.33	-	-	1	-	-	-	-	-	-	-	-	-	-
Wilson, J.W.	4	4	1	80	44*	26.67	-	-	1	-	152	135	3	45.00	50.67	5.33	-	-	2-21
Wiseman, P.J.	6	2	1	23	16	23.00	-	-	-	-	114	95	2	47.50	57.00	5.00	-	-	1-21
Wright, J.G.	149	148	1	3891	101	26.47	1	24	51	-	24	8	0	-	-	2.00	-	-	-
Young, B.A.	73	72	5	1644	74	24.54	-	9	28	-	-	-	-	-	-	-	-	-	-

PAKISTAN (124 PLAYERS)

Batting and Fielding

Player	M	Inns	NO	Runs	HS	Ave.	100s	50s	Ct	St	Balls	Runs	Wkts	Ave.	Stk Rt	Ec Rt	4wi	5wi	Best
Aamer Hameed	2	-	-	-	-	-	-	-	1	-	88	38	1	38.00	88.00	2.59	-	-	1-32
Aamer Hanif	5	4	2	89	36*	44.50	-	-	-	-	130	122	4	30.50	32.50	5.63	-	-	3-36
Aamer Malik	24	23	1	556	90	25.27	-	5	13	3	120	86	3	28.67	40.00	4.30	-	-	2-35
Aamir Nazir	9	3	2	13	2	13.00	-	-	-	-	417	346	11	31.45	37.91	4.98	-	-	3-43
Aamir Sohail	149	148	5	4651	134	32.52	5	31	49	-	4670	3547	82	43.26	56.95	4.56	1	-	4-22
Abdul Qadir	104	68	26	641	41*	15.26	-	-	21	-	5100	3453	132	26.16	38.64	4.06	4	2	5-44
Abdur Razzaq	13	10	2	101	46*	12.63	-	-	1	-	496	435	12	36.25	41.33	5.26	-	-	2-29
Akhtar Sarfraz	4	4	0	66	25	16.50	-	-	-	-	-	-	-	-	-	-	-	-	-
Akram Raza	49	25	14	193	33*	17.55	-	-	19	-	2601	1611	38	42.39	68.45	3.72	-	-	3-18
Anil Dalpat	15	10	3	87	37	12.43	-	-	13	2	-	-	-	-	-	-	-	-	-
Aqib Javed	163	51	26	267	45*	10.68	-	-	24	-	8012	5721	182	31.43	44.02	4.28	2	-	7-37
Arshad Khan	12	8	6	42	13*	21.00	-	-	3	-	564	437	10	43.70	56.40	4.65	-	-	3-70
Arshad Pervez	2	2	0	11	8	5.50	-	-	-	-	-	-	-	-	-	-	-	-	-
Ashfaq Ahmed	3	-	-	-	-	-	-	-	-	-	102	84	0	-	-	4.94	-	-	-
Ashraf Ali	16	9	5	69	19*	17.25	-	-	17	3	-	-	-	-	-	-	-	-	-
Asif Iqbal	10	8	2	330	62	55.00	-	5	7	-	592	378	16	23.63	37.00	3.83	1	-	4-56
Asif Mahmood	2	2	0	14	14	7.00	-	-	-	-	-	-	-	-	-	-	-	-	-

Batting and Fielding

Player	M	Inns	NO	Runs	HS	Ave.	100s	50s	Ct	St	Balls	Runs	Wkts	Ave.	Stk Rt	Ec Rt	4wi	5wi	Best
Asif Masood	7	3	1	10	6	5.00	-	-	1	-	402	234	5	46.80	80.40	3.49	-	-	2-9
Asif Mujtaba	66	55	14	1068	113*	26.05	1	6	18	-	756	658	7	94.00	108.00	5.22	-	-	2-38
Ata-ur-Rehman	30	13	6	34	11*	4.86	-	-	-	-	1492	1186	27	43.93	55.26	4.77	-	-	3-27
Azam Khan	6	5	0	116	72	23.20	-	1	2	-									
Azeem Hafeez	15	10	7	45	15	15.00	-	-	3	-	719	586	15	39.07	47.93	4.89	1	-	4-22
Azhar Mahmood	49	36	9	452	65*	16.74	-	2	16	-	2115	1682	34	49.47	62.21	4.77	-	-	3-34
Azmat Rana	2	2	0	42	22*	42.00	-	-	-	-									
Basit Ali	50	43	6	1265	127*	34.19	1	9	15	-	30	21	1	21.00	30.00	4.20	-	-	1-17
Fazl-e-Akbar	1	1	0	7	7	7.00	-	-	-	-	12	19	0			9.50	-	-	-
Ghulam Ali	3	3	0	53	38	17.67	-	-	-	-									
Haafiz Shahid	3	3	2	11	7*	11.00	-	-	3	-	127	112	3	37.33	42.33	5.29	-	-	2-56
Haroon Rashid	12	10	2	166	63*	20.75	-	1	-	-									
Hasan Jamil	6	5	0	111	28	22.20	-	-	1	-	232	154	8	19.25	29.00	3.98	-	-	3-18
Hasan Raza	11	9	0	122	46	13.56	-	-	1	-									
Ijaz Ahmed	215	198	26	5577	139*	32.42	9	30	79	-	621	464	4	116.00	155.25	4.48	-	-	2-31
Ijaz Ahmed jnr	2	1	1	3	3*	-	-	-	-	-	30	25	1	25.00	30.00	5.00	-	-	1-9
Ijaz Faqih	27	19	3	197	42*	12.31	-	-	2	-	1116	819	13	63.00	85.85	4.40	1	-	4-43
Imran Khan	175	151	40	3709	102*	33.41	1	19	37	-	7461	4845	182	26.62	40.99	3.90	3	1	6-14
Intikhab Alam	4	2	0	17	10	8.50	-	-	-	-	158	118	4	29.50	39.50	4.48	-	-	2-36
Inzamam-ul-Haq	171	161	21	5369	137*	38.35	5	37	46	-	40	52	2	26.00	20.00	7.80	-	-	1-4
Iqbal Qasim	15	7	1	39	13	6.50	-	-	3	-	664	500	12	41.67	55.33	4.52	-	-	3-13
Iqbal Sikander	4	1	1	1	1*	-	-	-	-	-	210	147	3	49.00	70.00	4.20	-	-	1-30
Ifran Bhatti	1	-	-	-	-	-	-	-	1	-	48	22	2	11.00	24.00	2.75	-	-	2-22
Jalaluddin	8	2	0	5	5	2.50	-	-	1	-	306	211	14	15.07	21.86	4.14	1	-	4-32
Javed Miandad	233	218	41	7381	119*	41.70	8	50	71	2	436	297	7	42.43	62.29	4.09	-	-	2-22
Javed Qadir	1	1	0	12	12	12.00	-	-	1	-									
Kabir Khan	7	3	2	7	5	7.00	-	-	1	-	239	197	7	28.14	34.14	4.95	-	-	2-23
Liaquat Ali	3	1	0	1	1	1.00	-	-	-	-	188	111	2	55.50	94.00	3.54	-	-	1-41
Mahmood Hamid	1	1	0	1	1	1.00	-	-	-	-									
Majid Khan	23	22	1	786	109	37.43	1	7	3	-	658	374	13	28.77	50.62	3.41	-	-	3-27
Mansoor Akhtar	41	35	1	593	47	17.44	-	-	14	-	138	110	2	55.00	69.00	4.78	-	-	1-7
Mansoor Rana	2	2	0	15	10	7.50	-	-	-	-	6	7	0			7.00	-	-	-
Manzoor Akhtar	7	5	1	97	44	24.25	-	1	1	-	199	184	5	36.80	39.80	5.55	1	-	4-50
Manzoor Elahi	54	46	13	741	50*	22.45	-	1	21	-	1743	1262	29	43.52	60.10	4.34	-	-	3-22
Maqsood Rana	1	1	0	5	5	5.00	-	-	-	-	12	11	0			5.50	-	-	-
Masood Iqbal	1	1	0	2	2	2.00	-	-	-	-									
Mohammad Akram	13	8	6	13	7*	6.50	-	-	5	-	522	434	12	36.17	43.50	4.99	-	-	2-28
Mohammad Hussain	14	11	6	154	31*	30.80	-	-	5	-	672	547	13	42.08	51.69	4.88	1	-	4-33

Batting and Fielding / **Bowling**

Player	M	Inns	NO	Runs	HS	Ave.	100s	50s	Ct	St	Balls	Runs	Wkts	Ave.	Stk Rt	Ec Rt	4wi	5wi	Best
Mohammad Nazir	4	3	3	4	2*	–	–	–	6	–	222	156	3	52.00	74.00	4.22	–	–	2-37
Mohammad Wasim	21	21	2	499	76	26.26	–	3	6	–	–	–	–	–	–	–	–	–	–
Mohammad Zahid	9	4	2	15	7*	7.50	–	–	–	–	392	288	7	41.14	56.00	4.41	–	–	2-20
Mohsin Kamal	19	6	3	27	11*	9.00	–	–	4	–	881	760	21	36.19	41.95	5.18	1	–	4-47
Mohsin Khan	75	75	5	1877	117*	26.81	2	8	13	–	12	5	1	5.00	12.00	2.50	–	–	1-2
Moin Khan	118	98	27	1684	69*	23.72	–	5	104	39	–	–	–	–	–	–	–	–	–
Moin-ul-Atiq	5	5	0	199	105	39.80	1	–	–	–	–	–	–	–	–	–	–	–	–
Mudassar Nazar	122	115	10	2653	95	25.27	–	16	21	–	4855	3432	111	30.92	43.74	4.24	1	1	5-28
Mujahid Jamshed	4	3	1	27	23	13.50	–	–	–	–	24	6	1	6.00	24.00	1.50	–	–	1-6
Mushtaq Ahmed	130	69	31	343	26	9.03	–	–	28	–	6727	4842	144	33.63	46.72	4.32	2	1	5-36
Mushtaq Mohammad	10	9	3	209	55	34.83	–	1	3	–	42	23	0	–	–	3.29	–	–	–
Nadeem Ghauri	6	3	2	14	7*	14.00	–	–	–	–	342	230	5	46.00	68.40	4.04	–	–	2-51
Nadeem Khan	2	1	0	2	2	2.00	–	–	–	–	96	81	0	–	–	5.06	–	–	–
Naeem Ahmed	1	1	1	0	0*	–	–	–	–	–	60	43	0	–	–	4.30	–	–	–
Naeem Ashraf	2	2	1	24	16	24.00	–	–	1	–	42	52	0	–	–	7.43	–	–	–
Naseer Malik	3	1	0	0	0*	–	–	–	–	–	180	98	5	19.60	36.00	3.27	–	–	2-37
Nasim-ul-Ghani	1	1	0	1	1	1.00	–	–	–	–	–	–	–	–	–	–	–	–	–
Naved Anjum	13	12	3	113	30	12.56	–	–	2	–	472	344	8	43.00	59.00	4.37	–	–	2-27
Parvez Mir	3	3	1	26	18	13.00	–	–	2	–	122	77	3	25.67	40.67	3.79	–	–	1-17
Qasim Omar	31	31	3	642	69	22.93	–	4	3	–	–	–	–	–	–	–	–	–	–
Ramiz Raja	198	197	15	5841	119*	32.09	9	31	33	–	6	10	0	–	–	10.00	–	–	–
Rashid Khan	29	15	7	110	17	13.75	–	–	3	–	1414	923	20	46.15	70.70	3.92	–	–	3-47
Rashid Latif	101	66	18	748	50	15.58	–	1	94	28	–	–	–	–	–	–	–	–	–
Rizwan-uz-Raman	3	3	0	20	14	6.67	–	–	2	–	–	–	–	–	–	–	–	–	–
Saadat Ali	8	7	1	184	78*	30.67	–	1	1	–	–	–	–	–	–	–	–	–	–
Sadiq Mohammad	19	19	1	383	74	21.28	–	2	5	–	27	29	2	14.50	13.50	6.44	–	–	2-24
Saeed Anwar	161	159	14	5852	194	40.36	15	27	29	–	38	26	2	13.00	19.00	4.11	–	–	2-20
Saeed Azad	4	4	0	65	31	16.25	–	–	2	–	188	167	3	55.67	62.67	5.33	–	–	1-9
Sajid Ali	13	12	0	130	28	10.83	–	–	1	–	–	–	–	–	–	–	–	–	–
Sajjad Akbar	2	1	0	5	5	5.00	–	–	–	–	60	45	2	22.50	30.00	4.50	–	–	2-45
Salim Altaf	6	2	1	25	21	25.00	–	–	1	–	285	151	5	30.20	57.00	3.18	–	–	2-7
Salim Elahi	18	18	1	509	102*	29.94	1	3	4	–	–	–	–	–	–	–	–	–	–
Salim Jaffer	39	13	11	36	10*	18.00	–	–	3	–	1900	1382	40	34.55	47.50	4.36	1	–	3-25
Salim Malik	276	250	37	7053	102	33.11	5	46	80	–	3493	2942	89	33.06	39.25	5.05	–	1	5-35
Salim Pervez	1	1	0	18	18	18.00	–	–	–	–	–	–	–	–	–	–	–	–	–
Salim Yousuf	86	62	19	768	62	17.86	–	4	81	22	–	–	–	–	–	–	–	–	–
Saqlain Mushtaq	88	50	15	415	30*	11.86	–	–	27	–	4609	3294	176	18.72	26.19	4.29	9	4	5-29
Sarfraz Nawaz	45	31	8	221	34*	9.61	–	–	8	–	2412	1463	63	23.22	38.29	3.64	4	–	4-27

Batting and Fielding / Bowling

Player	M	Inns	NO	Runs	HS	Ave.	100s	50s	Ct	St	Balls	Runs	Wkts	Ave.	Stk Rt	Ec Rt	4wi	5wi	Best
Shadab Kabir	3	3	0	0	0	0.00	-	-	1	-	-	-	-	-	-	-	-	-	-
Shafiq Ahmed	3	3	0	41	29	13.67	-	-	1	-	-	-	-	-	-	-	-	-	-
Shahid Afridi	71	68	2	1604	109	24.30	2	8	24	-	3095	2441	45	54.24	68.78	4.73	-	-	3-33
Shahid Anwar	1	1	0	37	37	37.00	-	-	-	-	-	-	-	-	-	-	-	-	-
Shahid Mahboob	10	6	1	119	77	23.80	-	1	1	-	540	382	7	54.57	77.14	4.24	-	-	1-23
Shahid Nazir	14	6	5	25	8	25.00	-	-	2	-	630	498	15	33.20	42.00	4.74	-	-	3-14
Shahid Saeed	10	10	0	141	50	14.10	-	1	2	-	222	159	3	53.00	74.00	4.30	-	-	2-20
Shakil Ahmed	2	2	0	61	36	30.50	-	-	-	-	-	-	-	-	-	-	-	-	-
Shakil Khan	1	1	0	0	0	0.00	-	-	-	-	54	50	1	50.00	54.00	5.56	-	-	1-50
Shoaib Akhtar	5	2	1	44	36	44.00	-	-	1	-	234	207	5	41.40	46.80	5.31	-	-	3-44
Shoaib Mohammed	63	58	6	1269	126*	24.40	1	8	13	-	919	725	20	36.25	45.95	4.73	-	-	3-20
Sikander Bakht	27	11	7	31	16*	7.75	-	-	4	-	1277	860	33	26.06	38.70	4.04	1	-	4-34
Sohail Fazal	2	2	0	56	32	28.00	-	-	1	-	6	4	0	-	-	4.00	-	-	-
Tahir Naqqash	40	23	9	210	61	15.00	-	1	11	-	1596	1240	34	36.47	46.94	4.66	-	-	3-23
Tanvir Mehdi	1	1	0	0	0	0.00	-	-	-	-	66	72	1	72.00	66.00	6.55	-	-	1-72
Taslim Arif	2	2	0	28	24	14.00	-	-	1	1	-	-	-	-	-	-	-	-	-
Tausif Ahmed	70	25	14	116	27*	10.55	-	-	10	-	3250	2247	55	40.85	59.09	4.15	1	-	4-38
Waqar Younis	172	85	31	537	37	9.94	-	-	19	-	8561	6545	283	23.13	30.25	4.59	11	9	6-26
Wasim Akram	254	200	36	2508	86	15.29	-	5	62	-	13112	8387	363	23.10	36.12	3.84	15	5	5-15
Wasim Bari	51	26	13	221	34	17.00	-	-	52	10	-	-	-	-	-	-	-	-	-
Wasim Haider	3	2	0	26	13	13.00	-	-	-	-	114	79	1	79.00	114.00	4.16	-	-	1-36
Wasim Raja	54	45	10	782	60	22.34	-	2	24	-	1036	687	21	32.71	49.33	3.98	1	-	4-25
Younis Ahmed	2	2	0	84	58	42.00	-	1	1	-	-	-	-	-	-	-	-	-	-
Yousuf Youhana	13	11	2	479	100	53.22	1	4	3	-	-	-	-	-	-	-	-	-	-
Zafar Iqbal	8	6	0	48	18	8.00	-	-	1	-	198	137	3	45.67	66.00	4.15	-	-	2-37
Zaheer Abbas	62	60	6	2572	123	47.63	7	13	16	-	280	223	7	31.86	40.00	4.78	-	-	2-26
Zahid Ahmed	2	2	1	3	3*	3.00	-	-	-	-	96	61	3	20.33	32.00	3.81	-	-	2-24
Zahid Fazal	19	18	3	348	98*	23.20	-	2	2	-	-	-	-	-	-	-	-	-	-
Zahoor Elahi	14	14	1	297	86	22.85	-	3	2	-	-	-	-	-	-	-	-	-	-
Zakir Khan	17	5	4	27	11*	27.00	-	-	-	-	646	494	16	30.88	40.38	4.59	1	-	4-19
Zulqarnain	16	6	3	18	11*	6.00	-	-	18	5	-	-	-	-	-	-	-	-	-

SOUTH AFRICA (55 PLAYERS)

Batting and Fielding

Player	M	Inns	NO	Runs	HS	Ave.	100s	50s	Ct	St	Bowling Balls	Runs	Wkts	Ave.	Stk Rt	Ec Rt	4wi	5wi	Best
Adams, P.R.	11	6	3	25	15*	8.33	-	-	3	-	498	377	14	26.93	35.57	4.54	-	-	3-26
Bacher, A.M.	8	8	0	168	45	21.00	-	1	3	-	-	-	-	-	-	-	-	-	-
Beckenstein, D.M.	7	7	3	188	69	47.00	-	1	1	-	-	-	-	-	-	-	-	-	-
Boje, N.	13	7	2	62	28	12.40	-	-	5	-	640	461	16	28.81	40.00	4.32	-	-	3-33
Bosch, T.	2	-	-	-	-	-	-	-	-	2	51	66	0	-	-	7.76	-	-	-
Boucher, M.V.	23	17	4	179	51	13.77	-	1	30	2	-	-	-	-	-	-	-	-	-
Bryson, R.E.	7	4	3	32	17*	32.00	-	-	1	-	378	323	7	46.14	54.00	5.13	-	-	2-34
Callaghan, D.J.	27	24	6	478	169*	26.56	1	-	6	-	444	365	10	36.50	44.40	4.93	-	-	3-32
Cook, S.J.	4	4	0	67	35	16.75	-	-	1	-	-	-	-	-	-	-	-	-	-
Cronje, W.J.	152	142	24	4695	112	39.79	2	33	60	-	4646	3347	98	34.15	47.41	4.32	1	-	5-32
Crookes, D.N.	24	17	4	243	54	18.69	-	1	16	-	863	688	15	45.87	57.53	4.78	-	1	3-30
Cullinan, D.J.	107	104	12	3197	124	34.75	3	20	45	-	168	120	5	24.00	33.60	4.29	-	-	2-31
Dawson, A.C.	1	-	-	-	-	-	-	-	-	-	54	51	1	51.00	54.00	5.67	-	-	1-51
de Villiers, P.S.	83	36	15	170	20*	8.10	-	-	15	-	4422	2636	95	27.75	46.55	3.58	2	-	4-27
Donald, A.A.	108	26	11	73	12	4.87	-	-	14	-	5754	3898	182	21.42	31.62	4.06	7	2	6-23
Eksteen, C.E.	6	2	1	6	6*	6.00	-	-	3	-	222	181	2	90.50	111.00	4.89	-	-	1-26
Elworthy, S.	11	2	1	14	14*	14.00	-	-	4	-	460	397	16	24.81	28.75	5.18	-	-	3-21
Gibbs, H.H.	22	22	0	485	125	22.05	1	-	11	-	-	-	-	-	-	-	-	-	-
Hall, A.J.	1	1	1	9	9*	-	-	-	1	-	42	38	0	-	-	5.43	-	-	-
Hayward, M.	1	-	-	-	-	-	-	-	-	-	24	35	0	-	-	8.75	-	-	-
Henry, O.	3	3	1	20	11	10.00	-	-	1	-	149	125	2	62.50	74.50	5.03	-	-	1-31
Hudson, A.C.	89	88	1	2559	161	29.41	2	18	17	-	6	3	0	-	-	3.00	-	-	-
Jack, S.D.	2	2	0	7	6	3.50	-	-	3	-	108	86	3	28.67	36.00	4.78	-	-	2-41
Kallis, J.H.	58	57	10	1804	113*	38.38	3	10	23	-	1405	1125	37	30.41	37.97	4.80	-	1	5-30
Kirsten, G.	96	96	9	3600	188*	41.38	8	20	32	-	30	23	0	-	-	4.60	-	-	-
Kirsten, P.N.	40	40	6	1293	97	38.03	-	9	11	-	183	152	6	25.33	30.50	4.98	-	-	3-31
Klusener, L.	43	35	6	1002	99	34.55	-	7	10	-	2079	1699	63	26.97	33.00	4.90	-	4	6-49
Koen, L.J.	2	2	0	22	22	11.00	-	-	-	-	-	-	-	-	-	-	-	-	-
Kuiper, A.P.	25	23	7	539	63*	33.69	-	3	3	-	588	518	18	28.78	32.67	5.29	-	-	3-33
Liebenberg, G.F.J.	4	4	0	94	39	23.50	-	-	9	-	-	-	-	-	-	-	-	-	-
Matthews, C.R.	56	22	9	141	26	10.85	-	-	9	-	3003	1975	79	25.00	38.01	3.95	3	-	4-10
McMillan, B.M.	78	52	16	840	127	23.33	1	-	42	-	3623	2589	70	36.99	51.76	4.29	1	-	4-32
Mpitsang, P.V.	1	1	1	1	1*	-	-	-	-	-	42	49	2	24.50	21.00	7.00	-	-	2-49
Ntini, M.	1	-	-	-	-	-	-	-	1	-	60	31	2	15.50	30.00	3.10	-	-	2-31
Palframan, S.J.	7	4	0	55	28	13.75	-	-	9	-	-	-	-	-	-	-	-	-	-

Batting and Fielding / Bowling

Player	M	Inns	NO	Runs	HS	Ave.	100s	50s	Ct	St	Balls	Runs	Wkts	Ave.	Stk Rt	Ec Rt	4wi	5wi	Best
Pollock, S.M.	63	48	17	960	75	30.97	-	4	14	-	3370	2184	92	23.74	36.63	3.89	3	1	6-35
Pringle, M.W.	17	8	3	48	13*	9.60	-	-	2	-	870	604	22	27.45	39.55	4.17	1	-	4-11
Rhodes, J.N.	146	135	28	3532	121	33.01	1	16	70	-	-	-	-	-	-	-	-	-	-
Rice, C.E.B.	3	2	0	26	14	13.00	-	-	-	-	138	114	2	57.00	69.00	4.96	-	-	1-46
Richardson, D.J.	122	77	33	868	53	19.73	-	1	148	17	-	-	-	-	-	-	-	-	-
Rindel, M.J.R.	22	22	1	575	106	27.38	1	2	8	-	270	242	6	40.33	45.00	5.38	-	-	2-15
Rundle, D.B.	2	2	0	6	6	3.00	-	-	3	-	96	95	5	19.00	19.20	5.94	1	-	4-42
Rushmere, M.W.	4	4	0	78	35	19.50	-	-	1	-	-	-	-	-	-	-	-	-	-
Schultz, B.N.	1	-	-	-	-	-	-	-	-	-	54	35	1	35.00	54.00	3.89	-	-	1-35
Shaw, T.G.	9	6	4	26	17*	13.00	-	-	2	-	504	298	9	33.11	56.00	3.55	-	-	2-19
Simons, E.O.	23	18	4	217	24	15.50	-	-	6	-	1212	810	33	24.55	36.73	4.01	1	-	4-42
Snell, R.P.	42	28	8	322	63	16.10	-	2	7	-	2095	1574	44	35.77	47.61	4.51	2	1	5-40
Stewart, E.L.R.	5	5	1	57	23*	14.25	-	-	3	-	-	-	-	-	-	-	-	-	-
Steyn, P.J.R.	1	1	0	4	4	4.00	-	-	-	-	-	-	-	-	-	-	-	-	-
Symcox, P.L.	77	53	13	694	61	17.35	-	3	22	-	3840	2622	72	36.42	53.33	4.10	1	-	4-28
Telemachus, R.	5	2	1	1	1*	-	-	-	-	-	262	174	12	14.50	21.83	3.98	1	-	4-43
van Zyl, C.J.P.G.	2	2	1	3	3*	3.00	-	-	-	-	108	93	0	-	-	5.17	-	-	-
Wessels, K.C.	55	54	4	1627	90	32.54	-	12	30	-	12	11	0	-	-	5.50	-	-	-
Williams, H.S.	1	1	1	1*	1*	-	-	-	-	-	48	55	0	-	-	6.88	-	-	-
Yachad, M.	1	1	0	31	31	31.00	-	-	1	-	-	-	-	-	-	-	-	-	-

SRI LANKA (98 PLAYERS)

Batting and Fielding / Bowling

Player	M	Inns	NO	Runs	HS	Ave.	100s	50s	Ct	St	Balls	Runs	Wkts	Ave.	Stk Rt	Ec Rt	4wi	5wi	Best
Ahangama, F.S.	1	1	1	-	-	-	-	-	-	-	18	23	0	-	-	7.67	-	-	-
Amalean, K.N.	8	3	1	15	9	7.50	-	-	-	-	318	207	9	23.00	35.33	3.91	1	-	4-46
Anurasiri, S.D.	45	18	12	62	11	10.33	-	-	10	-	2100	1464	32	45.75	65.63	4.18	-	-	3-40
Arnold, R.P.	3	2	0	14	11	7.00	-	-	2	-	24	24	0	-	-	6.00	-	-	-
Atapattu, M.S.	66	65	8	1972	132*	34.60	2	14	26	-	57	45	0	-	-	4.74	-	-	-
Bandaratilake, M.L.C.N.	3	1	0	0	0	0.00	-	-	-	-	144	112	2	56.00	72.00	4.67	-	-	2-35
Chandana, U.D.U.	47	36	7	466	50	16.07	-	1	23	-	1735	1405	44	31.93	39.43	4.86	2	-	4-31
Dassanayake, P.B.	16	10	2	85	20*	10.63	-	-	9	4	-	-	-	-	-	-	-	-	-
de Alwis, R.G.	31	27	8	401	59*	21.11	-	2	27	3	-	-	-	-	-	-	-	-	-
de Mel, A.L.F.	57	41	9	466	36	14.56	-	-	13	-	2735	2237	59	37.92	46.36	4.91	1	2	5-32
de Silva, A.M.	4	2	0	12	8	6.00	-	-	4	2	120	54	2	27.00	60.00	2.70	-	-	2-36
de Silva, D.L.S.	2	1	0	10	10	10.00	-	-	1	-	-	-	-	-	-	-	-	-	-
de Silva, D.S.	41	29	10	371	37*	19.53	-	-	5	-	2076	1557	32	48.66	64.88	4.50	-	-	3-29
de Silva, E.A.R.	28	20	6	138	19*	9.86	-	-	6	-	1374	967	17	56.88	80.82	4.22	-	-	3-38

Batting and Fielding Player	M	Inns	NO	Runs	HS	Ave.	100s	50s	Ct	St	Bowling Balls	Runs	Wkts	Ave.	Stk Rt	Ec Rt	4wi	5wi	Best
de Silva, G.N.	4	2	1	9	7	9.00	-	-	-	-	194	169	0	-	-	5.23	-	-	-
de Silva, G.R.A.	6	4	2	9	6*	4.50	-	-	2	-	305	262	9	29.11	33.89	5.15	-	-	3-41
de Silva, K.S.C.	33	15	9	35	13*	5.83	-	-	12	-	1466	1194	48	24.88	30.54	4.89	-	-	3-18
de Silva, P.A.	250	243	25	7863	145	36.07	11	53	76	-	3896	3192	81	39.41	48.10	4.92	1	-	4-45
de Silva, S.K.L.	11	6	3	161	57	53.67	-	2	9	6									
Dharmasena, H.D.P.K.	94	57	35	849	69*	26.53	-	4	26	-	4698	3499	92	38.03	51.07	4.47	1	-	4-37
Dias, R.L.	58	55	5	1573	121	31.46	2	11	16	-	56	70	3	23.33	18.67	7.50	-	-	3-25
Dunusinghe, C.I.	1	1	0	1	1	1.00	-	-	1	1									
Fernando, E.R.	3	3	0	47	22	15.67	-	-	-	-									
Fernando, E.R.N.S.	7	5	0	101	36	20.20	-	-	1	-									
Fernando, T.L.	1	1	0	8	8	8.00	-	-	-	-	18	16	1	16.00	18.00	5.33	-	-	1-16
Fernando, U.N.K.	2	2	2	22	20*	-	-	-	-	-									
Gamage, J.C.	4	2	2	8	7*	-	-	-	2	-	132	104	3	34.67	44.00	4.73	-	-	2-17
Goonasekara, Y.	3	3	0	69	35	23.00	-	-	-	-	36	35	1	35.00	36.00	5.83	-	-	1-24
Goonatillake, F.R.M.de	1	-	-	-	-	-	-	-	-	-	54	34	0	-	-	3.78	-	-	-
Goonatillake, H.M.	6	4	3	31	14*	31.00	-	-	-	4									
Gunawardene, A.	7	7	0	164	75	23.43	-	2	1	-									
Gunawardene, A.A.W.	1	1	0	2	2	2.00	-	-	-	-									
Gurusinha, A.P.	147	143	5	3902	117*	28.28	2	22	49	-	1585	1354	26	52.08	60.96	5.13	-	-	2-25
Hathurusinghe, U.C.	34	32	1	669	66	21.58	-	4	6	-	894	670	14	47.86	63.86	4.50	1	-	4-57
Heyn, P.D.	2	2	0	3	2	1.50	-	-	-	-									
Jayasekara, R.S.A.	2	1	0	17	17	17.00	-	-	-	-									
Jayasinghe, S.A.	2	1	0	1	1	1.00	-	-	1	-									
Jayasuriya, S.T.	178	170	7	4672	151*	28.66	7	29	59	-	6587	5350	152	35.20	43.34	4.87	4	2	6-29
Jayawardene, D.P.M.	16	16	2	319	120	22.79	1	1	7	-	204	187	1	187.00	204.00	5.50	-	-	1-24
Jeganathan, S.	5	4	1	25	20*	8.33	-	-	1	-	276	208	5	41.60	55.20	4.52	-	-	2-45
John, V.B.	45	19	10	84	15	9.33	-	-	5	-	2311	1655	34	48.68	67.97	4.30	-	-	3-28
Kalpage, R.S.	82	65	27	810	51	21.32	-	1	31	-	3756	2780	71	39.15	52.90	4.44	2	-	4-36
Kaluperuma, L.W.S.	4	3	3	33	14*	-	-	-	2	-	208	137	2	68.50	104.00	3.95	-	-	1-35
Kaluperuma, S.M.S.	2	2	0	11	7	5.50	-	-	-	-	6	3	0	-	-	3.00	-	-	-
Kaluwitharana, R.S.	112	108	6	1930	100*	18.92	1	12	76	47									
Karnain, S.H.U.	19	17	5	229	41*	19.08	-	1	7	-	635	505	16	31.56	39.69	4.77	-	1	5-26
Kuruppu, D.S.B.	54	52	1	1022	72	20.04	-	4	30	8									
Labrooy, G.F.	44	36	7	249	33	8.59	-	-	8	-	2308	1876	45	41.69	51.29	4.88	1	1	5-57
Liyanage, D.K.	15	10	2	142	43	17.75	-	-	6	-	606	487	9	54.11	67.33	4.82	-	-	3-49
Madugalle, R.S.	63	56	5	950	73	18.63	-	3	18	-	4	1	0	-	-	1.50	-	-	-
Madurasinghe, M.A.W.R	12	6	4	21	8*	10.50	-	-	3	-	480	358	5	71.60	96.00	4.48	-	-	1-11
Mahanama, R.S.	208	193	23	5027	119*	29.57	4	35	107	-	2	7	0	-	-	21.00	-	-	-

Batting and Fielding

Player	M	Inns	NO	Runs	HS	Ave.	100s	50s	Ct	St	Bowling Balls	Runs	Wkts	Ave.	Stk Rt	Ec Rt	4wi	5wi	Best
Mendis, L.R.D.	79	74	9	1527	80	23.49	-	7	14	-	-	-	-	-	-	-	-	-	-
Mendis, M.C.	1	1	1	3	3*	-	-	-	-	-	-	-	-	-	-	-	-	-	-
Munasinghe, M.	5	4	1	13	8	4.33	-	-	-	-	217	146	4	36.50	54.25	4.04	-	-	3-30
Muralitharan, M.	110	49	23	151	18	5.81	-	-	53	-	5973	4220	151	27.95	39.56	4.24	3	2	5-23
Nawaz, M.N.	1	1	0	5	5	5.00	-	-	-	-	253	180	5	36.00	50.60	4.27	-	-	3-31
Opatha, A.R.M.	5	3	0	29	18	9.67	-	-	3	-	28	20	0	-	-	4.29	-	-	-
Pasqual, S.P.	2	2	1	24	23*	24.00	-	-	-	-	12	15	0	-	-	7.50	-	-	-
Perera, K.G.	1	-	-	-	-	-	-	-	-	-	-	-	-	-	-	-	-	-	-
Perera, R.L.	2	2	0	3	3	1.50	-	-	-	-	120	126	3	42.00	40.00	6.30	-	-	3-55
Perera, S.A.	6	2	1	17	17	17.00	-	-	-	-	273	231	8	28.88	34.13	5.08	-	-	2-25
Pieris, H.S.M.	3	3	1	19	16	9.50	-	-	-	-	132	135	2	67.50	66.00	6.14	-	-	2-68
Pushpakumara, K.R.	29	8	5	36	14*	12.00	-	-	8	-	1328	1110	24	46.25	55.33	5.02	-	-	3-25
Ramanayake, C.P.H.	62	35	14	210	26	10.00	-	1	11	-	2864	2049	68	30.13	42.12	4.29	1	-	4-17
Ranasinghe, A.N.	9	8	1	153	51	21.86	-	1	-	-	324	281	2	140.50	162.00	5.20	-	-	1-21
Ranasinghe, S.K.	4	3	0	55	41	18.33	-	-	1	-	126	96	3	32.00	42.00	4.57	-	-	1-28
Ranatunga, A.	260	246	47	7248	131*	36.42	4	48	61	-	4710	3757	79	47.56	59.62	4.79	1	-	4-14
Ranatunga, D.	4	4	0	49	25	12.25	-	-	1	-	-	-	-	-	-	-	-	-	-
Ranatunga, N.	2	1	0	0	0	0.00	-	-	-	-	102	82	1	82.00	102.00	4.82	-	-	1-33
Ranatunga, S.	13	11	0	253	70	23.00	-	2	2	-	-	-	-	-	-	-	-	-	-
Ratnayake, N.L.K.	2	-	-	-	-	-	-	-	-	-	101	98	2	49.00	50.50	5.82	-	-	1-39
Ratnayake, R.J.	70	55	18	612	33*	16.54	-	-	11	-	3575	2712	76	35.68	47.04	4.55	1	1	5-32
Ratnayeke, J.R.	78	69	14	824	50	14.98	-	1	14	-	3573	2866	85	33.72	42.04	4.81	1	-	4-23
Samarasekara, M.A.R.	39	39	2	844	76	22.81	-	4	5	-	338	291	0	-	-	5.17	-	-	-
Samaraweera, D.P.	5	4	0	91	49	22.75	-	-	3	-	-	-	-	-	-	-	-	-	-
Samaraweera, T.T.	6	4	0	39	20	9.75	-	-	-	-	336	265	6	44.17	56.00	4.73	-	-	3-34
Senanayake, C.P.	7	7	0	126	27	18.00	-	-	2	-	-	-	-	-	-	-	-	-	-
Silva, K.J.	1	1	1	1	1*	-	-	-	-	-	48	55	0	-	-	6.88	-	-	-
Silva, S.A.R.	20	20	0	441	85	22.05	-	3	17	3	-	-	-	-	-	-	-	-	-
Tennekoon, A.P.B.	4	4	0	137	59	34.25	-	1	1	-	-	-	-	-	-	-	-	-	-
Tillakeratne, H.P.	176	149	36	3303	104	29.23	2	12	76	5	180	141	6	23.50	30.00	4.70	-	-	1-3
Tissera, M.H.	3	3	0	78	52	26.00	-	1	1	-	-	-	-	-	-	-	-	-	-
Upashantha, E.A.	3	2	1	11	8*	11.00	-	-	1	-	114	91	3	30.33	38.00	4.79	-	-	2-24
Vaas, W.P.U.C.J.	105	61	22	506	33	12.97	-	-	16	-	5050	3512	132	26.61	38.26	4.17	3	-	4-20
Vonhagt, D.M.	1	1	0	8	8	8.00	-	-	-	-	-	-	-	-	-	-	-	-	-
Warnapura, B.	12	12	0	180	77	15.00	-	1	5	-	414	316	8	39.50	51.75	4.58	-	-	3-42
Warnaweera, K.P.J.	6	3	3	1	1*	-	-	-	2	-	294	200	6	33.33	49.00	4.08	-	-	2-24
Weerakkody, A.P.	1	1	0	2	2	2.00	-	-	-	-	36	41	0	-	-	6.83	-	-	-
Weettimuny, M. de S.	1	1	0	2	2	2.00	-	-	-	-	-	-	-	-	-	-	-	-	-
Wettimuny, S.	35	33	1	786	86*	24.56	-	4	3	-	57	70	1	70.00	57.00	7.37	-	-	1-13

Batting and Fielding

Player	M	Inns	NO	Runs	HS	Ave.	100s	50s	Ct	St
Wettimuny, S.R. de S.	3	3	1	136	67	68.00	-	2	-	-
Wickremaratne, R.PA.H	3	2	0	4	3	2.00	-	-	-	-
Wickramasinghe, G.P.	107	46	16	234	21*	7.80	-	-	16	-
Wickremasinghe, A.G.D.	4	1	0	2	2	2.00	-	-	2	4
Wijegunawardene, K.I.W	26	12	5	20	8*	2.86	-	-	3	-
Wijesuriya, R.G.C.E.	8	3	2	18	12*	18.00	-	-	2	-
Zoysa, D.N.T.	9	4	2	9	4	4.50	-	-	-	-

Bowling

Player	Balls	Runs	Wkts	Ave.	Stk Rt	Ec Rt	4wi	5wi	Best
Wettimuny, S.R. de S.	-	-	-	-	-	-	-	-	-
Wickremaratne, R.PA.H	-	-	-	-	-	-	-	-	-
Wickramasinghe, G.P.	4537	3393	79	42.95	57.43	4.49	-	-	3-20
Wickremasinghe, A.G.D.	-	-	-	-	-	-	-	-	-
Wijegunawardene, K.I.W	1186	986	25	39.44	47.44	4.99	1	-	4-49
Wijesuriya, R.G.C.E.	312	287	8	35.88	39.00	5.52	-	-	2-25
Zoysa, D.N.T.	414	311	12	25.92	34.50	4.51	-	-	2-22

UNITED ARAB EMIRATES (16 PLAYERS)

Batting and Fielding

Player	M	Inns	NO	Runs	HS	Ave.	100s	50s	Ct	St
Arshad Laiq	6	6	1	101	43*	20.20	-	-	1	-
Azhar Saeed	7	7	0	61	32	8.71	-	-	2	-
Dukanwala, S.F.	5	4	2	84	40*	42.00	-	-	2	-
Imtiaz Abestasi	7	6	4	12	6*	6.00	-	-	4	2
Mazhar Hussein	7	7	0	179	70	25.57	-	1	1	-
Mehra, V.	6	6	1	92	43	18.40	-	-	1	-
Mohammad Aslam	4	4	0	38	23	9.50	-	-	1	-
Mohammad Ishaq	5	5	1	98	51*	24.50	-	1	1	-
Mylvaganam, G.	3	3	0	36	23	12.00	-	-	1	-
Poonawalla, R.	2	2	0	44	22	22.00	-	-	-	-
Saeed-al-Saffar	1	-	-	-	-	-	-	-	1	-
Salim Raza	6	6	0	159	84	26.50	-	1	-	-
Samarasekera, J.A	7	6	2	124	47*	31.00	-	-	1	-
Shahzad Altaf	2	-	-	-	-	-	-	-	-	-
Sohail Butt	2	2	1	8	6*	8.00	-	-	-	-
Sultan Zarawani	7	6	0	26	13	4.33	-	-	1	-

Bowling

Player	Balls	Runs	Wkts	Ave.	Stk Rt	Ec Rt	4wi	5wi	Best
Arshad Laiq	198	198	1	198.00	198.00	6.00	-	-	1-25
Azhar Saeed	271	213	6	35.50	45.17	4.72	-	-	3-45
Dukanwala, S.F.	198	153	6	25.50	33.00	4.64	-	1	5-29
Imtiaz Abestasi	-	-	-	-	-	-	-	-	-
Mazhar Hussein	48	60	0	-	-	7.50	-	-	-
Mehra, V.	-	-	-	-	-	-	-	-	-
Mohammad Aslam	-	-	-	-	-	-	-	-	-
Mohammad Ishaq	-	-	-	-	-	-	-	-	-
Mylvaganam, G.	-	-	-	-	-	-	-	-	-
Poonawalla, R.	-	-	-	-	-	-	-	-	-
Saeed-al-Saffar	18	25	0	-	-	8.33	-	-	-
Salim Raza	192	179	3	59.67	64.00	5.59	-	-	1-17
Samarasekera, J.A	294	235	4	58.75	73.50	4.80	-	-	1-17
Shahzad Altaf	78	37	1	37.00	78.00	2.85	-	-	1-15
Sohail Butt	78	79	2	39.50	39.00	6.08	-	-	2-52
Sultan Zarawani	264	257	5	51.40	52.80	5.84	-	-	2-49

WEST INDIES (91 PLAYERS)

Batting and Fielding

Player	M	Inns	NO	Runs	HS	Ave.	100s	50s	Ct	St
Adams, J.C.	74	57	20	1038	81*	28.05	-	7	48	5
Ambrose, C.E.L.	157	86	34	588	31*	11.31	-	-	42	-
Anthony, H.A.G.	3	3	0	23	21	7.67	-	-	-	-
Arthurton, K.L.T.	98	88	19	1871	84	27.12	-	9	27	-
Austin, R.A.	1	1	0	8	8	8.00	-	-	-	-

Bowling

Player	Balls	Runs	Wkts	Ave.	Stk Rt	Ec Rt	4wi	5wi	Best
Adams, J.C.	834	668	22	30.36	37.91	4.81	-	1	5-37
Ambrose, C.E.L.	8350	4939	210	23.52	39.76	3.55	6	4	5-17
Anthony, H.A.G.	156	143	3	47.67	52.00	5.50	-	-	2-47
Arthurton, K.L.T.	1186	990	40	24.75	29.65	5.01	3	-	4-31
Austin, R.A.	6	13	0	-	-	13.00	-	-	-

Batting and Fielding / **Bowling**

Player	M	Inns	NO	Runs	HS	Ave.	100s	50s	Ct	St	Balls	Runs	Wkts	Ave.	Stk Rt	Ec Rt	4wi	5wi	Best
Bacchus, S.F.A.F.	29	26	3	612	80*	26.61	-	3	10	-	-	-	-	-	-	-	-	-	-
Baptiste, E.A.E.	43	16	4	184	31	15.33	-	-	14	-	2214	1511	36	41.97	61.50	4.09	-	-	2-10
Benjamin, K.C.G.	26	13	7	65	17	10.83	-	-	4	-	1319	923	33	27.97	39.97	4.20	-	-	3-34
Benjamin, W.K.M.	85	52	12	298	31	7.45	-	-	16	-	4442	3079	100	30.79	44.42	4.16	-	1	5-22
Best, C.A.	24	23	4	473	100	24.89	1	2	5	-	19	12	0	-	-	3.79	-	-	-
Bishop, I.R.	84	44	19	405	33*	16.20	-	-	12	-	4332	3127	118	26.50	36.71	4.33	7	2	5-25
Boyce, K.D.	8	4	0	57	34	14.25	-	-	-	-	470	313	13	24.08	36.15	4.00	1	-	4-50
Browne, B.St A.	4	3	2	8	8*	8.00	-	-	-	-	180	156	2	78.00	90.00	5.20	-	-	2-50
Browne, C.O.	24	18	4	172	26	12.29	-	-	30	5	-	-	-	-	-	-	-	-	-
Campbell, S.L.	38	38	0	841	86	22.13	-	3	10	-	538	469	12	39.08	44.83	5.23	-	-	3-18
Chanderpaul, S.	61	57	3	1909	150	35.35	2	12	19	-	524	245	13	18.85	40.31	2.81	-	-	3-22
Clarke, S.T.	10	8	2	60	20	10.00	-	-	4	-	547	352	9	39.11	60.78	3.86	-	-	2-19
Croft, C.E.H.	19	6	4	18	8	9.00	-	-	1	-	1070	620	30	20.67	35.67	3.48	-	1	6-15
Cuffy, C.E.	11	7	3	25	17*	6.25	-	-	3	-	-	-	-	-	-	-	-	-	-
Cummins, A.C.	63	41	11	459	44*	15.30	-	-	11	-	3143	2246	78	28.79	40.29	4.29	2	1	5-31
Daniel, W.	18	5	4	49	16*	49.00	-	-	5	-	912	595	23	25.87	39.65	3.91	-	-	3-27
Davis, W.W.	35	5	3	28	10	14.00	-	-	1	-	1923	1302	39	33.38	49.31	4.06	1	1	7-51
Dhanraj, R.	6	2	1	8	8	8.00	-	-	1	-	264	170	10	17.00	26.40	3.86	1	-	4-26
Dillon, M.	11	2	1	5	5*	5.00	-	-	1	-	545	464	12	38.67	45.42	5.11	-	-	3-32
Drakes, V.	5	2	0	25	16	12.50	-	-	1	-	239	204	3	68.00	79.67	5.12	-	-	1-36
Dujon, P.J.L.	169	120	36	1945	82*	23.15	-	6	183	21	-	-	-	-	-	-	-	-	-
Foster, M.L.C.	2	1	0	25	25	25.00	-	1	1	-	30	22	2	11.00	15.00	4.40	-	-	2-22
Fredericks, R.C.	12	12	0	311	105	25.92	1	1	4	-	10	10	2	5.00	5.00	6.00	-	-	2-10
Gabriel, R.S.	11	11	0	167	41	15.18	-	-	1	-	-	-	-	-	-	-	-	-	-
Ganga, D.	2	2	0	1	1	0.50	-	-	1	-	-	-	-	-	-	-	-	-	-
Garner, J.	98	41	15	239	37	9.19	-	-	30	-	5330	2752	146	18.85	36.51	3.10	2	3	5-31
Gibbs, L.R.	3	1	1	0	0*	-	-	-	-	-	156	59	2	29.50	78.00	2.27	-	-	1-12
Gibson, O.D.	15	11	1	141	52	14.10	-	1	3	-	739	621	34	18.26	21.74	5.04	2	2	5-40
Gomes, H.A.	83	64	15	1415	101	28.88	1	6	14	-	1345	1045	41	25.49	32.80	4.66	2	-	4-31
Gray, A.H.	25	11	5	51	10*	8.50	-	-	3	-	1270	835	44	18.98	28.86	3.94	2	1	6-50
Greenidge, A.E.	1	1	0	23	23	23.00	-	-	-	-	-	-	-	-	-	-	-	-	-
Greenidge, C.G.	128	127	13	5134	133*	45.04	11	31	45	-	60	45	1	45.00	60.00	4.50	-	-	1-21
Griffith, A.F.G.	5	4	1	50	47	16.67	-	-	4	-	-	-	-	-	-	-	-	-	-
Harper, R.A.	105	73	20	855	45*	16.15	-	-	55	-	5175	3431	100	34.31	51.75	3.98	3	-	4-40
Haynes, D.L.	238	237	28	8648	152*	41.38	17	57	59	-	30	24	0	-	-	4.80	-	-	-
Haynes, R.C.	8	6	1	26	18	5.20	-	-	5	-	270	224	5	44.80	54.00	4.98	-	-	2-36
Headley, R.G.A.	1	1	0	19	19	19.00	-	-	-	-	-	-	-	-	-	-	-	-	-
Holder, R.I.C.	37	31	6	599	65	23.96	-	2	8	-	-	-	-	-	-	-	-	-	-

Batting and Fielding | | | | | | | | | | | **Bowling** | | | | | | | |

Player	M	Inns	NO	Runs	HS	Ave.	100s	50s	Ct	St	Balls	Runs	Wkts	Ave.	Stk Rt	Ec Rt	4wi	5wi	Best
Holder, V.A.	12	6	1	64	30	12.80	-	-	6	-	681	454	19	23.89	35.84	4.00	-	1	5-50
Holding, M.A.	102	42	11	282	64	9.10	-	2	30	-	5473	3034	142	21.37	38.54	3.33	5	1	5-26
Hooper, C.L.	177	161	36	4500	113*	36.00	6	25	85	-	7339	5320	160	33.25	45.87	4.35	3	-	4-34
Jacobs, R.D.	18	14	3	103	28*	9.36	-	-	18	6	-	-	-	-	-	-	-	-	-
Julien, B.D.	12	8	2	86	26*	14.33	-	-	4	-	778	463	18	25.72	43.22	3.57	2	-	4-20
Kallicharran, A.I.	31	28	4	826	78	34.42	-	6	8	-	105	64	3	21.33	35.00	3.66	-	-	2-10
Kanhai, R.B.	7	5	2	164	55	54.67	-	2	4	-	-	-	-	-	-	-	-	-	-
King, C.L.	18	14	2	280	86	23.33	-	1	6	-	744	529	11	48.09	67.64	4.27	1	-	4-23
King, R.D.	9	7	6	26	7	26.00	-	-	2	-	492	320	9	35.56	54.67	3.90	-	-	3-40
Lambert, C.B.	11	11	0	368	119	33.45	1	2	-	-	12	8	0	-	-	4.00	-	-	-
Lara, B.C.	137	135	13	5580	169	45.74	12	37	63	-	30	34	2	17.00	15.00	6.80	-	-	2-5
Lewis, R.N.	16	12	3	157	49	17.44	-	-	5	-	715	614	12	51.17	59.58	5.15	-	-	2-40
Lloyd, C.H.	87	69	19	1977	102	39.54	1	11	39	-	358	210	8	26.25	44.75	3.52	-	-	2-4
Logie, A.L.	158	133	36	2809	109*	28.96	1	14	61	-	24	18	0	-	-	4.50	-	-	-
Marshall, M.D.	136	83	19	955	66	14.92	-	2	15	-	7175	4233	157	26.96	45.70	3.54	6	-	4-18
Mattis, E.H.	2	2	0	86	62	43.00	-	1	2	-	-	-	-	-	-	-	-	-	-
McGarrell, N.C.	5	3	1	25	19	12.50	-	-	4	-	204	211	3	70.33	68.00	6.21	-	-	2-43
McLean, N.A.M.	16	11	0	69	23	6.27	-	-	4	-	707	590	16	36.88	44.19	5.01	-	-	3-41
Moseley, E.A.	9	6	2	7	2*	1.75	-	-	-	-	330	278	7	39.71	47.14	5.05	-	-	2-52
Murray, D.A.	10	7	2	45	35	9.00	-	-	16	-	-	-	-	-	-	-	-	-	-
Murray, D.L.	26	17	5	294	61*	24.50	-	2	37	1	-	-	-	-	-	-	-	-	-
Murray, J.R.	55	36	6	678	86	22.60	-	5	46	7	-	-	-	-	-	-	-	-	-
Parry, D.R.	6	5	1	61	32	15.25	-	-	8	-	330	259	11	23.55	30.00	4.71	-	-	3-47
Patterson, B.P.	59	20	15	44	13*	8.80	-	-	9	-	3050	2206	90	24.51	33.89	4.34	1	1	6-29
Payne, T.R.O.	7	4	0	126	60	31.50	-	1	6	-	-	-	-	-	-	-	-	-	-
Phillip, N.	1	1	0	0	0	0.00	-	-	-	-	42	22	1	22.00	42.00	3.14	-	-	1-22
Pydanna, M.R.	3	1	1	2	2*	-	-	-	2	1	-	-	-	-	-	-	-	-	-
Ramnarine, D.R.	1	1	1	2	2*	-	-	-	-	-	60	54	2	27.00	30.00	5.40	-	-	2-52
Reifer, F.L.	2	2	0	31	22	15.50	-	-	1	-	-	-	-	-	-	-	-	-	-
Richards, I.V.A.	187	167	24	6721	189*	47.00	11	45	101	-	5644	4228	118	35.83	47.83	4.49	1	2	6-41
Richardson, R.B.	224	217	30	6248	122	33.41	5	44	74	-	58	46	1	46.00	58.00	4.76	-	-	1-4
Roberts, A.M.E.	56	32	9	231	37*	10.04	-	-	6	-	3123	1771	87	20.36	35.90	3.40	2	1	5-22
Rose, F.A.	13	11	2	83	24	9.22	-	-	1	-	606	517	10	51.70	60.60	5.12	-	-	3-25
Rowe, L.G.	11	8	0	136	60	17.00	-	1	2	-	-	-	-	-	-	-	-	-	-
Samuels, R.G.	8	5	2	54	36*	18.00	-	-	3	-	-	-	-	-	-	-	-	-	-
Semple, K.F.	7	6	0	64	23	10.67	-	-	3	-	-	-	-	-	-	-	-	-	-
Shillingford, I.T.	2	2	0	30	24	15.00	-	-	2	-	132	121	3	40.33	44.00	5.50	-	-	2-35
Shivnarine, S.	1	1	1	20	20*	-	-	-	-	-	18	16	0	-	-	5.33	-	-	-

Batting and Fielding

Player	M	Inns	NO	Runs	HS	Ave.	100s	50s	Ct	St
Simmons, P.V.	133	130	10	3532	122	29.43	5	18	53	—
Small M.A.	2	1	0	0	0	0.00	—	—	1	—
Sobers, G.St A.	1	1	0	2	2	2.00	—	—	1	—
Thompson, P.I.T.	2	1	—	—	—	—	—	—	—	—
Tuckett, C.M.	1	—	—	—	—	—	—	—	—	—
Wallace, P.A.	26	26	0	554	103	21.31	1	2	8	—
Walsh, C.A.	185	68	29	289	30	7.41	—	—	27	—
Williams, D.	36	23	7	147	32*	9.19	—	—	35	10
Williams, L.R.	6	4	0	21	14	5.25	—	—	5	—
Williams, S.C.	46	46	4	1502	105*	35.76	1	12	11	—

Bowling

Player	Balls	Runs	Wkts	Ave.	Stk Rt	Ec Rt	4wi	5wi	Best
Simmons, P.V.	3505	2606	74	35.22	47.36	4.46	2	—	4-3
Small M.A.	84	54	1	54.00	84.00	3.86	—	—	1-40
Sobers, G.St A.	63	31	1	31.00	63.00	2.95	—	—	1-31
Thompson, P.I.T.	114	110	2	55.00	57.00	5.79	—	—	1-46
Tuckett, C.M.	48	41	2	20.50	24.00	5.13	—	—	2-41
Wallace, P.A.	—	—	—	—	—	—	—	—	—
Walsh, C.A.	9772	6312	204	30.94	47.90	3.88	5	1	5-1
Williams, D.	—	—	—	—	—	—	—	—	—
Williams, L.R.	203	173	8	21.63	25.38	5.11	—	—	3-16
Williams, S.C.	24	30	1	30.00	24.00	7.50	—	—	1-30

ZIMBABWE (55 PLAYERS)

Batting and Fielding

Player	M	Inns	NO	Runs	HS	Ave.	100s	50s	Ct	St
Arnott, K.J.	13	12	2	238	60	23.80	—	3	3	—
Brain, D.H.	23	18	4	117	27	8.36	—	—	5	—
Brandes, E.A.	54	38	9	330	55	11.38	—	1	10	—
Brent, G.B.	3	3	0	25	24	8.33	—	—	—	—
Briant, G.A.	5	5	2	39	16	13.00	—	—	—	—
Brown, R.D.	7	7	0	110	38	15.71	—	—	5	—
Bruk-Jackson, G.D.	1	1	0	12	12	12.00	—	—	—	—
Burmester, M.G.	8	7	1	109	39	18.17	—	—	2	—
Butchart, I.P.	20	16	2	252	54	18.00	—	1	4	—
Campbell, A.D.R.	92	89	9	2294	131*	28.68	3	13	35	—
Carlisle, S.V.	8	8	1	79	28	11.29	—	—	4	—
Crocker, G.J.	6	5	1	98	50	24.50	—	1	1	—
Curran, K.M.	11	11	0	287	73	26.09	—	2	1	—
Davies, S.G.	4	4	0	67	45	16.75	—	—	1	—
Dekker, M.H.	23	22	2	379	79	18.95	—	2	5	—
Duers, K.G.	6	2	1	7	5	7.00	—	—	2	—
Essop-Adam, E.A.	1	1	1	14	14*	—	—	—	2	—
Evans, C.N.	47	41	5	665	96*	18.47	—	1	11	—
Fletcher, D.A.G.	6	6	2	191	71*	47.75	—	2	—	—
Flower, A.	100	98	6	2940	115*	31.96	1	24	73	21
Flower, G.W.	87	85	4	2867	112	35.40	2	22	35	—
Goodwin, M.W.	26	26	0	722	111	27.77	1	4	7	—
Heron, J.G.	6	6	0	50	18	8.33	—	—	1	—

Bowling

Player	Balls	Runs	Wkts	Ave.	Stk Rt	Ec Rt	4wi	5wi	Best
Arnott, K.J.	1091	849	21	40.43	51.95	4.67	—	—	3-51
Brain, D.H.	2618	2089	67	31.18	39.07	4.79	1	2	5-28
Brandes, E.A.	116	108	1	108.00	116.00	5.59	—	—	—
Brent, G.B.	—	—	—	—	—	—	—	—	—
Briant, G.A.	—	—	—	—	—	—	—	—	—
Brown, R.D.	—	—	—	—	—	—	—	—	—
Bruk-Jackson, G.D.	—	—	—	—	—	—	—	—	—
Burmester, M.G.	209	213	5	42.60	41.80	6.11	—	—	3-36
Butchart, I.P.	702	640	12	53.33	58.50	5.47	—	—	3-57
Campbell, A.D.R.	225	179	4	44.75	56.25	4.77	—	—	2-22
Carlisle, S.V.	—	—	—	—	—	—	—	—	—
Crocker, G.J.	238	208	7	29.71	34.00	5.24	1	—	4-26
Curran, K.M.	506	398	9	44.22	56.22	4.72	—	—	3-65
Davies, S.G.	—	—	—	—	—	—	—	—	—
Dekker, M.H.	347	290	9	32.22	38.56	5.01	—	—	2-16
Duers, K.G.	300	256	3	85.33	100.00	5.12	—	—	1-17
Essop-Adam, E.A.	—	—	—	—	—	—	—	—	—
Evans, C.N.	862	717	18	39.83	47.89	4.99	—	—	3-11
Fletcher, D.A.G.	301	221	7	31.57	43.00	4.41	1	—	4-42
Flower, A.	30	23	0	—	—	4.60	—	—	—
Flower, G.W.	1460	1221	34	35.91	42.94	5.02	—	—	3-15
Goodwin, M.W.	206	173	3	57.67	68.67	5.04	—	—	1-12
Heron, J.G.	—	—	—	—	—	—	—	—	—

Batting and Fielding											Bowling								
Player	M	Inns	NO	Runs	HS	Ave.	100s	50s	Ct	St	Balls	Runs	Wkts	Ave.	Stk Rt	Ec Rt	4wi	5wi	Best
Hogg, V.R.	2	1	1	7	7*	-	-	-	-	-	90	49	0	-	-	3.27	-	-	-
Houghton, D.L.	63	60	2	1530	142	26.38	1	12	29	2	12	19	1	19.00	12.00	9.50	-	-	1-19
Huckle, A.G.	13	6	4	9	5*	4.50	-	-	3	-	594	476	3	158.67	198.00	4.81	-	-	2-27
James, W.R.	11	8	1	101	29	14.43	-	-	6	-	-	-	-	-	-	-	-	-	-
Jarvis, M.P.	12	5	3	37	17	18.50	-	-	1	-	601	451	9	50.11	66.78	4.50	-	-	2-37
Johnson, N.C.	9	9	0	351	103	39.00	1	2	5	-	417	372	5	74.40	83.40	5.35	-	-	2-37
Lock, A.C.I.	8	3	2	8	5	8.00	-	-	1	-	289	219	8	27.38	36.13	4.55	-	1	5-44
Madondo, T.N.	2	2	0	10	10	5.00	-	-	-	-	-	-	-	-	-	-	-	-	-
Martin, G.C.	5	4	0	31	16	7.75	-	-	1	-	132	95	2	47.50	66.00	4.32	-	-	1-15
Matambanadzo, E.	7	5	3	8	5*	4.00	-	-	-	-	297	217	11	19.73	27.00	4.38	1	-	4-32
Mbangwa, M.	13	7	2	24	11	4.80	-	-	2	-	655	545	7	77.86	93.57	4.99	-	-	2-24
Meman, M.A.	1	1	0	19	19	19.00	-	-	-	-	41	34	0	-	-	4.98	-	-	-
Nkala, M.	1	-	-	-	-	-	-	-	-	-	30	32	1	32.00	30.00	6.40	-	-	1-32
Olonga, H.K.	6	2	1	8	6	8.00	-	-	-	-	252	287	7	41.00	36.00	6.83	1	-	4-46
Paterson, G.A.	10	10	0	123	27	12.30	-	-	2	-	-	-	-	-	-	-	-	-	-
Peall, S.G.	21	15	1	91	21	6.50	-	-	1	-	900	678	8	84.75	112.50	4.52	-	-	3-54
Peckover, G.E.	3	3	1	33	16*	16.50	-	-	-	-	-	-	-	-	-	-	-	-	-
Pycroft, A.J.	20	19	2	295	61	17.35	-	2	6	-	-	-	-	-	-	-	-	-	-
Ranchod, U.	3	1	1	3	3*	-	-	-	1	-	174	130	1	130.00	174.00	4.48	-	-	1-44
Rawson, P.W.E.	10	8	3	80	24*	16.00	-	-	4	-	571	427	12	35.58	47.58	4.49	-	-	3-47
Rennie, G.J.	16	16	3	332	76	25.54	-	2	9	-	-	-	-	-	-	-	-	-	-
Rennie, J.A.	33	19	10	139	27	15.44	-	-	11	-	1425	1210	25	48.40	57.00	5.09	-	-	3-27
Shah, A.H.	28	28	2	437	60*	16.81	-	1	6	-	1077	812	18	45.11	59.83	4.52	1	-	3-33
Strang, B.C.	18	11	4	38	15	5.43	-	-	9	-	806	576	23	25.04	35.04	4.29	1	1	6-20
Strang, P.A.	69	58	20	955	47	25.13	-	-	21	-	3258	2287	72	31.76	45.25	4.21	2	1	5-21
Streak, H.H.	69	58	20	755	59	19.87	-	1	14	-	3520	2623	85	30.86	41.41	4.47	3	1	5-32
Traicos, A.J.	27	17	9	88	19	11.00	-	-	3	-	1524	987	19	51.95	80.21	3.89	-	-	3-35
Viljoen, D.P.	9	8	0	125	36	15.63	-	-	1	-	192	134	4	33.50	48.00	4.19	-	-	2-31
Waller, A.C.	39	38	3	818	83*	23.37	-	4	10	-	-	-	-	-	-	-	-	-	-
Whittall, A.R.	40	23	10	134	31	10.31	-	-	12	-	2024	1430	32	44.69	63.25	4.24	-	-	3-23
Whittall, G.J.	68	68	8	1360	83	22.67	-	8	18	-	2157	1859	49	37.94	44.02	5.17	-	-	3-43
Wishart, C.B.	39	34	2	644	102	20.13	1	1	13	-	12	12	0	-	-	6.00	-	-	-

World Cup

First held in 1975, cricket's World Cup takes place every four years between the Test-playing nations, usually joined by one or more ICC associate member countries. Matches in the first three World Cups held in England were played in a 60-overs per side format, then reduced to 50 overs per side in 1987, 1991/92 and 1995/96. Future World Cups will be hosted by England (1999), South Africa (2003) and the West Indies (2007).

THE MATCHES

1975 WORLD CUP IN ENGLAND

Match	Batted 1st	Batted 2nd	Result	Venue	Date
England v India	Eng 4-334	Ind 3-132	Eng by 202 runs	Lord's	7 June
New Zealand v East Africa	NZ 5-309	EAF 8-128	NZ by 181 runs	Birmingham	7 June
Australia v Pakistan	Aus 7-278	Pak 205	Aus by 73 runs	Leeds	7 June
West Indies v Sri Lanka	SL 86	WI 1-87	WI by 9 wkts	Manchester	7 June
England v New Zealand	Eng 6-266	NZ 186	Eng by 80 runs	Nottingham	11 June
India v East Africa	EAF 120	Ind 0-123	Ind by 10 wkts	Leeds	11 June
Australia v Sri Lanka	Aus 5-328	SL 4-276	Aus by 52 runs	The Oval	11 June
West Indies v Pakistan	Pak 7-266	WI 9-267	WI by 1 wkt	Birmingham	11 June
England v East Africa	Eng 5-290	EAF 94	Eng by 196 runs	Birmingham	14 June
New Zealand v India	Ind 230	NZ 6-233	NZ by 4 wkts	Manchester	14 June
Australia v West Indies	Aus 192	WI 3-195	WI by 7 wkts	The Oval	14 June
Pakistan v Sri Lanka	Pak 6-330	SL 138	Pak by 192 runs	Nottingham	14 June

Group A

Team	Played	Won	Lost	Pts
England	3	3	-	12
New Zealand	3	2	1	8
India	3	1	2	4
East Africa	3	-	3	-

Group B

Team	Played	Won	Lost	Pts
West Indies	3	3	-	12
Australia	3	2	1	8
Pakistan	3	1	2	4
Sri Lanka	3	-	3	-

Semi-finals

Match	Batted 1st	Batted 2nd	Result	Venue	Date
England v Australia	Eng 93	Aus 6-94	Aus by 4 wkts	Leeds	18 June
West Indies v New Zealand	NZ 158	WI 5-159	WI by 5 wkts	The Oval	18 June

Final

Match	Batted 1st	Batted 2nd	Result	Venue	Date
West Indies v Australia	WI 8-291	Aus 274	WI by 17 runs	Lord's	21 June

1979 WORLD CUP IN ENGLAND

Match	Batted 1st	Batted 2nd	Result	Venue	Date
West Indies v India	Ind 190	WI 1-194	WI by 9 wkts	Birmingham	9 June
New Zealand v Sri Lanka	SL 189	NZ 1-190	NZ by 9 wkts	Nottingham	9 June
England v Australia	Aus 9-159	Eng 4-160	Eng by 6 wkts	Lord's	9 June

Pakistan v Canada	Can 9-139	Pak 2-140	Pak by 8 wkts	Leeds	9 June
West Indies v Sri Lanka	*no result*			The Oval	13/14/15 June
New Zealand v India	Ind 182	NZ 2-183	NZ by 8 wkts	Leeds	13 June
Australia v Pakistan	Pak 7-286	Aus 197	Pak by 89 runs	Nottingham	13/14 June
England v Canada	Can 45	Eng 2-46	Eng by 8 wkts	Manchester	14 June
India v Sri Lanka	SL 5-238	Ind 191	SL by 47 runs	Manchester	16/18 June
West Indies v New Zealand	WI 7-244	NZ 9-212	WI by 32 runs	Nottingham	16 June
Australia v Canada	Can 105	Aus 3-106	Aus by 7 wkts	Birmingham	16 June
England v Pakistan	Eng 9-165	Pak 151	Eng by 14 runs	Leeds	16 June

Group A

Team	Played	Won	Lost	Pts
England	3	3	-	12
Pakistan	3	2	1	8
Australia	3	1	2	4
Canada	3	-	3	-

Group B

Team	Played	Won	Lost	NR	Pts
West Indies	3	2	-	1	10
New Zealand	3	2	1	-	8
Sri Lanka	3	1	1	1	6
India	3	-	3	-	-

Semi-finals

Match	Batted 1st	Batted 2nd	Result	Venue	Date
England v New Zealand	Eng 8-221	NZ 9-212	Eng by 9 runs	Manchester	20 June
West Indies v Pakistan	WI 6-293	Pak 250	WI by 43 runs	The Oval	20 June

Final

Match	Batted 1st	Batted 2nd	Result	Venue	Date
England v West Indies	WI 9-286	Eng 194	WI by 92 runs	Lord's	23 June

1983 WORLD CUP IN ENGLAND

Match	Batted 1st	Batted 2nd	Result	Venue	Date
England v New Zealand	Eng 6-322	NZ 216	Eng by 106 runs	The Oval	9 June
Pakistan v Sri Lanka	Pak 5-338	SL 9-288	Pak by 50 runs	Swansea	9 June
Australia v Zimbabwe	Zim 6-239	Aus 7-226	Zim by 13 runs	Nottingham	9 June
West Indies v India	Ind 8-262	WI 228	Ind by 34 runs	Manchester	9/10 June
England v Sri Lanka	Eng 9-333	SL 286	Eng by 47 runs	Taunton	11 June
New Zealand v Pakistan	NZ 9-238	Pak 186	NZ by 52 runs	Birmingham	11/12 June
West Indies v Australia	WI 9-252	Aus 151	WI by 101 runs	Leeds	11/12 June
India v Zimbabwe	Zim 155	Ind 5-157	Ind by 5 wkts	Leicester	11 June
England v Pakistan	Pak 8-193	Eng 2-199	Eng by 8 wkts	Lord's	13 June
New Zealand v Sri Lanka	SL 206	NZ 5-209	NZ by 5 wkts	Bristol	13 June
Australia v India	Aus 9-320	Ind 158	Aus by 162 runs	Nottingham	13 June
West Indies v Zimbabwe	Zim 7-217	WI 2-218	WI by 8 wkts	Worcester	13 June
England v New Zealand	Eng 234	NZ 8-238	NZ by 2 wkts	Birmingham	15 June
West Indies v India	WI 9-282	Ind 216	WI by 66 runs	The Oval	15 June
Pakistan v Sri Lanka	Pak 7-235	SL 224	Pak by 11 runs	Leeds	16 June
Australia v Zimbabwe	Aus 7-272	Zim 240	Aus by 32 runs	Southampton	16 June
England v Pakistan	Pak 8-232	Eng 3-233	Eng by 7 wkts	Manchester	18 June
New Zealand v Sri Lanka	NZ 181	SL 7-184	SL by 3 wkts	Derby	18 June
Australia v West Indies	Aus 6-273	WI 3-276	WI by 7 wkts	Lord's	18 June
India v Zimbabwe	Ind 8-266	Zim 235	Ind by 31 runs	Tunbridge Wells	18 June

England v Sri Lanka	SL 136	Eng 1-137	Eng by 9 wkts	Leeds	20 June
New Zealand v Pakistan	Pak 3-261	NZ 250	Pak by 11 runs	Nottingham	20 June
Australia v India	Ind 247	Aus 129	Ind by 118 runs	Chelmsford	20 June
West Indies v Zimbabwe	Zim 171	WI 0-172	WI by 10 wkts	Birmingham	20 June

Group A

Team	Played	Won	Lost	Pts	R-R
England	6	5	1	20	4.67
Pakistan	6	3	3	12	4.01
New Zealand	6	3	3	12	3.93
Sri Lanka	6	1	5	4	3.75

Group B

Team	Played	Won	Lost	Pts	R-R
West Indies	6	5	1	20	4.31
India	6	4	2	16	3.87
Australia	6	2	4	8	3.81
Zimbabwe	6	1	5	4	3.49

Semi-finals

Match	Batted 1st	Batted 2nd	Result	Venue	Date
India v England	Eng 213	Ind 4-217	Ind by 6 wkts	Manchester	22 June
Pakistan v West Indies	Pak 8-184	WI 2-188	WI by 8 wkts	The Oval	22 June

Final

Match	Batted 1st	Batted 2nd	Result	Venue	Date
India v West Indies	Ind 183	WI 140	Ind by 43 runs	Lord's	25 June

1987 WORLD CUP IN INDIA AND PAKISTAN

Match	Batted Ist	Batted 2nd	Result	Venue	Date
Pakistan v Sri Lanka	Pak 6-267	SL 252	Pak by 15 runs	Hyderabad (P)	8 Oct
India v Australia	Aus 6-270	Ind 269	Aus by 1 run	Chennai	9 Oct
England v West Indies	WI 7-243	Eng 8-246	Eng by 2 wkts	Gujranwala	9 Oct
New Zealand v Zimbabwe	NZ 7-242	Zim 239	NZ by 3 runs	Hyderabad (I)	10 Oct
Australia v Zimbabwe	Aus 9-235	Zim 139	Aus by 96 runs	Chennai	13 Oct
Pakistan v England	Pak 7-239	Eng 221	Pak by 18 runs	Rawalpindi (RC)	13 Oct
West Indies v Sri Lanka	WI 4-360	SL 4-169	WI by 191 runs	Karachi	13 Oct
India v New Zealand	Ind 7-252	NZ 8-236	Ind by 16 runs	Bangalore	14 Oct
Pakistan v West Indies	WI 216	Pak 9-217	Pak by 1 wkt	Lahore	16 Oct
India v Zimbabbwe	Zim 135	Ind 2-136	Ind by 8 wkts	Mumbai	17 Oct
England v Sri Lanka	Eng 4-296	SL 8-158	Eng by 108 runs	Peshawar	17 Oct
Australia v New Zealand	Aus 4-199	NZ 9-196	Aus by 3 runs	Indore	19 Oct
Pakistan v England	Eng 9-244	Pak 3-247	Pak by 7 wkts	Karachi	20 Oct
West Indies v Sri Lanka	WI 8-236	SL 8-211	WI by 25 runs	Kanpur	21 Oct
India v Australia	India 6-289	Aus 233	Ind by 56 runs	New Delhi	22 Oct
New Zealand v Zimbabwe	NZ 5-227	Zim 6-228	NZ by 4 wkts	Calcutta	23 Oct
Pakistan v Sri Lanka	Pak 7-297	SL 8-184	Pak by 113 runs	Faisalabad	25 Oct
Zimbabwe v India	Zim 7-191	Ind 3-194	Ind by 7 wkts	Ahmedabad (GS)	26 Oct
England v West Indies	Eng 5-269	WI 235	Eng by 34 runs	Jaipur	26 Oct
Australia v New Zealand	Aus 8-251	NZ 234	Aus by 17 runs	Chandigarh	27 Oct
Australia v Zimbabwe	Aus 5-266	Zim 6-196	Aus by 70 runs	Cuttack	30 Oct
England v Sri Lanka	SL 7-218	Eng 2-219	Eng by 8 wkts	Puna	30 Oct
Pakistan v West Indies	WI 7-258	Pak 9-230	WI by 28 runs	Karachi	30 Oct
India v New Zealand	NZ 9-221	Ind 1-224	Ind by 9 wkts	Nagpur	31 Oct

Group A

Team	Played	Won	Lost	Pts	R-R
India	6	5	1	20	5.39
Australia	6	5	1	20	5.19
New Zealand	6	2	4	8	4.88
Zimbabwe	6	-	6	-	3.76

Group B

Team	Played	Won	Lost	Pts	R-R
Pakistan	6	5	1	20	5.01
England	6	4	2	16	5.12
West Indies	6	3	3	12	5.16
Sri Lanka	6	-	6	-	4.04

Semi-finals

Match	Batted 1st	Batted 2nd	Result	Venue	Date
Pakistan v Australia	Aus 8-267	Pak 249	Aus by 18 runs	Lahore	4 Nov
India v England	Eng 6-254	Ind 219	Eng by 35 runs	Bombay	5 Nov

Final

Match	Batted 1st	Batted 2nd	Result	Venue	Date
Australia v England	Aus 5-253	Eng 8-246	Aus by 7 runs	Calcutta	8 Nov

1991/92 WORLD CUP IN AUSTRALIA AND NEW ZEALAND

Match	Batted 1st	Batted 2nd	Result	Venue	Date
New Zealand v Australia	NZ 6-248	Aus 211	NZ by 37 runs	Auckland	22 Feb
England v India	Eng 9-236	Ind 227	Eng by 9 runs	Perth	22 Feb
Zimbabwe v Sri Lanka	Zim 4-312	SL 7-313	SL by 3 wkts	New Plymouth	23 Feb
Pakistan v West Indies	Pak 2-220	WI 0-221	WI by 10 wkts	Melbourne	23 Feb
New Zealand v Sri Lanka	SL 9-206	NZ 4-210	NZ by 6 wkts	Hamilton	25 Feb
Australia v South Africa	Aus 9-170	SAF 1-171	SAF by 9 wkts	Sydney	26 Feb
Pakistan v Zimbabwe	Pak 4-254	Zim 7-201	Pak by 53 runs	Hobart (B)	27 Feb
West Indies v England	WI 157	Eng 4-160	Eng by 6 wkts	Melbourne	27 Feb
India v Sri Lanka	Ind 0-1	SL DNB	*No result*	Mackay	28 Feb
New Zealand v South Africa	SAF 7-190	NZ 3-191	NZ by 7 wkts	Auckland	29 Feb
West Indies v Zimbabwe	WI 8-264	Zim 7-189	WI by 75 runs	Brisbane	29 Feb
Australia v India	Aus 9-237	Ind 234	Aus by 1 run	Brisbane	1 Mar
England v Pakistan	Pak 74	Eng 1-24	*No result*	Adelaide	1 Mar
South Africa v Sri Lanka	SAF 195	SL 7-198	SAF by 3 wkts	Wellington	2 Mar
New Zealand v Zimbabwe	NZ 3-162	Zim 7-105	NZ by 48 runs	Napier	3 Mar
India v Pakistan	Ind 7-216	Pak 173	Ind by 43 runs	Sydney	4 Mar
South Africa v West Indies	SAF 8-200	WI 136	SAf by 64 runs	Christchurch	5 Mar
Australia v England	Aus 171	Eng 2-173	Eng by 8 wkts	Sydney	5 Mar
India v Zimbabwe	Ind 7-203	Zim 1-104	Ind by 55 runs	Hamilton	7 Mar
Australia v Sri Lanka	SL 9-189	Aus 3-190	Aus by 7 wkts	Adelaide	7 Mar
New Zealand v West Indies	WI 7-203	NZ 5-206	NZ by 5 wkts	Auckland	8 Mar
Pakistan v South Africa	SAF 7-211	Pak 8-173	SAf by 20 runs	Brisbane	8 Mar
England v Sri Lanka	Eng 6-280	SL 174	Eng by 106 runs	Ballarat	9 Mar
India v West Indies	Ind 197	WI 5-195	WI by 5 wkts	Wellington	10 Mar
South Africa v Zimbabwe	Zim 163	SAF 3-164	SAF by 7 wkts	Canberra	10 Mar
Australia v Pakistan	Pak 9-220	Aus 172	Pak by 48 runs	Perth	11 Mar
New Zealand v India	Ind 6-230	NZ 6-231	NZ by 4 wkts	Dunedin	12 Mar
England v South Africa	SAF 4-236	Eng 7-226	Eng by 3 wkts	Melbourne	12 Mar
Sri Lanka v West Indies	WI 8-268	SL 9-177	WI by 91 runs	Berri	13 Mar

Australia v Zimbabwe	Aus 6-265	Zim 137	Aus by 128 runs	Hobart (B)	14 Mar
New Zealand v England	Eng 8-200	NZ 3-201	NZ by 7 wkts	Wellington	15 Mar
India v South Africa	Ind 6-180	SAF 4-181	SAF by 6 wkts	Adelaide	15 Mar
Pakistan v Sri Lanka	SL 6-212	Pak 6-216	Pak by 4 wkts	Perth	15 Mar
New Zealand v Pakistan	NZ 166	Pak 3-167	Pak by 7 wkts	Christchurch	18 Mar
England v Zimbabwe	Zim 134	Eng 125	Zim by 9 runs	Albury	18 Mar
Australia v West Indies	Aus 6-216	WI 159	Aus by 57 runs	Melbourne	18 Mar

Final

Team	Played	Won	Lost	NR	Pts
New Zealand	8	7	1	-	14
England	8	5	2	1	11
South Africa	8	5	3	-	10
Pakistan	8	4	3	1	9
Australia	8	4	4	-	8
West Indies	8	4	4		8
India	8	2	5	1	5
Sri Lanka	8	2	5	1	5
Zimbabwe	8	1	7	-	2

Semi-finals

Match	Batted 1st	Batted 2nd	Result	Venue	Date
New Zealand v Pakistan	NZ 7-262	Pak 6-264	Pak by 4 wkts	Auckland	21 Mar
England v South Africa	Eng 6-252	SAF 6-232	Eng by 19 runs	Sydney	22 Mar

Final

Match	Batted 1st	Batted 2nd	Result	Venue	Date
England v Pakistan	Pak 6-249	Eng 227	Pak by 22 runs	Melbourne	25 Mar

1995/96 WORLD CUP IN INDIA, PAKISTAN AND SRI LANKA

Match	Batted 1st	Batted 2nd	Result	Venue	Date
England v New Zealand	NZ 6-239	Eng 9-228	NZ by 11 runs	Ahmedabad (GS)	14 Feb
South Africa v UAE	SAF 2-321	UAE 8-152	SAF by169 runs	Rawalpindi	16 Feb
Zimbabwe v West Indies	Zim 9-151	WI 4-155	WI by 6 wkts	Hyderabad (I)	16 Feb
New Zealand v Netherlands	NZ 8-307	Neth 7-188	NZ by 119 runs	Vadodara (IPCL)	17 Feb
Sri Lanka v Australia	*Australia forfeited*			Colombo (RPS)	17 Feb
India v Kenya	Ken 6-199	Ind 3-203	Ind by 7 wkts	Cuttack	18 Feb
UAE v England	UAE 136	Eng 2-140	Eng by 8 wkts	Peshawar	18 Feb
New Zealand v South Africa	NZ 9-177	SAF 5-178	SAF by 5 wkts	Faisalabad	20 Feb
Sri Lanka v Zimbabwe	Zim 6-228	SL 4-229	SL by 6 wkts	Colombo (SSC)	21 Feb
India v West Indies	WI 173	Ind 5-174	Ind by 5 wkts	Gwalor	21 Feb
England v Netherlands	Eng 4-279	Neth 6-230	Eng by 49 runs	Peshawar	22 Feb
Australia v Kenya	Aus 7-304	Ken 7-207	Aus by 97 runs	Visag	23 Feb
Pakistan v UAE	UAE 9-109	Pak I-112	Pak by 9 wkts	Gujranwala	24 Feb
Sri Lanka v West Indies	*West Indies forfeited*			Colombo (RPS)	25 Feb
South Africa v England	SAF 230	Eng 152	SAF by 78 runs	Rawalpindi (RC)	25 Feb
Pakistan v Netherlands	Neth 7-145	Pak 2-151	Pak by 8 wkts	Lahore	26 Feb
Zimbabwe v Kenya	Ken 134	Zim 5-137	Zim by 5 wkts	Patna	27 Feb
Australia v India	Aus 258	Ind 242	Aus by 16 runs	Mumbai	27 Feb
New Zealand v UAE	NZ 8-276	UAE 9-167	NZ by 109 runs	Faisalabad	27 Feb
Kenya v West Indies	Ken 166	WI 93	Ken by 73 runs	Pune	29 Feb
Pakistan v South Africa	Pak 6-242	SAF 5-243	SAF by 5 wkts	Karachi	29 Feb
Zimbabwe v Australia	Zim 154	Aus 2-158	Aus by 8 wkts	Nagpur	1 Mar
Netherlands v UAE	Neth 9-216	UAE 3-220	UAE by 7 wkts	Lahore	1 Mar
India v Sri Lanka	Ind 3-271	SL 4-272	SL by 6 wkts	Delhi	2 Mar

Pakistan v England	Eng 4-249	Pak 3-250	Pak by 7 wkts	Karachi	3 Mar
Australia v West Indies	Aus 6-229	WI 6-232	WI by 4 wkts	Jaipur	4 Mar
South Africa v Netherlands	SAF 3-328	Neth 8-168	SAF by 160 runs	Rawalpindi (RC)	5 Mar
Sri Lanka v Kenya	SL 5-398	Ken 7-254	SL by 144 runs	Kandy	6 Mar
India v Zimbabwe	Ind 5-247	Zim 207	Ind by 40 runs	Kanpur	6 Mar
Pakistan v New Zealand	Pak 5-281	NZ 9-235	Pak by 46 runs	Lahore	6 Mar

Group A

Team	Played	Won	Lost	Forfeit	Pts
Sri Lanka	5	5	-	-	10
Australia	5	3	1	1	6
India	5	3	2	-	6
West Indies	5	2	2	1	4
Zimbabwe	5	1	4	-	2
Kenya	5	1	4	-	2

Group B

Team	Played	Won	Lost	Pts
South Africa	5	5	-	10
Pakistan	5	4	1	8
New Zealand	5	3	2	6
England	5	2	3	4
United Arab Emirates	5	1	4	2
Netherlands	5	-	5	-

Quarter-finals

Match	Batted 1st	Batted 2nd	Result	Venue	Date
England v Sri Lanka	Eng 8-235	SL 5-236	SL by 5 wkts	Faisalabad	9 Mar
India v Pakistan	Ind 8-287	Pak 9-248	Ind by 39 runs	Bangalore	9 Mar
West Indies v South Africa	WI 8-264	SAF 245	WI by 19 runs	Karachi	11 Mar
New Zealand v Australia	NZ 9-286	Aus 4-289	Aus by 6 wkts	Chennai	11 Mar

Semi-finals

Match	Batted 1st	Batted 2nd	Result	Venue	Date
Sri Lanka v India	SL 8-251	Ind 8-120	SL by default	Calcutta	13 Mar
Australia v West Indies	Aus 8-207	WI 202	Aus by 5 runs	Mohali	14 Mar

Final

Match	Batted 1st	Batted 2nd	Result	Venue	Date
Sri Lanka v Australia	Aus 7-241	SL 3-245	SL by 7 wkts	Lahore	17 Mar

SUMMARY OF MATCHES BY COUNTRY

Team	First game	Versus	M	Won	Lost	NR	Win%
Australia	7 June 1975, Leeds	Pakistan	37	22	15[t]	-	59.5
Canada	9 June 1979, Leeds	Pakistan	3	-	3	-	-
East Africa	7 June 1975, Birmingham	New Zealand	3	-	3	-	-
England	7 June 1975, Lord's	India	40	25	14	1	64.1
India	7 June 1975, Lord's	England	36	18	17	1	51.4
Kenya	18 Feb 1996, Cuttack	India	5	1	4	-	20
Netherlands	17 Feb 1996, Baroda	New Zealand	5	-	5	-	-
New Zealand	7 June 1975, Birmingham	East Africa	35	19	16	-	54.2
Pakistan	7 June 1975, Leeds	Australia	37	21	15	1	58.3
South Africa	26 Feb 1992, Sydney	Australia	15	10	5	-	66.6
Sri Lanka	7 June 1975, Manchester	West Indies	34	12	20	2	37.5
UAE	16 Feb 1996, Rawalpindi	South Africa	5	1	4	-	20
West Indies	7 June 1975, Manchester	Sri Lanka	38	25	12[t]	1	67.5
Zimbabwe	9 June 1983, Nottingham	Australia	25	3	22	-	12

[t]does not include forfeits v Sri Lanka in Colombo during the 1995/96 World Cup

THE TEAMS

HIGHEST INNINGS TOTALS

Runs	Team	Batted 1st	Batted 2nd	Venue	Date
398	Sri Lanka	SL 5-398	Ken 7-254	Kandy	6 Mar 1996
360	West Indies	WI 4-360	SL 4-169	Karachi	13 Oct 1987
338	Pakistan	Pak 5-338	SL 9-288	Swansea	9 June 1983
334	England	Eng 4-334	Ind 3-132	Lord's	7 June 1975
333	England	Eng 9-333	SL 286	Taunton	11 June 1983
330	Pakistan	Pak 6-330	SL 138	Nottingham	14 June 1975
328	Australia	Aus 5-328	SL 4-276	The Oval	11 June 1975
328	South Africa	SAf 3-328	Neth 8-168	Rawalpindi (RC)	5 Mar 1996
322	England	Eng 6-322	NZ 216	The Oval	9 June 1983
321	South Africa	SAf 2-321	UAE 8-152	Rawalpindi (RC)	16 Feb 1996
320	Australia	Aus 9-320	Ind 158	Nottingham	13 June 1983

HIGHEST MATCH AGGREGATES

Runs	Match	Batted 1st	Batted 2nd	Venue	Date
652	Sri Lanka v Kenya	SL 5-398	Ken 7-254	Kandy	6 Mar 1996
626	Pakistan v Sri Lanka	Pak 5-338	SL 9-288	Swansea	9 June 1983
625	Zimbabwe v Sri Lanka	Zim 4-312	SL 7-313	New Plymouth	23 Feb 1992
619	England v Sri Lanka	Eng 9-333	SL 286	Taunton	11 June 1983
604	Australia v Sri Lanka	Aus 5-328	SL 4-276	The Oval	11 June 1975

LOWEST COMPLETED INNINGS TOTALS

Runs/Overs	Team	Batted 1st	Batted 2nd	Venue	Date
45 (40.3 overs)	Canada	Can 45	Eng 2-46	Manchester	14 June 1979
74 (40.2 overs)	Pakistan	Pak 74	Eng 1-24[t]	Adelaide	1 Mar 1992
86 (37.2 overs)	Sri Lanka	SL 86	WI 1-87	Manchester	7 June 1975
93 (36.2 overs)	England	Eng 93	Aus 6-94	Leeds	18 June 1975
93 (35.2 overs)	West Indies	Ken 166	WI 93	Pune	29 Feb 1996
94 (52.3 overs)	East Africa	Eng 5-290	EAf 94	Birmingham	14 June 1975

[t]match abandoned due to rain

LOWEST COMPLETED MATCH AGGREGATES

Runs	Match	Batted 1st	Batted 2nd	Venue	Date
91	England v Canada	Can 45	Eng 2-46	Manchester	14 June 1979
173	West Indies v Sri Lanka	SL 86	WI 1-87	Manchester	7 June 1975
187	England v Australia	Eng 93	Aus 6-94	Leeds	18 June 1975

LOWEST MATCH AGGREGATES WHERE BOTH TEAMS WERE DISMISSED

Runs	Match	Batted 1st	Batted 2nd	Venue	Date
259	England v Zimbabwe	Zim 134	Eng 125	Albury	18 Mar 1992
259	West Indies v Kenya	Ken 166	WI 93	Pune	29 Feb 1996

BIGGEST WINNING MARGINS (RUNS)

Runs	Team	Batted 1st	Batted 2nd	Venue	Date
202	England	Eng 4-334	Ind 3-132	Lord's	7 June 1975
196	England	Eng 5-290	EAf 94	Birmingham	14 June 1975
192	Pakistan	Pak 6-330	SL 138	Nottingham	14 June 1975
191	West Indies	WI 4-360	SL 4-169	Karachi	13 Oct 1987
181	New Zealand	NZ 5-309	EAF 8-128	Birmingham	7 June 1975
169	South Africa	SAF 2-321	UAE 8-152	Rawalpindi (RC)	16 Feb 1996
162	Australia	Aus 9-320	Ind 158	Nottingham	13 June 1983
160	South Africa	SAF 3-328	Neth 8-168	Rawalpindi (RC)	5 Mar 1996

BIGGEST WINNING MARGINS (10 WICKETS)

Wkts	Team	Batted 1st	Batted 2nd	Venue	Date
10	India	EAF 120	Ind 0-123	Leeds	11 June 1975
10	West Indies	Zim 171	WI 0-172	Birmingham	20 June 1983
10	West Indies	Pak 2-220	WI 0-221	Melbourne	23 Feb 1992

NARROWEST WINNING MARGINS (RUNS)

Runs	Team	Batted 1st	Batted 2nd	Venue	Date
1	Australia	Aus 6-270	Ind 269	Chennai	9 Oct 1987
1	Australia	Aus 9-237	Ind 234[†]	Brisbane	1 Mar 1992
3	New Zealand	NZ 7-242	Zim 239	Hyderabad (I)	10 Oct 1987
3	Australia	Aus 4-199	NZ 9-196	Indore	19 Oct 1987

[†]*target reduced to 236 due to rain*

NARROWEST WINNING MARGINS (WICKETS)

Wkts	Team	Batted 1st	Batted 2nd	Venue	Date
1	West Indies	Pak 7-266	WI 9-267	Birmingham	11 June 1975
1	Pakistan	WI 216	Pak 9-217	Lahore	16 Oct 1987
2	England	WI 7-243	Eng 8-246	Gujranwala	9 Oct 1987

ABANDONED MATCHES[†]

Match	Venue	Date
West Indies v Sri Lanka	The Oval	13/14/15 June 1979
India v Sri Lanka	Mackay	28 Feb 1992
Pakistan v England	Adelaide	1 Mar 1992

[†]*due to rain - no result*

FORFEITED MATCHES

Forfeit	Versus	Venue	Date
Australia	Sri Lanka	Colombo (RPS)	17 Feb 1996
West Indies	Sri Lanka	Colombo (RPS)	25 Feb 1996

THE PLAYERS

MOST APPEARANCES

Matches	Player	World Cups
33	Javed Miandad, Pakistan	1975, 1979, 1983, 1987, 1992, 1996
28	Imran Khan, Pakistan	1975, 1979, 1983, 1987, 1992
26	Kapil Dev, India	1979, 1983, 1987,1992
25	D.L. Haynes, West Indies	1979, 1983, 1987, 1992
25	A.R. Border, Australia	1979, 1983, 1987, 1992
25	A. Ranatunga, Sri Lanka	1983, 1987, 1992, 1996
25	S.R. Waugh, Australia	1987, 1992, 1996

YOUNGEST PLAYERS ON DEBUT

Years, days	Player	Versus	Venue	Date
17 years, 237 days	S.P. Pasqual, Sri Lanka	New Zealand	Nottingham	9 Jun 1979
17 years, 282 days	T. Odoyo, Kenya	India	Cuttack	18 Feb 1996
17 years, 364 days	Javed Miandad, Pakistan	West Indies	Edgbaston	11 Jun 1975
18 years, 304 days	S.R. Tendulkar, India	England	Perth	22 Feb 1992
18 years, 351 days	B. Zuiderent, Netherlands	New Zealand	Baroda	17 Feb 1996

OLDEST PLAYERS

Years, days	Player	Versus	Venue	Date
47 years, 256 days	N.E. Clarke, Netherlands	South Africa	Rawalpindi (RC)	5 Mar 1996
44 years, 306 days	A.J. Traicos, Zimbabwe	England	Albury	18 Mar 1992
43 years, 128 days	G.J.A.F. Aponso, Netherlands	South Africa	Rawalpindi (RC)	5 Mar 1996
43 years, 45 days	D.J. Pringle, East Africa	England	Birmingham	14 Jun 1975
42 years, 346 days	S.W. Lubbers, Netherlands	South Africa	Rawalpindi (RC)	5 Mar 1996

PLAYER OF THE TOURNAMENT

Year	Player
1975-87	*Not awarded*
1991/92	M.D. Crowe, New Zealand
1995/96	S.T. Jayasuriya, Sri Lanka

BATTING

LEADING RUN-SCORERS

Runs	Player	M	Inns	NO	HS	100s	50s	Ave
1083	Javed Miandad, Pakistan	33	30	5	103	1	8	43.42
1013	I.V.A. Richards, West Indies	23	21	5	181	3	5	63.31
897	G.A. Gooch, England	21	21	1	115	1	8	44.85
880	M.D. Crowe, New Zealand	21	21	5	100*	1	8	55.00
854	D.L. Haynes, West Indies	25	25	2	105	1	-	37.13
835	A. Ranatunga, Sri Lanka	25	24	8	88*	-	6	52.18
815	D.C. Boon, Australia	16	16	1	100	2	5	54.33
806	S.R. Tendulkar, India	15	14	2	137	2	6	67.16

MOST RUNS IN A TOURNAMENT

Runs	Player	World Cup	M	Inns	NO	HS	100s	50s	Ave.
523	S.R. Tendulkar, India	1995/96	7	7	1	137	2	3	87.16
484	M.E. Waugh, Australia	1995/96	7	7	1	130	3	1	80.66
471	G.A. Gooch, England	1987/88	8	8	-	115	1	4	58.87
456	M.D. Crowe, New Zealand	1991/92	9	9	5	100*	1	4	114
448	P.A. de Silva, Sri Lanka	1995/96	6	6	1	145	2	2	89.60
447	D.C. Boon, Australia	1987/88	8	8	-	93	-	5	55.88

HIGHEST INDIVIDUAL INNINGS

Runs	Player	Versus	Venue	Date
188*	G. Kirsten, South Africa	UAE	Rawalpindi (RC)	16 Feb 1996
181	I.V.A. Richards, West Indies	Sri Lanka	Karachi	13 Oct 1987
175*	Kapil Dev, India	Zimbabwe	Tunbridge Wells	18 June 1983
171*	G.M. Turner, New Zealand	East Africa	Birmingham	7 June 1975
161	A.C. Hudson, South Africa	Netherlands	Rawalpindi (RC)	5 Mar 1996
145	P.A. de Silva, Sri Lanka	Kenya	Kandy	6 Mar 1996
142	D.L. Houghton, Zimbabwe	New Zealand	Hyderabad(I)	10 Oct 1987
138*	I.V.A. Richards, West Indies	England	Lord's	23 June 1979
137	D.L. Amiss, England	India	Lord's	7 June 1975
137	S.R. Tendulkar, India	Sri Lanka	New Delhi	2 Mar 1996
131	K.W. Fletcher, England	New Zealand	Nottingham	11 June 1975
130	M.E. Waugh, Australia	Kenya	Visag	23 Feb 1996
130	D.I. Gower, England	Sri Lanka	Taunton	11 June 1983
130	C.Z. Harris, New Zealand	Australia	Chennai	11 Mar 1996
127*	S.R. Tendulkar, India	Kenya	Cuttack	18 Feb 1996
126	M.E. Waugh, Australia	India	Mumbai	27 Feb 1996
126*	G.R. Marsh, Australia	New Zealand	Chandigarh	27 Oct 1987
119	I.V.A. Richards, West Indies	India	The Oval	15 June 1983
119*	Ramiz Raja, Pakistan	New Zealand	Christchurch	18 Mar 1992
115	G.A. Gooch, England	India	Mumbai	5 Nov 1987
115*	A. Flower, Zimbabwe	Sri Lanka	New Plymouth	23 Feb 1992
114	G.M. Turner, New Zealand	India	Manchester	14 June 1975
114	Aamir Sohail, Pakistan	Zimbabwe	Hobart (B)	27 Feb 1992
113	Ramiz Raja, Pakistan	England	Karachi	20 Oct 1987
111	Aamir Sohail, Pakistan	South Africa	Karachi	29 Feb 1996
111	B.C. Lara, West Indies	South Africa	Karachi	1 1 Mar 1996
110	T.M. Chappell, Australia	India	Nottingham	13 June 1983
110	G.R. Marsh, Australia	India	Chennai	9 Oct 1987
110	R.B. Richardson, West Indies	Pakistan	Karachi	30 Oct 1987
110	P.V. Simmons, West Indies	Sri Lanka	Berri	13 Mar 1992
110	M.E. Waugh, Australia	New Zealand	Chennai	11 Mar 1996
107*	P.A. de Silva, Sri Lanka	Australia	Lahore	17 Mar 1996
106	V.G. Kambli, India	Zimbabwe	Kanpur	6 Mar 1996
106*	C.G. Greenidge, West Indies	India	Birmingham	9 June 1979
105*	C.G. Greenidge, West Indies	Zimbabwe	Worcester	13 June 1983
105	D.L. Haynes, West Indies	Sri Lanka	Karachi	13 Oct 1987
104*	G.A. Hick, England	Netherlands	Peshawar	22 Feb 1996
103*	Zaheer Abbas, Pakistan	New Zealand	Nottingham	20 June 1983
103*	S.M. Gavaskar, India	New Zealand	Nagpur	31 Oct 1987
103	Javed Miandad, Pakistan	Sri Lanka	Hyderabad (P)	8 Oct 1987
102	C.H. Lloyd, West Indies	Australia	Lord's	21 June 1975
102*	Imran Khan, Pakistan	Sri Lanka	Leeds	16 June 1983
102	A.J. Lamb, England	New Zealand	The Oval	9 June 1983
102*	Ramiz Raja, Pakistan	West Indies	Melbourne	23 Feb 1992

Runs	Player	Versus	Venue	Date
102	R.T. Ponting, Australia	West Indies	Jaipur	4 Mar 1996
101	A. Turner, Australia	Sri Lanka	The Oval	11 June 1975
101	N.J. Astle, New Zealand	England	Ahmedabad (GS)	14 Feb 1996
100	Salim Malik, Pakistan	Sri Lanka	Faisalabad	25 Oct 1987
100*	M.D. Crowe, New Zealand	Australia	Auckland	22 Feb 1992
100	D.C. Boon, Australia	New Zealand	Auckland	22 Feb 1992
100	D.C. Boon, Australia	West Indies	Melbourne	18 Mar 1992

HIGHEST INDIVIDUAL INNINGS FOR EACH BATTING POSITION

Pos.	Score	Batsman	Versus	Venue	Date
1	171*	G.M. Turner, New Zealand	East Africa	Birmingham	7 June 1975
2	188*	G. Kirsten, South Africa	UAE	Rawalpindi (RC)	16 Feb 1996
3	142	D.L. Houghton, Zimbabwe	New Zealand	Hyderabad(I)	10 Oct 1987
4	181	I.V.A. Richards, West Indies	Sri Lanka	Karachi	13 Oct 1987
5	130	C.Z. Harris, New Zealand	Australia	Chennai	11 Mar 1996
6	175*	Kapil Dev, India	Zimbabwe	Tunbridge Wells	18 June 1983
7	77	Shahid Mahboob, India	Sri Lanka	Leeds	16 June 1983
8	61	D.L. Murray, West Indies	Pakistan	Birmingham	11 June 1975
9	59	R.G. de Alwis, Sri Lanka	Pakistan	Swansea	9 June 1983
10	40	M.C. Snedden, New Zealand	Sri Lanka	Derby	18 June 1983
	40*	S.F. Dukanwala, UAE	South Africa	Rawalpindi (RC)	16 Feb 1996
11	37	J. Garner, West Indies	India	Manchester	9/10 June 1983

HIGHEST BATTING AVERAGES (minimum of 200 runs)

Batsman	Ave.	M	I	NO	Runs	HS	100s	50s
Saeed Anwar, Pakistan	82.25	6	6	2	329	83*	-	3
G. Kirsten, South Africa	78.20	6	6	1	391	188*	1	1
G. Fowler, England	72.00	7	7	2	360	81*	-	4
K.W.R. Fletcher	69.00	4	3	-	207	131	1	1
P.N. Kirsten, South Africa	68.33	8	8	2	410	90	-	4
S.R. Tendulkar, India	67.17	15	14	2	806	137	2	6
H.A. Gomes, West Indies	64.50	8	7	3	258	78	-	3
D.J. Cullinan, South Africa	63.75	6	6	2	255	69	-	2
G.P. Thorpe, England	63.50	6	6	2	254	89	-	2
I.V.A. Richards, West Indies	63.31	23	21	5	1013	181	3	5
M.E. Waugh, Australia	62.90	12	12	2	629	130	3	2
G.M. Turner, England	61.20	14	14	4	612	171*	2	2
D.L. Amiss, England	60.75	4	4	-	243	137	1	1
M.D. Crowe, New Zealand	55.00	21	21	5	880	100*	1	8
D.C. Boon, Australia	54.33	16	16	1	815	100	2	5
D.I. Gower, England	54.25	12	11	3	434	130	1	1
Ramiz Raja, Pakistan	53.85	16	16	3	700	119*	3	2
C.W.J. Athey, England	52.75	6	6	2	211	86	-	2
A. Ranatunga, Sri Lanka	52.19	25	24	8	835	88*	-	6
Majid Khan, Pakistan	51.28	7	7	-	359	84	-	5
S.G. Law, Australia	51.00	7	6	2	204	72	-	1
A.J. Lamb, England	50.46	19	17	4	656	102	1	3
B.C. Lara, West Indies	50.16	14	14	2	602	111	1	5

BATTED THROUGHOUT AN INNINGS

Batsman	Score	Total/Overs	Versus	Venue	Date
S.M. Gavaskar, India	36*	(3-132/60 overs)	England	Lord's	7 June 1975
G.M. Turner, New Zealand	171*	(5-309/60 overs)	East Africa	Birmingham	7 June 1975
G.R. Marsh, Australia	126*	(8-251/50 overs)	New Zealand	Chandigarh	27 Oct 1987
Ramiz Raja, Pakistan	102*	(2-220/50 overs)	West Indies	Melbourne	23 Feb 1992
A. Flower, Zimbabwe	115*	(4-312/50 overs)	Sri Lanka	New Plymouth	23 Feb 1992
G. Kirsten, South Africa	188*	(2-321/50 overs)	UAE	Rawalpindi (RC)	16 Feb 1996

MOST CENTURIES

No.	Player	World Cups
3	I.V.A. Richards, West Indies	1979 (1), 1983 (1), 1987 (1)
3	Ramiz Raja, Pakistan	1987 (1), 1992 (2)
3	M.E. Waugh, Australia	1996 (3)
2	G.M. Turner, New Zealand	1975 (2)
2	C.G. Greenidge, West Indies	1979 (1), 1983 (1)
2	G.R. Marsh, Australia	1987 (2)
2	D.C. Boon, Australia	1992 (2)
2	Aamir Sohail, Pakistan	1992 (1), 1996 (1)
2	S.R. Tendulkar, India	1996 (2)
2	P.A. de Silva, Sri Lanka	1996 (2)

CENTURY ON WORLD CUP DEBUT

Score	Player	Versus	Venue	Date
137	D.L. Amiss, England	India	Lord's	7 June 1975
171*	G.M. Turner, New Zealand	East Africa	Birmingham	7 June 1975
110	T.M. Chappell, Australia	India	Nottingham	13 June 1983
102	A.J. Lamb, England	New Zealand	The Oval	9 June 1983
110	G.R. Marsh, Australia	India	Chennai	9 Oct 1987
115*	A. Flower, Zimbabwe	Sri Lanka	New Plymouth	23 Feb 1992
101	N.J. Astle, New Zealand	England	Ahmedabad (SP)	14 Feb 1996
188*	G. Kirsten, South Africa	UAE	Rawalpindi (RC)	16 Feb 1996

YOUNGEST CENTURY-MAKERS

Years, days	Player	Score	Versus	Venue	Date
21 years, 76 days	R.T. Ponting, Australia	102	West Indies	Jaipur	4 Mar 1996
22 years, 300 days	S.R. Tendulkar, India	127*	Kenya	Cuttack	18 Feb 1996
23 years, 301 days	A. Flower, Zimbabwe	115*	Sri Lanka	New Plymouth	23 Feb 1992

FASTEST CENTURIES

Balls	Player	Versus	Venue	Date
72	Kapil Dev India	Zimbabwe	Tunbridge Wells	18 June 1983
82	C.H. Lloyd, West Indies	Australia	Lord's	21 June 1975
83	B.C. Lara, West Indies	South Africa	Karachi	11 Mar 1996
85	S.M. Gavaskar, India	New Zealand	Nagpur	31 Oct 1987

FASTEST HALF-CENTURIES

Balls	Player	Versus	Venue	Date
29	A. Ranatunga, Sri Lanka	Kenya	Kandy	6 Mar 1996
30	C.M. Old, England	India	Lord's	7 June 1975
30	Imran Khan, Pakistan	Sri Lanka	Swansea	9 June 1983
31	M.D. Crowe, New Zealand	Napier	Zimbabwe	3 Mar 1992
31	Inzamam-ul-Haq, Pakistan	New Zealand	Auckland	21 Mar 1992

NINETIES

Score	Batsman	Versus	Venue	Date
97	Zaheer Abbas, Pakistan	Sri Lanka	Nottingham	14 June 1975
97	M.D Crowe, New Zealand	England	The Oval	9 June 1983
96	S.O. Tikolo, Kenya	Sri Lanka	Kandy	6 Mar 1996
95*	I.V.A. Richards, West Indies	Australia	Lord's	18 June 1983
93	Zaheer Abbas, Pakistan	West Indies	The Oval	20 June 1979
93	R.B. Richardson, West Indies	England	Jaipur	26 Oct 1987
93	D.C. Boon, Australia	Zimbabwe	Cuttack	30 Oct 1987
93*	D.L. Haynes, West Indies	Pakistan	Melbourne	23 Feb 1992
93	M.A. Azharuddin, India	Australia	Brisbane	1 Mar 1992
93*	R.B. Richardson, West Indies	Australia	Jaipur	4 Mar 1996
93	N.S. Sidhu, India	Pakistan	Bangalore	9 Mar 1996
92*	D.I. Gower, England	New Zealand	Birmingham	15 June 1983
92	G.A. Gooch, England	West Indies	Jaipur	26 Oct 1987
92	R.G. Twose, New Zealand	UAE	Faisalabad	27 Feb 1996
91	R.A. Smith, England	India	Perth	22 Feb 1992
91	M.D. Crowe, New Zealand	Pakistan	Auckland	21 Mar 1992
91	P.A. de Silva, Sri Lanka	Zimbabwe	Colombo (SSC)	21 Feb 1996
90	C.G. Greenidge, West Indies	Australia	Lord's	18 June 1983
90	P.N. Kirsten, South Africa	New Zealand	Auckland	29 Feb 1992
90	D.M. Jones, Australia	India	Brisbane	1 Mar 1992
90	S.R. Tendulkar, India	Australia	Mumbai	27 Feb 1996

MOST SIXES IN AN INNINGS

No.	Player	Score	Versus	Venue	Date
6	Kapil Dev, India	175*	Zimbabwe	Tunbridge Wells	18 June 1983
6	I.V.A. Richards, West Indies	181	Sri Lanka	Karachi	13 Oct 1987
6	A.P. Gurusinha, Sri Lanka	87	Zimbabwe	Mumbai	21 Feb 1996

MOST FOURS IN AN INNINGS

No.	Player	Score	Versus	Venue	Date
18	D.L. Amiss, England	137	India	Lord's	7 June 1975
16	G.M. Turner, New Zealand	171*	East Africa	Birmingham	7 June 1975
16	Kapil Dev, India	175*	Zimbabwe	Tunbridge Wells	18 June 1983
16	I.V.A. Richards, West Indies	181	Pakistan	Karachi	13 Oct 1987

BATTING PARTNERSHIPS

HIGHEST PARTNERSHIPS

Runs	Wkt	Batsmen	Versus	Venue	Date
207	3rd	M.E. Waugh 130, S.R. Waugh 82, Australia	Kenya	Visag	23 Feb 1996
195	3rd	C.G. Greenidge 105*, H.A. Gomes 75*, WI	Zimbabwe	Worcester	13 June 1983
186	1st	G. Kirsten 83, A.C. Hudson 161, South Africa	Netherlands	Rawalpindi (RC)	5 Mar 1996
184	3rd	A.P. Gurusinha 84, P.A. de Silva 145, Sri Lanka	Kenya	Kandy	6 Mar 1996
182	1st	R.B. McCosker 73, A. Turner 101, Australia	Sri Lanka	The Oval	11 June 1975

RECORD WICKET PARTNERSHIPS

Wkt	Runs	Batsmen	Versus	Venue	Date
1st	186	A.C. Hudson 161, G. Kirsten 83, South Africa	Netherlands	Rawalpindi (RC)	5 Mar 1996
2nd	176	D.L. Amiss 137, K.W.R. Fletcher 68, England	India	Lord's	7 June 1975
3rd	207	S.R. Waugh 82, M.E. Waugh 130, Australia	Kenya	Visag	23 Feb 1996
4th	168	L.K. Germon 89, C.Z. Harris 130, New Zealand	Australia	Chennai	11 Mar 1996
5th	145*	A. Flower 115*, A.C. Waller 83, Zimbabwe	Sri Lanka	New Plymouth	23 Feb 1992
6th	144	Imran Khan 102, Shahid Mahboob 77, Pakistan	Sri Lanka	Leeds	16 June 1983
7th	75*	D.A.G. Fletcher 69, I.P. Butchart 34, Zimbabwe	Australia	Nottingham	9 June 1983
8th	117	D.L. Houghton 142, I.P. Butchart 54, Zimbabwe	New Zealand	Hyderabad (I)	10 Oct 1987
9th	126*	Kapil Dev 175*, S.M.H. Kirmani 24*, India	Zimbabwe	Tunbridge Wells	18 June 1983
10th	71	A.M.E. Roberts 37*, J. Gamer 37, West Indies	India	Manchester	10 June 1983

BOWLING

LEADING WICKET-TAKERS

Wkts	Bowler	M	Balls	Runs	Best	Ave.
34	Imran Khan, Pakistan	28	1017	655	4-37	19.26
30	I.T. Botham, England	22	1332	762	4-31	25.40
29	P.A.J. DeFreitas, England	22	1127	742	3-28	25.58
28	Kapil Dev, India	26	1422	892	5-43	31.85
28	Wasim Akram, Pakistan	22	1118	768	4-32	27.42
27	C.J. McDermott, Australia	17	876	587	5-44	22.57
26	Mushtaq Ahmed, Pakistan	15	810	549	3-16	21.11
26	A.M.E. Roberts, West Indies	16	1021	552	3-32	21.23

MOST WICKETS IN AN INNINGS

Wkts	Bowler	Versus	Venue	Date
7-51	W.W. Davis, West Indies	Australia	Leeds	11 June 1983
6-14	G.J. Gilmour, Australia	England	Leeds	18 June 1975
6-39	K.H. MacLeay, Australia	India	Nottingham	11 June 1983
5-21	A.G. Hurst, Australia	Canada	Birmingham	16 June 1979
5-21	P.A. Strang, Zimbabwe	Kenya	Patna	27 Feb 1996
5-25	R.J. Hadlee, New Zealand	Sri Lanka	Bristol	13 June 1983
5-29	S.F. Dukanwala, UAE	Netherlands	Lahore	1 Mar 1996
5-32	A.L.F. Del Mel, Sri Lanka	New Zealand	Derby	18 June 1983
5-34	D.K. Lillee, Australia	Pakistan	Leeds	7 June 1975
5-36	D.W. Fleming, Australia	India	Mumbai	27 Feb 1996
5-38	J. Garner, West Indies	England	Lord's	23 Jun 1979
5-39	A.L.F. Del Mel, Sri Lanka	Pakistan	Leeds	16 June 1983
5-39	V.J. Marks, England	Sri Lanka	Taunton	11 June 1983
5-43	Kapil Dev, India	Australia	Nottingham	13 June 1983
5-44	Abdul Qadir, Pakistan	Sri Lanka	Leeds	16 June 1983
5-44	C.J. McDermott, Australia	Pakistan	Lahore	4 Nov 1987
5-48	G.J. Gilmour, Australia	West Indies	Lord's	21 June 1975

HAT-TRICKS

Bowler	Batsmen	Venue	Date
C. Charma, India	K.R. Rutherford, I.D.S. Smith, E.J. Chatfield, New Zealand	Nagpur	31 Oct 1987

WICKET-KEEPING

MOST DISMISSALS IN AN INNINGS

Total	Player	Versus	Venue	Date
5 (5c)	S.M.H. Kirmani, India	Zimbabwe	Leicester	11 June 1983
5 (4c, 1st)	J.C. Adams, West Indies	Kenya	Pune	29 Feb 1996
5 (4c, 1st)	Rashid Latif, Pakistan	New Zealand	Lahore	6 Mar 1996

MOST DISMISSALS IN A CAREER

Total	Player	Matches	World Cups
22 (18c, 4st)	Wasim Bari, Pakistan	14	1975, 1979
21 (18c, 3st)	I.A. Healy, Australia	14	1992, 1996
20 (19c, 1st)	P.J. Dujon, West Indies	14	1983, 1987
18 (17c, 3st)	R.W. Marsh, Australia	11	1975, 1979, 1983
18 (17c, 3st)	K.S. More, India	14	1987, 1992

FIELDING

MOST CATCHES IN AN INNINGS

No.	Player	Versus	Venue	Date
3	C.H. Lloyd, West Indies	Sri Lanka	Manchester	7 June 1975
3	D.A. Reeve, England	Pakistan	Adelaide	1 Mar 1992
3	Ijaz Ahmed, Pakistan	Australia	Perth	11 Mar 1992
3	A.R. Border, Australia	Zimbabwe	Hobart (B)	14 Mar 1992
3	C.L. Cairns, New Zealand	UAE	Faisalabad	27 Feb 1996

MOST CATCHES IN A CAREER

No.	Player	Matches	World Cups
12	C.H. Lloyd, West Indies	17	1975, 1979, 1983
12	Kapil Dev, India	26	1979, 1983, 1987, 1992
12	D.L. Haynes, West Indies	25	1979, 1983, 1987, 1992
11	C.L. Cairns, New Zealand	11	1992, 1996
10	I.T. Botham, England	22	1979, 1983, 1987, 1992
10	A.R. Border, Australia	25	1979, 1983, 1987, 1992

ALL-ROUND PERFORMANCES

500 RUNS AND 20 WICKETS IN A CAREER

Runs	Wkts	Player	Matches	World Cups
669	28	Kapil Dev, India	26	1979, 1983, 1987, 1992
666	34	Imran Khan, Pakistan	29	1975, 1979, 1983, 1987, 1992
580	24	S.R. Waugh, Australia	23	1987, 1992, 1996

4 WICKETS AND 50 RUNS IN A MATCH

Runs	Wkts	Player	Versus	Venue	Date
69	4-42	D.A.G. Fletcher, Zimbabwe	Australia	Nottingham	9 June 1983
53	4-31	I.T. Botham, England	Australia	Sydney	5 Mar 1992

THE CAPTAINS

MOST MATCHES AS CAPTAIN

No.	Player	World Cups as captain
22	Imran Khan, Pakistan	1983, 1987, 1992
17	C.H. Lloyd, West Indies	1975, 1979, 1983
16	A.R. Border, Australia	1987, 1992
15	Kapil Dev, India	1983, 1987
15	M.A. Azharuddin, India	1992, 1996
14	R.B. Richardson, West Indies	1992, 1996
14	D.L. Houghton, Zimbabwe	1987, 1992

UMPIRES

MOST MATCHES AS UMPIRE

No.	Umpire	World Cups
18	H.D. Bird, England	1975, 1979, 1983, 1987
17	Khizer Hayat, Pakistan	1987, 1992, 1996
14	S.G. Randell, Australia	1992, 1996
12	D.J. Constant, England	1975, 1979, 1983
11	S.J. Woodward, New Zealand	1987, 1992

Other Tournaments and Series

ASIA CUP

The Asia Cup was inaugurated in 1983/84 and is now played every three or four years between the three Asian Test-playing nations and the winner of the ACC Trophy.

Year	Host nation	Winner	Runner-up	3rd	4th
1983/84	Sharjah	India	Sri Lanka	Pakistan	-
1985/86	Sri Lanka	Sri Lanka	Pakistan	Bangladesh	-
1988/89	Bangladesh	India	Sri Lanka	Pakistan	Bangladesh
1990/91	India	India	Sri Lanka	Bangladesh	-
1994/95	Sharjah	India	Sri Lanka	Pakistan	Bangladesh
1997/98	Sri Lanka	Sri Lanka	India	Pakistan	Bangladesh

SHARJAH TOURNAMENTS

A 12,000 seat stadium in Sharjah, one of the seven United Arab Emirates, opened in 1984 and since then various tournaments usually involving at least three teams, have been held twice a year, in April/May and October/November. The home side has only appeared in one tournament, playing two matches in the 1993/94 Austral-Asia Cup.

Austral-Asia Cup

Year	Winner	Runner-up	3rd	4th	5th	6th
1985/86	Pakistan	India	Sri Lanka	New Zealand	Australia	-
1989/90	Pakistan	Australia	New Zealand	Sri Lanka	India	Bangladesh
1993/94	Pakistan	India	Australia	New Zealand	Sri Lanka	UAE

Champions Trophy

Year	Winner	Runner-up	3rd	4th
1986/87	West Indies	Pakistan	India	Sri Lanka
1988/89	West Indies	Pakistan	India	-
1989/90	Pakistan	India	West Indies	-
1993/94	West Indies	Pakistan	Sri Lanka	-
1995/96	Sri Lanka	West Indies	Pakistan	-
1996/97	Pakistan	New Zealand	Sri Lanka	-
1997/98	England	West Indies	Pakistan	India
1998/99	India	Zimbabwe	Sri Lanka	

Sharjah Cup

Year	Winner	Runner-up	3rd	4th
1986/87	England	India	Pakistan	Australia
1987/88	India	New Zealand	Sri Lanka	-
1988/89	Pakistan	Sri Lanka	-	-
1990/91	Pakistan	Sri Lanka	-	-
1995/96	South Africa	India	Pakistan	-
1997/98	India	Australia	New Zealand	-

MISCELLANEOUS TOURNAMENTS

Year	Tournament	Host Nation	Winner	2nd	3rd	4th	5th	6th	7th
1984/85	World Championship of Cricket	Australia	India	Pak	WI	NZ	Aus	Eng	SL
1984/85	Four Nations Trophy	Sharjah	India	Aus	Pak	Eng	-	-	-
1985/86	Three Nations Trophy	Sharjah	West Indies	Pak	India	-	-	-	-
1985/86	John Player Tournament	Sri Lanka	Pakistan	NZ	SL	-	-	-	-
1986/87	America's Cup Challenge	Australia	England	Pak	WI	Aus	-	-	-
1989/90	Nehru Cup	India	Pakistan	WI	Eng	Ind	Aus	SL	-

Year	Tournament	Host Nation	Winner	2nd	3rd	4th	5th	6th	7th
1991/92	Wills Trophy	Sharjah	Pakistan	India	WI	-	-	-	-
1992/93	Wills Trophy	Sharjah	Pakistan	SL	Zim	-	-	-	-
1992/93	Total Triangular Series	South Africa	West Indies	Pak	SAF	-	-	-	-
1993/94	Hero Cup	India	India	WI	SAF	SL	Zim	-	-
1994/95	Wills Triangular Tournament	Pakistan	Australia	Pak	SAF	-	-	-	-
1994/95	Singer World Series	Sri Lanka	India	SL	Aus	Pak	-	-	-
1994/95	Centenary of New Zealand Cricket	New Zealand	Australia	NZ	SAF	Ind	-	-	-
1994/95	Wills World Series	India	India	WI	NZ	-	-	-	-
1994/95	Mandela Trophy	South Africa	South Africa	Pak	SL	NZ	-	-	-
1995/96	Singer Cup	Singapore	Pakistan	SL	Ind	-	-	-	-
1996/97	KCA Centenary Tournament	Kenya	South Africa	Pak	SL	Ken	-	-	-
1996/97	Singer World Series	Sri Lanka	Sri Lanka	Aus	India	Zim	-	-	-
1996/97	Singer-Akai Cup	Sharjah	Sri Lanka	Pak	Zim	-	-	-	-
1996/97	Titan Cup	India	India	SAF	Aus	-	-	-	-
1996/97	Independence Cup	India	Sri Lanka	Pak	Ind	NZ	-	-	-
1996/97	Standard Bank International Series	South Africa	South Africa	Ind	Zim	-	-	-	-
1997/98	Wills Quadrangular Tournament	Pakistan	South Africa	SL	Pak	WI	-	-	-
1997/98	President's Cup	Kenya	Zimbabwe	Ken	Ban	-	-	-	-
1997/98	Silver Jubilee Indepedence Cup	Bangladesh	India	Pak	Ban	-	-	-	-
1997/98	Standard Bank International Series	South Africa	South Africa	Pak	SL	-	-	-	-
1997/98	Pepsi Triangular Tournament	India	Australia	Ind	Zim	-	-	-	-
1997/98	Coca-Cola Cup	India	India	Ken	Ban	-	-	-	-
1997/98	Nihadas Independence Cup	Sri Lanka	India	SL	NZ	-	-	-	-
1998	Emirates Triangular Tournament	England	Sri Lanka	Eng	SAF	-	-	-	-
1998/99	Wills International Trophy	Bangladesh	South Africa	WI	Ind, SL, Aus, NZ, Pak, Eng, Zim				

ICC TROPHY

The ICC Trophy is held every four years between Associate Members of the International Cricket Conference, with the highest placed nations (marked [†]) gaining a place in the following World Cup.

Year	Host nation	Final result	3rd
1979	England	Sri Lanka[†] def Canada[†] by 60 runs	Denmark/Bermuda
1982	England	Zimbabwe[†] def Bermuda by 5 wickets	Papua New Guinea
1986	England	Zimbabwe[†] def Netherlands by 25 runs	Denmark
1990	Netherlands	Zimbabwe[†] def Netherlands by 6 wickets	Kenya/Bangladesh
1994	Kenya	UAE[†] def Kenya[†] by 2 wickets	Netherlands[†]
1997	Malaysia	Bangladesh[†] def Kenya[†] on run-rate	Scotland[†]

Note: Sri Lanka and East Africa were invited to take part in the first World Cup in 1975. Sri Lanka and Canada contested the ICC Trophy final in 1979 after being eliminated from the World Cup.

ONE-DAY SERIES FOR EACH COUNTRY

AUSTRALIA

A three-nation tournament has been held annually in Australia since 1979/80 featuring 12 preliminary games followed by a best-of-three match final. The tournament was known as the Benson & Hedges World Series Cup from 1979/80 to 1989/90, the Benson & Hedges World Series from 1990/91 to 1995/96 and was renamed the Carlton & United Series in 1996/97.

Season	Winner	Runner-up	3rd Team
1979/80	West Indies	England	Australia
1980/81	Australia	New Zealand	India
1981/82	West Indies	Australia	Pakistan
1982/83	Australia	New Zealand	England

1983/84	West Indies	Australia	Pakistan
1984/85	West Indies	Australia	Sri Lanka
1985/86	Australia	India	New Zealand
1986/87	England	Australia	West Indies
1987/88	Australia	New Zealand	Sri Lanka
1988/89	West Indies	Australia	Pakistan
1989/90	Australia	Pakistan	Sri Lanka
1990/91	Australia	New Zealand	England
1991/92	Australia	India	West Indies
1992/93	West Indies	Australia	Pakistan
1993/94	Australia	South Africa	New Zealand
1994/95[†]	Australia	Australia A	England
1995/96	Australia	Sri Lanka	West Indies
1996/97	Pakistan	West Indies	Australia
1997/98	Australia	South Africa	New Zealand
1998/99	Australia	England	Sri Lanka

[†]Zimbabwe also competed in 1994/95. Matches involving Australia A are not recognised by the ICC as official internationals.

Miscellaneous Series

Year Series	Winner	Runner-up	Result
1978/79 Benson & Hedges International Cup	Australia	England	2-1[†]

[†]One match was also abandoned.

CANADA

An annual five-match series between India and Pakistan has been held in Canada at the Toronto Skating, Curling and Cricket Club since 1996. The tournament is known as the Sahara "Friendship" Cup.

Year	Winner	Runner-up	Result
1996	India	Pakistan	3-2
1997	India	Pakistan	4-1[†]
1998	Pakistan	Pakistan	4-1

[†]One match was also abandoned.

ENGLAND

The Texaco Trophy is held regularly between England and one or two other touring teams, usually in a three match format. The series was known as the Prudential Trophy from 1972 until 1982 and was not played in the years that England hosted the World Cup; 1975, 1979 and 1983.

Year	Winner	Runner-up	Result
1972	England	Australia	2-1
1973	England	New Zealand	1-0
1973	West Indies[1]	England	1-1
1974	England	India	2-0
1974	Pakistan	England	2-0
1976	West Indies	England	3-0
1977	England	Australia	2-1
1978	England	Pakistan	2-0
1978	England	New Zealand	2-0
1980	West Indies[1]	England	1-1
1980	England	Australia	2-0
1981	Australia	England	2-1
1982	England	India	2-0
1982	England	Pakistan	2-0
1984	West Indies	England	2-1
1985	Australia	England	2-1

Year	Winner	Runner-up	Result
1986	India[1]	England	1-1
1986	New Zealand[1]	England	1-1
1987	England	Pakistan	2-1
1988	England	West Indies	3-0
1988	England	Sri Lanka	1-0
1989	England[1]	Australia	1-1[2]
1990	England[1]	New Zealand	1-1
1990	India	England	2-0
1991	England	West Indies	3-0
1992	England	Pakistan	4-1
1993	Australia	England	3-0
1994	England	New Zealand	1-0
1994	England	South Africa	2-0
1995	England	West Indies	2-1
1996	England	India	2-0[3]
1996	England	Pakistan	2-1
1997	England	Australia	3-0
1998	South Africa	England	2-1

[1]*Declared winners on superior run-rate.*
[2]*One match was also tied.*
[3]*One match was also abandoned.*

INDIA

The first limited-overs international wasn't played in India until 1981, however since then regular series between India and visiting teams have been held. The series was known as the Charminar Challenge Cup from 1983/84 to 1987/88, the Charms Cup in 1992/93 and the Pepsi Series in 1994/95. The 1984/85 series against Australia was known as the Ranji Trophy Golden Jubilee Series.

Year	Winner	Runner-up	Result
1981/82	India	England	2-1
1982/83	India	Sri Lanka	3-0
1983/84	India	Pakistan	2-0
1983/84	West Indies	India	5-0
1984/85	Australia	India	3-0[1]
1984/85	England	India	4-1
1986/87	India	Australia	3-2
1986/87	India	Sri Lanka	4-1
1986/87	Pakistan	India	5-0
1987/88	West Indies	India	6-1
1988/89	India	New Zealand	4-0
1990/91	India	Sri Lanka	3-0
1991/92	India	South Africa	2-1
1992/93	India drew series with England		3-3
1992/93	India	Zimbabwe	3-0
1993/94	India	Sri Lanka	2-1
1994/95	India	West Indies	4-1
1995/96	India	New Zealand	3-2
1997/98	India drew series with Sri Lanka		1-1[2]

[1]*Two matches were also abandoned.*
[2]*One match was also abandoned.*

NEW ZEALAND

New Zealand has hosted regular one-day series against a touring team in conjunction with a Test series since 1972/73. The series was known as the Rothmans Cup from 1981/82 until 1989/90 and the Bank of New Zealand Series from 1990/91 until 1993/94.

Year	Winner	Runner-up	Result
1972/73	New Zealand	Pakistan	1-0
1973/74	Australia	New Zealand	2-0
1974/75	New Zealand v England		No result[1]
1975/76	New Zealand	India	2-0
1979/80	New Zealand	West Indies	1-0
1980/81	New Zealand	India	2-0
1981/82	Australia	New Zealand	2-1
1982/83	New Zealand	England	3-0
1982/83	New Zealand	Sri Lanka	3-0
1983/84	England	New Zealand	2-1
1984/85	New Zealand	Pakistan	3-0[2]
1985/86	New Zealand drew series with Australia		2-2
1986/87	West Indies	New Zealand	3-0
1987/88	New Zealand drew series with England		2-2
1988/89	New Zealand	Pakistan	3-1
1989/90[3]	Australia	New Zealand	—
1990/91	New Zealand	Sri Lanka	3-0
1990/91	New Zealand	England	2-1
1991/92	England	New Zealand	3-0
1992/93	New Zealand	Pakistan	2-1
1992/93	Australia	New Zealand	3-2
1993/94	Pakistan	New Zealand	3-1[4]
1993/94	New Zealand drew series with India		2-2
1994/95	West Indies	New Zealand	3-0
1995/96	New Zealand drew series with Pakistan		2-2
1995/96	New Zealand	Zimbabwe	2-1
1996/97	New Zealand drew series with England		2-2[4]
1996/97	New Zealand drew series with Sri Lanka		1-1
1997/98	New Zealand	Zimbabwe	4-1
1997/98	New Zealand drew series with Australia		2-2
1998/99	New Zealand drew series with India		2-2[2]

[1]*Both matches were abandoned.*
[2]*One match was also abandoned.*
[3]*India also competed in 1989/90.*
[4]*One match was also tied.*

PAKISTAN

Pakistan's first limited-overs international at home was in 1976 and since then regular series, usually consisting of three matches, have been held against touring teams in conjunction with a Test series. The series was known as the Wills Series from 1980/81 until 1986/87 and the Wills Challenge in 1988/89 and 1989/90.

Year	Winner	Runner-up	Result
1976/77	New Zealand	Pakistan	1-0
1977/78	England	Pakistan	2-1
1978/79	Pakistan	India	2-1
1980/81	West Indies	Pakistan	3-0
1981/82	Pakistan	Sri Lanka	2-1
1982/83	Pakistan	Australia	2-0[1]
1982/83	Pakistan	India	3-1

Year	Winner	Runner-up	Result
1983/84	Pakistan drew series with England		1-1
1984/85	Pakistan	India	1-0[1]
1984/85	Pakistan	New Zealand	3-1
1985/86	Pakistan	Sri Lanka	4-0
1985/86	West Indies	Pakistan	3-2
1986/87	West Indies	Pakistan	4-1
1987/88	England	Pakistan	3-0
1988/89	Pakistan	Australia	1-0[2]
1989/90	Pakistan	India	2-0[1]
1990/91	Pakistan	New Zealand	3-0
1990/91	Pakistan	West Indies	3-0
1991/92	West Indies	Pakistan	2-0[3]
1991/92	Pakistan	Sri Lanka	4-1
1993/94	Pakistan	Zimbabwe	3-0
1995/96	Sri Lanka	Pakistan	2-1
1996/97	Pakistan	Zimbabwe	3-0
1996/97	Pakistan	New Zealand	2-1
1997/98	Pakistan	India	2-1
1998/99	Australia	Pakistan	3-0
1998/99	Pakistan	Zimbabwe	2-1

[1]*One match was also abandoned.*
[2]*Match tied, but Pakistan declared winners as they lost fewer wickets.*
[3]*One match was also tied.*

SOUTH AFRICA

Seven limited-overs internationals have been a regular feature of tours of South Africa by visiting teams in conjunction with a Test series since the Republic was re-admitted to the International Cricket Conference in 1991.

Year	Winner	Runner-up	Result
1992/93	South Africa	India	5-2
1993/94	South Africa drew series with Australia		4-4
1995/96	South Africa	England	6-1
1996/97	Australia	South Africa	4-3
1998/99	South Africa	West Indies	6-1

SRI LANKA

Three limited-overs internationals are usually played in Sri Lanka in conjunction with Test series. No matches were played between 1985/86 and 1992/93 due to civil unrest in the country.

Year	Winner	Runner-up	Result
1981/82	Sri Lanka drew series with England		1-1
1982/83	Sri Lanka	Australia	2-0[1]
1983/84	New Zealand	Sri Lanka	2-1
1984/85	Sri Lanka drew series with New Zealand		1-1
1985/86	Sri Lanka drew series with India		1-1[2]
1985/86	Pakistan	Sri Lanka	2-0[2]
1992/93	Sri Lanka	Australia	2-1
1992/93	Sri Lanka	New Zealand	2-0
1992/93	Sri Lanka	England	2-0
1993/94	Sri Lanka	India	2-1
1993/94	Sri Lanka drew series with South Africa		1-1[2]
1993/94	Sri Lanka drew series with West Indies		1-1
1994/95	Pakistan	Sri Lanka	4-1
1997/98	Sri Lanka	India	3-0[2]
1997/98	Sri Lanka	Zimbabwe	3-0

[1]*Two matches were also abandoned.*
[2]*One match also abandoned.*

WEST INDIES

Five match series have regularly played each season between the West Indies and a touring team since 1976/77 in conjunction with a Test series. The series was known as the Guinness Trophy in 1977/78 and the Cable & Wireless Series between 1987/88 and 1992/93.

Year	Winner	Runner-up	Result
1976/77	West Indies	Pakistan	1-0
1977/78	West Indies[1]	Australia	1-1
1980/81	West Indies	England	2-0
1982/83	West Indies	India	2-1
1983/84	West Indies	Australia	3-1
1984/85	West Indies	New Zealand	5-0
1985/86	West Indies	England	3-1
1987/88	West Indies	Pakistan	5-0
1988/89	West Indies	India	5-0
1989/90	West Indies	England	3-0[2]
1990/91	Australia	West Indies	4-1
1991/92	West Indies	South Africa	3-0
1992/93	West Indies drew series with Pakistan		2-2[3]
1993/94	West Indies	England	3-2
1994/95	West Indies	Australia	4-1
1995/96	West Indies	New Zealand	3-2
1996/97	West Indies	India	3-1
1996/97	West Indies	Sri Lanka	1-0
1997/98	West Indies	England	4-1

[1]*West Indies declared winners on superior run-rate.*
[2]*Two matches were also abandoned.*
[3]*One match was also tied.*

ZIMBABWE

Zimbabwe competed in three World Cups (1983, 1987/88 and 1991/92) but did not host their first one-day international until they were admitted as a full member of the International Cricket Conference in 1992. Three one-day internationals are usually played against touring teams in conjunction with a Test series.

Year	Winner	Runner-up	Result
1992/93	India	Zimbabwe	1-0
1992/93	New Zealand	Zimbabwe	2-0
1992/93	Pakistan	Zimbabwe	1-0
1994/95	Sri Lanka	Zimbabwe	2-1
1994/95	Zimbabwe drew series with Pakistan		1-1[†]
1995/96	South Africa	Zimbabwe	2-0
1996/97	Zimbabwe	England	3-0
1996/97	Zimbabwe	India	1-0
1997/98	Zimbabwe drew series with New Zealand		1-1[†]
1997/98	Pakistan	Zimbabwe	2-0
1998/99	India	Zimbabwe	2-1

[†] *One match was also tied.*

MISCELLANEOUS MATCHES

Year	Match	Result	Venue
1970/71	Australia v England[†]	Australia won by 5 wickets	Melbourne
1974/75	Australia v England	England won by 3 wickets	Melbourne
1975/76	Australia v West Indies	Australia won by 5 wickets	Adelaide
1982/83	Bushfire Appeal Challenge	New Zealand def Australia by 14 runs	Sydney
1987/88	Bicentennial One-Day International	Australia def England by 22 runs	Melbourne
1987/88	Indian Board Benevolent Fund Match	West Indies def India by 2 runs	Ahmedabad
1988/89	New Zealand v Pakistan[†]	New Zealand won by 8 wickets	Dunedin
1989/90	West Indies v England[†]	West Indies won by 7 wickets	Georgetown
1995/96	Queen's Park Oval Centenary	Sri Lanka def West Indies by 35 runs	Port-of-Spain
1996/97	Mohinder Armanath Benefit Match	India def South Africa by 74 runs	Mumbai

[†]*Replaced abandoned Test match*

Women's Limited-overs Internationals

THE TEAMS

HIGHEST INNINGS TOTALS

Total/Overs	Team	Versus	Venue	Date
5-455 (50 overs)	New Zealand	Pakistan	Christchurch	30 Jan 1997
3-412 (50 overs)	Australia	Denmark	Mumbai	16 Dec 1997
4-397 (50 overs)	Australia	Pakistan	Melbourne	7 Feb 1997
2-376 (50 overs)	England	Pakistan	Hyderabad (I)	12 Dec 1997
3-324 (50 overs)	England	Ireland	Pune	16 Dec 1997
4-301 (50 overs)	England	Denmark	Hyderabad (I)	14 Dec 1997
4-301 (50 overs)	India	Sri Lanka	Agra	31 Jan 1999
3-298 (50 overs)	India	Sri Lanka	Lucknow	27 Jan 1999
5-297 (60 overs)	New Zealand	Netherlands	Sydney	4 Dec 1988
5-297 (50 overs)	India	Sri Lanka	Lucknow	8 Feb 1999
5-294 (50 overs)	India	Sri Lanka	Kanpur	29 Jan 1999
3-286 (60 overs)	England	Denmark	Banstead	20 Jul 1993
1-284 (60 overs)	Australia	Netherlands	Perth	29 Nov 1988
6-284 (50 overs)	India	Sri Lanka	Lucknow	6 Feb 1999
4-282 (60 overs)	Australia	England	Christchurch	25 Jan 1992

HIGHEST INNINGS TOTAL BATTING SECOND

Total/Overs	Team	Versus	Venue	Date
8-254 (50 overs)	South Africa	England	Taunton	17 Aug 1997

HIGHEST INNINGS TOTAL FOR EACH TEAM

Team	Total/Overs	Versus	Venue	Date
Australia	3-412 (50 overs)	Denmark	Mumbai	16 Dec 1997
Denmark	8-185 (55 overs)	Ireland	Leicester	18 Jul 1990
England	2-376 (50 overs)	Pakistan	Hyderabad (I)	12 Dec 1997
India	4-301 (50 overs)	Sri Lanka	Agra	31 Jan 1999
International XI	5-163 (60 overs)	Jamaica	Leicester	14 Jul 1993
Ireland	7-242 (50 overs)	Pakistan	Gurgaon	18 Dec 1997
Jamaica	8-162 (55.4 overs)	International XI	Leicester	14 Jul 1973
Netherlands	9-172 (50 overs)	Ireland	Nottingham	19 Jul 1990
New Zealand	5-455 (50 overs)	Pakistan	Christchurch	30 Jan 1997
Pakistan	3-146 (47 overs)	England	Hyderabad (I)	12 Dec 1997
South Africa	7-258 (50 overs)	Pakistan	Vadodara (IPCL)	16 Dec 1997
Sri Lanka	8-181 (50 overs)	India	Agra	31 Jan 1999
Trinidad & Tobago	124 (45.3 overs)	Australia	Herts	30 Jun 1973
West Indies	6-208 (60 overs)	Ireland	Dorking	29 Jul 1993
Young England	6-174 (60 overs)	New Zealand	Eastbourne	21 Jul 1973

LOWEST INNINGS TOTALS (COMPLETED INNINGS)

Total/Overs	Team	Versus	Venue	Date
23 (24.1 overs)	Pakistan	Australia	Melbourne	7 Feb 1997
27 (13.4 overs)	Pakistan	Australia	Hyderabad (I)	14 Dec 1997
29 (25.1 overs)	Netherlands	Australia	Perth	29 Nov 1988
37 (35 overs)	India	New Zealand	Auckland	14 Jan 1982
40 (54.2 overs)	Netherlands	New Zealand	Lindfield	25 Jul 1993
46 (33 overs)	Denmark	England	Wit Haarlem	20 Jul 1991

Total/Overs	Team	Versus	Venue	Date
47 (29 overs)	Denmark	England	Wit Haarlem	19 Jul 1991
47 (33.5 overs)	Denmark	England	Banstead	20 Jul 1993
47 (23 overs)	Pakistan	New Zealand	Christchurch	30 Jan 1997
49 (37.5 overs)	India	New Zealand	Christchurch	2 Feb 1982
49 (25.5 overs)	Denmark	Australia	Mumbai	16 Dec 1997

LOWEST INNINGS TOTAL FOR EACH TEAM

Team	Total/Overs	Versus	Venue	Date
Australia	77 (51.3 overs)	New Zealand	Beckenham	29 Jul 1993
Denmark	46 (33 overs)	England	Wit Haarlem	27 Jul 1991
England	78 (43.5 overs)	India	Gauhati	14 Nov 1995
India	37 (35 overs)	New Zealand	Auckland	14 Jan 1982
International XI	60 (34.4 overs)	New Zealand	Auckland	12 Jan 1982
Ireland	77 (47.2 overs)	Australia	Belfast	28 Jun 1987
Jamaica	97 (51.5 overs)	Trinidad & Tobago	Ealing	4 Jul 1973
Netherlands	29 (25.1 overs)	Australia	Perth	29 Nov 1988
New Zealand	58 (56.3 overs)	Australia	Melbourne	7 Feb 1985
Pakistan	23 (24.1 overs)	Australia	Melbourne	7 Feb 1997
South Africa	134 (46.3 overs)	England	Lord's	20 Aug 1997
Sri Lanka	51 (47.4 overs)	Lucknow	Chandigarh	6 Feb 1999
Trinidad & Tobago	59 (45.5 overs)	England	Wolverhampton	20 Jul 1973
West Indies	88 (45.4 overs)	Netherlands	Meir Heath	21 Jul 1993
Young England	57 (31.1 overs)	Australia	Bournemouth	23 Jun 1973

HIGHEST MATCH AGGREGATES

Total/overs	Match	Batted 1st	Batted 2nd	Venue	Date
5-522 (97 overs)	Pakistan v England	Eng 2-376	Pak 3-146	Hyderabad(I)	12 Dec 1997
13-507 (100 overs)	England v South Africa	SAf 5-253	Eng 8-254	Taunton	17 Aug 1997

LOWEST MATCH AGGREGATES

Total/overs	Match	Batted 1st	Batted 2nd	Venue	Date
11-55 (19.5 overs)	Australia v Pakistan	Pak 27	Aus 1-28	Hyderabad (I)	14 Dec 1997
10-81 (67.4 overs)	Netherlands v New Zealand	Neth 40	NZ 0-41	Lindfield	25 Jul 1993

HIGHEST WINNING MARGINS (RUNS)

Runs	Team	Versus	Batted 1st	Batted 2nd	Venue	Date
408	New Zealand	Pakistan	NZ 5-455	Pak 47	Christchurch	30 Jan 1997
374	Australia	Pakistan	Aus 4-397	Pak 23	Melbourne	7 Feb 1997
363	Australia	Denmark	Aus 3-412	Den 49	Mumbai	16 Dec 1997
255	Australia	Netherlands	Aus 1-284	Neth 29	Perth	28 Nov 1988
239	England	Denmark	Eng 3-286	Den 47	Banstead	20 Jul 1993
233	India	South Africa	Ind 6-284	SL 51	Lucknow	6 Feb 1999
230	England	Pakistan	Eng 2-376	Pak 3-146	Hyderabad (I)	12 Dec 1997
210	New Zealand	Netherlands	NZ 5-297	Neth 87	Sydney	4 Dec 1988
208	England	Ireland	Eng 3-324	Ire 116	Pune	16 Dec 1997
206	England	Denmark	Eng 5-270	Den 64	Nottingham	19 Jul 1990

HIGHEST WINNING MARGINS (WICKETS)

Wkts	Team	Versus	Batted 1st	Batted 2nd	Venue	Date
10	Australia	Ireland	Ire 8-78	Aus 0-81	Sydney	4 Dec 1988
10	England	Ireland	Ire 9-109	Eng 0-110	Melbourne	13 Dec 1988
10	Australia	Ireland	Ire 88	Aus 0-89	Melbourne	16 Dec 1988
10	Australia	Netherlands	Neth 53	Aus 0-55	Warrington	20 Jul 1993
10	New Zealand	Netherlands	Neth 40	NZ 0-41	Lindfield	25 Jul 1993
10	New Zealand	Australia	Aus 77	NZ 0-78	Beckenham	29 Jul 1993
10	New Zealand	Pakistan	Pak 56	NZ 0-57	Christchurch	29 Jan 1997
10	Netherlands	Sri Lanka	SL 65	Neth 0-66	Kandy	2 Dec 1997
10	Australia	South Africa	SA 9-163	Aus 0-167	Bangalore	12 Dec 1997

NARROWEST WINNING MARGINS (RUNS)

Margin	Team	Versus	Batted 1st	Batted 2nd	Venue	Date
1 run	New Zealand	Australia	NZ 154	Aus 9-153	Wanganui	14 Feb 1995
2 runs	New Zealand	India	NZ 7-174	Ind 9-172	Delhi	19 Feb 1985
2 runs	New Zealand	Australia	NZ 9-183	Aus 181	Wellington	20 Jan 1986
3 runs	England	India	Eng 179	Ind 176	Finchampstead	22 Jan 1994
4 runs	Australia	New Zealand	Aus 6-211	NZ 9-207	Wellington	20 Jan 1986
4 runs	Netherlands	Denmark	Neth 126	Den 122	Wit Haarlem	16 Jul 1991
4 runs	Australia	New Zealand	Aus 9-164	NZ 8-160	Adelaide	3 Feb 1996
5 runs	Australia	New Zealand	Aus 5-169	NZ 9-164	Sydney	5 Nov 1997

TIED MATCHES

Match	Batted 1st	Batted 2nd	Venue	Date
New Zealand v England	NZ 9-147	Eng 8-147	Auckland	10 Jan 1982
Australia v England	Eng 8-167	Aus 167	Christchurch	2 Feb 1982
India v New Zealand	NZ 9-176	Ind 176	Indore	17 Dec 1997

THE PLAYERS

MOST APPEARANCES

No.	Player
91	D. Hockley, New Zealand
63	J. Brittin, England
60	K. Smithies, England
59	C. Campbell, New Zealand
58	Z. Goss, Australia
52	B. Clark, Australia
49	L. Larsen, Australia
47	C. Hodges, England
47	C. Matthews, Australia

BATTING

LEADING RUN-SCORERS

Player	M	Inns	NO	Runs	HS	Ave.	100s	50s
D. Hockley, New Zealand	91	91	14	3342	117	43.40	3	28
J. Brittin, England	63	59	9	2121	138*	43.29	5	7
B. Clark, Australia	52	49	6	2280	229*	53.02	3	14
D. Annetts, Australia	43	39	12	1126	100*	41.70	1	8
C. Hodges, England	47	39	6	1073	113	32.52	2	3
Z. Goss, Australia	58	45	10	1049	96*	29.97	0	7
L. Reeler, Australia	23	23	5	1034	143*	57.44	2	8

HIGHEST INDIVIDUAL INNINGS

Score	Player	Versus	Venue	Date
229*	B. Clark, Australia	Denmark	Mumbai	16 Dec 1997
173*	C. Edwards, England	Ireland	Pune	16 Dec 1997
166*	Chandrakanta Ahir, India	Sri Lanka	Agra	31 Jan 1999
156*	L. Keightley, Australia	Pakistan	Melbourne	7 Feb 1997
143*	L. Reeler, Australia	Netherlands	Perth	29 Nov 1988
142*	B. Daniels, England	Pakistan	Vijayawada	12 Dec 1997
142	B. Clark, Australia	New Zealand	Auckland	16 Feb 1997
138*	J. Brittin, England	International XI	Hamilton	14 Jan 1982
138	J. Brittin, England	Pakistan	Vijayawada	12 Dec 1997
135*	K. Le Comber, New Zealand	Ireland	Pembroke	19 Jul 1996
134	L. Thomas, England	International XI	Hove	23 Jun 1973
131	B. Clark, Australia	Pakistan	Melbourne	7 Feb 1997
123	Chandrakanta Ahir, India	Sri Lanka	Kanpur	29 Jan 1999
122	J. Kennare, Australia	England	Melbourne	2 Feb 1985
118	E. Bakewell, England	Australia	Birmingham	28 Jul 1973
118	H. Plimmer, England	Ireland	Reading	24 Jul 1993
117	D. Hockley, New Zealand	England	Durham	18 Jun 1996
114*	M. P. Moore, Ireland	Denmark	Dublin	18 Jul 1985
114	R. Heyhoe Flint, England	Young England	Ilford	18 Jul 1973
114	N. Turner, New Zealand	Netherlands	Sydney	4 Dec 1988
113*	K. Rolton, Australia	New Zealand	Wellington	23 Feb 1997
113*	L. Keightley, Australia	England	Lord's	21 Jul 1998
113	C. Hodges, England	Ireland	Reading	24 Jul 1993
108*	L. Reeler, Australia	New Zealand	Melbourne	10 Dec 1988
107*	W. Watson, England	Ireland	Okley	22 Jul 1990
106	L. Hill, Australia	England	Canterbury	1 Aug 1976
105*	C. Hodges, England	Australia	Guildford	26 Jul 1993
105*	R. Buckstein, Australia	Netherlands	Melbourne	14 Dec 1988
105	M. Lewis, New Zealand	Pakistan	Christchurch	30 Jan 1997
104	J. Brittin, England	Denmark	Banstead	20 Jul 1993
102	C. Edwards, England	South Africa	Taunton	17 Aug 1997
102	Chandrakanta Ahir, India	Sri Lanka	Lucknow	6 Feb 1999
101*	E. Bakewell, England	International XI	Hove	23 Jun 1973
101*	Mithali Raj, India	Sri Lanka	Lucknow	8 Feb 1999
101	B. Bevege, New Zealand	International XI	Auckland	12 Jan 1982
101	J. Brittin, England	New Zealand	Hastings	24 Jun 1984
100*	J. Kennare, Australia	England	Melbourne	3 Feb 1985
100*	D. Annetts, Australia	England	Christchurch	25 Jan 1992
100*	D. Hockley, New Zealand	Sri Lanka	Chandigarh	13 Dec 1997
100	R. Buckstein, Australia	Netherlands	Perth	29 Nov 1988
100	J. Brittin, England	India	Finchampstead	25 Jul 1993
100	D. Hockley, New Zealand	West Indies	Chandigarh	15 Dec 1997

HIGHEST INDIVIDUAL INNINGS FOR EACH TEAM

Team	Player	Score	Versus	Venue	Date
Australia	B. Clark	229*	Denmark	Mumbai	16 Dec 1997
Denmark	J. Jonsson	53	Ireland	Dublin	18 Jul 1995
England	C. Edwards	173*	Ireland	Pune	16 Dec 1997
India	F. Khaleeli	88	England	Wanganui	20 Jan 1982
International XI	L. Thomas	70*	India	Napier	17 Jan 1982
Ireland	M.P. Moore	114*	Denmark	Dublin	18 Jul 1985
Jamaica	V. Latty Scott	61	Young Eng	Sittingbourne	30 Jun 1973
Netherlands	P. Te Beest	62	West Indies	Meir Heath	21 Jul 1993
New Zealand	K. Le Comber	135*	Ireland	Pembroke	19 Jul 1996
Pakistan	Sharmeen Khan	48	South Africa	Vadodara (IPCL)	16 Dec 1997
South Africa	H. Davies	64	England	Bristol	15 Aug 1997
Sri Lanka	V. Bowen	38	England	Mohali	21 Dec 1997
Trinidad & Tobago	L. Browne	50*	Jamaica	Ealing	4 Jul 1973
West Indies	E. Caesar	78	Ireland	Dorking	29 Jul 1993
Young England	G. Davies	65	International XI	Bletchley	7 Jul 1973

HIGHEST CAREER BATTING AVERAGES (minimum 500 runs)

Player	M	Inns	NO	Runs	HS	Ave.	100s	50s
R. Heyhoe Flint, England	23	20	9	643	114	58.45	1	4
C. Edwards, England	14	13	2	639	173*	58.09	2	3
L. Reeler, Australia	23	23	5	1034	143*	57.44	2	8
B. Calver, Australia	34	21	11	534	81*	53.40	-	3
B. Clark, Australia	52	49	6	2280	229*	53.02	3	14
W. Watson, England	23	22	6	768	107*	48.00	1	5
L. Thomas, England	24	22	4	821	134	45.61	1	3
J. Kennare, Australia	19	19	1	789	122	43.83	2	3
D. Hockley, New Zealand	91	91	14	3342	117	43.40	3	28
J. Brittin, England	63	58	9	2121	138*	43.29	5	7
L. Oliver, South Africa	15	15	3	512	78*	42.66	-	6
R. Buckstein, Australia	16	14	2	511	105*	42.58	2	1
L. Keightley, Australia	27	26	6	843	156*	42.15	2	6
D. Annetts, Australia	43	39	12	1126	100*	41.70	1	8
D. Emerson, Australia	21	21	1	820	84	41.00	-	8

MOST CENTURIES

No.	Player
5	J. Brittin, England
3	Chandrakanta Ahir, India
3	B. Clark, Australia
3	D. Hockley, New Zealand
2	E. Bakewell, England
2	R. Buckstein, Australia
2	C. Hodges, England
2	L. Reeler, Australia
2	J. Kennare, Australia
2	C. Edwards, England
2	L. Keightley, Australia

BATTING PARTNERSHIPS

HIGHEST PARTNERSHIPS

Runs	Wkt	Players	Versus	Venue	Date
246	1st	E. Bakewell 101*, L. Thomas 134, England	International XI	Hove	23 Jun 1973
220	1st	R. Buckstein 100, L. Reeler 143*, Australia	Netherlands	Perth	29 Nov 1988
219	1st	B. Clark 131, L. Keightley 156*, Australia	Pakistan	Melbourne	7 Feb 1997
213	3rd	C. Hodges 113, H. Plimmer 118, England	Irleand	Reading	24 Jul 1993
203	2nd	J. Brittin 138, B. Daniels 142*, England	Pakistan	Vijayawada	12 Dec 1997

RECORD WICKET PARTNERSHIPS

Wkt	Runs	Players	Versus	Venue	Date
1st	246	E. Bakewell 101*, L.Thomas 134, England	International XI	Hove	23 Jun 1973
2nd	203	J. Brittin 138, B.Daniels 142*, England	Pakistan	Vijayawada	12 Dec 1997
3rd	213	C. Hodges 113, H.Plimmer 118, England	Ireland	Reading	24 Jul 1993
4th	131*	C. Edwards 173*, J.Cassar 50*, England	Ireland	Pune	16 Dec 1997
	131	Chandrakanta Ahir 68, Hemlata Kala 88*, India	Sri Lanka	Mujjpurnagar	2 Feb 1999
5th	151*	J. Broadbent 82*, B Calver 81*, Australia	Ireland	Dublin	24 Jul 1998
6th	100	S. Tredea 69, Z.Goss 47, Australia	England	Sydney	3 Dec 1988
7th	73*	S. Rattray 60*, D.Caird16*, New Zealand	England	Bristol	21 Jul 1984
8th	64	R. Thompson 50*, L.Fullston 27, Australia	International XI	Palmerston North	20 Jan 1982
9th	58	K.Gunn 49, S.McLauchlan 29, New Zealand	Australia	Wellington	19 Jan 1992
10th	36	L.Thomas 70*, S.Braganza 9, International XI	India	Napier	17 Jan 1992

BOWLING

LEADING WICKET-TAKERS

Player	O	M	Runs	Wkts	Ave.	Best	5wi	Ec Rt
L. Fullston, Australia	394.2	80	971	73	13.30	5-27	2	2.45
K. Smithies, England	436.5	110	1147	63	18.21	3-6	-	2.79
J. Harris, New Zealand	414.2	98	1124	61	18.42	4-8	-	2.71
C. Hodges, England	367.5	93	874	58	15.07	4-3	-	2.38
Z. Goss, Australia	431.4	90	1169	57	20.51	3-26	-	2.71
C. Fitzpatrick, Australia	303.3	60	820	54	15.18	5-47	1	2.70
K. Brown, Australia	414	117	869	52	16.71	4-4	-	2.09

MOST WICKETS IN AN INNINGS

Wkts	Bowler	Versus	Venue	Date
7-8	J. Chamberlain, England	Denmark	Wit Haarlem	19 Jul 1991
6-10	J. Lord, New Zealand	India	Auckland	14 Jan 1982
6-20	G. Page, New Zealand	Trinidad & Tobago	St Albans	23 Jun 1973
5-5	J. Turner, New Zealand	Netherlands	Lindfield	25 Jul 1993
5-10	J. Broadbent, Australia	New Zealand	Lismore	13 Jan 1993
5-14	T. Macpherson, Australia	Young England	Bournemouth	23 Jun 1973
5-15	S. Gill, England	Denmark	Nottingham	19 Jul 1990
5-18	J. Chamberlain, England	Ireland	Nykobing Mors	21 Jul 1989
5-22	K. Gunn, New Zealand	Australia	Lower Hutt	10 Feb 1990
5-27	S. Bray, Ireland	Denmark	Leicester	18 Jul 1990
5-27	L. Fullston, Australia	New Zealand	Melbourne	18 Jan 1982
5-28	L. Fullston, Australia	Netherlands	Wellington	14 Dec 1988
5-29	J. Owens, Australia	Ireland	Dublin	1 Jul 1987
5-30	G. Smith, England	Australia	Guildford	26 Jul 1993
5-36	C. Singh, West Indies	Ireland	Dorking	29 Jul 1993
5-47	C. Fitzpatrick, Australia	England	Lord's	21 Jul 1998

BEST CAREER AVERAGES (minimum 20 wickets)

Player	Overs	Mdns	Runs	Wkts	Ave.	Best	5w	Ec Rt
G. Smith, England	253.3	74	514	41	12.54	5-15	2	2.02
J. Lord, New Zealand	132.3	25	318	25	12.72	6-10	1	2.40
L. Fullston, Australia	394.2	80	971	73	13.30	5-27	2	2.45
D. Martin, Australia	181	65	376	27	13.93	3-8	-	2.07
K. Rolton, Australia	129.1	13	445	29	15.34	3-9	-	3.45
C. Hodges, England	367.5	93	874	58	15.07	4-3	-	2.37
C. Fitzpatrick, Australia	303.3	60	820	54	15.18	5-47	1	2.70
S. Brown, England	170	63	308	20	15.40	3-34	-	1.81
C. Mason, Australia	182.1	33	560	36	15.56	4-18	-	3.07
P. Rau, India	174.3	25	545	35	15.57	4.26	-	3.12
S. Tredrea, Australia	280	88	521	32	16.28	4-25	-	1.86
J. Chamberlain, England	321.2	68	805	49	16.43	7-8	2	2.50
J. Broadbent, Australia	216.3	44	610	37	16.49	5-10	-	2.82
O. Magno, Australia	218.2	44	582	35	16.63	4-10	-	2.67
K. Brown, Australia	414	117	869	52	16.71	4-4	-	2.09
D. Edulji, India	326.5	76	775	46	16.85	4-12	-	2.37
K. Smithies, England	436.5	110	1147	63	18.21	3-6	-	2.79

WICKET-KEEPING

MOST DISMISSALS

No.	Player	Catches	Stumpings	Matches
49	C. Matthews, Australia	35	14	47
48	S. Illingworth, New Zealand	27	21	37
47	J. Cassar, England	24	23	36
35	S. Hodges, England	20	15	26
33	I. Jagersma, New Zealand	24	9	34

WOMEN'S CRICKET WORLD CUP

The first Women's Cricket World Cup was held in 1973, preceding the men's World Cup by two years. The tournament featured seven teams in 60 overs per side format. New Zealand will host the seventh World Cup in 2000.

Year	Host Nation	Final Result	Venue
1973	England	England	*NA*
1978	India	Australia	*NA*
1982	New Zealand	Australia def England by 3 wickets	Christchurch
1988	Australia	Australia def England by 8 wickets	Melbourne
1993	England	England def New Zealand by 67 runs	Lord's
1997	India	Australia def New Zealand by 5 wickets	Calcutta

Note: No final was played in 1973 and 1978, the winner being the team that finished at the top of the table in each tournament.

VII Cricket World Cup
Match Schedule

14 May – 20 June 1999

GROUP A

England, India, Kenya, South Africa, Sri Lanka, Zimbabwe

Date	Match	Venue
14 May	England v Sri Lanka	Lord's
15 May	India v South Africa	Hove
15 May	Zimbabwe v Kenya	Taunton
18 May	England v Kenya	Canterbury
19 May	Sri Lanka v South Africa	Northampton
19 May	India v Zimbabwe	Leicester
22 May	England v South Africa	The Oval
22 May	Zimbabwe v Sri Lanka	Worcester
23 May	Kenya v India	Bristol
25 May	England v Zimbabwe	Trent Bridge
26 May	Sri Lanka v India	Taunton
26 May	South Africa v Kenya	Amsterdam
29 May	England v India	Edgbaston
29 May	Zimbabwe v South Africa	Chelmsford
30 May	Sri Lanka v Kenya	Southampton

GROUP B

Australia, Bangladesh, New Zealand, Pakistan, Scotland, West Indies

Date	Match	Venue
16 May	Australia v Scotland	Worcester
16 May	West Indies v Pakistan	Bristol
17 May	New Zealand v Bangladesh	Chelmsford
20 May	Australia v New Zealand	Cardiff
20 May	Pakistan v Scotland	Chester-Le-Street
21 May	West Indies v Bangladesh	Dublin
23 May	Australia v Pakistan	Headingley
24 May	West Indies v New Zealand	Southampton
24 May	Scotland v Bangladesh	Edinburgh
27 May	West Indies v Scotland	Leicester
27 May	Australia v Bangladesh	Chester-Le-Street
28 May	New Zealand v Pakistan	Derby
30 May	West Indies v Australia	Old Trafford
31 May	Scotland v New Zealand	Edinburgh
31 May	Pakistan v Bangladesh	Northampton

SUPER SIX

Date	Match	Venue
4 June	Group A 2nd v Group B 2nd	The Oval
5 June	Group A 1st v Group B 1st	Trent Bridge
6 June	Group A 3rd v Group B 3rd	Headingley
8 June	Group A 2nd v Group B 1st	Old Trafford
9 June	Group A 3rd v Group B 2nd	Lord's
10 June	Group A 1st v Group B 3rd	Edgbaston
11 June	Group A 3rd v Group B 1st	The Oval
12 June	Group A 2nd v Group B 3rd	Trent Bridge
13 June	Group A 1st v Group B 2nd	Headingley

SEMI-FINALS

16 June	Team 1 v Team 4	Old Trafford
17 June	Team 2 v Team 3	Edgbaston

FINAL

20 June		Lord's

Reproduced with the kind permission of the 1999 Cricket World Cup.

Note: these dates are subject to change.

Bibliography

Armstrong, G. and Gately, M. 1994, *The People's Game – Australia in One-day Cricket,* Pan Macmillan, Sydney.

Benaud, Richie (ed.) *Cricket Yearbook 1984-96*, Hamlyn Australia, Melbourne.

Benaud, Richie, *Lights, Camera, Action! An Illustrated History of the World Series*, Hamlyn Australia, Melbourne.

Brooke, Robert and Matthews, Peter 1988, *Guinness Cricket Firsts*, Guinness Publishing Limited, London.

Cashman, Richard (ed.) 1996, *The Oxford Companion to Australian Cricket*, Oxford University Press, Melbourne.

Cashman, Richard and Weaver, Amanda 1991, *Wicket Women: Cricket and Women in Australia*, NSW University Press, Sydney.

Dawson, Graham and Wat, Charlie 1998, *Test Cricket Lists (4th edn)*, The Five Mile Press, Melbourne.

Dawson, Marc 1993, *The Bumper Book of Cricket Extras*, Kangaroo Press, Melbourne.

Dawson, Marc 1994, *Cricket Extras 2,* Kangaroo Press, Melbourne.

Frindall, Bill (ed) 1996, *Playfair Cricket World Cup Guide*, Headline Publishing, London.

Frindall, Bill 1997, *Limited-overs International Cricket: The Complete Record,* Headline Book Publishing, London.

John Wisden and Co. 1972-97, *Wisden Cricketers Almanack*, (various eds), London.

Lemmon, David (ed) 1980-98, *Benson & Hedges Cricket Yearbook,* Bloomsbury Publishing, London.

Smith, Patrick 1992, *The Age World Cup Cricket 1992: The Complete Record,* The Five Mile Press, Melbourne.

Waugh, Steve 1996, *Steve Waugh's World Cup Diary*, HarperCollins Publishers, Sydney.

Magazines

The Cricketer, Inside Edge, Wisden's Cricket Monthly

Newspapers

The Times, London; *The Daily Telegraph,* Sydney; *The Sydney Morning Herald; The Australian*

Internet sites

CricInfo (www.cricket.org); Khel.com (www.khel.com); HowzStat! (http://mullara.met.unimelb.edu.au:8080/howzstat)

Notes

Notes